Energy Resources and Systems

Tushar K. Ghosh • Mark A. Prelas

Energy Resources and Systems

Volume 1: Fundamentals and Non-Renewable
Resources

 Springer

Tushar K. Ghosh
Nuclear Science & Engineering Institute
University of Missouri-Columbia
E 2434 Lafferre Hall
Columbia MO 65211
USA

Mark A. Prelas
Nuclear Science & Engineering Institute
University of Missouri-Columbia
E 2434 Lafferre Hall
Columbia MO 65211
USA

ISBN: 978-90-481-2382-7   e-ISBN: 978-90-481-2383-4

Library of Congress Control Number: 2009928307

Printed on acid-free paper

9 8 7 6 5 4 3 2 1

springer.com

Dedication

This book is dedicated to Alexander Prelas, a young man who in his fight for life has shown great courage and determination. Our hope is that Alex's generation will show the same courage and determination in solving the energy crisis.

This book is also dedicated to our kids who will be challenged more than any other previous generations to find stable and affordable energy resources without harming the mother earth.

PREFACE

In the lifetimes of the authors, the world and especially the United States have received three significant "wake-up calls" on energy production and consumption. The first of these occurred on October 15, 1973 when the Yom Kippur War began with an attack by Syria and Egypt on Israel. The United States and many western countries supported Israel. Because of the western support of Israel, several Arab oil exporting nations imposed an oil embargo on the west. These nations withheld five million barrels of oil per day. Other countries made up about one million barrels of oil per day but the net loss of four million barrels of oil production per day extended through March of 1974. This represented 7% of the free world's (i.e., excluding the USSR) oil production. In 1972 the price of crude oil was about $3.00 per barrel and by the end of 1974 the price of oil had risen by a factor of 4 to over $12.00. This resulted in one of the worst recessions in the post World War II era. As a result, there was a movement in the United States to become energy independent. At that time the United States imported about one third of its oil (about five million barrels per day). After the embargo was lifted, the world chose to ignore the "wake-up call" and went on with business as usual.

The second "wake-up call" occurred on November 4, 1979 when the new government of Iran allowed "students" to take United States embassy employees hostage. At that point in time the United States was importing about 41% of its oil (about seven million barrels per day). During the 444 day crisis United States oil imports dropped to about four million barrels per day and the world had another tailspin into a deep recession. Oil prices went from $14 per barrel to $35 per barrel in 1981. There was a great deal of discussion about energy independence but when the hostage crisis abated, the world chose to go back to business as usual.

By the time of the First Gulf War which began on August 2, 1990 with Iraq's invasion of Kuwait, the United States was importing about seven million barrels of oil per day or about 42% of its oil. By the Second Gulf War, March 20, 2003, the United States was importing about 9.6 million barrels of oil (about 63% of its usage). Neither war stirred the embers of a significant energy independence movement because oil was still relatively cheap (under $30 per barrel in 2003).

The third "wake-up call" began in 2004 when the price of oil first rose to over $40 per barrel, then $50 and finally by August of 2005 it hit $60. In mid-2006 it hit a high of $75 per barrel but dropped back by the end of the year to $60. In 2007 prices continued to rise and hit $92 per barrel by October and $99 by December. In February 2008, it hit $103 per barrel and then by July hit an all time high of $147.02. The price of oil was finally tempered by a financial collapse in the fall of 2008 when it dropped below $40 per barrel by the end of the year. No one should take comfort. It took a financial collapse of the magnitude of the great depression of the 1930s to bring oil prices down. Oil prices will rise as economic activity picks up again. The question is, which countries will take this respite to invest in the energy infrastructure required to give them a competitive edge after the inevitable recovery.

The authors began working on this project in 1996 while revamping the curriculum for a course titled Energy Systems and Resources. This course was started by the late Prof. Walt Meyer in the 1970s after the oil embargo crisis. The course adopted the book Learning about Energy by David J. Rose in 1986. What became clear to us early on in the project was that in the 10 years since the publication of Rose's book a great deal had changed. Additionally, we decided that the course needed to encompass the depth and breadth of energy resources and the depth and breadth of the links between energy resources to social structure, environment, economy, food, medicine, health, terrorism, war and a host of other global human interactions. To tackle the problem of presenting these complex interactions in the course and eventually as a text, we began by closely examining every potential energy resource and began looking at systems that could be used to glean useful energy from the resource and the broader implications of these systems to the human condition.

This is the first volume of a three volume series. In this volume, Basics and Nonrenewable Sources, the focus is on the basic tools required to understand the complex interactions of energy and society (economy, population, finance, etc.), fundamentals (thermodynamics, heat transfer, etc.) as well as nonrenewable energy sources (coal, oil, natural gas and nuclear).

The second volume, Renewable and Other Potential Sources, discusses wind, solar, hydropower, geothermal, ocean, biomass, ethanol, fusion, space based power systems, hydrogen, advanced systems and fuel cells.

The third volume, Environmental Effects, Remediation, and Policies, looks at the impact of energy on the environment (e.g., acid rain, ozone depletion, global warming, emissions, pollution, etc.), green technologies (e.g., conservation, hybrid cars, electric vehicles, hydrogen economy, distribution systems etc.), policies (e.g., deregulation) and future trends.

This is perhaps the most opportunistic time in history to seriously address the world's energy problems. The lessons learned from 2004 to 2008 and the rise and fall of oil prices are that over dependence on a single energy resource is a recipe for disaster. Albeit, oil is unique in that it is a high energy density liquid fuel which is highly portable. It has fueled the economic development of the world from the great depression to the present and it permeates our lives in numerous ways (food production, chemicals, pharmaceuticals, transportation, world wide travel and freedom). It has made the United States the envy of the world and a role model for economic development. It has fueled the economic growth of South East Asia and has been the ambassador of globalization. It has been a source of greed, envy and conflict. It is a finite resource and even though there is money to be made in exploiting it until it runs dry, there is no wisdom to succumbing to greed. Oil's main benefit to mankind is that it is a treasure trove of complex organic molecules that should be used to produce critical chemicals and pharmaceuticals for generations to come. Yet, oil's main use today is in transportation where it is burned causing global warming and climate change.

Be optimistic in the fact that there are solutions to the energy independence problem. The solutions are not easy and will take leadership, vision and time to implement. There are technologies that can address one of the most significant issues on the table-the replacement of petroleum based transportation. There are technologies which change the way petroleum is used such as hybrid vehicles and plug in hybrid vehicles. There are technologies which eliminate petroleum such as the fuel cells, the electric vehicle, compressed air vehicles and fly wheel powered vehicles. Many of these concepts depend on enhancement of electrical generation resources. Political decisions will soon be made that will shape the future of countries, the world and world order. It is a mistake to think that any one single energy resources (e.g., wind or solar) or any group of energy resources (such as renewable) will lead to a stable solution to the world's energy problems. If the need for diversity in energy resources has not yet been recognized by our leaders after the near disasters caused by oil price volatility, than prepare for the worst because society will be doomed to make the same mistakes over and over again. It is important to be realistic- renewable energy resources are an important part of the solution but not the whole solution. The solution will also require a mix of nuclear energy, oil, natural gas and coal.

Do not forget that global climate change may cause drastic shifts in the weather patterns of regions where at present wind or solar are economical. Twenty or 30 years from now these regions might not be very economical for wind or solar energy. Having a stable electrical power base load to counter the whims of weather is a critical part of the solution to the energy problem.

This is an exciting time and a time where clear thinking and vision will determine winners and losers in the twenty-first century. We can only hope that our leaders show the wisdom that comes from lessons learned from the past and that they will not pander to special interests.

Tushar K. Ghosh
and
Mark A. Prelas

CONTENTS

1 INTRODUCTION

Abstract

The effect of energy in our life and society is enormous. Energy basically controls everyday aspects of our lives. Its impact on economy both at the local and global level is discussed in this chapter. Energy is necessary in two forms: liquid fuel, mainly for transportation, and electricity for computers, lighting, TV, air conditioners, and appliances that we use in our everyday life. The cross-over is possible, but often costly and technologically challenging to meet our current life style. Various general aspects of energy usage, their effect on environment, economy, and how it relates to population are discussed in this chapter.

1.1 Energy Sources

Energy is the lifeline of the economy for any country. Economic growth and development depend on the availability of cheap and affordable energy. The standard of living of citizens can be directly correlated to the use of energy. The demand for energy will only grow as we try to improve our quality of life. Energy can be defined as the ability to do work. Energy is used to do all types of work which is manifested in the form of movement, displacement, or light. Energy is available in various forms – gaseous, liquid and solid – from a variety of sources. However, these energy sources must be transformed into usable forms, such as mechanical (e.g., motion), electrical (e.g., electricity), heat, or light for practical use. For example, automobiles, airplanes, boats, and various machineries use gasoline, diesel, or other forms of petroleum products to generate heat which is then converted to mechanical energy to move or do work. The energy sources are generally classified into two categories:

1. Non-Renewable Energy Sources
2. Renewable Energy Sources

T.K. Ghosh and M.A. Prelas, *Energy Resources and Systems:*
Volume 1: Fundamentals and Non-Renewable Resources, 1–22.

A non-renewable energy source can be defined as a resource that is not replaced on a continuous basis or is replaced only very slowly, but dependent completely on natural processes. Fossil fuels that are considered non-renewable may continually be produced by the decay of plant and animal matter, but as shown in Table 1.1, the rate of their production is so slow that they are not going to be replaced in the next hundred million years, therefore, should be considered "used up", not available to us again. The following energy sources are considered non-renewable:

- Petroleum (Oil)
- Coal
- Natural Gas
- Uranium and Thorium (Nuclear Energy)

Table 1.1. Estimated geological-time for formation of anthracite coal in three USA deposits.

Formation	Age $(10^6$ years)	Average Formation Temperature (°C)
Upper Carboniferous, Oklahoma	270	100
Jurassic, Texas	160	175
Pliocene/Pleistocene, Salton Geo-thermal Fields, California	<2	290–300

Source: Adapted from [1].

Renewable energy is considered as any energy resource that is available naturally on a continuous basis or can be continually generated over a short period of time; which may be on a daily basis, or over several days, or several years. The renewable energy sources are derived directly from the sun (such as thermal, photo-chemical, and photoelectric), indirectly from the sun (such as wind, hydropower, and photosynthetic energy stored in biomass), or from other natural phenomena of the environment (such as geothermal and tidal energy). The most common renewable energy sources are:

- Solar energy
- Wind energy
- Hydropower energy
- Geothermal energy
- Ocean energy
- Biomass energy

As can be seen from Fig. 1.1, oil has been the world's foremost energy source for the last several decades, and it is expected to remain the dominant energy source worldwide at least through 2025. International Energy Outlook, 2008 projects [2] that the world use of oil and other liquids will increase at an annual rate of about 1.5%, or from 83.6 million barrels per day in 2005 to 95.7 million barrels per day by 2015 and to 112.5 million barrels per day in 2030. The question remains whether the world has enough reserves of oil to meet this demand.

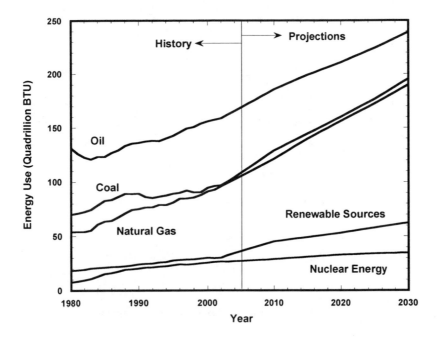

Fig. 1.1. World marketed energy use by fuel type [2].

1.2 Energy and Economy

The profound effect of energy on the economy is not properly understood by the general population. We feel the price shock of energy only at the gas station when filling up our cars. The increasing cost of energy affects every sector of the economy including food, transportation, petroleum based products, textile, steel, to name a few. Most of the equipment, machinery, manufacturing plants and office buildings could not function without an available supply of energy resources such as oil, natural gas, coal or electricity. Energy is such an important component to manufacturing and production that its availability has a direct impact on the GDP for the USA and the overall economic health of a country. The close relationship between energy and GDP is shown in Fig. 1.2. A similar relationship exists for all other countries.

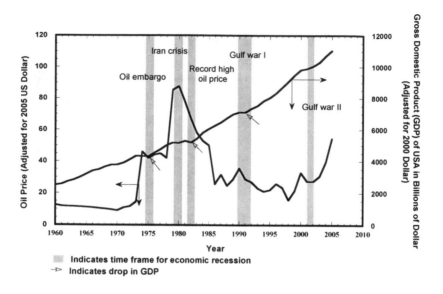

Fig. 1.2. Effect of oil price in the Gross Domestic Product (GDP) of USA [3, 4].

1.2.1 How Energy Price Shocks Affect the Economy

The events of the past several decades have shown us that the price and availability of a single energy resource – oil – can significantly affect the world economy [5–14]. It has been noted that when oil price rises, companies whose production methods depend on oil as the primary fuel tend to either reduce the number of goods manufactured or close the operation until oil price drops back to an affordable level. They might even initiate a reduction in the workforce at their manufacturing plants. Some companies may search for other sources of energy that are less expensive, but this option is not easy to implement in the short term. Often, it is difficult for companies to purchase machines and equipment that use other fuels. Since all prices are interrelated, oil price also determines the material manufacturing costs that will be used for developing other energy sources and their transportation costs. As a result, prices for alternative sources of energy tend to rise when oil prices increase. Some companies may decide to maintain current production levels while increasing the prices of the products. Combined, these factors can cause both recessionary and inflationary pressures on the economy, particularly for an oil importing country, such as the USA. However, it should be noted that the extent of the effect of an oil shock depends on a number of other factors too, such as, the length of the shock, the dependency of the economy on oil, and the policy response of monetary and fiscal authorities. Figure 1.3 shows that the USA and world experienced ten such recessions over the last 30 years due to oil price shock. However, as noted by the Federal Reserve Bank of Dallas [15], nine of the ten post-World War II recessions were preceded by sharply rising oil prices. Although the oil price yielded four false signals during the 1980's and 1990's, historical data still raises concerns about the relationship between oil price shock and recession.

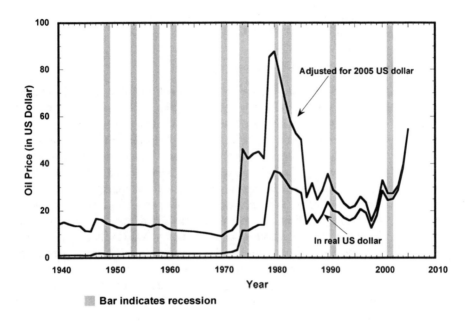

Fig. 1.3. Effect of global events on oil price and its subsequent impact on global economy [4, 15].

Events that affected these recessions are listed below.

- 1947: End of great depression
- 1951–1953: Korean war
- 1957: EEC formed
- 1959: Eisenhower imposes import quotas
- 1965: Vietnam troop increase begins
- 1971: US market control ends, Rail Road Commission of Texas (Texas RRC) 100% proration
- 1973: US import quotas ease to six million barrel per day (MMBPD)
- 1974–1975: US and global recession was triggered by the tripling of the price of oil following the Yom Kippur war and the following oil embargo of 1973
- 1980–1981: US and global recession was triggered by a spike in the price of oil following the Iranian revolution in 1979
- 1980–1988: Iran–Iraq war

- 1990–1991: US recession was partly caused by the spike in the price of oil following the Iraqi invasion of Kuwait in the summer of 1990
- 1997–1998: East Asian crisis
- 2001: US and global recession was partly caused by the sharp increase in the price of oil in 2000 following the California energy crisis and the tensions in the Middle East (the beginning of the second intifada). But other factors were more important: the bust of the internet bubble, the collapse of real investment and, in smaller measure, the Fed tightening between 1999 and 2000
- 2002: Venezuela civil unrest
- 2003: Gulf War II
- 2005: Effect of Rita/Katrina hurricanes

There is one notable exception to the oil price shock that did not lead to recession. In 2003, although the Gulf War II caused a spike in the oil price, it did not lead to recession, in part due to the short duration of the spike.

A sharp energy price drop, on the other hand, such as the one that occurred in the mid-1980s, stimulates the overall economy. Most producers and consumers benefit from lower energy costs. Both the cost of products decrease and the buying power of consumers' increases since less money is spend on energy.

The recent increase in the oil price (starting 2006) is no longer considered a price shock. It is rather based on the laws of supply and demand. The oil price is expected to rise as the demand increases and the supply is dwindling. As a consequence, business and industry are viewing this increase in oil price as permanent and making adjustments to compensate for higher energy prices.

The direct connection between energy and the economy of industrialized countries is evident from a number of other indicators: increase use of energy, stock market data, and inflation data. Increased electricity demand could be a direct measure of the health of the economy too. The growing use of electric-based technologies, such as telecommunications devices, computers and internet-oriented equipment, is an indicator of growth of the country's economy. For example, each percentage increase in real GDP between 1970 and 2000 has, in general, resulted in over 1% rise in the demand for electricity. The energy use and GDP of various countries are given in Appendix I.

A comparison of historical data (Fig. 1.4) of the Dow Jones Industrial Average and New York Stock Exchange (NYSE) with that of oil prices clearly shows a dip in the stock market when the oil price goes up. In most cases, the drop in the stock market is delayed by an average of 12 months (Table 1.2) due to a variety of reasons. One of the main reasons is that the effect of high oil price does not affect the economy immediately. The refineries and companies maintain a stock of crude petroleum for 6–8 months and it takes about 12 months for the refined or finished products to appear in the market.

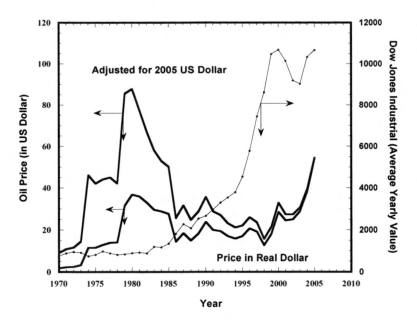

Fig. 1.4. Effect of oil price on Dow Jones Industrial [4, 16].

Table 1.2. Delay between oil price rise and New York Stock Exchange decline.

Oil peak	NASD peak	Months delay
Jul-74	Sep-75	14
Dec-79	Mar-81	15
Jul-87	Sep-87	2
Oct-90	Oct-91	12
Oct-96	Mar-98	17
Feb-00	Sep-00	7
Ave. # Months		~12

Source: Adapted from [17].

Another notable impact of oil price is on inflation. As shown in Fig. 1.5, the consumer price index, which is an indication of inflation, reacts sharply with the increase of oil price. One way to fight inflation is to slow down the economy by raising the interest rate, which generally has a negative impact on the economy.

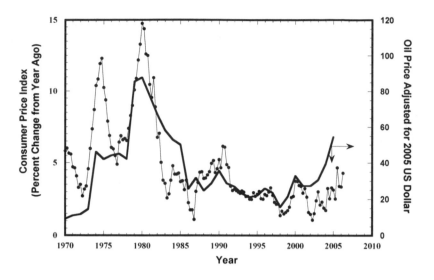

Fig. 1.5. Effect of oil price on consumer price index [4, 18].

1.2.2 Energy Dollar

Jobs and business activities are essential elements of a local economy and are often used to measure its health. Some local governments have realized the importance of "energy dollars" and how they relate to local economic health [19]. The annual energy bill for an entire community, i.e., all the money a community spends on energy purchases – the residential, commercial, industrial, agricultural, and institutional users – represents its energy dollars. Usually, a community's total utility bills (e.g., electric, gas) and petroleum product purchases (e.g., gasoline, fuel oil) represent the majority of energy dollars. If a community does not have its own energy sources, it must be purchased from other sources outside the community, resulting in energy dollars generated in the community leaving the community or state. The consequences are:

- Loss of economic power, community's economic health, and dependence on other states or countries for energy who in turn might try to manipulate the community's way of life.
- Loss of "economic multiplier" benefit that energy dollars could generate.

The economic multiplier, also known as the multiplier effect, is a measure of how much economic activity can be generated in a community by different combinations of purchasing and investment. For example, in Osage Beach, Missouri,

USA, a $1.00 purchase of ordinary consumer goods in a local store generates $1.90 of economic activity in the local economy. This occurs as the dollar is respent; the store pays its employees, who purchase more goods, all with the same original dollar. Petroleum products generate a multiplier of about $1.51; utility services, $1.66; and energy efficiency, $2.23. A higher economic multiplier will lead to greater economic vitality due to increased business activity and creation of new jobs. Economic growth is enhanced when expenditures with a good economic multiplier are implemented. This leads to growth in the local tax base and a healthier fiscal picture. Once energy dollars leave the community they can't be used to foster additional economic activity.

1.3 Energy and Population

Energy is one of the most basic needs of humans. We need energy to heat and air-condition our living spaces, to cook food, for transportation, and to generate electricity for a myriad purpose. Energy use is closely tied to health and well-being – low energy users have high infant mortality rates, low literacy rates and low life expectancies [20–22]. Worldwide, two billion people do not have access to electricity and use wood or dung for cooking and heating. Figure 1.6 shows the world population based on 2005 data. Although the world's population is projected to grow at just under 1% per year, the population by 2030 is expected to be approximately eight billion. This will put tremendous pressure on the energy needs of the world. First, we must meet the needs of the existing two billion people, who currently do not have access to suitable energy resources, and on top of that, the world has to meet the needs of energy for an additional two billion people that will be added to the existing population in the next 2 decades. As shown in Table 1.3, Europe will have negative growth, and North America will grow at less than 1% annually. Most of the growth is expected to be in developing non-Organization for Economic Cooperation and Development (non-OECD) regions. A significant population growth will occur in Africa, Latin America and Asia Pacific. More than 90% of the world's population growth will be in the developing world. As a consequence, the energy demand for the future as shown in Table 1.4 is expected to be highest in developing non-OECD regions.

(The Organization for Economic Cooperation and Development (OECD) consists of Australia, Austria, Belgium, Canada, Czech Republic, Denmark, Finland, France, Germany, Greece, Hungary, Iceland, Ireland, Italy, Republic of Korea, Japan, Luxembourg, Mexico, the Netherlands, New Zealand, Norway, Poland, Portugal, Slovak Republic, Spain, Sweden, Switzerland, Turkey, the United Kingdom and the United States).

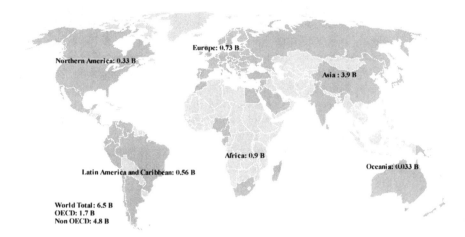

Fig. 1.6. World population distribution based on 2005 data [23].

Table 1.3. Project population growth in billions in different regions of the world [23].

Region	2005	Projection of Population Growth					% Change from 2005 to 2030
		2010	2015	2020	2025	2030	
Africa	0.905	1.006	1.115	1.228	1.344	1.463	61.65
Asia	3.905	4.130	4.351	4.554	4.728	4.872	24.76
Europe	0.728	0.725	0.721	0.714	0.707	0.698	− 4.12
Latin America and the Caribbean	0.561	0.598	0.634	0.667	0.697	0.722	28.69
Northern America	0.330	0.346	0.361	0.375	0.388	0.400	21.21
Oceania	0.033	0.035	0.037	0.038	0.041	0.042	27.27
World	6.464	6.842	7.219	7.577	7.905	8.199	26.84

Table 1.4. World Primary Energy Consumption (Quadrillion Btu), 2000–2004 (Quadrillion, 10^{15} Btu) [24].

Region/Country	2000	2001	2002	2003	2004
Bermuda	0.007	0.007	0.008	0.008	0.008
Canada	13.05	12.82	13.07	13.52	13.60
Greenland	0.008	0.008	0.008	0.008	0.008
Mexico	6.322	6.258	6.333	6.514	6.609
Saint Pierre and Miquelon	0.001	0.001	0.001	0.001	0.001
United States	98.97	96.49	97.96	98.27	100.41
North America	**118.36**	**115.59**	**117.39**	**118.32**	**120.64**
Antarctica	0.003	0.003	0.003	0.003	0.003
Antigua and Barbuda	0.007	0.007	0.007	0.008	0.008
Argentina	2.664	2.608	2.469	2.664	2.788
Aruba	0.013	0.013	0.013	0.014	0.014
Bahamas, The	0.047	0.046	0.047	0.056	0.057
Barbados	0.024	0.023	0.023	0.023	0.024
Belize	0.010	0.013	0.013	0.013	0.014
Bolivia	0.162	0.145	0.157	0.204	0.198
Brazil	8.582	8.502	8.601	8.709	9.078
Cayman Islands	0.005	0.005	0.005	0.005	0.005
Chile	1.014	1.052	1.080	1.137	1.181
Colombia	1.186	1.211	1.163	1.214	1.193
Costa Rica	0.151	0.156	0.165	0.171	0.186
Cuba	0.456	0.463	0.464	0.471	0.469
Dominica	0.001	0.002	0.002	0.002	0.002
Dominican Republic	0.262	0.251	0.274	0.307	0.301
Ecuador	0.344	0.360	0.364	0.375	0.383
El Salvador	0.108	0.114	0.113	0.123	0.123
Falkland Islands	0.0004	0.0004	0.0004	0.0004	0.0005
French Guiana	0.014	0.014	0.014	0.015	0.015
Grenada	0.002	0.003	0.003	0.003	0.004
Guadeloupe	0.026	0.026	0.027	0.028	0.028
Guatemala	0.155	0.167	0.166	0.175	0.180
Guyana	0.023	0.024	0.024	0.023	0.024
Haiti	0.024	0.026	0.026	0.026	0.027
Honduras	0.086	0.098	0.106	0.104	0.101
Jamaica	0.146	0.147	0.151	0.157	0.158
Martinique	0.028	0.028	0.029	0.030	0.032

(Continued)

Table 1.4. (Continued)

Region/Country	2000	2001	2002	2003	2004
Montserrat	0.001	0.001	0.001	0.001	0.001
Netherlands Antilles	0.155	0.157	0.150	0.144	0.153
Nicaragua	0.057	0.061	0.063	0.065	0.069
Panama	0.206	0.203	0.202	0.197	0.209
Paraguay	0.430	0.377	0.394	0.424	0.420
Peru	0.528	0.537	0.545	0.556	0.577
Puerto Rico	0.440	0.478	0.477	0.517	0.550
Saint Kitts and Nevis	0.001	0.001	0.001	0.002	0.002
Saint Lucia	0.005	0.005	0.005	0.006	0.006
Saint Vincent/Grenadines	0.003	0.003	0.003	0.003	0.003
Suriname	0.035	0.037	0.038	0.039	0.038
Trinidad and Tobago	0.420	0.473	0.500	0.539	0.593
Turks and Caicos Islands	NA	0.0002	0.0002	0.0002	0.0002
Uruguay	0.164	0.162	0.168	0.164	0.173
Venezuela	2.766	3.028	2.931	2.721	2.884
Virgin Islands, U.S.	0.138	0.199	0.198	0.231	0.244
Virgin Islands, British	0.001	0.001	0.001	0.001	0.001
Central & South America	**20.895**	**21.230**	**21.189**	**21.673**	**22.517**
Albania	0.096	0.091	0.094	0.114	0.114
Austria	1.382	1.441	1.445	1.505	1.456
Belgium	2.693	2.674	2.644	2.724	2.784
Bosnia and Herzegovina	0.211	0.208	0.220	0.222	0.215
Bulgaria	0.869	0.911	0.885	0.886	0.846
Croatia	0.376	0.384	0.378	0.398	0.387
Czech Republic	1.668	1.677	1.652	1.743	1.770
Denmark	0.876	0.887	0.854	0.895	0.864
Faroe Islands	0.010	0.010	0.010	0.010	0.011
Finland	1.219	1.240	1.261	1.318	1.346
France	10.871	11.092	11.007	11.125	11.250
Germany	14.261	14.620	14.339	14.585	14.693
Gibraltar	0.093	0.051	0.052	0.053	0.054
Greece	1.338	1.355	1.359	1.437	1.446
Hungary	1.027	1.056	1.056	1.079	1.065
Iceland	0.133	0.136	0.141	0.142	0.148
Ireland	0.597	0.625	0.625	0.612	0.637
Italy	7.634	7.682	7.704	7.981	8.265
Luxembourg	0.154	0.160	0.170	0.179	0.200

Region/Country	2000	2001	2002	2003	2004
Macedonia	0.115	0.106	0.106	0.116	0.112
Malta	0.039	0.033	0.039	0.039	0.041
Netherlands	3.794	3.929	3.939	4.001	4.103
Norway	1.955	1.871	1.936	1.825	1.941
Poland	3.628	3.458	3.449	3.618	3.667
Portugal	1.070	1.086	1.083	1.118	1.111
Romania	1.584	1.713	1.683	1.630	1.644
Serbia and Montenegro	0.627	0.663	0.745	0.743	0.772
Slovakia	0.798	0.816	0.819	0.799	0.797
Slovenia	0.293	0.300	0.303	0.301	0.330
Spain	5.531	5.786	5.867	6.178	6.402
Sweden	2.200	2.349	2.221	2.147	2.317
Switzerland	1.293	1.345	1.279	1.298	1.287
Turkey	3.161	2.892	3.146	3.311	3.533
United Kingdom	9.680	9.817	9.693	9.879	10.038
Europe	**81.277**	**82.464**	**82.204**	**84.013**	**85.647**
Armenia	0.162	0.164	0.164	0.175	0.180
Azerbaijan	0.519	0.520	0.614	0.612	0.655
Belarus	1.051	0.968	0.907	0.984	0.967
Estonia	0.197	0.205	0.204	0.224	0.223
Former U.S.S.R.	NA	NA	NA	NA	NA
Georgia	0.137	0.127	0.148	0.133	0.143
Kazakhstan	1.938	2.112	2.190	2.287	2.331
Kyrgyzstan	0.241	0.228	0.184	0.189	0.170
Latvia	0.153	0.160	0.153	0.160	0.172
Lithuania	0.296	0.317	0.338	0.353	0.356
Moldova	0.112	0.109	0.120	0.134	0.127
Russia	27.458	27.703	27.928	28.763	30.062
Tajikistan	0.241	0.247	0.251	0.270	0.272
Turkmenistan	0.401	0.502	0.584	0.759	0.808
Ukraine	5.755	5.646	5.833	6.260	6.486
Uzbekistan	1.941	2.033	2.088	2.120	2.227
Eurasia	**40.604**	**41.041**	**41.706**	**43.422**	**45.179**
Bahrain	0.365	0.377	0.397	0.408	0.414
Cyprus	0.103	0.112	0.110	0.111	0.114
Iran	5.006	5.380	5.880	6.171	6.449

(Continued)

Table 1.4. (Continued)

Region/Country	2000	2001	2002	2003	2004
Iraq	1.082	1.131	1.143	1.009	1.207
Israel	0.844	0.873	0.890	0.852	0.873
Jordan	0.224	0.220	0.230	0.249	0.280
Kuwait	0.908	0.919	0.886	0.990	1.061
Lebanon	0.234	0.224	0.228	0.232	0.238
Oman	0.341	0.347	0.360	0.356	0.374
Qatar	0.645	0.502	0.521	0.584	0.706
Saudi Arabia	4.845	5.130	5.375	5.751	6.100
Syria	0.791	0.761	0.815	0.813	0.824
United Arab Emirates	1.796	1.936	2.088	2.180	2.336
Yemen	0.143	0.147	0.152	0.159	0.164
Middle East	**17.324**	**18.060**	**19.075**	**19.864**	**21.139**
Algeria	1.237	1.254	1.275	1.292	1.239
Angola	0.091	0.119	0.127	0.135	0.141
Benin	0.024	0.024	0.026	0.030	0.030
Botswana	0.056	0.051	0.051	0.052	0.053
Burkina Faso	0.017	0.016	0.017	0.018	0.018
Burundi	0.007	0.007	0.007	0.008	0.008
Cameroon	0.081	0.082	0.078	0.084	0.086
Cape Verde	0.003	0.002	0.002	0.002	0.002
Central African Republic	0.005	0.005	0.006	0.006	0.006
Chad	0.003	0.003	0.003	0.003	0.003
Comoros	0.001	0.001	0.001	0.001	0.002
Congo (Brazzaville)	0.013	0.016	0.015	0.017	0.017
Congo (Kinshasa)	0.091	0.081	0.080	0.082	0.087
Cote d'Ivoire (IvoryCoast)	0.132	0.109	0.109	0.111	0.110
Djibouti	0.025	0.025	0.025	0.026	0.026
Egypt	2.007	2.255	2.271	2.454	2.523
Equatorial Guinea	0.004	0.004	0.049	0.006	0.006
Eritrea	0.009	0.010	0.010	0.011	0.011
Ethiopia	0.065	0.067	0.074	0.079	0.084
Gabon	0.037	0.038	0.038	0.039	0.040
Gambia, The	0.004	0.004	0.004	0.004	0.004
Ghana	0.143	0.141	0.131	0.125	0.142
Guinea	0.022	0.022	0.022	0.022	0.023
Guinea-Bissau	0.005	0.005	0.005	0.005	0.005
Kenya	0.143	0.145	0.150	0.165	0.175

Region/Country	2000	2001	2002	2003	2004
Lesotho	0.006	0.006	0.006	0.007	0.005
Liberia	0.006	0.007	0.007	0.007	0.007
Libya	0.629	0.666	0.696	0.683	0.749
Madagascar	0.031	0.033	0.037	0.035	0.036
Malawi	0.021	0.022	0.023	0.023	0.024
Mali	0.010	0.010	0.011	0.011	0.011
Mauritania	0.050	0.050	0.048	0.049	0.051
Mauritius	0.049	0.055	0.050	0.051	0.055
Morocco	0.445	0.480	0.488	0.491	0.444
Mozambique	0.092	0.100	0.133	0.125	0.139
Namibia	0.042	0.047	0.050	0.053	0.055
Niger	0.015	0.015	0.016	0.017	0.017
Nigeria	0.808	0.911	0.934	0.981	1.012
Reunion	0.042	0.044	0.044	0.044	0.044
Rwanda	0.012	0.012	0.012	0.013	0.013
Saint Helena	0.0003	0.0002	0.0002	0.0002	0.0002
Sao Tome and Principe	0.001	0.001	0.001	0.001	0.001
Senegal	0.063	0.063	0.064	0.064	0.067
Seychelles	0.008	0.008	0.012	0.012	0.012
Sierra Leone	0.013	0.013	0.014	0.014	0.014
Somalia	0.010	0.010	0.010	0.010	0.010
South Africa	4.551	4.637	4.519	4.889	5.119
Sudan	0.103	0.130	0.134	0.148	0.148
Swaziland	0.021	0.021	0.021	0.021	0.021
Tanzania	0.058	0.068	0.075	0.076	0.072
Togo	0.023	0.016	0.021	0.033	0.034
Tunisia	0.301	0.336	0.338	0.330	0.333
Uganda	0.033	0.035	0.037	0.039	0.041
Western Sahara	0.004	0.004	0.004	0.004	0.004
Zambia	0.096	0.112	0.111	0.118	0.122
Zimbabwe	0.210	0.192	0.193	0.195	0.204
Africa	**11.976**	**12.591**	**12.685**	**13.320**	**13.706**
Afghanistan	0.023	0.017	0.018	0.015	0.016
American Samoa	0.008	0.008	0.008	0.008	0.008
Australia	4.833	4.993	5.097	5.093	5.266
Bangladesh	0.503	0.552	0.584	0.623	0.658
Bhutan	0.017	0.018	0.018	0.018	0.020
Brunei	0.065	0.073	0.085	0.090	0.100

(Continued)

Table 1.4. (Continued)

Region/Country	2000	2001	2002	2003	2004
Burma	0.166	0.163	0.178	0.194	0.202
Cambodia	0.008	0.008	0.008	0.008	0.008
China	38.798	40.835	42.381	49.727	59.573
Cook Islands	0.001	0.001	0.001	0.001	0.001
East Timor	NA	NA	NA	NA	NA
Fiji	0.017	0.017	0.024	0.028	0.028
French Polynesia	0.011	0.011	0.011	0.013	0.013
Guam	0.039	0.042	0.029	0.033	0.034
Hawaiian Trade Zone	NA	NA	NA	NA	NA
Hong Kong	0.804	0.856	0.923	0.957	1.091
India	13.554	13.973	13.965	14.436	15.417
Indonesia	4.097	4.456	4.634	4.696	4.686
Japan	22.448	22.177	21.990	22.204	22.624
Kiribati	0.0003	0.0004	0.0004	0.0004	0.0004
Korea, North	0.859	0.882	0.847	0.871	0.891
Korea, South	7.922	8.018	8.423	8.691	8.985
Laos	0.046	0.047	0.047	0.049	0.050
Macau	0.022	0.024	0.026	0.027	0.032
Malaysia	1.871	2.106	2.245	2.459	2.519
Maldives	0.007	0.007	0.013	0.015	0.015
Mongolia	0.082	0.085	0.092	0.091	0.093
Nauru	0.002	0.002	0.002	0.002	0.002
Nepal	0.058	0.062	0.059	0.061	0.063
New Caledonia	0.026	0.025	0.028	0.028	0.028
New Zealand	0.865	0.860	0.899	0.871	0.884
Niue	0.00004	0.00004	0.00004	0.00004	0.00004
Pakistan	1.854	1.823	1.873	1.976	1.986
Papua New Guinea	0.046	0.046	0.061	0.069	0.075
Philippines	1.251	1.224	1.244	1.260	1.310
Samoa	0.002	0.002	0.002	0.002	0.002
Singapore	1.518	1.561	1.588	1.800	1.936
Solomon Islands	0.002	0.003	0.003	0.003	0.003
Sri Lanka	0.189	0.186	0.190	0.195	0.197
Taiwan	3.768	3.853	4.014	4.202	4.399
Thailand	2.577	2.697	2.940	3.227	3.423
Tonga	0.002	0.002	0.002	0.002	0.002
U.S. Pacific Islands	0.004	0.004	0.004	0.004	0.004
Vanuatu	0.001	0.001	0.001	0.001	0.001

Region/Country	2000	2001	2002	2003	2004
Vietnam	0.748	0.812	0.901	0.977	0.948
Wake Island	0.019	0.019	0.019	0.019	0.019
Asia & Oceania	**109.134**	**112.553**	**115.475**	**125.046**	**137.613**
World Total	399.574	403.534	409.726	425.663	446.442

Data for the most recent year are preliminary. Total primary energy consumption reported in this table includes the consumption of petroleum, dry natural gas, coal, and net hydroelectric, nuclear, and geothermal, solar, wind, and wood and waste electric power. Total primary energy consumption for each country also includes net electricity imports (electricity imports minus electricity exports). Electricity net imports are included because the net electricity consumption by energy type data, noted above, are really net electricity generation data that have not been adjusted to include electricity imports and exclude electricity exports. Total primary energy consumption for the United States also includes the consumption of geothermal, solar, and wood and waste energy not used for electricity generation. Sum of components may not equal total due to independent rounding.

Although the population growth in India, China, and other Asian countries is expected to be modest, the economy in terms of GDP is expected to grow at a much faster rate (Fig. 1.7). The global economy is expected to have a growth rate of 2.7% per year. The annual growth rate of China, India, Indonesia and Malaysia, is expected to be on average more than 5%. Their combined economic output can become equal or greater than that of Europe. Average annual growth in GDP of various countries in the last several years and the projections for the future growth is given in Table 1.5.

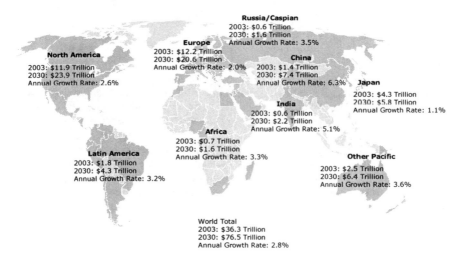

Fig. 1.7. Project GDP of various region of the world by 2030 [25].

Table 1.5. Average Annual Growth in World Gross Domestic Product by Selected Countries and Regions, 1973–2030 (Percent per year) [26].

Region	History				Projections		
	1978-2003	2003	2004	2005	2005–2015	2015–2030	2003–2030
OECD North America	2.9	2.5	4.1	3.5	3.1	2.9	3.1
United States	2.9	2.7	4.2	3.6	3.1	2.9	3.0
Canada	2.8	2.0	2.9	2.9	2.6	1.8	2.2
Mexico	2.9	1.4	4.4	3.1	4.0	4.1	4.1
OECD Europe	2.4	1.4	2.6	1.9	2.3	2.1	2.2
OECD Asia	3.0	1.9	3.0	2.6	2.3	1.6	1.9
Japan	2.5	1.4	2.6	2.4	1.7	1.0	1.4
South Korea	6.7	3.1	4.7	4.0	4.7	2.8	3.6
Australia/New Zealand	3.3	3.2	3.6	2.3	2.5	2.4	2.5
Total OECD	2.7	2.0	3.4	2.7	2.7	2.4	2.6
Non-OECD Europe and Eurasia	- 0.3	7.7	8.1	6.5	4.9	3.7	4.4
Russia	- 0.5	7.3	7.2	6.1	4.2	3.3	3.9
Other	0.2	8.0	9.5	7.0	5.9	4.0	5.1
Non-OECD Asia	6.7	7.6	7.8	7.5	5.8	4.9	5.5
China	9.4	9.1	9.5	9.2	6.6	5.2	6.0
India	5.3	8.5	6.9	6.8	5.5	5.1	5.4
Other	5.4	4.8	6.0	5.4	4.9	4.3	4.6
Middle East	2.6	4.8	6.4	6.7	4.4	3.7	4.2
Africa	2.9	4.8	5.1	4.9	4.8	4.1	4.4
Central and South America	2.3	2.1	5.9	4.5	3.8	3.5	3.8
Brazil	2.5	0.5	4.9	2.7	3.7	3.3	3.5
Total Non-OECD	3.7	6.4	7.2	6.7	5.3	4.5	5.0
Total World							
Purchasing Power Parity Rates	3.1	4.0	5.1	4.6	4.0	3.6	3.8
Market Exchange Rates	2.8	3.5	4.1	3.1	3.1	2.6	3.0

All regional real GDP growth rates presented in this table are based on 2000 purchasing power parity weights for the individual countries in each region, except for the final line in the table, which presents world GDP growth rates based on 2000 market exchange rate weights for all countries.

Sources: International Energy Outlook 2006, Report # DOE/EIA-0484 (2006); Historical Growth Rates: Global Insight, Inc., World Overview (Lexington, MA, Various issues). Projected GDP Administration, Annual Energy Outlook 2006, DOE/EIA-0383 (2006) (Washington DC, February 2006). GDP growth rates for China and India were adjusted downword based on the analyst's judgment.

As mentioned earlier, the increase in economic development or growth is tied to the increase use of energy. The need of energy for the world will increase from 205 MBDOE in 2000 to nearly 335 MBDOE in 2030. The regional increase in energy need is given in Table 1.6.

Table 1.6. World Marketed Energy Consumption by Country Grouping, 2003–2030 in Quadrillion Btu [26].

Region	2003	2010	2015	2020	2025	2030	Average Annual Percent Change, 2003–2030
OECD	234.3	256.1	269.9	281.6	294.5	308.8	1.0
North America	118.3	131.4	139.9	148.4	157.0	166.2	1.3
Europe	78.9	84.4	87.2	88.7	91.3	94.5	0.7
Asia	37.1	40.3	42.8	44.4	46.1	48.0	1.0
Non-OECD	186.4	253.6	293.5	331.5	371.0	412.8	3.0
Europe and Eurasia	48.5	56.5	62.8	68.7	74.0	79.0	1.8
Asia	83.1	126.2	149.4	172.8	197.1	223.6	3.7
Middle East	19.6	25.0	28.2	31.2	34.3	37.7	2.4
Africa	13.3	17.7	20.5	22.3	24.3	26.8	2.6
Central and South America	21.9	28.2	32.5	36.5	41.2	45.7	2.8
Total World	420.7	509.7	563.4	613.0	665.4	721.6	2.0

Most of the energy requirement will be in the form of electricity, which is expected to grow at 2% per year. Because of this strong demand for electricity, the use of natural gas and coal is expected to experience the highest rates of growth, at 1.8% annually each. Much of the growth in coal will take place in Asia, where there are large supplies. Other forms of energy, such as nuclear, hydropower, wind, biomass and other renewable sources, together will grow at 1.6% annually. The increase in energy usage is expected to be in all four sectors as shown in Fig. 1.8. However, most of the growth is expected to be in industrial sectors. The uses of energy in various sectors in the USA from various resources are given in Appendix I.

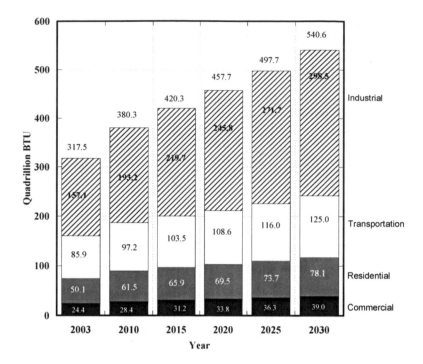

Fig. 1.8. Increase in energy demand by various sectors in 2030 [26].

1.4 Energy and Environment

Energy use and protection of environment go hand-to-hand and is essential for sustainable economic development. Lack of access to clean, affordable energy services can cause environmental degradation, such as climate change, loss of biodiversity and ozone layer depletion. These issues are global and cannot be addressed by countries acting alone. The effect of energy use on the environment is discussed in detail in Volume 3 of this book series. Suffice it to say, that the cost of energy does not price in the environmental impact of the energy source with one exception, nuclear energy. Nuclear energy as part of its cost includes long-term waste disposal as well as decommissioning of the plant. Eventually the cost of carbon emissions may be accounted for through international agreements. The Kyoto Protocol is a first step in what may be sweeping changes motivated by global warming.

1.5 Energy and Food Price

The availability of energy and its price is beginning to affect both the supply and price of food worldwide. The cost of fertilizer, transportation of raw materials, and the use of machinery for both planting and harvesting of agricultural products depend on the cost and availability of energy. Additionally, the use of corn for the production of ethanol was encouraged by the USA energy policy. The consequence of this policy is that it has put enormous strain on worldwide grain supplies. These issues are discussed in details in Volume 3 of the book series.

References

1. Lopatin NV, Bostick NH (1973) Nature of organic matter in recent and fossil sediments. Nauka Press, Moscow
2. Energy Information Administration (EIA) www.eia.doe.gov/iea/
3. National Economic Accounts, Bureau of Economic Analysis, US Department of Commerce, bea.gov/bea/dn/home/gdp.htm.
4. Energy Information Administration (2006) Spot prices for crude oil and petroleum products. tonto/eia/doe/gov/dnav/pet/pet_pri_spt_s1_d.htm.
5. Perron P (1989) The Great crash, the oil price shock, and the unit root hypothesis. Econometrica 57(6): 1361–1401
6. Zivot E, Andrews DWK (1992) Further evidence on the great crash, the oil-price shock, and the unit-root hypothesis. Journal of Business & Economic Statistics, 10(3): 251–270
7. Bernanke BS, Gertler M, Watson M, Sims CA, Friedman BM (1997) Systematic Monetary Policy and the Effects of Oil Price Shocks. Brookings Papers on Economic Activity 91–157
8. Sadorsky P (1999) Oil price shocks and stock market activity. Energy Economics 21(5): 449–469
9. Jones DW, Leiby PN, Paik IK (1998) Oil Price Shock and The Macroeconomy: What Has Been Learned Since 1996. The Findings of the DOE Workshop on Economic Vulnerability to Oil Price Shocks: Summary and Integration with Previous Knowledge Oak Ridge National Laboratory September
10. Jones CM, Kaul G (1996) Oil and the stock market. Journal of Finance 51: 463–491
11. Kaul G, Seyhun HN (1990) Relative price variability, real shocks, and the stock market. Journal of Finance 45: 479–496
12. Keane MP, Prasad ES (1996) The employment and wage effects of oil price changes: a sectoral analysis. Review of Economics and Statistics 78: 389–399
13. Kim I-M, Loungani P (1992) The role of energy in real business cycles. Journal of Monetary Economics 29: 173–189
14. Cobo-Reyes R, Pérez Quirós G (2005) The effect of oil price on industrial production and on stock returns. The Papers 05/18, Department of Economic Theory and Economic History of the University of Granada

15. Brown SPA (2004) Do Energy Price Threaten the Recovery? Southwest Economy. Federal Reserve Bank of Dallas, 3
16. Dow Jones Industrial Average Index (2006). http://finance.yahoo.com/q/hp?s=%5EDJI, 12/12/2006
17. McMahon T, Is Oil Predicting a Stock Market Crash? Financial Trend Forcaster, http://www.fintrend.com/ftf/Articles/OilCorrelation.asp
18. U.S. Department of Labor Bureau of Labor Statistics (2006) Consumer Price Indexes. www.bls.gov 12/12/06
19. Hope M (2006) 2000 Energy dollar flow analysis for the state of Arizona, Arizona Department of Commerce Energy Office. 12/12/06 http://www.azcommerce.com/doclib/energy/az%202000%20dollar%20flow%20analysis.pdf
20. Darmstadter J (2003) Energy and Population in Encyclopedia of Population, 1, Eds. P. Demeny and G. McNicoll, Macmillan Reference, USA
21. Duncan RC (2001) World energy production, population growth, and the road to the Olduvai Gorge. Population & Environment 22(5): 503–522
22. Holdren JP (1991) Population and the energy problem, Population & Environment. 12(3): 231–255
23. United Nations Population Division (2006) World Population Prospects: The 2004 Revision Population Database. http://esa.un.org/unpp/p2k0data.asp, 12/12/2006
24. Energy Information Administration (2006) International Energy Annual 2004. http://www.eia.doe.gov/pub/international/iealf/tablee1.xls July 2006
25. Gardner DJ (2005) The Outlook for Energy: A 2030 View, Corporate Planning Department. ExxonMobil Asilomar Conference August 24, 2005
26. Energy Information Administration, International Energy Outlook 2006, DOE/EIA-0484 (2006), June 2006

Problems

1. What is oil price shock and how does it affect the local and global economy?
2. Can the oil price increase of 2005–2007 be considered a price shock? Does this price increase have the same effect as other oil price increases?
3. What is an energy dollar? Determine the value of an energy dollar of your community.
4. What are the consequences of population growth? Can the world meet the energy needs of the anticipated world population in 2030?

2 ENGINEERING ECONOMICS

Abstract

Engineers involved in construction and evaluation of a project should have a basic understanding of engineering economics. For most of the large projects, such as construction of a power plant, money is borrowed from investors or banks. A cost-benefit analysis, rate of return, pay out period, etc. must be performed before venturing into a project. Among several other factors, the project director must be familiar with the cash flow, interest on the borrowed money, and timely completion of the project. Familiarity with interest rates, depreciation rates, and salvage values of equipment are equally important in understanding the economic viability of a project. All these topics are discussed in this chapter.

2.1 Introduction

The decision to construct any plant depends on two major issues: technical feasibility and economical feasibility of the system. Once the technical feasibility of the system is determined, economical feasibility is addressed. This approach is the same if one is constructing a coal power plant or buying a piece of equipment. Before purchasing or replacing a major piece of equipment, engineers must conduct a detailed cost analysis. The questions that need to be answered include, should one take a loan, what will be the interest rate, how long it will take to pay off for the new equipment, what will be the cash flow during this time period, what should be the rate of depreciation, what should be the salvage value, etc. Figure 2.1 shows the concept of cash flow for an industrial operation. Once this information become available, the design engineer must analyze the costs and profits of the particular project before making a decision to go ahead with the investment. A capital investment is required for any industrial operation and a cost-benefit analysis is usually done before investing any capital. The investment may be in the form of purchasing equipment, construction of a plant, or getting

T.K. Ghosh and M.A. Prelas, *Energy Resources and Systems:*
Volume 1: Fundamentals and Non-Renewable Resources, 23–76.

equipment on loan. The total investment for any project should include fixed capital investment, working capital, purchasing or stocking of raw materials and handling, cost for maintaining an inventory of finished products, etc.

As shown in Fig. 2.1, input to the capital sink can be in the form of loans, stock issues, bond releases or any other funding opportunities. Output from the capital source generally includes total capital investments, dividends to stock holders, repayment of debts or loans. Another item that must be kept in mind is the depreciation, which must be recognized as a cost before income tax charges are made and before net profit is reported to the relevant parties.

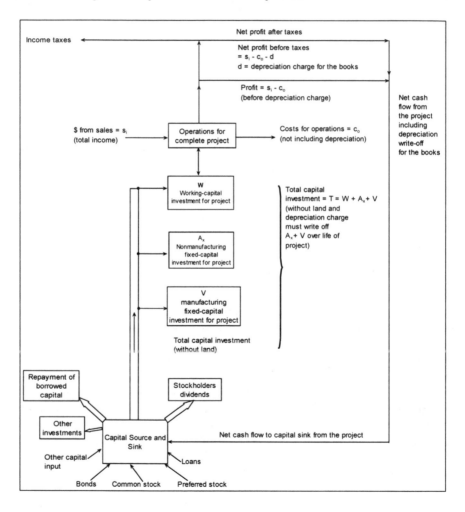

Fig. 2.1. Cash flow diagram for industrial operations (Printed with permission from [1]).

Symbols

A	Uniform amount per interest period, or annual amount, $
B	Present worth of all benefits, $
BV_j	Book value at the end of jth year , $
C	Cost or present worth of all costs, $
d	Declining balance, or depreciation rate, decimal
D	Depreciation, $
DR	Present worth of after-tax depreciation recovery, %
e	Constant inflation rate, decimal
E	Initial amount for exponentially growing cash flow, $
EAA	Equivalent uniform annual cost, $
EUAC	Equivalent uniform annual cost, $
f	Federal income tax rate, decimal
F	Future worth, value or amount, $
g	Exponential growth rate, decimal
G	Uniform gradient amount per interest period, $
i	Effective rate per period, decimal
i'	Effective rate per period corrected for inflation, decimal
k	Member of compounding, per year
m	Integer, or number of compounding periods per year
n	Number of compounding periods, or life of asset
P	Present worth, value, or amount, $
r	Nominal rate per year, decimal
ROI	Return on investment, $
ROR	Rate of return, decimal
s	State income tax rate, decimal
S_n	Expected salvage value in year n, $
t	Composite tax rate, decimal
t	Time, years
TC	Tax credit, $
i_e	Effective interest rate per period, decimal

Subscripts

j	at time j
n	at time n
t	at time t

2.2 Cash Flow Diagrams

A cash flow diagram is a pictorial representation of financial transaction that shows all cash inflows and outflows when plotted along a horizontal line that presents the time [2–8]. The pictorial representation is shown in the examples to follow. The horizontal line (see Example 2.1) is divided into equal time intervals. Depending on the time line of cash flow, the horizontal line may be divided into days, weeks, or years. Each cash flow, such as a payment or receipt, is plotted along this line at the beginning or end of the period in which it occurs. Funds that are paid out are considered negative cash flows and are represented by arrows which extend downward from the time line. Funds that are received, such as income or profits, are represented by arrows extending outward from the line. This is explained further in the following examples.

Example 2.1

A mechanical device will cost $20,000 when purchased. The maintenance cost is $1,000/year. The device will generate $5,000 each year for 5 years. The expected salvage value is $7,000. Show the transactions using a cash flow diagram.

Solution

All the cash transactions are shown in the diagram.

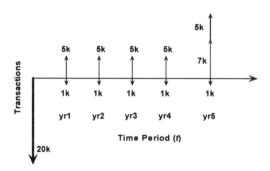

The equivalent cash flow diagram can be drawn as follows.

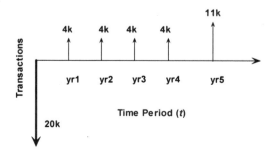

Example 2.2

Assume a nuclear power plant costs 5 billion dollars, rate income is 1.0 billion/year, interest payments/year is 0.3 billion, labor costs 0.2 billion/year, refueling costs 0.1 billion/year, plant lifetime is 50 years and decommissioning cost after 50 years is 1 billion. Present this information in a cash flow diagram.

Solution

All the cash flows are as follows.

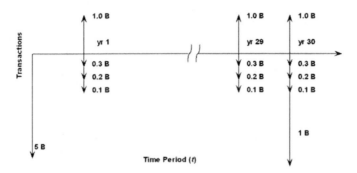

The equivalent cash flow diagram is as follows.

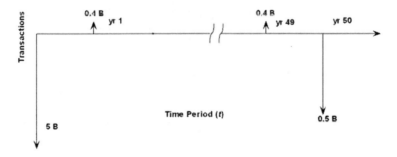

2.3 Types of Cash Flow

Cash flow may be divided into five categories depending on how the payments are made through the time period of interest.

(a) Single payment cash flow
(b) Uniform series cash flow
(c) Gradient series cash flow

(d) Exponential gradient cash flow

(e) Irregular series cash flow

Several assumptions are made when developing these cash flow diagrams and these are:

- Year-end convention is applied, i.e., all cash flow transactions are placed at the end of an interest period.
- There is no inflation now or at any time during the lifetime of the project.
- A before-tax analysis is needed.
- The effective interest rate is constant.
- Non-quantifiable factors can be disregarded.
- Funds invested in a project are available.
- Excess funds earn interest.

(a) *A single payment cash flow*: It can begin at $t = 0$, $t = n$ or at any t in between. The cash flow is denoted by P and is shown below.

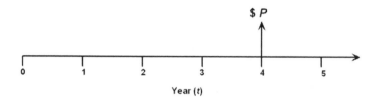

Year (t)

(b) *The uniform series cash flow*: It consists of a series of equal transactions starting at $t = 1$ and ending at $t = n$. The amount of each individual cash flow may be represented by P.

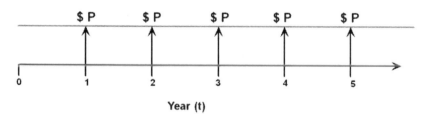

Year (t)

(c) *The gradient series cash flow*: It assumes the total time period (t) as n. The cash flow starts at $t = 1$ as shown below and increases by G each year until $t = n$, at which time the final cash flow is $(n - 1)G$.

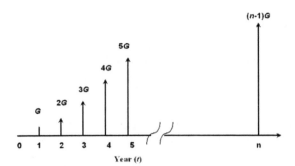

(d) *An exponential gradient cash flow*: It is based on a phantom value (E_0) at $t = 0$ and grows or decays exponentially:

Cash flow at time $t = E_t = E_0(1+g)^t$ (2.1)

where, $t = 1, 2, 3,....n$
g = exponential growth rate

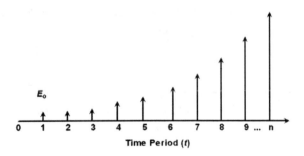

(e) *Irregular series cash flow:* As the name suggests, the cash flow can occur at any time and also the amount can vary.

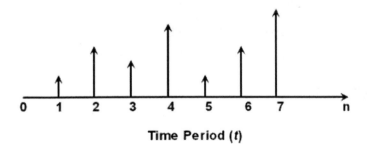

2.4 Simple and Compound Interest

When money is borrowed, a fee called "interest" is charged by the lender for the use of that money for a given period of time. The borrower has to pay back both the original amount borrowed (the principal) and the interest that will be accumulated during the borrowing period. The amount of interest depends on the interest rate, the amount of money borrowed (principal) and the length of time that the money is borrowed. Similarly, when one deposits money in a bank, the bank pays interest to the deposited amount. In this case, the bank is the borrower and the individual deposited the money is the lender. The interest can be *simple interest* or *compound interest*. The difference between these two interest rates is explained below.

Simple Interest: In the case of simple interest, the interest earned or charged is directly proportional to the principal involved in the process.

A mathematical formula for Simple Interest can be written as:

$$Interest = Principle \times Rate \times Time \tag{2.2}$$

Compound Interest: Interest which is calculated not only on the initial principal but also the accumulated interest of prior periods.

Example 2.3

One hundred dollars have been deposited in a bank account that gives 5% compound interest. Calculate the total amount at the end of 3 years.

Solution

Year 0	$100
Year 1	$100 + ($100)(0.05) = ($100) (1.05) = $105
Year 2	($105) (1.05) = $110.25
Year 3	($110.25) (1.05) = $115.76

Here interest was earned on both principal and interest from previous years.

2.5 Equivalence

2.5.1 Economic Equivalence

Economic equivalence is the concept of linking different cash flows to different alternatives so that comparisons based on economic worth can be made [9]. Total money generated at different points in time must be compared when evaluating investment alternatives. In order to make this evaluation, all the characteristics of cash flow need to be analyzed on an equivalent basis. The following three factors are involved in determining the economic equivalence:

- The amount of money
- The time of occurrence
- The rate of interest

Suppose a bank has an interest rate of 5%. One can put $100 in the bank at $t = 0$. After 1 year the money increases to $105. After 2 years the money increases to $110.25. The equivalent cash flow diagrams for these cases are shown below.

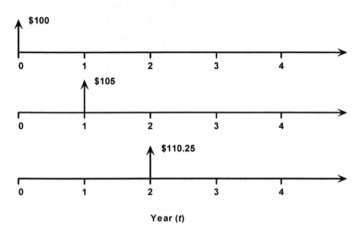

Year (t)

Example 2.4

Suppose the bank has an interest rate of 5%. You would like to invest $1000 over 10 years. You have two alternatives; either put all $1,000 now at $t = 0$, or invest $100 each year over the next 10 years. Which investment is better?

Solution

We will make some assumption to simplify the problem. All the interest is paid at the end of the year. The money is invested at the beginning of the year and does not get any interest until the end of the year. A comparison of the two investments is presented in Table 2.1

Table 2.1. Comparison of two investments.

	Cash accumulation at the end of each year						
	0	1	2	4	6	8	10
Investment 1	1,000	1,050	1,102.5	1,215.50	1,340.10	1,477.45	1,628.90
Investment 2	100	205	315.25	552.56	814.20	1,102.65	1,420.68

Investment 1 is better than investment 2. It should be noted that in making this evaluation, we have used the same time period (10 years) and the interest rate remained the same over the 10 years and was same for both $100 and $1000 investment. It should be noted that although investment 1 is better, if the same amount is invested in stocks, because of the fluctuations, investment 2 may be better.

2.5.2 Single Payment Equivalence

In the previous problem, we calculated the cash accumulation on year by year basis. The same calculation can be performed using a mathematical formula and is discussed below. The equivalence of any present amount P at $t = 0$ to any future amount F at $t = n$ is called future worth. The following expression provides the relationship between P, F, time period (t), and interest rate (i).

$$F = P(1+i)^n \tag{2.3}$$

Inversely,

$$P = F(1+i)^{-n} = \frac{F}{(1+i)^n} \tag{2.4}$$

where, $(1+i)^{-n}$ = single payment present worth factor, and i = effective interest rate over the time period.

Example 2.5

If you have a savings account with an effective annual rate of 10%, how much would you put in to have $10,000 after 5 years?

Solution

Here, the future worth $F = 10000$, $i = 0.1$, and $n = 5$. Therefore, the present worth (P) or the amount that needs to be deposited now is given by:

$$P = F(1+i)^{-n} = \frac{F}{(1+i)^n} = \frac{10000}{(1+0.1)^5}$$

Or, $P = \$6,209.21$

The problem can be represented by the cash flow diagram as follows

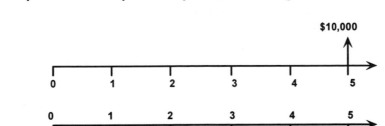

2.6 Minimum Attractive Rate of Return

Often times the interest rate at which a project should be evaluated needs to be established. A target rate or a cut-off rate should be determined. This rate is called the Minimum Attractive Rate of Return (MARR). A company may have an established policy to set a MARR on all of its investment. For example, if a bank has a rate of return of 5% in a simple account, the company may decide that 5% is the MARR.

2.7 Various Algebraic Expressions or Formulas

In Engineering Economics, various special notations are used to describe a problem mathematically. These are described below. The future worth (F) is described as:

$$F = P\left(F/_P, i\%, n\right) \tag{2.5}$$

If P is given, this formula finds F.

Similarly, if F is given, P can be found from the following expression.

$$P = F(P/_F, i\%, n) \tag{2.6}$$

In general, the notation meaning is as follows,

(What you want to find/what you are given, $i\%$, n)

This notation can be more easily grasped if you consider the following algebraic approach. If you know the formula for the ratio of F/P, then you can find F by multiplying the ratio by P,

$$F = P \times \frac{F}{P} \tag{2.7}$$

Suppose that you also know the ratio of (P/A). Then, if you want to find the ratio (F/A) you can calculate it by using the ratio of P/A and F/P.

$$\left(\frac{F}{P}\right) \times \left(\frac{P}{A}\right) = \frac{F}{A} \tag{2.8}$$

where A is annual cash flow. We see then that the notation introduced previously, can be used in the same way that algebraic ratios are used. For example, if we want to find A, and if we are given a uniform gradient then we may use the formula for $(P/G, i\%, n)$ and $(A/P, i\%, n)$ as shown below,

$$A = G\left(\frac{P}{G}, i\%, n\right) \left(\frac{A}{P}, i\%, n\right) \tag{2.9}$$

Various conversion factors for other cases can be generated in the same manner and are given in Table 2.2. In this table a number of common conversion factors are given that show the symbol equivalent and the corresponding formula. These conversion factors can be used to solve a wide variety of problems in economics and specifically in engineering economics.

Table 2.2. Formula for calculating various factors.

Factor name	Converts	Symbol	Formula
Single payment compound amount	P to F	(F/P, i%, n)	$(1+i)^n$
Single payment present worth	F to P	(P/F, i%, n)	$(1+i)^{-n}$
Uniform series sinking fund	F to A	(A/F, i%, n)	$\dfrac{i}{(1+i)^n - 1}$
Capital recovery	P to A	(A/P, i%, n)	$\dfrac{i(1+i)^n}{(1+i)^n - 1}$
Uniform series compound amount	A to F	(F/A, i%, n)	$\dfrac{(1+i)^n - 1}{i}$

Factor name	Converts	Symbol	Formula
Uniform series present worth	A to P	(P/A, i%, n)	$\dfrac{(1+i)^n-1}{i(1+i)^n}$
Uniform gradient present worth	G to P	(P/G, i%, n)	$\dfrac{(1+i)^n-1}{i^2(1+i)^n}-\dfrac{n}{i(1+i)^n}$
Uniform gradient future worth	G to F	(F/G, i%, n)	$\dfrac{(1+i)^n-1}{i^2}-\dfrac{n}{i}$
Uniform gradient uniform series	G to A	(A/G, i%, n)	$\dfrac{1}{i}-\dfrac{n}{(1+i)^n-1}$

In the following example, we demonstrate the use of the notation and formula given in Table 2.2.

Example 2.6

What factor will convert a gradient cash flow ending at $t = 8$? What is $(F/G, i\%, n)$? The effective annual interest rate is 10%.

Solution

From the table, $(F/G, 10\%, 8) = \dfrac{(1+i)^n-1}{i^2}-\dfrac{n}{i}$

$$(F/G, 10\%, 8) = \frac{(1+0.1)^8-1}{(0.1)^2}-\frac{8}{0.1} = 34.3589$$

The cash flow diagram for this problem is shown below.

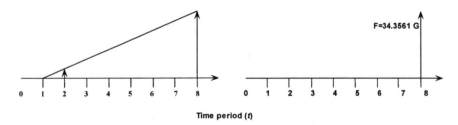

Time period (t)

2.8 Use of Formula for Cash Flow Calculation

2.8.1 Gradient Cash Flow

It is common to see uniformly increasing cash flow. However, the gradient series cash flow involves an increase of a fixed amount in the cash flow at the end of each period. The present worth of such a cash flow can be found by using the uniform gradient factor,

$$\left(P/_{G}, i\%, n\right) \tag{2.10}$$

This factor finds the present worth of a uniform gradient cash flow that starts in year 2 *not* in year 1.

1. This assumes that the increasing cost begin at the end of year 1 because of the year end convention. After year 1, costs begin to increase. (*P/G*) find the relative worth of only the increasing part of the annual expenses. The present worth of the base expense incurred at $t = 1$ and must be found separately with (*P/A*).
2. (*P/G*, *i%*, *n*) has only $n - 1$ actual cash flow. *n* must be defined as the last period number in which the last gradient cash flow occurs, *not* the number of gradient cash flow.
3. The sign convention used with a gradient cash flow is as follows: if an expense increases each year, the gradient is negative. If the revenue increases each year, the gradient is positive.

Example 2.7

Maintenance on an old machine is $100 this year but is expected to increase $25 per year thereafter. What is the present worth of 5 years of maintenance if $i = 10\%$?

Solution

The cash flow diagram is shown below.

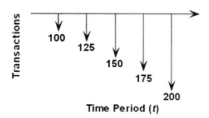

The cash flow can be broken down into two parts as follows:

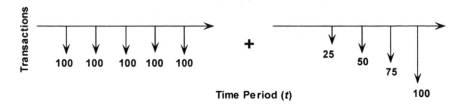

$$P = A(P/A, i\%, n) + G(P/G, i\%, n)$$

where, $i = 10\%$, $n = 5$

$$P = (-100)\frac{(1+i)^n - 1}{i(1+i)^n} + (-25)\left(\frac{(1+i)^n - 1}{i^2(1+i)^n} - \frac{n}{i(1+i)^n}\right)$$

$$P = (-100)\frac{(1+0.1)^5 - 1}{0.1 \times (1+0.1)^5} + (-25)\left(\frac{(1+0.1)^5 - 1}{(0.1)^2(1+0.1)^5} - \frac{5}{0.1 \times (1+0.1)^5}\right)$$

$$P = (-100)(3.7908) - 25(6.8618)$$

$$P = -\$551$$

2.8.2 Stepped Cash Flow

Use superposition of cash flow as we did in the previous example.

Example 2.8

An investment costing $1,000 returns $100 for the first 5 years, and returns $200 for the following 5 years. Find present worth.

Solution

The transactions for this investment can be described by the following cash flow diagram.

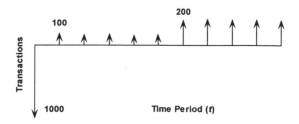

Using the superposition method, the same problem can be divided into two sub problems with equal amount of cash flow for the said time period.

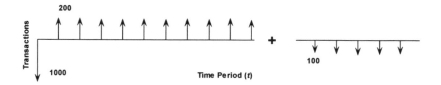

The present worth may be calculated from the following formula.

$$P = -1000 + 200(P/A, i\%, 10) - 100(P/A, i\%, 5)$$

Problems may arise when the cash flow does not match the standard models. For example, how to handle a missing or extra part of cash flow is shown in the figure below?

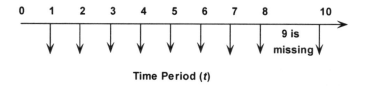

The way to do this is to superimpose two series so that the result adds up to the non-standard cash flow such as the one shown above. This type of problem can be solved by adding the present worth for the entire time period and then subtracting a single future payment for the missing year. The above problem may be expressed as follows. The expression for the present worth is given by:

$$P = A(P/A, i\%, 10) - A(P/F, i\%, 9)$$

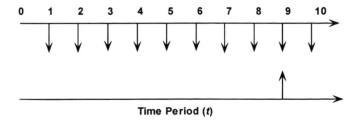

Time Period (*t*)

The same series can be represented by finding the present worth with an annual series over 8 years and then adding the present worth of a single payment in the 10th year. In this case the present worth is given by:

$$P = A(P/A, i\%, 8) + A(P/F, i\%, 10)$$

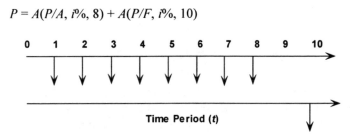

Time Period (*t*)

2.8.3 Delayed and Premature Cash Flow

In the delayed and premature cash flow problem, the present worth is first referenced to year 2. The cash flow diagram for $P' = -75 (P/A, i\%, 7)$ can be expressed as:

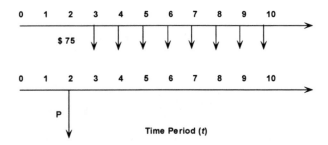

Time Period (*t*)

In this case, first find the present worth of future value P' referenced to $t = 0$ by:

$$P = P' (P/F, i\%, 2) = -75 (P'/A, i\%, 7) (P/F, i\%, 2)$$

The cash flow diagram will look like the one shown below.

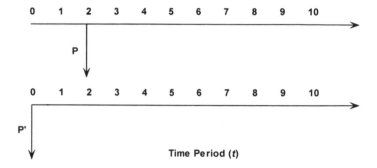

2.8.4 Use of Superposition Method for Cash Flow

Consider that a deposit of $300 at the beginning of each year is made for a total of ten payments. First payment occurs at $t = 0$, and there is no payment at $t = 10$. The cash transactions can be expressed by the following diagram.

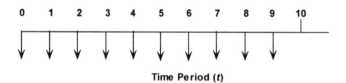

Since there is no transaction at $t = 10$, the problem can be separated into two sub-problems as follows.

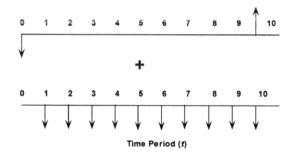

Now the cash transactions can be expressed by the following expression.

$$F = 300 \ (F/P, \ i\%, \ 10) + 300 \ (F/A, \ i\%, \ 10) - 300$$

Example 2.9

Suppose that someone asks you to loan him $100 and that at the end of 1 year he will pay you $5 in interest. Is this a good deal if bank also gives 5% interest?

Solution

We will assume that you make a comparison to a bank account. If you put $100 in a 5% bank account it will yield $105 at the end of the year. So a 5% interest rate is the standard for comparison. The following cash flow diagram is developed for comparison purpose.

This is analyzed by subtracting the loan amount of $100. Then add the $105 that will be paid at the end of the year. However, a conversion of this future value to a present value should be done and is shown below.

$$P = \ -100 + 105 \ (P/F, \ 5\%, \ 1)$$

$$= \ -100 + 105 \ (0.9524) = 0$$

In this example, the present worth stays the same. The bank account will generate the same and furthermore, keeping money in the bank will be safer than giving the loan. No risk is involved in keeping the money in the bank. This is not a good deal.

Example 2.10

If you are offered $120 for the loan of $100 over 1 year, what is the amount of money that you make above a normal bank account if the interest is 5%?

Solution

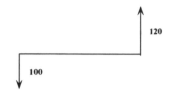

$$P = -100 + 120 \ (P/F, 5\%, 1)$$

$$P = -100 + (120) \ (0.9524) = \$14.29$$

2.9 Uniform Series Factors

A cash flow that repeats each year for n years without change in the amount is called a uniform series cash flow. An example of where the uniform series can be used is for a piece of equipment that requires maintenance at a constant cost per year. Each of the n amounts can be calculated and then summed. You can use the uniform series factor to calculate the future value of the maintenance costs as shown below:

Example 2.11

Your car's warranty has run out. In your experience, your maintenance costs have averaged $100/month. After 5 years what is the future value of car maintenance costs?

Solution

Using an effective annual interest rate of 10%, you can find the future value by using the A to F conversion factor given in Table 2.2.

$$F = A \ (F/A, i\%, n) = A \ \frac{(1+i)^n - 1}{i}$$

$$F = A \ \frac{(1.008333)^{60} - 1}{0.008333} = \$100 \times 77.437 = \$7,743.70$$

The cash flow diagram for the problem will be as follows.

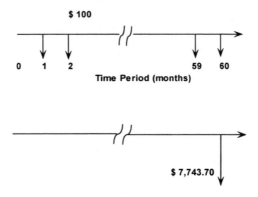

2.10 Gradient Series Cash Flow Factor

This involves periodic payments that increases or decreases by a constant amount (G) from one payment period to another period. General convention is to start the origin of gradient series at the end of first period. Therefore, the cash flow at A_n^{th} period is $A_n = (n-1)\,G$. Based on the value of G, a gradient series may be called an increasing gradient series (if $G > 0$) or a decreasing gradient series (if $G < 0$).

Consider the following problem:

A chemical company has just purchased a pump that has useful life of 5 years. Maintenance costs during the first year are $100. Maintenance costs are expected to increase as the pump ages at the rate of $150 per year over the remaining life. Assume that maintenance costs occur at the end of each year. Maintenance account earns 8% annual interest. How much does the company have to deposit in the account now?

Before solving the problem, we need to understand the *sinking fund* concept. A company generally creates an account or fund for the maintenance or to pay for the debt and is called sinking fund.

2.11 Sinking Fund

Sinking fund is defined as a fund or account into which annual deposits A are made in order to accumulate F at $t = n$ in the future. This fund may be used to pay for the debt, maintenance, etc., of the company.

The annual deposit is

$$A = F\left(A/F, i\%, n\right)$$ (2.11)

A/F is the sinking fund factor.

Example 2.12

I want to buy a car for $25,000 in 5 years. If I can get a CD rate of 6%, what should my monthly deposit be over 5 years to get a future value of $25,000?

Solution

$A = 25{,}000\ (A/F, 0.5\%, 60)$

Note that for 1 month $i = 6\%/12 = 0.5\%$

$$A\ =\ 25{,}000\ \frac{i}{(1+i)^n - 1} = 25{,}000\ \frac{0.005}{(1.005)^{60} - 1}$$

$$=\ 25{,}000\ (0.014332801) = \$358.32$$

The cash flow diagram for the above case is shown below.

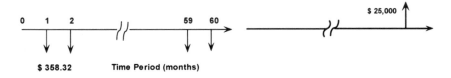

Students now should try to solve the problem described earlier using the above example.

2.12 Annuity (Present Worth Factor)

In engineering problems, cash flow is determined at a given point of time by calculating either its present worth or its future worth. The cash flow can be for one time (a single amount) or an annuity which is defined as a series of equal payments (A) occurring at equal time intervals. In the simplest case of an annuity that starts at the end of the first year and continues for n years, the present worth, also called purchase price P, is given by:

$$P = A\left(P/_A, i\%, n\right) \qquad (2.12)$$

An example of how an annuity is used can be seen in reporting lottery prizes. A $10,000,000 lottery prize is typically a 30-year annuity. Suppose for argument sake that you use an annual interest rate of 10%. What would the yearly payment, A, be to the prizewinner.

$i = 10\%/12 = 0.8333\%$ per month

$A = P(A/P, i\%, n) =$

$$10,000,000\frac{i(1+i)^n}{(1+i)^n - 1} = 10,000,000\frac{0.008333(1.008333)^{30}}{(1.008333)^{30} - 1}$$

$$= \$10,000,000(0.037797611) = \$377,976.12$$

The cash flow diagram for the problem is shown below.

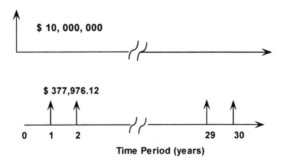

Time Period (years)

2.13 Determination of Various Factors for Economic Evaluation of a Project

2.13.1 Equivalent Uniform Annual Cost (EUAC)

When purchasing a new piece of equipment, the company does not necessarily pay immediately the cost of construction, maintenance, upkeep, and all of the other expenses that will incur over the life time of the equipment. Instead, the company generally borrows the money from a lender to make the initial purchase and pay annual expenses as they occur. An economic analysis should be carried out to evaluate various investment or payment options. One of these analyses is net present value analysis which provides an evaluation between investments by summing the present value of all future incomes and expenses. In another investment strategy, instead of paying up front for all the future costs of installation, maintenance, and operation of the equipment, the payments of a fixed amount could be made over the life of the equipment. The later method of evaluation is called the equivalent uniform annual cost (EUAC) method. When comparing EUACs for competing equipment, the life of the equipment should be close to each other and may not differ by more than 3–4 years. The annual amount that is equivalent to all of the cash flows is the other alternative. Consider the following problem.

Example 2.13

A machine has a maintenance cost of $250/year. What is the present worth of these maintenance costs over a 12 year period if $i = 8\%$?

Solution

$$P = A\,(P/A,\ 8\%,\ 12) = -250\ \frac{(1+i)^n - 1}{i(1+i)^n}$$

$$= -250\ \frac{(1.08)^{12} - 1}{0.08 \times (1.08)^{12}} = \frac{2.51817 - 1}{0.08 \times (2.51817)}$$

$$= -\$1884$$

The cash flow diagram is shown below.

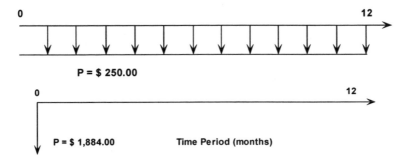

P = $ 250.00

P = $ 1,884.00   Time Period (months)

2.13.2 Finding a Past Value

How do you determine an amount in the past equivalent to some current (or future) amount? Place $t = 0$ at time of original investment and then calculate the past amount as a P value.

Example 2.14

I purchased a new car in 1984. My monthly payment was $179 for 60 months at an interest rate of 8%. What is the current value of the purchased price?

Solution

The first step is to calculate the purchased price of the car. All the transactions are shown in the cash flow diagram.

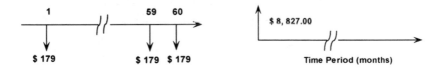

$ 179 $ 179 $ 179   Time Period (months)

P' is the present value of the car in 1984:

$$P' = A (P/A, i\%, n)$$

$$P' = \$179 \frac{(1+i)^n - 1}{i(1+i)^n} = \$179 \frac{(1.00667)^{60} - 1}{0.00667 \times (1.00667)^{60}}$$

$$= \$179 \; \frac{(1.4901)-1}{0.00667 \times (1.4901)} = \$8,827 \; \text{(in 1,984 dollars)}$$

Step two of the problem is to project the current value 15 years in the future to 1999. Make an assumption that the inflation rate is 3% per year. P is the present value of the car in 1999.

$$P = P'(P/P', 3\%, 15) = \$8,827 \, (1+i)^n = \$8,827 \, (1.03)^{15}$$

$$P = \$8,827 \, (1.558) = \$13,752.18.$$

The cash flow diagram is

2.14 Doubling Time

Whenever we talk about the population growth, investment, or any kind of future projection, it is easy to attract somebody's attention by describing the doubling time, which is the time that it will take for a population, an investment, or other quantity to double in size if it were growing exponentially at a constant rate. Exponential growth can be both beneficial and detrimental. If we are investing money, significant gains can be made by simply relying on exponential growth over time. The dramatic increase due to exponential growth is demonstrated in Fig. 2.2. An investment of $1,000 will grow to $ 64,000 in 60 years if the annual rate of return is 7%. The same dramatic increase will happen if we let the population grow or consume resources such as coal and oil at the same rate of 7%.

2.14.1 Calculation of Doubling Time

The basic differential equation for exponential growth can be written as

$$\frac{dN}{dt} = i \, N \tag{2.13}$$

where N is the quantity growing and i is the rate of growth.

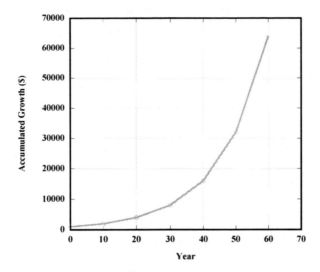

Fig. 2.2. The behavior of the exponential growth function.

Integration of Eq. (2.13) between a specific time period starting at $t = 0$ to $t = t$, the time period in question, provides the following solution

$$N(t) = N(0) \times e^{it} \tag{2.14}$$

In Eq. (2.14), $N(t)$ is the value of the quantity N after t time interval, $N(0)$ is the initial value of the quantity N.

Equation (2.14) is rearranged to calculate the doubling time.

$$\ell n \left(\frac{N(t)}{N(0)} \right) = it \tag{2.15}$$

The quantity $N(t)$ becomes twice of $N(0)$ at the doubling time t_2. Therefore, Eq. (2.15) becomes

$$\ell n \left(\frac{2N(0)}{N(0)} \right) = it, \quad or, \quad \ell n\, 2 = it_2, \quad or, \quad 0.693 = it_2$$

$$or, \ t_2 = \frac{0.693}{i} \approx \frac{70}{i \times 100} = \frac{70}{i\%}$$

The doubling time can also be approximated in the following manner

An investment doubles when

$$\frac{F}{P} = 2 = (1+i)^{t_2} \tag{2.16}$$

$$t_2 = \frac{\ell n(2)}{\ell n(1+i)} \approx \frac{69.3}{i \times 100} \approx \frac{70}{i\%}$$

Note, $\ell n(1+i) \approx i$ if $i \ll 1$

2.15 Tripling Time

We can calculate the tripling time in the same manner. The tripling time is the time that it will take to triple the original quantity.

$$\frac{F}{P} = 3 = (1+i)^{t_3} \tag{2.17}$$

$$t_3 = \frac{\ell n(3)}{\ell n(1+i)} \approx \frac{109}{i x 100} \approx \frac{110}{i\%}$$

2.16 Rate of Return (ROR)

Rate of Return (ROR), also called Return on Investment (ROI) is the ratio of money gained or lost on an investment to the amount of money invested. Essentially, effective annual interest rate at which an investment accrues income is the rate of return [10, 11].

Suppose we look at the previous problem. The interest was 5%. Thus the present worth of $100 invested at 5% is $100 regardless of n. A working definition of ROR would be the effective annual interest rate that makes the present worth of the investment zero.

Suppose you have a $100 investment that pays back at $75 at the end of each of the first 2 years.

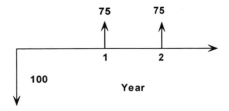

$$P = 0 = (-100) + 75 \times (1+i)^{-1} + 75(1+i)^{-2}$$

This is a quadratic equation. The order of the polynomial depends on n, and the polynomial must be solved to find the roots or the value of the interest rate, i.

The solution to this problem is, $i = 31.87\%$

The ROR can be also found by a trial and error method and is demonstrated in the example below.

Example 2.15

What is the ROR on a capitol investment of $1,000 at $t = 0$ when $500 is returned in year 4, and $1,000 returned in year 8?

Solution

The cash flow diagram of the problem is drawn first.

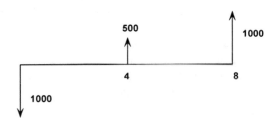

To find out, the interest rate for the given present worth, a trial and error method is used. A value of i is assumed and the present worth is calculated as follows. For iteration 1, i = 5% is used.

$$P = -1000 + 500 \ (P/F, 5\%, 4) + 1000 \ (P/F, 5\%, 8)$$
$$= -1000 + (500)(0.8227) + (1,000) \ (0.6768)$$
$$= \$88$$

5% is too low, now try 10%

$$P = -1000 + 500 \ (P/F, \ 10\%, \ 4) + 1000 \ (P/F, \ 10\%, \ 8)$$
$$= -1000 + (500) \ (0.6830) + (1,000) \ (0.4665)$$
$$= -\$162$$

10% is too high, now try 6%

You will find that 6% is too low but close to zero. So the next step is to try $i = 7\%$. Next try 6.1%, and so on. Continuing this iteration procedure, it should be noted that a solution is obtained for $i = 6.37\%$.

2.17 Rate on Investment (ROI)

ROR is the effective annual interest rate % per year, where as Rate on Investment (ROI) is the dollar amount.

2.18 Characteristics of Engineering Economy Problems

Depending on the type of projects, the economic evaluation will be different [12–16]. The first step is to determine all the items that will impact the cash flow of the operation. For most of the projects, several alternatives are available. Once all the information is gathered for all the possible alternatives, an evaluation should be carried out. At the minimum, the following information should be available.

- An interest rate will be given
- Two or more alternatives will compete for funding
- Each alternative will have its own cash flow
- It is the best alternative that must be found

Consider the following case:

Investment A cost \$10,000 today and pays back \$11,500 in 2 years. Investment B costs \$8,000 today and pays back \$4,500 each year. Which is the best investment? The method for determining the best investment is described below.

2.18.1 Present Worth Method

The present worth or present value of a future amount may be defined as the present principal, which must be deposited at a certain interest rate (or present interest rate) that will yield the amount desired at certain time in the future. Therefore, to determine the best investment of the above problem, the present worth for both the investment should be calculated as follows.

$$
\begin{aligned}
P(A) &= -10{,}000 + 11{,}500 \ (P/F,\ 5\%,\ 2) \\
&= -10{,}000 + 11{,}500 \ (0.9070) \\
&= \mathbf{\$431} \\
P(B) &= -8{,}000 + 4{,}500 \ (P/F,\ 5\%,\ 2) \\
&= -8{,}000 + 4{,}500 \ (1.8594) \\
&= \mathbf{\$367}
\end{aligned}
$$

A is better than B.

2.18.2 Capitalization Cost Method

Another way of making a decision is to look at the capitalized cost or life cycle costs. Capitalized cost is the amount of money at $t = 0$ needed to perpetually support the project or the earned interest only. One assumes infinite life in making the comparisons. In such a case, either (A/P) approaches the interest rate or n becomes large. Since (A/P) and (P/A) are reciprocal, one can divide an *infinite* series of equal cash flows by the interest rate to calculate the present worth of the *infinite* series.

Capital Costs = initial Cost + (Annual Costs/i)   (2.18)

This assumes a constant annual cost.

If the costs vary from year to year, you must determine a cash flow of equal annual amounts (EAA) that is equivalent.

$$
\begin{aligned}
\text{Capital Costs} &= \text{initial cost} + (\text{EAA}/i) \\
&= \text{initial cost} + \text{present worth of all expenses}
\end{aligned}
$$
    (2.19)

Example 2.16

What is the capitalized cost of a public works project that will cost $25,000,000 now and will require $2,000,000 in maintenance annually?

Solution

Assume $i = 12\%$
Use the units of millions of dollars (M)
Capital Costs $\quad = \quad 25M + 2M\ (P/A,\ 12\%,\ \infty)$
$\qquad\qquad\quad = \quad 25M + (2M/0.12) = \$41.67M$

The cash flow diagram will be as follows.

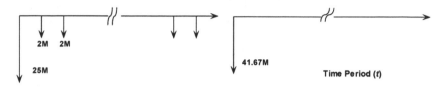

2.18.3 Annual Cost Method

Suppose that two projects have unequal lives. One can use the annual cost method to examine the alternatives. (Also called the annual return method or capital recovery method.) This method is described below through an example.

Assume that a project has a life of 10 years (Case I) and an alternative projects has 5 years of life time (Case II). The cash flow diagram of the two methods is shown below. When comparing these two methods, two life cycles for Case II should be considered.

Case I

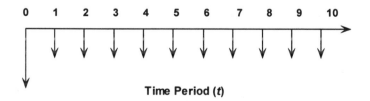

Case II

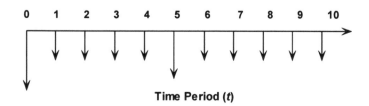

2.19 Life Cycle Cost Analysis

Engineers will be frequently involved in evaluating different alternatives for various infrastructure projects. In order to determine the best or most cost effective alternative, a Life Cycle Cost Analysis (LCCA) that involves calculating the total costs to construct and maintain an asset over a designated time period should be performed. The following factors are generally given for such an analysis.

LCCA equates all present and future costs (and benefits) over the life of a project by accounting for the value of money over time. LCCA results can be presented in several ways. The two most common methods are present worth and equivalent uniform annual cost.

2.19.1 Present Worth Method

For the life cycle cost analysis, present worth is the sum of all costs (and benefits) over the project life in today's dollars. It combines initial costs with discounted future maintenance costs, rehabilitation costs, and a salvage value. The future costs are discounted to account for the time value of money using the discount (real interest) rate. Present worth analysis is limited to comparing alternatives with equal analysis periods.

2.19.2 Equivalent Uniform Annual Cost

Equivalent uniform annual cost spreads the cost of all items (initial startup costs, user fees, maintenance, and anticipated rehabilitation costs) annually over the life cycle of the project. An analysis using equivalent uniform annual cost more effectively compares alternates with different service lives. However, when making such comparisons, the user must understand that during analysis it is assumed that the same set of activities will be repeated indefinitely. EUAC is the calculated annual cost.

Example 2.17

Consider the finish on a building being either brick or wood. Over 30 years and $i = 7\%$ which alternative is superior?

	Alternative A	Alternative B
Type	Brick	Wood
Life	30 years	10 years
Initial cost	$1,800	$450
Maintenance	$5/year	$20/year

Solution

$$
\begin{aligned}
\text{EUAC }(A) \quad &= \quad 1{,}800 \ (A/P, \ 7\%, \ 30) + 5 \\
&= \quad 1{,}800 \ (0.0806) + 5 \\
&= \quad \$150
\end{aligned}
$$

$$
\begin{aligned}
\text{EUAC }(B) \quad &= \quad 450 \ (A/P, \ 7\%, \ 10) + 20 \\
&= \quad 450 \ (0.1424) + 20 = \$84
\end{aligned}
$$

Therefore, *B* is cheaper than *A*. It is assumed that for wood, over 30 years it will be replaced at year-10 and year-20.

2.20 Benefit–Cost Ratio Analysis

One can also use the Benefit–Cost ratio when evaluating two projects [17]. This method is typically used in municipal projects where benefits and costs accrue for different segments of the community. The present worth of all benefits is divided by the present worth of all costs.

One tries to achieve a benefit to cost ratio that is greater than one in the analysis.

$B/C > 1.0$

Usually the system to be evaluated already exists (such as a highway). The objective is to determine if an improvement to the existing system is beneficial from the point of view of investment or costs associated with the project. In such a case, *B/C* is defined as follows:

$$
{}^{B}\!\!/\!{}_{C} = \frac{\Delta user\ benefit}{\Delta investment\ \cos t + \Delta ma\mathrm{int}\ enance - \Delta residual\ value} \tag{2.20}
$$

Example 2.18

A community wants to build a bridge over a river in order to take time off of a route that goes through the mountains. Benefits are decreased travel time, fewer accidents, reduced gas usage, etc. Should the bridge be built?

Solution

An engineer makes the following estimates. Note that the number of lives saved has an economic value, and is factored in annual user benefits.

	$ Millions
Initial Cost	40
Annual maintenance	12
Annual user benefits	49
Residual value	0

$$\frac{B}{C} = \frac{49}{40 + 12 + 0} = 0.942 , \text{ or } \frac{B}{C} \le 1$$

Since B/C is less than one, the benefit to cost ratio of the project does not justify the costs of the project. The minimum attractive ROR (MARR) can also be used for comparison purposes.

Ranking Mutually Exclusive Multiple Projects

If you have two projects and need to rank their relative economic benefits, you can rank the projects by the following method,

$$\frac{B_2 - B_1}{C_2 - C_1} \ge 1 \tag{2.21}$$

If this ratio is greater than 1, the project 2 has a higher benefit to cost ratio than project 1.

Alternatives with Different Lifetimes

Suppose that you have a choice between two cars.

Car A has a 3-year projected lifetime
Car B has a 5-year projected lifetime

The first question you ask is how long do you need a car? The length of need is the parameter that will allow you to evaluate the alternatives properly. The following issues should be addressed before making the final decision.

(A) A finite time line will require some additional considerations: For example, if your need is for 3 years and you choose the car with a 5 year lifetime, after 3 years your car will have a salvage value. If you have a 5-year need and you chose a car with a 3-year life, you must get 2 years of service from another source such as a rental car.

(B) A finite lifetime with an integer multiple of lifetime: Your need might be 15 years. No car will have this type of lifetime. But you can purchase 5 Car – *As* over 15 years or 3 – car *Bs* over 15 years.
(C) An infinite lifetime: You simply cost out the best alternative when it is required.

Opportunity Costs

An opportunity cost would be something like a trade-in allowance. In the case of a car, you can negotiate a trade-in value for your used car when you buy a new car.

Replacement Studies

If you decide to replace some equipment, you need to investigate the costs of retiring the equipment. In these types of studies, the existing equipment is called the "defender" and the new piece of equipment is called the "challenger."

Salvage Value

Since most defenders have a market value when you decide to retire them, they will have a salvage value that needs to be considered.

By convention, the salvage value is subtracted from the defender's present cost.

The Equivalent Uniform Annual Cost of the defender can be calculated from the following expression.

EUAC   = Next Year's Maintenance Cost + $(1+ i)$ × Current Salvage Value
         – Next Year's Salvage Value

2.21 Economic Life

As an asset grows older, the maintenance value increases. Additionally, the amortized cost of the purchase price decreases. An example would be a car. When does it make sense to replace the car?

The maintenance cost and the salvage value should be evaluated and the point where the sum of the maintenance cost and the salvage value is a minimum should be the economic life of the equipment. This is shown in Fig. 2.3.

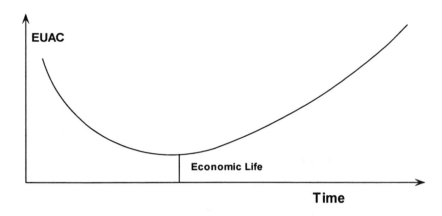

Fig. 2.3. Determination of economic life of equipment.

Example 2.19

Let's assume that a City has purchased a bus for $120,000. The projected maintenance cost and salvage value of the bus are known from prior experience with this model of bus and given below.

Solution

Year	Maintenance cost $	Salvage value $
1	35,000	60,000
2	38,000	55,000
3	43,000	45,000
4	50,000	25,000
5	65,000	15,000

Find the present worth and amortize the maintenance costs. Assume an interest rate of 8%.

EUAC (year 1) = 120,000(A/P, 8%, 1) + 35,000(A/F, 8%, 1) − 60,000(A/F, 8%, 1)
     = 120,000(1.08) + 35,000(1) − 60,000(1)
     = $104,600

EUAC (year 2) = [120,000+35,000(P/F, 8%, 1)] (A/P, 8%, 2) +
       (38,000 − 55,000)(A/F, 8%, 2)
     = [120,000 + 35,000(0.9259)] (0.5608) +
       (38,000 − 55000)(0.4808)
     = $77,300

EUAC (year 3) = [120,000 + 35,000(P/F, 8%, 1) + 38,000(P/F, 8%, 2)](A/P, 8%, 3)
        + (43,000 − 45,000)(A/F, 8%, 3)
    = [120,000 + 35,000(0.9259) + 38,000(0.8573)](0.3880)
        − 2,000(0.308)
    = $71,200

EUAC (year 4) = [120,000 + 35,000(P/F, 8%, 1) + 38,000(P/F, 8%, 2) +
        43,000(P/F, 8%, 3)](A/P, 8%, 4) + (50,000 − 25,000)(A/F, 8%, 4)
    = [120,000 + 35,000(0.9259) + 38,000(0.8573) +
        43,000(0.79383)](0.3019) + (25,000)(0.2219)
    = $71,699

EUAC (year 5) = [120,000 + 35,000(P/F, 8%, 1) + 38,000(P/F, 8%, 2)
        + 43,000(P/F, 8%, 3) + 65,000(P/F, 8%, 4)](A/P, 8%, 5)
        + (65,000-15,000)(A/F,8%,5)
    = [120,000+35,000(0.9259) + 38,000(0.8573)
        + 43,000(0.79383) + 65,000(0.680583)](0.2504)
        + 50,000(0.170456)
    = $74,467

The EUAC data are plotted versus the year in the following graph. As can be seen from the graph (Fig. 2.4), the minimum occurs at year 3.

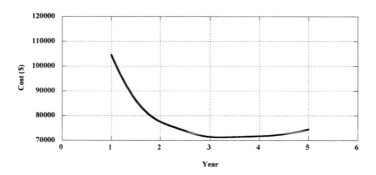

Fig. 2.4. Plot of annual cost (EUAC) for the bus at different year.

Capitalized Assets versus Expenses

For a business, each and every expenditure, even an asset purchase, can be labeled as an expense. This will reduce profits and lower income tax. Also, the asset can be capitalized by dividing the cost of the asset into parts and only one part is taken as an expense each year.

2.22 Depreciation

The value of physical assets decreases with age and a business is allowed to take this into consideration when analyzing costs and profits for a particular operation. The decrease in the value may be due to several factors including physical deterioration, technological advances, and economic changes which may cause to the retirement of the property. Depreciation is a method used for accounting the cost of the asset when income is determined for tax purposes. According to the Internal Revenue Service of the U.S. Department of the Treasury

"Depreciation is an income tax deduction that allows a taxpayer to recover the cost or other basis of certain property. It is an annual allowance for the wear and tear, deterioration, or obsolescence of the property.

Most types of tangible property (except, land), such as buildings, machinery, vehicles, furniture, and equipment are depreciable. Likewise, certain intangible property, such as patents, copyrights, and computer software is depreciable.

In order for a taxpayer to be allowed a depreciation deduction for a property, the property must meet all the following requirements:

- The taxpayer must own the property. Taxpayers may also depreciate any capital improvements for property the taxpayer leases.
- A taxpayer must use the property in business or in an income-producing activity. If a taxpayer uses a property for business and for personal purposes, the taxpayer can only deduct depreciation based only on the business use of that property.
- The property must have a determinable useful life of more than one year. Even if a taxpayer meets the preceding requirements for a property, a taxpayer cannot depreciate the following property:
- Property placed in service and disposed of in same year.
- Equipment used to build capital improvements. A taxpayer must add otherwise allowable depreciation on the equipment during the period of construction to the basis of the improvements.
- Certain term interests.

Depreciation begins when a taxpayer places property in service for use in a trade or business or for the production of income. The property ceases to be depreciable when the taxpayer has fully recovered the property's cost or other basis or when the taxpayer retires it from service, whichever happens first." The lifetime of various properties is given in Appendix II.

2.23 Methods for Calculating Depreciation

Depreciation costs can be determined by a number of methods; however, one must be familiar with the rules and regulations when calculating depreciation. Depreciation methods may be divided into two categories: (1) arbitrary methods that do not take into account the interest rates, such as straight line, declining balance, sum-of-the-year-digits methods, and (2) methods that take into account the interest rate, such as sinking fund and the present worth methods. The purchase price of an asset or property is generally spread over a number of years. The following notations are used in describing various depreciation methods.

C = purchase price
S_n = Salvage value
Depreciation basis = $C - S_n$

2.23.1 Straight Line Method

In the straight line method, it is assumed that the value of the property decreases linearly with time. Equal amounts are depreciated each year throughout the life time of the property. The depreciation cost may be expressed by the following expression.

$$D = \frac{C - S_n}{n} \tag{2.22}$$

where, D is the annual depreciation (\$/year) and n is the service life in years. Because of its simplicity, straight line method is widely used for determining depreciation cost.

Constant percentage

In this method, a fixed percentage of the purchase price is retired every year until it becomes zero or reaches the service life.

D = (depreciation fraction) (depreciation basis)
D = (depreciation fraction) $(C - S_n)$ $\tag{2.23}$

2.23.2 Sum-Of-the-Years-Digits (SOYD) Method

This is an arbitrary method for determining depreciation, but larger amounts are allowed to depreciate during the early life of the property. This method does allow the purchase price to decrease to zero at the end of the service life.

Sum of the digits, T, for an asset with useful life n is calculated from the following expression.

$$T = \frac{1}{2}n(n+1) \tag{2.24}$$

The annual depreciation in a particular year j is given by,

$$D_j = \frac{(C - S_n)(n - j + 1)}{T} \tag{2.25}$$

The accumulated depreciation at the end of year j can be calculated from the following expression.

$$\sum_{j=1,j} D_j = \frac{jn - [j(j-1)/2]}{T}(C - S_n) \tag{2.26}$$

2.23.3 Double Declining Balance (DDB)

In this method, the annual depreciation cost is a fixed percentage of the property value at the beginning of the particular year. The fixed percentage factor remains constant throughout the service life of the asset. Therefore, the annual depreciated amount is different for each year. In the double declining balance method, double the straight line depreciation amount is taken in the first year. Therefore, the depreciation rate is given by

$$d = \frac{2}{n} \tag{2.27}$$

The depreciated amount at the end of first year is given by.

$$D_1 = \frac{2C}{n} \tag{2.28}$$

The accumulated depreciation at the end of year j can be expressed as:

$$D_{Total} = \sum_{K=1}^{j} D_K \qquad (2.29)$$

The depreciated amount at any particular year j may be calculated from the following equation.

$$D_j = \frac{2(C - \sum_{m=1}^{j-1} D_m)}{n} \qquad (2.30)$$

The same expression in terms of depreciation rate, d, can be written as:

$$D_j = dC(1-d)^{j-1} \qquad (2.31)$$

Statutory depreciation

A number of businesses would like to recover the cost of their assets at an accelerated rate. Accelerated depreciation methods are popular for writing-off equipment that might be replaced before the end of its useful life since the equipment might be obsolete (e.g. computers). These methods provide a greater write-off allowing a better tax shield than straight line depreciation. Two methods for accelerated depreciation are generally used: (1) Accelerated Cost Recovery System (ACRS) and (2) the Modified Accelerated Cost Recovery System (MACRS). ACRS Depreciation methods applied to limited partnership assets placed in service in 1986 or before. This was replaced by the MACRS which is applied to assets placed in service after 1986.

ACRS was implemented from 1981–1986 in the United States, under the Economic Recovery Tax Act (ERTA) of 1981. Under ACRS property class lives were established, calculations were based on an estimated salvage value of zero, and shorter recovery periods were used to calculate annual depreciation.

Depreciation under ACRS = 2 × Straight Line Depreciation   (2.32)

MACRS replaced ACRS in the United States in 1986 with the passing of the Tax Reform Act of 1986 (TRA-86). In MACRS, the number of property classes was expanded; a half year convention was added to the code for the first and final years of a property's recovery life. MACRS allows for more depreciation towards the beginning of the life of the capital asset (similar to double declining balance).

The service life and depreciation methods allowed under the TRA-86 act for some selected equipment are given in Appendix II.

Production on service output

If the value of a property depends more on the number of operations performed than on calendar year time, the unit-of-production or service output method may be used for depreciation cost determination. For example, for a car, depreciation based on miles traveled may be more appropriate if the car is used heavily for transportation. Similarly, the depreciation may be based on number of units (pieces) produced, other measurable service output, and resource depletion as in the mining industry. The depreciation cost can be expressed by the following expression.

$$D_j = (C - S_n) \frac{actual\,output\,in\,year\,j}{estimated\,lifetime\,output} \tag{2.33}$$

2.24 Sinking Fund Method

The sinking fund method uses compound interest in calculating depreciation costs. The method depreciates a property value as if the company were to make a series of annual deposits whose value at the end of the service life would be equal to the cost of replacement of the original property. The amount in the sinking fund at the end of year j is the accumulated depreciation to date and is given by

$$D_j = (C - S_n)\,(A/F,\,i\%,\,n)\,(F/P,\,i\%,\,n) \tag{2.34}$$

A number of other methods have been proposed based on the sinking fund methods and their formulas are listed below.

Sinking fund plus interest on first cost

$$D = (C - S_n)\,(A/F,\,i\%,\,n) + C_i \tag{2.35}$$

Straight line plus interest on first cost

$$D = \frac{1}{n}(C - S_n) + C_i \tag{2.36}$$

Straight line plus average interest method

$$D = \frac{(C - S_n)}{n}[1 + \frac{i(n+1)}{d}] + iS_n \tag{2.37}$$

Example 2.20

An asset costs $9,000. The economic life is 10 years. The salvage value, $S_{10} = $200. Find the depreciation from $n = 1$ to 3 using straight line, double declining balance, and sum of the years digit methods.

Solution

Straight Line:

$$D = \frac{9,000 - 200}{10} = \$880/year$$

Double Declining Balance:

$$D_1 = \frac{2 \times 9,000}{10} = \$1,800/year$$

$$D_2 = \frac{2 \times (9,000 - 1,800)}{10} = \$1,440/year$$

$$D_3 = \frac{2 \times (9,000 - 1,800 - 1,440)}{10} = \$1,152/year$$

Sum-Of-the-Years-Digits:

$$T = \frac{1}{2}(10)(11) = 55$$

$$D_1 = \frac{10}{55}(9,000 - 200) = \$1,600/year$$

$$D_2 = \frac{9}{55}(9,000 - 200) = \$1,440/year$$

$$D_3 = \frac{8}{55}(9,000 - 200) = \$1,280/year$$

A comparison of various depreciation methods is shown in Fig. 2.5.

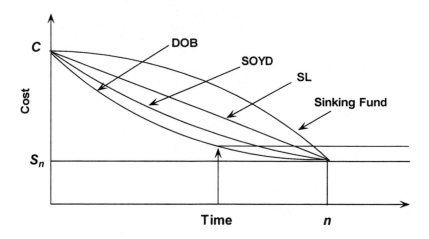

Fig. 2.5. Characteristics of various depreciation methods.

2.25 Finding Book Value

The Book Value (BV) of an asset can be determined at any particular year using the depreciation cost calculated by the above methods. The expressions for determining the book value by various methods are given below.

Straight line method

$$BV_j = C - \frac{j(C - S_n)}{n} = C - jD \tag{2.38}$$

SOYD

$$BV_j = (C - S_n)(1 - \frac{j(2n+1-j)}{n(n+1)}) + S_n \tag{2.39}$$

DDB

$$BV_j = C(1 - d) \tag{2.40}$$

Sinking fund

$$BV_j = C - (C - S_n)(A/F, i\%, n)(F/A, i\%, n) \tag{2.41}$$

Method of successive subtractions

$$BV_j = C - \sum_{m=1}^{j} D_m \tag{2.42}$$

Example 2.21

With a book value of $9,000 in the beginning, find the *BV* after 3 years by SOYD. $S_{10} = \$200$ (for an item that depreciates in 10 years). Also, use the method of successive subtractions.

Solution

$$BV_j = C - \sum_{m=1}^{j} D_m$$

where, $D_m = \dfrac{(C - S_n)(n - j + 1)}{T}$

$$T = \frac{1}{2}n(n + 1)$$

For, $n = 3$

$$T = \frac{1}{2}10(10 + 1) = 55$$

$$D_1 = \frac{(10 - 1 + 1)}{55}(9,000 - 200) = 1,600$$

$$D_2 = \frac{(10 - 2 + 1)}{55}(9,000 - 200) = 1,440$$

$$D_3 = \frac{(10 - 3 + 1)}{55}(9,000 - 200) = 1,280$$

$BV_1 = 9,000 - D_1 = 9,000 - 1,600 = 7,400$
$BV_2 = 9,000 - BV_1 = 5,960$
$BV_3 = 9,000 - BV_2 = 4,680$

2.26 Amortization

Amortization is similar to depreciation. Both the terms are often used interchangeably. Both the terms divide up base cost or value of an asset. Amortization spreads cost of the asset. Amortization is usually associated with a definite period of cost distribution, while depreciation usually deals with an unknown or estimated period over which the assets are distributed. The factor can be time, units of production, number of customers, etc. The asset can be tangible like a truck or building. Here the standard is time.

The asset can be intangible like goodwill or a patent. Here the variable can be different from time.

Example 2.22

A company purchases patent rights to an invention for $1,200,000. The market for the invention will be 1,200 units total. What is the amortization rate in dollars per unit?

Solution

$$\frac{\$1,200,000}{1,200} = \$1,000 \,/\, unit$$

2.27 Depletion

Depletion is referred to a resource that is continuously depleted such as in mining and oil deposits, since the capacity was lost due to materials actually consumed. Depletion cost equals to initial cost times the ratio of amount of materials used to original amount of materials purchased.

2.28 Income Tax

Companies are also required to pay various taxes to federal, state or local governments based on their income. The total income minus the total production cost gives the gross earnings made by the particular operation. The tax rate applicable to gross earning can be calculated as follows:

$$t = \text{tax rate} = s + f - sf \tag{2.43}$$

where, f = fraction of profits as federal income tax, and s = fraction of profits as state income tax (state taxes are deductible in federal income tax). The following basic rules must be followed when calculating tax rate.

1. Initial purchase expenditures are unaffected by income taxes.
2. Salvage revenues are unaffected by income taxes.
3. Deductible expenses are operating cost, maintenance costs, and interest payments. These are reduced by the fraction t.
4. Revenues are reduced by a fraction t.
5. Depreciation is handled as an operating expense and is deductible.

Example 2.23

A corporation pays 53% of its profit in income tax. The corporation invests $10,000 in an asset that will produce $3,000 annually for 8 years. The annual expense is $700, the S_8 = $500, and i = 9%. What is the after tax worth? Disregard depreciation.

Solution

The cash flow diagram is shown below.

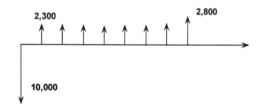

The after tax worth can be calculated from the following expression.

$$P = -10{,}000 + 3{,}000 \ (P/A, 9\%, 8)(1 - 0.53) - 700(P/A, 9\%, 8) \ (1 - 0.53)$$
$$+ \ 500(P/F, 9\%, 8)$$
$$= -10{,}000 + 3{,}000 \ (5.5348) \ (0.47) - 700 \ (5.5348) \ (0.47) + 500 \ (0.5019)$$
$$= -\$3{,}766$$

Tax Credit (TC)

Often federal, state, or local governments may give a tax break or tax credit for one time against income tax to companies as incentives. The tax credit is defined as follows:

$$TC = \text{fraction x initial cost} \tag{2.44}$$

Calculation of gain or loss on sale of depreciated asset

The calculation procedure is explained through the following example.

One year a corporation makes a $5,000 investment in an old building. The investment is not depreciable, but qualifies for a one time 20% tax credit. The revenue in year 1 is $45,000, and expenses are $25,000. The income tax rate is 53%. What is the after tax present worth of the corporation's investment if $i = 10\%$?

The tax credit, $TC = 0.2(5,000) = \$1,000$, and the cash flow diagram is given by:

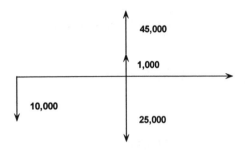

The after tax present worth is calculated as follows.

$$
\begin{aligned}
P &= -5,000 + (45,000 - 25,000)\,(1 - 0.53)\,(P/F,\,10\%,\,1) + 1,000\,(P/F,\,10\%,\,1) \\
&= -5,000 + 20,000\,(0.47)\,(0.9091) + 1,000\,(0.9091) \\
&= \$4,455
\end{aligned}
$$

2.29 Depreciation Recovery

When a business stops its function, sell or dispose of business assets should be taken into account when making an adjustment in the end of year tax return to account for the gain or loss. A gain is included as gross income and a loss (except buildings) as an allowable deduction. Given the tax rate, t, the depreciation recovery (DR) can be expressed as:

$$
DR = t \sum_{j=1}^{n} D_j \left(P/F, i\%, n \right)
\tag{2.45}
$$

The same methods that are used to calculate depreciation can be used to determine depreciation rate and are given below.

2.29.1 Straight Line Depreciation Rate

$$DR = t\,D\!\left(P\!\!\Big/_{\!A},i\%,n\right) \tag{2.46}$$

where, $D = \dfrac{C - S_n}{n}$

2.29.2 Sum of the Year's Digits Depreciation Rate

$$DR = t\,\frac{C - S_n}{T}\left[n\!\left(P\!\!\Big/_{\!A},i\%,n\right) - \left(P\!\!\Big/_{\!G},i\%,n\right)\right] \tag{2.47}$$

2.29.3 Double Declining Balance

If the $BV_n > S_n$

$$DR = t\,C\!\left(\frac{d}{1-d}\right)\!\left(P\!\!\Big/_{\!E}G, z-1, n\right) \tag{2.48}$$

where, $\left(P\!\!\Big/_{\!E}G, z-1, n\right) = \dfrac{z^n - 1}{z^n (z-1)}$ \hfill (2.49)

and $z = \dfrac{1+i}{1-d}$ \hfill (2.50)

Example 2.24

An asset is purchased for \$9,000, the salvage value after 10 years is \$200, interest rate is 6%, and income tax rate is 48%. Find *DR* by the SL and SOYD methods.

Solution

SL

$$
\begin{aligned}
DR &= 0.48\,[(9{,}000 - 200)/10]\,(P/A, 6\%, 10)\\
   &= 0.48(880)(7.3601)\\
   &= \$3{,}109
\end{aligned}
$$

SOYD

$$DR = \left[t\left(\frac{C - S_n}{T} \right) \right]\left[\left(n\left(P/_A, 6\%, 10 \right) \right) - \left(P/_G, 6\%, 10 \right) \right]$$

$T = 0.5\ (10)\ (11) = 55$

$DR = (0.48(9,000 - 200)/55)\ [10(7.3601) - (29.6023)]$
$ = \$3,379$

References

1. Peters MS, Timmerhaus KD (1980) Plant Design and Economics for Chemical Engineers. 3rd Ed, McGraw–Hill, New York
2. Newnan G, Eschenbach TG, Lavelle JP (2004) Engineering Economic Analysis. Oxford University Press, Oxford
3. Sullivan WG, Wicks EM, Luxhoj J (2002) Engineering Economy. 12th Ed. Prentice Hall, New Jersey
4. Sepulveda JA, Souder WE, Gottfried BS (1984) Schaum's Outline of Engineering Economics. McGraw-Hill, New York
5. Park CS (2003) Fundamentals of Engineering Economics. Prentice Hall, New Jersey
6. White JA, Case KE, Pratt DB, Agee MH (2001) Principles of Engineering Economic Analysis. 4th Ed. Wiley, New York
7. Park CS, Sharp-Bette GP (1990) Advanced Engineering Economics. Wiley, New York
8. Foster JE (2004) Engineering Economics. Stipes Pub Lic USA
9. Holland FA, Yaws CL (1978) Project cash flow-description and interpretation. Hydrocarbon Process 57(3): 77
10. Kapier WH (1969) Appraising rate of return methods. Chem Eng Progr 65(11): 55
11. Haskett CE (1972) Evaluation by rate of return or present value. Pet Eng 8(45): 48
12. Scott NR, Minott S (2003) Feasibility of Fuel Cells for Energy Conversion on the Dairy Farm. Final Report The New York State Energy Research and Development Authority, Agreement No. 6243, NYSERDA 6243-1, March 2003
13. Sahirman S, Creese RC, Setyawati BR (2003) Evaluation of the Economic Feasibility of Fiber-Reinforced Polymer (FRP) Bridge Decks. ISPA/SCEA International Joint Conference, 2003 Annual Meeting, Orlando, FL, June 2003
14. Ebly RW (1973) Comparison of methods for evaluating capital equipment eeplacement. Trans Am Assoc Cost Eng 23
15. Sohtaoglu NH (2000) Investigation of the Effects of Differing Investment Programs and Macroeconomics Parameters on Long Term Power Transmission Planning: Part I. Model, 10th Mediterranean Electrotechnical Conf., MEleCon 2000, Vol III, 1015–1018
16. Camargo I, Figueiredo F, De Oliveira M (2001) Economic choice of optimum feeder cable considering risk analysis. CIRED2001 18–21 June 2001 Conference Publication No. 482 IEE Paper No. 5.15

17. Sugden R, Williams A (1978) The Principles of Practical Cost-Benefit Analysis. Oxford University Press, Oxford

Problems

1. A company deposited $50,000 in a bank account and withdrew $60,000 after exactly 1 year. Calculate the interest rate paid by the bank.
2. Calculate the simple interest rate if $300 is earned in 6 months on an investment of $10,000.
3. Assume that you have deposited $1,000 in a bank account at 6% simple interest per year for 5 years. At the end of the 5 years, all the money earned was put into fixed deposit for another 5 years at compound interest rate of 8%. What will be the total amount at the end of 10 years?
4. How much money will be required 4 years from today to repay a $10,000 loan that is made today at (a) 8% simple interest and (b) 8% compound interest.
5. You would like to borrow $30,000 from the bank for a period of 1 year at an annual interest rate of 7%. How much will you have to pay to the bank after 1 year? Draw the cash flow diagram.
6. You would like to invest $1116.47 in the bank at 6% for 7 years. However, you would like to withdraw cash each year in equal amounts until your account is depleted. How much can you withdraw each year? Show all the transactions in a cash flow diagram.
7. How much money do we need to invest today, at 6%, to be able to withdraw $0 at the end of year 1, $100 at the end of year 2, $200 at the end of year 3, and so on, and $700 at the end of year 8? Draw the cash flow diagram.
8. How much money could you take out of the bank after 5 years if you are willing to invest $100 today, $200 at the end of the first year, $300 at the end of the second year, $400 at the end of the third year, $500 at the end of the fourth year, and $600 at the end of the fifth year? Use a 6% interest rate. Draw the cash flow diagram.
9. Use the formulas given in Table 2.2 to solve the following problems.

    (a) A deposit of $3,000 is made to a bank account that pays 8% interest per year, compounded annually. If all the money is allowed to accumulate, how much will be earned at the end of 10 years and 15 years?
    (b) How much money should be deposited in a account so that $5,000 can be withdrawn 10 years hence, if the interest rate is 6% per year, compounded annually and if all the interest is allowed to accumulate?
    (c) You want to create a future college education fund for a 4-year old child. You identify a bank that is willing to pay 7% interest compounded annually. You want to make equal payment from the 5th birthday through the 18th. In order to withdraw $20,000 annually for 4 years starting at the 19th birthday, what equal monthly payment must be made?

(d) Mr. Z plans to make a series of gradient type withdrawals from his savings account over a 10-year period, beginning at the end of second year. What equal amount withdrawal would be equivalent to a withdrawal of $1,000 at the end of the second year, $2,000 at the end of the third year, and so an, and $9,000 at the end of the 10th year, if the bank pays 8% per year, compounded annually?

(e) Suppose $10,000 is deposited in a savings account that pays interest at 8% per year, compounded annually. If no withdrawals are made, how long will it take to accumulate $15,000?

(f) Evaluate

    (i)   (F/P, 10%, 40)

    (ii) (A/F, 5%, 35)

    (iii) Find (A/F, i%, n) from (F/P, i%, n); (P/F, i%, n); (A/P, i%, n)

10. A community would like to build a recreation center. Land for the project will cost $350,000, construction costs will be $800,000, and annual maintenance will be $25,000/year. Annual benefits expected from this project = $250,000 per year. Determine the Benefit-Cost ratio assuming a rate of 6% and a life of 20 years.

11. Consider a series of 10 annual payments of $3,000 which is equivalent to two equal payments, one at the end of 15 years and the other at the end of 20 years. The interest rate is 8%, compounded annually. What is the amount of the two equal payments?

12. Find the uniform annual series of 8 payments that would be equivalent to the following gradient series: $1,000 initially, with an increment of $100 per year, for a total of 8 years. The interest rate is 10%, compounded annually.

13. Determine the present worth of the following cash flows, based on an interest rate of 10% per year, compounded annually: End of year 0 – $0, year 1 – $1,500, year 2 – $3,000, year 3 – $4,500, year 4 – $5,000, year 5 – $6,000.

14. A college student borrows $2,500 during his senior year from a bank with the arrangement that the loan is to be repaid in 20 equal quarterly installments. The interest rate is 5% per year with the first payment to be made 3 years after the date of the loan. What will be the approximate amount of the quarterly payment?

15. A $10,000 loan is to be repaid at the rate of $200 per month, with an annual effective interest rate of 10% charged against the unpaid balance. What principal remains to be paid after the each payment and how long it will take to repay the loan amount?

16. One type of road surface will cost $15,000 per unit distance. The average annual maintenance is estimated at $500, with resurfacing required every 12 years at a cost of $7,000. Calculate the capitalized cost of perpetual service, using an effective annual interest of 3.5%.

17. A piece of machinery costs $900. After 5 years, the salvage value is $300. Annual maintenance costs are $50. If the interest rate is 8%, find the equivalent uniform annual cost.

18. Maintenance expenditures for a building with a 20-year life will be disbursed in the following manner: $1,000 at the end of the 5th year, $2,000 at the end of the 10th year, and $3,500 at the end of the 15th year. Using an annual interest rate of 10%, find the equivalent uniform annual cost for the 20-year period.

19. An engineering firm needs a particular machine. The firm is given two options. In Option 1 the firm can buy the machine for $50,000, and pay a maintenance contract of $1,000 per year. The salvage value of the machine after 10 years is expected to be $10,000. In Option 2, the machine may be leased at $7,000 per year and pay no maintenance, but receive no salvage. Assume that the machine will generate an income of $8,000 per year. Which option will be best for the firm?

20. Assume that the tax on $1,000,000 in 1 year is 50% and the tax on $50,000 per year is only 25%. This means that the present value of the $1,000,000 is only $500,000, and that the annual payment of the $50,000 is only $37,500. Calculate the equivalent annual payment for the $500,000 and compare it to the $37,500. Also calculate the present value of the $37,500 payment option.

21. A machine costs $10,000 and is expected to have salvage value of $1,500 whenever it is retired. The operating disbursements for the first year are expected to be $2,000 and they will then increase $500 per year. If the MARR is 15%, determine the machines's economic life?

22. A Construction Company is considering acquisition of a new earthmover. The mover's basic price is $100,000 and it will cost another $20,000 to buy other accessories necessary to make it more useful for the company. Find the MACRS class for this equipment. It can be sold after 4 years for $80,000. The earthmover purchase will have no effect on revenues, but it is expected to save the firm $32,000 per year in before-tax operating costs, mainly labor. The firm's marginal tax rate (federal plus state) is 40% and its MARR is 15%. Is this project acceptable based on the most-likely estimates given in the problem?

23. A cost of a rental property is $350,000. Annual income from rentals will be $55,000 and that annual expenditure for maintenance of the property, other than income taxes, will be about $15,000. The property is expected to appreciate at the annual rate of 6%. After 20 years once it is acquired, it will be depreciated based on the 39-year real property class (MACRS), assuming that the property would be placed in service on January 1. What would be the minimum annual total of rental income that would make the investment break even if the tax rate is 30% and the MARR is 15%?

24. A $60,000 asset will be depreciated over a 10-year period. No salvage value is expected. If the tax rate is 50%. Calculate the depreciation by straight line method and compare with the sum-of-years-digit method given a 10% after tax MARR.

25. Equipment is purchased for $1,000 and it is expected to be in use for 10 years. The estimated salvage value is $500. Using various depreciation methods discussed in the chapter, determine which method may be the best and also fine the book value at the end of each year.

3 UNITS AND UNIT CONVERSIONS

Abstract

The type of units used to describe the energy content of a resource depends on the resource itself. As a consequence, a variety of units are used in the energy industry. The conversion of one unit to another unit is essential for comparison purpose and also to prevent various mishaps. Scientists and engineers working in the energy related industry should know how to convert gallons to liters, and vice versa. The difference between energy content and power output should be clear to all professionals in the energy field. This chapter addresses various units used in the energy industry and their conversion from one unit to another unit.

3.1 Introduction

One of the most important endeavors of an engineer is to understand the units used in describing, evaluating, and comparing various systems. Two systems of units exist in science and engineering. These two systems are Système International d'unités (in short SI system) and British system. The SI system is also known as the Metric System. Currently, the United States, Liberia, and Myanmar are the only countries yet to adopt the metric system officially. In 1866, the use of the metric system was made legal but not mandatory in the United States by the Metric Act of 1866 (P.L. 39-183) [1]. Since then various other laws were passed in the U.S. Congress to promote the use of metric systems [2, 3].

From a historical perspective, energy has been measured by British units. The energy system may be the only system that was affected significantly when implementation of the metric system occurred. For example, Joules, the common measurement used in the metric system is seldom used in measuring energy resources in our day to day life. As can be seen from Table 3.1, the most common units used to measure various energy resources are still in British Units.

T.K. Ghosh and M.A. Prelas, *Energy Resources and Systems:*
Volume 1: Fundamentals and Non-Renewable Resources, 77–87.

Table 3.1. Common measuring units used to describe common energy sources.

Energy source	Common measuring units
Oil	Million barrels
Coal	Million tonnes
Natural Gas	Billion standard cubic feet
Uranium	Thousand tonnes
Wood	Cord

The units for measuring energy sources and their conversion factors are given in Table 3.2. The conversion factors of various other units are given in Appendix III.

Table 3.2. Conversion factors for energy related units.

Unit	Multiply by	To obtain
Barrels of oil (bbl)	42	US gallons (gal)
Barrels of oil (bbl)	34.97	Imperial gallons (UK gal)
Barrels of oil (bbl)	0.136	Tonnes of oil equivalent (toe)
Barrels of oil (bbl)	0.1589873	Cubic meter (m^3)
Barrels of oil equivalent (boe)	5,658.53	Cubic feet (ft^3) of natural gas
Tonnes of oil equivalent (toe)	7.33*	Barrels of oil equivalent (boe)
Cubic yards (yd^3)	0.764555	Cubic meter (m^3)
Cubic feet (ft^3)	0.02831685	Cubic meter (m^3)
Cubic feet (ft^3) of natural gas	0.0001767	Barrels of oil equivalent (boe)
US gallons (gal)	0.0238095	Barrels (bbl)
US gallons (gal)	3.785412	Liters (l)
US gallons (gal)	0.8326394	Imperial gallons (UK gal)
Imperial gallons (UK gal)	1.201	US gallon (gal)
Imperial gallons (UK gal)	4.545	Liters (l)
Short tons	2,000	Pounds (lb)
Short tons	0.9071847	Metric tonnes (t)
Long tons	1.016047	Metric tonnes (t)
Long tons	2,240	Pounds (lb)
Metric tonnes (t)	1,000	Kilograms (kg)
Metric tonnes (t)	0.9842	Long tons
Metric tonnes (t)	1.102	Short tons
Pounds (lb)	0.45359237	Kilograms (kg)
Kilograms (kg)	2.2046	Pounds (lb)
Acres	0.40469	hectares (ha)
Square miles (mi^2)	2.589988	square kilometers (km^2)
Square yards (yd^2)	0.8361274	square meters (m^2)
Square feet (ft^2)	0.09290304	square meters (m^2)
Square inches (in^2)	6.4516	square centimeters (cm^2)
British Thermal Units (Btus)	1,055.05585262	joules (J)
Calories (cal)	4.1868	joules (J)
Kilowatt hours (kWh)	3.6	Megajoules (MJ)
Therms	100,000	British thermal units (Btus)

Unit	Multiply by	To obtain
Tonnes of oil equivalent	10,000,000	Kilocalories (kcal)
Tonnes of oil equivalent	396.83	Therms
Tonnes of oil equivalent	41.868	Gigajoules (GJ)
Tonnes of oil equivalent	11,630	Kilowatt hours (kWh)
Cubic feet (ft^3) of natural gas	1,025	British Thermal Units (Btus)

* This conversion can range from 6.5 to 7.9 depending on the type of crude oil

It is important to understand both the units and how to convert British units to metric units and vice versa. Various units used in energy systems and businesses are explained below and their conversion factors are given in Appendix III.

3.2 Basic Energy Units

British Thermal Unit (BTU)

The *BTU* is defined as the amounts of energy required to raise one pound of water at its maximum density, which occurs at a temperature of 39.1 degrees Fahrenheit (°F) by 1°F at sea level.

Calorie (Cal)

Calorie is the equivalent of BTU in SI or Metric system of units. Calorie is defined as the amounts of energy required to raise 1 g of water by one degree Celsius (1°C) from 14.5°C to 15.5°C at sea level.

Joule (J)

Joule is the unit of electrical, mechanical, and thermal energy in the SI system of units. Depending on its use, its definition or interpretation is different.

As a unit of electrical energy, joule is the energy equal to the work done when a current of 1 ampere is passed through a resistance of 1 ohm for 1 s.

As a unit of mechanical energy, it is the energy equal to the work done when a force of 1 Newton acts through a distance of 1 m in the direction the force is applied. This is also a unit of work which is equal to 10^7 units of work in the Centimeter, the Gram, and the Second (CGS) system of units (ergs, the unit of work or energy in the CGS system, equal to the work done by a force of 1 dyne acting through a distance of 1 cm).

As a unit of thermal energy, it is defined as the amount of energy required to raise the temperature of 1 kg of water by 1°C.

In terms of kinetic energy, one joule is equal to the energy of a mass of 2 kg moving at a velocity of one meter per second.

1 J/s = W

The conversion factors between these units are given below.

1 BTU	=	251.9 cal
	=	0.2519 kcal
	=	1055 J
	=	1.055 kJ

1 cal	=	3.9698×10^{-3} BTU
	=	4.1868 J

1 J	=	0.2388 cal
	=	$9.4786\ 10^{-4}$ BTU

3.2.1 Other Energy Units

Quad

A Quad is used when measuring large amounts of energy.

1 Quad = 10^{15} BTUs.

The United States used 101.6 quads per year in 2007.

Therm

A Therm is another energy unit mainly used to describe energy content of natural gas.

1 Therm = 100,000 BTU

Often a number of prefixes are used with the regular units to describe large amounts of energy. This is most common with the SI units. Some of these prefixes used to describe energy units are given in Table 3.3.

Table 3.3. Prefixes used to describe large energy units.

Unit	Equivalent
Kilowatt (kW)	1,000 (One Thousand) Watts
Megawatt (MW)	1,000,000 (One Million) Watts
Gigawatt (GW)	1,000,000,000 (One Billion) Watts
Terawatt (TW)	1,000,000,000,000 (One Trillion) Watts
Kilowatt-hours (kWh)	1,000 (One Thousand) Watt-hours
Megawatt-hours (MWh)	1,000,000 (One Million) Watt-hours
Gigawatt-hours (GWh)	1,000,000,000 (One Billion) Watt-hours
Terawatt-hours (TWh)	1,000,000,000,000 (One Trillion) Watt-hours

Source: Energy Information Administration, Office of Coal, Nuclear, Electric and Alternate Fuels, Electric Power Division [4].

Cord

A Cord is the unit of measure of wood that is equivalent to a pile of round wood 4 ft wide, 8 ft long and 4 ft high. It contains 128 ft^3 of wood and space. It may contain approximately 80–90 ft^3 of solid wood. A common, but fairly meaningless conversion is 500 board feet per cord.

3.3 Energy Content

It is important to understand the energy content of various energy resources that are available throughout the world. Various countries in the world are rich in certain resources. For example, the United States has very large coal reserves, it is rich in uranium reserves, it has a large amount of natural gas, it has a very good resource base of wind energy, it has a rich resource base of hydro, it has a large amount of land mass and therefore has access to solar energy, and it has a moderate amount of oil reserves. Other countries are not as well off as the United States. For example, France has a very poor energy resource base. It has chosen to go to an all nuclear energy economy. Japan has a very poor energy resource base and, like France, it too has chosen to go to an all nuclear energy economy. Other countries such as Canada and Russia are rich in resources like the United States. Countries in the Middle East are very rich in oil reserves. In order to compare the values of these resources, energy content of all the resources is described by a common unit, called *tonne of oil equivalent* (*toe*) or *tonne of coal equivalent* (*tce*). However, the use of *toe* is more common than *tce*. The Statistics Division of the United Nations Secretariat and the International Energy Agency defines one tonne of oil equivalent as 10^7 kcal, net calorific value (equivalent to 41.868 GJ). The *toe* of various energy sources is shown below.

1 t of crude oil = about 7.3 barrels
1 t of natural gas liquids = 45 GJ (net calorific value)
1,000 standard cubic meters of natural gas = 36 GJ (net calorific value)
1 t of uranium = 10,000–16,000 toe
1 t of peat = 0.2275 toe
1 t of fuelwood = 0.3215 toe

The average energy content of various energy sources in a common unit, such as BTU are given below.

- One barrel of crude oil equals to 42 gallons of crude oil, or 5.8 million BTUs
- One cubic foot (ft^3)of natural gas equals to 1032 BTUs
- One tonne of coal equals to 24 to 28 million BTUs
- One cord of wood equals to 15–24 million BTUs
- Solar heat is capable of providing 0.06 million BTUs per square foot per year
- A 10 m or 33 ft in diameter windmill located in the Great Plains region of the USA with an average wind speed of 20 mph can produce 49,000 kWh per year or 167 million BTUs per year.
- 1 kg of U-235 can produce 78,000 million BTUs.

Example 3.1

How many barrels of crude oil are needed to supply the USA's energy needs for the year 2007?

Solution

Data: US uses about 101.6 quad energy per year.
     1 quad = 10^{15} BTU
     1 barrel of oil contents about 5.8×10^6 BTU of energy

$$\# barrels = \frac{101.6 \times 10^{15}\ BTUs}{5.8 \times 10^6\ BTU/barrel} = 1.752 \times 10^{10}\ barrels$$

Example 3.2

How many cubic feet of gas are needed to supply the USA's energy needs for the year 2007?

Solution

$$\begin{aligned} \#Cubic\ feet &= 101.6 \times 10^{15}\ BTUs /(1.032 \times 10^3\ BTU/ft^3) \\ &= 9.845 \times 10^{13}\ ft^3 \end{aligned}$$

Example 3.3

How many tons of coals are needed to supply the USA's energy needs for the year 2007?

Solution

$$\#\text{Tons} = 101.6 \times 10^{15} \text{ BTUs}/(24 \times 10^6 \text{ BTU/t}) = 4.233 \times 10^9 \text{ t}$$

Example 3.4

How many square feet of land for solar energy are needed to supply the USA's energy needs for the year 2007 (not considering the thermal energy conversion efficiency)?

Solution

$$\begin{aligned}\#\text{Square Feet} \quad &= \quad 101.6 \times 10^{15} \text{ BTUs }/(0.06 \times 10^6 \text{ BTU/ft}^2) \\ &= \quad 1.693 \times 10^{12} \text{ ft}^2\end{aligned}$$

This is about 61,101 square miles (Note: This is a square of about 247 by 247 miles.

The energy conversion problem is significant. The most cost effective solar cells are less than 10% efficient. Assuming 10% efficiency, to produce 101.6 Quads of electrical energy by solar cells would take a land area of 611,010 square miles (or a square of 782 by 782 miles). This is about the equivalent land area of Arizona, New Mexico, Colorado, Utah, Nevada and Idaho (Arizona covers 114,006 square miles, New Mexico covers 121,598 square miles, Colorado covers 104,100 square miles, Utah covers 84,904 square miles, Nevada covers 110,567, and Idaho covers 83,574 square miles), or alternatively we could choose Texas, California, Nevada and Utah (Texas covers 26,8601 square miles and California, covers 163,707 square miles).

Example 3.5

How many kg of U-235 are needed to supply the USA's energy needs for the year 2007?

Solution

$$\begin{aligned}\#\text{kg} \quad &= \quad 101.6 \times 10^{15} \text{ BTUs}/(78,000 \times 10^6 \text{ BTU/kg}) = 1.295 \times 10^6 \text{ kg} \\ &= \quad 1.426 \times 10^3 \text{ t}\end{aligned}$$

Example 3.6

In 2007 the energy used by the US for transportation was 29.10 quads. How many nuclear power plants would it take to produce enough hydrogen to provide the energy needed for transportation? Assume that the conversion efficiency from electricity to hydrogen using electrolysis is 50%. A typical nuclear power plant produces about 1,200 MW electric. Assume that a nuclear power plant operates at 90% of its capacity (capacity factor) for the year. The first step is to calculate the number of BTUs that a nuclear power plant produces in a year.

$$\text{Energy Produced Per Plant} = 0.9 \times 1{,}200 \times 10^6 \text{ W} \times 1 \text{ J/s-W} \times 1 \text{ year} \times 365$$
$$\text{day/year} \times 24 \text{ h/day} \times 60 \text{ min/h} \times 60 \text{ s/min}$$
$$\times 9.4786 \ 10^{-4} \text{ BTU/J}$$
$$= 3.228 \times 10^{13} \text{ BTU/Power Plant}$$

The next step is to calculate the energy in hydrogen converted by electrolysis using the electricity of the nuclear power plant.

Hydrogen Energy Produced per Power Plant = $0.5 \times 3.228 \times 10^{13}$ BTU/Power Plant = 1.614×10^{13} BTU-Hydrogen/Power Plant

Number of Power Plants Needed for Transportation = 29.10×10^{15} BTU/1.614×10^{13} BTU/Power Plant = **1, 803 Power Plants**

3.4 Power

We are involved every day with energy and power. For example, automobiles and electrical motors are rated by Horsepower, light bulbs are sold by Watts, the price of natural gas is set by Therms, the consumption of electricity is defined by kilo-watt-hours, and air conditioners are sold by Tons or BTUs per hour. Some of these are described by energy units, while others are by power unit. Energy is a funda-mental unit. From fundamental units, one can derive other essential parameters. An example of this is power. Power is the rate at which energy is used. Power is defined as the energy per unit time. The units of power are:

• Kilowatt
• BTUs per hour – British Thermal Units per hour

Kilowatt

Kilowatt-hour (kWh) is the metric unit of energy. It may be defined as the work or energy equal to that expended by 1 kW in 1 h. One kilowatt-hour is equal to 3,600,000 J or 3.6 MJ, or 3,413 BTUs. Kilowatt, on the other hand, is the unit of power. It is an energy use rate of 1,000 J per second.

MMB/D

MMB/D (equivalent to a million barrels of oil per day) – if all of the energy used by the US, 101.6 quads in 2007, were from oil than the United States uses about 48 MMB/D.

Tara Watt

Tara Watt = TW = 1 trillion watts

Example 3.7

How many kilowatt-hours does a 1 GWe nuclear power plant produce in a year? Assume a capacity factor of 90%.

Solution

1 year = 1 year $\times$ 365 days/year $\times$ 24 h/day = 8,760 h

Energy = 1 $\times$ 10^6 kW $\times$ 0.90 $\times$ 8,760 h = 7.884 $\times$ 10^9 kWh

Example 3.8

How many BTUs is 7.884 $\times$ 10^9 kWh?

Solution

Energy = 3,413 BTUs/kWh $\times$ 7.884 $\times$ 10^9 kWh = 2.668 $\times$ 10^{13} BTUs

Example 3.9

How many Quads are in 2.668 $\times$ 10^{13} BTUs?

Solution

Energy = 2.668 × 10^{13} BTUs/(10^{15} BTUs/quad) = 2.668 × 10^{-2} quad

Example 3.10

How many MMB/D are in 2.668 × 10^{-2} quad?

Solution

Energy = 2.668 × 10^{-2} quad /(2.1 quad/MMB/D) = 1.284 × 10^{-2} MMB/D

Example 3.11

What percentage of the US energy use does a 1 GWe nuclear plant produce?

Solution

% of US Energy Produced = 100 × 1.284 × 10^{-2} MMB/D/(48 MMB/D) = 0.02675%

Example 3.12

It is given that a light bulb has a power rating 100 W. This is a rate at which the bulb uses energy. What will be the energy consumption of ten, 100 W bulbs in 1 h in British units?

Solution

Ten 100 W light bulbs turned on for 1 h is equivalent to:

100 W × 10 light bulbs × 1 h   = 1,000 W hours = 1 kWh = 3,413 BTU

Example 3.13

How many 100 W light bulbs will be required to consume 101.6 quads of energy per year?

Solution

From the previous problem, one 100 W light bulb consumes 341.3 BTU per hour. There are 24 h in a day. There are 365 days in a year and therefore 8,760 h per year. Thus a single 100 W light bulb will use 2,989,788 BTUs per year if it is on for the whole year.

Number of light bulbs = 101.6 × 10^{15}/2.989788 × 10^6 = 34 billion light bulbs

References

1. Metric Act of 1866, Public Law 39-183, U.S. Congress, 28 July 1866.
2. U.S. Metric Study Act of 1968, Public Law 90-472, U. S. Congress, 9 August 1968.
3. Metric Conversion Act of 1975, Public Law 94-168, U. S. Congress, 23 December 1975.
4. Energy Information Administration, Office of Coal, Nuclear, Electric and Alternate Fuels (3/23/2009) Electric Power.

Problems

1. The universal Gas-law constant in cal/(gmol K) is 1.987. What is its value in cubic centimeters atm/(gmol K), (lb.in^2) (ft^3)/(lbmol°R), (atm ft^3)/(lbmol°R), and (lb/ft^2) (ft^3)/ (lbmol°R)?
2. The unit of viscosity in SI units is generally given in centipoise (g/(s cm). Convert 1 centipoise to British units (lb/(s ft).
3. Thermal conductivity of water at 32°F in British units is 0.32 Btu/(h)(ft^3)(°F/ft). Convert this to SI unit.
4. Calculate the energy content of (a) one barrel of crude oil (b) one cubic foot of natural gas (c) one short ton of coal (d) one cord of wood (e) 1 kg of U 235 in the following units (1) calorie, (2) joules, (3) ft-lb, and (4) kWh.

4 THERMODYNAMIC CYCLES

Abstract

Energy sources such as coal, natural gas, or petroleum cannot be used directly to perform a work. These sources are burned to generate heat which is then converted to mechanical or electrical energy. These processes are governed by thermodynamic cycles and the efficiency of the overall process depends mainly on the choice or efficiency of the cycle. A number of thermodynamic cycles using various working fluids have been suggested. The description and analysis of these cycles are presented in this chapter.

4.1 Introduction

The energy resources available in nature such as coal, natural gas, petroleum, and uranium cannot be used directly for most of the applications. These resources have to be transformed into a useful form such as heat or electricity before their use. For example, coal must first be burned or combusted to generate heat which is then used to produce steam for space heating or electricity generation. Similarly, crude petroleum must first be refined to obtain gasoline or diesel. In automobiles, gasoline or diesel is first burned to generate heat which is then converted to mechanical energy to move the automobiles. Air is generally used as the carrier of heat. The conversion of heat energy to mechanical or other forms of energy is governed by a series of thermodynamic processes.

A thermodynamic cycle is a series of thermodynamic processes at the end of which the system returns to its initial state. Properties depend only on the thermodynamic state which varies during the operations of the process. During the process, heat is added in certain stages and work is obtained from other stages, but obeys the first law of thermodynamics, which states that the net heat input is equal to the net work output over any cycle. The repeating nature of the process path allows for continuous operation. Thermodynamic cycles are discussed in details in a

T.K. Ghosh and M.A. Prelas, *Energy Resources and Systems:*
Volume 1: Fundamentals and Non-Renewable Resources, 89–140.

number of text books [1–9]. Two primary classes of thermodynamic cycles are power cycles and refrigeration cycles. Power cycles are cycles that convert a heat input into a work output, while refrigeration cycles transfer heat from low to high temperatures using work input. In this chapter the emphasis will be on power cycles.

The Carnot cycle is considered an ideal thermodynamic cycle. It is the most efficient cycle possible for converting a given amount of thermal energy into work or, conversely, for using a given amount of work for refrigeration purposes. Any cycle operating between temperatures T_H and T_C, cannot exceed the efficiency of a Carnot cycle. The temperatures are expressed in Kelvin (K) or Rankine (R). Further discussion on Carnot engine efficiency is given by Curzon and Ahlborn [10].

4.2 Carnot Cycle

The Carnot cycle was first studied by Nicolas Léonard Sadi Carnot in the 1820s. Benoit Paul Émile Clapeyron in the 1830s and work in the 1940s further investigated the Carnot cycle.

A Carnot cycle acting as a heat engine is shown in Fig. 4.1 on a temperature (T)-entropy (s) diagram. The cycle takes place between a hot reservoir at temperature T_H and a cold reservoir at temperature T_C. The Carnot cycle consists of the following steps:

Reversible isothermal expansion of the gas at the "hot" temperature, T_H (Isothermal heat addition): During this step (1 to 2 in Fig. 4.1) the expanding gas causes the piston to do work on the surroundings. The gas expansion is propelled by absorption of heat from the high temperature reservoir.

Reversible adiabatic expansion of the gas: For this step (2 to 3 in Fig. 4.1) it is assumed that the piston and cylinder are thermally insulated, so that no heat is gained or lost. The gas continues to expand, doing work on the surroundings. The gas expansion causes it to cool to the "cold" temperature, T_C.

Reversible isothermal compression of the gas at the "cold" temperature, T_C (Isothermal heat rejection): This step is shown as 3–4 in Fig. 4.1. Now the surroundings do work on the gas, causing heat to flow out of the gas to the low temperature reservoir.

Reversible adiabatic compression of the gas: This is Step 4 to 1 in Fig. 4.1. Once again it is assumed that the piston and cylinder are thermally insulated. During this step, the surroundings do work on the gas, compressing it and causing the temperature to rise to T_H. At this point the gas is in the same state as at the start of Step 1.

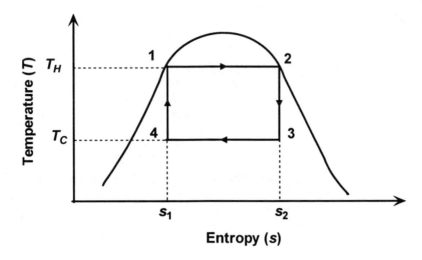

Fig. 4.1. The *T-s* diagram of the Carnot cycle.

4.2.1 Efficiency of Carnot Engine

The amount of energy transferred as work is given by;

$$\Delta W = \int P\, dv = (T_H - T_C)(s_B - s_A) \tag{4.1}$$

where W is the work done per unit mass, P is the pressure, v is the specific volume, and s_1 and s_2 are entropies corresponding to State 1 and State 2, respectively. The total amount of thermal energy transferred between the hot reservoir and the system will be:

$$\Delta Q_H = T_H(s_B - s_A) \tag{4.2}$$

The total amount of thermal energy transferred between the system and the cold reservoir will be:

$$\Delta Q_C = T_C(s_B - s_A) \tag{4.3}$$

The efficiency η is defined as the amount of work done divided by the heat input to the system from the hot reservoir (T in absolute temperature units, Kelvins):

$$\eta = \frac{\Delta W}{\Delta Q_H} = 1 - \frac{T_C}{T_H} \tag{4.4}$$

For a heat engine, this efficiency represents the fraction of the heat energy extracted from the hot reservoir and converted to mechanical work. For a refrigeration cycle, it is the ratio of energy input to the refrigerator divided by the amount of energy extracted from the hot reservoir.

Example 4.1

An engine is operating based on a Carnot cycle. The temperatures of the hot and cold reservoirs are 200°C and 20°C, respectively. Calculate the thermal efficiency of the cycle. If the work output from the engine is 15 kW, how much heat should be rejected from the condenser?

Solution

The thermal efficiency of the Carnot Cycle is given by

$$\eta = 1 - \frac{T_C}{T_H} = 1 - \frac{20 + 273.15}{200 + 273.15} = 1 - \frac{293.15}{473.15} = 0.38$$

The heat input to the cycle is calculated based on per unit time basis.

$$Q_H = \frac{W}{1 - T_c / T_H} = \frac{15}{0.38} = 39.47 \text{ kW}$$

The heat rejected to the condenser is

$$Q_L = Q_H - W = 39.47 - 15 = 24.47 \text{ kW}$$

In reality it is not possible to build an ideal thermodynamically reversible engine based on the Carnot cycle. Therefore, real heat engines based on real thermodynamic cycles are less efficient than the Carnot cycle. A number of real thermodynamic cycles have been designed based on the process needs. Thermodynamic cycles that are widely used in various day-to-day operations include the following.

(A) Brayton Cycle
    1. Open (gas turbine)
    2. Closed
        (i) Inert working fluid
        (ii) Active working fluid

   (B)   Otto Cycle (spark ignition)
      1. Reciprocating ("gas" engine)
         (i) 4-stroke cycle
         (ii) 2-stroke cycle
      2. Rotary
      3. Homogeneous Charge Compression Ignition (HCCI)
   (C)   Diesel Cycle (compression ignition)
      1. Reciprocating
         (i) 4-stroke cycle
         (ii) 2-stroke cycle
      2. Rotary
   (D)   Dual Cycle
   (E)   Rankine Cycle
      1. Reheat
      2. Regenerative
         (i) Open feed water
         (ii) Closed feed water
      3. Supercritical
   (F)   Combined Brayton and Rankine Cycle
   (G)   Stirling Cycle
   (H)   Ericsson Cycle
   (I)   Atkinson Cycle
   (J)   Miller Cycle
   (K)   Kalina Cycle

4.3 Brayton Cycle

The Brayton cycle is used for gas turbines only where both the compression and expansion processes take place in rotating machinery. The two major application areas of gas-turbine engines are aircraft propulsion and electric power generation. Gas turbines are used in stationary power plants to generate electricity as stand-alone units or in conjunction with steam power plants on the high-temperature side.

The Brayton cycle may be operated either as an open cycle or as a closed cycle. Gas turbines usually operate on an open cycle, as shown in Fig. 4.2. Fresh air at ambient conditions is drawn into the compressor, where its temperature and pressure are raised. The high-pressure air proceeds into the combustion chamber, where the fuel is burned at constant pressure. The resulting high-temperature gases then enter the turbine, where they expand to the atmospheric pressure through a row of nozzle vanes. This expansion causes the turbine blade to spin, which then turns a shaft inside a magnetic coil. When the shaft is rotating inside the magnetic coil, electrical current is produced. The exhaust gases leaving the turbine in the open cycle are not re-circulated.

The open gas-turbine cycle can be modeled as a closed cycle, as shown in Fig. 4.3, by utilizing the air-standard assumptions. Here the compression and expansion processes remain the same, but a constant-pressure heat-rejection process to the ambient air replaces the combustion process. The working fluid undergoes four internally reversible processes in this closed loop Brayton cycle.

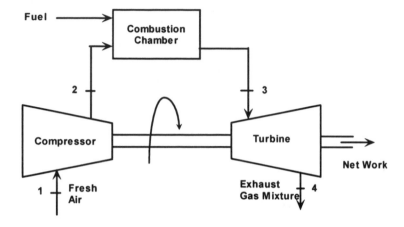

Fig. 4.2. An open cycle gas turbine engine.

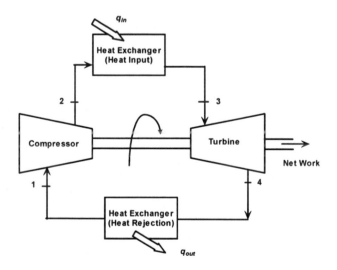

Fig. 4.3. A closed cycle gas turbine engine.

The *P-v* and *T-s* diagrams of an ideal Brayton cycle are shown in Figs. 4.4 and 4.5, respectively. Various stages of the Brayton cycle are as follows:

1–2: Isentropic compression (in a compressor)
2–3: Constant pressure heat addition
3–4: Isentropic expansion (in a turbine)
4–1: Constant pressure heat rejection

However, as shown in Fig. 4.4, during actual operation, the process follows 1–2'–3–4'–1 path.

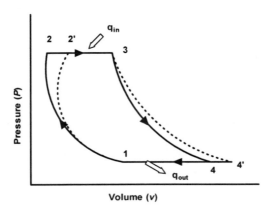

Fig. 4.4. The P-v diagram of the Brayton cycle.

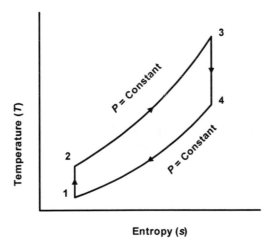

Fig. 4.5. The *T-s* diagram of the Brayton cycle.

The heat balance equation for the system can be written as

$$(q_{in} - q_{out}) + (W_{in} - W_{out}) = h_{out} - h_{in} \tag{4.5}$$

where q_{in} is the amount of heat added at the boiler and q_{out} is the amount of heat removed from the condenser (in the case of the closed cycle system) or heat carried away by the exhaust stream (in the case of the open cycle). W_{in} is the work input to the pump and W_{out} is the work output from the turbine. The enthalpy of the stream is given by h. Heat transfers to and from the working fluid can be expressed by:

$$q_{in} = h_3 - h_2 = C_P(T_3 - T_2) \tag{4.6}$$

$$q_{out} = h_4 - h_1 = C_P(T_4 - T_1) \tag{4.7}$$

where, C_p is the specific heat at constant pressure and T represents the temperature in Kelvin (K). The thermal efficiency of an ideal Brayton cycle may be expressed as

$$
\begin{aligned}
\eta &= \frac{w_{net}}{q_{in}} \\
&= 1 - \frac{q_{out}}{q_{in}} \\
&= 1 - \frac{C_P(T_4 - T_1)}{C_P(T_3 - T_2)} \\
&= 1 - \frac{T_1\left(\dfrac{T_4}{T_1} - 1\right)}{T_2\left(\dfrac{T_3}{T_2} - 1\right)}
\end{aligned} \tag{4.8}
$$

Processes 1–2 and 3–4 are isentropic. For an adiabatic quasiequilibrium process involving an ideal gas, the following relationships hold:

$$Tv^{k-1} = constant, \quad TP^{\left(\frac{1-k}{k}\right)} = constant, \quad Pv^k = constant$$

where, k is the ratio of specific heats ($k = C_p/C_v$). C_p is the specific heat at constant pressure and C_v is the specific heat at constant volume. Since, $P_2 = P_3$, and $P_4 = P_1$, the temperature ratios may be expressed in terms of pressure (P) as:

$$\frac{T_2}{T_1} = \left(\frac{P_2}{P_1}\right)^{\frac{k-1}{k}}$$

$$\frac{T_3}{T_4} = \left(\frac{P_3}{P_4}\right)^{\frac{k-1}{k}}$$

(4.9)

From Fig. 4.5,

$$\frac{P_2}{P_1} = \frac{P_3}{P_4}$$

(4.10)

This suggests that:

$$\frac{T_4}{T_1} = \frac{T_3}{T_2}$$

(4.11)

Using Eqs. (4.9–4.11), the efficiency may be expressed by the following expression.

$$\eta = 1 - \frac{1}{\left(\dfrac{P_2}{P_1}\right)^{\frac{k-1}{k}}}$$

(4.12)

Equation (4.12) suggests that the efficiency of the cycle may be increased by increasing the pressure ratio and the specific heat ratio of the working fluid (if different from air). Various aspects of Brayton cycles have been studied by a number of investigators [11–18]. Applications of Brayton cycles have been explored for a number of new systems, including power plants [19–22], nuclear power plants [23–30], space power applications [31–36], coal gasification plants [37], waste heat recovery system [38], automobile engines [39–42], and using other working fluids [43–50]. Discussion on Brayton cycle efficiency and how it can be improved has been discussed by Sahin et al. [51], Wu et al. [52–56], and Cheng and Chen [57, 58].

Example 4.2

Air enters the compressor of a gas turbine operating on a Brayton Cycle at ambient conditions (100 kPa and 25°C). It leaves the compressor and combustor at 500 kPa and 850°C, respectively. Calculate the temperature at various stages of the cycle and the thermal efficiency.

Solution

The following information is given:

T_1 = 25 + 273.15 = 298.15 K, and T_3 = 850 + 273.15 = 1123.15 K, P_1 = 100 kPa, and P_2 = 500 kPa. The value of k for air is 1.4.

From Eq. (4.9),

$$T_2 = T_1 \left(\frac{P_2}{P_1} \right)^{\left(\frac{k-1}{k} \right)} = 298.15 \, (5)^{0.286} = 472 \, K$$

Similarly,

$$T_4 = T_3 \left(\frac{P_4}{P_5} \right)^{\left(\frac{k-1}{k} \right)} = 1123.15 \left(\frac{1}{5} \right)^{0.286} = 709.0 \, K$$

The thermal efficiency calculated from Eq. (4.12) is 0.369 or 36.9%

4.4 The Otto Cycle

All internal combustion engines are operated based on the Otto thermodynamic cycle. The process is shown on the *P-v* diagram in Fig. 4.6.

The movement and location of the piston in the cylinder during the cycle is shown in Fig. 4.7. The diameter of the piston is called the bore and the distance the piston travels in a direction is called the stroke. During the intake stroke, the piston does not travel all the way to the bottom of the cylinder. When the piston moves to the lowest allowable point at the bottom, known as Bottom Dead Center (BDC), the air occupies the maximum volume. Similarly, the piston moves only to a specified distance during the compression stroke. At the end of the compression stroke, the volume occupied by the air in the cylinder is at a minimum and called Top Dead Center (TDC). This volume is the clearance volume.

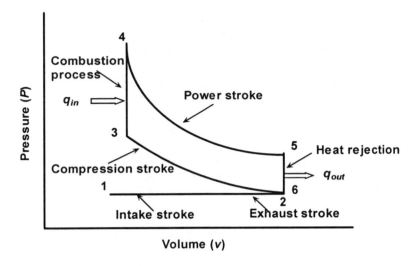

Fig. 4.6. The *P-v* diagram of the Otto cycle.

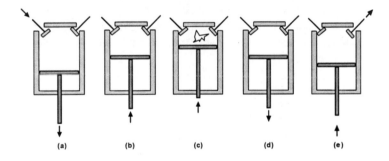

Fig. 4.7. Position of pistons in the cylinder for a 4-stoke Otto engine.

The cycle proceeds as follows:

Stage 1: The intake valve opens and a mixture of fuel and air is drawn into the cylinder. The piston is pulled towards the crankshaft, as shown in Fig. 4.7a, at constant pressure. In the *P-v* diagram, 1–2 is Stage 1 and is the beginning of the intake stroke.

Stage 2: At the end of the intake stroke, the intake valve is closed and the piston is moved back towards the combustion chamber (Fig. 4.7b). The pressure and temperature are increased by the adiabatic compression (Step 2–3 in the *P-v* diagram). Stage 2 is the beginning of the compression stroke.

Stage 3: At the end of the compression stroke, the spark plug in the engine, which generates an electric spark, ignites the fuel-air mixture (Fig. 4.7c). Stage 3 is the beginning of the combustion process and is Step 3–4 in the P-v diagram.

Stage 4: This is called the power stroke and is shown in Step 4–5 in the P-v diagram. Combustion occurs very quickly at constant volume in the combustion chamber in an Internal Combustion (IC) engine. The high pressure forces the piston back towards the crankshaft as shown in Fig. 4.7d.

Stage 5: This is the end of the power stroke, and heat is rejected to the surroundings as shown in Step 5–6 in the P-v diagram.

Stage 6: Following heat rejection, the exhaust valve is opened and the residual gas is forced out into the surroundings to prepare for the next intake stroke (Fig. 4.7e). Stage 6 is the beginning of the exhaust stroke.

Work is done on the gas by the piston between Stages 2 and 3. Work is done by the gas on the piston between Stages 4 and 5. Therefore, the area enclosed by the cycle on a P-v diagram is proportional to the work produced by the cycle. The work times the rate of the cycle (cycles per second) is equal to the power produced by the engine. For calculation of the efficiency of an Otto cycle, first an ideal cycle should be considered in which there is no heat entering (or leaving) the gas during the compression and power strokes, no friction losses, and instantaneous burning occurring at constant volume. In actual operation, there are many losses associated with each process. These losses are taken into account by introducing efficiency factors. The ideal efficiency of the cycle may be calculated using the following simplified P-v diagram (Fig. 4.8).

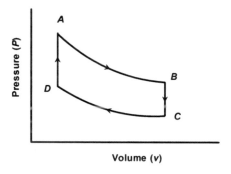

Fig. 4.8. A simplified P-v diagram of the Otto cycle.

The work done by the air-standard Otto cycle may be determined by a total energy balance.

$$W = q_{DA}\left(\frac{q_{DA} + q_{BC}}{q_{DA}}\right) \tag{4.13}$$

The heat input or rejection may be described in terms of temperature as follows.

$$q_{DA} = C_v(T_A - T_D)$$
$$q_{BC} = C_v(T_C - T_B) \tag{4.14}$$

where Cv is the heat capacity at constant volume. The efficiency, therefore, can be expressed as

$$\eta = \frac{W}{q_{DA}} = \frac{C_v(T_A - T_D) - C_v(T_B - T_C)}{C_v(T_A - T_D)} \tag{4.15}$$

$$\eta = 1 - \frac{T_B - T_C}{T_A - T_D} \tag{4.16}$$

As mentioned earlier, for the adiabatic reversible processes, the following relationship holds for air as it can be assumed to behave as an ideal gas

$$Pv^k = cons\,tan\,t \tag{4.17}$$

Using this relationship, the temperature at various point of the cycle can be expressed as follows.

$$T_B = \frac{P_B v_B}{R} = \frac{P_B v_C}{R}$$
$$T_C = \frac{P_C v_C}{R}$$
$$T_A = \frac{P_A v_A}{R} = \frac{P_A v_D}{R} \tag{4.18}$$
$$T_D = \frac{P_D v_D}{R}$$

Therefore,

$$P_A v_D^k = P_B v_C^k$$
$$P_C v_C^k = P_D v_D^k \tag{4.19}$$

By defining the compression ratio as the ratio of the volume occupied by the air at BDC to the volume occupied by air at TDC, the following expression is obtained.

$$r = \frac{v_C}{v_D}$$ (4.20)

The efficiency for the cycle can be written as

$$\eta = 1 - \left(\frac{1}{r}\right)^{\gamma-1}$$ (4.21)

The work W can be expressed by the temperatures as follows

$$W = C_v\left[(T_4 - T_3) - (T_5 - T_2)\right]$$ (4.22)

The work times the rate of the cycle (cycles per second, cps) is equal to the power produced by the engine.

$$Power = W \bullet cps$$ (4.23)

The mean effective pressure (MEP) is another quantity that can be used to rate piston-cylinder engines and is given by the following expression.

$$W_{cycle} = (MEP)(v_{BDC} - v_{TDC})$$ (4.24)

As noted by Mandl [59], for a car with $r = 10$, the theoretical expression gives an efficiency of 0.6, but the practical efficiency is more like 0.3. A table of thermal efficiencies and peak cylinder pressure and combustion temperature is given by Anderson [60]. Thermodynamic analysis of the Otto cycle has been performed by a number of investigators using first and second law analysis method [61–73]. An attempt has also been made to use the Otto cycle for solar collectors [74].

4.5 Diesel Cycle

In diesel engines, the fuel and air are compressed separately and brought together at the time of combustion. In this arrangement, fuel is injected into the cylinder which contains compressed air at a higher temperature than the self-ignition temperature of the fuel. Once injected, the fuel ignites on its own and does not need an ignition system. It should be noted that the upper limit of compression ratio is limited in spark ignition engines due to the self-ignition temperature of the fuel. Therefore, diesel engines are not limited by the fuel to air compression ratio.

The diesel cycle is similar to the Otto cycle; the main difference is in the process of heat addition. In the diesel cycle, the heat addition takes place at constant pressure whereas in the Otto cycle it is at a constant volume. For this reason, the diesel cycle is often referred to as the constant-pressure cycle. The P-v and T-s diagrams of the diesel cycle are shown in Figs. 4.9 and 4.10, respectively.

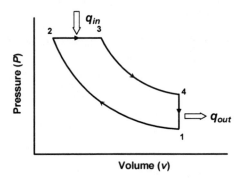

Fig. 4.9. The P-v diagram of the diesel cycle.

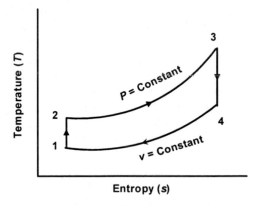

Fig. 4.10. The T-s diagram of the diesel cycle.

The diesel cycle is an ideal air standard cycle consisting of the following four processes:

1–2: Isentropic compression
2–3: Reversible constant pressure heating
3–4: Isentropic expansion
4–1: Reversible constant volume cooling

The maximum theoretical efficiency of a diesel engine can be calculated in the same way as described earlier for Carnot or Brayton cycles. The efficiency of the diesel cycle can be expressed as:

$$\eta = 1 - \frac{1}{k} \frac{r_e^k - 1}{r_c^{k-1}(r_e - 1)}$$

(4.25)

where k is the ratio of the specific heats. The expansion ratio (r_e) and compression ratio (r_c) are given by the following expressions.

$$r_e = \frac{v_3}{v_2}$$

(4.26)

$$r_c = \frac{v_1}{v_2}$$

(4.27)

The performance of a diesel engine under various conditions has been investigated by several researchers [75–79]. One of the main concerns of diesel engines is emission of pollutants. Several approaches including direct water injection have been explored for reduction of pollutants from a diesel engine [80–82].

Example 4.3

A diesel cycle operates on air with a pressure of 200 kPa and 200°C. The compression ratio is 15. If 1,000 kJ/kg of work output is desired, determine the thermal efficiency of the cycle. What is the MEP for the cycle? What will be the efficiency of an Otto cycle under similar operating conditions?

Solution

Determine the compression ratio, r_c. Assume ideal gas law:

$$v_1 = \frac{RT_1}{P_1} = \frac{(0.287)(200 + 273)}{200} = 0.6788 \text{ m}^3/\text{kg}$$

The compression ratio, r_c, is given by

$$r_c = \frac{v_1}{v_2} = 15, \text{ therefore, } v_2 = 0.6788/15 = 0.04525 \text{ m}^3/\text{kg}$$

Since process 1 to 2 is isentropic, it can be shown that

$$T_2 = T_1\left(\frac{v_1}{v_2}\right)^{k-1} = (200 + 273)(15)^{0.4} = 1397.3 \text{ K}$$

In terms of pressure, the relationship is given by,

$$P_2 = P_1\left(\frac{v_1}{v_2}\right)^{k} = 200(15)^{1.4} = 8862.5 \text{ kPa}$$

The net work done by the cycle can be calculated as

$$w_{net} = q_{net} = q_{2-3} + q_{4-1} = C_p(T_3 - T_2) + C_v(T_1 - T_4)$$

Substituting the values for *Wnet*, C_p, C_v, T_1, and T_2, we get

$$1000 = 1.00(T_3 - 1397.3) + 0.717(473 - T_4)$$

T_3 and T_4 are unknown, but can be expressed in terms of v_3 by using the following expressions.

$$T_3 = v_3\frac{T_2}{v_2} = 30879.5 v_3$$

$$T_4 = T_3\left(\frac{v_3}{v_4}\right)^{k-1} = T_3\left(\frac{v_3}{0.6788}\right)^{0.4} = 1.1676\, T_3 v_3^{0.4} = 36054.97\, v_3^{1.4}$$

It may be noted that $v_4 = v_1$. Substitution of T_4 and T_3 provides the following expression

$$1000 = (30879.5\, v_3 - 1397.3) + 0.717(473 - 36054.97 v_3^{1.4})$$

This equation must be solved by a trial and error method. The solution provides the following values:

$v_3 = 0.1$ m³/kg, $T_3 = 3087.95$ K, and $T_4 = 1435.4$ K.

The cut off ratio r_e is given by

$$r_e = \frac{v_3}{v_2} = \frac{0.1}{0.04525} = 2.21$$

The thermal efficiency is given by Eq. (4.13) and is 0.60 or 60%. The MEP can be calculated as follows.

$$MEP = \frac{W_{net}}{v_1 - v_2} = \frac{1000}{0.6788 - 0.04525} = 1578.4 \, kPa$$

Under similar conditions, the efficiency of an Otto cycle can be calculated from Eq. (4.27). However, the compression ratio, r_c, of Otto cycle is given by

$$r_{c,Otto} = \frac{v_1}{v_3} = \frac{0.6788}{0.1} = 6.788$$

$$\eta_{Otto} = 1 - \left(\frac{1}{r_{Otto}}\right)^{k-1} = 1 - \left(\frac{1}{6.788}\right)^{0.4} = 0.5351 \text{ or } 53.51\%.$$

4.6 The Dual Cycle

A dual cycle approximates an ideal cycle better during the actual performance of a compression-ignition engine. In this cycle, the combustion process is modeled by two heat-addition processes: a constant volume process and a constant pressure process. The process is shown in Fig. 4.11.

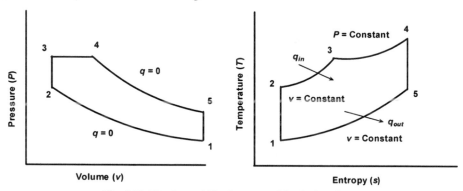

Fig. 4.11. The *P-v* and *T-s* diagrams of the dual cycle.

The thermal efficiency in terms of temperature can be expressed by the following expression:

$$\eta = 1 - \frac{T_5 - T_1}{T_3 - T_2 + k(T_4 - T_3)} \tag{4.28}$$

In terms of pressure, the thermal efficiency may be expressed as

$$\eta = 1 - \left(\frac{1}{r^{k-1}}\right)\left(\frac{r_p r_c^k - 1}{k r_p (r_c - 1) + r_p - 1}\right) \tag{4.29}$$

where, $r_P = \dfrac{P_3}{P_2}$. $\tag{4.30}$

The effect of working fluid on dual cycle efficiency has been studied by Chen et al. [83] and Zheng et al. [84]. Dual cycles have been developed for a variety of applications including its use in gas turbines [85], coal gasification units [86], and boiling water reactors for power generation using nuclear energy [87, 88].

4.7 Rankine Cycle

Rankine cycles describe the operation of steam turbines used in power generation plants [89–93]. This is also known as the vapor power cycle as the working fluid changes phase from a liquid to a vapor within the system. A schematic of a Rankine cycle is shown in Fig. 4.12 and the *T-s* diagram of the process is shown in Fig. 4.13. There are four processes or steps in the Rankine cycle. These states are identified by number in the diagram below.

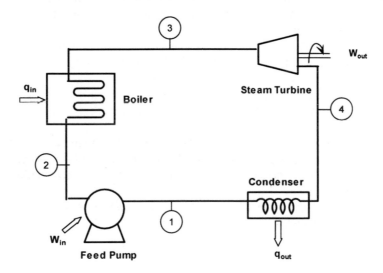

Fig. 4.12. The schematic of the Rankine cycle.

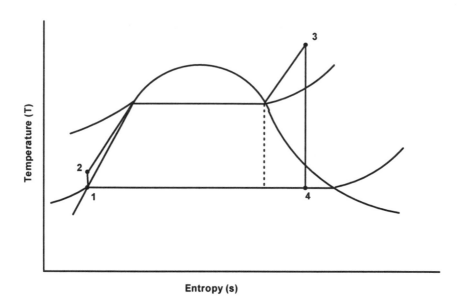

Fig. 4.13. The *T-s* diagram of the Rankine cycle.

Process 1–2: The working fluid is pumped or pressurized isentropically from low to high pressure by a pump. Pumping requires a power input (for example mechanical or electrical).

Process 2–3: The high pressure liquid enters a boiler where it is heated at constant pressure to saturated vapor. Heat sources for power plant systems could be coal, natural gas, or nuclear power.

Process 3–4: The saturated vapor expands through a turbine to generate power output. Ideally, this expansion is isentropic. This decreases the temperature and pressure of the vapor.

Process 4–1: The vapor then enters a condenser where it is cooled to saturated liquid. This liquid then re-enters the pump and the cycle repeats.

In a real Rankine cycle, the compression by the pump and the expansion in the turbine are not isentropic. This increases the power required by the pump and decreases the power generated by the turbine. It also makes calculations more involved and difficult.

Work output of the cycle (Steam turbine), W_{out}, and work input to the cycle (Pump), W_{in}, are given by:

$$W_{out} = \dot{m}(h_3 - h_4) \tag{4.31}$$

$$W_{in} = v_1 (P_2 - P_1)$$ (4.32)

where $\dot{m}$ is the mass flow of the cycle. Heat supplied to the cycle (boiler), q_{in} and heat rejected from the cycle (condenser), q_{out} are:

$$q_{in} = \dot{m}(h_3 - h_2)$$ (4.33)

$$q_{out} = \dot{m}(h_4 - h_1)$$ (4.34)

The net work output of the cycle is:

$$W = W_{out} - W_{in}$$

The thermal efficiency of a Rankine cycle is:

$$\eta = \frac{W}{q_{in}} = \frac{W_{out} - W_{in}}{q_{in}} \approx \frac{W_{out}}{q_{in}}, \text{ since } W_{in} << W_{out}$$ (4.35)

The efficiency of the Rankine cycle is not as high as the Carnot cycle but the cycle has less practical difficulties and is more economical. Two main variations of the basic Rankine cycle are used in modern practice.

4.7.1 Rankine Cycle With Reheat

One of the major issues with a Rankine cycle with a high boiler pressure or a low condenser pressure is the formation of liquid droplets in the low pressure side of the turbine. The reheat cycle is often used to prevent liquid droplet formation. The first turbine accepts vapor from the boiler at high pressure. After the vapor has passed through the first turbine, it re-enters the boiler and is reheated before passing through a second, lower pressure turbine. Among other advantages, this prevents the vapor from condensing during its expansion which can seriously damage the turbine blades. The reheat cycle does not significantly influence the thermal efficiency of the cycle, but it does increase the work out. The reheat cycle requires additional investment for equipment and also increases the maintenance costs. An economic analysis should be preformed to justify the reheat cycle. A schematic diagram of the reheat Rankine cycle is given in Fig. 4.14 and various thermodynamic states are given in Fig. 4.15.

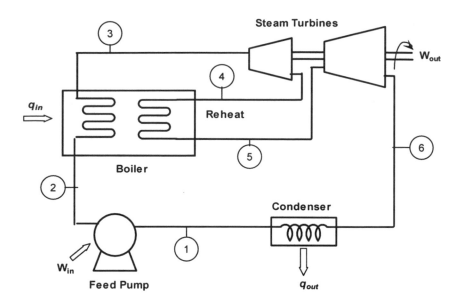

Fig. 4.14. Schematic of a reheat Rankine cycle.

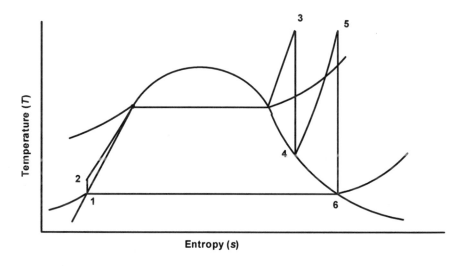

Fig. 4.15. The *T-s* diagram of a reheat Rankine cycle.

The total heat input to the cycle is given by

$$q_{in} = q_{primary} + q_{reheat} = (h_5 - h_4) + (h_3 - h_2) \tag{4.36}$$

The total work output is the combination of the work output from both the turbines and is given by

$$W_{out} = W_{turbine1} + W_{turbine2} = (h_5 - h_6) + (h_3 - h_4)$$ (4.37)

The thermal efficiency is expressed as

$$\eta = \frac{W_{out}}{q_{in}}$$ (4.38)

4.7.2 Regenerative Rankine Cycle

In the regenerative Rankine cycle, the working fluid, water, after emerging from the condenser possibly as a subcooled liquid is heated by steam tapped from the hot portion of the cycle. This can reduce the energy required to heat the high pressure water to its saturation temperature in the boiler. This would avoid the necessity of condensing all of the steam. A cycle which utilizes this type of reheating is called a regenerative cycle and a schematic diagram of the major elements of the cycle is shown in Fig. 4.16. The *T-s* diagram of such a cycle is shown in Fig. 4.17.

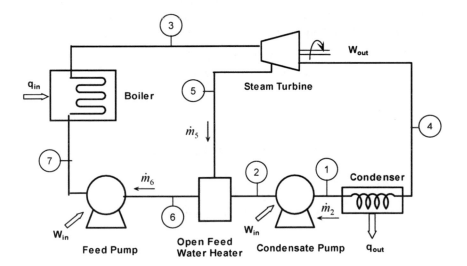

Fig. 4.16. Schematic of a regenerative Rankine cycle with an open feed water heater.

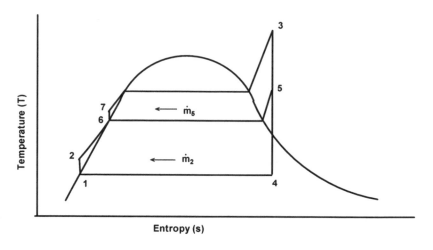

Fig. 4.17. The T-s diagram of the regenerative Rankine cycle.

The water entering the boiler is generally referred to as feedwater and the device used to mix the extracted steam and the condenser water is called a feedwater heater. Two types of schematics can be used for the feedwater heater:

- Open feedwater heater: In this scheme, condensate is mixed directly with the steam in a mixing chamber.
- Closed feedwater heater: In this arrangement, mixing of the two streams is not allowed. The feedwater heater rather is a heat exchanger in which water passes through tubes and the steam condenses on the outer surface of the tubes.

Analysis of a Rankine cycle with an open feedwater heater requires a mass balance of the control volume surrounding the feedwater heater. The mass balance equation is given by,

$$\dot{m}_6 = \dot{m}_5 + \dot{m}_2 \tag{4.39}$$

An energy balance equation assuming no heat loss can be written as

$$\dot{m}_6 h_6 = \dot{m}_5 h_5 + \dot{m}_2 h_2 \tag{4.40}$$

Therefore, the mass input to the feedwater pump is given by

$$\dot{m}_6 = \frac{(h_5 - h_2)}{(h_6 - h_2)} \dot{m}_5 \tag{4.41}$$

If it is assumed that $\dot{m}_6 = 1$, then the total heat input to the cycle is given by;

$$q_{in} = h_3 - h_7 \tag{4.42}$$

and, work output from the turbine is given by;

$$W_{out} = h_3 - h_5 + \dot{m}_2 \left(h_5 - h_4 \right) \tag{4.43}$$

Therefore, the efficiency can be expressed by;

$$\eta = \frac{W_{out}}{q_{in}} = \frac{h_3 - h_5 + \dot{m}_2 \left(h_5 - h_4 \right)}{\left(h_3 - h_7 \right)} \tag{4.44}$$

The schematic of the regenerative Rankine cycle with a closed feed water heater is explained in Fig. 4.18. In this configuration, part of the stream from the turbine is mixed directly with that from the condenser. In general, the more feed-water heaters, the better is the cycle efficiency.

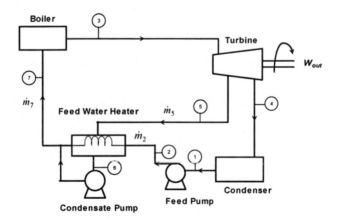

Fig. 4.18. Schematic of a regenerative Rankine cycle with a closed feed water heater.

4.8 Supercritical Rankine Cycle

New materials are allowing the use of much higher temperature in power plants [94, 95]. As discussed in Chapter 6, a number of supercritical power plants are now in operations world wide, which use a supercritical Rankine cycle [96–105]. A pressure of 30 MPa and a temperature greater than 600°C are generally used in supercritical power plants. The *T-s* diagram of the cycle is shown in Fig. 4.19.

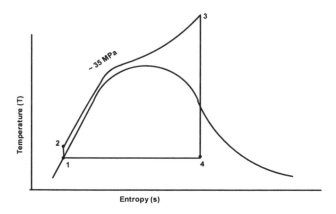

Fig. 4.19. The *T-s* diagram of a Rankine cycle operating under supercritical condition of steam.

4.9 Combined Reheat and Regenerative Rankine Cycle

The regenerative cycle generally has problems with water droplets at the low pressure side of the turbines. To overcome this problem, several power plants combine a reheat cycle with a regenerative cycle. This increases the thermal efficiency. A typical combined cycle is shown in Fig. 4.20 and the *T-s* diagram of the process is shown in Fig. 4.21.

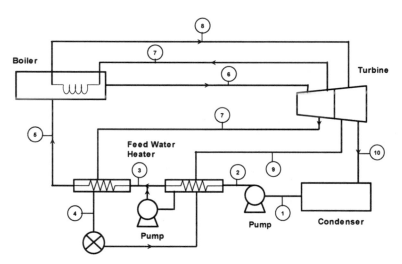

Fig. 4.20. Schematic of a reheat-regenerative Rankine cycle Numbers in the figure refer to various thermodynamic states that are shown in the *T-s* diagram below.

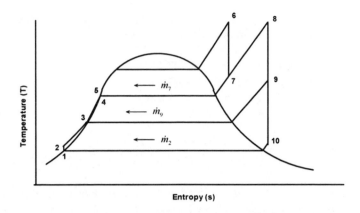

Fig. 4.21. The *T-s* diagram of a reheat-regenerative Rankine cycle.

Example 4.4

A supercritical Rankine cycle operates between pressures of 30 MPa and 10 kPa with a maximum temperature of 600°C. The cycle contains two reheat stages and two open feedwater heaters. The high pressure turbine operates between 30 MPa and 4 MPa. A portion of the steam is reheated to 600°C and expanded in another turbine to 200 kPa. A portion of the extracted steam is again reheated to 350°C and finally expanded to 10 kPa in the final low pressure turbine. Show the cycle in a *T-s* diagram and calculate the efficiency of the cycle.

Solution

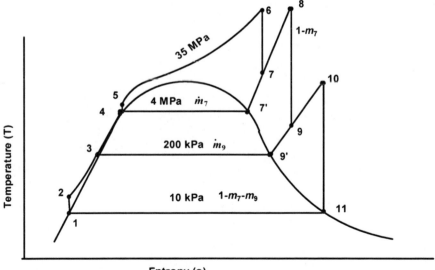

Using a steam table (Appendix IV), the following values for enthalpy, and entropy are obtained. The condition of the steam is noted in the parenthesis.

h_1 (Saturated water at 10 kPa) = h_2 = 191.8 kJ/kg
h_3 (Saturated water at 200 kPa) = 504.7 kJ/kg
h_4 (Saturated water at 4 MPa) = h_5 = 1087.3 kJ/kg
h_6 (Superheated steam at 30 MPa, 600°C) = 3443.9 kJ/kg
h_8 (Superheated steam at 4 MPa, 600°C) = 3674.4 kJ/kg
h_{10} (Superheated steam at 200 kPa, 350°C) = 3174.3 kJ/kg
$s_6 = s_7$ = 6.2331 kJ/kg.K; $s_8 = s_9$ = 7.3696 kJ/kg.K; $s_{10} = s_{11}$ = 8.0636 kJ/kg.K

The values of h_7 and h_9 are determined by interpolation as follows.
To find, h_7, the data is interpolated between stage 6 and saturated stage 7'. Similarly, h_9 was found by interpolation between stage 8 and saturated stage 9'.

$$h_7 = \left(\frac{6.2339 - 6.0709}{6.3622 - 6.0709} \right)(2961 - 2801) + 2801 = 2891\,\text{kJ/kg}$$

$$h_9 = \left(\frac{7.3696 - 7.2803}{7.5074 - 7.2803} \right)(2870 - 2769) + 2769 = 2809\,\text{kJ/kg}$$

The fraction of the steam at stage 11, is calculated as follows.

$$x_{11} = \frac{8.0636 - 0.6491}{7.5019} = 0.9883$$

$$h_{11} = 191.8 + (0.9883)(2393) = 2557\,\text{kJ/kg}$$

The mass flow rates in the high and low pressure heaters are calculated as follows.

$$h_5 = h_7 \dot{m}_7 + (1 - \dot{m}_7)h_3, \quad \dot{m}_7 = \frac{h_5 - h_3}{h_7 - h_3} = 0.2439\,\text{kg/s}$$

$$(1 - \dot{m}_7)h_3 = \dot{m}_9 h_9 + (1 - \dot{m}_7 - \dot{m}_9)h_2, \quad \dot{m}_9 = \frac{(1 - \dot{m}_7)h_3 - h_2 - \dot{m}_7 h_2}{h_9 - h_2}$$

Substituting values, $\dot{m}_9 = 0.0904$ kg/s

The power from the turbine is given by

$$\dot{W}_T = 1(h_6 - h_7) + (1 - \dot{m}_7)(h_8 - h_9) + (1 - \dot{m}_7 - \dot{m}_9)(h_{10} - h_{11})$$

Or,

$$\dot{W}_T = (3444 - 2891) + (1 - 0.2439)(3674 - 2809) +$$
$$\quad (1 - 0.2439 - 0.0904)(3174 - 2557)$$
$$= 1,609 \text{ KW}$$

The energy input to the boiler is given by

$$q_{in} = 1(h_6 - h_5) + (1 - \dot{m}_7)(h_8 - h_7) + (1 - \dot{m}_7 - \dot{m}_9)(h_{10} - h_9)$$
$$= (3444 - 1087) + (1 - 0.2439)(3674 - 2891) +$$
$$\quad (1 - 0.2439 - 0.0904)(3174 - 2809)$$
$$= 3,192 \text{KW}$$

The efficiency of the cycle is

$$\eta = \frac{1609}{3192} = 0.504 \text{ , or } 50.4\%$$

4.10 Combined Cycles in Stationary Gas Turbine for Power Production

The gas temperature at the inlet point of a gas turbine operating in a Brayton cycle is considerably higher than the peak steam temperature used in the steam turbine. Depending on the compression ratio of the gas turbine, the exhaust temperature from the gas turbine could be high enough to permit economic generation of steam and run a steam turbine. A configuration such as this is known as the combined Brayton-Rankine cycle. The schematic of such a combined cycle is shown in Fig. 4.22, and the T-s diagram of the cycle is illustrated in Fig. 4.23.

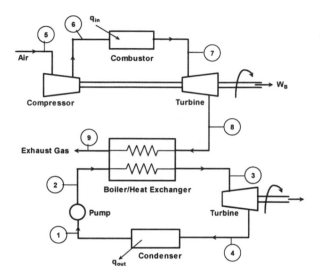

Fig. 4.22. Gas turbine-steam combined cycle.

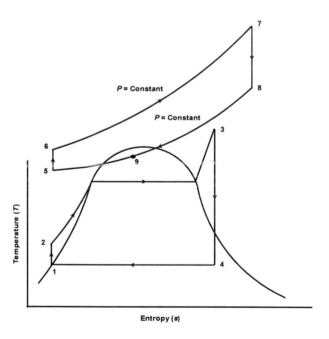

Fig. 4.23. The *T-s* diagram of the combined cycle.

A thermal efficiency analysis of the combined cycle can be carried out as follows. The heat input to the gas turbine can be designated as q_{in}, and the heat rejected to the atmosphere as q_{out}. The heat out of the gas turbine is denoted as q_{GT}. If it is assumed that the heat exchanger is 100% efficient, then the heat input to the Rankine cycle can be denoted as q_{GT} too. The overall combined cycle efficiency can be expressed as

$$\eta_{cc} = \frac{W_{out,Total}}{q_{in}} = \frac{W_B + W_R}{q_{in}} \tag{4.45}$$

where η_{cc} is the overall efficiency of the combined cycle, W_B is the work done by the Brayton cycle and W_R is the work done by the Rankine cycle. Eq. (4.45) can be rearranged as follows:

$$\eta_{cc} = \frac{(q_{in} - q_{GT}) + (q_{GT} - q_{out})}{q_{in}} = \left(1 - \frac{q_{GT}}{q_{in}}\right) + \left(1 - \frac{q_{out}}{q_{GT}}\right)\left(\frac{q_{GT}}{q_{in}}\right) \tag{4.46}$$

The efficiencies of a Brayton cycle and a Rankine cycle can be expressed as follows:

$$\eta_B = 1 - \frac{q_{GT}}{q_{in}}$$
$$\eta_R = 1 - \frac{q_{out}}{q_{GT}} \tag{4.47}$$

Therefore, the combined cycle efficiency becomes

$$\eta_{cc} = \eta_B + \eta_R - \eta_B \eta_R \tag{4.48}$$

The efficiency of a gas turbine cycle is generally on the order of 40%. If we assume that the Rankine cycle efficiency for the combined system will be in the order of 30%, the combined cycle efficiency would be 58%, which is a very large increase over either of the two simple cycles. Some representative efficiencies and power outputs for different cycles are shown in Fig. 4.24.

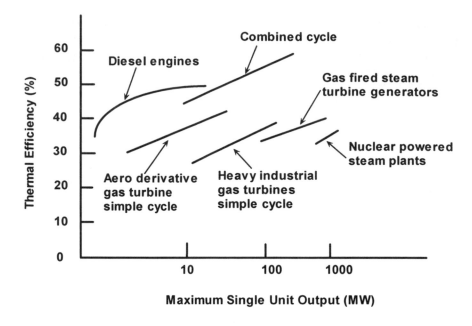

Fig. 4.24. Comparison of efficiency and power output of various power products [106].

Example 4.5

Consider a combined Brayton-Rankine cycle. The gas turbine of the Brayton cycle takes in air at 100 kPa and 25°C, has a pressure ratio of 5 and the temperature of the exhaust steam is 850°C. The gas turbine exhaust provides the energy input to the boiler of the Rankine cycle. The exhaust gas temperature from the boiler is 75°C. It may be assumed that the Rankine cycle is operating between 10 kPa and 4 MPa with a maximum temperature of 400°C. Assume that the total power output from the steam turbine is 100 MW. Calculate the efficiency of individual cycle, and that of the combined cycle.

Solution

First calculate the efficiency of the Rankine cycle

The *T-s* diagram of the combined cycle is shown in Fig. 4.23. The following values are obtained from the steam table.

h_1 (saturated liquid at 10 kPa) = 191.8 kJ/kg
$h_2 = h_1$ (neglecting work input to the pump) = 191.8 kJ/kg
h_3 (superheated steam, 400°C and 4 MPa) = 3214 kJ/kg
s_3 (superheated steam, 400°C and 4 MPa) = 6.7698 kJ/kg.

In State 4, both vapor and liquid exist. Therefore, we need to calculate the quality of the steam, x_4.

$$x_4 = \frac{s_4 - s_f}{s_{fg}} = \frac{7.7698 - 0.6491}{7.5019} = 0.8159$$

$$h_4 = h_f - x_4\, h_{fg} = 191.8 + 0.8159 \times 2393 = 2144 \text{ kJ/kg}$$

Heat input to the boiler

$$q_B = h_3 - h_2 = 3214 - 191.8 = 3022.2 \text{ kJ/kg}$$

Work output by turbine

$$w_T = h_3 - h_4 = 3214 - 2144 = 1070 \text{ kJ/kg}$$

The thermal efficiency

$$\eta_{Rankine} = \frac{1070}{3022.2} = 0.3541 \text{, or } 35.41\%$$

The thermal efficiency of the Brayton cycle is given by

$$\eta_{Brayton} = 1 - r^{1-k/k} = 1 - (5)^{1-1.4/1.4} = 0.369 \text{ or } 36.9\%$$

Efficiency of the Combined Cycle

We need to calculate the power output from the gas turbine. In order to calculate this, mass flow rate of air to the gas turbine compressor should be calculated first.

Steam mass flux is calculated from the following expression.

$$\dot{w}_{Steam} = \dot{m}_s (h_3 - h_4); \quad 100\,000 = \dot{m}_s (3214 - 2144); \quad \dot{m}_s = 93.46 \text{ kg/s}$$

Temperatures at various location of the Brayton cycle are calculated next.

$$T_6 = T_5 \left(\frac{P_6}{P_5} \right)^{k-1/k} = (25 + 273)(5)^{\frac{1.4-1}{1.4}} = 472 \text{ K}$$

$$T_8 = T_7 \left(\frac{P_8}{P_7}\right)^{k-\frac{1}{k}} = (850 + 273)\left(\frac{1}{5}\right)^{\frac{1.4-1}{1.4}} = 709\,\text{K}$$

Heat balance in the boiler provides

$$\dot{m}_s \left(h_3 - h_2\right) = \dot{m}_a C_p \left(T_8 - T_9\right)$$
$$93.46 \times (3214 - 191.8) = \dot{m}_a \times 1.0 \times \left[709 - (75 + 273)\right]$$

$$\dot{m}_a = 786\,\text{kg/s}$$

The output of the gas turbine is given by

$$\dot{W}_{gas\,turbine} = \dot{m}_a C_p \left(T_7 - T_8\right) = 786 * 1.0 \times (1123 - 709) = 325.5\,\text{MW}$$

The input work to compressor is:

$$\dot{W}_{compressor} = \dot{m}_a C_p \left(T_6 - T_5\right) = 136.9\,\text{MW}$$

The net output from the gas turbine,

$$\dot{W}_{Total} = \dot{W}_{gas\,turbine} - \dot{W}_{compressor} = 325.5 - 136.9 = 188.6\,\text{MW}$$

The energy input to the combustion chamber,

$$q_{in} = \dot{m}_a C_p \left(T_7 - T_6\right) = 786.5 \times 1.0 \times (1123 - 472) = 512\,\text{MW}$$

The efficiency of the combined cycle

$$\eta = \frac{100 + 188.6}{512} = 0.564 \text{ , or } 56.4\%$$

4.11 Stirling Cycle

The components of a Stirling cycle are shown in Fig. 4.25.

The Stirling cycle has several advantages when used in a Stirling engine, also known as the hot air engine. A Stirling engine is a heat engine. The heat-exchange process allows for near-ideal efficiency for conversion of heat into mechanical energy by following the Carnot cycle as closely as is practically possible with the given materials [107–111]. During the transfer stroke, the regenerator can rapidly transfer the heat to the working fluid reducing the amount of heat necessary from the external source. This has a positive effect on the thermal efficiency. Also, substitution of two isentropic processes with two constant volume processes results in increasing the work done as evident from the *P-v* diagram (Fig. 4.26). The *T-s* diagram is shown in Fig. 4.27.

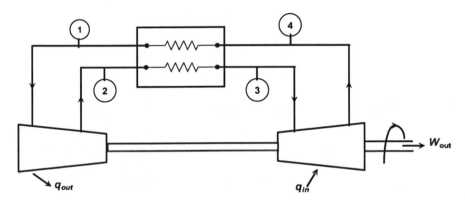

Fig. 4.25. Schematic diagram of a Stirling or Erricson Cycle.

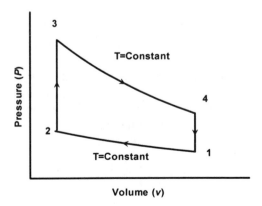

Fig. 4.26. *P-v* diagram of the Stirling cycle.

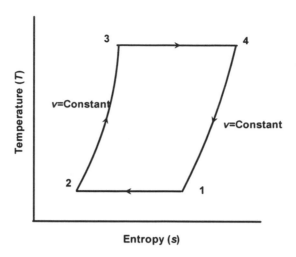

Fig. 4.27. *T-s* diagram of the Stirling cycle.

4.11.1 Efficiency of the Stirling Cycle

For an air-standard Stirling cycle, Kongtragool and Wongwises [112] derived an expression for calculating the thermal efficiency. The amounts of heat added and rejected per unit mass of working fluid can be expressed by the following expression [113]:

$$q_{in} = xC_v\left(T_H - T_C\right) + RT_H \, \ell n \frac{v_1}{v_2} \tag{4.49}$$

$$q_{out} = xC_v\left(T_C - T_H\right) + RT_C \, \ell n \frac{v_2}{v_1} \tag{4.50}$$

The parameter x is defined as the fractional deviation from the ideal regeneration ($x = 1$ for no regeneration and $x = 0$ for ideal regeneration), C_v is the specific heat capacity at constant volume in J/(kg K), T_H is the source temperature in the Stirling cycle in K, T_C is the sink temperature in K, R is the gas constant in J/(kg K), v_1 and v_2 are specific volumes of the constant-volume regeneration processes of the cycle in m³/kg, and v_2/v_1 is the volume compression ratio. With these parameters, the Stirling cycle efficiency can be expressed as:

$$\eta_s = \frac{1 - {T_C}\big/{T_H}}{1 + \left(\dfrac{x c_v}{R \ell n \dfrac{v_1}{v_2}} \right)\left(1 - \dfrac{T_C}{T_H}\right)}$$

(4.51)

4.12 Ericssion Cycle

The Ericsson engine, which is based on the Ericsson cycle, is also known as an "external combustion engine", because it is externally heated [114–118]. To improve efficiency, the engine has a recuperator or regenerator between the compressor and the expander. The engine can be run either as an open cycle or as a closed cycle.

The Ericsson Cycle is often compared to the Stirling Cycle, since the engines based on these cycles are both external combustion engines with regenerators. Theoretically, both of these cycles have so called *ideal* efficiency, and it is estimated from the following expression:

$$\eta = 1 - \frac{T_C}{T_H}$$

(4.52)

The Ericsson Engine comprises of an air compressor that pumps air into a tank. The heat loss from the tank essentially maintains a constant temperature, thus approximating isothermal compression. From the tank, the compressed air passes through the regenerator and picks-up heat on the way to the heated power cylinder. The air is expanded in the cylinder at a constant temperature. Before the air is released as exhaust, it is passed back through the regenerator, thus heating the air for the next cycle. The *P-v* and *T-s* diagrams of the cycle are shown below in Figs. 4.28 and 4.29, respectively.

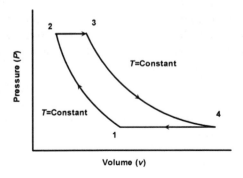

Fig. 4.28. *P-v* diagram of the Ericsson cycle.

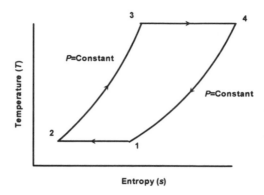

Fig. 4.29. *T-s* diagram of the Ericsson cycle.

4.13 Miller Cycle

Internal combustion engine based on Miller cycle was first used in ships and stationary power-generating plants, but recently was adapted by Mazda for their *KJ-ZEM*-V6, Millenia sedan. Subaru has also combined a Miller cycle flat-4 with a hybrid driveline for their "Turbo Parallel Hybrid" car, known as the Subaru *B5-TPH*.

Assuming constant specific heats, the efficiency of the Miller cycle can be expressed as

$$\eta = 1 - r^{(1-k)} \tag{4.53}$$

Miller [119] proposed a different Otto cycle with unequal compression and expansion strokes. The basic Miller cycle is very much like the Otto cycle that utilizes the four-stroke method. The difference is in the compression stroke. Figure 4.30 is the *P–v* diagram of the four-stroke Miller cycle without supercharger. In this figure, process 1–2 is an isobaric process; process 2–3 is an isobaric process if the intake valve is closed late; process 3–4 is an isentropic compression process; process 4–5 is an isochoric heating process; 5–6 is an isentropic expansion process; process 6–7 is an isochoric cooling process; and process 7–1 is an isobaric cooling process with the exhaust valve open.

Miller cycle efficiency may be enhanced by a number of methods [120, 121] including the use of a variable valve timing scheme during the combustion process [122]. Recently the emphasis is to reduce the emission from Miller engines by using a lean burn engine [123–129].

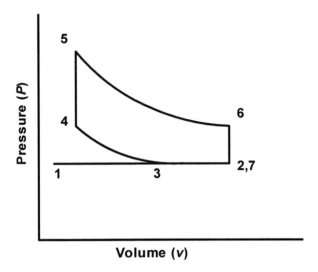

Fig. 4.30. The *P-v* diagram of a four-stroke Miller cycle (intake valve closed late).

4.14 Atkinson Cycle

The Atkinson cycle [130–136] is also refered to as a four stroke piston engine in which the intake valve is held open longer than normal to allow a reverse flow of intake air into the intake manifold. This modification resulted in improved fuel economy over the Otto cycle, because the compression ratio in a spark ignition engine is limited by the octane rating of the fuel used. The disadvantage of the four-stroke Atkinson cycle engine versus the more common Otto cycle engine is reduced power density. The Atkinson cycle is increasingly used in modern hybrid electric cars. The engine is only run at high powers intermittently, and the power of the engine is supplemented by an electric motor during times when high power is needed. This forms the basis of an Atkinson cycle based hybrid electric drive-train. Currently, Toyota's Prius and Camry, and Ford's Escape hybrid electric cars utilize Atkinson cycle.

The Atkinson cycle is internally reversible, but externally irreversible, since there is external irreversibility of heat transfer during the processes of constant volume heat addition and constant pressure heat rejection. The *T-s* diagram of the Atkinson cycle is shown in Fig. 4.31.

The Atkinson cycle starts with adiabatic compression of a vapor to an intermediate pressure and heating it at a constant volume to a high pressure P_3 at temperature T_3. Following this, an adiabatic expansion takes place to produce work from P_3 to P_4, and then cooling occurs at constant pressure P_4 to complete the cycle.

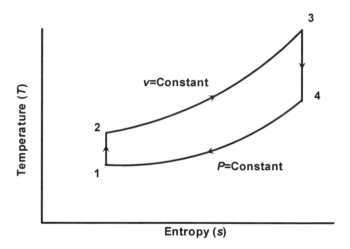

Fig. 4.31. The *T-s* diagram of the Atkinson cycle.

The thermal efficiency can be calculated from the following expression:

$$\eta = 1 - k\left(\frac{1}{r_c}\right)^{k-1} \frac{r-1}{\left(r^k - 1\right)} \tag{4.54}$$

where, r is the ratio of expansion ratio to compression ratio ($r = r_e/r_c$), r_c is compression ratio, and r_e is the expansion ratio and are given by the following expressions, respectively:

$$r_c = \left(\frac{v_1}{v_2}\right) = \left(\frac{P_2}{P_1}\right)^{1/k} = \left(\frac{T_2}{T_1}\right)^{\frac{1}{k-1}}$$

$$\tag{4.55}$$

$$r_e = \left(\frac{v_4}{v_3}\right) = \left(\frac{P_3}{P_4}\right)^{1/k} = \left(\frac{T_3}{T_4}\right)^{\frac{1}{k-1}}$$

4.15 Kalina Cycle

The Kalina cycle [137–154], which uses an ammonia-water mixture, has a higher energy efficiency than a conventional Rankine cycle by about 10–20%. The increased efficiency resulted from the use of ammonia/water mixture as the working fluid, rather than the pure water or pure ammonia that is used in a standard Rankine cycle. The Kalina cycle is found to be more appropriate and efficient for use in Ocean Thermal Energy Conversion (OTEC) systems. For OTEC power systems, almost 80% increase in the efficiency over previous closed-cycle designs have been claimed. The Kalina cycle takes advantage of the variable boiling and condensing temperatures of ammonia/water mixtures.

The OTEC Kalina cycle uses the four typical Rankine cycle phases: evaporation, expansion, condensation and feed. An additional piece of equipment, the recuperator, recovers heat from the warm, but unvaporized, liquid leaving the separator vessel. A simplified schematic diagram of the system is shown in Fig. 4.32.

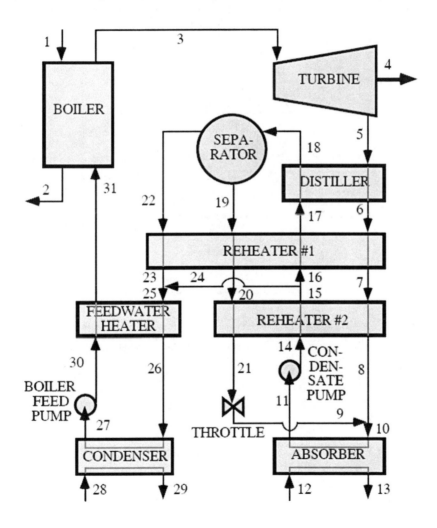

Fig. 4.32. The schematic diagram of a Kalina Cycle.

The Kalina cycle may be considered as a bottoming cycle feed, where the exhaust gases is fed to the boiler (1–2) to obtain superheated ammonia-water vapor (3), which is expanded in a turbine to generate work (4). The turbine exhaust (5) goes through a series of heat exchanger for cooling (6, 7, 8). The exhaust is diluted with ammonia-poor liquid (9, 10) and condensed (11) in the absorber by cooling water (12, 13). The saturated liquid leaving the absorber is compressed (14) to an intermediate pressure and heated (15, 16, 17, and 18). The saturated mixture is separated into an ammonia-poor liquid (19) which is cooled (20, 21) and depressurized in a throttle, and ammonia-rich vapor (22) is cooled (23) and some of the original condensate (24) is added to the nearly pure ammonia vapor to obtain an ammonia concentration of about 70% in the working fluid (25). The mixture is then cooled (26), condensed (27) by cooling water (28, 29), compressed (30), and sent to the boiler via regenerative feedwater heater (31). The T-s diagram of the cycle is shown in Fig. 4.33.

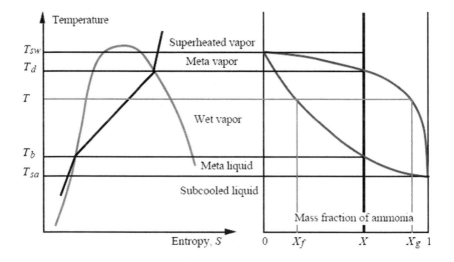

Fig. 4.33. The Kalina cycle in T-s diagram and corresponding thermodynamic state of ammonia-water mixture.

References

1. Zemansky MW (1968) Heat and Thermodynamics: An Intermediate Textbook. 5th ed. New York, McGraw-Hill
2. Van Ness HC (1983) Thermodynamics. Dover Publications, Inc.
3. Sonntag RE, Borgnakke C, Van Wylen GJ (1998) Fundamentals of Thermodynamics. 6th ed. New York, Wiley

4. Van Wylen GJ, Sonntag RE (1973) Fundamentals of Classical Thermodynamics. New York, Wiley
5. Schmidt PS, Ezekoye O, Howell JR, Baker D (2005) Thermodynamics: An Integrated Learning System. 1st ed. New York, Wiley
6. Shapiro M (2004) Fundamentals of Engineering Thermodynamics, 5th ed, New York, Wiley
7. Kaminski D, Jensen MK (2005) Introduction to Thermal and Fluid Engineering. New York, Wiley
8. Pulkrabek WW (1997) Engineering Fundamentals of the Internal Combustion Engine. New Jersey, Prentice Hall
9. Heywood JB (1997) Internal Combustion Engine Fundamentals. New York, McGraw-Hill
10. Curzon FL, Ahlborn B (1975) Efficiency of Carnot engine at maximum power output. Am J Phys 43: 22–24
11. Roco JMM, Velasco S, Medina A, Hernandez AC (1997) Optimum performance of a regenerative Brayton thermal cycle. Journal of Applied Physics 82(6): 2735–2741
12. Doty FD, Jones JD (1990) A new look at the closed Brayton cycle. Proceedings of the Intersociety Energy Conversion Engineering Conference 25th, 2: 166–172
13. Decher R (1987) Power density optimization of Brayton cycle engines. Proceedings of the Intersociety Energy Conversion Engineering Conference, 22: 1359–1363
14. Hiller CC (1979) Sensitivity study of Brayton cycle power plant performance. NTIS Report (1978), (SAND-78-8020), Energy Res. Abstr. 4(3), Abstr. No. 5518, 1979
15. Pietsch A (1969) Closed Brayton cycle power system applications, Proc. Intersoc. Energy Convers. Eng. Conf 4th, pp. 642–651
16. Stewart WL (1967) Brayton cycle technology, NASA (Nat. Aeronaut. Space Admin.), Access. (1966), (NASA-SP-131), pp. 95–145. From: Sci. Tech. Aerospace Rept. 5(1), N67-10266, 1967
17. Chen L, Ni N, Cheng G, Sun F, Wu C (1999) Performance analysis for a real closed regenerated Brayton cycle via methods of finite-time thermodynamics. International Journal of Ambient Energy 20(2): 95–104
18. Brokaw RS (1961) Thermal conductivity and chemical kinetics. Journal of Chemical Kinetics 35, 1569–1580
19. Schleicher R, Raffray AR, Wong CP (2001) An assessment of the Brayton cycle for high performance power plants. Fusion Technology, 39(2, Pt. 2): 823–827
20. Negri di Montenegro G, Bettocchi R, Cantore G, Borghi M, Naldi G (1988) A comparative study on the ways of converting steam power plants to steam-gas combined cycle power plants. Ist. Macch Proceedings of the Intersociety Energy Conversion Engineering Conference, 23rd 1: 301–306
21. Schwarz N (1984) Increasing the efficiency of thermal power stations, Oesterr. Forschungszent. Seibersdorf, [Ber.] OEFZS (OEFZS BER. No. 4261), 20 pp
22. Krasin K and Nesterenko V. B (1971) Dissociating gases: a new class of coolants and working substances for large power plants, Atomic Energy Review, 9, 177–194
23. Peterson PF (2003) Multiple-reheat Brayton cycles for nuclear power conversion with molten coolants. Nuclear Technology 144(3): 279–288
24. Fenech H, Saunders RJ (1989) Application of heat storage reservoirs to improve the performance of Brayton cycle nuclear power plants with atmospheric heat rejection. Annals of Nuclear Energy 16(4): 203–209

25. Walter A (2006) System modeling and simulation of HTR circuits with Brayton cycle for operational and accidental conditions. Wissenschaftliche Berichte - Forschungszentrum Karlsruhe (FZKA 7155), pp. 181–186.
26. Walter A, Alexander S, Guenter L (2006) Comparison of two models for a pebble bed modular reactor core coupled to a Brayton cycle. Nuclear Engineering and Design 236(5–6): 603–614
27. Frye PE, Robert A, Rex D (2005) Brayton power conversion system study to advance technology readiness for nuclear electric propulsion - phase I. AIP Conference Proceedings (2005), 746 (Space Technology and Applications International Forum–STAIF 2005), pp. 727–737
28. Wang J, Gu Y (2005) Parametric studies on different gas turbine cycles for a high temperature gas-cooled reactor. Nuclear Engineering and Design 235(16): 1761–1772
29. Wang H, Wang C (2005) A closed cycle helium gas turbine plant used for a high-temperature gas cooled reactor-based electric power generation unit. Reneng Dongli Gongcheng 20(4): 337–341
30. Lipinski RJ, Wright SA, Dorsey DJ, Peters CD, Brown N, Williamson J, Jablonski J (2005) A gas-cooled-reactor closed- Brayton – cycle demonstration with nuclear heating. AIP Conference Proceedings 746 (Space Technology and Applications International Forum--STAIF 2005): 437–448
31. Chaudourne S (1990) Optimization of a heat pipe radiator for a 20-kWe Brayton cycle space power system. Proc. Symp. Space Nucl. Power Syst 7th 2: 633–638
32. Tilliette ZP, Proust E, Carre F (1987) Progress in investigating Brayton cycle conversion systems for future French Ariane 5 space power applications. Proceedings of the Intersociety Energy Conversion Engineering Conference (1987), 22nd 1: 438–443
33. Barrett MJ, Johnson PK (2005) Performance and mass modeling subtleties in closed-Brayton – cyclespace power systems. NASA/TM (2005), (2005-213985), i, 1–12
34. Barrett MJ, Reid BM (2004) System mass variation and entropy generation in 100-kWe closed- Brayton – cycle space power systems. NASA/TM (2004), (NASA/TM-2004-212741): 1–8
35. El-Genk, MS, Tournier, J-M (2006) High temperature water heat pipes radiator for a Brayton space reactor power system. AIP Conference Proceedings (2006), 813(Space Technology and Applications International Forum–STAIF 2006): 716–729
36. Joyner CR II, Fowler B, Matthews J (2003) A closed Brayton power conversion unit concept for nuclear electric propulsion for deep space missions. AIP Conference Proceedings (2003), 654(Space Technology and Applications International Forum–STAIF 2003): 677–684
37. Stasa FL, Osterle F (1981) The thermodynamic performance of two combined cycle power plants integrated with two coal gasification systems. Journal of Engineering for Power 103(3): 572–581
38. Iles TL, Ruder JM (1982) Brayton cycle waste heat recovery system. Proc Int Gas Res Conf 2nd: 1069–1080
39. Amann CA (1999) Evaluating alternative internal combustion engines: 1950–1975, Journal of Engineering for Gas Turbines and Power, 121: 540–545
40. Rogers C, McDonald CF (1997) Automotive turbogenerator design considerations and technology evolution, Society of Automotive Engineers. Technical Paper 972673.11, 1997
41. Wilson DG (1997) A New approach to low-cost high efficiency automotive gas turbines, society of automotive engineers. Technical Paper 970234

42. Wilson DG (1978) Alternative automobile engines, Scientific American, 239(1): 39–49
43. McDonald F, Etzel K.T (1995) The closed Brayton cycle - a fuel neutral gas turbine to meet energy user's needs in the Pacific Rim nations. Proceedings of the American Power Conference 57(1): 382–387
44. Mason JL (1967) Working gas selection for the closed Brayton cycle, AGARDograph, Volume Date 1964(81): 223–252
45. Kesavan K, Osterle JF (1982) Split-flow nuclear gas turbine cycle using dissociating N_2O_4, Paper 82–GT–181, The American Society of Mechanical Engineers, New York
46. Krasin K (1975) Dissociating Gases as Heat-Transfer Media and Working Fluids in Power Installations, AEC-tr-7295, translated and published for the Atomic Energy Commission and the National Science Foundation by Amerind Publishing, New Delhi
47. Lighthill MJ (1957) Dynamics of a dissociating gas Part I equilibrium flow. Journal of Fluid Mechanics 2: 1–32
48. Stochl RJ (1979) Potential performance improvement using a reacting gas (Nitrogen Tetroxide) as the working fluid in a closed Brayton cycle, NASA TM–79322
49. Dostal V, Hejzlar P, Driscoll MJ (2006) The supercritical carbon dioxide power cycle: comparison to other advanced power cycles. Nuclear Technology 154(3): 283–301
50. Dostal V, Hejzlar P, Driscoll MJ (2006) High-performance supercritical carbon dioxide cycle for next-generation nuclear reactors. Nuclear Technology 154(3): 265–282
51. Sahin B, Kodal A, Yavuz H (1995) Efficiency of a Joule–Brayton engine at maximum power density. Journal of Physics Series D: Applied Physics 28: 1309–1313
52. Wu C, Chen L, Sun F (1996) Performance of regenerative Brayton heat engines. Energy International Journal 21(2): 71–76
53. Cheng CY, Chen CK (1997) Ecological optimization of an irreversible Carnot heat engine. Journal of Physics Series D: Applied Physics 30: 1602–1609
54. Cheng CY, Chen CK (1998) Ecological optimization of an endoreversible Brayton cycle. Energy Conversion and Management 39: 33–44
55. Wu C, Chen L, Chen J (1999) Recent Advances in Finite-Time Thermodynamics. New York, Nova Science
56. Chen L, Zheng J, Sun F, Wu C (2001) Power density optimization for an irreversible regenerated closed variable temperature heat reservoir Brayton cycle. Journal of Physics Series D: Applied Physics 34(11): 1727–1739
57. Chen L, Zheng J, Sun F, Wu FC (2001) Power density analysis and optimization of a regenerated closed Brayton cycle. Physica Scripta 64(3): 184–191
58. Chen L, Zheng J, Sun F, Wu C (2002) Performance comparison of an endoreversible closed variable temperature heat reservoir Brayton cycle under maximum power density and maximum power conditions. Energy Conversion and Management 43:33–43.
59. Akash BA (2001) Effect of heat transfer on the performance of an air-standard diesel cycle. International Communications in Heat and Mass Transfer 28(1): 87–95
60. Pirouzpanah V, Kashani BO (1999) A diesel engine cycle model for prediction of performance and pollutants emission, in Energy and the Environment, Editor(s): I. Dincer and T. Ayhan, Proceedings of the Trabzon International Energy and Environment Symposium, 2nd, Trabzon, Turkey, July 26–29: 101–105
61. Harris WD (1997) An external combustion, open-diesel cycle heat engine. Proceedings of the Intersociety Energy Conversion Engineering Conference, 32nd: 967–972
62. Blank DA, Wu C (1993) The effect of combustion on a power optimized endoreversible diesel cycle. Energy Conversion and Management 34(6): 493–498

63. Klein SA (1991) An explanation for observed compression ratios in internal combustion engines. Journal of Engineering for Gas Turbines and Power 113(4): 511–513
64. Hellen G (1994) Controlling NOx emissions at diesel power plants. Proceedings of the Institution of Mechanical Engineers, IMechE Conference (7): 107–112
65. Melton RB Jr, Lestz SJ, Quillian RD Jr, Rambie EJ (1975) Direct water injection cooling for military engines and effects on the diesel cycle. Symposium (International) on Combustion, Proceedings, 15: 1389–1399
66. Wang Y, Zeng S, Huang J, He Y, Huang X, Lin L, Li S (2005) Experimental investigation of applying Miller cycle to reduce NOx emission from diesel engine, Proceedings of the Institution of Mechanical Engineers, Part A: Journal of Power and Energy 219(A8): 631–638
67. Chen L, Ge Y, Sun F. Wu C (2006) Effects of heat transfer, friction and variable specific heats of working fluid on performance of an irreversible dual cycle. Energy Conversion and Management 47(18–19): 3224–3234
68. Zheng T, Chen L, Sun F, Wu C (2004) Finite time thermodynamic performance for an irreversible Dual cycle. Advances in Finite Time Thermodynamics: 51–61
69. Kokubu (1998) Development of dual fluid cycle gas turbine. Proceedings of the International Gas Research Conference, 5: 804–816
70. Juneja MN, Biswas DK, Majumder A, Singh S (1978) Coal gasification for dual cycle power generation. Chemical Engineering World 13(3): 45–49
71. Elliott VA, Trocki T (1957) Power conversion systems for dual-cycle boiling reactor. Selected Papers 1st Nuclear Eng. Sci. Congr, Cleveland, 1955, 1: 285–291
72. Untermyer S (1955) Dual cycle improves boiling-water reactors. Nucleonics 13(7): 34–35
73. Mandl F (1989) Statistical Physics, 2nd ed, Chichester, England, Wiley, pp. 121–123
74. Anderson HL (Ed.-in-Chief) (1989) A Physicist's Desk Reference, American Institute of Physics, New York.
75. Ge Y, Chen L, Sun F, and Wu C (2005) Thermodynamic simulation of performance of an Otto cycle with heat transfer and variable specific heats of working fluid. International Journal of Thermal Sciences 44(5): 506–511
76. Vinokurov VA, Kaminskii VA, Frost VA, Kolesnikov IM (2000) Modeling of combustion processes in internal combustion engines. Chemistry and Technology of Fuels and Oils (Translation of Khimiya i Tekhnologiya Topliv i Masel) 36(6): 408–415
77. Boggs DL, Hilbert HS, Schechter MM (1995) The Otto-Atkinson cycle engine-fuel economy and emissions results and hardware design. Society of Automotive Engineers, [Special Publication] SP, SP-1108 (Futuristic Concepts in Engines and Components): 47–59
78. Angulo-Brown F, Rocha-Martinez JA, and Navarrete-Gonzalez TD (1996) A non-endoreversible Otto cycle model: improving power output and efficiency. Journal of Physics D: Applied Physics 29(1): 80–83
79. Klimstra J, Bijma BJ, Westing JE (1993) Efficiency determination of turbochargers for Otto-cycle engines. Society of Automotive Engineers, [Special Publication] SP, SP-993 (Gaseous Fuel Technology For The Nineties): 43–55
80. Rakopoulos CD (1993) Evaluation of a spark ignition engine cycle using first and second law analysis techniques. Energy Conversion and Management 34(12): 1299–1314
81. Wu C, Blank DA (1993) Optimization of the endoreversible Otto cycle with respect to both power and mean effective pressure. Energy Conversion and Management 34(12) 1315–1318

82. Wu C, Blank DA (1992) The effects of combustion on work-optimized endo-reversible Otto cycle. Journal of the Institute of Energy 65(463): 86–89

83. Maly R (1990) Improved Otto cycle by enhancing the final phase of combustion, Comm. Eur. Communities, [Rep.] EUR (EUR 12467)

84. Patrick RS (1989) Air-fuel ratio estimation in an Otto cycle engine: two methods and their performance, Ph.D. Dissertation, Stanford University, Stanford, CA, USA

85. Lior N, Rudy GJ (1988) Second-law analysis of an ideal Otto cycle. Energy Conversion and Management 28(4): 327–334

86. Brown GG (1938) A thermodynamic analysis of the rate of rise of pressure in the Otto cycle. Chemical Reviews 22: 27–49

87. Rosecrans CZ, Felbeck GT (1925) A thermodynamic analysis of gas engine tests. Univ. Ill. Eng. Expt. Sta, Bull.150

88. Eldighidy SM (1993) Optimum outlet temperature of solar collector for maximum work output for an Otto air-standard cycle with ideal regeneration. Solar Energy 51(3): 175–182

89. Lee WY, Kim SS (1991) Analytical formula for the estimation of a Rankine-cycle heat engine efficiency at maximum power. International Journal of Energy Research 15: 149–159

90. Bejan A (1988) Advanced Engineering Thermodynamics. New York, Wiley

91. El-Wakil MM (1984) Powerplant Technology, New York, McGraw-Hill

92. Wood BD (1969) Applications of Thermodynamics. Reading, MA, Addison-Wesley

93. Bernard DW (1969) Application of Thermodynamics. Reading, MA, Addison-Wesley

94. Kern T.-U, Wieghardt K., Kirchner H (2005) Material and design solutions for advanced steam power plants. Advances in Materials Technology for Fossil Power Plants, Proceedings from the International Conference, 4th, Hilton Head Island, SC, United States, Oct. 25–28, 2004 Meeting Date 2004: 20–34

95. Ellis FV, Wright IG, Maziasz PJ (2005) Review of turbine materials for use in ultra - supercritical steam cycles. Advances in Materials Technology for Fossil Power Plants, Proceedings from the International Conference, 4th, Hilton Head Island, SC, United States, Oct. 25–28, 2004 Meeting Date 2004: 535–551

96. Macmillan JH (1965) Nuclear power and supercritical steam cycles. Proceedings of the American Power Conference 27: 243–247

97. Potter JH (1969) Totally supercritical steam cycle. Journal of Engineering for Power 91(2): 113–120

98. Szewalski R (1974) New high-efficiency steam power cycle for supercritical steam conditions. Prace Instytutu Maszyn Przeplywowych, Polska Akademia Nauk 64: 3–20.

99. Sedler B (1975) Application of a regenerative heat exchanger for supercritical parameters in steam and water cycle of a steam power plant. Prace Instytutu Maszyn Przeplywowych, Polska Akademia Nauk 66: 29–43

100. Reuter FD (1993) Steam generator for power plant concepts with high efficiency. VDI-Berichte 1029: 124–140

101. Miyashita K (1997) Overview of advanced steam plant development in Japan. IMechE Conference Transactions (2, Advanced Steam Plant): 17–30

102. Swanekamp R (2001) Supercritical steam cycle delivers efficient and reliable performance. Power 145(4): 87–88

103. De S, Nag PK (2000) Thermodynamic analysis of a partial gasification pressurized combustion and supercritical steam combined cycle. Proceedings of the Institution of Mechanical Engineers, Part A: Journal of Power and Energy 214(A6): 565–574

104. Dostal V, Hejzlar P, Todreas NE, Buongiorno J (2004) Medium-power lead-alloy fast reactor balance-of-plant options. Nuclear Technology 147(3): 388–405

105. Tsiklauri G, Talbert R, Schmitt B, Filippov G, Bogoyavlensky R, Grishanin E (2005) Supercritical steam cycle for nuclear power plant. Nuclear Engineering and Design 235(15): 1651–1664

106. Dominic B (1997) Comparison of efficiency and power output of various power products, Keynote talk, 1997 International Gas Turbine Institute (IGTI) Turbo Expo

107. Simon TW, Seume JR (1990) The Stirling engine: an engine that requires high-flux heat exchange under oscillating flow conditions, In: R. K. Shah, A. D. Kraus, and D. Metzger (Eds), Compact Heat Exchangers. New York, Hemisphere Publishing, pp. 567–626

108. Walker G (1980) Stirling Engines. Oxford, Clarendon Press

109. West CD (1986) Principles and Applications of Stirling Engines. New York, Van Nostrand Rheinhold

110. Allan J (1992) Thermodynamics and Gas Dynamics of the Stirling Cycle Machine. Cambridge, Cambridge University Press

111. Urieli, A, Berchowitz DM (1984) Stirling Cycle Engine Analysis. Bristol, Adam Higler Ltd.

112. Kongtragool B, Wongwises S (2003) A review of solar-powered stirling engines and low temperature differential Stirling engines. Renewable and Sustainable Energy Reviews 7: 131–154

113. Howell JR, Bannerot RB (1977) Optimum solar collector operation for maximizing cycle work output. Solar Energy 19: 149–153

114. Erbay LB, Sisman A, Yavuz H (1996) Analysis of Ericsson cycle at maximum power density conditions. ECOS'96, Stockholm, June 25–27: 175–178

115. Cataldo RS (1979) Modified Ericsson cycle engine, US Patent 4133172

116. Corey JA (1991) Ericsson cycle machine, US Patent 4984432

117. Blank DA, Chih W (1996) Power limit of an endoreversible Ericsson cycle with regeneration. Energy Conversion and Management, 37(1): 59–66(8)

118. Berrin L, Sisman A, and Yavuz H (1996) Analysis of Ericsson cycle at maximum power density conditions. ECOS: 25–27

119. Miller RH (1947) Supercharging and internally cooling for high output. ASME Transactions 69: 453–464

120. Al-Sarkhi J, Jaber O, Probert SD (2006) Efficiency of a Miller engine. Applied Energy 83(4): 343–351

121. Ge Y, Chen L, Sun F, Wu C (2005) Effects of heat transfer and friction on the performance of an irreversible air-standard Miller cycle. International Communications in Heat and Mass Transfer 32(8): 1045–1056

122. Fontana G, Galloni E, Palmaccio R, Torella E (2006) The influence of variable valve timing on the combustion process of a small spark-ignition engine. Proceedings of Automotive Engineers, [Special Publication] SP, SP-2011(Multi-Dimensional Engine Modeling 2006): 151–160

123. Kesgin U (2005) Efficiency improvement and NOx emission reduction potentials of two-stage turbocharged Miller cycle for stationary natural gas engines. International Journal of Energy Research 29(3): 189–216

124. Shimoda H, Kakuhama Y, Noguchi T, Endo H, Tanaka K (2004) High efficiency miller cycle gas engine generator with clean and low carbon dioxide emission. Mitsubishi Juko Giho 41(1): 24–25

125. Kakuta A, Shimoda H, Takaishi T (2003) Mitsubishi lean-burn gas engine of the highest thermal efficiency in the world. Mitsubishi Juko Giho 40(4): 246–249

126. Fujiwaka T, Kakuhama Y (2001) Development of lean burn Miller cycle gas engine. Proceedings of the International Gas Research Conference RCP31/1-RCP31/14

127. Tsukida N, Abe T, Okamoto K, Takemoto T (1999) Development of Miller cycle gas engine for cogeneration. AES (American Society of Mechanical Engineers) 39(Proceedings of the ASME Advanced Energy Systems Division–1999): 453–457

128. Fujiwaka T, Tsurusaki M, Shimoda H, Endo H (1998) Development of the Miller cycle lean burn gas engine. Proceedings of the International Gas Research Conference, 4: 336–345

129. Okamoto K, Zhang F-R, Shimogata S, and Shoji F (1997) Development of a late intake-valve closing (LIVC) Miller cycle for stationary natural gas engines - effect of EGR utilization. Society of Automotive Engineers, [Special Publication] SP, SP-1305(Preparing Mixtures for Diesel and SI Engines): 87–99

130. Bussing T, Pappas G (1994) An Introduction to Pulse Detonation Engines. Paper AIAA 94-0263, The American Institute of Aeronautics and Astronautics, Washington, D.C

131. Heywood JB (1988) Internal Combustion Engine Fundamentals. New York, McGraw-Hill

132. Kailasanath K, Patrick G, Li C (1999) Computational Studies of Pulse Detonation Engines – A Status Report. Paper AIAA 99-2634, The American Institute of Aeronautics and Astronautics, Washington, D.C

133. Wilson DG, Korakianitis T (1998) The Design of High-Efficiency Turbomachinery and Gas Turbines, 2nd ed. New Jersey, Prentice-Hall

134. Wilson MW (1999) Efficiency enhanced turbine engine. U. S. Patent Number 5966927, October 19

135. Chen L, Lin J, Sun F, Wu C (1998) Efficiency of an Atkinson engine at maximum power density. Energy Conversion and Management 39(3/4): 337

136. Wang P-Y, Hou S-S (2005) Performance analysis and comparison of an Atkinson cycle coupled to variable temperature heat reservoirs under maximum power and maximum power density conditions. Energy Conversion and Management 46: 2637–2655

137. Amano Y, Kawanishi K, Hashizume T (2005) Experimental investigations of oscillatory fluctuation in an ammonia-water mixture turbine system, AES (American Society of Mechanical Engineers), 45(Proceedings of the ASME Advanced Energy Systems Division–2005): 391–398

138. Prisyazhniuk VA, Holon I (2006) Strategies for emission reduction from thermal power plants. Journal of Environmental Management 80(1): 75–82

139. Borgert JA Velasquez JA (2004) Exergoeconomic optimisation of a Kalina cycle for power generation, International Journal of Energy 1(1): 18–28

140. Jonsson M (2003) Advanced power cycles with mixtures as the working fluid, PhD Dissertation, Kungliga Tekniska Hogskolan, Stockholm, Sweden

141. DiPippo R (2004) Second Law assessment of binary plants generating power from low-temperature geothermal fluids. Geothermics 33(5): 565–586

142. Bisio G, Rubatto G (2001) Marangoni effects and heat transfer variations in steam condensation by employing Kalina cycles. Proceedings of the Intersociety Energy Conversion Engineering Conference, 36th 2: 1171–1176

143. Dejfors C, Thorin E, and Svedberg G (1998) Ammonia-water power cycles for direct-fired cogeneration applications. Energy Conversion and Management 39(16–18): 1675–1681

144. Mlcak HA (1996) An introduction to the Kalina cycle, PWR (American Society of Mechanical Engineers), 30(Proceedings of the International Joint Power Generation Conference, 2: 765–776

145. Nag PK, Gupta AVSSKS (1998) Energy analysis of the Kalina cycle. Thermal Engineering 18(6): 427–439

146. Enick RM, Donahey GP, Holsinger M (1998) Modeling the high-pressure ammonia-water system with WATAM and the Peng-Robinson equation of state for Kalina cycle studies. Industrial & Engineering Chemistry Research 37(5): 1644–1650

147. Enick RM, Gale T, Klara J (1997) Modeling the application of Kalina cycle to LEBS power plants. Proceedings of the International Technical Conference on Coal Utilization & Fuel Systems, 22: 209–220

148. Rogdakis ED (1996) Thermodynamic analysis, parametric study and optimum operation of the Kalina cycle. International Journal of Energy Research, 20(4): 359–370

149. Marston CH, Sanyal Y (1994) Optimization of Kalina cycles for geothermal application, AES (American Society of Mechanical Engineers), 33 (Thermodynamics and the Design, Analysis, and Improvement of Energy Systems 1994): 97–104

150. Lazzeri L, Diotti F, Bruzzone M, Scala M (1995) Applications of Kalina cycle to geothermal applications. Proceedings of the American Power Conference 57(1): 370–373

151. Marston CH, Hyre M (1995) Gas turbine bottoming cycles: triple-pressure steam versus Kalina. Journal of Engineering for Gas Turbines and Power 117(1): 10–15

152. Kalina A, Leibowitz HM (994) Applying Kalina cycle technology to high-enthalpy geothermal resources. Transactions - Geothermal Resources Council, 18, Restructuring the Geothermal Industry: 531–536

153. Rumminger MD, Dibble RW, Lutz AE, Yoshimura AS (1994) An integrated analysis of Kalina cycle in combined cycles. Proceedings of the Intersociety Energy Conversion Engineering Conference, 29TH(PT.2), 974–979

154. Ibrahim MB, Kovach RM (1993) A Kalina cycle application for power generation. Energy (Oxford, United Kingdom) 18(9): 961–969

Problems

1. Steam enters the turbine of a power plant operating on the Rankine cycle at 3,300 kPa and leaves at 50 kPa. Determine the thermal efficiency of the cycle and the quality of the exhaust stream from the turbine for turbine-inlet stream temperatures of:
   (a) 475°C; (b) 550°C; and (c) 600°C.

   What effect will an increase in the turbine inlet stream temperature have on the following?

   (i) The thermal efficiency and
   (ii) The quality of the exhaust stream exiting the turbine

   If the turbine had an efficiency of 0.80, determine its impact on the thermal efficiency of the process at your temperature and its effect on the sizing of the equipment (the boiler, condenser, etc.).

2. Electrical power is to be produced from a steam turbine connected to a nuclear reactor. Steam is obtained from the reactor at 800 °F and 700 psia and exits a turbine at 50 psia. The turbine operates adiabatically. Compute the maximum work per pound of steam that can be obtained from the turbine. Also show the process in a P-v and a T-s diagram. Note: use steam tables.

3. Electrical power is to be produced from a steam turbine connected to a nuclear reactor. Steam can be obtained from the reactor at 500 °F and 600 psia and exits the turbine at 20 psia. The turbine operates adiabatically. Compute the maximum work per pound of steam that can be obtained from the turbine.

Assume that the single turbine considered above is replaced by two adiabatic turbines with a reheat loop. In this modified process, the steam exiting from the first turbine is returned to the reactor, where it is reheated at constant pressure to 500 °F, and then fed to the second stage of the turbine. Draw a process flow sheet for this suggested operation with labeled streams, where P' is the pressure for the stream exiting the first turbine.

(a) Determine the maximum work obtained per pound of steam if the two turbine process is used and the exhaust pressure from the first turbine is P' = 310 psia.
(b) Compute the maximum work obtained per pound of steam if the two turbine process is used and the exhaust pressure from the first turbine is P' = 35 psia.
(c) Compute the heat adsorbed per pound of steam in the reheating steps in parts (a) and (b).
(d) Show the process in a P-v and a T-s diagram.
Note: use steam tables.

4. Consider the following air-standard thermodynamic cycle. Assume all processes are quasi-static and air behaves as an ideal gas.
Air undergoes a quasi-static thermodynamic cycle 1–2–3–4–1 as shown above. Various conditions are given in the figure. The conditions at state 1 are p_1 = 100 kPa, T_1 =300 K. The pressure ratio (p_2/p_1) over process 1–2 is 10 and the peak temperature of the cycle is 1,500 K. Assume that c_p = 1.0035 kJ/kg-K and c_v = 0.7165 kJ/kg-K are constants, and that R = 0.287 kJ/kg-K.

(a) For each section of the cycle determine the heat flow, whether the heat added to the system, q_{in}, and the work done by the system, W_{in} and W_{out}.
(b) For each section of the cycle calculate the work and heat transfer, the change in internal energy and the change in enthalpy.
(c) What is the net work of the cycle?
(d) What is the thermal efficiency of the cycle?

5. A Carnot heat engine produces power of 2.5 kW. It rejects heat to a river that is flowing at 2 kg/s, resulting in a temperature increase of 2°C. The average temperature of the river is 20°C. Determine

(a) The heat transfer input required for the heat engine
(b) The efficiency of the heat engine
(c) The temperature at which heat transfer occurs to the engine

6. A device has an inlet flow of air at 20°C, 300 kPa, and 5 kg/s and two outlet flows, air at 60°C, 270 kPa, and 2 kg/s and air at 0°C, 270 kPa, and 3 kg/s. Verify if there is no work or heat transfer under these conditioned.

7. Determine the power output of an adiabatic turbine with isentropic efficiency 0.83 that has a steam input of 15 MPa and 650°C and an outlet pressure of 50 kPa.

8. Consider a steam power plant operating on a Rankine cycle with two open feedwater heaters. Steam leaves the boiler at 20 MPa and 670°C. The first high pressure open feedwater heater operates at 4 MPa, the low pressure open feedwater heater operates at 0.4 MPa, and the condenser operates at 0.004 MPa. Determine:

   (a) thermal efficiency of the plant
   (b) mass flow rate of steam leaving the boiler required to produce 60 MW of power.

9. Consider an internal combustion engine operating on the ideal Dual cycle with the following conditions: Two cylinder, four stroke engine with displacement of 1.6 l; Compression ratio of 7.5; Cutoff Ratio of 1.7; Combustion temperature of 1,700 K; Engine speed of 1,300 rpm. The initial temperature and pressure are taken to be 150 kPa and 315 K due to turbocharging of the intake air. Just before the final process (constant volume cooling) 85% of the air is extracted and is used to power a turbine that supplies power to the intake compressor (i.e. the turbocharger). Determine:

   (a) Engine thermal efficiency
   (b) Engine power output
   (c) Engine MEP
   (d) Exhaust turbine power

5 FUNDAMENTALS OF HEAT TRANSFER

Abstract

Energy from most resources is extracted in the form of heat by combustion. The heat or thermal energy is then transferred to other media, such as water to generate steam or a gas to heat it up. Steam is used to run a steam turbine, and hot gas is used in a gas turbine. The heat transfer mechanism should be understood in order to design such a system. Various heat transfer mechanisms and factors that affect the transfer of heat from one medium to another are discussed in this chapter.

5.1 Introduction

The goal of heat transfer is to predict the rate at which energy is transferred between various bodies of material. This energy transfer is calculated in terms of heat. There are three modes of heat transfer: conduction, convection, and radiation. Generally all three modes of heat transfer are important when calculating energy transfer. In any normal situation, all three modes of heat transfer may not occur simultaneously, or one mode may dominate other modes of heat transfer. Unless the temperatures are high, the effect of radiative heat transfer will be minimal. We will first consider these three modes of heat transfer separately and then will integrate them for a system.

5.2 Thermal Conduction

The flow of heat by conduction occurs when atoms and molecules within a substance collide with each other resulting in a transfer of kinetic energy that manifest in the form of heat. This transfer of kinetic energy from the hot to the cold side is called a flow of heat through conduction. Therefore, the thermal conduction

T.K. Ghosh and M.A. Prelas, *Energy Resources and Systems:*
Volume 1: Fundamentals and Non-Renewable Resources, 141–157.

occurs between parts of a continuum. Different materials transfer heat by conduction at different rates, which is measured by the material's **thermal conductivity**.

The heat transfer rate is usually expressed by the symbol "q". We first look at conduction heat transfer rate and its mathematical representation. If a temperature gradient exists in a body, there will be energy transfer from the high-temperature region to the low temperature region. It should be noted that although we are interested in total heat transfer, heat is not a directly measurable quantity. It is estimated from the knowledge of temperature which can be measured directly using various instruments such as a thermocouple. The energy that is transferred by conduction per unit area is proportional to the temperature gradient.

$$\frac{q}{A} \propto \frac{dT}{dx} \tag{5.1}$$

When a constant is inserted in the above equation it becomes:

$$q = -kA \frac{dT}{dx} \tag{5.2}$$

where

q = Heat transfer rate, Btu/h or W

k = Thermal conductivity, Btu/(h ft F) or W/(m C)

A = Area normal to the heat flow, ft^2 or m^2

T = Temperature, °F or °C

$\frac{dT}{dx}$ = Temperature gradient, °F/ft or °C/m.

Equation (5.2) is best known as the Fourier equation that expresses steady state heat conduction in one dimension. Equation (5.2) incorporates a negative sign because q flows in the positive direction of x when dT/dx is negative.

Consider a wall of thickness L whose two sides are assumed to be at uniform temperatures T_1 and T_2 (see Fig. 5.1). If the thermal conductivity, the heat transfer rate, and the area are constant, Eq. (5.2) may be integrated to obtain the rate of heat flow across the wall as follows:

$$\int_{x_1}^{x_2} q \, dx = \int_{T_1}^{T_2} -k \, A \, dT \tag{5.3}$$

$$q(x_2 - x_1) = -k \, A \, (T_2 - T_1) \tag{5.4}$$

$$q = \frac{-k \, A \, (T_2 - T_1)}{(x_2 - x_1)} \tag{5.5}$$

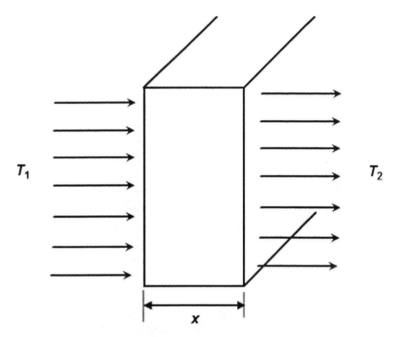

Fig. 5.1. Heat transfer through a solid object.

Example 5.1

What is the rate of heat loss per unit area of a 0.3 inch thick window if the room temperature is 20°C and the outside temperature is 0°C.

Solution

Assume that the problem is one dimensional and the window is made out of regular single pane glass. This is a good assumption since the window thickness is much less than the area of the window. In Table 5.1, the thermal conductivity of glass is given as 0.78 W/m °C. Thus the rate of heat loss per unit area is:

$$\frac{q}{A} = -k\frac{\partial T}{\partial x} \approx -k\frac{\Delta T}{\Delta x} = -0.78\,W/(mC)\frac{20-0}{0.00762} = -2047.24\,\frac{W}{m^2}$$

Table 5.1. Thermal conductivity of various materials.

Material	k(W/m °C)	k(Btu/h ft °F)
Aluminum	202	117
Copper	385	223
Iron	73	54
Lead	35	25
Nickel	93	54
Silver	410	237
Steel	43	20.3
Glass	0.78	0.45
Marble	2.08	1.2
Wood	0.17	0.096
Water	0.556	0.327
Air	0.0242	0.0139
CO_2	0.0146	0.00844
Helium	0.141	0.081
Hydrogen	0.175	0.101
H_2O (v)	0.0206	0.0119

Thermal conductivity for various building materials is given in Appendix V.

5.3 Modeling of Heat Transfer by Conduction

If a body of material has a temperature that is changing with time which may or may not be due to heat sources within the body, then one can model the system by using a detailed energy balance. The heat can flow in all three directions depending on the system. First, the energy balance equation is derived by considering heat flow in all three directions. This equation then can be simplified to address heat flow in a one-dimensional body. A rectangular parallelepiped volume element shown in Fig. 5.2 is considered for the energy balance. Assume that the solid thermal conductivity (k), specific heat (c), and the density (ρ) are independent of temperature. A small volume element of dimension $\Delta x \times \Delta y \times \Delta z$ is considered for energy balance. The energy balance equation of this element gives:

Rate of heat input + Rate of heat generation = Rate of heat output + Rate of accumulation of heat.

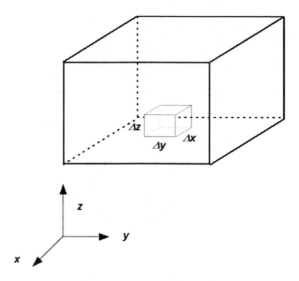

Fig. 5.2. Three dimensional heat transfers by conduction in a parallelogram.

The rate at which heat flows across an infinitesimal area in a direction normal to the area element is given by the Fourier equation (Eq. (5.2)). If the temperature gradient in the x direction is given by $\partial x/\partial T$, then the rate of heat flow in the direction of x across a plane of area $\Delta y \times \Delta z$ normal to the axis of x and passing through the mid-point of the volume element is given by:

$$q_{xx}\big|_x = -k(\Delta y \times \Delta z)\frac{\partial T}{\partial x}\bigg|_x \tag{5.6}$$

Similarly, the rates of heat flow in y and z directions are given by Eqs. (5.7) and (5.8), respectively.

$$q_{yy}\big|_y = -k(\Delta z \times \Delta x)\frac{\partial T}{\partial y}\bigg|_y \tag{5.7}$$

$$q_{zz}\big|_z = -k(\Delta x \times \Delta y)\frac{\partial T}{\partial z}\bigg|_z \tag{5.8}$$

The rate of heat flow out of the element in x, y, and z directions can be expressed by the following equations.

$$q_{xx}\big|_{x+\Delta x} = -k(\Delta y \times \Delta z)\frac{\partial T}{\partial x}\bigg|_{x+\Delta x} \tag{5.9}$$

$$q_{yy}\big|_{y+\Delta y} = -k(\Delta z \times \Delta x)\frac{\partial T}{\partial y}\bigg|_{y+\Delta y} \tag{5.10}$$

$$q_{zz}\big|_{z+\Delta z} = -k(\Delta x \times \Delta y)\frac{\partial T}{\partial z}\bigg|_{z+\Delta z} \tag{5.11}$$

If the heat generation is assumed to be $\ddot{q}$ per unit volume, then the total heat generation within the control element is given by

$$Heat\ generation = \ddot{q}(\Delta x \times \Delta y \times \Delta z) \tag{5.12}$$

The heat accumulation within the body is expressed as:

$$Accumulation = \rho c_p \Delta x\, \Delta y\, \Delta z\, \frac{\Delta T}{\Delta t} \tag{5.13}$$

After substitution of these terms into the energy balance equation, we get

$$q_{xx}\big|_x + q_{yy}\big|_y + q_{zz}\big|_z + \ddot{q}(\Delta x \times \Delta y \times \Delta z) =$$
$$q_{xx}\big|_{x+\Delta x} + q_{yy}\big|_{y+\Delta y} + q_{zz}\big|_{z+\Delta z} + \rho c_p \Delta x\, \Delta y\, \Delta z\, \frac{\Delta T}{\Delta t} \tag{5.14}$$

Rearranging,

$$\left(q_{xx}\big|_x - q_{xx}\big|_{x+\Delta x}\right) + \left(q_{yy}\big|_y - q_{yy}\big|_{y+\Delta y}\right) + \left(q_{zz}\big|_z - q_{zz}\big|_{z+\Delta z}\right)$$
$$+ \ddot{q}(\Delta x \times \Delta y \times \Delta z) = \rho c_p \Delta x\, \Delta y\, \Delta z\, \frac{\Delta T}{\Delta t} \tag{5.15}$$

Substitution of q by Eq. (5.2), and rearranging, the following expression is obtained.

$$k(\Delta y \times \Delta z)\left(\left.\frac{\partial T}{\partial x}\right|_{x+\Delta x} - \left.\frac{\partial T}{\partial x}\right|_x\right) + k(\Delta z \times \Delta x)\left(\left.\frac{\partial T}{\partial y}\right|_{y+\Delta y} - \left.\frac{\partial T}{\partial y}\right|_y\right)$$

$$+ k(\Delta x \times \Delta y)\left(\left.\frac{\partial T}{\partial z}\right|_{z+\Delta z} - \left.\frac{\partial T}{\partial z}\right|_z\right) + \ddot{q}(\Delta x \times \Delta y \times \Delta z) \tag{5.16}$$

$$= \rho c_p \, \Delta x \, \Delta y \, \Delta z \, \frac{\Delta T}{\Delta t}$$

Dividing both sides by $\Delta x \times \Delta y \times \Delta z$, Eq. (5.16) becomes

$$k\frac{\left(\left.\frac{\partial T}{\partial x}\right|_{x+\Delta x} - \left.\frac{\partial T}{\partial x}\right|_x\right)}{\Delta x} + k\frac{\left(\left.\frac{\partial T}{\partial y}\right|_{y+\Delta y} - \left.\frac{\partial T}{\partial y}\right|_y\right)}{\Delta y} + k\frac{\left(\left.\frac{\partial T}{\partial z}\right|_{z+\Delta z} - \left.\frac{\partial T}{\partial z}\right|_z\right)}{\Delta z} + \ddot{q} = \rho c_p \frac{\Delta T}{\Delta t} \tag{5.17}$$

Using the first principle of calculus and in the limit of $\Delta x \to 0$, $\Delta y \to 0$, $\Delta z \to 0$, and $\Delta t \to 0$, the above equation becomes

$$\frac{\partial}{\partial x}\left(\frac{\partial T}{\partial x}\right) + \frac{\partial}{\partial y}\left(\frac{\partial T}{\partial y}\right) + \frac{\partial}{\partial z}\left(\frac{\partial T}{\partial z}\right) + \ddot{q} = \frac{1}{\alpha}\frac{\partial T}{\partial t} \tag{5.18}$$

where

$$\alpha = \frac{k}{\rho c_p} \text{ , and is called the thermal diffusivity.}$$

Equation (5.18) can be further rewritten as:

$$\frac{\partial^2 T}{\partial x^2} + \frac{\partial^2 y}{\partial y^2} + \frac{\partial^2 z}{\partial z^2} + \ddot{q} = \frac{1}{\alpha}\frac{\partial T}{\partial t} \tag{5.19}$$

For one dimensional heat transfer, say in the direction of x and in the absence of any internal heat generation, Eq. (5.19) can be written as:

$$\frac{\partial^2 T}{\partial x^2} = \frac{1}{\alpha}\frac{\partial T}{\partial t} \tag{5.20}$$

Solution of Eq. (5.20) under various initial and boundary conditions is given by a number of researchers [1–5].

5.4 Convective Heat Transfer

When a solid material is interfaced with a gaseous or liquid medium, the heat transfer at the boundary between these two materials differs from conduction. In the interface between two materials of different phases, such as a solid and gas, the rate of collisions between gas molecules in the solid surface determines the rate of heat transfer from the interface. In the very thin layer, generally known as a boundary layer, the heat transfer may be by conduction. However, in the bulk fluid, the mixing is the dominant energy transfer mechanism. The higher the velocity of the gas molecules, the larger is the rate of heat transfer. This mechanism of heat transfer is called convective heat transfer. The mathematical model for convective heat transfer is given by Newton's law of cooling.

$$q = hA(T_g - T_w) \tag{5.21}$$

where

q = Heat transfer rate from fluid to wall, Btu/h or W
h = Convective heat-transfer coefficient or film coefficient, Btu/(h-ft^2-F) or W/(m^2-s)
T_g = Bulk fluid or gas temperature, °F or °C
T_w = Wall temperature, °F or °C

The convective heat transfer coefficient (h) is generally obtained experimentally or from an empirical formula that is obtained by considering various factors that affect the heat transfer and fitting the experimental data [6, 7]. The values for convective heat transfer coefficient for various media are given in Table 5.2.

Example 5.2

What is the heat transfer rate of a container filled with boiling water? The area is 1 m^2. The wall temperature is 200°C.

Solution

Here, T_w = 200°C, and T_g (boiling point of water) = 100°C.

$$q = -hA(T_w - T_g) = -2,500(200 - 100) = -250,000 \, W \, [44,000 BTU]$$

Table 5.2. Convective coefficient for various systems.

Material	k(W/m²-°C)	k(Btu/h-ft²-°F)
Free covection, ΔT = 30°C, vertical plate, 0.3 m high in air	4.5	0.79
Horizontal cylinder, 5-cm diameter, in air	6.5	1.14
Free Convection Horizontal cylinder, 2 cm diameter, in water	890	157
Forced Convection, airflow at 2 m/s over 0.2 m square plate	12	2.1
Forced Convection, airflow 35 m/s over 0.75 m square plate	75	13.2
Forced Convection, air at 2 atm. Flowing in 2.5 cm diameter tube at 10 m/s	65	11.4
Forced convection, water at 0.5 kg/s flowing in 2.5 cm diameter tube	3500	616
Airflow across 5 cm diameter cylinder with velocity of 50 m/s	180	32
Boiling Water in a container	2,500–35,000	440–6200
Boiling Water in a tube	5,000–10,0000	880–17,600
Condensation of H₂O (v), 1 atm	4,000–11,300	700–2000

5.5 Radiative Heat Transfer

All matter emits electromagnetic radiation depending on its temperature. Thus, energy transfer can occur between two bodies with different temperatures through the exchange of photons. An ideal radiator has a net heat exchange rate that is proportional to the difference in T^4 and is given by

$$q = \sigma A(T_1^4 - T_2^4) \tag{5.22}$$

where,

q = Heat transfer rate

σ = Stefan-Boltzmann constant, 5.669×10^{-8} W/m²-K⁴

A = Area of heat transfer, m²

T_1 = Temperature of the body 1, K

T_2 = Temperature of the body 2, K.

This equation is also known as the Stefan–Boltzmann law of thermal radiation.

This formula only applies to black bodies. A blackbody is a body which is in thermodynamic equilibrium and radiates energy according to the Stefan-Boltzmann law of thermal radiation. A body may not emit as much energy as a blackbody, but it may still follow the T^4 law. Such a body is called a "gray" body. Additionally, the emitting surface radiates in all directions. The body to which it radiates may only pick up a small fraction of the energy. This is due to geometrical factors in the line of site of the gray body to the receiving body (see Fig. 5.3).

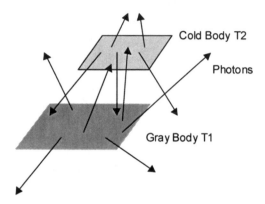

Fig. 5.3. Mechanism of radiative heat transfer. Photons travel in a straight line (the "ray" model), thus the number of photons which intersect the cold body depends upon the solid angle which the gray body sees. The geometrical view factor therefore plays an important role.

Introducing geometric view factor, the rate of heat transfer by radiation becomes:

$$q = F_e F_G \sigma A (T_1^4 - T_2^4) \tag{5.23}$$

where F_e is the emissivity function, F_G is the geometric "view factor."

Example 5.3

Two infinite black plates in deep space at 800°C (1073 K) and 300°C (573 K) exchange heat by radiation. Calculate the heat transfer per unit area.

Solution:

$$\frac{q}{A} = \sigma (T_1^4 - T_2^4) = 5.669 x 10^{-8} (1073^4 - 573^4)$$

$$\frac{q}{A} = 69.03 \frac{kW}{m^2} \left[21{,}884 \frac{BTU}{h\,ft^2} \right]$$

Example 5.4

A 10% efficient, 1 kW$_e$ nuclear battery is used in a deep space mission. This means that 90% of the energy produced by the battery must be transferred away from the battery. In deep space, the only means of transferring heat is by radiation. If the radiating surface is a 1 m^2 black body what is the equilibrium temperature of the nuclear battery? Deep space has a background temperature of 4 K.

Solution

Thermal energy rating = 1kW$_e$/0.1 = 10 kW$_{th}$

Energy that must be radiated = Δq = 10 kW-1 kW = 9 kW

Or, Δq = 9 kW

$$\frac{\Delta q}{A} = 9 \frac{kW}{m^2} = \sigma(T_1^4 - T_2^4) = 5.669x10^{-8}(T^4 - 4^4)$$

$$T^4 - 256 = \frac{9}{5.660x10^{-8}}$$

$$T^4 = 1.5876x10^8 + 256 \approx 1.5876x10^8$$

$$T \approx 112.24\ K$$

5.6 Thermal Resistance

Materials with a large thermal conductivity will transfer large amounts of heat over time for a given temperature difference. Such materials include metals such as copper, aluminum, etc. and are called thermal conductors. Conversely, materials with low thermal conductivities will transfer small amounts of heat over time, such as ceramic materials, and are known as poor thermal conductors. Home insulation is thus a poor thermal conductor, which keeps as much heat in as possible. Instead of being rated in terms of thermal conductivity, insulation is therefore usually rated in terms of its **thermal resistance**.

In a steady-state conduction problem, it is possible to model heat transfer by a technique called thermal resistance. This method is analogous to electrical resistance.

The heat conduction Eq. (5.2) can be written in another form using the concept of thermal resistance.

$$q = -\frac{(T_2 - T_1)}{R'} \tag{5.24}$$

where R' is called the thermal resistance and is defined by

$$R' = \frac{x_2 - x_1}{kA} = \frac{\Delta x}{kA} \tag{5.25}$$

In Eq. (5.24), $(T_2 - T_1)$ may be assumed as the thermal potential and is responsible for heat flow.

Thus, one can define heat flow by:

$$Heat\ Flow = \frac{Thermal\ Potential}{Thermal\ Resistance} \tag{5.26}$$

Thermal resistance (R') is analogous to electrical resistance, and q and $(T_2 - T_1)$ may be viewed as the current and potential difference in Ohm's law, respectively. Like an electrical circuit, the thermal resistance may be in series and thus provides a very useful method of analyzing heat transfer through a composite wall or slab made up of layers of dissimilar material. In Fig. 5.4 is shown a wall constructed of three different materials. The heat transferred by conduction through this wall is given by Eq. (5.27):

$$R' = R_A + R_B + R_C = \frac{\Delta x_1}{k_1 A} + \frac{\Delta x_2}{k_2 A} + \frac{\Delta x_3}{k_3 A} \tag{5.27}$$

The thermal resistance model works much like the electrical resistance model. In Fig. 5.4, the thermal resistances are in series. We can also apply the concept of thermal resistances in parallel as shown in Fig. 5.5. The application of parallel network is also analogous to the electrical model.

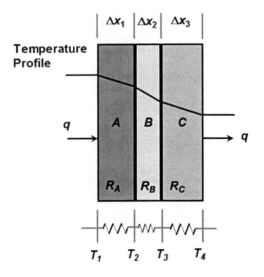

Fig. 5.4. One dimensional heat flow through a composite wall with the corresponding electrical analog.

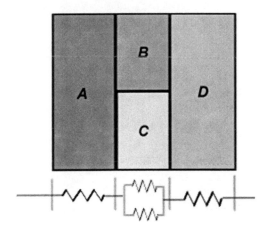

Fig. 5.5. The thermal equivalent of parallel resistance.

Equation (5.2) is developed for Cartesian coordinates (x-y-z). The application of Eq. (5.2) is restricted to a plane wall where the cross-sectional area is a constant. However, Eq. (5.2) can be extended to both polar and spherical coordinate system. Consider a long, hollow cylinder whose cross section is shown in Fig. 5.6. In this case, area A is a function of radius r. Therefore, Eq. (5.1) can be written as

$$\dot{q}_r = -k(2\pi r L)\frac{dT}{dr}$$

(5.28)

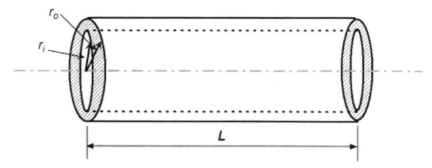

Fig. 5.6. A cylinder considered for heat transfer.

where,

r = Radius of the cylinder
L = Length of the cylinder

Integration of Eq. (5.28) yields

$$q_r = \frac{2\pi k L}{\ell n\left(\dfrac{r_0}{r_i}\right)}(T_i - T_0)$$

(5.29)

Equation (5.29) can be written in terms of thermal resistance

$$q_r = \frac{(T_i - T_0)}{R'}$$

(5.30)

where,

$$R' = \frac{\ell n\left(\dfrac{r_0}{r_i}\right)}{2\pi k L}$$

5.7 R Values

Insulation industry uses the concept of R-values to describe the thermal resistance of insulations [8–10]. It should be noted that R-values are not defined in the same manner as the thermal resistance. An R-value is defined as:

$$R = \frac{\Delta T}{q/A} \tag{5.31}$$

The heat flow on a per unit area basis is used in this equation.

Example 5.5

What is the difference in heat flow per unit area for insulation with an R value of 13 versus 19? Assume that the temperature indoors is 70°F and outdoors is 50°F.

Solution

$$q/A = \frac{\Delta T}{R} \ \text{Btu/h-ft}^2$$

$$q/A = \frac{20}{13} = 1.538 \ \text{Btu/h-ft}^2$$

$$q/A = \frac{20}{19} = 1.053 \ \text{Btu/h-ft}^2$$

$$\Delta \frac{q}{A} = 1.538 - 1.053 = 0.485 \ \text{Btu/h-ft}^2$$

References

1. Ozisik MN (1993) Heat Condustion. New York, Wiley-Interscience
2. Carslaw HS, Jaeger JC (1986) Conduction of Heat in Solids. New York, Oxford University Press
3. Crank J (1980) The Mathematics of Diffusion. New York, Oxford University Press
4. Cussler EL (1997) Diffusion: Mass Transfer in Fluid Systems, 2nd ed. Cambridge, Cambridge University Press
5. Bird RB, Stewart WE, Lightfoot EN (2006) Transport Phenomena, 2nd ed. New York, Wiley
6. ASHRAE Handbook (2001) Fundamentals. American Society of Heating, Refrigerating and Air-Conditioning Engineers, Atlanta, GA
7. Parker JD, Boggs JH, Blick EF (1969) Introduction to Fluid Mechanics and Heat Transfer, Reading, MA, Addison-Wesley
8. NBS Special Publication 548 (1974) Summer Attics and Whole-house Ventilation, US Department of Commerce, National Bureau of Standards, Washington, DC

9. Parker DS, Fairey PW, Gu L (1991) A Stratified Air Model for Simulation of Attic Thermal Performance, Insulation Materials: Testing and Applications, Volume 2, ASTM STP 1116, R. S. Graves and D. C. Wysocki, Eds., American Society of Testing and Materials, Philadelphia, PA
10. McQuiston FC, Parker JD (1988) Heating Ventilating and Air Conditioning Analysis and Design, 3rd ed. New York, Wiley

Problems

1. Aluminum has a specific heat of 0.902 J/g x °C. How much heat is lost when a piece of aluminum with a mass of 23.984 g cools from a temperature of 415.0°C to a temperature of 22.0°C?
2. The temperature of a sample of water increases by 69.5°C when 24,500 J are applied. The specific heat of liquid water is 4.18 J/g x °C. What is the mass of the sample of water?
3. 850 calories of heat are applied to a 250 g sample of liquid water with an initial temperature of 13.0°C. Find (a) the change in temperature and (b) the final temperature. (Remember, the specific heat of liquid water, in calories, is 1.00 cal/g x °C.)
4. When 34,700 J of heat are applied to a 350 g sample of an unknown material the temperature rises from 22.0°C to 173.0°C. What is the specific heat of this material?
5. The wall of a furnace is comprised of three layers as shown in the figure. The first layer is refractory (whose maximum allowable temperature is 1,400°C) while the second layer is insulation (whose maximum allowable temperature is 1,093°C). The third layer is a plate of 6.35 mm thick steel [thermal conductivity = 45 W/(m K)]. Assume the layers to be in very good thermal contact.

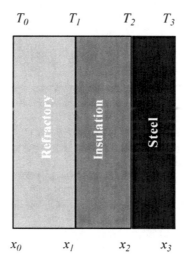

The temperature T_0 on the inside of the refractory is 1370°C, while the temperature T_3 on the outside of the steel plate is 37.8°C. The heat loss through the furnace wall is expected to be 15,800 W/m^2. Determine the thickness of refractory and insulation that results in the minimum total thickness of the wall.

Given thermal conductivities in W/(m K):

Layer	k at 37.8°C	k at 1,093°C
Refractory	3.12	6.23
Insulation	1.56	3.12

6 COAL

Abstract

Coal is the primary source of energy for most of the countries in the world. Although the main use of coal is in the generation of electricity, recently synthesis of liquid fuel from coal is becoming attractive, although coal liquefaction is a very old and well known process that was developed just after World War I. This may relieve pressure on petroleum as the only source of automobile fuel. However, a major concern in the use of coal is emissions of various pollutants including gases that cause acid rain and CO_2 emissions – a major contributor to global warming. Two approaches are pursued to reduce emissions from coal power plants. Most of the recent coal power plants are designed to produce supercritical steam, increasing the efficiency to about 50%. Another approach is to develop zero emission coal power plants. In this chapter, a comprehensive discussion on the use of coal and associated issues are presented.

6.1 Introduction

Coal has a long and rich history. The commercial use of coal can be traced back to 1000 BC by China. However, there is evidence that coal has been used for heating by the cave men. Archeologists have also found evidence that the Romans in England used coal in the second and third centuries (100–200 AD). The first scientific reference to coal may have been made by the Greek philosopher and scientist Aristotle, who referred to a charcoal like rock. It was during the Industrial Revolution in the 18th and 19th centuries that demand for coal surged. The introduction of the steam engine by James Watt in 1769 was largely responsible for the growth in coal use.

Coal was discovered in the United States by explorers in 1673. However, the Hopi Indians used coal for cooking, heating and to bake the pottery during the 1300s. Commercial coal mines started operation around 1740s in Virginia. During

T.K. Ghosh and M.A. Prelas, *Energy Resources and Systems:*
Volume 1: Fundamentals and Non-Renewable Resources, 159–279.

the Civil War, weapons factories were beginning to use coal. By 1875, coke (which is made from coal) replaced charcoal as the primary fuel for iron blast furnaces to make steel.

The use of coal for electricity generation started around the nineteenth century. The first practical coal-fired electricity generating station, developed by Thomas Edison, went into operation in New York City in 1882, supplying electricity for household lights.

Coal was the primary source of energy until 1960s. The use of oil for transportation overtook coal as the largest source of primary energy in the 1960s. However, coal still plays a vital role in the world's primary energy mix, providing 24.4% of global primary energy needs in 2003 and 40.1% of the world's electricity. The production and consumption of coal by various regions and some selected countries are given in Tables 6.1 and 6.2. As can be seen from Table 6.2, the use of coal world wide is increasing slowly. In Table 6.3 shows how long the coal will last at the current rate of use and with modest increase in the next few years.

Table 6.1. Yearly coal production of selected countries in million tonnes.[a]

Countries	Years				Share of the World (%)
	2003	2004	2005	2006	
USA	972.3	1008.9	1026.5	1053.6	19.3
Canada	62.1	66.0	65.3	62.9	1.1
Mexico	9.7	9.9	10.0	11.1	0.2
Total North America	**1044.1**	**1084.8**	**1101.8**	**1127.7**	**20.5**
Brazil	4.7	5.4	6.3	6.3	0.1
Colombia	50.0	53.7	60.6	65.6	1.4
Venezuela	7.0	8.1	8.1	8.1	0.2
Other S. & Cent. America	0.5	0.3	0.8	0.7	–
Total S. & Cent. America	**62.2**	**67.5**	**75.7**	**80.7**	**1.7**
Bulgaria	27.3	26.6	26.4	27.5	0.2
Czech Republic	63.9	62.0	62.0	62.4	0.8
France	2.2	0.9	0.6	0.5	–
Germany	204.9	207.8	202.8	197.2	1.6
Greece	71.0	71.6	70.6	70.6	0.3
Hungary	13.3	11.5	9.6	10.0	0.1
Kazakhstan	84.9	86.9	86.6	96.3	1.6

Countries	Years				Share of the World (%)
	2003	2004	2005	2006	
Poland	163.8	162.4	159.5	156.1	2.2
Romania	33.1	31.8	31.1	35.1	0.2
Russian Federation	276.7	281.7	298.5	309.2	4.7
Spain	20.5	20.5	19.4	18.4	0.2
Turkey	49.3	49.9	61.7	63.4	0.4
Ukraine	80.2	81.3	78.7	80.5	1.4
United Kingdom	28.3	25.1	20.5	18.6	0.4
Other Europe & Eurasia	66.2	65.2	63.9	66.7	0.5
Total Europe & Eurasia	**1185.7**	**1185.1**	**1192.0**	**1212.4**	**14.5**
Total Middle East	**1.0**	**1.1**	**1.1**	**1.1**	**–**
South Africa	237.9	243.4	244.4	256.9	4.7
Zimbabwe	2.8	3.8	2.9	2.9	0.1
Other Africa	2.0	2.0	1.8	1.8	–
Total Africa	**242.7**	**249.2**	**249.0**	**261.6**	**4.8**
Australia	351.5	366.1	378.8	373.8	6.6
China	1722.0	1992.3	2204.7	2380.0	39.4
India	375.4	407.7	428.4	447.3	6.8
Indonesia	114.3	132.4	146.9	195.0	3.9
Japan	1.3	1.3	1.1	1.3	–
New Zealand	5.2	5.2	5.3	5.8	0.1
Pakistan	3.3	3.3	3.5	4.3	0.1
South Korea	3.3	3.2	2.8	2.8	–
Thailand	18.8	20.1	20.9	19.4	0.2
Vietnam	19.3	26.3	32.6	38.9	0.7
Other Asia Pacific	37.5	40.0	41.9	43.1	0.7
Total Asia Pacific	**2651.8**	**2997.7**	**3267.0**	**3511.7**	**58.5**
TOTAL WORLD	**5187.6**	**5585.3**	**5886.7**	**6195.1**	**100.0**

[a]Commercial solid fuels only, i.e. bituminous coal and anthracite (hard coal), and lignite and brown (sub-bituminous) coal.

Annual changes and shares of total are based on data expressed in tonnes oil equivalent. Because of rounding some totals may not agree exactly with the sum of their component parts.
Source: Reference [1].

Table 6.2. World coal consumption by regions and of selected countries.

Region/Country	2002	2003	2004	% of World in 2004
World Total	5,262.80	5,698.15	6,098.78	
Asia & Oceania	2,448.45	2,795.88	3,190.25	52.31
North America	1,151.89	1,182.43	1,182.53	19.39
Europe	1,030.01	1,052.40	1,036.30	16.99
Eurasia	398.01	413.30	429.40	7.04
Africa	184.44	200.33	205.83	3.37
Central & South America	35.92	37.57	38.21	0.63
Middle East	16.07	16.23	16.27	0.27
China	1,412.96	1,720.24	2,062.39	33.82
United States	1,065.84	1,094.86	1,107.25	18.16
India	434.44	448.62	478.16	7.84
Germany	278.98	277.29	279.95	4.59
Russia	240.23	243.43	257.52	4.22
Japan	173.47	185.24	203.72	3.34
South Africa	169.56	186.60	195.14	3.20
Australia	145.37	142.64	150.09	2.46
Poland	149.45	155.49	153.10	2.51
Ukraine	71.51	75.39	77.50	1.27
Korea, South	81.47	83.13	90.56	1.48
Greece	76.81	78.16	80.34	1.32
Turkey	73.16	70.65	69.59	1.14
Canada	72.21	68.88	57.76	0.95
Kazakhstan	66.24	72.32	72.86	1.19
Czech Republic	64.65	65.58	63.43	1.04
United Kingdom	64.17	68.78	67.16	1.10
Taiwan	56.32	60.67	62.90	1.03
Spain	50.53	46.68	48.67	0.80
Korea, North	31.99	32.58	33.07	0.54
Other Countries				8.00

Source: Reference [1].

Table 6.3. Years coal will last at various consumption rate.

Country	Current consumption (2004)	Total reserve	Consumption time in year with the following growth rate annually							
			0%	2%	2.50%	3.00%	3.50%	4%	4.50%	5%
China	2,062.39	126,215	61.20	40.36	37.59	35.26	33.28	31.56	30.05	28.72
United States	1,107.25	271,677	245.36	89.69	79.57	71.84	65.71	60.70	56.53	52.99
India	478.16	93,031	194.56	80.16	71.63	65.03	59.75	55.40	51.75	48.63
Germany	279.95	72,753	259.88	92.12	81.58	73.56	67.21	62.04	57.73	54.08
Russia	257.52	173,074	672.08	134.84	116.61	103.26	93.01	84.85	78.19	72.64
Japan	203.72	852	4.18	4.06	4.03	4.00	3.97	3.94	3.92	3.89
South Africa	195.14	54,586	279.73	95.25	84.18	75.78	69.14	63.76	59.28	55.49
Australia	150.09	90,489	602.90	129.75	112.47	99.77	89.99	82.19	75.81	70.48
Poland	153.1	24,427	159.55	72.36	65.09	59.39	54.78	50.97	47.75	44.98
Ukraine	77.5	37,647	485.77	119.77	104.32	92.88	84.02	76.92	71.09	66.21
Greece	80.34	3,168	39.43	29.36	27.78	26.41	25.21	24.14	23.18	22.32
Turkey	69.59	4,066	58.43	39.09	36.47	34.26	32.37	30.73	29.28	28.01
Canada	57.76	7,251	125.54	63.42	57.52	52.83	48.99	45.78	43.04	40.68
Kazakhstan	72.86	37,479	514.40	122.39	106.47	94.70	85.60	78.32	72.34	67.34
Czech Republic	63.43	6,259	98.68	55.03	50.35	46.56	43.42	40.76	38.48	36.50
UK	67.16	1,653	24.61	20.21	19.42	18.71	18.06	17.47	16.94	16.44
Spain	48.67	728	14.96	13.22	12.87	12.54	12.24	11.96	11.69	11.45
Korea, North	33.07	661	19.99	16.98	16.41	15.89	15.42	14.98	14.58	14.20

6.2 Origin of Coal

Two main theories have been suggested by scientists on the origin of coal or how coal is formed [2–4]. According to the first theory, coal formed in situ, where the vegetation grew and fell, and such a deposit is said to be autochthonous in origin. The starting constituents of coal are believed to be plant debris, trees, and bark that accumulated and settled in swamps. Composition of coals differs throughout the world due to the kinds of plant materials involved in the formation (type of coal), in the degree of metamorphism or coalification (rank of coal), and in the type of impurities included (grade of coal). However, there is a great controversy on the bearing of plant constituents, particularly cellulose and lignin, on coal formation.

The unconsolidated accumulation of plant remains is called peat. The beginning of most coal deposits started with thick peat bogs where the water was nearly stagnant and plant debris accumulated. The plant debris converted into peat by microbiological action. Over the years, these layers of peat became covered with sediment and were subjected to heat and pressure from the subsidence of the swamps. The cycles of accumulation and sediment deposition continued and were followed by diagenetic (i.e., biological) and tectonic (i.e., geological) actions and, depending upon the extent of temperature, time, and forces exerted, formed the different ranks of coal observed today [5–19]. A number of researchers concluded that cellulose in plants was the main path towards the ultimate formation of coal [20–28]. Both the theories were reviewed by several groups and their applicability to various deposits around the world was discussed. However, it became certain from these reviews that one single theory could not be applied to explain all the deposits [29–48].

A metamorphic process, called coalification as shown in Fig. 6.1, eventually formed the coal. The metamorphic process is thought to have occurred in several stages and the factors assumed to affect the content, makeup, quality, and rank of the coal are given below.

- Temperature
- Pressure
- Time
- Layering process
- Fresh water/sea water
- Swamp acidity
- Types of plant debris
- Types of sediment cover

Plant materials are first converted to peat that has high moisture content and a relatively low heating value. However, as the process of coalification continues under greater pressure and temperature, peat starts to loose moisture and other types of coal formed.

Fig. 6.1. Coal formation process. (Adapted from [49]).

The mineral content in coal comes from the salts that were part of the body of water. This generally leads to different mineral contents in various coal deposits. Ash content is due to the mud (may be considered as a mixture of mineral) that was deposited along with the plant matter. Different bodies of water had different rates of mud deposit.

In the USA, eastern coal is the oldest and formed from the organic debris in a shallow sea. Eastern coal is high in sulfur because the seas it formed in were high in sulfur salts. Nearly all eastern coal is bituminous. There is a small amount of anthracite in the east. Western coal is relatively young. It formed mostly in fresh water swamps. It contains less sulfur because there was relatively little sulfur salts in the water. It has more ash because the rate of mud deposit in a swamp is high. Western coal is mostly sub-bituminous or lignite.

The second theory stipulates that coal formed through the accumulation of vegetal matter that has been transported by water to another location [3, 4]. According to this theory (i.e., allochthonous origin), the fragments of plants were carried away by streams and deposited on the bottom of the sea or in lakes where they build up strata, which later became compressed into coal. Major coal deposits were formed in every geological period since the Upper Carboniferous Period, 350–270 million years ago. The main coal-forming periods are shown in Fig. 6.2, which shows the relative ages of the world's major coal deposits.

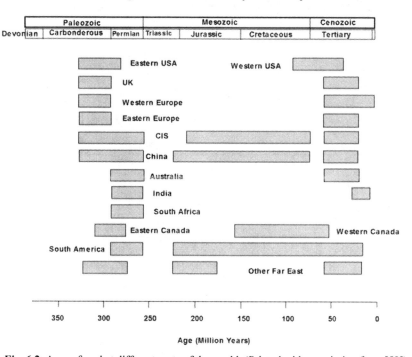

Fig. 6.2. Ages of coal at different parts of the world. (Printed with permission from [50]).

6.3 Classification

Coal is generally divided into two main categories: Anthracite (or Hard Coal) and Bituminous (or Soft Coal). The classification is mainly based on the carbon content and moisture content of the coal. As the coalification process continues the rank of the coal increases. The rank of coal is defined as the degree of changes (metamorphism) that occurs as a coal matures from peat to anthracite. The coal may be classified in a number of ways as described below. There are a number of subdivisions within these categories too.

1. By ash content
   Low ash (<5%)
   High ash (>20%)
2. Its structure
   Anthracite (nearly pure carbon)
   Bituminous (more bound hydrogen)
   Sub-Bituminous (less bound hydrogen)
   Lignite
3. Heating values
   Anthracite: 22–28 x 10^6 BTU/ton
   Bituminous: 25 x 10^6 BTU/ton
   Lignites: 12 x 10^6 BTU/ton
4. Sulfur content
   Low (<1%)
   High (about 7%)
5. Coke grade
   Metallurgical coke (premier grade)
   Non metallurgical coke (low grade)
6. Caking properties
   Caking
   Non-caking

The American Society of Testing and Material (ASTM) has a standard classification of coals by ranks and is provided in their D388-84, which is given in Table 6.4.

The four main constituents of coal are volatile matters, hydrogen, carbon, and oxygen. The percentage of these elements determines the heating value of coal rank. The C/H and (C+H)/O ratios are also important for determining combustion characteristics of coal. These values for different ranks of coal are shown in Table 6.5.

Table 6.4. Classification of coal by rank according to ASTM standard 388.

Class	Group	Fixed carbon limits (%) (dry mineral matter free basis)		Volatile matter limits (%) (dry, mineral matter free basis)		Calorific value limits (BTU/lb) (moist mineral matter free basis)		Agglomerating character
		Equal to or greater than	Less than	Greater than	Equal to or less than	Equal to or greater than	Less than	
I. Anthracite	1. Meta-anthracite	98	–	–	2	–	–	Non-agglomerating
	2. Anthracite	92	98	2	8	–	–	
	3. Semi-anthracite	86	92	8	14	–	–	
II. Bituminous	1. Low volatile bituminous coal	78	86	14	22	–	–	Commonly agglomerating
	2. Medium volatile bituminous coal	69	78	22	31	–	–	
	3. High volatile A bituminous coal	–	69	31	–	14,000	–	
	4. High volatile B bituminous coal	–	–	–	–	13,000	14,000	
	5. High volatile C bituminous coal	–	–	–	–	11,500	13,000	
						10,500	11,500	Agglomerating
III. Subbituminous	1. Subbituminous A coal	–	–	–	–	10,500	11,500	Non-agglomerating
	2. Subbituminous B coal	–	–	–	–	9,500	10,500	
	3. Subbituminous C coal	–	–	–	–	8,300	9,500	
IV. Lignite	1. Lignite A	–	–	–	–	6,300	8,300	Non-agglomerating
	2. Lignite B	–	–	–	–	–	6,300	

(a) This classification applies to coals composed mainly of volatile: coals rich in liptinite or inertinite do not fit into this classification system.

(b) Standard units for ASTM classification for calorific value are BTU/lb. To convert to SI units of kJ/kg, multiply BTU/lb by 2.326.

(c) Moist refers to coal containing its natural inherent moisture but not including visible water on the surface of the coal.

(d) If agglomerating, classify in low-volatile group of the bituminous class.

(e) Coals having 69% or more fixed carbon on a dry, mineral matter free basis are classified according to fixed carbon only, regardless of calorific value.

(f) It is recognized that there may be non-agglomerating varieties in these groups of bituminous class, and that there are notable exceptions in the high volatile C bituminous group.

(g) Agglomerating coals in the range 10,500–11,500 BTU/lb are classed as high volatile C bituminous coal.

Source: ASTM Standard D388-84 (1984).

Table 6.5. Classification profile chart.

	Volatile matter (%)	Hydrogen (wt%)	Carbon (wt%)	Oxygen (wt%)	Heating value (kJ/kg)	C/H ratio	(C+H)/O ratio
				Average analysis-moisture and ash free basis			
Anthracite							
Meta	1.8	2.0	94.4	2.0	34,425	46.0	50.8
Anthracite	5.2	2.9	91.0	2.3	35,000	33.6	42.4
Semi	9.9	3.9	91.0	2.8	35,725	23.4	31.3
Bituminous							
Low-vol.	19.1	4.7	89.9	2.6	36,260	19.2	37.5
Med-vol.	26.9	5.2	88.4	4.2	35,925	16.9	25.1
High-vol. A	38.8	5.5	83.0	7.3	34,655	15.0	13.8
High-vol. B	43.6	5.6	80.7	10.8	33,330	14.4	8.1
High-vol. C	44.8	4.4	77.7	13.5	31,910	14.2	6.2
Sub-bituminous							
Sub-bitu. A	44.7	5.3	76.0	16.4	30,680	14.3	5.0
Sub-bitu. B	42.7	5.2	76.1	16.6	30,400	14.7	5.0
Sub-bitu. C	44.2	5.1	73.9	19.2	29,050	14.6	4.2
Lignite							
Lignite A	46.7	4.9	71.2	21.9	28,305	14.5	3.6

To convert kJ/kg to BTU/lb, divide by 2.326
Source: Reference [51]

The use of coal depends on its rank and their use is summarized in Table 6.6.

Table 6.6. Use of coal depending on its rank.

Types of coal	% of World reserves	Uses
Low rank coals		
Lignite	17	Mainly power generation
Sub-bituminous	30	Power generation
		Cement manufacture
		Industrial uses
Hard coal		
Bituminous	52	
Thermal steam coal		Power generation
		Cement manufacture
		Industrial uses
Metallurgical coking coal		Manufacture of iron and steel
Anthracite	1	Domestic/Industrial uses
		Smokeless fuel

Source: Reference [52].

The reserve of different ranks of coal in various countries is given in Table 6.7.

Table 6.7. Coal: proved reserves at the end 2006 (in million tones).

Country	Anthracite and bituminous	Sub-bituminous and lignite	Total	Share of world total	R/P ratio
USA	111,338	135,305	246,643	27.1%	234
Canada	3,471	3,107	6,578	0.7%	105
Mexico	860	351	1,211	0.1%	109
Total North America	**115,669**	**138,763**	**254,432**	**28.0%**	**226**
Brazil	–	10,113	10,113	1.1%	*
Colombia	6,230	381	6,611	0.7%	101
Venezuela	479	–	479	0.1%	60
Other S. & Cent. America	992	1,698	2,690	0.3%	*
Total S. & Cent. America	**7,701**	**12,192**	**19,893**	**2.2%**	**246**
Bulgaria	4	2,183	2,187	0.2%	80
Czech Republic	2,094	3,458	5,552	0.6%	89

(Continued)

Table 6.7. (Continued)

Country	Anthracite and bituminous	Sub-bituminous and lignite	Total	Share of world total	R/P ratio
France	15	–	15	◆	30
Germany	183	6,556	6,739	0.7%	34
Greece	–	3,900	3,900	0.4%	55
Hungary	198	3,159	3,357	0.4%	337
Kazakhstan	28,151	3,128	31,279	3.4%	325
Poland	14,000	–	14,000	1.5%	90
Romania	22	472	494	0.1%	14
Russian Federation	49,088	107,922	157,010	17.3%	*
Spain	200	330	530	0.1%	29
Turkey	278	3,908	4,186	0.5%	66
Ukraine	16,274	17,879	34,153	3.8%	424
United Kingdom	220	–	220	◆	12
Other Europe & Eurasia	1,529	21,944	23,473	2.6%	352
Total Europe & Eurasia	**112,256**	**174,839**	**287,095**	**31.6%**	**237**
South Africa	48,750	–	48,750	5.4%	190
Zimbabwe	502	–	502	0.1%	176
Other Africa	910	174	1,084	0.1%	*
Middle East	419	–	419	◆	399
Total Africa & Middle East	**50,581**	**174**	**50,755**	**5.6%**	**194**
Australia	38,600	39,900	78,500	8.6%	210
China	62,200	52,300	114,500	12.6%	48
India	90,085	2,360	92,445	10.2%	207
Indonesia	740	4,228	4,968	0.5%	25
Japan	359	–	359	◆	268
New Zealand	33	538	571	0.1%	99
North Korea	300	300	600	0.1%	20
Pakistan	–	3,050	3,050	0.3%	*
South Korea	–	80	80	◆	28
Thailand	–	1,354	1,354	0.1%	70
Vietnam	150	–	150	◆	4
Other Asia Pacific	97	215	312	◆	7
Total Asia Pacific	**192,564**	**104,325**	**296,889**	**32.7%**	**85**
TOTAL WORLD	**478,771**			**100.0%**	**147**

Country	Anthracite and bituminous	Sub-bituminous and lignite	Total	Share of world total	R/P ratio
European Union 25	17,424	17,938	35,362	3.9%	65
European Union 27	17,450	20,593	38,043	4.2%	63
OECD	172,363	20,0857	373,220	41.1%	177
Former Soviet Union	94,513	132,741	227,254	25.0%	464
Other EMEs	211,895	96,695	308,590	33.9%	86

*More than 500 years.
♦Less than 0.05%.
Proved reserves of coal – Generally taken to be those quantities that geological and engineering information indicates with reasonable certainty can be recovered in the future from known deposits under existing economic and operating conditions.

Reserves/Production (R/P) ratio – If the reserves remaining at the end of the year are divided by the production in that year, the result is the length of time that those remaining reserves would last if production were to continue at that rate.
Source: References [1, 53].

The exports and imports of coal by various countries are given in Appendix VI.

6.4 Coal Properties and Structure

The analysis of coal is carried out not only to determine its rank, but also its combustion characteristics. The results of these analyses can be used to predict coal behavior and the corresponding environmental impact during its use. Analysis of coal must be carried out using established protocols and standard methods described by American Society for Testing and Materials (ASTM), International Organization for Standardization (ISO) and British Standards Institution (BSI) test method numbers. These standards are listed in Table 6.8. Descriptions and objectives of these analyses are described in Table 6.9.

Table 6.8. ASTM and corresponding ISO methods for coal analysis.

Parameter	ASTM method	ISO method	BSI
Ultimate analysis		ISO 17247:2005	BS 1016-6
Proximate	D-5142	ISO 17246	BS 1016 P104
Sulfur	D-4239	ISO 334 and ISO 351	BS 1016 P106 S106.4.2
Carbon & hydrogen	D-5373	ISO 609 and 625	BS 1016 P106 SS106.1.1

(Continued)

Table 6.8. (Continued)

Parameter	ASTM method	ISO method	BSI
Nitrogen	D-5373	ISO 333	BS 1016 P106 S106.2
BTU	D-2015		
Forms of sulfur	D-2492	ISO 157	BS 1016 P106 S106.5
HGI	D-409		
Trace elements by ICP	D-6357		
Trace elements by rf-source GDMS	N/A		
Moisture	D-1412	ISO 589	BS 1016 P104 S104.1
Specific gravity	D-167		
Sulfur in ash	D-5016		
Ash fusion temp.	D-1857	ISO 540	BS 1016 P113
Mineral ash	D-4326	ISO 1171	
Sieve analysis	D-4749		BS 1016 P109
Sample prep.	D-2013		BS1017 P1
Washability	D-4371		
Chloride	D-4208		
Mercury	D-3684	ISO 15237	
Arsenic		ISO 601	BS 1016 P10
Phosphorous		ISO 622	BS 1016-9
Petrographic analysis		ISO 7404	BS 6127
Mineral matter		ISO 602	
Abrasiveness		ISO 12900	BS1016 P111

Table 6.9. Description and objectives of various coal analysis techniques.

Properties	Description of the analysis
Chemical properties	
Proximate analysis	Determination of the "approximate" overall composition of a coal, i.e., moisture, volatile matter, ash, and fixed carbon content.
Ultimate analysis	Absolute measurement of the elemental composition of coal excluding ash elements.
Atomic ratio	The H/C and O/C chemical analysis of coal.
Elemental analysis	Measurement of elements in coal including ash elements.
Sulfur forms	Chemically bonded sulfur in coal: organic, sulfide, or sulfate.
Physical properties	
Density	True density measured by helium displacement, minimum of 1.3 g/mL at 85–90% C.

Properties	Description of the analysis
Specific gravity	Apparent density – use of fluid that does not penetrate pores.
Pore structure	Specification of the porosity of coals and nature of pore structure between macro, micro, and transitional pores.
Surface area	Determination of surface area by nitrogen or carbon dioxide adsorption.
Reflectivity	Useful in petrographic analyses.
Mechanical properties	
Elasticity	Quality of regaining original shape after deformation: rheology, deformation, flow.
Strength	Specification of compressibility strength in psi.
Hardness/abrasiveness	Scratch and indentation hardness by Vickers hardness number: abrasiveness of coal
Friability	Ability to withstand degradation in size on handling, tendency toward breakage, two tests: tumbler test and drop shatter test.
Grindability	Relative amount of work needed to pulverize coal against a standard, measured by Hardgrove grindability index.
Dustiness index	Dust produced when coal is handled in a standard manner: index of dutiness
Thermal properties	
Calorific value	Indication of energy content in coal.
Heat capacity	Heat required to raise the temperature of a unit amount of coal by 1°.
Thermal conductivity	Rate of heat transfer through unit area, unit thickness, unit temperature difference.
Plastic/agglutinating	Changes in a coal upon heating and caking properties of coal, measured by Gieseler plastometer test.
Agglomerating index	Grading based on nature of residue from 1 g sample when heated at 950°C: Roga index
Free-swelling index	Measure of the increase in volume when a coal is heated without restriction, indication of plastic and caking properties.
Electrical properties	
Electrical resistivity	Electrical resistivity of coal in ohm-cm, coal is considered a semiconductor.
Dielectric constant	Electrostatic polarizability, related to the π electrons of aromatic rings.
Magnetic susceptibility	Diamagnetic, paramagnetic and ferromagnetic characteristics of coal.
Ash properties	
Elemental analysis	Major elements found in coal ash, 90% of ash is made up of SiO_2, Al_2O_3, and Fe_2O_3.
Mineralogical analysis	Analysis of the mineral content in coal ash.

(Continued)

Table 6.9. (Continued)

Properties	Description of the analysis
Trace element analysis	Analysis of trace elements found in coal, 22 elements occur in most samples, averages show some enrichment in ash.
Ash fusibility	Temperature at which ash passes through defined stages of fusing and flow.
Petrographic properties	
Maceral composition	Specification of the maceral components of coal, important to describing how a coal will react in coal conversion and what coal products will be given off.
Vitrinite reflection	Important to maceral analysis and rank calculation
Sample information	
Sample history	Sampling date and agency, sample type.
Mine information	Mine life expectancy, reserves, annual production and mining method.
Sample location	Country, state, county, township, city, coal, province, and region.
Seam information	Age of seam, group, formation and seam thickness.

Source: Reference [54].

6.5 Coal Structure

The structure of coal is extremely complex and depends on the origin, history, age, and rank of the coal. The molecular (chemical) and conformational structures of coal are studied to determine its reactivity during combustion, pyrolysis, and liquefaction processes [55–120]. Structures were derived using data obtained from various analyses including coal atomic composition, analysis of product from chemical reactions, coal liquefaction, and pyrolysis. Molecular models derived by various researchers for bituminous coal are shown in Fig. 6.3. Carlson [58] studied the three dimensional structures of coal using computer simulation and further analyzed the structures suggested by Given [121], Solomon [122], Shinn [123], and Wiser [124].

(a) Given [121]

(b) Solomon [122]

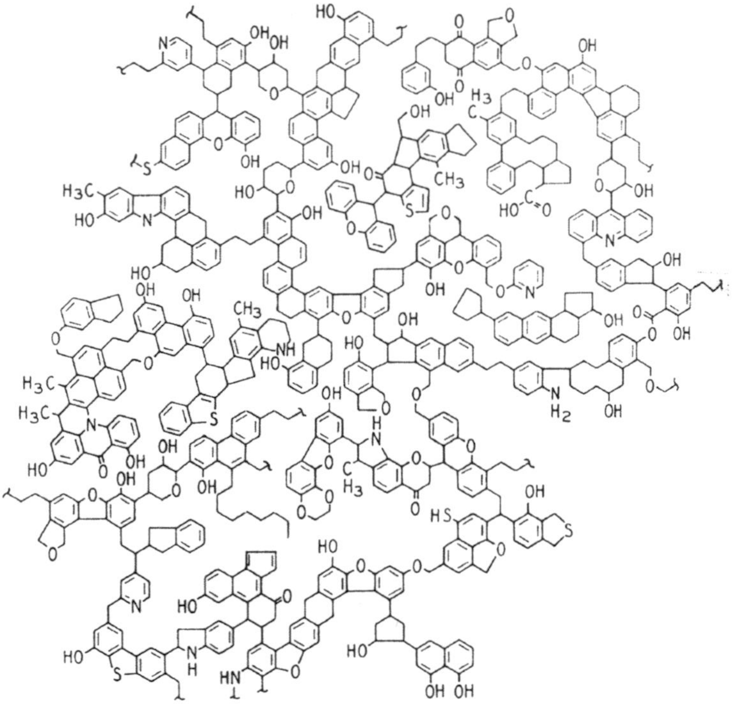

(c) Shinn [123]

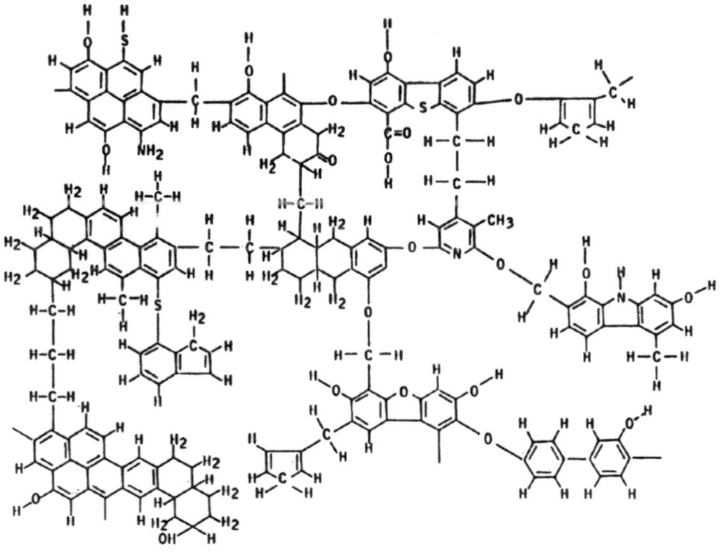

(d) Wiser [124]

Fig. 6.3. Structures of coal as suggested by various researchers.

6.6 Coal Mining

The mining techniques used for extraction of coal depend on the quality, depth of the coal seam, and the geology of the coal deposit. The coal mining process can be classified into two categories depending on the mode of operation.

1. Surface Mining
    (a) Strip mining
    (b) Mountain top mining
2. Underground Mining
    (a) Room and Pillar mining
    (b) Longwall mining

A schematic depiction and various terminology associated with coal mining is given in Fig. 6.4.

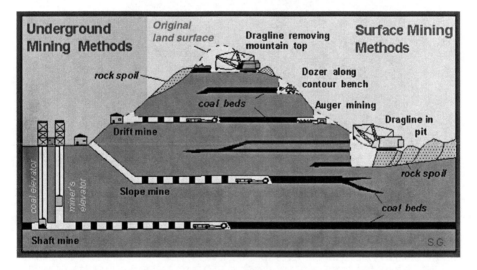

Fig. 6.4. A Schematic depiction of the range of different surface and underground types of coal mining, illustrating types of access to coal deposits and mining terminology [125].

6.6.1 Surface Mining

Surface mining is the most common type of mining of coal in the world. It is called strip mining. It accounts for around 80% of production in Australia, while in the USA it is used for about 67% of production. It is similar to open-pit mining in many regards. Surface mining is used when a coal seam is usually within 200 feet of the surface. The layer of soil and rock covering the coal (called the "overburden") is first removed from the surface to expose the coal, but is stored near the site

(Fig. 6.5). A variety of heavy equipment including draglines, power shovels, bull-dozers, and front-end loaders are used to expose the coal seam for mining. After the surface mining, the overburden is replaced; it is graded, covered with topsoil, fertilized and seeded to make the land useful again for crops, wildlife, recreation, or commercial development. About 32% of coal in the USA can be extracted by surface mining, and about 63% of all U.S. coal is mined using this method today. Surface mining is typically much cheaper than underground mining.

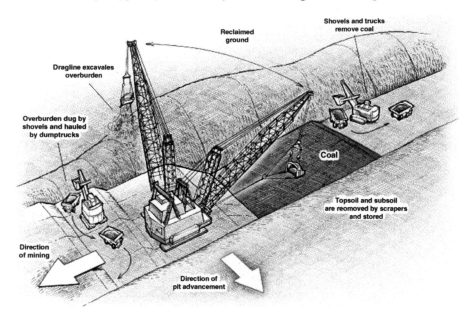

Fig.6.5. A schematic representation of surface mining. (Adapted from [126]).

Another type of surface mining is called mountain top mining. This type of mining is a relatively new process for coal mining from a depth of about 1,000 ft below the surface. In this process, the land is first clear-cut and then leveled by explosives. Dozens of seams are exposed on a single mountain by the blasts, lowering the mountain's height each time, sometimes by hundreds of feet [127]. Most mountain top mining in the United States occurs in West Virginia and Eastern Kentucky, and together they use more than 1,000 t of explosives per day for surface mining [128].

6.6.2 Underground Mining

Underground mining is used when the coal seam is several hundred feet below the surface. A vertical "shaft" or a slanted tunnel is constructed, called a "slope", to get the machinery and people down to the mine. Mine shafts may be as much as 1,000 ft deep.

6.6.2.1 Room and Pillar Mining

In room-and-pillar mining, a significant amount of coal is left behind to support the mine's roofs and walls (Fig. 6.6). Sometimes, this amount could be as much as half of the coal mined. Large column formations are necessary to keep the mine from collapsing. In this method, a set of entries, usually between 3 and 8, are driven into a block of coal. These entries are connected by cross-cuts, which are usually at right angle to the entries. The entries are commonly spaced from 50 to 100 ft apart, and the cross cuts are usually about 50–150 ft apart.

In the conventional room and pillar method, several operations known as undercutting, drilling, blasting, loading and roof bolting operations are performed to get to the coal. Recent advancement includes continuous room and pillar method that eliminates undercutting, drilling and blasting. The cutting and loading functions are performed by a mechanical machine – the continuous miner. The coal is loaded onto coal transport vehicles and then dumped onto a panel-belt conveyor for further transport out of the mine. Once the coal has been cut, the strata above the excavated coal seam are supported by roof bolts.

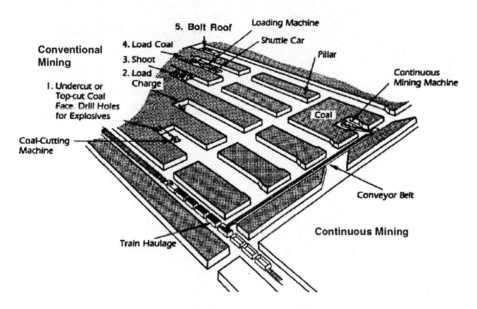

Fig.6.6. A schematic representation of room and pillar mining. (Adapted from [129]).

6.6.2.2 Longwall Mining

In this method, a mined-out area is allowed to collapse in a controlled manner (EIA [130]). Huge blocks of coal, up to several hundred feet wide, can be removed and high recovery and extraction rates are feasible (Fig. 6.7). However, the coal bed should be relatively flat-lying, thick, and uniform. The block of coal is further cut into small pieces using a high-powered cutting machine (the shearer). The sheared, broken coal is continuously hauled away by a floor-level conveyor system.

The use of longwall mining in underground production has been growing in the USA both in terms of amount and percentages, increasing from less than 10% of underground production (less than 10 million annual tons) in the late 1960s, to about 50% of underground production (over 200 million annual tons).

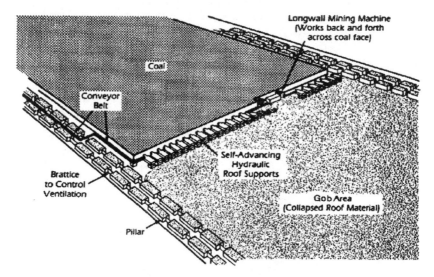

Fig. 6.7. A schematic representation of logwall mining. (Adapted from [131]).

Underground mining currently accounts for about 60% of world coal production, although in several important coal producing countries surface mining is more common.

6.7 Cost of Coal and Its Mining

A number of costs are associated with coal mining and its delivery price. The mining of coal involves various types of costs. However, with the use of modern and more efficient equipment, the cost of mining has gone down significantly. Some of the activities that are associated with the cost of coal mining include restoration of the land, mine drainage, and water usage. All these factors determine the cost of coal that is delivered to end users. The average price of coal at various regions in the USA and the price to the end users are given in Table 6.10.

The production cost of coal depends on the method of mining and also varies from region to region. In Table 6.11 is shown the cost of coal at various states in the USA for different mining methods.

Table 6.10. Average price of coal delivered to end use sector by census division and state, 2005, 2004 (dollars per short ton).

Census division and state	2005			2004			Annual percent change		
	Electric utility plants	Other industrial plants	Coke Plants	Electric utility plants	Other industrial plants	Coke plants	Electric utility plants	Other industrial plants	Coke plants
New England	65.39	85.57	–	52.14	65.54	–	25.40	30.60	–
Middle Atlantic	51.97	W	W	42.92	W	W	21.10	15.60	28.5
East North Central	30.45	53.89	89.97	26.69	41.22	63.30	14.10	30.70	42.1
West North Central	16.47	24.00	–	15.34	21.93	–	7.40	9.50	–
South Atlantic	51.21	W	W	43.29	W	W	18.30	25.60	36.8
East South Central	36.91	W	W	32.22	W	59.16	14.60	28.80	W
West South Central	21.55	W	–	20.72	W	–	4.00	12.70	–
Mountain	23.30	35.93	–	21.87	31.92	–	6.50	12.60	–
Pacific	21.33	50.62	–	19.91	42.94	–	7.10	17.90	–
US Total	31.22	47.63	83.79	27.30	39.30	61.50	14.40	21.20	36.2

W = Withheld to avoid disclosure of individual company data.

Includes manufacturing plants only.

Source: References [132–134].

Table 6.11. Average open market sales price of coal by state and underground mining method, 2005 (Dollars per short ton).

Coal producing state	Continuous[a]	Conventional[b]	Longwall[c]	Other[d]	Total
Alabama	W	–	W	–	54.75
Colorado	W	–	W	–	21.69
Illinois	W	–	W	–	29.18
Indiana	33.17	–	–	–	33.17
Kentucky Total	W	38.71	W	–	38.70
Eastern	W	W	W	–	43.55
Western	W	W	–	–	27.48
Maryland	W	–	–	–	W
Montana	W	–	–	–	W
New Mexico	–	–	W	–	W
Ohio	W	–	W	–	25.25
Oklahoma	W	–	–	–	W
Pennsylvania Total	46.07	40.17	W	W	36.23
Anthracite	W	W	–	W	46.74
Bituminous	W	W	W	–	36.18
Tennessee	49.89	–	–	–	49.89
Utah	25.17	–	21.02	–	21.45
Virginia	42.47	63.89	W	–	48.01
West Virginia Total	46.54	W	W	–	41.99
Northern	31.88	W	32.60	–	32.52
Southern	47.85	–	53.00	–	49.06
Wyoming	–	–	–	–	–
U.S. Total	**39.04**	**W**	**33.90**	**W**	**36.42**

[a]Mines that produce greater than 50% of their coal by continuous mining methods.

[b]Mines that produce greater than 50% of their coal by conventional mining methods.

[c]Mines that have any production from longwall mining method. A typical longwall mining operation uses 80% longwall mining and 20% continuous mining.

[d]Mines that produce coal using shortwall, scoop loading, hand loading, or other mining methods, or a 50/50% percent conventional/conventional split in mining method.

W = Withheld to avoid disclosure of individual company data.

Open market includes all coal sold on the open market to other coal companies or consumers. An average open market sales price is calculated by dividing the total free on board (f.o.b) rail/barge value of the open market coal sold by the total open market coal sold. Excludes mines producing less than 10,000 short tons, which are not required to provide data. Excludes silt, culm, refuse bank, slurry dam, and dredge operations. Totals may not equal sum of components because of independent rounding.

Source: References [135, 136].

Cost of coal is also different in different countries, particularly for the coal importers. In this case, the cost includes that of raw materials, insurance and freight. The cost in US dollar for Europe and Japan is given in Table 6.12.

Table 6.12. Coal price in other countries.

US dollars per tonne	Northwest Europe marker price †	US Central Appalachian coal spot price index[a]	Japan coking coal import cif price	Japan steam coal import cif price
1987	31.30	–	53.44	41.28
1988	39.94	–	55.06	42.47
1989	42.08	–	58.68	48.86
1990	43.48	31.59	60.54	50.81
1991	42.80	29.01	60.45	50.30
1992	38.53	28.53	57.82	48.45
1993	33.68	29.85	55.26	45.71
1994	37.18	31.72	51.77	43.66
1995	44.50	27.01	54.47	47.58
1996	41.25	29.86	56.68	49.54
1997	38.92	29.76	55.51	45.53
1998	32.00	31.00	50.76	40.51
1999	28.79	31.29	42.83	35.74
2000	35.99	29.90	39.69	34.58
2001	39.29	49.74	41.33	37.96
2002	31.65	32.95	42.01	36.90
2003	42.52	38.48	41.57	34.74
2004	71.90	64.33	60.96	51.34
2005	61.07	70.14	89.33	62.91
2006	63.67	62.98	93.46	63.04

[a]Price is for CAPP 12,500 BTU, 1.2 SO2 coal, fob.

cif = cost + insurance + freight (average prices); fob = free on board.

Source: Reference [137].

6.8 Transportation of Coal

The electric power sector uses more than 90% of the coal produced in the United States and is transported to more than 400 coal-burning power plant sites. About 58% of coal is transported by rail, 17% by water-ways, 10% by trucks, 3% are mine mouth plants with conveyor systems and the rest 12% by other methods (This includes barge) [138, 139]. However, these numbers do not include mode of transportation of coals to main transportation ports. The EIA figures report methods by which coals are delivered to its final destination (see Table 6.13), and do not describe how many tons may have traveled by other means along the way – almost one third of all coal delivered to power plants is subject to at least one transloading along the transportation chain [138]. For example, the U.S. Army Corps of Engineers reported that 223 million tons of domestic coal and coke were carried by water at some point in the transport chain in 2004 [140].

Recently transportation of coal as a slurry through pipelines has been explored. This type of transportation method not only requires water for transportation, but also need a number of pumping station to boost the pressure in the pipeline. It requires about 1 ton of water for 1 ton of coal and a booster pump for every 100 km when flowing at a velocity of 1–2 m/s.

Table 6.13. Mode of transportation of coal to end users (thousands short tons).

Delivery methods	Electricity generation	Coke plant	Industrial (except coal)[a]	Residential/ commercial	Total
Great Lakes	8,644	1,144	1,341	–	11,128
Railroad	625,830	10,414	46,031	1,975	684,249
River	71,062	3,722	7,915	406	83,105
Tidewater Piers	3,391	–	530	–	3,936
Tramway, Conveyor and Slurry Pipeline	79,997	1,014	31,975	–	115,262
Truck	73,441	453	50,266	2,741	128,900
Others	–	–	–	–	28,005
Total	863,802	17,095	150,309	5,122	1,064,348

[a]This category includes coal that is transported to plants that transform it into 'synthetic' coal that is then distributed to the final end-user – a substantial component goes to electricity generation plants.
Source: Reference [139].

6.9 Coal Cleaning

The objectives of coal cleaning are to remove ash, rock, and moisture from coal to reduce transportation costs and improve the power plant efficiency. Coal cleaning is now also focused on removing sulfur to reduce acid-rain-related emissions. The benefits of coal cleaning are:

- Removal of substantial quantities of sulfur (chlorine in coal is a problem too)
- Increase of carbon content in the clean coal resulting in a higher BTU value
- Removal of ash that can result in a reduction of pollutant emissions and disposable costs
- Reduction in concentration of trace elements that can reduce emissions of toxic heavy metals, and
- Uniform coal quality for improve process control

Coal cleaning processes may be categorized as either physical cleaning or chemical cleaning. Physical coal cleaning processes involve the mechanical separation of coal from its contaminants using differences in density. Chemical coal cleaning processes involve removing organic sulfur. Their performance and costs under commercial setting of these processes are yet to be determined.

A typical process flow diagram for a coal cleaning plant is shown in Fig. 6.8. It generally varies from plants to plants due to the characteristics of the coal. Most coal cleaning plants are consisted of four basic stages: initial preparation stage, fine coal processing stage, coarse coal processing stage, and final preparation stage.

In the first stage of coal cleaning, the raw coal is unloaded, stored, conveyed, and crushed to 50 mm diameter particles, followed by screening into coarse, intermediate and fine coal fractions. Crushing liberates ash-forming minerals and inorganic sulfur (e.g., pyrites, FeS_2). Higher separation occurs if grinding results into smaller particles. The size fractions are then conveyed to their respective cleaning processes.

Fine coal processing and coarse coal processing take advantage of the differences of the specific gravity of the particles. The primary difference is in the operating parameters. The majority of coal cleaning processes uses upward currents or pulses of a fluid such as water to fluidize a bed of crushed coal and impurities. Because mineral matter has a higher density than coal particles, it can be separated from the coarse and intermediate particles of coal by jigs, dense-medium baths, cyclone systems, and concentrating tables (Table 6.14). The lighter coal particles rise and are removed from the top of the bed. The heavier impurities are removed from the bottom. Coal cleaned in the wet processes then must be dried in the final preparation processes. Reviews of various coal cleaning processes have been carried out by a number of researchers [144–156].

The next stage involves removal of water and moisture from coal, thereby reducing freezing problems and weight, and raising the heating value. During dewatering a major portion of water is removed by the use of screens, thickeners, and cyclones. The moisture can be removed by forced drying, achieved by any one of three dryer types: fluidized bed, flash, and multi-louvered.

Various advanced cleaning methods have been proposed including advanced physical cleaning, aqueous phase pretreatment, selective agglomeration, and organic phase pretreatment; however, these methods are mostly in the development or demonstration stages. These methods are summarized in Table 6.15.

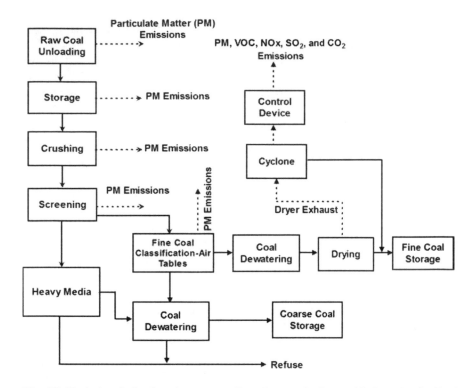

Fig. 6.8. Typical coal cleaning plant process flow diagram. Background Information for Establishment of National Standards of Performance For New Sources: Coal Cleaning Industry, EPA Contract No. CPA-70-142, Environmental Engineering, Inc., Gainesville, FL, July 1971 [141]. Air Pollutant Emissions Factors, Contract No. CPA-22-69-119, Resources Research Inc., Reston, VA, April 1970 [142]. Second Review Of New Source Performance Standards For Coal Preparation Plants, EPA-450/3-88-001, U.S. Environmental Protection Agency, Research Triangle Park, NC, February 1988 [143].

Table 6.14. Conventional physical coal-cleaning technologies.

Technology type	Process
Crushing [157–163]	Grinders pulverize coal, which is then screened into coarse (£50 mm diameter), intermediate, and fine (<0.5 mm) particles. The crushing liberates the nonorganically bound mineral particles from the coal. Because these mineral particles are denser than the organically rich coal, they can be separated from the coal by further processing (see next items).
Jigs (G) [164–169]	For coarse to intermediate particles
Dense-medium baths (G) [170–182]	For coarse to intermediate particles
Cyclones (G) [183–190]	For coarse to intermediate particles

Froth flotation (G)	Froth flotation is a process for separating fine-size particles by selective
Technology type	**Process**
[191–226]	attachment of air bubbles to coal particles, causing them to be buoyed up into a forth while leaving the refuse particles in water.
	For fines; relies on the different surface properties of ash (hydrophilic) vs. coal (hydrophobic); high potential, but current technologies do not handle the small particles efficiently.
Wet concentration Table [227]	The rapid shaking motion causes particles of different densities to migrate to different zones on the table's periphery. Specific gravity of pyrite is about 5.0 and that of coal is about 1.8
Concentration spiral [228–239]	Coal pulp is fed from the top of the spiral and it flows downword. Centrifugal force causes the separation
Electrokinetics [240–241]	Physical cleaning is accomplished by using elctrophoresis method. Electrophoresis is defined as the migration of electrokinetically charged particles in a liquid toward an electrode of opposite charge in a dc electrical field.

G = Gravity-(density)-based separation.

Table 6.15. Various advanced cleaning processes.

Technology type	Process
Advanced physical cleaning	Advanced froth floatation (S) [242–249] Electrostatic (S) [250–260] Heavy liquid cycloning (G) [261–265]
Aqueous phase pretreatment	Bioprocessing [266–271] Hydrothermal [272–275] Ion exchange [276]
Selective agglomeration	Otisca [277–280] LICADO [281–287] Spherical agglomeration aglofloat [288–308]
Organic phase pretreatment	Depolymerization [309–321] Alkylation [322–343] Solvent swelling [344–352] Catalyst addition (e.g., carbonyl) [353] Organic sulfur removal [354–362]
Other processes	Microwave [363–366] Microbial desulfurization [367–390] Fluidized bed [391–399] Sonic [400–401] LFBC [402–404] Chemical processes [405–420] Dry beneficiation [421–427] HGMS [428–436]

G = Gravity-(density)-based separation; S = surface-effect-based separation.

The above cleaning processes can remove ash by 60% and total sulfur by 10–40%. The percentage of coal retained after cleaning is generally in the range of 60–90%, but the thermal recovery (percent of heating value retained) is 85–98%.

6.10 The Use of Coal

Although the main use of coal is for electricity generation, a number of other industry and products depend heavily on coal. These are listed below.

- Iron and steel production
- Coal and cement
- Liquid from coal
- Activated carbon – used in filters for water and air purification and in kidney dialysis machines
- Carbon fiber – an extremely strong but light weight reinforcement material used in construction, mountain bikes and tennis rackets
- Silicon metal – used to produce silicones and silanes, which are in turn used to make lubricants, water repellents, resins, cosmetics, hair shampoos and tooth-pastes

Other important users of coal include alumina refineries, paper manufacturers, and the chemical and pharmaceutical industries. Several valuable chemicals can be produced from by-products of coal. Refined coal tar is used in the manufacture of chemicals, such as creosote oil, naphthalene, phenol, and benzene. Ammonia gas recovered from coke ovens is used to manufacture ammonia salts, nitric acid and agricultural fertilizers. Thousands of different products have coal or coal by-products as components: soap, aspirins, solvents, dyes, plastics and fibers, such as rayon and nylon.

6.10.1 Electricity Production from Coal

Steam coal, also known as thermal coal, is used in power stations to generate electricity. Coal provides the majority of the electricity needs for countries such as Poland (96%), South Africa (90%), China (81%), Greece (70%), India (75%), USA (56%), and Germany (51%). In Fig. 6.9 shows the top 12 countries that generate electricity from coal.

Thomas Edison's Pearl Street Generating Plant in New York City, USA, based on coal came online in 1882. Its efficiency was about 2.5%. By the 1920s, they were achieving 20% efficiency. Today the efficiency of the most coal-fired power plant is between 30% and 40%. The improvement in the efficiency was due to several factors:

- Continuous improvements in the design of the furnace for coal combustion that made the largest impact on efficiencies
- Invention of the steam turbine
- Improvements in materials used to construct boilers and piping allowed increase of the temperatures and pressures of the water and steam
- Different ways of handling coal allowed it to combust more rapidly and evenly

Majority of the coal-fired power plants are subcritical power plant. The steam properties are below the critical point of water. Some of the characteristics of subcritical power plants are as follows.

- Efficiencies are usually around 33%
- Use relatively cheap fuel
- Several expensive flue gas clean up (pollution control) systems are necessary
- Use water at subcritical condition
- Use steam turbines as the only source to generate electrical power
- Require coal with relatively low amounts of ash
- Initial cost is around $1,200 per kW of electricity produced

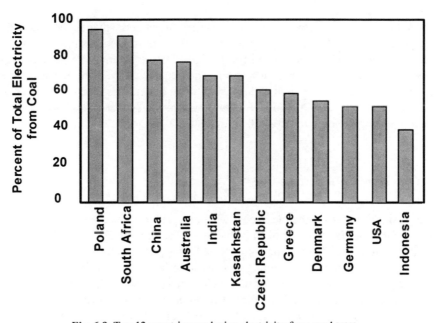

Fig. 6.9. Top 12 countries producing electricity from coal [437].

Basic steps of generating electricity by burning coal are shown in Fig. 6.10.

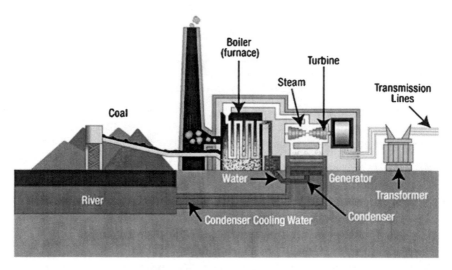

Fig. 6.10. A coal fired power plant. (Adapted from [438]).

In the modern coal power plants, coal is first pulverized which is then burned in a combustion chamber of the furnace. Water, flows through tubes lined in the furnace, is heated to produce superheated, high pressure steam. The high pressure steam is passed into a steam turbine to generate electricity. The exhaust steam from the turbine is condensed and returned to the boiler. The electricity generated is transformed up to 400,000 V for transmission via power line grids, which is then transformed down to 100–250 V for domestic use.

6.11 Clean Coal Technology

The main objective of the clean coal technology is to reduce emission of pollutants from a coal-fired power plant including carbon dioxide. This may be achieved by using improved flue gas clean-up technologies and increasing the efficiency of the power plant. Significant improvements have been made in both areas. Clean coal technologies are a family of new technological innovations that are environmentally superior to the technologies in common use today. Most are the products of research that has been conducted over the last 20 years or more. Clean coal technologies can be new combustion processes, such as fluidized bed combustion, and low-NOx burners that remove pollutants, or prevent them from forming while coal burns. Clean coal technologies can also involve new pollution control devices – such as advanced scrubbers – that clean pollutants from flue gases before they exit a plant's smokestack. Still other clean coal technologies can convert coal into fuel forms that can be cleaned before being burned. For example, a clean coal plant may convert coal into a gas that has the same environmental characteristics as clean-burning natural gas. The clean coal technologies may be grouped into two categories

- Power plant efficiency improvement technologies
- Pollution control technologies

To improve the efficiency of the power plant the following systems have been developed over the years.

- Supercritical Pulverized Coal Power Plant
- Atmospheric Circulating Fluidized Bed Combustion (ACFBC)
- Pressurized Circulating Fluidized Bed Combustion (PCFBC)
- Integrated Gasification Combined Cycle (IGCC)

6.11.1 Supercritical Pulverized Coal Power Plant

The efficiency of the power plant was enhanced by increasing the temperature and pressure of the steam generated from the boiler. Depending on the steam conditions, the power plants could be categorized into three groups as shown in Table 6.16. Worldwide, more than 400 supercritical plants are in operation. Supercritical coal fired power plants with efficiencies of 45% have much lower emissions than subcritical plants for a given power output [439–446]. Although early experience with supercritical plants in the US suggests that these plants may not be as reliable as subcritical plants, several other countries including Japan, China, South Africa, and European countries using once through boilers plants indicated that these plants are just as reliable as subcritical plants [447–450]. Supercritical cycles are operated at pressure of greater than 22.1 MPa in the evaporator part of the boiler. Therefore the steam is in a single phase fluid with homogeneous properties and there is no need to separate steam from water in a drum. Once-through boilers are used in supercritical cycles. The use of supercritical cycles became possible due to the advancement of materials [451–489].

Table 6.16. Temperatures and pressures for different types of plant using bituminous coal.

Operating conditions	Temperature (°C)	Pressure (bar)
Subcritical	538	167
Supercritical	540–566	250
Ultra-supercritical	580–620	270–285

Source: World Coal Institute, London, UK.

Advanced steels allow construction of once-through boilers, operating at pressures up to 30 MPa, and other components such as the live steam and hot reheat steam piping that are in direct contact with steam under these conditions.

Figure 6.11 shows a supercritical cycle arrangement. Advantages of supercritical cycles are high thermal efficiency and use of proven design, components, and materials. The increase in the efficiency with the increase of steam conditions is shown in Fig. 6.12.

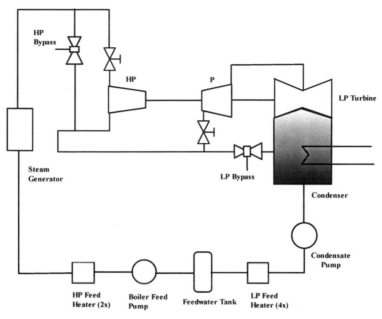

Fig. 6.11. A schematic diagram of a supercritical steam cycle. Design features: supercritical steam parameters: 30 MPa/540°C/560°C and condensate polishing.

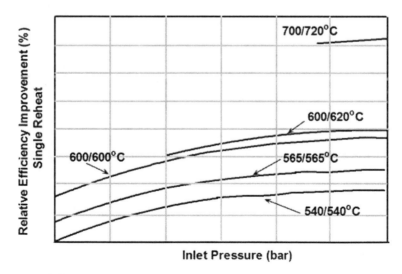

Fig. 6.12. Effect of steam properties on cycle efficiency for single reheat units (http://www.dti.gov.uk/files/file30703.pdf) [490].

Europe and Asia are using supercritical boiler-turbine technology in their recent plants and China has made this standard on all new plants 600 MWe and upwards. In China, more than 60 GW of SC units were ordered over 2004–2005 and by the end of 2006, the total number of large SC units was 26. China is currently constructing around two SC units a week In India, the first of three 660 MWe SC units are under construction by Doosan at Sipat. Several other pithead SC projects are also under consideration. India has announced plans for a series of ~4,000 MW 'ultra-mega' power projects using SC technology. There are currently over 20 new SC projects proposed or in the pipeline in the USA. Many are due to come on line 2009–2011. Other countries currently using or proposing to adopt SC/USC include Canada, Czech Republic, Denmark, Germany, Italy, Japan, Mexico, Poland, Russia, South Africa, South Korea, Chinese Taipei and the UK. Operating conditions of some coal plants using supercritical steam are given in Table 6.17. To achieve even higher efficiencies, potentially up to around 50%, ultra-supercritical conditions are proposed. However, the main obstacle is the materials of construction. Research is focusing on the development of new steels for boiler tubes and on high alloy steels that minimize corrosion under ultra supercritical conditions.

Table 6.17. A list of coal power plants around the world using supercritical steam cycle.

Country	Power plant	Unit rating MWe net (gross)	Steam press (bar)	Main steam Temp (°C)	Reheat RH1 steam temp (°C)	Reheat RH2 steam temp (°C)	Effi-ciency (% net LHV)
Denmark	Avedorevaerket 2	390	300	580	600	–	48.3
Denmark	Nordjyland 3	411	285	580	580	580	47
Denmark	Skaerbaek 3	411	290	582	580	580	49
Holland	Hemweg 8	630	260	540	568	–	42
Finland	Meri Pori	550	244	540	560	–	45
Germany	Staudinger	509	262	545	562	–	43
Germany	Niederaussem K	965	275	580	600	–	45.2
Japan	Tachibanawan	1,050	250	600	610	–	43.5
Japan	Isogo	600	266	600	610	–	NA
China	Changshu	600	259	569	569	–	42
China	Wangqu	600	247	571	569	–	43
USA	Tanners Creek	580	241	538	552	566	39.8
USA	Duke Power	(1,120)	241	538	538	–	NA

Source: Reference [490].

As shown in Fig. 6.13 below, the use of supercritical cycles can reduce the pollution level significantly. One percent increase in efficiency reduces emissions of CO_2, NO_x, SO_x and particulates by about 2%.

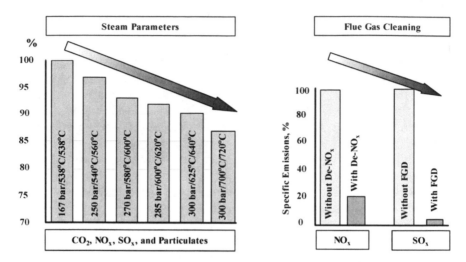

Fig. 6.13. Emission levels corresponding to steam parameters of supercritical plants and with and without flue gas cleaning systems (http://www.worldbank.org/html/fpd/em/supercritical/supercritical/supercritical.htm) [491].

Advantages of ultra-supercritical over subcritical pulverized power plants are:

- Efficiencies of around 50%
- No need to separate steam from water
- No boiler blowdown, less water makeup
- Many components are still the same
- Not as much pollution to remove due to higher efficiencies

Disadvantages of Ultra-supercritical over Subcritical PC Power Plants

- Still require same pollution controls as subcritical power plants
- Require much higher strength materials for some plant components
- Still limited to coal with relatively low ash content
- Technology will not be ready for commercialization until about 2015

The disadvantages of a supercritical power plant are: (1) its initial cost, which can be around $1,450 per kW, (2) the plant still requires the same pollution control devices as subcritical power plants (its not pollution free operation), (3) it requires higher strength materials for some plant components increasing the initial capital investment, and (4) the use of coals with relatively low ash content.

6.11.2 Atmospheric Circulating Fluidized Bed Combustion (ACFBC)

ACFBC system [492–517] is generally used in power plants of capacity of around 250–300 MWe. However, there are designs for units up to 600 MWe in size. In fluidized beds, solid fuels are suspended by an upward-blowing jets of air during the combustion process. The result is a turbulent mixing of gas and solids allowing more effective chemical reactions and heat transfer. An atmospheric pressure fluidized bed combustion system can be both bubbling (BFBC) and circulating (CFBC) bed type. They are used mainly with subcritical steam turbines, together with sorbent injection for SO_2 reduction and particulates removal from flue gases.

Combustion takes place at temperatures from 800°C to 900°C resulting in reduced NOx formation compared with pulverized coal combustion process. Sulfur dioxide emissions can be reduced by the injection of a sorbent, such as limestone, into the bed and subsequent removal of ash together with reacted sorbent. The direct injection of limestone into the bed offers the possibility of economic SO_2 removal without the need for flue gas desulphurization. The turbulent actions reduce the temperature of the combustion process below the threshold where large amounts of NOx form. Fluidized bed systems can reduce sulfur dioxide by 90–95% and nitrogen oxides by 90% or more.

CFBCs are designed for the particular coal to be used. The method is principally of value for low grade, high ash coals which are difficult to pulverize, and which may have variable combustion characteristics. It is also suitable for co-firing coal with low grade fuels, including some waste materials. A schematic diagram of a power plant using ACFBC is shown in Fig. 6.14.

The advantages of ACFBC based power plants over subcritical pulverized coal (PC) power plants may be summarized as follows:

- Efficiencies are around 36%
- More complete combustion of coal
- Better heat transfer properties
- Much lower emissions of sulfur oxides and nitrogen oxide
- No need for the expensive pollution controls of subcritical plants
- Fuel flexible (coal and municipal waste)
- Smaller in size for same power output

Some of the disadvantages of ACFBC over Subcritical PC Power Plants are (1) initial cost which is around $1,500 per kW, (2) complex combustion process requiring more control of the system and skilled labor, (3) not many models available for combustion process yet as it is relatively new technology and less industry experience, and (4) availability of limestone or dolomite can also be an issue.

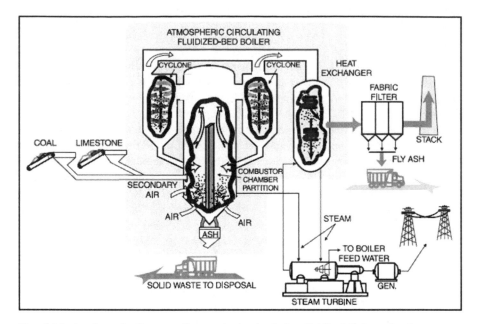

Fig. 6.14. A schematic diagram of atmospheric circulating fluidized bed combustion system. (Adapted from Clean coal technology demonstration program (1992) DOE/FE/0247P, US Department of Energy, Washington DC, USA).

6.11.3 Pressurized Fluidized Bed Combustion (PCFBC)

The first-generation PCFBC system used a sorbent and jets of air to suspend the mixture of sorbent and burning coal during combustion. Since the systems operate at elevated pressures, they produce a high-pressure gas stream at temperatures that can drive a gas turbine [518–533]. Steam generated from the heat in the fluidized bed can run a steam turbine, creating a highly efficient combined cycle system. In the second-generation PFBC systems, a pressurized carbonizer converts coal into fuel gas and char. The char is burned to produce steam and to heat combustion air for the gas turbine. The fuel gas from the carbonizer burns in another combustor to heat the gases so that the temperature of the feed gas to the gas turbine reaches the turbine's rated firing temperature. Heat is recovered from the gas turbine exhaust to produce steam, which is used to drive a conventional steam turbine, resulting in a higher overall efficiency for the combined cycle power output. These systems are also called APFBC, or advanced circulating pressurized fluidized-bed combustion combined cycle systems. An APFBC system is entirely coal-fueled. A typical schematic of the APFBC is shown in Fig. 6.15.

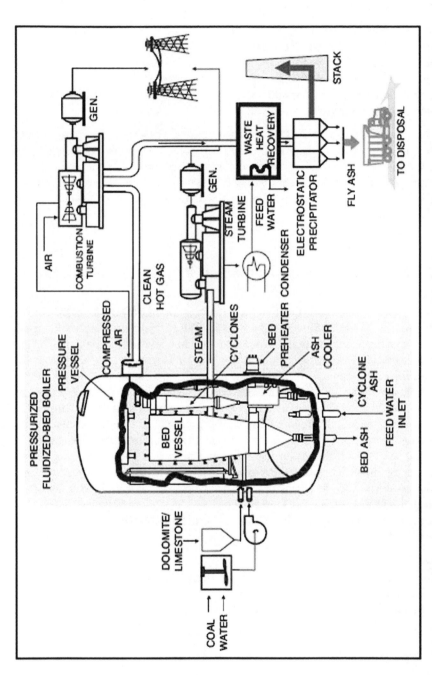

Fig. 6.15. A schematic diagram of a pressurized fluidized bed combustion system. (Adapted from Clean coal technology demonstration program (1992) DOE/FE/0247P, US Department of Energy, Washington DC, USA).

Advantages of APFBC based power plants over subcritical pulverized coal power plants can be summarized as follows:

- Efficiencies of around 42%
- More complete combustion of coal
- Better heat transfer properties
- Much lower emissions of sulfur oxides and nitrogen oxide
- No need for the expensive pollution controls devices for subcritical plants
- Smaller in size for same power output

The disadvantages of an APFBC over a subcritical pulverized coal power plants, are: (1) initial cost which is around $1500 per kW, (2) complex combustion process requiring more control of the system and skilled labor, (3) not many models available for combustion process yet as it is relatively new technology and less industry experience, (4) availability of limestone or dolomite can also be an issue, and (5) less fuel flexibility.

6.11.4 Integrated Gasification Combined Cycle Coal Power Plant

These systems depart from direct coal combustion based power plants [534–553]. In this process, coal is converted into a gas, called Synthetic Gas (or Syngas), which is cleaned of its impurities, almost to the same level as natural gas. The gas is further burned to run a gas turbine to generate electricity. Exhaust from the gas turbine is hot enough to produce steam to drive a steam turbine for further electricity generation. Initial gasification-based plants could boost efficiencies by as much as 20% over conventional coal-burning power plants, and improved versions might eventually double today's efficiencies. Gasification combined cycle technologies are among the cleanest ways to generate electricity from coal. As much as 95–99% of the sulfur and nitrogen impurities in the coal gas can be removed by known chemical processes. These pollutants can be converted into useable products, such as chemicals and fertilizers. The schematic diagram of the integrated system is shown in Fig. 6.16.

Some of the advantages of IGCC over subcritical pulverized coal power plants can be listed as follows:

- Efficiencies are around 45%
- Fuel flexibility (coal, biomass, municipal waste)
- Uses a proven combined cycle layout
- Very low emissions of sulfur oxides and nitrogen oxide

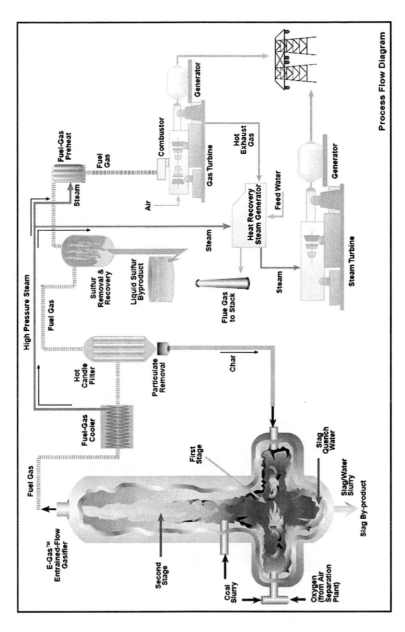

Fig. 6.16. An integrated coal gasification combined cycle coal power plant lay-out. (Adapted from the US Department of Energy).

IGCC process also have several disadvantages over subcritical pulverized coal power plants. They can be summarized as follows.

- Initial cost is around $1,800 per kW
- Syngas will still have some impurities in it
- Combustion turbines need to be able to handle syngas
- Will not be cost competitive until around 2008
- New technology

6.11.5 Integrated Coal Gasification: Fuel Cells for Power Generation

An integrated coal gasification process can be combined with fuel cells to increase the overall efficiency of the process. Fuel cell technology is discussed in Volume 2. Advantages of coal gasification with fuel cells over subcritical pulverized coal power plants are:

- No moving parts (in the fuel cell)
- Efficiencies of around 50%
- Very quiet
- Fuel cell heat can be useful
- Operate cleanly
- Fuel flexible (any fossil fuel, biomass, municipal waste)

And the disadvantages are mainly:

- This is not a proven technology, and
- Materials used to create fuel cells are still relatively expensive

A summary of coal power plants using various technologies is provided in Table 6.18.

6.11.6 Zero Emission Coal Power Plant

Zero emissions of greenhouse gases and all other pollutants are a goal of the coal industry [554–569]. A number of cutting edge research programs are actively pursuing this vision.

Table 6.18. A summary of various types of coal power plants using advanced and proposed steam cycles.

	Subcritical pulverized	Supercritical pulverized coal	Ultra-supercritical pulverized coal	Atmospheric circulating fluidized bed-circulation	Pressurized circulating fluidized bed combustion	Integrated gasification combined cycle	Coal gasification with fuel cells
Efficiency	33%	38–43%	50%	36%	42%	45%	50%
Fuel flexibility	Require low ash coals	Require low ash coals	Require low ash coals	Coal, municipal wastes	Coal, municipal wastes	Coal, biomass, municipal wastes	Coal, biomass, municipal wastes
Cost, US$	$1200/kW	$1450/kW	–	1,500/kW	1,700/kW	$1800/kW	–
Commercial availability	Yes	Yes	No	Yes	Yes	Yes	No
Emission control	Many expensive controls	Many expensive controls	Many expensive controls	Mainly particulates	Mainly particulates	Very few if any	Very few if any
Most sulfur and nitrogen pollutants removed in boiler section	No	No	No	Yes	Yes	Yes	Yes
Proven technology	Yes	Yes	No	Yes	No	No	No
When it will be ready for full commercialization	Now	Now	2015	Now	2006	2008	–

One example is the United States Department of Energy's Vision 21 Program, which aims to develop the ultimate energy facility. The Vision 21 plant will have zero emissions and no net discharges of wastewater, solid waste, sulfur dioxide, nitrous oxide or carbon dioxide. If required, the plant will capture and store (sequester) carbon dioxide to achieve zero emissions.

In this concept, hydrogen is produced from coal and water in the absence of air or oxygen. The hydrogen is used to produce electricity in a solid oxide fuel cell. The carbonation of calcium oxide (CaO) to calcium carbonate ($CaCO_3$) sequesters CO_2 and assists in increasing the hydrogen yield. The calcium carbonate is dissociated back into calcium oxide and a concentrated stream of carbon dioxide (CO_2) by the waste heat from the fuel cell. The carbon dioxide can then be injected into ocean, or other geological reservoir, such as used-up natural gas reservoir. Also calcium carbonate can be stored as solid waste. The basic schematic of a hypothesized zero emission coal power plant is shown in Fig. 6.17.

6.12 Pollution Control from Coal Combustion

The major pollutants emitted during coal combustions are SO_2, NOx, and particulates. However, one of the objectives of clean coal technology is to capture CO_2 too. Sulfur compounds present in coal convert to SO_2 during the combustion process. Although attempts have been made to remove sulfur compounds from coal prior to combustion, post combustion flue gas desulphurization appears to be more economical and technologically less challenging. Sulfur present in coal may be broadly grouped into the following three categories:

- Organic
    30–70% of the total sulfur in coal are in this form and cannot be removed by direct physical separation.
- Sulfate
    Less than 0.05% of total sulfur in coal is present as sulfates, which are generally soluble in water.
- Pyritic
    0.5–3% of total sulfur in coal is in this form and is generally removed from the coal during cleaning process and size reduction using gravity separation.

6.12.1 Removal of Organic Sulfur

Organic sulfur species in coals are mainly thiols, sulfides, disulfides, thiophenes and their derivatives. A number of methods have been explored for removal of organic sulfur prior to combustion. These include:

1. Solvent partitioning
2. Neutralization method
3. Hydrogenation reaction or sulfur reduction
4. Thermal decomposition
5. Oxidation
6. Sodium hydroxide treatment or nucleophilic displacement, and
7. Microbial removal

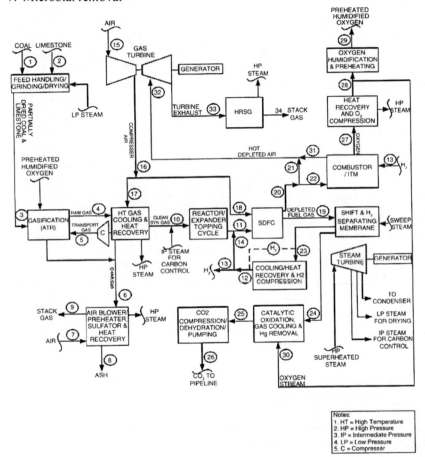

Fig. 6.17. Conceptual system for zero emission coal power plant. (Printed with permission from [560]).

6.12.1.1 Solvent Partitioning

In this method, an organic solvent is used to dissolve the organic portion of the sulfur compounds that are present in the coal. The solvent is regenerated and recycled for economic operation. A number of solvents have been tested for removal of organic sulfur and are listed in Table 6.19. Some of the solvents were also used at supercritical conditions to enhance the extraction process.

Table 6.19. Solvents proposed for removal of organic sulfur by solvent partitioning method.

Solvent	Operating temperature	% of organic sulfur removed
n-Propanol [571]	30	43–61%
Tetrachloroethylene [572][a]	120	43
Tetrachloroethylene [573]	120	50
Hydrogen peroxide (15%) [574]	15–40	76% pyritic, 70% sulfate, 5% organic
Hydogen peroxide + 0.1N H_2SO_4 [574]	15–40	~100% pyritic, ~100% sulfate, 26% organic
Methanol/water and methanol/KOH [575]	–	33–62 total sulfur
Methanol [576]	500	86% total, 90% organic
Perchloroethylene [577–581]	120	5–30% fresh coal
		30–60% weathered coal
Perchloroethylene [582]	120	70
Trichloroethane [583]		
Potassium permanganate (6%) [584]	Room temp	90% pyritic; 87% organic
Methanol/KOH (5% wt) [585]	350	>90%
Methanol and ethanol [586, 587]	Supercritical	–
Acetone+water [588]	Supercritical	61
Methanol + water and ethanol + water [589]	Supercritical	60% pyritic; 97% sulfate; 28% organic
CO_2	450 (supercritical CO_2)	50 Total
CO_2 + H_3PO_4		80 Total
CO_2 + methanol (10%) [590][b]		60% Organic

Source: Reference [570].
[a]Process involved copper chloride oxidation followed by tetrachloroethylene extraction.
[b]Supercritical extraction under pyrolysis condition.

6.12.1.2 Neutralization Method

Thiols and mercaptans may be neutralized using an alkaline solution due to the acidic nature of these two compounds. However, it should be noted that other organic sulfur compounds, such as sulfides and disulfides, cannot be removed by this method [591].

6.12.1.3 Hydrogenation Reaction

Sulfur compounds react with hydrogen producing hydrogen sulfide, which is then scrubbed from the gas stream using an acid gas treatment process. The chemical reactions of hydrogen with thiol compounds are shown below [591].

Ethanethiol: $CH_3CH_2SH + H_2 \rightarrow CH_3CH_3 + H_2S$
2-Propanethiol: $(CH_3)_2CHSH + H_2 \rightarrow CH_3CH_2CH_3 + H_2S$

6.12.1.4 Thermal Decomposition

In this method, coal is heated to a high temperature in the absence of oxygen. Sulfur containing compounds undergo the decomposition reaction liberating sulfur as SO_2 or H_2S. In most of the cases, H_2S is released. A number of researchers proposed the use of a catalyst to lower the decomposition temperature for sulfur compounds. Other compounds present in the coal are found to decompose at this temperature [592–598].

Ethanethiol: $CH_3CH_2SH \rightarrow CH_2=CH_2 + H_2S$
2-Propanethiol: $(CH_3)_2CHSH \rightarrow CH_3CH=CH_2 + H_2S$

6.12.1.5 Oxidation Reaction

Sulfur compounds may be reacted directly with oxygen or other oxidizing agents to convert them to water soluble sulfate compounds [599–601].

$$RSH + \frac{1}{2}O_2 \rightarrow RSO_2OH \text{ (sulfonic acid)}$$

where 'R' represents CH_3CH_2 or $(CH_3)_2CH$ groups.

6.12.1.6 Reaction with Sodium Hydroxide

Sodium hydroxide can react with sulfur compounds forming water soluble sodium sulfide. A typical reaction with NaOH is shown below [602–607].

$$RSH + NaOH \rightarrow Na_2S + 2H_2O + R'CH=CH_2$$

6.12.1.7 Microbial Removal

Certain microorganisms have the potential to remove sulfur from coal [608–622]. Microbial desulfurization of coal has shown various advantages including a higher pyrite removal efficiency and lower coal wastage compared to physical methods. The costs are also lower compared to chemical methods because microbial methods operate at ambient conditions with fewer chemicals. However, microbial processes are slower, requiring days to complete. The best known pyrite-oxidizing bacteria is *Thiobacillus ferrooxidans*, a gram-negative iron-, sulfur and metal sulfide-oxidizing bacterium. Certain thermophilic bacteria have also shown to remove pyritic sulfur from coal. These include *Sulfolobus acidocaldarius*. *Sulfolobus*, a member of archaebacteria, oxidizes pyrite, elemental sulfur, certain metal sulfides and organic compounds at temperature of up to 85°C. Other microorganisms capable of desulfurization of coal include *Thiobacillus thiooxidans* and *Leptospirillum ferrooxidans*.

6.12.2 Removal of Pyritic Sulfur

Pyritic sulfur can be removed from coal prior to combustion by reacting it with hydrogen, NaOH, or oxygen. The hydrogenation Reaction can be written as:

$FeS_2 + H_2 \rightarrow FeS + H_2S$: occurs at 230°C
$FeS + H_2 \rightarrow Fe + H_2S$: not a favorable reaction

Oxidation Reaction

$FeS_2 + O_2 \rightarrow FeSO_4 + SO_2$: $FeSO_4$ soluble in water

Reaction with sodium hydroxide (NaOH)

$FeS_2 + NaOH \rightarrow Fe_2O_3 + Na_2S + Na_2S_2O_3 + H_2O$

Various other methods have been proposed to remove sulfur from coal prior to combustion, however, all these processes still would require a post combustion flue gas clean up system. As a result most of the current focus is to develop a better flue gas desulfurization system to capture sulfur dioxide in the combustor as soon as it is released.

6.12.3 Sulfate Sulfur

Most of the coals contain a very small percentage of sulfur in the sulfate form. Most of the sulfates are also water soluble and generally are removed during the coal cleaning process.

6.13 Flue Gas Desulfurization and NOx Removal

A number of technologies have been proposed for flue gas cleaning. Several processes are already in use commercially. A review of these processes has been provided by a number of researchers [623–627]. Figure 6.18 shows these processes. Based on the working principles of these technologies, they can be classified first into two main categories: Once Through and Regenerable.

In the Once Through process, SO_2 reacts with the sorbent, which is generally disposed of as a waste. Most of the processes generate $CaSO_4$, or better known as gypsum, that can be used for other applications, such as soil treatment and plaster.

In the regenerable processes, sorbent is regenerated and recycled back to the system. However, the main issue with the regenerable processes is how to store the released SO_2.

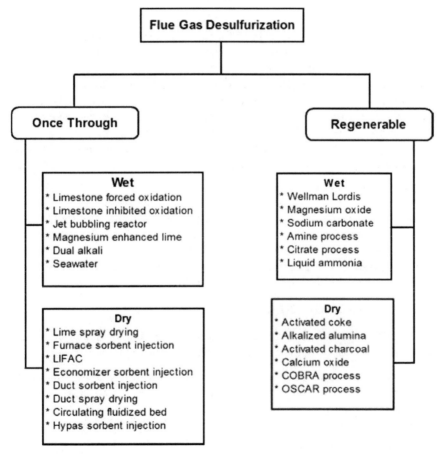

Fig. 6.18. Various methods for flue gas desulfurization. (Adapted with permission from [623]).

Among the processes mentioned in Fig. 6.18, the following processes have been employed commercially so far. The other processes are either in the experimental or pilot plant stage. The Flue Gas Desulfurization (FGD) methods currently used in the industry are listed below.

- Lime and limestone FGD
- Spray dryer absorption
- Furnace injection of calcium sorbent (LIMB)
- Calcium silicate injection (ADVACATE)
- Combined spray drying and electrostatic precipitator (E-SOx)
- Combined SO_2/NOx removal processes

6.13.1 Wet Scrubber (Lime and Limestone FGD)

This method was introduced in 1970 for flue gas desulfurization [628–630]. Wet scrubbers are the most widely used technology for SO_2 control throughout the world. Generally, a slurry mixture of lime and limestone is used in a scrubber to remove the sulfur dioxide. These are favored because of their availability and relative low costs. However, sodium- and ammonium-based sorbents have also been used in a slurry mixture. The slurry is injected into a specially designed vessel where it reacts with the SO_2 in the flue gas. The preferred sorbent in operating wet scrubbers is limestone followed by lime. The chemical reaction that takes place with limestone or lime sorbent is shown below.

$$SO_2 + CaCO_3 = CaSO_3 + CO_2$$

Calcium sulfite ($CaSO_3$) produced in the reaction is further oxidized to calcium sulfate (gypsum). The excess oxygen (from excess air) in the flue gas can initiate the oxidation reaction. In some design, a forced oxidation step, in situ or ex situ (in the scrubber or in a separate reaction chamber), involving the injection of air is carried out. The chemical reaction is shown below.

$$SO_2 + CaCO_3 + \tfrac{1}{2}O_2 + 2H_2O = CaSO_4.2H_2O + CO_2$$

A variety of scrubbers have been designed to carry out the above two reactions and a brief description of their operating principle is given below.

Spray tower: Spray nozzles atomize the pressurized scrubbing liquid into the reaction chamber providing large particle surface area for efficient contact and subsequent reaction.

Plate tower: The scrubber consists of a number of plates stacked at a certain interval. The flue gas is dispersed through several opening or slots in the plate holding the scrubbing liquid, which also provides large sorbent surface area.

Impingement scrubber: In this design, a vertical chamber incorporates perforated plates with openings that are partially covered by target plates. The plates are flooded with the sorbent slurry and the flue gas is accelerated upwards through the perforations. The flue gas and sorbent liquid make contact around the target plate, creating a turbulent frothing zone to provide the desired reaction contact.

Packed tower: A tower is packed with inert packings. The flue gas flows upward through the packing material in the counter-current direction to the liquid sorbent flow which is introduced at the top of the packing through a distributor.

Commercial wet scrubbing systems are available in many variations and proprietary designs. Systems currently in operation include:

- Lime/limestone/sludge wet scrubbers
- Lime/limestone/gypsum wet scrubbers
- Wet lime, fly ash scrubbers, and
- Other wet scrubbers that utilize seawater, ammonia, caustic soda, sodium carbonate, potassium and magnesium hydroxide based scrubbing solution

Wet scrubbers can achieve removal efficiencies as high as 99%. It is expected that wet scrubbers, where the end product is gypsum, will become a more popular FGD technology, since disposal of waste faces increasingly stricter governmental regulations. However, wet scrubbing technology still needs to treat the waste water before disposal. A flow diagram of the process is shown in Fig. 6.19.

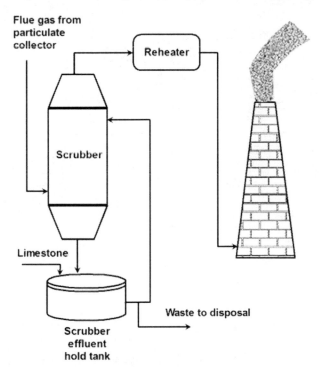

Fig. 6.19. A schematic diagram of wet scrubbing system for flue gas desulfurization.

Generally a high liquid to gas ratio is used to avoid scaling. In some units forced oxidation was also tried to avoid scaling. A thiosulfate-forming additive is mixed with the slurry to facilitate the removal of scales that might deposit on the wall. It was also noted that by maintaining a certain pH, using an organic acid buffer, SO_2 removal could be enhanced.

6.13.2 Dry Sorbent Injection Method

This method for flue gas desulfurization evolved from spray drying technology. This method of SO_2 emission control relies on the atomization of a sorbent – most commonly an aqueous lime slurry – in a reaction chamber upstream of a particulate collection device. A basic schematic diagram of the process is shown in Fig. 6.20. Two processes are currently practiced commercially for capture of SO_2 from the flue gas: Furnace injection and Duct injection.

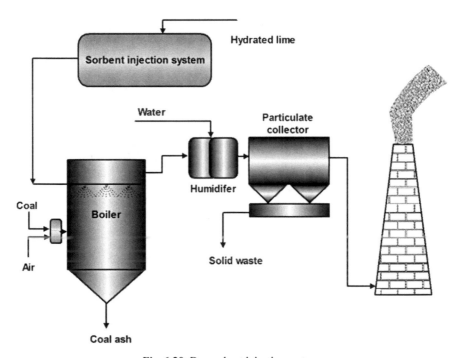

Fig. 6.20. Dry sorbent injection system.

6.13.2.1 Furnace Injection

Furnace injection systems are typically designed to operate at 15–25°C (27–45°F) approach to the adiabatic saturation temperature of the flue gas. Dry sorbent is injected directly into the section of the furnace where temperature ranges between 950°C and 1,000°C. The fine droplets absorb SO_2 and form the product calcium sulfite and sulfate as the water evaporates. A downstream electrostatic precipitator (ESP) or baghouse collects the dry salts along with fly ash present in the flue gas. Use of a baghouse enhances the performance of the dry scrubber because additional SO_2 absorption occurs as the flue gas passes through the accumulation.

The reactions taking place in the furnace are as follows:

Calcination: $CaCO_3 \rightarrow CaO + CO_2$

Sulfation: $CaO + SO_2 + 1/2\ O_2 \rightarrow CaSO_4$

To avoid CO_2 release, dry powder of calcium oxide is mainly used as the sorbent. However, a lime slurry, also called lime milk, can be atomized/sprayed into the reactor vessel in a cloud of fine droplets. Water is evaporated by the heat of the flue gas, thus does not require any waste water treatment facility. About 10 s of residence time in the reactor is sufficient to allow for the SO_2 and the other acid gases such as SO_3 and HCl to react simultaneously with the hydrated lime to form a dry mixture of calcium sulfate/sulfite. The unreacted lime is recycled and mixed with fresh lime slurry to enhance sorbent utilization. Other factors that may affect the performance include flue gas temperature, SO_2 concentration in the flue gas and the size of the atomized or sprayed slurry droplets. The absorber construction material is usually carbon steel making the process less expensive in capital costs compared with wet scrubbers. However, the necessary use of lime in the process increases its operational costs.

Spray dry scrubbers are the second most widely used FGD technology. However, their application is limited to flue gas volume from about 200 MWe plants on average. Larger plants require the use of several modules to deal with the total flue gas flow. This is why in general the technology is used in small to medium sized coal-fired power plants. Spray dry scrubbers in commercial use have achieved a removal efficiency in excess of 90% with some suppliers claiming >95% SO_2 removal efficiency under certain conditions.

The Babcock & Wilcox Company (B&W) designed a limestone injection multistage burner (LIMB) system to improve the efficiency of the system [631–637]. The description of the system is shown in Fig. 6.21. Humidification of the flue gas before it enters an ESP is necessary to maintain normal ESP operation and to enhance SO_2 removal. The goal of LIMB process was to remove more than 50% SO_2 and NOx from the flue gas. Combinations of three bituminous coals (1.6, 3.0, and 3.8% sulfur) and four sorbents were tested and overall removal efficiency in the range of 50–63% was reported when using lingo lime. B&W further modified the design and called it the *coolside* process.

In the coolside process, dry sorbent is injected into the flue gas downstream of the air preheater, followed by flue gas humidification (see Fig. 6.22). Humidification enhances ESP performance and SO_2 absorption. SO_2 absorption is improved

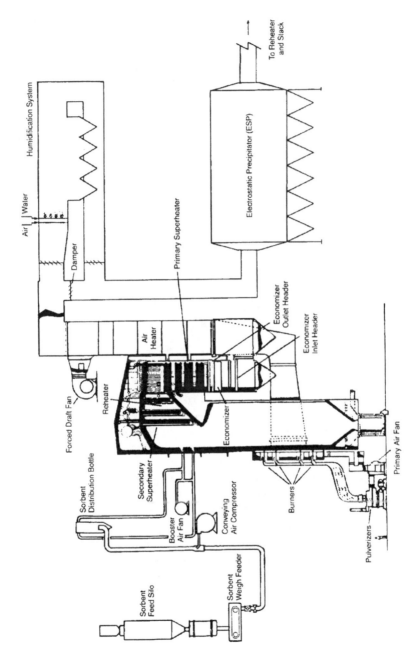

Fig. 6.21. A limestone injection multistage burner (LIMB) designed by Babcock & Wilcox Co. (Adapted from [638]).

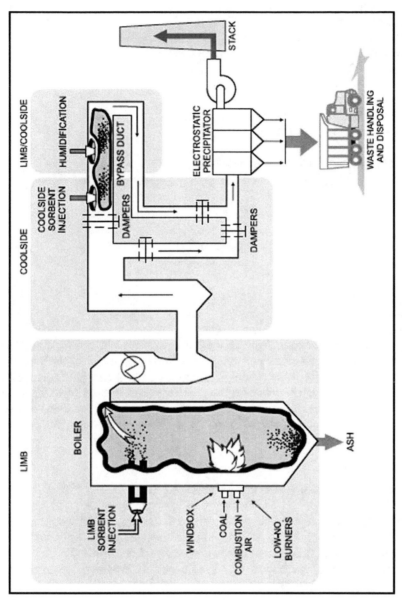

Fig. 6.22. The coolside process that couples flue gas humidification with hydrated lime injection into the duct. (Adapted from [639]).

by dissolving sodium hydroxide (NaOH) or sodium carbonate (Na_2CO_3) in the humidification water. The spent sorbent is collected with the fly ash, as in the LIMB process. Bituminous coal with 3.0% sulfur was used in testing, and SO_2 removal of 70% was reported. SO_2 capture takes place according to the following reactions:

Calcination: $Ca(OH)_2 + heat \rightarrow CaO + H_2O$

Sulfation: $CaO + SO_2 + 0.5\ O_2 \rightarrow CaSO_4 + heat$

Hydration: $CaO + H_2O \rightarrow Ca(OH)_2 + heat$
$\qquad\qquad CaSO_4 + 2H_2O \rightarrow CaSO_4 \cdot 2H_2O + heat$

The additional reactions involving NaOH are as follows:

$2NaOH + SO_2 \rightarrow Na_2SO_3 + H_2O + heat$
$2NaOH + SO_2 + 0.5\ O_2 \rightarrow Na_2SO_4 + H_2O + heat$

6.13.2.2 Duct Injection

In this process, dry sorbent is injected in the flue gas duct between the air preheater and particulate collector. Most commonly used sorbent is hydrated lime, however, sodium bicarbonate has been also used. Approximately 50–60% SO_2 is captured with lime, and the capture efficiency may be increased to 80% by using sodium bicarbonate. It is primarily used for those applications where a moderate degree of desulfurization is required at low capital cost. However, sodium bicarbonate is relatively expensive [640].

6.13.2.3 Calcium Silicate Injection (ADVACATE)

An advanced version of duct spray injection is the ADVAanced siliCATE (ADVACATE) process [641]. ADVACATE uses an advanced silicate that is more absorbent than lime. This process removes 90–95% of the sulfur dioxide and other acidic gases from stacks of any coal-fired boiler. A schematic diagram of the process is given in Fig. 6.23.

This dry duct injection system utilizes a fly ash-based throwaway sorbent to remove sulfur dioxide. High surface area calcium silicate hydrates are made by slurrying $Ca(OH)_2$ (calcium hydroxide) with fly ash and recycled sorbents in water at elevated temperatures. The resulting sorbent has the handling properties of a dry powder while maintaining moisture levels of up to 50–76% by weight.

The dry powder is injected into the duct, where sulfur dioxide removal takes place. Some removal of SO_2 also takes place in the particulate collection device. Sulfur dioxide captured by dry powder is collected with the fly ash and is separated into waste and recycle streams.

The calcium silicate formed has a large surface area capable of adsorbing a large amount of water. Sulfur dioxide dissolves into the water to react with calcium ions. The final products are calcium sulfite and calcium sulfate. Calcium sulfite is the main product. The ADVACATE absorbent has been tested in a 10 MW pilot plant, and 89% of SO_2 removal and 61% of lime utilization were achieved [642].

The Electric Power Research Institute estimates that the new process will cost $85 per kW versus $215 per kW for conventional flue gas scrubbing.

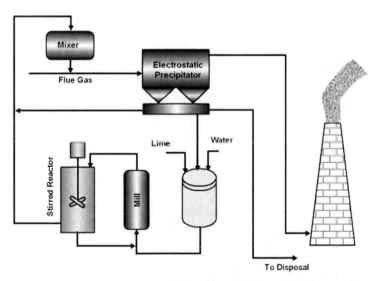

Fig. 6.23. A schematic representation of ADVAanced siliCATE (ADVACATE) process.

6.13.2.4 Combined Spray Drying and Electrostatic Precipitator (E-SOx)

The E-SOx technology combines improved electrostatic precipitation technology with conventional spray drying FGD techniques for better efficiency [643, 644]. A schematic diagram of the process is shown in Fig. 6.24.

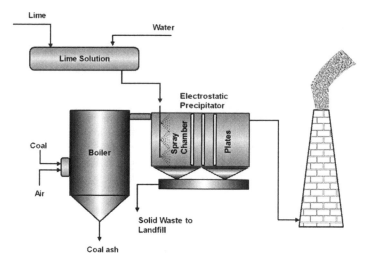

Fig. 6.24. The E-SOx process for enhancing flue gas desulfurization.

6.13.2.5 SOx -NOx Rox Box (SNRB)

This process combines hydrated lime and ammonia injection upstream of a hot, catalytic baghouse (Box), where the solid products calcium sulfite and sulfate and particulate (Rox) are removed, and the NOx is reduced to nitrogen and water. The design of the burner is shown in Fig. 6.25.

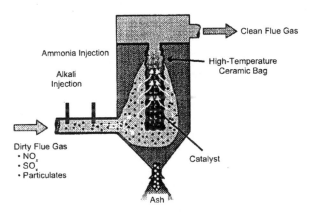

Fig. 6.25. The burner configuration for simultaneous removal of SOx-NOx-ROx-BOx. (Adapted from [638]).

A comparison of costs among various flue gas desulfurization methods is shown in Table 6.20

Table 6.20. A comparison of costs of various flue gas desulfurization processes.

Process	Plant capacity (MWe)	Sulfur content of coal (%)	Targeted SO$_2$ reduction (%)	Capital costs ($/kW)	Annual levelized costs ($/t of SO$_2$ removed)
Wet limestone scrubber					
Forced oxidation	300	1.7	90	209	540
Wallboard gypsum	300	2.6	90	243	476
Inhibited oxidation	300	2.6	90	234	476
Dibasic acid (additive)	300	2.6	90	211	463
Magnesium enhanced	300	2.6	90	189	477
Lime spray drying	300	1.7	90	160	490
	300	2.6	90	173	439
Dry sorbent injection					
Furnace injection	300	2.6	50	94	751
Duct injection	300	2.6	50	98	768
LIMB	100–500	1.5–3.5	60	31–102	392–791
Coolside	100–500	1.5–3.5	70	69–160	482–943
ADVACATE	300	2.6	90	84	327

6.14 Iron and Steel Production

Coal is one of the main constituents of iron and steel and is also used as the energy source during their production. About 66% of steel production worldwide comes from iron made in blast furnaces which use coal. World crude steel production was 1,129 million tonnes (Mt) in 2005, using around 664 Mt of coal. First iron is produced in a blast furnace that uses a mixture of iron ore, coke (made from specialist coking coals) and small quantities of limestone. Some furnaces use cheaper steam coal known as pulverized coal injection (PCI) process in order to save costs. Air is heated to about 1,200°C and is blown into the furnace through nozzles in the lower section to heat the mixture.

To produce coke, the coking coal is first crushed and washed. It is then carbonized in a series of coke ovens, called batteries. During this process, by-products are removed and coke is produced.

The iron ore is reduced to molten iron by various chemical reactions in the furnace. A tap at the bottom of the furnace is periodically opened to remove molten iron and slag. It is next taken to a basic oxygen furnace (BOF) where steel scrap and more limestone are added and 99% pure oxygen is blown onto the mixture. The reaction with the oxygen raises the temperature up to 1,700°C, oxidizes the impurities, and produces almost pure liquid steel. Around 0.63 t (630 kg) of coke produces 1 t (1,000 kg) of steel.

In PCI technology coal is injected directly into the blast furnace. A wide variety of coals can be used in PCI, including steam coal.

In 2004, about 214 Mt of coking coal was traded internationally, which represented 28% of total world hard coal trade. The coking coal trade increased by 8% to 227 Mt by 2005. The top coking coal exporting countries in 2005 are given in Table 6.21, and major importers of coking coals are listed in Table 6.22.

Table 6.21. Top coking coal exporters (2005).

Country	Amount exported in 2004 (Mt)	Amount exported in 2005 (Mt)
Australia	112	125
Canada	25	16
USA	24	26
Indonesia	17	19
Russia	14	12
PR China	6	6

Source: Reference [645].

Table 6.22. Major coking coal importers (2005).

Country	Amount imported (Mt)	Country	Amount imported (Mt)
Japan	63	Chinese Taipei	7
South Korea	21	Turkey	7
India	20	PR China	7
Brazil	15	Germany	7

Source: Reference [645].

6.14.1 Pulverized Coal Injection (PCI) Process

In this process, coal is injected directly into the blast furnaces during steel making. Coals used for pulverized coal injection into blast furnaces have more narrowly defined qualities than steam coal used in electricity generation. The use of PCI is slowly increasing world wide as one tonne of PCI is equivalent to about 1.4 t of coking coal. Table 6.23 shows the use of PCI world wide and Table 6.24 lists the countries that use most of PCI.

Table 6.23. PCI coals used in blast furnaces.

Year	Total consumption (Mt)	Year	Total consumption (Mt)
2004	29	2001	25
2003	26	2000	24
2002	25	1995	18

Source: Reference [645].

Table 6.24. Major consumers of PCI Coals (2004e).

Country	Consumption (Mt)	Country	Consumption (Mi)
Japan	8	India	3
South Korea	5	Germany	3
USA	3	France	3

Source: Reference [645].

6.15 Use of Coal in Cement Production

Coal is used as an energy source in cement production. Large amounts of energy are required to produce cement. Kilns usually burn coal in the form of powder and consume around 450 g of coal for about 900 g of cement produced. Coal is likely to remain an important input for the global cement industry for many years to come.

6.16 Liquid Fuels from Coal

A variety of chemicals can be produced from coals (see Fig. 6.26). It can be a significant source of liquid fuel for use in transportation and starting raw materials for a number of other chemicals [646–648]. Liquid fuels derived from coal have several advantages:

- Coal-derived fuels are ultra-clean: sulfur-free, low in particulates, with low levels of oxides of nitrogen.
- Carbon dioxide emissions, over the full fuel cycle, can be reduced by as much as 20%, compared to conventional oil products, through the use of carbon capture and storage [649].
- Coal is mined in over 50 countries and at present over 70 infrastructure systems exist for utilizing this resource to provide liquid fuels.
- Ultra-clean coal-derived fuels can be used for transportation, cooking and stationary power generation, and as a feedstock for the chemical industry.
- Largely proven technology for the manufacture of useful liquid products.
- Ability to manufacture transportation fuels from abundant coal.
- Insurance against depleting oil stocks and oil supply problems.

A number of methods have been proposed for liquefaction of coal. These methods can be classified as below:

- Carbonization and Pyrolysis
- Direct Coal Liquefaction Process
- Indirect Liquefaction Process

The processes that have been explored for liquefaction of coal are shown in Table 6.25. Plants that are planned in the USA and around the world are listed in Appendix VI.

6.16.1 Carbonization and Pyrolysis

In this method [651–658], coal is heated at a high temperature in the absence of oxygen during which hydrocarbon liquid is produced as a byproduct. The main product is coke. The yield of liquid depends mainly on the temperature: a yield of less than 5% occurs when the temperature is around 950°C.

About 15–20% yield of liquid fuel can be achieved using mild pyrolysis conditions, which consist of heating the coal to a temperature in the range of 450–650°C. Under this condition, not only volatile matters from the original coal are released, but also other volatile organic compounds are formed by thermal decomposition of higher molecular weight hydrocarbons. The main product is a char with a reduced hydrogen and heteroatom content. The USA has led the development of this process, primarily as a means to upgrade low-rank sub-bituminous

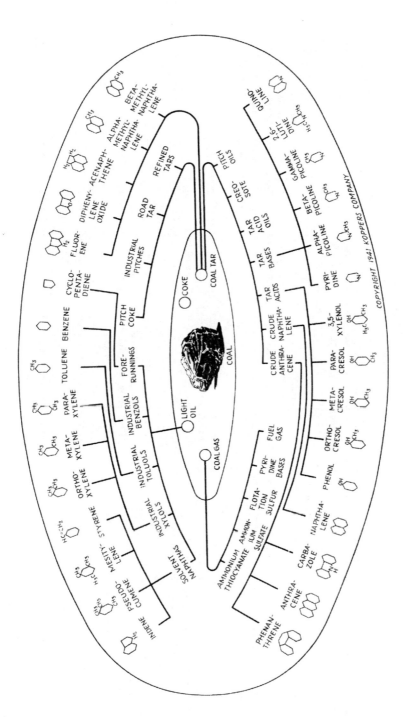

Fig. 6.26. Chemicals from coal. (Printed with permission from Shreve RN (1967) Chemical Process Industries. McGraw-Hill).

Table 6.25. A listing of processes explored for liquefaction of coal.

Mild pyrolysis	Single-stage direct liquefaction	Two-stage direct liquefaction	Co-processing and dry hydrogenation	Indirect liquefaction
Liquids from Coal (LFC) Process – Encoal	Solvent Refined Coal Processes (SRC-I and SRC-II) – Gulf Oil	Consol Synthetic Fuel (CSF) Process	MITI Mark I and Mark II Co-Processing	Sasol
Coal Technology Corporation	Exxon Donor Solvent (EDS) Process	Lummus ITSL Process	Cherry P Process – Osaka Gas Co.	Rentech
	H-Coal Process – HRI	Chevron Coal Liquefaction Process (CCLP)	Solvolysis	Syntroleum
University of North Dakota Energy and Environmental Center (EERC)/AMAX R&D Process	Imhausen High-Pressure Process	Kerr-McGee ITSL Work	C-Processing – Mitsubishi	Mobil Methanol-to-Gasoline (MTG) Process
	Conoco Zinc Chloride Process	Mitsubishi Solvolysis Process	Mobil Co-Processing	Mobil Methanol-to-Olefins (MTO) Process
	Kohleoel Process – Ruhrkohle	Pyrosol Process – Saarbergwerke	Pyrosol Co-Processing – Saabergwerke	Shell Middle Distillate Synthesis (SMOS)
Institute of Gas Technology	NEDO Process	Catalytic Two-Stage Liquefaction Process – DOE and HRI	Chevron Co-Processing	
		Liquid Solvent Extraction (LSE) Process – British Coal	Lummus Crest Co-Processing	
Char, Oil Energy Development (COED)		Brown Coal Liquefaction (BCL) Process – NEDO	Alberta Research Council Co-Processing	
		Amoco CC-TSL Process	CANMET Co-Processing	
		Supercritical Gas Extraction (SGE) Process – British Coal	Rheinbraun Co-Processing	
			TUC Co-Processing	
			UOP Slurry-Catalysed Co-Processing	
			HTI Co-Processing	

Source: Reference [651].

coals and lignites, to increase calorific value (CV) by rejection of the coal's oxygen as carbon dioxide (CO_2) and reduce the sulfur content. At least one process has been developed to a semi-commercial scale.

A higher yield of liquids can be obtained by rapid pyrolysis of coal at temperatures up to 1,200°C, at a residence time of few seconds at most. Rapid pyrolysis is aimed at producing chemical feedstocks rather than liquid fuels, and process economics are not favorable for production of liquid fuels. There also appear to be unresolved engineering difficulties. Most of the recent interest in these processes has been in the USA as a method for upgrading coals.

Encoal Corporation, Gillette, Wyoming, USA, built a mild pyrolysis demonstration plant with support from the United States Department of Energy's (USDOE's) Clean Coal Technology Demonstration Program based on the technology developed by SMC and SGI International. The process, called the Liquids from Coal (LFC) process [659], has been in commercial-scale operation since 1992. The flow diagram of the LFC process is shown in Fig. 6.27. Two main products were produced for marketing: a low-sulfur, high heating-value solid known as 'Process-Derived Fuel' (PDF) and a hydrocarbon liquid known as 'Coal-Derived Liquid' (CDL). PDF yields are considerably higher than CDL yields.

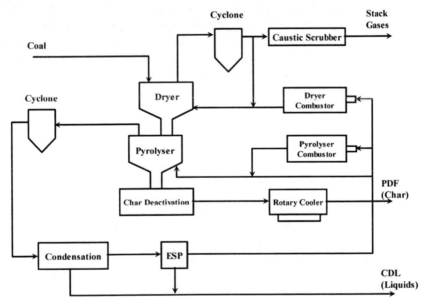

Fig. 6.27. A schematic diagram of the liquid from coal process developed by Encol (Coal Liquefaction, Technology Status Report 010, Department of Trade and Industry, www.dti.gov.uk/ent/coal, 1999 [660]).

The plant had a maximum capacity of 1,000 t/day of sub-bituminous Powder River Basin coal with a high moisture and low sulfur content. The coal is crushed and screened and then heated by a hot gas stream on a rotary grate dryer. The solid bulk temperature is controlled so that the coal is only dried. The dried coal is then fed into the main rotary grate pyrolyzer where it is heated to ~540°C by a hot recycled gas stream. Both the temperature and residence time is controlled accurately to maximize the yield. The PDF from the pyrolyzer is further stabilized by slight oxidation. The gas stream leaving the pyrolyzer is cooled in a quench tower, condensing CDL but leaving water in the gas phase. The residual gas is recycled to the pyrolyzer. The remaining gas is burned in the dryer combustor and passes into the dryer gas recycle loop. The purge from this loop is wet-scrubbed to remove particulates and sulfur oxides. The PDF is shipped by rail to power plants. CDL, roughly equivalent to a No. 6 fuel oil, is shipped by rail to a fuel oil distributor.

6.16.2 Direct liquefaction

In the direct liquefaction processes [661–674], coal is dissolved in a solvent at elevated temperature and pressure, followed by the hydro-cracking of the dissolved coal with H_2 and a catalyst. Liquid yields in excess of 70% by weight of the dry, mineral matter-free coal feed have been demonstrated for some processes, and overall thermal efficiencies for modern processes are generally in the range of 60–70% if allowance is made for generating losses and other non-coal energy imports. The liquid products from direct liquefaction processes are of better quality than those from pyrolysis processes and can be used unblended for most stationary fuel applications. For use as transportation fuels, further upgrading is required. Direct liquefaction processes can be divided into two groups.

- Single-stage direct liquefaction process
- Two-stage direct liquefaction process

6.16.2.1 Single-Stage Direct Liquefaction Process

The development of single-stage direct liquefaction processes started mainly in 1960s. The emergence of petroleum as the transportation fuel made most of these processes expensive. The research and development continued for a few processes. With the current increases in the oil price and the dwindling supply, there is a renewed interest in these processes. The single-stage processes that were developed furthest are:

- Kohleoel (Ruhrkohle, Germany)
- NEDOL (NEDO, Japan)
- H-Coal (HRI, USA)
- Exxon Donor Solvent (EDS) (Exxon, USA)
- SRC-I and II (Gulf Oil, USA)
- Imhausen high-pressure (Germany)
- Conoco zinc chloride (Conoco, USA)

Among these processes only the Kohleoel and NEDOL processes were advanced enough to be considered ready for commercialization. These two processes are discussed below.

The Kohleoel Process

The Kohleoel process shown in Fig. 6.28 has been developed by Ruhrkohle AG and VEBA OEL AG of Germany, and was used on a commercial scale in Germany until 1945 [660]. Two units, one of 0.5 t/day capacity, a 0.2 t/day continuous unit at Bergbau-Forschung (now DMT) and another one of 200 t/day at Bottrop were constructed. The Bottrop plant operated from 1981 to 1987, producing over 85,000 t of distillate products from 170,000 t of coal over approximately 22,000 operating hours. In this process pulverized coal is added to a solvent to make a slurry into which is added a 'red mud' of disposable iron catalyst. The mixture is pressurized and preheated and hydrogen is introduced.

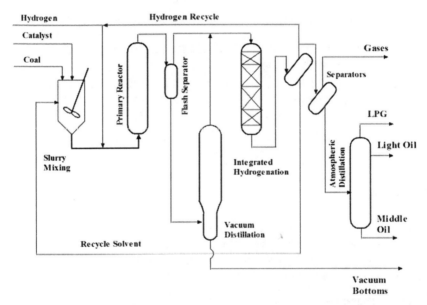

Fig. 6.28. The Kohleoel process for liquefaction of coal (Coal Liquefaction, Technology Status Report 010, Department of Trade and Industry, www.dti.gov.uk/ent/coal, 1999 [660]).

The overhead products from this separator remain in the gas phase and are further hydrotreated at a temperature of 350–420°C in a fixed-bed reactor at 300 bar. The hydrotreated products are depressurized, cooled, and separated in separators. The liquid product from the flash separator passes through an up-flow tubular reactor, operating at 300 bar and 470°C. The specific coal feed rate to this reactor is in the range 0.5–0.65 t/m^3/h. The solvent from the second stage separator is recycled to the mixer. The liquid product from the second stage separator is distilled at atmospheric pressure, yielding a light oil (C5 – 200°C bp) and a medium oil (200–325°C bp) product. A vacuum distillation column is also used to recover distillable liquids. The vacuum column bottoms consist of pitch, mineral matter, unreacted coal and catalyst. Greater than 90% conversion can be obtained when processing bituminous coals, with liquid yields in the range 50–60% on dry ash-free coal. Process yields and quality, when using Prosper, a German bituminous coal, are summarized in Tables 6.26 and 6.27, respectively.

Table 6.26. Yields with prosper coal from Kohleoel process.

Process yields	Yield (%)
Hydrocarbon gases (C_1–C_4)	19.0
Light oil (C_5–200°C)	25.3
Medium oil (200–325°C)	32.6
Unreacted coal and pitch	22.1

Table 6.27. Product quality with prosper coal from Kohleoel process.

Product quality	Light oil	Medium oil
Hydrogen (%)	13.6	11.9
Nitrogen (ppm)	39	174
Oxygen (ppm)	153	84
Sulfur (ppm)	12	<5
Density (kg/m^3)	772	912

Source: Reference [660].

The NEDOL Process

The NEDOL process was developed by a Japanese consortium managed by the New Energy and Industrial Technology Development Organization (NEDO) [675]. Figure 6.29 shows a process flow diagram of the NEDOL process. The NEDOL process consists of four units:

• Slurry preparation
• Liquefaction
• Distillation, and
• Solvent hydrogenation

Coal is dried and pulverized and prepared as a slurry by mixing the coal with recycle solvent and catalyst. This mixture is fed into liquefaction reactors, where coal is liquefied. Products from the reactors are separated into product oils and recycle solvent. The solvent is hydrogenated in a hydrogenation reactor to improve its quality. The composition of the catalysts is given in Table 6.28. The process parameters are listed in Table 6.29. The composition of the liquid fuel depends on the original coal composition. The characteristics of liquid fuel from Tanito Harum coal of Indonesia before and after hydrogenation treatment are shown in Table 6.30.

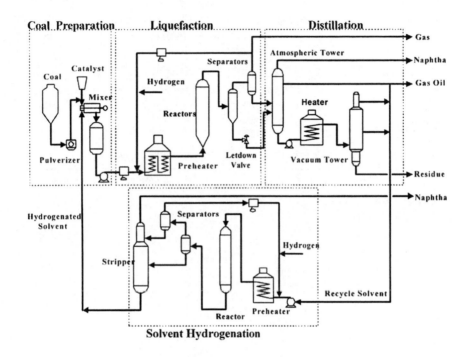

Fig. 6.29. The NEDOL Process [675].

Table 6.28. Characteristics of catalysts used in NEDOL process.

Catalyst properties	
Liquefaction catalyst	**Hydrogenation catalyst**
Catalyst composition	Catalyst composition, Ni-Mo/γ
Fe (wt%) 48.2	Al$_2$O$_3$
S (wt%) 51.0	Specific surface area (m^2/g) 190
Other (wt%) 0.8	Micropore volume (ml/g) 0.7
Specific surface area (m^2/g) 6.1	Mean micropore size (nm) 14.5
Size of pulverized catalyst (D50, μm) 0.7–0.8	

Table 6.29. Reaction conditions typical of the NEDOL process.

Various condition for liquefaction reaction			
Temperature:	450°C	Slurry concentration:	40 wt% (dry coal basis)
Pressure:	170 kg/cm².G		
Catalyst type:	Iron based	Slurry retention time:	60 min
fine powder		Gas/slurry ratio:	700 Nm³/t
Amount of catalyst: 3 wt% (dry coal basis)		Hydrogen concentration	
		In recycle gas:	85 vol%
Solvent hydrogen reaction			
Temperature:	320°C	Gas/solvent ratio:	500 N m³/t
Pressure:	110 kg/cm2.G	Hydrogen concentration	
Catalyst type:	Ni-Mo-Al₂O₃	In recycle gas:	85 vol%
LHSV:	1 h⁻¹		

Table 6.30. Characteristics of coal derived liquid.

	Crude	Primary hydrogenated liquid
Specific gravity (g/cm³)	0.8994	0.8204
Elemental analysis		
C (wt%)	84.7	
H (wt%)	10.9	
N (ppm)	6,400	1
S (ppm)	500	5
O (wt%)	3.5	
Yield at the temperature range (vol%)		
−180°C	18.3	35.8
180–240°C	40.2	39.2
240–340°C	41.5	25.0

The H-Coal Process [676, 677]

The H-Coal process was developed by Hydrocarbon Research Incorporated (HRI) (now Hydrocarbon Technologies Incorporated, HTI) based on H-Oil process that was used to upgrade heavy oils. A pilot plant of 200 tons/day capacity was built at Catlettsburg, Kentucky, USA, in 1980 and operated until 1983. The H-Coal process remained the basis of most of the subsequent process development sponsored by the USDOE and was incorporated into the Catalytic Two-stage Liquefaction (CTSL) process.

The Exxon Donor Solvent (EDS) Process [678]

Exxon Corporation started the EDS process development in the 1970s and progressed to the construction of a 250 t/day pilot plant at Baytown, Texas, USA, in 1980. The pilot plant was operated until 1982, with further research continued until at least 1985.

The SRC-I and SRC-II Processes [679, 680]

The Solvent Refined Coal (SRC) processes were developed to produce cleaner boiler fuels from coal. Two pilot plant units, one at Wilsonville (SRC-I, 6 t/day) and another one at Fort Lewis, Washington (SRC-I, 50 t/day) were constructed for testing of the process. The Fort Lewis plant was later converted to a SRC-II unit, because of the more severe conditions required for SRC-II, the capacity was downgraded to about 25 t/day. The objective of the SRC-II process is to produce distillate products.

The Imhausen High-pressure Process [681]

The operating conditions of the Imhausen high-pressure process (470–505°C and 600–1,000 bar) were considered to be rather high for commercialization. As a result no further work after 1984 was reported.

The Conoco Zinc Chloride Process [682]

Although the Conoco zinc chloride process, which uses molten zinc chloride to hydrocrack coal directly, provided good yields of gasoline in a single step, the corrosive nature of zinc chloride hindered further development of the process. This process is one of the very few direct liquefaction processes that is not a direct derivative of prewar technology. The process was taken to the 1 t/day pilot plant scale, although this was operated for only a short period and with limited success. However, the development of new and better materials that can withstand corrosion from chloride salts may help to overcome some of these problems.

6.16.2.2 Two-Stage Direct Liquefaction Processes

Most two-stage direct liquefaction processes were developed in response to the oil crisis of the early 1970s. A number of processes were developed by various countries throughout the world, however, only few processes were developed beyond the laboratory scale. These processes are given below. The current increase of oil price is renewing the interest of these processes again.

- Catalytic Two-Stage Liquefaction (CTSL) (USDOE and HRI, now HTI, USA) [683, 684]
- Liquid Solvent Extraction (LSE) (British Coal Corporation, UK)
- Brown Coal Liquefaction (BCL) (NEDO, Japan) [685]
- Consol Synthetic Fuel (CSF) (Consolidation Coal Co, USA) [686, 687]
- Lummus Integrated Two-Stage Liquefaction (ITSL) (Lummus Crest, USA) [688–692]
- Chevron Coal Liquefaction Process (CCLP) (Chevron, USA) [693]
- Kerr-McGee ITSL (Kerr-McGee, USA) [694]
- Mitsubishi Solvolysis (Mitsubishi Heavy Industries, Japan) [695]
- Pyrosol (Saarbergwerke, Germany) [696]
- Amoco Close-Coupled Two-Stage Liquefaction (CC-TSL) (Amoco, USA) [697]
- Supercritical Gas Extraction (SGE) (British Coal Corporation, UK). [698]

Among these processes, CTSL, LSE and BCL processes are most advanced and are discussed below.

6.16.3 The Catalytic Two-Stage Liquefaction (CTSL) Process

The CTSL process is the extension of the H-Coal single-stage process. The CTSL process has evolved into a baseline process for the liquefaction development work funded by the USDOE in the 1980s and 1990s. A schematic diagram for the most recent version of the process is shown in Fig. 6.30.

Coal slurry is prepared by using recycled solvent, preheated, mixed with H_2 and fed to the bottom of an ebullating bed reactor. This reactor contains a supported catalyst, generally nickel-molybdenum on alumina, which is fluidized in the reactor.

The first stage reactor operates at about 400°C and 170 bar to re-hydrogenate the solvent when processing bituminous coals. With sub-bituminous coals, higher temperatures may be required. The products from the first reactor are fed directly to the second, ebullating-bed reactor, operating also at 170 bar, but at a higher temperature (~430–440°C). This reactor also contains a supported catalyst, generally but not necessarily the same as that in the first reactor. After separation and depressurization steps, the products from the second reactor enter an atmospheric distillation column, where distillate products boiling up to 400°C are removed. Distillate product yields of 65% or higher on dry ash-free coal can be obtained, although the product has relatively high boiling point. The residue is unconverted coal and the heavy asphalt.

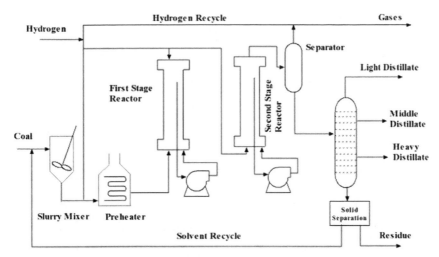

Fig. 6.30. A schematic flow diagram of the CSTL process (Coal Liquefaction, Technology Status Report 010, Department of Trade and Industry, www.dti.gov.uk/ent/coal, 1999 [660]).

The Liquid Solvent Extraction (LSE) Process

The LSE process was developed by British Coal Corporation between 1973 and 1995. A 2.5 t/day pilot plant was built and operated for four years at Point of Ayr, North Wales. Figure 6.31 shows a schematic diagram of the process. Coal slurry prepared using recycled solvent, is preheated and passed to a non-catalytic diges-tion step, which consists of two or more continuous-stirred tank reactors in series. These reactors operate at a temperature of 410–440°C and a pressure of 10–20 bar.

The digester product is partially cooled and filtered in a vertical-leaf pressure filter to remove unreacted coal and ash. The filter cake is washed with a light recycle oil fraction to recover product and dried under vacuum. The filtered coal extract passes to a distillation column to recover the light oil wash solvent and is then preheated, mixed with H_2 and fed to one or more ebullating-bed reactors in series. The reactors operate at: ~200 bar, 400–440°C and a space velocity in the range of 0.5–1.0 h^{-1} (kg feed per kg catalyst per hour). The reactor products are cooled, depressurized and fed to the atmospheric distillation column to recover various primary distillate products. Primary product quality is summarized in Table 6.31. To further enhance the product yield, a vacuum distillation column is also used. The total distillate product yield is in the range of 60–65% (dry ash-free coal), most of which boils below 300°C. The total filter cake yield includes ~7% of undistillable pitch.

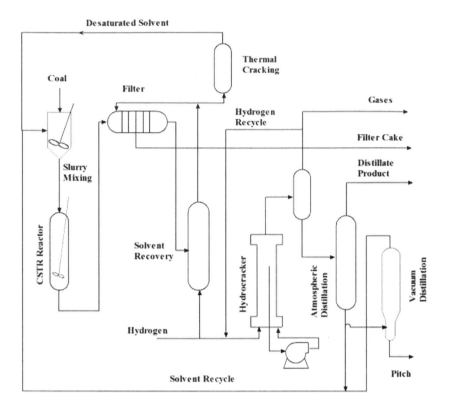

Fig. 6.31. A flow diagram of liquid solvent extraction (LSE) process (Coal Liquefaction, Technology Status Report 010, Department of Trade and Industry, www.dti.gov.uk/ent/coal 1999 [660]).

Table 6.31. LSE process conditions, yields and product quality using Point of Ayr coal.

Operating conditions	
Solvent to coal ratio	2.2
Digestion pressure (bar)	15
Digestion temperature (°C)	431
Nominal residence time (min)	50
Hydrocracking pressure (bar)	200
Hydrocracking temperature (°C)	434
Space velocity (kg feed/kg cal/h)	0.76
Product yield	
C_1-C_4 Hydrocarbon gases (% daf coal)	15.4
C_5–300°C Distillate product (% daf coal)	49.9
300–450°C Solvent surplus (% daf coal)	12.4

Pitch (>450°) (% daf coal)	0.8
Filter cake organics (% daf coal)	23.9
Product analysis	
Hydrogen (wt%)	12.14
Nitrogen (wt%)	0.14
Sulfur (wt%)	0.04

daf: dry ash free

The Brown Coal Liquefaction (BCL) Process

The BCL process shown in Fig. 6.32 was developed by NEDO of Japan at Morwell in Victoria, Australia that was capable of processing 50 t/day coal. The process is designed specifically to handle very low-rank coals containing >60% moisture. A critical aspect of the process is the efficient drying of the coal. An improved version of BCL process consists of a slurry de-watering unit, a liquefaction system, an in-line hydrotreating unit, and a de-ashing system. The other characteristics of the process include the use of a high-active and inexpensive catalyst such as limonite ore, the use of a heavy fraction solvent (bp 300–420°C) and recycling of coal liquid bottom (bp > 420°C).

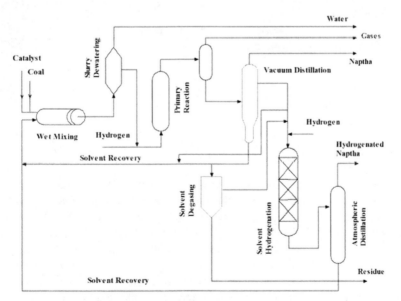

Fig. 6.32. Schematic flow diagram of the BCL process (Coal Liquefaction, Technology Status Report 010, Department of Trade and Industry, www.dti.gov.uk/ent/coal, 1999 [660]).

6.16.4 Co-processing

Co-processing [660] involves simultaneous upgrading of coal and of a non coal-derived liquid hydrocarbon. The liquid hydrocarbon is used to make the slurry for the coal. The non coal-derived liquid includes bitumen, any ultra-heavy crude oil, a distillation residue, or tar from conventional crude oil processing. There is no solvent recycle loop. One of the disadvantages of co-processing is that the non coal-derived solvents are both poor physical solvents for coal and poor hydrogen donors. This results in a relatively low conversion of the coal to liquid products. The economics of co-processing systems are yet to be determined, however, a number of co-processing methods have been proposed and are listed below.

- MITI Mark I (Japan)
- MITI Mark II (Japan)
- The Cherry P Process (Osaka Gas Co., Japan)
- Solvolysis (Mitsubishi Heavy Industries, Japan)
- Mobil (USA)
- Pyrosol (Saarbergwerke, Germany)
- Chevron (USA)
- Lummus Crest (USA)
- Alberta Research Council (ARC, Canada)
- CANMET AOSTRA (Canada)
- Rheinbraun (Germany)
- TUC (Technical University of Clausthal, Germany)
- UOP Slurry-catalysed (UOP, USA)
- HTI (USA).

Among these methods, the ARC, CANMET, HTI and Lummus Crest appear to be most promising commercially.

6.16.4.1 Lummus Crest Co-processing

Lummus Crest Co-processing involves hydrogenating the petroleum heavy oil residue prior to use as the solvent for making the coal slurry, which is reacted in an uncatalyzed, short contact time reactor at a temperature of 430–450°C and a hydrogen pressure of 140 bar [699]. The reactor products pass directly to a second stage ebullated-bed reactor, which operates at the same pressure and temperature containing a supported hydrotreating catalyst. About 90% of the coal is dissolved in the first stage on a dry ash-free basis, with overall conversions approaching 95%. The overall conversion of heavy material in the petroleum residue is 70–80%. The total net yield of distillable products is in the range 50–55% on the basis of fresh feed.

6.16.4.2 Alberta Research Council (ARC) Co-processing

The ARC co-processing was developed by Canadian Energy Developments for co-processing subbituminous coals with bitumen [700]. The process uses carbon monoxide and water in the first satge in a counter flow reactor. The first stage has been tested at a scale of 0.25 t/day for co-processing and 5 t/day for bitumen alone. Coal slurry containing bitumen, water and a disposable alkali metal catalyst is fed to the top of the counter-flow reactor, which operates at 380–400°C and 87 bar. The reaction generates H_2 in situ. The high oxygen content of sub-bituminous coals is reduced by use of CO and steam and the process is claimed to be more effective and has lower cost than the direct use of H_2. The second stage reactor system operates at ~420–480°C and 175 bar. Either H_2 or CO and steam could be used in this stage. The conversion of the coal depends primarily on the coal characteristics, but conversions of up to 98% on dry, ash-free coal have been reported. The overall product yield from the two stages is approximately 70% on the basis of combined weight, dry ash-free coal and bitumen-fed.

6.16.4.3 CANMET Co-processing

The CANMET hydrocracking process [701–703] was developed to hydrocrack heavy oils. A 5,000 barrels (bbl)/day commercial scale unit was constructed at the Petro Canada, Montreal, refinery in 1985. A 0.5 t/day pilot plant was constructed by a consortium formed by Rheinbraun AG, Amoco Corporation and the Alberta Oil Sands Technology and Research Authority (AOSTRA). In this process, coal, a disposable coal-based catalyst, and bitumen are mixed to make the slurry. The slurry along with hydrogen was fed to a single-stage upflow reactor. Typical operating temperature ranged from 440°C to 460°C, pressures from 10–15 MPa with feedstock coal concentrations of 30–40 wt% (mineral matter-free basis). About 98% of coal on a dry ash-free basis was converted by this process. The distillable oil yields of up to 80% on dry ash-free slurry feed are reported.

6.16.4.4 HTI Co-processing

HTI (previously HRI) co-processing [704] is a simplified version of the two-stage direct CTSL coal liquefaction process. It differs only in that there is no recycle solvent loop. Using GelCat™, an iron-based dispersed catalyst, coal conversions of up to 91% (dry ash-free basis) have been reported. The distillable product yield was in the range of 77–86% by weight on the basis of total feed.

6.16.5 Indirect Liquefaction Processes

The first step of the indirect liquefaction process [705, 706] involves the gasification of coal with steam to produce a mixture of carbon monoxide (CO) and hydrogen (H_2). The ratio of CO and H_2 is further adjusted and any sulfur is removed from the stream, as sulfur can poison the catalyst. The resulting 'synthesis gas' is reacted over a catalyst at relatively low pressure and temperature. The products may be paraffins, olefinic hydrocarbons or alcohols (particularly methanol), depending on the catalyst selected and the reaction conditions used.

The only commercial-scale coal liquefaction process currently in operation is the indirect Sasol process of South Africa. Sasol produces gasoline, diesel fuel and a wide range of chemical feedstocks and waxes from three plants. Two other processes were developed: one by Mobil and another one by Shell that have been put into commercial-scale operation and are discussed below.

6.16.5.1 The Sasol Process

The Sasol process [707–714] was developed in Germany around 1930–1940 based on the Fischer-Tropsch (FT) liquefaction process. The synthesis gas was produced from coal by the Lurgi gasification process. However, the first commercial scale plant was constructed at Sasolburg, South Africa, called Sasol 1, in the mid-1950s with a capacity of ~6,000 bbl/day of gasoline. Two more units, Sasol 2 and 3 plant, were completed at Secunda in 1980 and 1982, respectively. These plants were each designed to produce 50,000 bbl/day of gasoline, together with substantial quantities of other products for use as chemical feedstocks, from the processing of 30,000 t/day of coal. A schematic diagram of the Sasol process, based on the Sasol 2 and 3 plant, is shown in Fig. 6.33.

Currently, Sasol process uses both low-temperature Fischer Tropsch (LTFT) and high-temperature Fischer Tropsch (HTFT) for synthesis reaction. The LTFT process operates at 200–250°C and 20–30 bar and produces paraffins and waxes, where as the HTFT process operates at 300–350°C and 20–30 bar and produces a lighter, more olefinic product slate including gasoline, petrochemicals and oxygenated chemicals. Both the processes use an iron based catalyst.

The pulverized coal is wet-screened into two fractions: and the coal particles of greater than 5 mm are directed to the steam boiler whilst the particles less than 5 mm fraction goes to the Lurgi gasifiers. Raw-gas clean-up on both sites is carried out using conventional Lurgi Rectisol method with cold methanol as the wash medium. The gasoline produced by upgrading the primary products is of particularly good quality.

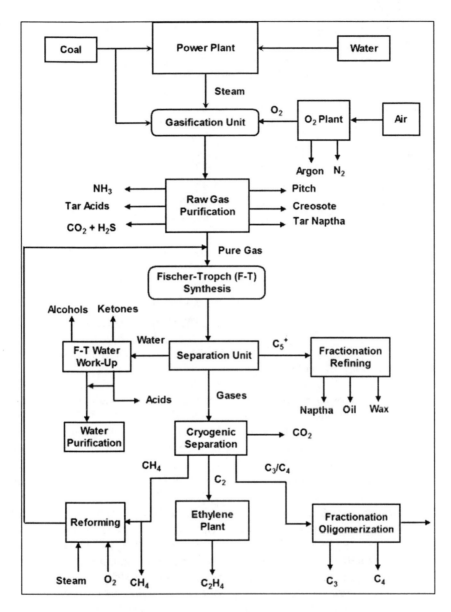

Fig. 6.33. Various product streams from the Sasol process [715].

The fuel quality produced by the Sasol process is given in Table 6.32.

Table 6.32. Typical Sasol fuels analyses.

	Gasoline			Diesel fuel	
	Sasol	Specification		Sasol	Specification
Reid vapor pressure (kPa)	63	65 max	Flash point (°C)	60	55 min
Octane: RON	93	93 min	Kin viscosity (40°C, cSt)	2.3	1.7–5.5
MON	84	83 min			
R100	85	83 min			
Pb (kg/m^3)	0.4	0.4 max	Cold filter plugging point (°C)	< − 6	−4 (winter)
Potential gum (mg/100 ml)	1	4 max	Ramsbottom (%)	0.1	0.2 max
Copper corrosion	1	1 max	Total acid (mg KOH/g)	0.01	0.25 max
			Cetane number	47	45 min

6.16.5.2 The Mobil MTG Process

The Mobil methanol-to-gasoline (MTG) process produces gasoline from coal or natural gas in two steps [716–724]. A commercial scale plant of 12,500 bbl/day capacity has been constructed at Maui field, New Zealand. The plant is currently used for methanol production, for which the economics are currently more favorable. Synthesis gas produced by steam reforming of natural gas or by coal gasification is reacted over a copper-based catalyst to produce methanol having almost 100% yield. The reaction is carried out at 260–350°C and 50–70 bar. To produce other hydrocarbon products, methanol is first converted to dimethyl ether by partial dehydration of methanol at 300°C and 22 bar over an activated alumina catalyst, followed by reaction over a fixed-bed zeolite ZSM-5 catalyst. Methanol further reacts with dimethyl ether producing olefins and other saturated hydrocarbons. Yields of material in the gasoline boiling range represent ~80% of the total hydrocarbon product. With alkylation of by-product propane and butane, total gasoline yields of 90% at 93.7 RON (octane number) were achieved at the New Zealand plant. Further modification of the process involved the use of a fluidized-bed reactor, which provided better temperature control (near isothermal condition) and constant catalytic activity. The fluidized bed reactor could be operated at 410°C and 3 bar. Primary, gasoline-range liquid yields are lower, but there is little difference in final gasoline yields after alkylation.

6.16.5.3 The Shell SMDS Process

The Shell Middle Distillate Synthesis (SMDS) process produces a high quality diesel fuel from natural gas [725–727]. However, it is concluded that synthesis gas produced by coal gasification can also be used to produce same quality liquid fuel. A schematic diagram of the process is shown in Fig. 6.34.

In this process, synthesis gas is reacted over a proprietary Shell catalyst in a fixed-bed tube-bundle reactor that is cooled by boiling water. The product is almost exclusively paraffinic. The reactor operates at 300–350°C and 30–50 bar. A high degree of product recycle is used to minimize the production of light products. The product distribution can be adjusted to give up to 60% diesel, with 25% kerosene and 15% naphtha. If desired, process parameters can be changed to produce up to 50% kerosene.

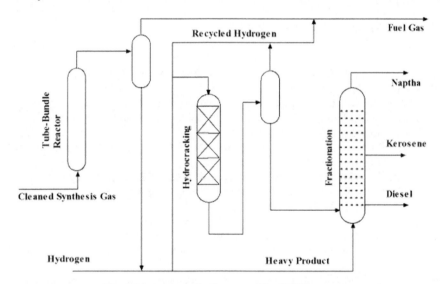

Fig. 6.34. A schematic diagram of the SMDS process.

Coal will certainly remain a dominant energy resource worldwide. However, the environmental issues must be addressed, since we no longer can ignore global warming. Various new technologies are addressing the carbon capture and storage. The effort is also underway to build more coal liquefaction plants, however, it should be noted that the burning of coal derived liquid will not eliminate CO_2 emission. The use of supercritical or ultra supercritical steam will enhance the efficiency of the coal-fired power plant in the range of 50%, which will help to reduce emissions of various pollutants in the atmosphere.

References

1. Statistical review of world energy 2007, British Petroleum, http://www.bp.com/ productlanding.do?categoryId=6848&contentId=7033471
2. Moore ES (1922) Coal: Its Properties, Analysis, Classification, Geology, Extraction, Uses, and Distribution. Wiley, New York, 124
3. Jeffrey EC (1915) The mode of origin of coal. J Geol 23: 218–231
4. Jeffrey EC (1924) Origin and organization of coal. Mem Am Acad Arts Sci 15: 1–52
5. Potonie H (1908) The origin of coal and related products, including petroleum. Ber Dent Pharm Ges 70: 180–223
6. Boudouard O (1911) Action of physical and chemical agents on wood, peat and lignite: formation of coal. Rev Metal 8: 38–46
7. Runner JJ (1919) Origin of coal. Pahasapa Quart 8: 74–83
8. Urbasch S (1922) The origin of coal, Naturwissenschaftliche Umschau der Chemiker-Zeitung 11: 38–41
9. Fischer F (1925) Origin of coal. Z deut geol Ges 77A: 534–550
10. Schrader H (1926) Recent English work on the constitution of coal. Brennstoff-Chemie 7: 155–157
11. Marcusson J (1927) Lignin and oxycellulose theory (of the origin of coal) Angewandte Chemie 40: 48–50
12. Strache H (1927) Lignitic origin of coal. Brennstoff-Chemie 8: 21–22
13. Lieske R (1930) Origin of coal according to the present position of biological investigation. Brennstoff-Chemie 11: 101–105
14. Liesye R (1930) Lignin theory of the origin of coal from the biological point of view. Brennstoff-Chemie 11: 86–90
15. Potonie R (1929) The origin of coal. Intern Bergwirt and Bergtech 22: 395–398
16. Fuchs W (1930) Origin of coal according to the present position of chemical investigation. Brennstoff-Chemie 11: 106–112
17. Schopf JM (1952) Was decay important in origin of coal? J Sediment Petrol 22: 61–69
18. Hatcher PG, Breger IA, Szeverenyi N, Maciel GE (1982) Nuclear magnetic resonance studies of ancient buried wood – II. Observations on the origin of coal from lignite to bituminous coal. Org Geochem 4: 9–18
19. Fischer F, Schrader H. Old and new ideas about the original coal substance. Ges Abh Kenninis der Kohle 5: 543–552
20. Stach E (1970) Significance of cellulose for the origin of coal. Fortschritte in der Geologie von Rheinland und Westfalen 17: 439–460
21. Sagui CL (1933) Origin of coal. Rev Geol 14: 316
22. Sagui CL (1931) Origin of coal. Bollettino della Societa Geologica Italiana 50: 227–228
23. Terres E (1932) The origin of coal and petroleum. Proc 3rd Int Conf Bituminous Coal 2: 797–808
24. Bode H (1930) The lignin theory and the origin of coal. Kohle und Erz 27: 652–656, 681–656, 711–614
25. Berl E, Schmidt A, Koch H (1930) The origin of coal. Angewandte Chemie 43: 1018–1019
26. Bode H (1930) Lignin theory [of the origin of coal]. Brennstoff-Chemie 11: 81–86
27. Donath E (1924) The question of the origin of coal. Brennstoff-Chemie 5: 136–138

28. Potonie R (1922) The lignin origin of coal: a geologic and palaeontologic impossibility. Braunkohle (Duesseldorf) 21: 365–369
29. White D (1913) Origin of coal. US Bur Mines Bull 38: 1–4
30. Schwarz H, Laupper G (1922) The origin of coal. Vierteljahrsschrift der Naturforschenden Gesellschaft in Zuerich 67: 268–371
31. Petraschek W (1923) Geology of coal in the Austrian states. II. The general geology of coal. Montanistische Rundschau 15: 37–160
32. Obst W (1928) The origin of coal. Chemiker-Zeitung 52: 629
33. Pieters HAJ (1930) Composition and origin of coal. Het Gas 50: 289–289
34. Fuchs W, Horn O (1931) The origin of coal. Angewandte Chemie 44: 180–184
35. Stadnikov G (1931) The origin of coal strata. Kolloid-Zeitschrift 57: 221–225
36. Berl E, Schmidt A, Koch H (1932) The origin of coal. Angew Chem 45: 517–519
37. Berl E (1932) The origin of coal, oil and asphalt. Montanistische Rundschau 24: 1–10
38. Stach E (1933) The origin of coal vitrite. Angew Chem 46: 275–278
39. Galle RR (1935) The origin of coals. Khimiya Tverdogo Topliva (Leningrad) 6: 683–694
40. Stadnikov GL (1937) Constitution and the origin of coal. Brennstoff-Chemie 18: 108–110
41. Hendricks TA (1945) The origin of coal. Chemistry of Coal Utilization. Wiley, New York, vol 1, pp 1–24
42. Fuchs W (1946) The origin of coal and the change of rank in coal fields. Fuel 25: 132–134
43. Fuchs W (1952) Recent investigations on the origin of coal. Chemiker-Zeitung 76: 61–66
44. Fujita A (1961) The origin of coal. Kagaku no Ryoiki 15: 239–241
45. Krejci-Graf K (1962) Origin of coal and petroleum. Freiberger Forschungshefte A C123: 5–34
46. Schobert HH (1989) The geochemistry of coal. I. The classification and origin of coal. J Chem Educ 66: 242–244
47. Scott AC (2002) Coal petrology and the origin of coal macerals: a way ahead? Int J Coal Geol 50: 119–134
48. Ritz M (2007) Identification of origin of coal from the Ostrava-Karvina Mining District by infrared spectroscopy and discriminant analysis. Vib Spectrosc 43: 319–323
49. Coal origin and properties www.coaleducation.org/Ky_Coal_Facts/coal_resources/coal_origin.htm
50. Walker S (2000) Major Coalfields of the World. IEA Coal Research, London, 2000
51. Hensel RP (1981) Coal: Classification, Chemistry and Combustion. Coal fired industrial boilers workshop, Raleigh, NC, USA
52. World Coal Institute, Richmond-upon-Thames, UK
53. Survey of Energy Resources 2004, World Energy Council, London, UK
54. Smith KL, Smoot LD (1990) Characteristics of commonly used US coals – towards a set of standard research coals. Prog Energy Combust Sci 16(1): 1–53
55. Bhatia SK (1987) Modeling the pore structure of coal. AIChE J 33: 1707–1718
56. Brusset H (1949) The most recent view of the structures of coal. Memoires ICF 102: 69–74
57. Carlson GA (1991) Molecular modeling studies of bituminous coal structure. Preprints of Papers – American Chemical Society, Division of Fuel Chemistry 36: 398–404

58. Carlson GA (1992) Computer simulation of the molecular structure of bituminous coal. Energy Fuels 6: 771–778
59. Carlson GA, Faulon JI (1994) Applications of molecular modeling in coal research. Preprints of Papers – American Chemical Society, Division of Fuel Chemistry 39: 18–21
60. Chung KE (1989) Fundamental chemical structure of coal. Final report, Electr Power Res Inst, Palo Alto, CA, USA, p 47
61. Crussard L (1938) Recent data on the structure of coal. Rev Ind Minerale No. 422: 331–350
62. Davidson RM (1980) Molecular Structure of Coal. IEA Coal Research, London, UK
63. Davidson RM (1980) Molecular Structure of Coal. IEA Report No. ICTIS/TR08. London, UK, p 86
64. Davidson RM (1982) Molecular structure of coal. Coal Sci 1: 83–160
65. Dryden IGC (1953) Chemical structure of coal. Fuel 32: 395–396
66. Dryden IGC (1955) Chemical interpretation of x-ray studies of the ultrafine structure of coal. Fuel 34: S29–S35
67. Dryden IGC (1956) The molecular structure of coal: comparison of results based on organochemical methods and infrared studies. Brennstoff-Chemie 37: 42–46
68. Fischer F, Schrader H (1921) The origin and chemical structure of coal. Brennstoff-Chemie 2: 37–45
69. Fischer F, Schrader H (1922) Observations on the origin and chemical structure of coal. Brennstoff-Chemie 3: 65–72
70. Gagarin SG, Skripchenko GB (1986) Modern concepts of the chemical structure of coals. Khimiya Tverdogo Topliva (Moscow, Russian Federation): 3–14
71. Gillet AC (1947) The molecular structure of coal. Chaleur et Industrie 28: 274–275
72. Gillet AC (1938) Formation and chemical constitution of coal, lignites and peat. Revue Universelle des Mines, de la Metallurgie, de la Mecanique, des Travaux Publics, des Sciences et des Arts Appliques a l'Industrie 14: 782–786
73. Green TK (1984) The macromolecular structure of coal: 184
74. Green TK (1987) The macromolecular structure of coal. J Coal Qual 6: 90–93
75. Grigoriew H (1990) Diffraction studies of coal structure. Fuel 69: 840–845
76. Grigoriew H, Cichowska G (1990) Spatial coal structure models. J Appl Crystallogr 23: 209–210
77. Grimes WR (1982) The physical structure of coal. Coal Science 1: 21–42
78. Harris LA, Yust CS (1979) Ultrafine structure of coal determined by electron microscopy. Oak Ridge Natl Lab, Oak Ridge, TN: 8
79. Heredy LA, Wender I (1980) Model structure for a bituminous coal. Preprints of Papers – American Chemical Society, Division of Fuel Chemistry 25: 38–45
80. Hower J, Suarez-Ruiz CI, Mastalerz M, Cook AC (2007) The investigation of chemical structure of coal macerals via transmitted-light FT-IR microscopy by X. Sun. Spectrochimica acta. Part A, Molecular and biomolecular spectroscopy 67: 1433–1437
81. Inouye K (1953) Structural skeleton in a bituminous coal. Nature (London, UK) 171: 487–488
82. Kasatochkin VI, Razumova LL (1956) X-ray analysis of the molecular structure of anthracite and coke. Isvest Akad Nauk S.S.S.R Ser. Fiz. 20: 751–754
83. Kemp NC (1924) The X-ray analysis of coal. Iron and Coal Trades Rev 108: 295–296
84. Kessler MF (1956) New conceptions of the molecular coal structure. Uhli 6: 376–380
85. King JG, Wilkins ET (1944) The internal structure of coal. Proc Conf Ultra-fine Structure of Coals and Cokes, Brit Coal Utilisation Research Assoc: 46–56

86. Kitazaki U (1953) The structure of coal. J Geol Soc Jpn 59: 241–255
87. Ladner WR, Stacey AE (1961) Possible coal structures. Fuel 40: 452–454
88. Larsen JW (1978) Some thoughts on the organic structure of bituminous coal. Proc Coal Chem Workshop: 39–51
89. Larsen JW (1988) Macromolecular structure and coal pyrolysis. Fuel Process Technol 20: 13–22
90. Larsen JW (1992) The physical and macromolecular structure of coals. NATO ASI Series, Ser C: Math Phys Sci 370: 1–14
91. Lazarov L (1982) Modern conceptions of the molecular structure of coal. Freiberger Forschungshefte A A 668: 37–56
92. Lomax J (1913) Microscopic structure of coal and its constituents. J Soc Chem Indus, London 32: 276
93. Lomax J (1913) Microscopic structure of coal and its constituents. J Gas Lighting, Water Supply Sanitary Improvement 121: 601
94. Lynch LJ (1987) Molecular properties of coals. Chem Aust 54: 244–246
95. Marzec A (1981) Molecular structure of coal. Chemia Stosowana 25: 381–389
96. Neavel RC (1979) Coal structure and coal science: overview and recommendations. Preprints of Papers – American Chemical Society, Division of Fuel Chemistry 24: 73–82
97. Neavel RC (1981) Coal structure and coal science: overview and recommendations. Adv Chem Ser 192: 1–13
98. Nomura M, Iino M, Sanada Y, Kumagai H (1994) Advanced studies on coal structure. Enerugi, Shigen 15: 177–184
99. Nomura M, Murata S, Miyake M, Miura M (1993) An approach to chemical structure of coal. Nippon Enerugi Gakkaishi 72: 321–329
100. Ohuchi K (1980) Structure of coal. Petrotech (Tokyo, Japan) 3: 513–519
101. Orchin M (1953) Chemical structure of coal. Ohio State Univ Eng Expt Sta News 25: 25–31
102. Riley HL (1947) Molecular structure of coal. Science Progress (St. Albans, UK) 35: 590–604
103. Riley HL (1948) Macromolecular structure of bituminous coal. Bulletin des Societes Chimiques Belges 57: 400–415
104. Sanada Y (1980) Macromolecular structure of coal seen from viewpoint of chemical application. Kagaku Kogyo 31: 241–245
105. Schrauth W (1923) The chemical structure of coal. J Chem Soc, Abstracts 124: 502–503
106. Shapiro MD, Al'terman LS, Macromolecular structure of coals and their technological properties. Khimiya Tverdogo Topliva (Moscow, Russian Federation): 17–22
107. Smirnov RN (1959) Modern concepts of the structure of coal. Uspekhi Khimii 28: 826–849
108. Smirnov RN (1979) Polymeric structure of coal. Khimiya Tverdogo Topliva (Moscow, Russian Federation): 40–45
109. Stopes MC, Wheeler RV (1916) The structure of coal, Colliery Guardian 112: 464
110. Szklarska-Olszewska Z (1951) Structure of coal and coke. Prace Glownego Inst Met 3: 161–172
111. Takanohashi T (1994) Cross-link structure of coal. Tohoku Daigaku Hanno Kagaku Kenkyusho Hokoku 4: 19–40
112. Thiessen R (1913) Microscopic study of coal. Bull 38: 187–379

113. van Krevelen DW (1947) The structure of coal, the coalification and the carbonization process. Chemisch Weekblad 43: 20–27
114. van Krevelen DW (1959) Chemical structure of coal. Fuel 38: 245–247
115. Vorres KS (2004) Coal. Kirk-Othmer Encyclopedia of Chemical Technology (5th Edition) 6: 703–771
116. Whitaker A (1955) The ultimate structure of coal. J Inst Fuel 28: 218–223
117. Whitehurst DD (1978) A primer on the chemistry and constitution of coal. ACS Symp Ser 71: 1–35
118. Xuguang S (2005) The investigation of chemical structure of coal macerals via transmitted-light FT-IR microspectroscopy, Spectrochim Acta A Mol Biomol Spectrosc 62: 557–564
119. Yokono T, Shibuya T, Sanada Y (1978) Nuclear magnetic relaxation and x-ray diffraction studies of the structure of coal. Nippon Kagaku Kaishi: 1132–1136
120. Zwietering P, van Krevelen DW (1954) Chemical structure and properties of coal. IV. Pore structure. Fuel 33: 331–337
121. Given PH (1960) The distribution of hydrogen in coals and its relation to coal structure. Fuel 39: 147–153
122. Solomon PR (1981) New approaches in coal chemistry. ACS Symposium Series No. 169, American Chemical Society, Washington, DC: 61–71
123. Shinn JH (1984) From coal to single stage and two stage products: a reactive model to coal structure. Fuel 63, 1187–1196
124. Wiser WH (1984) Conversion of bituminous coal to liquids and gases: chemistry and representative processes. NATO ASI Series C, 124, 325–350
125. KGS (Kentucky Geological Survey) (2006) Methods of Mining. www.uky.edu/kgs/coal/coal_mining.htm
126. United Mine Workers of America (UMWA) http: //www.umwa.org/mining/surmine.shtml
127. Burns SS (2005) Bringing Down the Mountains: The Impact of Mountaintop Removal Surface Coal Mining on Southern West Virginia Communities. Ph.D. dissertation. West Virginia University.
128. Kramer DA (2001) Explosives, US Geological Survey Mineral Handbook, 25-1, 25-6
129. United Mine Workers of America (UMWA) www.umwa.org/mining/ugmine.shtml
130. EIA (Energy Information Administration) (2007) Glossary: Longwall Mining. www.eia.doe.gov/glossary/glossary_l.htm
131. United Mine Workers of America (UMWA) www.umwa.org/mining/lwmine.shtml
132. Federal Energy Regulatory Commission, FERC Form 423, Monthly Report of Cost and Quality of Fuels for Electric Plants
133. EIA (Energy Information Administration) Form EIA-3, Quarterly Coal Consumption and Quality Report, Manufacturing Plants
134. EIA (Energy Information Administration) Form EIA-5, Quarterly Coal Consumption and Quality Report, Coke Plants.
135. EIA (Energy Information Administration) Form EIA-7A, Coal Production Report
136. US Department of Labor, Mine Safety and Health Administration, Form 7000-2, Quarterly Mine Employment and Coal Production Report
137. McCloskey Coal Information Service. www.coal-ink.com
138. NCC (National Coal Council) (2006) Coal: America's Energy Future, Volumes I. Washington, DC, National Coal Council: 132

139. EIA (Energy Information Administration) (2006) Average Contract Coal Transportation Rate per Ton-Mile by Transportation Mode, 1979–1997. Washington, DC, U.S. Department of Energy. www.eia.doe.gov/cneaf/coal/ctrdb/tab37.html

140. USACE (U.S. Army Corps of Engineers) (2006) Waterborne Commerce of the United States, Calendar Year 2004. Part 5-National Summaries. www.iwr.usace.army.mil/ndc/wcsc/pdf/wcusnatl04.pdf

141. Background Information for Establishment of National Standards of Performance for New Sources: Coal Cleaning Industry, EPA Contract No. CPA-70-142, Environmental Engineering Inc, Gainesville, FL, July 1971

142. Air Pollutant Emissions Factors, Contract No. CPA-22-69-119, Resources Research, Inc Reston, VA, April 1970

143. Second Review of New Source Performance Standards for Coal Preparation Plants, EPA-450/3-88-001, US Environmental Protection Agency, Research Triangle Park, NC, February 1988

144. Ahmad S, Saeed MT, Taj F (2005) Developments in coal desulphurization – a review. Part-I: pre-combustion desulphurization. Pakistan Journal of Science 57: 19–27

145. Atherton LF (1985) Chemical coal beneficiation of low-rank coals. Proc. – Int. Conf. Coal Sci.: 553–556

146. Gupta V, Mohanty MK (2006) Coal preparation plant optimization: a critical review of the existing methods. Int J Mineral Process 79: 9–17

147. Fonseca AG (1995) Challenges of coal preparation. Mining Engineering (Littleton, CO) 47: 828–834

148. Liu F (2003) Comprehensive review on coal preparation technology, Xuanmei Jishu: 1–13

149. McCandless LC, Onursal AB, Moore JM (1986) Assessment of coal cleaning technology. Final report, Versar Inc Springfield, VA, USA: 209

150. Okazaki TA (2000) survey of coal cleaning technologies (coal preparation) Nippon Enerugi Gakkaishi 79: 267–284

151. Onursal AB, Buroff J, Strauss J (1986) Evaluation of conventional and advanced coal cleaning techniques. Versar Inc Springfield, VA, USA: 385

152. Osborne DG (1986) Fine coal cleaning by gravity methods: a review of current practice. Coal Prep (London, UK) 2: 207–241

153. Osborne DG, Fonseca AG (1992) Coal preparation – the past ten years. Coal Preparation (London, UK) 11: 115–143

154. Parekh BK (1996) Coal Preparation. Coal Preparation (Gordon & Breach) 17: 1

155. Picard JL (1985) Coal preparation washing processes: a technology review. CANMET Report 85-2E: 87

156. Swanson A (2001) Australian coal preparation – A 2000 review. J South African Institute of Mining & Metallurgy 101: 107–113

157. Jeffrey Specialty Equipment Corporation, Woodruff, SC, USA, www.jeffreycorp.com

158. Pennsylvania Crusher Corporation, Broomall, PA, USA, www.penncrusher.com

159. Taylor JCP (1959) Advances in impact crushing techniques as related to coal. Inst Mining, Met Petrol Engrs Proc A.I.M.E 18: 29–30

160. Sharma MK, Chaudhuri AJ, Prasad S, Prasad BN, Das AK, Parthasarthy L (2007) Development of new coal blend preparation methodologies for improvement in coke quality. Coal Preparation (Philadelphia, PA, USA) 27(1–3): 57–77

161. Kimura H (1982) Properties and crushing of coal. Funtai to Kogyo 14(11): 21–28

162. Zbraniborski O (1965) Apparatus for crushing and reducing coal samples. Koks, Smola, Gaz 10(2): 64–66
163. Banaszewski T (1996) Classification and crushing techniques used in coal preparation. Recent Adv Coal Process 1: 25–29
164. Mohanty MK, Honaker RQ, Patwardhan A (2001) Altair centrifugal jig: an in-plant evaluation for fine coal cleaning. Proceedings – Annual International Pittsburgh Coal Conference 18th: 2849–2872
165. Mohanty MK, Honaker RQ, Patwardhan A (2002) Altair jig: an in-plant evaluation for fine coal cleaning. Mineral Eng 15: 157–166
166. Olajide O, Cho EH (1987) Study of the jigging process using a laboratory-scale Baum jig. Minerals Metallurgical Process 4: 11–14
167. Peng FF, Dai Q, Yang DC (2002) Analysis of packed column jig for fine coal separation. Coal Prep (London, UK) 22: 199–217
168. Sanders GJ, Ziaja D, Kottmann J (2002) Cost-efficient beneficiation of coal by ROM-JIGs and BATAC Jigs. Coal Prep (London, UK 22: 181–197
169. Yang DC, Bozzato P (2003) Multi-cell jigging for fine coal cleaning. Proceedings of the International Technical Conference on Coal Utilization & Fuel Systems 28th: 881–892
170. Anuprienko TA, Nikitin IN (1996) Methods for preparing and monitoring of heavy media in coal beneficiation. Obogashchenie Rud (Sankt-Peterburg): 11–12
171. Atwood GA, Leehe HH (1992) Perchloroethylene coal beneficiation. Coal Prep (London, UK) 11: 77–86
172. Cho H, Klima MS (1994) Application of a batch hindered-settling model to dense-medium separations. Coal Preparation (London, UK) 14: 167–185
173. Dardis, K.A The design and operation of heavy medium recovery circuits for improved medium recovery, Coal Prep (London, UK) 7: 119–157 (1989)
174. de Korte GJ (2002) Dense-medium beneficiation of fine coal revisited. Symposium Series – South African Institute of Mining and Metallurgy S29: 43–46
175. de Korte GJ (2003) Comments on the use of tracers to test dense-medium plant efficiency, Coal Preparation (Philadelphia, PA, USA) 23: 251–266
176. Honaker RQ, Singh N (1999) The application of dense medium in an enhanced gravity separator for fine coal cleaning. Proceedings – Annual International Pittsburgh Coal Conference 16th: 1737–1754
177. Honaker RQ, Singh N, Govindarajan B (2000) Application of dense-medium in an enhanced gravity separator for fine coal cleaning. Mineral Eng 13: 415–427
178. Kalabukhov ML, Glukhikh SG (2002) Technology and techniques for coal beneficiation in heavy-medium. Koks i Khimiya: 5–9
179. Miller GM (1989) Design of medium recovery and heavy medium management circuits – a different approach. Coal Prep (London, UK) 7: 175–182
180. Senftle FE, Thorpe AN, Davis D, Glasgow V, Akers D (1994) Determination of magnetite in dense-medium coal cleaning plants by the use of a Davis Tube. Coal Prep (London, UK) 14: 185–197
181. Klima MS, Luckie PT (1990) Use of an unsteady-state pulp-partition model to investigate variable interactions in dense-medium separators. Coal Prep (London, U K) 8: 185–193
182. van Dyk JC (2003) Effect of coal particle size and dense medium beneficiation on yields, carbon and sulphur content of Secunda coal. Proceedings – Annual International Pittsburgh Coal Conference 20th: 1909

183. Barraza JM, Caicedo MR, Botache CA (2000) Colombian coals beneficiation using hydrocyclone separation. Proceedings – Annual International Pittsburgh Coal Conference 17th: 2167–2175
184. Blaschke Z (2000) Evolution of the effectiveness of beneficiation and desulfurization of coal slurries in spiral concentrators. Inzynieria Mineralna 1: 33–36
185. Firth B, O'Brien M (2003) Hydrocyclone circuits. Coal Prep (Philadelphia, PA, USA) 23: 167–183
186. Hornsby DT, Watson SJ, Clarkson CJ (1993) Fine coal cleaning by spiral and water washing cyclone. Coal Prep (London, UK) 12: 133–161
187. Hredzak S (1999) Selected results of Slovak steam coal preparation in hydrocyclones. Gospodarka Surowcami Mineralnymi 15: 221–228
188. Jakabsky S, Lovas M, Hredzak SR, Turcaniova L (1998) Application of water only cyclone in Slovak steam coal preparation. Proceedings – Annual International Pittsburgh Coal Conference 15th: 1600–1607
189. Jenkins KA, He DX, Gargis AL, Chiang SH (1994) Development and use of a Taylor-vortex column for fine coal cleaning. Adv Filtrat Sep Technol 8: 444–447
190. Yang J, Zhang W, Wang Y (1999) Coal desulphurization by cyclonic whirl. Proceedings – Annual International Pittsburgh Coal Conference 16th: 46–51
191. Andrews GF, Noah KS (1997) The slurry-column coal beneficiation process. Fuel Process Technol 52: 247–266
192. Angadi SI, Suresh N (2005) A kinetic model for the prediction of water reporting to the froth products in batch flotation. Transactions of the Institutions of Mining and Metallurgy, Section C: Mineral Processing and Extractive Metallurgy 114: C225–C232
193. Arnold BJ (2000) The 'Grab and Run' revisited – improving selectivity between organic and inorganic components in conventional coal froth flotation. Int J Mineral Process 58: 119–128
194. Attia YA, Conkle HN, Krishnan SV (1984) Selective flocculation coal cleaning for coal slurry preparation. Coal Slurry Combust Int Symp 6th: 571–597
195. Attia YA, Yu S, Vecci S (1987) Selective flocculation cleaning of Upper Freeport coal with a totally hydrophobic polymeric flocculant. Process Technol Proc 4: 547–564
196. Behl S, Moudgil BM (1992) Fine coal cleaning by selective flocculation. Coal Prep (London, UK) 11: 35–49
197. Bennett AJ, Bustamante RH, Shibaoka M, Telfer A, Warren LJ, Woods G (1983) Coal cleaning by flotation. Dev Demonstration Counc Natl Energy Res, Canberra, Australia: 149
198. Bhattacharya S, Roy J, Sinha S (2002) Effect of seasonal variation of temperature on coal flotation. Symposium Series – South African Institute of Mining and Metallurgy S29: 359–364
199. Borts MA, Bochkov YN, Ryabchenko AN (1990) New flocculants for the coal industry. Perspekt. Napravleniya Nauch. Issled. po Razvitiyu Obogashch. Uglei. Kompleks. N-i. i Proekt.-Konstr. In-t Obogashch. Tverd. Goryuch. Iskop (IOTT) Lyubertsy: 128–139
200. Zhu H, Yang J, Shen Y, Ou Z, Zhao Y (1999) Coal desulfurization in flotation by electrochemical control. Proceedings – Annual International Pittsburgh Coal Conference 16th: 52–55
201. Yoon RH, Luttrell GH, Adel GT, Mankosa MJ (1992) The application of Microcel column flotation to fine coal cleaning. Coal Prep (London, UK) 10: 177–188

202. Yang DC (1984) Static tube flotation for fine coal cleaning. Coal Slurry Combust Int Symp 6th: 582–597

203. Yang DC (1990) Packed-bed column flotation of fine coal. Part II. Technical-economic feasibility and scale-up considerations. Coal Prep (London, UK) 8: 37–48

204. Yang DC (1990) Packed-bed column flotation of fine coal. Part I. Laboratory tests and flotation circuit design. Coal Prep (London, UK) 8: 19–36

205. Sun J, Long Z, Wang J, Fan Z (2002) Application of flotation reagent emulsion station in coal cleaning production. Xuanmei Jishu: 28–29

206. Song S, Zhang Y, Wu K, Lopez-Valdivieso A, Lu S (2004) Flotation of coal fines as hydrophobic flocs for ash rejection. J Dispers Sci Technol 25: 75–81

207. Polat H, Chander S (1995) Improved efficiency of coal cleaning using a flotation-regrinding-flotation process. Processing of Hydrophobic Minerals and Fine Coal, Proceedings of the UBC-McGill Bi-Annual International Symposium on Fundamentals of Mineral Processing, 1st, Vancouver, BC, Aug. 20–24, 1995: 179–189

208. Petukhov VN (1986) Improvement of technology for flotation of coals using modifier reagents. Flotatsionnye Reagenty: 201–203

209. Parekh BK, Bland AE, Groppo JG, Yingling J (1990) A parametric study of column flotation for fine coal cleaning. Coal Prep (London, UK) 8: 49–60

210. Parekh BK, Groppo JG, Datta RS (1992) A column flotation technique for cleaning ultra-fine coal. Adv Filtrat Sep Technol 5: 130–136

211. Ofori P, O'Brien G, Firth B, Jenkins B (2005) Flotation diagnostics and modeling by coal grain analysis. Publications of the Australasian Institute of Mining and Metallurgy 5/2005: 769–774

212. Ofori P, O'Brien G, Firth B, Jenkins B (2006) Flotation process diagnostics and modelling by coal grain analysis. Minerals Eng 19: 633–640

213. Munirathinam M, Groppo JG, Parekh BK, Cleaning of coal using an integrated grinding-flotation column system. Fuel Sci Technol 13: 119–129

214. Luttrell GH, Yoon RH (1994) Commercialization of the Microcel column flotation technology. Proceedings – Annual International Pittsburgh Coal Conference 11th: 1503–1508

215. Lalvani SB (1990) Coal flotation and flocculation in the presence of humic acids. Final report, January 1, 1989–August 31, 1990, Dep. Mech. Eng. Energy Process, South Illinois Univ Carbondale, IL, USA

216. Kawatra SK, Eisele TC (1995) Baffled-column flotation of a coal plant fine-waste stream. Minerals Metallurg Process 12: 138–142

217. Kawatra SK, Eisele TC, Baffled-column flotation of a coal plant fine-waste stream. Transactions of Society for Mining, Metallurgy, and Exploration, Inc. 298: 138–142/Section 133

218. Davis VL Jr, Bethell PJ, Stanley F, Luttrell GH, Mankosa MJ, Yoon RH (1993) Application of Microcel column flotation technology for fine coal recovery. Proceedings – Annual International Pittsburgh Coal Conference 10th: 90–96

219. Firth BA (1999) Australian coal flotation practice, Advances in Flotation Technology. Proceedings of the Symposium Advances in Flotation Technology held at the SME Annual Meeting, Denver, Mar. 1–3, 1999: 289–307

220. Hasuda T, Ogawa K, Arai S (1991) Advanced coal cleaning-deashing and desulfurization of coal by microbubble column flotation. Sekitan Riyo Gijutsu Kaigi Koenshu 1st: 254–263

221. Humeres E, Debacher NA (2002) Kinetics and mechanism of coal flotation. Colloid Polym Sci 280: 365–371
222. Kikkawa H, Takezaki H, Ootani Y, Shoji K (1988) Preparation of clean coal and water mixtures by efficient froth flotation. Kagaku Kogaku Ronbunshu 14: 755–761
223. Lehmkuhl J, Seifert G (1985) New aspects of the use of flocculants in coal preparation. Aufbereitungs Technik (1960–1989) 26: 645–651
224. Rubinstein JB, Linev BI, Hall ST (1998) Multisectional flotation column in coal preparation. Innovations in Mineral and Coal Processing, Proceedings of the International Mineral Processing Symposium, 7th, Istanbul, September 15–17, 1998: 345–350
225. Sekine OY, Sato D, Yamaguchi D, Kikuchi E, Matsukata M (2001) Effect of the distribution of hydrophilicity/hydrophobicity of coal on column flotation results. Sekitan Kagaku Kaigi Happyo Ronbunshu 38th: 307–310
226. Venkatadri R, Markuszewski R, Wheelock TD, Walters AB (1989) Flocculation of coal and mineral particles with a polyanionic biopolymer. Coal Prep (London, UK) 6: 207–225
227. Kawatra SK, Eisele TC (2001) Coal Desulfurization: High Efficiency Preparation Methods. Taylor & Francis
228. Shah CL, MacNamara L, Miles NJ, Hall ST (1997) Optimizing spiral separators and froth flotation in fine coal preparation circuits. DGMK Tagungsbericht 9702: 527–530
229. Zeilinger JE, Deurbrouck AW (1976) Physical desulfurization of fine-size coals on a spiral concentrator. US Bur Mines, Rep Invest RI 8152
230. Mellor GH (1979) Using Humphreys spirals for recovery of minus 4 mesh coal. Papers presented before the Symposium on Coal Preparation and Utilization: 35–41
231. Alexis J (1980) Cleaning coal and refuse fines with the Humphreys spiral concentrator. Mining Engineering (Littleton, CO, USA) 32(8): 1224, 1226–1228
232. Richards RG, Hunter JL, Holland-Batt AB (1985) Spiral concentrators for fine coal treatment. Coal Prep (London, UK) 1(2): 207–229
233. Sivamohan R, Forssberg E (1985) Principles of spiral concentration. Int J Mineral Process 15(3): 173–81
234. Davies POJ, Goodman RH, Deschamps JA (1991) Recent developments in spiral design, construction and application. Miner Eng 4(3–4): 437–456
235. Subasinghe GKNS, Kelly EG (1991) Model of a coal washing spiral. Coal Prep (London, UK) 9(1–2): 1–11
236. King RP, Juckes AH, Stirling PA (1992) A quantitative model for the prediction of fine coal cleaning in a spiral concentrator. Coal Prep (London, UK) 11(1–2): 51–66
237. Bohle B (1994) Environmental applications of spiral concentrators in Europe. Prog Miner Process Technol Proc Int Miner Process Symp 5th: 65–70
238. Honaker RQ, Wang D, Ho K (1996) Application of the Falcon Concentrator for fine coal cleaning. Miner Eng 9(11): 1143–1156
239. Blaschke Z (2000) Evolution of the effectiveness of beneficiation and desulfurization of coal slurries in spiral concentrators. Inzynieria Mineralna 1(2): 33–36
240. Lalvani SB (1989) Coal flotation and flocculation in the presence of humic acids. Final report, January 1–December 31, 1988. DOE/PC/88861-T6; Order No. DE89009573
241. Jessop RR, Stretton JL (1969) Electrokinetic measurements on coal and a criterion for its hydrophobicity. Fuel 48(3): 317–320
242. Yoon RH, Luttrell GH (1995) Advanced froth flotation techniques for fine coal cleaning, Coal Fines: The Unclaimed Fuel. Annual Technical Conference 20th, Clearwater, Fl. March 20–23, 1995: 65–75

243. Meenan GF (1999) Modern coal flotation practices. Advances in flotation technology. Proceedings of the Symposium Advances in Flotation Technology held at the SME Annual Meeting, Denver, March 1–3, 1999: 309–319
244. Li B, Tao D, Ou Z, Liu J (2003) Cyclo-microbubble column flotation of fine coal. Sep Sci Technol 38: 1125–1140
245. Lai R (2002) Cyclonic flotation column for minerals beneficiation. Mining Eng (Littleton, CO, USA) 54: 51–52
246. Honaker RQ, Mohanty MK (1996) Enhanced column flotation performance for fine coal cleaning. Miner Eng 9: 931–945
247. Feris LA, De Leon AT, Santander M, Rubio J (2004) Advances in the adsorptive particulate flotation process. International J Miner Process 74: 101–106
248. Feris LA, Souza ML, Rubio J (2002) Sorption of Heavy Metals on a Coal Beneficiation Tailing Material: II. Adsorptive Particulate Flotation. Coal Prep (London, UK) 22: 235–248
249. Shevchenko TV, Osadchii VL, Yakovchenko MA, Ul'rikh EV (2004) Use of super-high-molecular-weight flocculants in coal beneficiation processes. Khimicheskaya Promyshlennost Segodnya: 38–41
250. Agus M, Carbini P, Ciccu R, Ghiani M (1990) Triboelectric coal cleaning and desulfurization with the turbocharger separator. Coal Sci Technol 16: 311–320
251. Baek SH, Jeon HS, Han OH (2005) Development of new techniques of electrostatic separation for using of clean coal. Chawon Rissaikuring 14: 54–61
252. Ban H, Schaefer JL, Saito K, Stencel JM (1994) Particle tribocharging characteristics relating to electrostatic dry coal cleaning. Fuel 73: 1108–1113
253. Ban H, Schaefer JL, Stencel JM (1993) Size and velocity effects on coal particle triboelectrification and separation efficiency. Proceedings – Annual International Pittsburgh Coal Conference 10th: 138–143
254. Baek SH, Jeon HS, Han OH (2005) Development of new techniques of electrostatic separation for using of clean coal. Chawon Rissaikuring 14: 54–61
255. Finseth D, Newby T, Elstrodt R (1993) Dry electrostatic separation of fine coal. Coal Sci Technol 21: 91–98
256. Lewowski T (1990) Electrostatic desulfurization of hard steam coals. Mater Sci 16: 55–59
257. Masuda S, Toraguchi M, Takahashi T, Haga K (1981) Electrostatic beneficiation of coal using a cyclone-tribocharger. Conference Record – IAS Annual Meeting: 1001–1005
258. Mazumder MK, Tennal KB, Lindquist D (1994) Electrostatic beneficiation of coal. Annual Coal Preparation, Utilization, and Environmental Control Contractors Conference, Proceedings, 10th, Pittsburgh, July 18–21, 1994 1: 111–116
259. Mills O Jr, Chen ZY (1993) Electrostatic coal beneficiation – potential applications and research needs. Proceedings of the International Technical Conference on Coal Utilization & Fuel Systems 18th: 577–589
260. Wang FX (1993) Dry fine coal beneficiation utilizing open-system triboelectrostatic separator. Proceedings – Annual International Pittsburgh Coal Conference 10th: 211–216
261. Klima MS, Polat M, Chander S, Ahuja G (1994) An integration of dense-medium cycloning and froth flotation for fine-coal cleaning. Proceedings – Annual International Pittsburgh Coal Conference 11th: 1267–1272

262. Lathioor RA, Osborne DG (1984) Dense medium cyclone cleaning of fine coal. Hydrocyclones. Pap Int Conf 2nd: 233–252
263. Qi Z (2003) Review on coal cleaning by dense medium cyclone, Xuanmei Jishu: 19–25
264. Turek ML, Klima MS (2003) Dense-medium cycloning of fine coal refuse material. Coal Prep (Philadelphia, PA, USA) 23: 267–284
265. Zalar JL (1983) Evaluation of low gravity dense media cyclone performance in cleaning fine coal. Bitum Coal Res Inc Monroeville, PA, USA
266. Murty MVS, Bhattacharyya D, Aleem MIH (1994) Recent advances in bioprocessing of coal. Biol Degrad Biorem Toxic Chem: 470–492
267. Bos P, Boogerd FC, Gijs KJ (1992) Microbial desulfurization of coal. Environ Microbiol 375–403
268. Khalid AM, Aleem MIH, Kermode RI, Bhattacharrya D (1989) Bioprocessing of coal and oil-water emulsions and microbial metabolism of dibenzothiophene (DBT). Proc – Bioprocess. Fossil Fuels Workshop, CONF-890884--DE90 007955: 55–78
269. Khalid AM, Bhattacharyya D, Hsieh M, Kermode RI, Aleem MIH (1990) Biological desulfurization of coal. Coal Sci Technol 16 (Process Util High-Sulfur Coals 3): 469–480
270. Isbister JD, Wyza RE, Lippold J, DeSouza A, Anspach G (1988) Bioprocessing of coal. Basic Life Sci 45 (Environ Biotechnol): 281–293
271. Olson GJ, Brinckman FE (1986) Bioprocessing of coal. Fuel 65(12): 1638–1646
272. Stambaugh EP (1977) Hydrothermal coal process. ACS Symp Ser 64 (Coal Desulfurization) 198–205
273. Stambaugh EP, Levy A, Giammar RD, Sekhar KC (1976) Hydrothermal coal desulfurization with combustion results. Energy Environ (Dayton) 4: 386–394
274. Wang Z-C, Shui H-F, Zhang D-X, Gao J-S (2006) Effect of hydrothermal treatment on coal properties of Shenhua, China. Ranliao Huaxue Xuebao 34(5): 524–529
275. Ross DS, Hirschon AS, Tse DS, Loo BH (1990) The effects of hydrothermal treatment on Wyodak coal. Preprints of Papers – American Chemical Society, Division of Fuel Chemistry 35(2): 352–363
276. Ito M, Ando T, Yamashita T, Shinozaki S (2001) Removal of alkali and alkaline earth metals for hyper coal production. Sekitan Kagaku Kaigi Happyo Ronbunshu 38th 239–242
277. Smith CD (1979) Coal cleaning by the Otisca Process. Otisca Ind Ltd LaFayette, NY, USA: 623–636
278. Simmons FJ, Keller DV Jr (1984) Heavy-liquid beneficiation of fine coal, Phase II. Final report, OTISCA Ind Ltd Syracuse, NY, USA
279. Keller DV Jr, Simmons FJ (1983) Heavy-liquid beneficiation of fine coal. OTISCA Ind Ltd, Syracuse, NY, USA
280. Keller DV Jr, Simmons FJ (1983) Heavy-liquid beneficiation of fine coal. OTISCA Ind. Ltd Syracuse, NY, USA
281. Chi SM, Morsi BI, Klinzing GE, Chiang SH (1989) LICADO process for fine coal cleaning – mechanism. Coal Prep (London, UK) 6: 241–263
282. Chiang SH, Klinzing GE, He DX, Feng YR, Yu SN, Jenkins K, Diffendal G (1994) Update of the LICADO coal cleaning process. Annual Coal Preparation, Utilization,

and Environmental Control Contractors Conference, Proceedings, 10th, Pittsburgh, July 18–21, 1994 1: 67–74

283. He DX, Araujo G, Morsi B, Klinzng G, Venkatadri R, Chiang SH, Cooper MH (1989) Development of the Licado coal cleaning process. Proceedings – Annual International Pittsburgh Coal Conference 6th: 882–889

284. He DX, Araujo G, Morsi BI, Klinzing GE, Venkatadri R, Chiang SH (1990) Application of Licado process to high-sulfur bituminous coals. Coal Sci Technol 16: 247–253

285. Jenkins KA (1997) Using fuzzy logic and genetic algorithms to model the LICADO separation process (coal): 223

286. Feng YR, He DX, Chiang SH, Klinzing GE, Mulik PR, Yang WC (1994) Further study of the LICADO coal cleaning process. Proceedings-Annual International Pittsburgh Coal Conference 11th: 582–587

287. Cooper MH, Muenchow HO, Chiang SH, Klinzing GE, Morsi B, Venkatadri R (1990) The LICADO coal cleaning process: a strategy for reducing sulfur dioxide emissions from fossil-fueled power plants. Proceedings of the Intersociety Energy Conversion Engineering Conference 25th: 137–142

288. Alonso MI, Valdes AF, Martinez-Tarazona RM, Garcia AB (1999) Coal recovery from coal fines cleaning wastes by agglomeration with vegetable oils: effects of oil type and concentration. Fuel 78: 753–759

289. Bandopadhyay P (1984) Oil agglomeration-the emerging technique for fine coal beneficiation. Urja 16: 377–380, 384

290. Baruah MK, Kotoky P, Baruah J, Bora GC (2000) Cleaning of Indian coals by agglomeration with xylene and hexane. Sep Purif Technol 20: 235–241

291. Capes CE, Coleman RD, Thayer WL (1981) Selective oil agglomeration: an answer to fine coal treatment problems. Coal: Phoenix '80s, Proc. CIC Coal Symp 64th 1: 209–216

292. Carbini P, Ciccu R, Ghiani M, Satta F, Tilocca C (1996) Oil agglomeration using water jets, Changing Scopes in Mineral Processing. Proceedings of the International Mineral Processing Symposium, 6th, Kusadasi, Turk September 24–26, 1996: 693–698

293. Choi WZ, Chung HS, Yang JI, Kim SB (1992) Shear coagulation process for selective upgrading of ultrafine coals. Han'guk Chawon Konghak Hoechi 29: 165–171

294. Honaker RQ, Yoon RH, Luttrell GH (2005) Ultrafine coal cleaning using selective hydrophobic coagulation. Coal Prep (Philadelphia, PA, USA) 25: 81–97

295. Kim S, Morsi BI, Araujo G, Chiang SH, Blachere J, Sharkey A (1991) Effect of grinding conditions on the performance of a selective agglomeration process for physical coal cleaning. Coal Prep (London, UK) 9: 141–153

296. Mang JT, Oder RR (1990) Coal beneficiation by electrostatic coalescence. Coal Sci Technol 16: 341–350

297. Mukherjee DK, Das SK, Sanyal JM, Rudra SR, Choudhury DP, Jha GS, Chattopadhyay PC (1991) An integrated concept for chemical comminution and selective agglomeration of coal. Fuel Sci Technol 10: 113–114

298. Shen M, Wheelock TD (2000) Coal agglomeration with microbubbles. Coal Prep (Gordon & Breach) 21: 277–298

299. Shen M, Wheelock TD (2001) Development and scale-up of a gas-promoted oil agglomeration process for coal beneficiation. Minerals Metallurg Process 18: 87–94

300. Skarvelakis C, Hazi M, Antonini G (1995) Investigations of coal purification by selective oil agglomeration. Sep Sci Technol 30: 2519–2538

301. Song S, Haidari S, Trass O (1995) Flotation of oil-agglomerated coal for ash and py-rite removal. Processing of Hydrophobic Minerals and Fine Coal, Proceedings of the UBC-McGill Bi-Annual International Symposium on Fundamentals of Mineral Proc-essing, 1st, Vancouver, B. C August 20–24, 1995: 223–234

302. Song S, Perkson A, Trass O (1996) Flotation of oil-agglomerated coal for ash and py-rite removal-simultaneous grinding and agglomeration. Proceedings of the Interna-tional Technical Conference on Coal Utilization & Fuel Systems 21st: 339–351

303. Sparks BD, Farnand JR, Capes CE (1982) Agglomerative separations in organic me-dia. J Sep Process Technol 3: 1–15

304. Szymocha K (2003) Industrial applications of the agglomeration process. Powder Technol 130: 462–467

305. Trass O, Bajor O (1984) Improved oil agglomeration process for coal beneficiation. Coal Slurry Combust Int. Symp 6th: 639–648

306. Uenal I, Ersan MG (2007) Factors Affecting the Oil Agglomeration of Sivas-Divrigi Ulucayir Lignite. Energy Sources, Part A: Recovery, Utilization, and Environmental Effects 29: 983–993

307. Yang Q, Liu L, Shi X (2001) Research on the deashing agent during selective oil ag-glomeration. Proceedings – Annual International Pittsburgh Coal Conference 18th: 2891–2897

308. Rahmani AA (1996) Spherical oil agglomeration (SOA)/colloidal gas aphrons (CGA) flotation. Int J Eng 9: 211–220

309. Silva-Stenico ME, Vengadajellum CJ, Janjua HA, Harrison STL, Burton SG, Cowan, DA (2007) Degradation of low rank coal by Trichoderma atroviride ES11. J Indus Mi-crobiol Biotechnol 34(9): 625–631

310. Shimizu K, Kawashima H (1999) Comparison of superacid-catalyzed depolymeriza-tion and thermal depolymerization of bituminous coal-catalysis by superacid HF/BF3 and synthetic pyrite. Energy Fuels 13(6): 1223–1229

311. Shimizu K, Saito I (1998) Depolymerization of subbituminous coal under mild condi-tions in the presence of aromatic hydrocarbon with recyclable superacid HF/BF3. En-ergy Fuels 12(1): 115–119

312. Hofrichter M, Ziegenhagen D, Sorge S, Bublitz F, Fritsche W (1997) Enzymic de-polymerization of low-rank coal (lignite) DGMK Tagungsbericht 9704 Proceedings ICCS '97 3: 1595–1598

313. Hofrichter M, Ziegenhagen D, Sorge S, Ullrich R, Bublitz F, Fritsche W (1999) Deg-radation of lignite (low-rank coal) by ligninolytic basidiomycetes and their manganese peroxidase system. Appl Microbiol Biotechnol 52(1): 78–84

314. Tomita K, Isoda T, Kusakabe K, Morooka S, Hayashi J (1996) Depolymerization of coal by oxidation and alkylation. Sekitan Kagaku Kaigi Happyo Ronbunshu 33rd 323–326

315. Shimizu K, Miki K, Saito I (1997) Superacid-catalyzed depolymerization of several coal model compounds and subbituminous coal : catalysis by trifluoromethanesulfonic acid. Proceedings of the International Technical Conference on Coal Utilization & Fuel Systems 22nd 59–69

316. Sakanishi K, Honda K, Mochida I, Okuma O (1993) Coal pretreatments for deminer-alization and acceleration of depolymerization. Proceedings – Annual International Pittsburgh Coal Conference 10th: 198–203

317. Silva-Stenico ME, Vengadajellum CJ, Janjua HA, Harrison STL, Burton SG, Cowan DA (2007) Degradation of low rank coal by Trichoderma atroviride ES11. J Indus microbiol Biotechnol 34(9): 625–631

318. Hessley RK (1985) Co-oxidative depolymerization of coal. EPRI-AP-4105 Order No. TI85920721

319. Mastral AM, Membrado L, Rubio B (1988) Depolymerization as a pretreatment in coal liquefaction. Proceedings – Annual International Pittsburgh Coal Conference 5th 605–612

320. Shabtai J, Zhang Y, White R (1990) Recent progress in the development of a low-temperature coal depolymerization -liquefaction procedure. Proceedings – Annual International Pittsburgh Coal Conference 7th: 701–708

321. Lalvani SB (1992) Lignin-assisted coal depolymerization: Technical report, December 1, 1991–February 29, 1992. Report DOE/PC/91334-T62; Order No. De92018351

322. Kozlowski M (2001) Two-stage reduction and reductive alkylation of coal using deuterium-labelled modifying agents. Fuel 80(7): 937–943

323. Kozlowski M, Wachowska H, Yperman, J (2003) Composition of extraction products from alkylated high-sulphur coals. Central Eur J Chem 1(4): 366–386

324. Fujimaki T, Kato T, Yoneyama Y (1998) A study on mechanism of coal solubilization by alkylation. Sekitan Kagaku Kaigi Happyo Ronbunshu 35th: 23–26

325. Nosyrev IE, Cagniant D, Gruber R, Fixari B (1997) Influence of chemical treatments on the behavior of a bituminous coal in thermal analyses. Analusis 25(9–10): 313–318

326. Tomita K, Isoda T, Kusakabe K, Morooka S, Hayashi J (1996) Depolymerization of coal by oxidation and alkylation. Sekitan Kagaku Kaigi Happyo Ronbunshu 33rd: 323–326

327. Hayashi J, Kusakabe K, Morooka S (1993) Improvement of coal structure and reactivity by pretreatment. Nippon Enerugi Gakkaishi 72(5): 338–345.

328. Baldwin RM, Kennar DR, Nguanprasert O, Miller RL (1991) Liquefaction reactivity enhancement of coal by mild alkylation and solvent swelling techniques. Fuel 70(3): 429–433

329. Chatterjee K, Miyake M, Stock LM (1990) Coal solubilization through C- alkylation. Preprints of Papers – American Chemical Society, Division of Fuel Chemistry 35(1): 46–50

330. Miller RL, Armstrong ME, Baldwin RM (1989) The effect of mild alkylation pretreatment on liquefaction reactivity of Argonne coals. Preprints of Papers – American Chemical Society, Division of Fuel Chemistry 34(3): 873–880.

331. Stock LM (1987) Coal alkylation and pyrolysis. Preprints of Papers – American Chemical Society, Division of Fuel Chemistry 32(1): 463–470

332. Stefanova MD, Lang I (1986) Fractionation of soluble portion of reductively alkylated bituminous coals. Collection of Czechoslovak Chemical Communications 51(5): 1071–1082

333. Bimer J, Witt I (1985) Reactivity in the reductive alkylation of coal. Koks Smola Gaz 30(1): 9–12

334. Kalra RL, Choudhury R, Sarkar MK (1982) Liquid-phase alkylation of Assam (Baragolai) coal. Fuel 61(12): 1286–1288

335. Miyake M, Uematsu R, Nomura M (1984) High efficacy of ultrasound-promoted reductive alkylation of coal. Chem Lett (4): 535–538.

336. Liotta R, Rose K, Hippo E (1981) O-Alkylation chemistry of coal and its implications for the chemical and physical structure of coal. J Org Chem 46(2): 277–283

337. Schlosberg RH, Neavel RC, Maa PS, Gorbaty ML (1980) Alkylation: a beneficial pretreatment for coal liquefaction. Fuel 59(1): 45–47

338. Baldwin RM, Miller RL (1991) Process and analytical studies of enhanced low severity co-processing using selective coal pretreatment: Final technical report. Report DOE/PC/88812-T15; Order No. DE93004915

339. Shams KG, Miller RL, Baldwin RM (1992) Enhancing low severity coal liquefaction reactivity by using mild chemical pretreatment. Fuel 71(9): 1015–23.

340. Miller RL, Baldwin RM, Nguanprasert O, Kenner DR (1991) Effect of mild chemical pretreatment on liquefaction reactivity of Argonne coals. ACS Symp Ser 461(Coal Sci 2) 260–272

341. Miller RL, Shams K, Baldwin RM (1991) Mild coal pretreatment to enhance liquefaction reactivity. Preprints of Papers – American Chemical Society, Division of Fuel Chemistry 36(1): 1–6

342. Sharma DK (1987) Chemical pretreatment of coals for enhanced solubilization (extractability) and coal pyrolysis. J Sci Indus Res 46(5): 224–229

343. Schlosberg RH, Neavel RC, Maa PS, Gorbaty ML (1980) Alkylation: a beneficial pretreatment for coal liquefaction. Fuel 59(1): 45–47

344. Agun N, Yagmur E, Simsek E, Togrul T (2005) The effect of swelling pretreatment on the coal liquefaction in Tetralin with microwave energy. Energy Sources 27(12): 1105–1115

345. Yokoyama T, Sako T, Gao H, Kidena K, Nomura M, Murata S (2001) The effects of pretreatment on the rate of solvent swelling of single coal particles. Sekitan Kagaku Kaigi Happyo Ronbunshu 38th: 47–50

346. Onal Y, Akol S (2003) Influence of pretreatment on solvent – swelling and extraction of some Turkish lignites. Fuel 82(11): 1297–1304.

347. Bai J, Wang Y, Hu H, Guo S, Chen G (2000) Effect of swelling pretreatment on pyrolysis and liquefaction characteristics of Zalainuer lignite. Meitan Zhuanhua 23(4): 50–54

348. Hu HQ, Sha GY, Guo SC (1997) Swelling pretreatment of coal for improved liquefaction at less severe conditions. DGMK Tagungsbericht 9704 (Proceedings ICCS '97, Volume 3) 1465–1468

349. Pinto F, Gulyurtlu I, Lobo LS, Cabrita I (1999) Effect of coal pre-treatment with swelling solvents on coal liquefaction. Fuel 78(6): 629–634

350. Mae K, Inoue S, Miura K (1996) Flash Pyrolysis of Coal Modified through Liquid Phase Oxidation and Solvent Swelling. Energy Fuels 10(2): 364–70

351. Torres-Ordonez RJ, Quinga EM, Cronauer DC (1993) Solvent and pretreatment effects on coal swelling. Preprints of Papers – American Chemical Society, Division of Fuel Chemistry 38(3): 1039–1044

352. Artok L, Davis A, Mitchell GD, Schobert HH (1992) Swelling pretreatment of coals for improved catalytic liquefaction. Fuel 71(9): 981–991

353. Hulston CKJ, Redlich PJ, Jackson WR, Larkins FP, Marshall M (1997) Hydrogenation of a brown coal pretreated with water-soluble nickel/molybdenum and cobalt/molybdenum catalysts. Fuel 76(14/15): 1465–1469

354. Luo D, Liu J (2005) Organic sulfur removal from coal in alkaline system by electrolysis. Mei Huagong 33(3): 29–31, 62

355. Zhao W, Zhu H, Yan X-h (2003) Organic sulfur removal from coal by copper chloride oxidation and tetrachloroethylene extraction. Ranliao Huaxue Xuebao 31(5): 390–394

356. Li D-x, Gao J-s, Yue G-x, Lu J-f (2002) Mechanism of organic sulfur removal from coal by electrolysis. Ranshao Kexue Yu Jishu 8(5): 421–425
357. Sugawara K, Abe K, Sugawara T (1995) Organic sulfur removal from coal by rapid pyrolysis with alkali leaching and density separation. Coal Sci Technol 24 (Coal Science, Vol. 2): 1709–1712
358. Runnion K, Combie JD (1993) Organic sulfur removal from coal by microorganisms from extreme environments. FEMS Microbiol Rev 11(1–3): 139–144
359. Vishnubhatt P, Lee S (1993) Effect of filtration temperature on organic sulfur removal from coal by perchloroethylene coal cleaning process. Fuel Sci Technol Int 11(8): 1081–1093
360. Vishnubhatt P, Thome T, Lee S (1993) Effect of pyritic sulfur and mineral matter on organic sulfur removal from coal. Fuel Sci Technol Int 11(7): 923–936.
361. Wapner PG, Lalvani SB, Awad G (1988) Organic sulfur removal from coal by electrolysis in alkaline media. Fuel Process Technol 18(1): 25–36
362. Joshi JB, Shah YT (1981) Kinetics of organic sulfur removal from coal by oxydesulfurization. Fuel 60(7): 612–614
363. TRW Space and Technology Group (1985) Development of a microwave coal cleaning process. Energy Div Redondo Beach, CA, USA
364. TRW Space and Technology Group (1986) Development of a microwave coal cleaning process. Appl Technol Div Redondo Beach, CA, USA
365. Kusakabe K, Morooka S, Aso S (1988) Chemical coal cleaning with molten alkali hydroxides in the presence of microwave radiation. Fuel Process Technol 19: 235–242
366. Gunasekaran S, Mutunayagam S (2003) Sulphur reduction in coal by microwave treatment and its spectral analysis. Indian J Environ Protect 23: 188–194
367. Acharya C, Kar RN, Sukla LB (2001) Bacterial removal of sulphur from three different coals, Fuel 80: 2207–2216
368. Gupta A, Saroj KK, Thakur DN (1977) Microbial desulfurization of pyritic coal. Chemical Era 13(8): 238–243
369. Detz CM, Barvinchak G (1979) Microbial desulfurization of coal. Mining Congr J 65(7): 75–82, 86
370. Kargi F, Robinson JM (1982) Microbial desulfurization of coal by thermophilic microorganism Sulfolobus acidocaldarius. Biotechnol Bioeng 24(9): 2115–2121
371. Vaseen VA (1985) Commercial microbial desulfurization of coal. Coal Sci Technol 9 (Process. Util. High Sulfur Coals): 699–715.
372. Isbister JD, Kobylinski EA (1985) Microbial desulfurization of coal. Coal Sci Technol 9 (Process. Util. High Sulfur Coals) 627–641
373. Dugan PR (1986) Microbiological desulfurization of coal and its increased monetary value. Biotechnol Bioeng Symp 16 (Biotechnol. Min. Met.-Refin. Fossil Fuel Process. Ind.) 185–203
374. Kargi F, Weissman JG (1987) Kinetic parameter estimation in microbial desulfurization of coal. Biotechnol Bioeng 30(9): 1063–1066
375. Eligwe CA (1988) Microbial desulfurization of coal. Fuel 67(4): 451–458
376. Hoene HJ, Beyer M, Ebner HG, Klein J, Juentgen H (1987) Microbial desulfurization of coal – development and application of a slurry reactor. Chem Eng Technol 10(3): 173–179
377. Kargi F (1990) Use of Sulfolobus acidocaldarius for microbial desulfurization of coal. Bioprocess Biotreat Coal: 603–605.

378. Ohmura N, Kitamura K, Saiki H (1992) Microbial desulfurization from coal. Bio Indus 9(2): 108–116

379. Ju LK (1992) Microbial desulfurization of coal. Fuel Sci Technol Int 10(8): 1251–1290

380. Bos P, Boogerd FC, Gijs KJ (1992) Microbial desulfurization of coal. Environ Microbiol 375–403

381. Andrews GF, Dugan PR, McIlwain ME, Stevens CJ (1992) Microbial desulfurization of coal. Report EGG-2669; Order No. DE92008975

382. Olsson G, Pott B-M, Larsson L, Holst O, Karlsson HT (1994) Microbial desulfurization of coal by Thiobacillus ferrooxidans and thermophilic archaea. Fuel Process Technol 40(2+3): 277–282

383. Klein J, van Afferden M, Pfeifer F, Schacht S (1994) Microbial desulfurization of coal and oil. Fuel Process Technol 40(2+3): 297–310

384. Larsson L, Olsson G, Karlsson HT, Holst O (1994) Microbial desulfurization of coal with emphasis on inorganic sulfur. Biol Degrad Biorem Toxic Chem 493–505

385. Juszczak A, Domka F, Kozlowski M, Wachowska H (1995) Microbial desulfurization of coal with Thiobacillus ferrooxidans bacteria. Fuel 74(5): 725–728

386. Raman VK, Pandey RA, Bal AS (1995) Reactor systems for microbial desulfurization of coal: an overview. Crit Rev Environ Sci Technol 25(3): 291–312

387. Durusoy T, Bozdemir T, Yurum Y (1999) Recent advances in coal biodesulfurization. Rev Process Chem Eng 2(1): 39–52

388. Najafpour GD, Azizan A, Harun A (2002) Microbial desulfurization of Malaysian coal in batch process using mixed culture. Int J Eng, Trans B: Appl 15(3): 227–234.

389. Acharya C, Sukla LB, Misra VN (2004) Biodepyritisation of coal. J Chem Technol Biotechnol 79(1): 1–12

390. Pandey RA, Raman VK, Bodkhe SY, Handa BK, Bal AS (2004) Microbial desulphurization of coal containing pyritic sulphur in a continuously operated bench scale coal slurry reactor. Fuel 84(1): 81–87

391. Choung J, Mak C, Xu Z (2005) Fine coal beneficiation using an air dense medium fluidized bed. Coal Prep (Philadelphia, PA, USA) 26: 1–15

392. Luo Z, Chen Q (2001) Dry beneficiation technology of coal with an air dense-medium fluidized bed. Int J Miner Process 63: 167–175

393. Luo Z, Zhao Y, Tao X, Fan M, Chen Q, Wei L (2003) Progress in dry coal cleaning using air-dense medium fluidized beds. Coal Prep (Philadelphia, PA, USA) 23: 13–20

394. Honaker RQ, Das A (2004) Ultrafine coal cleaning using a centrifugal fluidized-bed separator. Coal Prep (Philadelphia, PA, USA) 24: 1–18

395. Honaker RQ, Paul BC, Wang D, Huang M (1995) Application of centrifugal washing for fine-coal cleaning. Miner Metallurg Process 12: 80–84

396. Honaker RQ, Paul BC, Wang D, Huang M (1996) Application of centrifugal washing for fine-coal cleaning. Transactions of Society for Mining, Metallurgy, and Exploration, Inc. 298: 80–84/Section 83

397. Oshitani J, Tani K, Takase K, Tanaka Z (2004) Fluidized bed medium separation (FBMS) for dry coal cleaning. Funtai Kogaku Kaishi 41: 334–341

398. Sahan RA (1997) Coal cleaning performance in an air fluidized bed. Energy Sources 19: 475–492

399. Sahan RA, Kozanoglu B (1996) Use of an air fluidized bed separator in a dry coal cleaning process. Energy Conv Manag 38: 269–286

400. Buttermore WH, Slomka BJ, Dawson MR (1988) Sonic enhancement of the physical cleaning of coal. Proceedings – Annual International Pittsburgh Coal Conference 5th: 431–443
401. Fairbanks HV, Morton W, Wallis J (1986) Separation processes aided by ultrasound. Filtration+Separation 23: 236–237
402. Calo JM, Hu X, Logan T, Choi D, Apicello J (2002) Coal cleaning via liquid-fluidized bed classification (LFBC) with selective particle modification. Preprints of Symposia – American Chemical Society, Division of Fuel Chemistry 47: 645–646
403. Calo JM, Hu X, Logan T, Choi D, Apicello J (2003) Coal cleaning via liquid-fluidized bed classification (LFBC) with selective particle modification. J Sep Sci 26: 1429–1435
404. Calo JM, Lilly WD, Hradil G, Mohsen P (1996) Separation of waste plastic particles via liquid-fluidized bed classification (LFBC) Adv Filtrat Sep Technol 10: 399–404
405. Chriswell CD, Kaushik SM, Shah ND, Markuszewski R (1989) Chemical cleaning of coal by molten caustic leaching after pretreatment by low-temperature devolatilization. US Patent 88-24499 4859212
406. Chriswell CD, Shah ND, Markuszewski R (1988) Recovery and regeneration of caustic for use in cleaning of coal by the molten caustic leaching process. Proceedings – Annual International Pittsburgh Coal Conference 5th: 446–459
407. Clements JL, Dadyburjor DB (1991) Hydrotreatment reactions with a disposable catalyst. Fuel 70: 747–751
408. Contos GY, Frankel IF, McCandless LC (1978) Assessment of coal cleaning technology: an evaluation of chemical coal cleaning processes, Versar, Inc Springfield, VA, USA: 299
409. Hart WD (1982) Chemical coal cleaning. USA: 66–75
410. Maijgren B, Huebner W (1983) Coal cleaning by molten caustics. Proc. – Int. Conf. Coal Sci.: 256–259
411. McCormick RL, Jha MC (1995) Effect of Catalyst Impregnation Conditions and Coal Cleaning on Caking and Gasification of Illinois No. 6 Coal. Energy Fuels 9: 1043–1050
412. Meyers RA (1979) Introduction to chemical coal cleaning, TRW Syst Energy, Redondo Beach, CA, USA: 923–933
413. Nowak MA, Meyers RA (1993) Molten-caustic leaching (MCL) process integration. Coal Sci Technol 21: 305–315
414. Oder RR, Murthy BN, McGinnis EL (1983) Chemical coal cleaning assessments at Gulf. Sep SciTechnol 18: 1371–1393
415. Oki T, Owada S, Harada T (1991) Research trend of chemical coal cleaning. Sekitan Riyo Gijutsu Kaigi Koenshu 1st: 147–160
416. Palmer SR, Hippo EJ, Dorai XA (1994) Chemical coal cleaning using selective oxidation. Fuel 73: 161–169
417. Palmer ST (1991) Chemical coal cleaning using selective oxidation. Technical report March 1, 1991–May 31, 1991, South Illinois Univ Carbondale, IL, USA
418. Ruether JA (1979) Chemical coal cleaning. Combustion (New York, 1929) 51: 25
419. Sharma DK, Singh SK (1995) Advanced process for the production of clean coal by chemical leaching technique. Energy Sources 17: 485–493
420. Steel KM, Patrick JW (2003) The production of ultra clean coal by sequential leaching with HF followed by HNO3. Fuel 82: 1917–1920

421. Dwari RK, Rao KH (2007) Dry beneficiation of coal – a review. Miner Process Extract Metallurg Rev 28: 177–234

422. Fan M, Chen Q, Zhao Y, Luo Z (2002) dry coal separation by magnetically stabilized fluidized-bed. Xuanmei Jishu: 6–8

423. Qingru C, Yufen Y (2002) Current status in the development of dry beneficiation technology of coal with air-dense medium fluidized bed in China. Symposium Series – South African Institute of Mining and Metallurgy S29: 429–432

424. Tanaka Z (1986) Dry coal preparation. Nippon Kogyo Kaishi 102: 730–731

425. Tanaka Z (1996) Dry-cleaning coal by fluidized-bed. Kemikaru Enjiniyaringu 41: 218–221

426. Tanaka Z, Oshitani J, Kubo Y (2002) Dry coal cleaning process with fluidized heavy media. Symposium Series – South African Institute of Mining and Metallurgy S29: 425–428

427. Wei L, Chen Q, Zhao Y (2003) Formation of double-density fluidized bed and application in dry coal beneficiation. Coal Prep (Philadelphia, PA, USA) 23: 21–32

428. Kelland DR (1984) Continuous heavy medium recovery by high gradient magnetic separation (HGMS). IEEE Trans Magnet MAG-20: 1180–1182

429. Kelland DR, Dobby GS, Maxwell E (1981) Efficient HGMS for highly magnetic materials. IEEE Transactions on Magnetics MAG-17: 3308–3310

430. Kelland DR, Maxwell E (1978) Improved magnetite recovery in coal cleaning by HGMS. IEEE Trans Magnet MAG-14: 401–403

431. Liu YA, Oak MJ (1983) Studies in magnetochemical engineering. Part III: Experimental applications of a practical model for high-gradient magnetic separation to pilot-scale coal beneficiation. AIChE J 29: 780–789

432. Luo Z-f, Fan M-m, Chen Q-r (2001) Stability of magnetically fluidized bed, Zhongguo Kuangye Daxue Xuebao 30: 350–353

433. Oda T, Kunisue Y, Fujita T, Masuda S (1982) Coal powder beneficiation by dry-type HGMS. Nippon Oyo Jiki Gakkaishi 6: 159–162

434. Oder RR, R.E. Jamison, and E.D. Brandner (2001) Dry coal cleaning with a MagMill. Mining Eng (Littleton, CO, USA) 53: 47–51

435. Oder RR, Jamison RE, Reichner TW, Davis JR (1995) Coal cleaning in a Mag-Mill. Proceedings – Annual International Pittsburgh Coal Conference 12th: 306–311

436. Zhou S, Garbett ES, Boucher RF (1996) Gravity-enhanced magnetic (HGMS) coal cleaning. Indus Eng Chem Res 35: 4257–4263

437. Coal Resource: A Comprehensive Overview of Coal, World Coal Institute. www.worldcoal.org

438. Tennessee Valley Authority (1/9/2009) Coal fired power plant. www.tva.gov/power/coalart.htm

439. Fogelholm C-J, Tuominen M, Saeed LH (1998) Comparison between IGCC and supercritical power plant processes. Proceedings – Annual International Pittsburgh Coal Conference 15th: 66–77.

440. Tagishi A, Nakamura S (2000) Advanced technology on coal-fired power generation systems. Editor(s): Cheng, Ping. Proceedings of Symposium on Energy Engineering in the 21st Century, Hong-Kong, China, January 9–13, 2000 4: 1715–1721

441. Klebes J (2007) High efficiency coal-fired power plant based on proven technology. VGB PowerTech 87(3): 80–84.

442. Gasteiger G, Stamatelopoulos G-N (2002) State-of-the-art and perspectives of coal-fired power plants. Stahl und Eisen 122(5) 29–36.

443. Gorokhov VA, Ramezan M, Ruth LA, Kim SS (1999) Worldwide supercritical power plants: status and future. Proceedings of the International Technical Conference on Coal Utilization & Fuel Systems 24th: 25–37.
444. Blum R, Hald J (1998) High efficiency USC power plant – present status and future potential. VTT Symp 184: 13–27.
445. Tokuda K, Hashimoto A, Fujioka Y, Kaneko S (1998) Progress of advanced coal power plant technology. Mitsubishi Juko Giho 35(6): 378–379.
446. Loh HP, Ruether J, Dye R (1998) Advanced technologies for power generation from coal with reduced carbon dioxide emissions. Greenhouse Gas Mitigation: Technologies for Activities Implemented Jointly, Proceedings of Technologies for Activities Implemented Jointly, Editor(s): Riemer PWF, Smith AY, Thambimuthu KV, Vancouver, BC, May 26–29, 1997: 567–572
447. Muramatsu K (1999) Development of ultra-super critical plant in Japan, Advanced Heat Resistant Steels for Power Generation. Conference Proceedings, Editor(s): Viswanathan R, Nutting JW, San Sebastian Spain, April 27–29, 1998: 543–559.
448. Blum R, Hald J (1998) High efficiency USC power plant – present status and future potential. VTT Symp 184: 13–27.
449. Miyashita K (1997) Overview of advanced steam plant development in Japan. IMechE Conf Trans (2, Advanced Steam Plant) 17–30.
450. Blum HJR, Hald J (1997) Development of high-efficiency USC power plants in Denmark. IMechE Conf Trans (2, Advanced Steam Plant) 3–16
451. Clarke PD, Morris PF, Cardinal N, Worrall MJ (2003) Factors influencing the creep resistance of martensitic alloys for advanced power plant applications. In Parsons 2003: Engineering Issues in Turbine Machinery, Power Plant and Renewables. Strang A, Conroy RD, Banks WM, Blackler M, Leggett J, McColvin GM, Simpson S, Smith M, Starr F, Vanstone RW, Eds. Inst Mater Miner Mining: 333–345
452. Birks N (1995) Selection of materials for advanced heat exchangers. Report to Pittsburgh Energy Technology Center
453. Hottenstine RD (1999) An investigation of the role of super nine material in supercritical plant development. Parsons Infrastructure and Technology Group, Inc Position Paper PZ-401-03
454. Viswanathan R, Bakker WT (2000) Materials for ultra-supercritical fossil power plants. EPRI Report No. TR-114750
455. Kaplan A, Miyazaki A (1986) Advanced 12Cr steel for high-temperature rotors. Proc First EPRI Intl. Conf. on Improved Coal-Fired Power Plants, Electric Power Research Institute, Palo Alto, CA
456. Watanabe O, Ganesh S (1986) High-purity NiCrMoV steel for low-pressure rotors. Proc First EPRI Intl. Conf. on Improved Coal-Fired Power Plants, Electric Power Research Institute, Palo Alto, CA
457. Mayer K-H, Konig H (1986) High-temperature bolting. Proc First EPRI Intl. Conf. on Improved Coal-Fired Power Plants, Electric Power Research Institute, Palo Alto, CA
458. Mayer K-H, Gysel W (1986) Cast components. Proc First EPRI Intl. Conf. on Improved Coal-Fired Power Plants, Electric Power Research Institute, Palo Alto, CA
459. Vanstone R (2000) Advanced 700°C pulverized fuel power plant. In Proc 5th International Charles Parsons Turbine Conference: Parsons 2000: Advanced Materials for 21st Century Turbine and Power Plants. Strang A, Banks WM, Conroy RD, McColvin GM, Neal JC, Simpson S, Eds. IOM Communications, Ltd., London, Book 736: 91–97

460. Viswanathan R (2004) Materials for USC plant—a DOE project update. Proc 29th Int Technical Conference on Coal Utilization & Fuel Systems, National Energy Technology Laboratory

461. Armor AF, Preston GT (1985) A study of coal-fired power plants in Japan. Am Power Conf 47: 72–80

462. Muramatsu K (1999) Development of ultra-supercritical plant in Japan. In Advanced Heat- Resistant Steel for Power Generation, Viswanathan R, Nutting J, Eds, IOM Communications Ltd Book No. 708: 543–559

463. Masuyama F (2001) History of power plants and progress in heat-resistant steels. ISJI Int 41(6): 612–625

464. Viswanathan R, Bakker WT (2001) Materials for ultra-supercritical coal power plants—turbine materials: Part II. J Mater Eng Perform 10(1): 96–101

465. Shingledecker JP, Swindeman RW, Klueh RL, Maziasz PJ (2004) Mechanical properties and analysis of ultra-supercritical steam boiler materials. Proc. 29th Int. Technical Conference on Coal Utilization & Fuel Systems, National Energy Technology Laboratory

466. Harlow JH (1963) Metallurgical experience with the Eddystone 5000lb/in2 1200°F Unit No. 1. In Proc Joint International Conference on Creep. The Institution of Mechanical Engineers, London, Paper No. 10: 7–11–7–20

467. Chamberlain HG (July 1983) The Eddystone experience: an overview of experience in the first twenty-four years. Presented at the EPRI Advanced Pulverized Coal Power Plant Utility Advisory Committee Meeting, Washington, DC

468. Abe F, Horiuchi T, Taneike M, Sawada S (2003) Improvement of creep strength by boron and nanosize nitrides for tempered martensitic 9Cr-3W-3Co-Vnb steel at 650°C. Parsons 2003: Engineering Issues in Turbine Machinery, Power Plant and Renewables, Strang A, Conroy RD, Banks WM, Blackler M, Leggett J, McColvin GM, Simpson S, Smith M, Starr F, Vanstone RW, Eds. Inst Mater Miner Mining: 389–396

469. Muneki S, Okubo H, Okada H, Igarashi M, Abe F (2003) A study of new carbon-free martensitic alloys with superior creep properties at elevated temperatures over 973 K. Parsons 2003: Engineering Issues in Turbine Machinery, Power Plant and Renewables, Strang A, Conroy RD, Banks WM, Blackler M, Leggett J, McColvin GM, Simpson S, Smith M, Starr F, Vanstone RW, Eds. Inst Mater Miner Mining: 570–582.

470. Kure-Jensen J, Morson A, Schilke P (1993) Large steam turbines for advanced steam conditions. In Vol. 1 Proc EPRI Intl Symp on Improved Technology for Fossil Power Plants – New and Retrofit Applications

471. Seth B (1999) U.S. developments in advanced steam turbine materials. In Advanced Heat- Resistant Steel for Power Generation, Viswanathan R, Nutting J, Eds. IOM Communications Ltd Book No. 708: 519–542

472. Staubli ME, Mayer K-H, Kern TU, Vanstone RW (2000) COST 501–522: The European collaboration in advanced steam turbine materials for ultra-efficient, low-emissions steam power plant. In Proc 5th International Charles Parsons Turbine Conference: Parsons 2000 Advanced Materials for 21st Century Turbine and Power Plants, Strang A, Banks WM, Conroy RD, McColvin GM, Neal JC, Simpson S, Eds. IOM Communications, Ltd, London, Book 736: 98–122

473. Mayer K-H, Kern TU, Staubli ME, Tolksdorf E (2000) Long-term investigation of specimens of 24 production components manufactured from advanced martensitic 10%Cr steels for 600°C turbines. In Proc 5th International Charles Parsons Turbine Conference: Parsons 2000 Advanced Materials for 21st Century Turbine and Power

Plants, Strang A, Banks WM, Conroy RD, McColvin GM, Neal JC, Simpson S, Eds. IOM Communications, Ltd, London, Book 736: 372–385

474. Blum R, Vanstone RW (2003) Materials development for boilers and steam turbines operating at 700°C. In Parsons 2003: Engineering Issues in Turbine Machinery, Power Plant and Renewables, Strang A, Conroy RD, Banks WM, M. Blackler, J. Leggett, G.M. McColvin, S. Simpson, M. Smith, F. Starr, and R.W. Vanstone, Eds. Maney for the Inst. of Materials, Minerals, and Mining: 489–510

475. Maziasz PJ, Pollard M (2003) High-temperature cast stainless steel. Adv Mater Process 161: (10) 57

476. Knödler R, Scarlin B (2002) Oxidation of advanced ferritic/martensitic steels and of coatings in flowing steam at 650°C. In Proc. Materials for Adv Power Eng 2002, Lecomte- Beckers J, Carton M, Schubert F, Ennis PJ. Eds. Forschungszentrum Julich GmbH: 1601–1611

477. Mayer K-H (1992) New materials for advanced steam turbines. Volume 5 of Survey of Superalloy Bolt Failures in High-temperature Service, EPRI Report No. TR100979

478. Hidaka K, Shiga M, Nakamura S, Fukui Y, Shimizu N, Kaneko R, Watanabe Y, Fujita T (1994) Development of 12Cr steel for 650°C USC steam turbine rotors. In Materials for Advanced Power Engineering 1994, Coutsouradis D, Davidson JH, Ewald J, Greenfield P, Khan T, Malik M, Meadowcroft DB, Regis V, Scarlin RB, Schubert F, Thornton DV, Eds. Kluwer: 281–290

479. Thornton DV, Meyer K-H (1994) European high-temperature materials development for advanced steam turbine. In Materials for Advanced Power Engineering, Coutsouradis D, Davidson JH, Ewald J, Greenfield P, Khan T, Malik M, Meadowcroft DB, Regis V, Scarlin RB, Schubert F, Thornton DV, Eds. Kluwer: 349–364

480. Miyazaki M, Yamada M, Tsuda Y, Ishii R (1994) Advanced heat-resistant steels for steam turbines. In Materials for Advanced Power Engineering, Coutsouradis D, Davidson JH, Ewald J, Greenfield P, Khan T, Malik M, Meadowcroft DB, Regis V, Scarlin RB, Schubert F, Thornton DV, Eds. Kluwer: 574–585

481. Distefano JR, DeVan JH, Fuller LC (1988) Assessment of materials requirements for advanced steam cycle systems (>1100°F). ORNL Report No. TM-10489

482. Pint BA, Rakowski JM (2000) Effect of water vapor on the oxidation resistance of stainless steels. Paper No. 00259, NACE/Corrosion 2000, Orlando, Florida

483. Woodford DA (1993) Test methods for accelerated development, design, and life assessment of high temperature materials. Mater Design 14(4): 231

484. Viswanathan R, Coleman K, Rao U (2006) Materials for ultra – supercritical coal-fired power plant boilers. Int J Pressure Vessels Piping 83(11–12): 778–783

485. Viswanathan R, Sarver J, Tanzosh JM (2006) Boiler materials for ultra – supercritical coal power plants -steam-side oxidation. J Mater Eng Perform 15(3): 255–274

486. Caminada S, Cumino G, Cipolla L, Di Gianfrancesco A (2005) Long term creep behaviour and microstructural evolution of ASTM grade 91 steel. Advances in Materials Technology for Fossil Power Plants, Proceedings from the International Conference, 4th, Hilton Head Island, SC, USA, October 25–28, 2004: 1071–1085

487. Viswanathan R, Henry JF, Tanzosh J, Stanko G, Shingledecker J, Vitalis B, Purgert R (2005) U.S. program on materials technology for ultra – supercritical coal power plants. J Mater Eng Perform 14(3): 281–292

488. Chen Q, Scheffknecht G (2003) New boiler and piping materials design. Consideration for advanced cycle conditions. VGB PowerTech 83(11): 91–98

489. Knezevic V, Sauthoff G, Vilk J, Inden G, Schneider A, Agamennone R, Blum W, Wang Y, Scholz A, Berger C, Ehlers J, Singheiser L (2002) Martensitic/ferritic super heat-resistant 650°C steels-design and testing of model alloys. ISIJ Int 42(12): 1505–1514

490. Advanced power plant using high efficiency boiler/turbine www.dti.gov.uk/files/file30703. pdf

491. The World Bank. www.worldbank.org/html/fpd/em/supercritical/supercritical.htm

492. Abroell GH, Bade K, Bietz H, Jahn P (1991) Largest fluidized-bed combustion power plant unit for electricity and heat supply in Berlin. VGB Kraftwerkstechnik 71: 1020–1030

493. Ahr O (1993) Successful operation of the atmospheric circulating fluidized-bed firing system of the Emile Huchet power plant. VGB Kraftwerkstechnik 73: 446–449

494. Anders R, Plass L, Beisswenger H (1989) Clean energy by Lurgi circulating fluidized-bed combustion (ZWS) technology. Industriefeuerung 48: 34–38

495. Basu P (2001) Revamping of a 120 MWe pulverized coal fired boiler with circulating fluidized bed firing. Proceedings of the International Conference on Fluidized Bed Combustion 16th: 881–891

496. Dreher I (1990) Two chosen circulating fluidized-bed combustors of power station boilers. Brennstoff-Waerme-Kraft (1949–1999) 42: 493–494, 497–498, 501–492

497. Forster M, Krumm W (1999) Theoretical investigations on the operational behavior of circulating pressurized fluidized bed combustion. VDI-Berichte 1492: 159–165

498. Furuya O, Takayama K (2000) Outline of circulating fluidized bed combustion boiler and improvement on steam cycle. Boira Kenkyu 299: 13–18

499. Girard R, Semedard JC (1988) Circulating fluidized bed combustion at the Emile Huchet power plant. Revue Generale de Thermique 27: 111–114

500. Glasmacher-Remberg C, Fett FN (1999) A dynamic simulation model for power plants with atmospheric and pressurized circulating fluidized bed combustion – interactions of plant components and design studies. Proceedings of the International Conference on Fluidized Bed Combustion 15th: 1429–1452

501. Hafke C, Plass L, Bierbach H (1988) Power stations based on circulating fluidized bed combustion. Chemie Ingenieur Technik 60: 686–690

502. Isaka H, Hyvarinen KH, Morita A, Yano K, Ooide M (1989) Conceptual design of a 350-MWe circulating fluidized-bed power generating plant. Proceedings of the International Conference on Fluidized Bed Combustion 10th: 783–791

503. Jarboe TB, Wen H (1988) Circulating fluidized-bed power plants offer improved technology for burning low-grade coals. Mining Engineering (Littleton, CO, USA) 40: 1021–1023

504. Jukkola G, Liljedahl G, ya Nsakala N, Morin JX, Andrus H (2005) An ALSTOM vision of future CFB technology based power plant concepts. Proceedings of the International Conference on Fluidized Bed Combustion 18th: 109–120

505. McIlveen-Wright D, Pinto RF, Armesto L, Caballero MA, Aznar MP, Cabanillas A, Huang Y, Franco C, Gulyurtlu I, McMullan JT (2006) A comparison of circulating fluidized bed combustion and gasification power plant technologies for processing mixtures of coal. biomass and plastic waste, Fuel Process Technol 87: 793–801

506. Nag PK, Raha D (1995) Thermodynamic analysis of a coal-based combined-cycle power plant. Heat Recover Syst CHP 15: 115–129

507. Nielsen PT, Hebb JL, Aquino R (1998) Large-scale CFB combustion demonstration project. Proceedings of the International Technical Conference on Coal Utilization & Fuel Systems 23rd: 23–34

508. Nowak W (1997) Fluidized-bed coal combustion. Part III. Steam power plants with pressurized fluidized-bed boilers. Gospodarka Paliwami i Energia 45: 2–10

509. Oakes EJ, Swartz KF (1988) Circulating fluidized bed combustion technology achieves commercial status – Colorado-Ute and Mt. Poso cogeneration company. Energy Technology 15: 83–92

510. Plass L, Daradimos G, Beisswenger H, Lienhard H (1986) Concepts and experience in the operation of power plants with circulating fluidized bed combustion. VGB Kraftwerkstechnik 66: 801–807

511. Plass L, Daradimos G, Lienhard H (1985) Power plants with circulating fluidized-bed combustion. Plant designs and operating experience, VDI-Berichte 574: 125–143

512. Rajaram S (1999) Next generation CFBC. Chem Eng Sci 54: 5565–5571

513. Rajaram S (1999) Design features and operating experience of circulating fluidized bed boilers firing high ash coals in India. Proceedings of the International Conference on Fluidized Bed Combustion 15th: 832–844

514. Reddy DN, Sethi VK (2006) Refurbishment of an old PC boiler confronted with coal quality degradation by a CFBC boiler – a case study. Proceedings – Annual International Pittsburgh Coal Conference 23rd: 33 34/31–33 34/15

515. Schafer J, Renz U, Paul S (1999) Mathematical modeling of a circulating fluidized bed steam generator with the objective of a real-time simulation. VGB Kraftwerkstechnik 79: 48–53

516. Stamatelopoulos G-N, Seeber J (2005) Fluidized-bed technology for the capacity range 400 to 600 MWe. VGB PowerTech 85: 38–43

517. Wein WH, Hoeffgen K, Maintok H, Daradimos G (1982) Steam generator with circulating atmospheric fluidized-bed combustion. Stadtwerke Duisburg A.-GDuisburg Fed Rep Ger

518. Bockamp S (2002) Dynamic operating behavior of combined cycle power plants with circulating pressurized fluidized bed firing. Fortschritt-Berichte VDI, Reihe 6: Energietechnik 478: i–iii, v–xiv, 1–204

519. Bockamp S, Krumm W (2001) Studies regarding dynamic load change behavior of a combined cycle power plant based on pressurized fluidized bed combustion with the aid of a simulation model. VDI-Berichte 1629: 161–171

520. Chalupnik RW, Krautz HJ, Schulze H, Stuhlmuller F, Thielen W (1999) Plant studies and experiments for a lignite-fired combined-cycle power plant using circulating pressurized fluidized bed combustion. Proceedings of the International Conference on Fluidized Bed Combustion 15th: 1409–1428

521. Derdiger JA, Saliga JJ, Koza H (1985) An assessment of modularized turbocharged PFBC plants. Proceedings of the American Power Conference 47: 96–103

522. Forster M, Bockamp S, Krumm W (2000) Mathematical modelling of pressurized fluidized bed systems – simulation of a combined cycle power plant. Recents Progres en Genie des Procedes 14: 559–567

523. Hashimoto H (1998) Development of a pressurized internally circulating fluidized-bed boiler and its further development for a gasifier, Dennetsu Kenkyu 37: 54–59

524. Heinbockel I, Fett FN (1995) Simulation of a combined cycle power plant based on a pressurized circulating fluidized bed combustor, Heat Recov Syst CHP 15: 171–178

525. Holley EP, Lewnard JJ, Richardson KW, von Wedel G, Domeracki WF, Carpenter LK (1994) Demonstration of the advances pressurized circulating fluid bed combustion process at the Four Rivers Project, Proceedings – Annual International Pittsburgh Coal Conference 11th: 1334–1339

526. Holley EP, Lewnard JJ, von Wedel G, Richardson KW, Morehead HT (1995) Four rivers second generation pressurized circulating fluidized bed combustion project, Proceedings of the International Conference on Fluidized Bed Combustion 13th: 919–924

527. Krautz HJ, Schierack F, Wirtz M, Priesmeier U (2003) Initial operation of the test facility with pressurized circulating fluidized bed combustion 2. Generation and experimental results in Cottbus, VDI-Berichte 1750: 87–92

528. McKinsey RR, Wheeldon JM, Brown RA (1996) Preliminary results of an engineering and economic evaluation of Lurgi-Lentjes-Babcock's circulating PFBC power plant design, Proceedings – Annual International Pittsburgh Coal Conference 13th: 261–266

529. Weinstein RE, Tonnemacher GC (1999) APFBC repowering could help meet Kyoto Protocol CO2 reduction goals, Proceedings of the International Technical Conference on Coal Utilization & Fuel Systems 24th: 873–884

530. O'Donnell JJ (1990) A combined cycle power plant based on pressurized circulating fluid bed gasification and combustion. Proceedings – Annual International Pittsburgh Coal Conference 7th: 879–889

531. Schierack F, Krautz HJ (2001) Development of a new brown coal fired combined-cycle power plant using CPFBC. 2nd generation, Proceedings – Annual International Pittsburgh Coal Conference 18th: 1352–1362

532. Weinstein RE, Goldstein HN, White JS, Travers RW, Killen DC, Tonnemacher GC (1997) Repowering an existing steam plant with advanced circulating pressurized fluidized bed combustion (APFBC). Proceedings of the International Conference on Fluidized Bed Combustion 14th: 551–559

533. Wheeldon JM, Bonsu AK, Foote JP, Morton FC, Romans DE, Zoldak FD, Longanbach JR, McClung JD, Lock DT (2001) Commissioning of the circulating PFBC in the Foster Wheeler advanced PFBC train at the PSDF. Proceedings of the International Conference on Fluidized Bed Combustion 16th: 1466–1485

534. Amick P, Geosits R, Herbanek R, Kramer S, Tam S (2002) A large coal IGCC power plant. Proceedings – Annual International Pittsburgh Coal Conference 19th: 436–463

535. Amick P, Geosits R, Herbanek R, Kramer S, Tam S (2003) An advanced IGCC coal power plant, Proceedings – Annual International Pittsburgh Coal Conference 20th: 410–430 (2003)

536. Anand A, May P, Wotzak G, Jandrisevits M, Yackly K (2005) Gas turbine cycle optimization for an IGCC plant, Proceedings – Annual International Pittsburgh Coal Conference 22nd: 188/181-188/114 (2005)

537. Banda BM, Evans TF, Thompson BH, Vierrath H (1985) Assessment of an IGCC power plant using British Gas/Lurgi gasifier. Proceedings of the American Power Conference 47: 244–249

538. Chen C-s, Chiu Y-p, Tsai Y-h, Huang C-c, Chen W-c, Chen B-c (2007Development status of integrated gasification combined cycle (IGCC) power plant. Nengyuan Jikan 37: 83–92

539. Freier MD, Jewell DM, Motter JW, Pinon P (1996) An advanced IGCC demonstration. Proceedings of the American Power Conference 58: 363–368

540. Frey HC, Zhu Y (2006) Improved System Integration for Integrated Gasification Combined Cycle (IGCC) Systems. Environ Sci Technol 40: 1693–1699

541. Hu T-X, Zhang B-S, Xu G-S, Ai C-S (2003) General development of integral gasification combined cycle (IGCC) technology, Heilongjiang Dianli 25: 50–55

542. Imamoto T, Suzaki M, Shinada O, Ikegami T, Koyama T (2002) Development of integrated coal gasification combined cycle (IGCC) Mitsubishi Juko Giho 39: 124–127
543. Khan SR, Wayland RJ, Schmidt LJ (2005) Environmental impact comparisons IGCC vs. PC plants. Proceedings – Annual International Pittsburgh Coal Conference 22nd: 176/171–176/117
544. Korobov D (2003)Study of the efficiency potentials of IGCC power plant concepts. Freiberger Forschungshefte A A876: i–vi, 1–210
545. Korobov D, Ogriseck S, Meyer B (2005) Investigation of new IGCC concepts with high efficiency. Proceedings – Annual International Pittsburgh Coal Conference 22nd: 64/61–64/20
546. Marion JL, Liljedahl GN, Black S (2004) A review of the state-of-the-art and a view of the future for combustion-based coal power generation, Proceedings of the International Technical Conference on Coal Utilization & Fuel Systems 29th: 601–612
547. Mirolli MD, Doering EL (1998) ASME PTC 47- IGCC performance testing: gasification island thermal performance testing. PWR (American Society of Mechanical Engineers) 33: 377–381
548. Nagai T, Kajitani S (2007) Development of IGCC demonstration plant – from 200 t/d pilot plant to 250 mw demonstration plant. J Jpn Inst Energy 86: 315–320
549. Nizamoff AJ, Kramer S, Lau FS, Olson S, Roberts M, Tam S, Zabransky R (2005) Lignite-fueled IGCC power plant. Proceedings – Annual International Pittsburgh Coal Conference 22nd: 173/171–173/118
550. Predick P, Rice D, Lauzze K (2006) Comparison of IGCC and pulverized coal technologies, Annual Convention Proceedings – Gas Processors Association 85th: predick paul1/1-predick paul1/17
551. Schellberg W (1998First results of the PRENFLO based IGCC power plant in Puertollano/Spain. Proceedings – Annual International Pittsburgh Coal Conference 15th: 455–463
552. Seliger B, Hanke-Rauschenbach R, Hannemann F, Sundmacher K (2006) Modelling and dynamics of an air separation rectification column as part of an IGCC power plant. Sep Purif Technol 49: 136–148
553. Stahl K, Neergaard M (1999) Experiences from the Varnamo IGCC Demonstration Plant. VTT Symp 192: 73–86
554. Belova AG, Yegulalp TM (2007) Thermodynamic optimization of hydrogen production for a coal-based power plant with zero emissions. Transactions of Society for Mining, Metallurgy, and Exploration, Inc. 320: 6–10.
555. Bancalari Ed, Chan P, Diakunchak IS (2006) Advanced hydrogen turbine development. Proceedings – Annual International Pittsburgh Coal Conference 23rd: 29.2/1–29.2/16.
556. Corrado A, Fiorini P, Sciubba E (2006) Environmental assessment and extended exergy analysis of a "zero CO_2 emission", high-efficiency steam power plant. Energy (Oxford, UK) 31(15): 3186–3198.
557. Verma A, Rao AD, Samuelsen GS (2006) Sensitivity analysis of a Vision 21 coal based zero emission power plant. J Power Source 158(1): 417–427.
558. Lackner KS, Yegulalp T (2005) Thermodynamic foundation of the zero emission concept. Miner Metallurg Process 22(3): 161–167.
559. Giove J III, Daniels, J, Der VK (2004) FutureGen zero emission power plant of the future. Proceedings – Annual International Pittsburgh Coal Conference 21st 38.1/1–38.1/11.

560. Rao AD, Samuelsen GS, Yi Y (2005) Gas turbine based high-efficiency 'Vision 21' natural gas and coal central plants. Proceedings of the Institution of Mechanical Engineers, Part A: J Power Energy 219(A2): 127–136

561. Martinez-Frias J, Aceves SM, Smith JR, Brandt H (2003) A coal-fired power plant with zero atmospheric emissions. AES (American Society of Mechanical Engineers) 43 (Proceedings of the ASME Advanced Energy Systems Division – 2003): 411–422

562. Koehler D, Krammer T, Schwaerzer M (2003) Zero emission coal process. BWK 55(3): 63–66

563. Ruth LA (2003) Advanced clean coal technology in the USA. Mater High Temp 20(1): 7–14

564. Schreurs HCE (2002) Potential for CO2-sequestration in the Netherlands. Proceedings – Annual International Pittsburgh Coal Conference 19th : 724–742

565. Anderson RE, Brandt H, Pronske K, Viteri F (2002) Near-term potential for power generation from coal with zero atmospheric emissions. Proceedings of the International Technical Conference on Coal Utilization & Fuel Systems 27th 1: 51–62

566. Anderson RE, Brandt H, Viteri F (2001) Power generation from coal with zero atmospheric emissions. Proceedings – Annual International Pittsburgh Coal Conference 18th: 940–951

567. Ziock H-J, Lackner KS, Harrison DP (2001) Zero Emission Coal power, a new concept. http://www.netl.doe.gov/publications/proceedings/01/carbon_seq/2b2.pdf

568. Ziock H-J, Lackner KS (1998–2000) Zero-emission coal technology. Earth and Environmental Sciences Progress Report 1998–2000: 52–55

569. Lozza G, Romano M (1/12/2008) A thermodynamic study of a novel zero emission power plant, based on hydrogasification of coal. http://www.ieacoal.org.uk/publishor/system/component_view.asp?LogDocId=81714&PhyDocId=6369

570. Meyers RA (1977) Coal Desulfurization. Marcel Dekker

571. Xu L, Zou D, Cheng Y (2006) Study on removal of organic sulfur in coal with n-propanol. Meitan Zhuanhua 29(4): 13–16

572. Zhao W, Zhu H, Yan X-h (2003) Organic sulfur removal from coal by copper chloride oxidation and tetrachloroethylene extraction. Ranliao Huaxue Xuebao 31(5): 390–394

573. Zhao J, Zhang Y, Wang H, Chen Q (2002) Desulfurization of high organic sulfur coal by tetrachloroethylene extraction. Meitan Zhuanhua 25(1): 48–51

574. Mukherjee S, Mahiuddin S, Borthakur PC (2001) Demineralization and desulfurization of subbituminous coal with hydrogen peroxide. Energy Fuels 15(6): 1418–1424

575. Ratanakandilok S, Ngamprasertsith S, Prasassarakich P (2001) Coal desulfurization with methanol/water and methanol/KOH. Fuel 80(13): 1937–1942

576. Wang G, Trass O (1997) Coal beneficiation-sulfur removal using methanol. Proceedings of the International Technical Conference on Coal Utilization & Fuel Systems 22nd: 513–520

577. Lee S, Kulik C (1996) A novel precombustion coal desulfurization process. Recent Adv Coal Process 1 (New Trends in Coal Preparation Technologies and Equipment): 293–298, 306–307

578. Tartamella T, Fullerton K, Lee S, Fish R (1996) Ligand assisted desulfurization of lignite using the perchloroethylene coal refining process. Fuel Sci Technol Int 14(4): 503–509

579. Thome TL, Fullerton KL, Lee S (1994) Design and operation of a mini-pilot plant for the removal of sulfur from coal using the perchloroethylene process. Proceedings – Annual International Pittsburgh Coal Conference 11th 2: 1075–1080

580. Azzam FO, Lee S (1993) A comparison of alcohol-water blends in their supercritical desulfurization efficiency of Midwestern U.S. bituminous coals. Fuel Sci Technol Int 11(7): 951–73

581. Vishnubhatt P, Lee S (1993) Perchloroethylene extraction desulfurization of low sulfate coals. Fuel Sci Technol Int 11(3–4): 529–39

582. Chou MIM, Lytle JM, Ruch RR, Kruse CW, Chaven C, Hackley KC, Hughes RE, Harvey RD, Frost JK (1992) Sulfur removal from high-sulfur Illinois coal by low-temperature perchloroethylene (PCE) extraction. Technical report, December 1, 1991– February 29, 1992, NTIS. Report (DOE/PC/91334-T57; Order No. DE92018296)

583. Lee S, Vishnubhatt P, Kulik CJ (1994) Selective removal of organic sulfur from coal by trichloroethane extraction. Fuel Sci Technol Int 12(2): 211–28

584. Attia YA, Lei W (1987) Removal of organic sulfur from high sulfur coals by mild chemical oxidation using potassium permanganate. Editor(s): Chugh YP, Caudle RD. Process Util High Sulfur Coals, Proc Int Conf 2nd: 202–12

585. Muchmore CB, Chen JW, Kent AC, Liszka M (1987) Removal of organic sulfur from coal by sequential treatment with alcohols. Coal Sci Technol 11(Int Conf Coal Sci: 439–42

586. Muchmore CB, Chen JW, Kent AC, Tempelmeyer KE (1985) Removal of organic sulfur from coal by supercritical extraction with alcohols, Preprints of Papers – American Chemical Society, Division of Fuel Chemistry 30(2): 24–34.

587. Muchmore CB, Chen JW, Kent AC, Tempelmeyer KE (1986) Removal of organic sulfur from coal by reaction with supercritical alcohols. ACS Symp Ser 319 (Fossil Fuels Util.): 75–85.

588. Azzam FO, Fullerton KL, Kesavan S, Lee S (1992) Supercritical extraction of organosulfur from coal using acetone-water mixtures. Fuel Sci Technol Int 10(3): 347–69.

589. Azzam FO, Lee S (1993) A comparison of alcohol-water blends in their supercritical desulfurization efficiency of Midwestern U.S. bituminous coals. Fuel Sci Technol Int 11(7): 951–73.

590. Louie PKK, Timpe RC, Hawthorne SB, Miller DJ (1994) Sulfur removal from coal by analytical-scale supercritical fluid extraction (SFE) under pyrolysis conditions. Fuel 73(7): 1173–1178

591. Kawatra SK, Eisele TC (2001) Coal desulfurization high efficiency preparation methods. Taylor & Francis

592. Sun L-B, Zong Z-M, Kou J-H, Yu G-Y, Chen H, Liu C-C, Zhao W, Wei X-Y, Lee CW, Xie K-C, Li C-Q, Takanohashi T, Li L-Y (2005) Thermal release and catalytic removal of organic sulfur compounds from upper free port coal. Energy Fuels 19: 339–342

593. Sugawara T, Sugawara K (1991) Desulfurization from solid phase by rapid hydropyrolysis of coal. Sekiyu Gakkaishi 34: 500–509

594. Sugawara K, Sugawara T, Shirai M (1999) Sulfur behavior in rapid pyrolysis of coals with chemical pretreatments, Japanese Journal of Applied Physics, Part 1: Regular Papers, Short Notes & Review Papers 38: 608–611

595. Sugawara K, Abe K, Sugawara T (1995) Organic sulfur removal from coal by rapid pyrolysis with alkali leaching and density separation. Coal Sci Technol 24: 1709–1712

596. Hippo EJ (1991) Mild pyrolysis of selectively oxidized coals. Technical report September 1–November 30, 1991 Energy Process South Illinois Univ Carbondale, IL, USA

597. Gryglewicz G (1996) Effectiveness of high temperature pyrolysis in sulfur removal from coal. Fuel Process Technol 46: 217–226
598. Chen H, Li B, Zhang B (2000) Decomposition of pyrite and the interaction of pyrite with coal organic matrix in pyrolysis and hydropyrolysis. Fuel 79: 1627–1631
599. Joshi JB, Shah YT (1981) Kinetics of organic sulfur removal from coal by oxydesulfurization. Fuel 60: 612–614
600. Palmer SR, Hippo EJ, Dorai XA (1994) Chemical coal cleaning using selective oxidation. Fuel 73: 161–169
601. Jorjani E, Rezai B, Vossoughi M, Osanloo M, Abdollahi M (2004) Oxidation pretreatment for enhancing desulfurization of coal with sodium butoxide. Miner Eng 17: 545–552
602. Zhao JC, Hu WD, Long YH, Gao JS (1994) Study on the coal desulfurization by dilute alkali/acid treatment and its mechanism. Fuel Sci Technol Int 12: 1183–1191
603. Xiong F, Li W, Jiang Y (1993) Desulfurization of coal using molten caustic leaching. Meitan Zhuanhua 16: 67–75
604. Prassassarakich P, Thaweesri T (1996) Kinetics of coal desulfurization with sodium benzoxide. Fuel 75: 816–820
605. Mukherjee S, Borthakur PC (2001) Chemical demineralization/desulphurization of high sulphur coal using sodium hydroxide and acid solutions. Fuel 80: 2037–2040
606. Mukherjee S (2003) Demineralization and desulfurization of high-sulfur assam coal with alkali treatment. Energy Fuels 17: 559–564
607. Li W, Cho EH (2005) Coal desulfurization with sodium hypochlorite. Energy Fuels 19: 499–507
608. Zhang X, Su X, Ding Y, Wang S, Tao X (2005) Mechanism and strategy of biodesulfurization by chemoautotrophic Thiobacillus. Xiandai Huagong 25: 7–10
609. Runnion K, Combie JD (1993) Organic sulfur removal from coal by microorganisms from extreme environments. FEMS Microbiol Rev 11: 139–144
610. Otaka Y (1993) Microbial removal of organic sulfur from coal. Nippon Enerugi Gakkaishi 72: 142–150
611. Olsson G, Larsson L, Holst O, Karlsson HT (1993) Kinetics of coal desulfurization by Acidianus brierleyi. Chemical Eng Technol 16: 180–185
612. Kurane R (1993) Biodesulfurization of hard-to-remove organic sulfur compounds by microorganism under microaerobic condition. Nippon Enerugi Gakkaishi 72: 151–157
613. Kilbane JJ II (1990) Microbial removal of organic sulfur from coal: current status and research needs. Bioprocess Biotreat Coal: 487–506
614. Kargi F, Robinson JM (1986) Removal of organic sulfur from bituminous coal. Use of the thermophilic organism Sulfolobus acidocaldarius. Fuel 65: 397–399
615. Hossain SKM, Anantharaman N (2005) Biodesulfurization of coal using Thiobacillus ferrooxidans strain M-1. Chem Eng World 40: 101–104
616. Hossain SKM, Das M, Anantharaman N (2004) Studies of biodesulfurization of coal using thiobacillus ferrooxidans. Process Plant Eng 22: 85–88
617. He D-W, Liang Y-J, Chai L-Y, Wang Y-Y, Jin Y, Peng B (2006) Desulphurization of coal by fungus. Advanced Processing of Metals and Materials, Sohn International Symposium, Proceedings, San Diego, CA, USA, August 27–31 2: 163–170
618. Gullu G, Durusoy T, Ozbas T, Tanyolac A, Yurum Y (1992) Biodesulfurization of coal. NATO ASI Series. Ser C: Math Phys Sci 370: 185–205

619. Fecko P, Sitavancova Z, Cvesper L, Koval L (2006) Application of bacteria thiobacillus ferrooxidans by desulphurization of coal. Proceedings – Annual International Pittsburgh Coal Conference 23rd: 48 42/41–48 42/44
620. ElSawy A, Gray D (1991) A critical review of biodesulfurization systems for removal of organic sulfur from coal. Fuel 70: 591–594
621. Boyer YN, Crooker SC, Kitchell JP, Nochur SV (1991) Enzymatic desulfurization of coal. Final report Revision Dyna Gen Inc Cambridge, MA, USA
622. Acharya C, Kar RN, Sukla LB (2004) Microbial desulfurization of different coals. Appl Biochem Biotechnol 118: 47–63
623. Mobley JD, Dickerman JC (1984) Commercial utility flue gas desulfurization systems. US Environmental Protection Agency, Washington, DC, EPA/600/J-84/084. Mech Eng 106(7): 62–71
624. Srivastava RK (2000) Controlling SO2 emissions: a review of technologies. US Environmental Protection Agency, Washington, DC, EPA/600/R-00/093 (NTIS PB2001-101224)
625. Wet Flue Gas Desulfurization (FGD) www.worldbank.org/html/fpd/em/power/EA/mitigatn/aqsowet.stm
626. US Environmental Protection Agency. Lesson 9 Flue Gas Desulfurization (Acid Gas Removal) Systems. yosemite.epa.gov/oaqps/EOGtrain.nsf/fabbfcfe2fc93dac85256afe00483cc4/d4ec501f07c0e03a85256b6c006caf64/$FILE/si412c_lesson9.pdf
627. IEA Clean Coal centre. Clean Coal Technologies, Flue gas desulfurization (FGD) for SO2 control. www.iea-coal.org.uk/site/ieacoal/home
628. Anderson K, Barrier J, O'Brien W, Tomlinson S (1981) Definitive SOx control process evaluations: limestone, lime, and magnesia FGD processes. US Environmental Protection Agency, Washington, DC, EPA/600/7-80/001
629. Black & Veatch Consulting Engineers (1983) Lime FGD Systems Data Book. 2nd ed. EPRI, Publication No. CS-2781
630. Hance SB, Kelly JL (1991) Status of flue gas desulfurization systems. Paper presented at the 84th Annual Meeting of the Air and Waste Management Association. Paper No. 91-157.3
631. Babcock & Wilcox Company (1987) LIMB Demonstration Project Extension. Comprehensive Report to Congress, DOE Clean Coal Technology Program, Babcock & Wilcox Company.
632. Clark J, Koucky R, Gogineni M, Kwasnik A (1994) Demonstration of sorbent injection technology on a tangentially coal-fired utility boiler (Yorktown LIMB demonstration). US Environmental Protection Agency, Washington, DC, EPA/600/R-94/184 (NTIS PB95105881)
633. LIMB Demonstration Project Extension and Coolside Demonstration. A DOE Assessment, DOE/NETL-2000/1123, U.S. Department of Energy, National Energy Technology Laboratory
634. DePero MJ, Goots TR, Nolan PS (1992) Final Results of the DOE LIMB and Coolside Demonstration Projects. Babcock & Wilcox Company, Presented at First Annual Clean Coal Technology Conference, Cleveland, OH, November 1992
635. Electric Power Research Institute (1989) TAG™ Technical Assessment Guide, Report P-6587-l, Electric Power Research Institute, Palo Alto, CA

636. Goots TR, DePero MJ, Nolan PS (1992) LIMB Demonstration Project Extension and Coolside Demonstration -Final Report. Babcock & Wilcox Company. DOE/PC/79798-T27 (NTIS DE93005979

637. McCoy DC, Scandrol RO, Statnick RM, Stouffer MR, Winschel RA, Withum JA, Wu MM, Yoon H (1992) The Edgewater Coolside Process Demonstration: A Topical Report, report to Babcock & Wilcox Company, Consolidation Coal Company. DOE/PC/79798-T26 (NTIS DE93001722)

638. Nolan PS (1996) Emission control technologies for coal fired power plants. BR-1607, Babcock & Wilcox Co., Ohio, USA

639. Clean coal technology demonstration program (1992) DOE/FE/0247P, US Department of Energy, Washington DC, USA

640. Shiomoto GH, Smith RA, Muzio LJ, Hunt T (1994) Integrated dry NOx/SO2 emissions control system calcium-based dry sorbent injection. Test report, April 30–November 2, 1993, DOE/PC/90550–T14

641. Sedman C, Maxwell M, Jozewicz W, Chang J (1990) Commercial development of the advacate process for flue gasdesulfurization. US Environmental Protection Agency, Washington, DC, EPA/600/D-90/147

642. Lepovitz LR, Brown CA, Pearson TE, Boyer JF, Burnett TA, Norwood VM, Puschaver EJ, Sedman CB, TooleO'Neil B (1993) 10 MW Demonstration of the ADVACATE Flue Gas Desulfurization Process. EPRI, 1993 SO_2 Control Symposium, Boston, MA, 1993

643. Drehmel DC, Princiotta FT (1988) Research in a regulatory environment. PB-88-239058/XAB;EPA-600/D-88/173

644. Sparks LE, Durham NP (1987) Combined electrostatic precipitator and acidic gas removal system, US Patent 4, 885, 139

645. World Coal Institute (1/9/2009) Coal statistics. www.worldcoal.org

646. Shadle LJ, Berry DA, Syamlal M (2004) Coal Liquefaction. Kirk-Othmer Encyclopedia of Chemical Technology. Wiley-Interscience

647. Lee S, Speight JG, Loyalka SK (2007) Handbook of Alternative Fuel Technologies. CRC Press, Boca Raton, FL

648. Okuma O, Sakanishi K (2004) Liquefaction of Victorian Brown Coal. Advances in the Science of Victorian Brown Coal. Elsevier Science

649. Williams RH, Larson ED (2003) A comparison of direct and indirect liquefaction technologies for making fluid fuels from coal. Energy for Sustainable Development VII(4).

650. Miller CL (2007) Coal Conversion – A Rising Star. 23rd Intl Pittsburgh Coal Conference, September 25–28, 2006. Coal Conversion – Pathway to Alternate Fuels Office of Fossil Energy U.S. Department of Energy, Congressional Briefing Washington, DC

651. US Department of Energy (1977) Assessment of Technology for Liquefaction of Coal. www.fischer-tropsch.org/DOE/DOE_reports/12163/fe12163_toc.htm

652. Ahmed MM (1979) Solvent Refined Coal (SRC) Process. Development of a Process for producing an Ashless, Low Sulfur Fuel from Coal. Volume IV. Product Studies. Part 9: An Investigation of the Activity of Two Cobalt-Molybdenum-Alumina Catalysts for hydrodesulfurization of a Coal-Derived Liquid. FE-O496-T9

653. US Department of Energy (1978) Environmental Development Plan (EDP) Coal Liquefaction Program. DOEIEUP-O012

654. Weinstein NJ (1977) Fundamental data Needs for Coal Conversion Technology. US Department of Energy C00/4059-1

655. O'Hara JB, Jentz NE, Syverson HT, Hervey GH, Teeple RV (1977) Project POGO: Total Coal Utilization COG Refining Design Criteria. US Department of Energy FE-1775-11

656. US Department of Energy (1978) Clean Coke Process: Process Development Studies. FE-1220-39, vol. 1–3, pts. 1 and 2

657. Epstein M, Chen TP, Ghaly MA (1978) Analysis of coal hydrogasification processes. FE-2565-14

658. Fallon P, Steinberg H (1977) Flash hydropyrolsis of coal; The design, construction, operation and initial results of a flash hydropyrolysis experimental unit. BNL 50698

659. Encoal Corporation (1997) Encoal mild coal gasification project. DOE/MC/27339-5798 (DE98002007)

660. Department of Trade and Industry, UK (1999) Coal Liquefaction, Technology Status Report 010 www.dti.gov.uk/ent/coal

661. Derbyshire F, Hager T (1994) Coal liquefaction and catalysis. Fuel 73(7): 1087–1092

662. Lumpkin RE (1988) Recent progress in the direct liquefaction of coal. Science 19 February 1988, 239(4842): 873–877

663. Donath EE (1977) Early Coal hydrogenation catalysts. Fuel Process Technol 1: 3–20

664. Lee ES (1979) Coal liquefaction. In: Coal Conversion Technology, Wen CY, Lee ES, Eds. Addison-Wesley, Reading, MA, Chap. 5, 428–545

665. Elliott MA (1981) Chemistry of Coal Utilization. Second Supplementary Volume, Elliott MA, ed. Wiley, New York

666. Derbyshire FJ (1988) Catalysis in coal liquefaction. IEACR/08, IEA Coal Research, London, UK

667. DOE COLIRN Panel, 1989, DOE COLIRN Panel (1989) Coal liquefactions – A research and development needs assessments. DOE Report No. DE- AC0187,ER30110, Final Report, Vol. 1 and Vol. 2, US Department of Energy, Pittsburgh, PA

668. van Krevelen D W (1993) Coal. Topology-Physics-Chemistry-Constitution. 3rd ed. Elsevier, Amsterdam

669. Weller S W (1994) Catalysis and catalyst dispersion in coal liquefaction. Energy Fuels 8(2): 415–420

670. Mochida I, Sakanishi K (1994) Catalysis in coal liquefaction. Adv Catal 40: 39–85

671. Chianelli RR, Lyons JE, Mills GA (1994) Catalysts for liquid transportation fuels from petroleum, coal, residual oil and biomass. Catal Today 22: 261–396

672. Comolli AG, Lee LK, Pradhan VR, Stalzer RH (1995) The direct liquefaction proof of concept program. Proceedings of US DOE Coal liquefaction and Gas Conversion Contractors Review Conference, August 29–31, 1995, Pittsburgh, PA: 25–36

673. Comolli AG, Zhou P (2000) The direct liquefaction proof of concept facility. Hydrocarbon Technologies Inc Final Report to US DOE, AC22-92PC92148, US Department of Energy, National Energy Technology Laboratory, Pittsburgh, PA

674. S Wasaka. Securing liquid fuels in the 21st century. Achievements in development of the NEDOL coal liquefaction process. www.apec-egcfe.org/7thtech/p42.pdf

675. Kydd PH, Chervenak MC, DeVaux GR (1983) H-Coal process and plant design. US Patent 4400263

676. Johnson CA, Chervenak MC, Johanson ES, Stotler HH (1973) Present status of the H-coal® process. In Clean Fuel from Coal, Institute of Gas Technology Symposium, Chicago, September 10–14 1973: 549

677. Neavel RC, Knights CF, Schulz H (1981) Exxon Donor Solvent Liquefaction Process [and Discussion]. New Coal Chemistry, Philosophical Transactions of the Royal Society of London. Ser A, Math Phys Sci 300(1453): 141–156

678. Schmid BK, Jackson DM (1980) SRC-II process. CONF-800528-1

679. Jackson DM, Schmid BK (1978) Commercial Scale Development of the SRC-II Process. Fifth Annual International Conference on Commercialization of Coal Gasification, Liquefaction, and Conversion to Electricity. Pittsburgh, USA, August 1–3: 22

680. Imhausen KH (1981) The joint Australia/Federal Republic of Germany feasibility study on the conversion of Australian coals into liquid fuels in Australia. Final Report Imhausen-Chemie G.m.b.H Lahr (Germany, F.R.)

681. Gorin E (1981) Method for hydrocracking a heavy polynuclear hydrocarbonaceous feedstock in The presence of a molten metal halide catalyst. US Patent 4247385

682. Comolli, A.G., Johanson, E.S., Karolkiewicz, W.F., Lee, L.K., Stalzer, R.H., Smith, T.O (1993) Catalytic Two-Stage Liquefaction (CTSL) process bench studies with bituminous coal. Final report [October 1, 1988–December 31, 1992], DOE/PC/88818–T3

683. Wright CW, Later DW (1985) HRI catalytic two-stage liquefaction (CTSL) process materials: chemical analysis and biological testing. PNL-5605

684. Li CZ (2004) Advances in the Science of Victorian Brown Coal. Elsevier

685. Bodie WW, Vyas KC (1974) Clean fuels from coal. Oil Gas J 72(34): 73–88

686. Project gasoline (1970) Volume IV, Book 3. Pilot-scale development of the CSF process. Interim report, July 1968–December 1970 PB-234131 OCR-39-(Vol. 4-Bk.3)

687. Simone AA, Long RH, Peluso M (1979) The C-E Lummus clean fuel from coal process. Presented at Coal Technology '79, Houston, TX, November 1979, 3: 263–287

688. Peluso M, Schiffer AN, Schindler HD (1981) The integrated two stage liquefaction process (ITSL) Presented at Coal Technology '81, Houston, 4: 353–379

689. Schiffer AN, Peluso M, Chen J, Schindler HD, Potts JD (1982) An update of the integrated two-stage liquefaction process (ITSL) Presented at the National Meeting of the Am Inst Chem Eng February–March 1982, Orlando, FL

690. Schindler HD, Chen JM, Peluso M, Moroni EC, Potts JD (1982) The integrated two stage liquefaction process (ITSL) Chem Econom Eng Rev 14(3): 15–20

691. Schiffer AN, Peluso M, Chen J, Schindler HD (1982) Integrated two-stage coal liquefaction. Energy Prog 2(4): 220–223

692. Rosenthal JW, Dahlberg AJ, Kuehler CW, Cash DR, Freedman W (1982) The Chevron coal liquefaction process (CCLP). Fuel 61(10): 1045–1050

693. Brule MR (1983) Process for the liquefaction of coal. US Patent 4,374,015

694. Honda H, Kakiyama H (1979) Solvolysis liquefaction of coal. Energy Dev Jpn 1(3) 255–266

695. Würfel H (1986) Pyrosol, the new coal liquefaction process of Saarbergwerke AG Erdoel Erdgas. 102(1): 45–48

696. Nalitham RV, Lee JM, Davies OL, Pinkston TE, Jeffers ML, Prasad A (1988) Catalytic close-coupled two-stage liquefaction process development with a bituminous coal. Fuel Proc Tech 18, 161

697. Geoff MK. A History of Coal Liquefaction in United Kingdom. 1967–1992 www.anl.gov/PCS/acsfuel/preprint%20archive/Files/Merge/Vol-42_1-0003.pdf

698. Greene M, Gupta A, Moon W (1986) Coal liquefaction/resid hydrocracking via two-stage integrated co-processing. Prepr Pap Am Chem Soc Div Fuel Chem 31(4): 192. American Chemical Society national meeting September 7, 1986, Anaheim, CA, USA: 208–215

699. Lee LK, Ignasiak B (1988) The behavior of Highvale and Vesta coals under co-processing conditions. CONF-8806312, Preprints of Papers, American Chemical Society, Division of Fuel Chemistry 33(1) Symposium on coal-derived fuels – coprocessing, June 5–10, 1988, Toronto (Canada): 20–26

700. Rahimi PM, Fouda SA, Kelly JF. Coprocessing using H_2 as a promoter. http://www.anl.gov/PCS/acsfuel/preprint%20archive/Files/31_4_ANAHEIM_09-86_0192.pdf

701. Fouda SA, Kelly JF (1985) CANMET coprocessing of low-rank Canadian coals' Division Report ERP/ERL 85-63(0PJ) CANMET, Energy Mines and Resources Canada, Presented at the US Dept of Energy Direct Liquefaction Contractors' Review Meeting, Pittsburg, PA, November 19–21, 1985

702. Kelly JF, Fouda SA, Rahimi PM, Ikura M (1984) CANMET coprocessing – A status report. Proceedings o f the Coal Conversion Contractors' Review Meeting, Calgary, Alberta, 1984; Kelly JF (ed)

703. Comolli AG, Lee TLK, Hu J, Karolkiewicz WF, Parfitt DS, Popper G, Zhou PZ (1998) Direct liquefaction proof-of-concept program. DE-92148-TOP-10

704. Larson ED, Tingjin R (December 2003) Synthetic fuel production by indirect coal liquefaction. Energy Sust Dev VII(4)

705. Eastman Chemical and Air Products and Chemicals Inc (Eastman) (2003) Project Data on Eastman Chemical Company's Chemicals-from-Coal Complex in Kingsport, TN, for USDOE/NETL contract DE-FC22-92PC90543, Kingsport, Tennessee, March.

706. Derbyshire F, Hager T (1994) Coal liquefaction and catalysis. Fuel 73(7): 1087–1092

707. Dry ME (1983) The Sasol Fischer-Tropsch processes. Appl Ind Catal 2: 167–213

708. Dry ME (1988) The Sasol route to chemicals and fuels. Stud Surf Sci Catal 36: 447–456

709. Joiner JR, Kovach JJ (1982) Sasol Two and Sasol Three. Energy Prog 2: 66–68

710. Mako PF, Van Oeveren P (1982) Coal liquefaction. Sasol technology. Proc – Int Symp: Large Chem Plants: Energy, Feedstocks, Processes, 5th: 89–98

711. McIver AE (1975) SASOL: processing coal into fuels and chemicals for the South African Coal, Oil and Gas Corporation. Annu Symp Coal Gasif, Liquefaction, Util: Best Prospects Commer, [Proc], 2nd: IX, 24 pp

712. Mullowney JF (1980) Sasol – coal to synfuels now. Fuels Future, Pap Altern Fuels/Refin Tech Stream Sess: 31–34

713. Papic MM (1981) Coal liquefaction via Sasol Fischer-Tropsch synthesis. CIM Bulletin 74: 60–64

714. Samuel WA (1981) Sasol – a proven prescription to convert tons to barrels. Energy Technology 8th: 704–711

715. Dry ME, Erasmus HBW (1987) Update of the Sasol synfuels process. Ann Rev Energy 12: 1–46

716. Wham RM, Fisher JF, Forrester RC III, Irvine AR, Salmon R, Singh SPN, Ulrich WC (1981) Liquefaction technology assessment. Phase I: indirect liquefaction of coal to methanol and gasoline using available technology. Report ORNL-5664

717. Coal liquefaction technology assessments, phase I (1980) Report ORNL/Sub-80/24707/1

718. Coal Liquefaction Technology Assessment Phase II. Texaco gasifications. Final report (1984) Report ORNL/Sub-81/24707/2; Order No. DE84010163

719. Grimmer HR, Thiagarajan N, Nitschke E (1988) Conversion of methanol to liquid fuels by the fluid bed Mobil process (a commercial concept) Stud Surf Sci Catal 36 (Methane Convers): 273–291
720. Yurchak S (1988) Development of Mobil 's fixed-bed methanol-to-gasoline (MTG) process. Stud Surf Sci Catal 36 (Methane Convers): 251–272
721. Lee S, Gogate M, Kulik CJ (1995) Methanol-to-gasoline vs. DME-to-gasoline. II. Process comparison and analysis. Fuel Sci Technol Int 13(8): 1039–1057
722. Chang CD (1997) MTG: from concept to commercial reality. Book of Abstracts, 214th ACS National Meeting, Las Vegas, NV, September 7–11, PETR-097
723. Keil FJ (1999) Methanol-to-hydrocarbons: process technology. Microporous Mesoporous Mater 29(1–2): 49–66
724. Chang CD (2000) The methanol-to-hydrocarbons reaction: a mechanistic perspective. ACS Symp Ser 738 (Shape-Selective Catalysis): 96–114
725. Hoek A, Kersten LBJM (2004) The Shell Middle Distillate Synthesis process: technology, products and perspective. Stud Surf Sci Catal 147 (Natural Gas Conversion VII): 25–30
726. Senden M, McEwan M (2000) The Shell Middle Distillate Synthesis experience. Proceedings of the World Petroleum Congress 16th, 4: 7–10
727. Eilers J, Posthuma SA, Sie ST (1990) The Shell middle distillate synthesis process (SMDS) Catal Lett 7(1–4): 253–269

American Standard and Testing Materials (ASTM)

D-167-93(2004)E1 Standard Test Method for Apparent and True Specific Gravity and Porosity of Lump Coke
D-409 Standard Test Method for Grindability of Coal by the Hardgrove-Machine Method
D-1412-07 Standard Test Method for Equilibrium Moisture of Coal At 96–97% Relative Humidity and 30°C
D-1857-04 Standard Test Method for Fusibility of Coal and Coke Ash
D-2013-07 Standard Practice for Preparing Coal Samples for Analysis
D-2015 Standard Test Method for Gross Calorific Value of Coal and Coke by the Adiabatic Bomb Calorimeter
D-2492-02(2007) Standard Test Method for forms of Sulfur in Coal
D-3684-01 (2006) Standard Test Method for Total Mercury in Coal by The Oxygen Bomb combustion/Atomic Absorption Method
D-4208 Standard Test Method for Total Chlorine in Coal by The Oxygen Bomb Combustion/Ion Selective Electrode Method
D-4239-08 Standard Test Methods for Sulfur in the Analysis Sample of Coal and Coke Using High-Temperature Tube Furnace Combustion Methods
D-4326-04 Standard Test Method for Major and Minor Elements in Coal and Coke Ash by X-Ray Fluorescence
D-4371-06 Standard Test Method for Determining the Washability Characteristics of Coal
D-4749-87 (2007) Standard Test Method for Performing the Sieve Analysis of Coal and Designating Coal Size
D-5016-08 Standard Test Method for Total Sulfur in Coal and Coke Combustion Residues Using A High-Temperature Tube Furnace Combustion Method With Infrared Absorption
D-5142-04 Standard Test Methods for Proximate Analysis of the Analysis Sample of Coal and Coke by Instrumental Procedures

D-5373-08 Standard Test Methods for Instrumental Determination of Carbon, Hydrogen, and Nitrogen In Laboratory Samples of Coal

D-6357-04 Test Methods for Determination of Trace Elements In Coal, Coke, & Combustion Residues From Coal Utilization Processes by Inductively Coupled Plasma Atomic Emission, Inductively Coupled Plasma Mass & Graphite Furnace Atomic Absorption Spectrometries

International Organization for Standardization

ISO 17247: 2005 Coal – Ultimate Analysis

ISO 17246: 2005 Coal – Proximate Analysis

ISO 334: 1992 Solid Mineral Fuels – Determination of Total Sulfur – Eschka Method

ISO 351: 1996solid Mineral Fuels – Determination of Total Sulfur – High Temperature Combustion Method

ISO 609: 1996 Solid Mineral Fuels – Determination of Carbon and Hydrogen – High Temperature Combustion Method

ISO 625: 1996 Solid Mineral Fuels – Determination of Carbon and Hydrogen – Liebig Method

ISO 333: 1996 Coal – Determination of Nitrogen – Semi-Micro Kjeldahl Method

ISO 157: 1996 Coal – Determination of forms of Sulfur

ISO 589: 2008 Hard Coal – Determination of Total Moisture

ISO 540: 2008 Hard Coal and Coke – Determination of Ash Fusibility

ISO 1171: 1997 Solid Mineral Fuels – Determination of Ash Content

ISO 15237: 2003 Solid Mineral Fuels – Determination of Total Mercury Content of Coal

ISO 601: 1981 Solid Mineral Fuels – Determination of Arsenic Content Using the Standard Silver Diethyldithiocarbamate Photometric Method of ISO 2590

ISO 622: 1981 Solid Mineral Fuels – Determination of Phosphorus Content – Reduced Molybdophosphate Photometric Method

ISO 7404 Methods for the Petrographic Analysis of Bituminous Coal and Anthracite

ISO 602: 1983 Coal – Determination of Mineral Matter

ISO 12900: 1997 Hard Coal – Determination of Abrasiveness

British Standards Institution

BS 1016-6: 1997 Methods for Analysis and Testing of Coal and Coke. Ultimate Analysis of Coal

BS 1016 P104 Methods for Analysis and Testing of Coal and Coke-Part 104: Proximate Analysis-Section 104.1: Determination of Moisture Content of the General Analysis Test Sample

BS 1016 P106 S106.4.2 Methods for Analysis Testing of Coal and Coke – Part 106: Ultimate Analysis of Coal and Coke – Section 106.4: Determination of Total Sulfur Content – Subsection 106.4.2: High Temperature Combustion Method.

BS 1016 P106 Ss106.1.1 Methods for Analysis and Testing of Coal and Coke – Part 106: Ultimate Analysis of Coal and Coke – Section 106.1 Determination of Carbon and Hydrogen Content – Subsection 106.1.1 High Temperature Combustion Method

BS 1016 P106 S106.2 Methods for Analysis and Testing of Coal and Coke – Part 106: Ultimate Analysis of Coal and Coke – Section 106.2: Determination of Nitrogen Content

BS 1016 P106 S106.5 Methods for Analysis and Testing of Coal and Coke – Part 106: Ultimate Analysis of Coal and Coke – Section 106.5 Determination of forms of Sulfur in Coal

BS 1016 P104 S104.1 Methods for Analysis and Testing of Coal and Coke – P. 104: Proximate Analysis – S. 104.1: Determination of Moisture Content of The General Analysis Test Sample

BS 1016 P113 Methods for Analysis and Testing of Coal and Coke – Part 113. Determination of Ash and Fusibility

BS 1016 P109 Methods for Analysis and Testing of Coal and Coke – Part 109. Size Analysis of Coal

BS 1017 P1 Sampling of Coal and Cole Part 1. Methods for Sampling of Coal

BS 1016 P10 Arsenic in Coal and Coke

BS 1016-9 Phosphorus in Coal and Coke

BS 6127 Petrographic Analysis of Bituminous Coal and Anthracite Part 1. Glossary of Terms Relating to The Petrographic Analysis of bituminous Coal and Anthracite

BS 1016 P111 Analysis and Testing of Coal and Coke – Part 111. Determination of abrasion Index of Coal

Problems

1. What are the likely future scenarios for the role of coal-fired generation in the U.S.?
2. What are the environmental and regulatory challenges associated with the future use of coal for power generation?
3. What technological improvements in coal use are most important to pursue? What financial and/or regulatory mechanisms are necessary to bring these technological improvements to market?
4. What improvements in existing transportation or transmission infrastructure are needed to improve the use of coal for power generation?
5. What is the state-of-the-art in coal combustion
6. Discuss the impact of carbon tax on the coal industry.
7. Determine the approximate cost to build a coal-to-liquid power plant?
8. How much carbon dioxide does the average coal-burning power plant release into the atmosphere in a year? Assume a capacity of the plant.
9. Will carbon capture and storage (CCS) technologies eliminate CO_2 emission? Discuss.
10. Is zero emission coal technology possible?
11. Discuss various carbon capture and sequestration technologies and their long term implications.
12. Are there advantages of coal use compared to other fossil fuels?
13. How is sulfur formed in coal? Why it is necessary to remove sulfur from coal and how is it done?
14. During the 1970s, following the oil embargo, various agencies and experts suggested that the US had enough coal for 600–700 years. However, the recent forecasts are that the US has enough coal for 250 years. Explain this deference in the predictions. First verify these predictions and the assumptions made. Were those assumptions correct?

7 NATURAL GAS

Abstract

Natural gas is considered as one of the primary energy sources of the world. It mainly contains methane (CH_4) and is colorless and odorless. Natural gas has many uses and can be used in most energy sectors: residential, commercial, and industrial. In this chapter, we have discussed its total reserve worldwide, its origin, processing, transportation, and storage. Natural gas from the well head has to go through various processing steps before its final use. Like every other commodities, natural gas is also traded internationally and transported through pipelines across the countries. However, its transportation through pipe lines is limited and as a result its movement is generally confined among neighboring countries. Recently, natural gas is liquefied, called liquefied natural gas (LNG), and is transported via sea to distant countries. Consequently, natural gas is becoming a dominant energy source.

7.1 Introduction

Worldwide consumption of natural gas in 2005 was 104 trillion cubic feet and it is expected to increase to 182 trillion cubic feet in 2030. This represents a worldwide increase of 2.5% annually. Natural gas is considered to be one of the cleanest energy sources as it can be burned more efficiently compared to coal and petroleum. The worldwide reserve of natural gas and its production and consumption rate is shown in Fig. 7.1. As shown in Table 7.1, the use of natural gas in the USA is expected to increase in all sectors; however, the main increase is expected to be in industrial sectors, such as for fertilizer production, and electricity generation. The two top users of the natural gas are the USA and China. In Table 7.2 the production and consumption rate of various countries in the last five years along with

T.K. Ghosh and M.A. Prelas, *Energy Resources and Systems:*
Volume 1: Fundamentals and Non-Renewable Resources, 281–381.

their reserve are given. Although the data show that a considerable amount of natural gas is available, its trade or use is more regional as delivery of the natural gas through pipeline from one region to another region is costly. The international trade of natural gas among various countries is given in Tables 7.3–7.5. At the current rate of consumption, natural gas is expected to last about 65 years, unless new reserves are discovered.

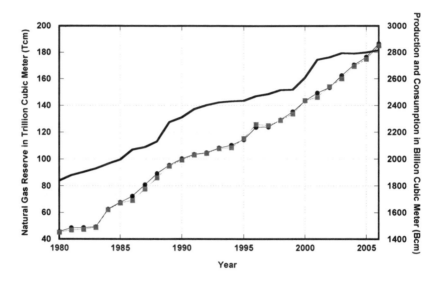

Fig. 7.1. Reserve, production, and consumption of natural gas worldwide [1].

Table 7.1. Increase of natural gas use by various sectors in the USA (in trillion cubic feet).

Consump- tion sectors	Year								
	2005	2006	2007	2008	2010	2015	2020	2025	2025
Residential	4.83	4.37	4.73	4.83	4.81	5.01	5.15	5.19	5.17
Commercial	3.00	2.83	3.02	3.05	2.96	3.20	3.37	3.53	3.67
Industrial	6.60	6.49	6.60	6.64	6.95	7.00	6.93	6.96	6.87
Electric power	5.87	6.24	6.78	6.83	6.70	6.56	5.92	5.30	4.99
Total	22.01	21.66	22.90	23.12	23.25	23.66	23.33	22.99	22.72

Source: Reference [2].

Table 7.2. Proven reserves, consumption, and percent change of natural gas use.

Countries	Reserve at the end of 2006		Share of total	R/P ratio	Production in 2006 bcm	% Change from 2005	Consumption in 2006 bcm	% Change from 2005
	Cubic feet	Cubic meter						
USA	209.15	5.93	3.3%	11.3	524.1	2.3%	619.7	-1.7%
Canada	58.77	1.67	0.9%	8.9	187.0	0.6%	96.6	5.7%
Mexico	13.70	0.39	0.2%	8.9	43.4	10.6%	54.1	13.6%
Total North America	281.62	7.98	4.4%	10.6	754.4	2.3%	770.3	0.1%
Argentina	14.65	0.42	0.2%	9.0	46.1	1.0%	41.8	3.5%
Bolivia	26.12	0.74	0.4%	66.3	11.2	7.2%	–	–
Brazil	12.28	0.35	0.2%	30.2	11.5	1.3%	21.1	6.1%
Chile	–	–	–	–	–	–	7.6	-11.5%
Colombia	4.34	0.12	0.1%	16.9	7.3	7.6%	7.3	7.6%
Ecuador	–	–	–	–	–	–	0.3	3.8%
Peru	12.00	0.34	0.2%	*	–	–	1.8	17.0%
Trinidad & Tobago	18.71	0.53	0.3%	15.1	35.0	15.6%	–	–
Venezuela	152.32	4.32	2.4%	*	28.7	-1.0%	28.7	-1.0%
Other South & Central America	2.40	0.07	□	14.3	4.8	5.0%	22.1	14.0%
Total South & Central America	242.83	6.88	3.8%	47.6	144.5	4.7%	130.6	3.9%
Austria	–	–	–	–	–	–	9.4	-6.0%
Azerbaijan	47.66	1.35	0.7%	*	6.3	18.0%	9.6	8.1%
Belarus	–	–	–	–	–	–	19.6	3.4%

(Continued)

Table 7.2. (Continued)

Countries	Reserve at the end of 2006		Share of total	R/P ratio	Production in 2006 bcm	% Change from 2005	Consumption in 2006 bcm	% Change from 2005
	Cubic feet	Cubic meter						
Belgium & Luxembourg	–	–	–	–	–	–	17.0	2.4%
Bulgaria	–	–	–	–	–	–	3.0	3.1%
Czech Republic	–	–	–	–	–	–	8.5	-0.3%
Denmark	2.72	0.08	–	7.4	10.4	-0.3%	5.1	1.8%
Finland	–	–	–	–	–	–	4.3	7.7%
France	–	–	–	–	–	–	45.2	-1.5%
Germany	5.47	0.16	0.1%	9.9	15.6	-1.2%	87.2	1.1%
Greece	–	–	–	–	–	–	3.2	15.2%
Hungary	–	–	–	–	–	–	12.5	-4.9%
Iceland	–	–	–	–	–	–	–	–
Ireland	–	–	–	–	–	–	4.5	15.6%
Italy	5.63	0.16	0.1%	14.5	11.0	-9.0%	77.1	-2.1%
Kazakhstan	105.90	3.00	1.7%	*	23.9	2.7%	20.2	3.3%
Lithuania	–	–	–	–	–	–	3.3	0.1%
The Netherlands	47.55	1.35	0.7%	21.8	61.9	-1.6%	38.3	-3.0%
Norway	102.09	2.89	1.6%	33.0	87.6	3.1%	4.4	-1.4%
Poland	3.67	0.10	0.1%	24.4	4.3	-1.3%	13.7	0.6%
Portugal	–	–	–	–	–	–	4.1	-3.9%
Romania	22.17	0.63	0.3%	51.7	12.1	0.2%	17.0	-1.7%
Russian Federation	1,682.07	47.65	26.3%	77.8	612.1	2.4%	432.1	6.7%
Slovakia	–	–	–	–	–	–	5.5	-16.0%

Countries	Reserve at the end of 2006		Share of total	R/P ratio	Production in 2006 bcm	% Change from 2005	Consumption in 2006 bcm	% Change from 2005
	Cubic feet	Cubic meter						
Spain	–	–	–	–	–	–	33.4	3.2%
Sweden							0.8	7.1%
Switzerland								–3.7%
Turkey	100.96	2.86	1.6%	46.0	62.2	5.9%	30.5	13.5%
Turkmenistan	38.83	1.10	0.6%	57.7	19.1	–1.7%	18.9	14.0%
Ukraine	100.96	2.86	1.6%	46.0	62.2	5.9%	66.4	–8.8%
UK	16.98	0.48	0.3%	6.0	80.0	–8.6%	90.8	–4.5%
Uzbekistan	66.01	1.87	1.0%	33.7	55.4	0.8%	43.2	–1.9%
Other Europe & Eurasia	15.99	0.45	0.2%	41.4	10.9	7.8%	14.7	0.7%
Total Europe & Eurasia	2,263.69	64.13	35.3%	59.8	1,072.9	1.2%	1,146.3	1.9%
Bahrain	3.18	0.09	☐	8.1	11.1	3.2%	–	–
Iran	992.99	28.13	15.5%	*	105.0	4.1%	105.1	2.7%
Iraq	111.90	3.17	1.7%	*	–	–	–	–
Kuwait	62.83	1.78	1.0%	*	12.9	4.9%	12.9	4.9%
Oman	34.59	0.98	0.5%	39.0	25.1	27.0%	–	–
Qatar	895.24	25.36	14.0%	*	49.5	8.1%	19.5	4.3%
Saudi Arabia	249.68	7.07	3.9%	96.0	73.7	3.5%	73.5	3.5%
Syria	10.24	0.29	0.2%	52.3	5.5	3.3%	–	–
United Arab Emirates	213.95	6.06	3.3%	*	47.4	0.9%	41.7	1.0%
Yemen	17.12	0.49	0.3%	*	–	–	–	–

(Continued)

Table 7.2. (Continued)

Countries	Reserve at the end of 2006			R/P ratio	Production in 2006 bcm	% Change from 2005	Consumption in 2006 bcm	% Change from 2005
	Cubic feet	Cubic meter	Share of total					
Other Middle East	1.80	0.05	□	9.0	5.6	28.1%	36.4	17.5%
Total Middle East	2,593.53	73.47	40.5%	*	335.9	5.8%	289.3	4.5%
Algeria	159.00	4.50	2.5%	53.3	84.5	-4.3%	23.7	2.2%
Egypt	68.48	1.94	1.1%	43.3	44.8	29.3%	28.7	11.4%
Libya	46.45	1.32	0.7%	88.9	14.8	31.0%	–	–
Nigeria	183.91	5.21	2.9%	*	28.2	25.9%	–	–
Other Africa	42.82	1.21	0.7%	*	8.2	–	23.3	2.3%
Total Africa	500.67	14.18	7.8%	78.6	180.5	9.5%	75.8	5.5%
Australia	91.96	2.61	1.4%	67.0	–	–	28.6	3.4%
Bangladesh	15.36	0.44	0.2%	28.6	15.2	7.1%	15.2	7.1%
Brunei	11.83	0.34	0.2%	27.3	12.3	6.5%	–	–
China	86.45	2.45	1.3%	41.8	58.6	17.2%	55.6	21.6%
Hong Kong	–	–	–	–	–	–	2.4	13.2%
India	37.95	1.08	0.6%	33.9	31.8	-1.0%	39.7	4.3%
Indonesia	92.91	2.63	1.5%	35.6	74.0	0.3%	39.6	5.6%
Japan	–	–	–	–	–	–	84.6	7.0%
Malaysia	87.54	2.48	1.4%	41.2	60.2	0.4%	40.3	2.5%
Myanmar	18.99	0.54	0.3%	40.1	13.4	3.1%	–	–
New Zealand					3.9	2.2%	3.7	6.4%

Countries	Reserve at the end of 2006			R/P ratio	Production in 2006 bcm	% Change from 2005	Consumption in 2006 bcm	% Change from 2005
	Cubic feet	Cubic meter	Share of total					
Pakistan	28.17	0.80	0.4%	26.0	30.7	4.8%	30.7	4.8%
Philippines							2.6	-13.8%
Singapore							6.6	–
South Korea							34.2	1.4%
Papua New Guinea	15.36	0.44	0.2%	*	–	–		
Taiwan							11.9	12.1%
Thailand	10.63	0.30	0.2%	12.4	24.3	2.8%	30.6	2.3%
Vietnam	14.12	0.40	0.2%	57.1	7.0	1.6%	–	–
Other Asia Pacific	11.90	0.34	0.2%	48.8	6.9	-5.4%	12.1	6.3%
Total Asia Pacific	523.15	14.82	8.2%	39.3	377.1	4.0%	438.5	6.5%
TOTAL WORLD	6,405.48	181.46	100%	60.3	2,865.3	3.0%	2,850.8	2.5%
of which: European Union 25	85.66	2.43	1.3%	12.8	190.0	-4.9%	467.4	-1.4%
European Union 27					202.7	-4.6%	487.4	-1.3%
OECD	561.29	15.90	8.8%	14.7	1,078.5	1.1%	1,419.8	0.3%
Former Soviet Union	2,051.28	58.11	32.0%	74.6	779.3	2.5%	621.1	4.0%
Other EMSs					1,007.5	5.6%	809.9	5.3%

More than 100 years. ^ Less than 0.05. Less than 0.05%. n/a not available.

#Excludes Estonia, Latvia and Lithuania prior to 1985 and Slovenia prior to 1991.

Annual changes and shares of total are calculated in million tonnes oil equivalent figures.

As far as possible, the data above represent standard cubic metres (measured at 15°C and 1,013 mbar); as they are derived directly from tones of oil equivalent using an average conversion factor, they do not necessarily equate with gas volumes expressed in specific national terms.

The difference between these world consumption figures and the world production statistics is due to variations in stocks at storage facilities and liquefaction plants, together with unavoidable disparities in the definition, measurement or conversion of gas supply and demand data.

Table 7.3. Natural gas trading by countries via pipeline in 2006 in North America and South & Central America (billions of cubic meter).

To	From			Total imports
	USA	Canada	Mexico	
North America				
USA	–	99.75	0.08	99.83
Canada	9.37			9.37
Mexico	9.85			9.85
Total imports	19.22	99.75	0.08	

To	From		Total imports
	Argentina	Bolivia	
South and Central America			
Argentina	–	1.80	1.80
Brazil	0.46	9.00	9.46
Chile	5.56	–	5.56
Uruguay	0.12	–	0.12
Total imports	6.14	10.80	

Source: Energy Information Administration, USA

Table 7.4. Natural gas trading by countries via pipeline in 2006 in Europe (billions of cubic meter).

To	From									Total imports
	Belgium	Denmark	Germany	The Netherlands	Norway	UK	Russian Fed.	Turkmenistan	Other Europe & Eurasia	
Austria	–	–	1.10	–	0.78	–	6.85	–	–	8.73
Belgium	–	–	1.00	7.60	8.50	0.64	0.63	–	–	18.37
Bulgaria	–	–	–	–	–	–	2.85	–	–	2.85
Croatia	–	–	–	–	–	–	0.75	–	0.40	1.15
Czech Republic	–	–	–	–	2.35	–	7.13	–	–	9.48
Finland	–	–	–	–	–	–	4.52	–	–	4.52
France	1.90	–	0.10	9.50	14.50	0.20	9.50	–	–	35.70
Germany	–	1.92	–	21.30	26.80	3.08	36.54	–	1.20	90.84
Greece	–	–	–	–	–	–	2.40	–	–	2.40
Hungary	–	–	0.83	–	–	–	8.32	–	1.80	10.95
Ireland	–	–	–	–	–	3.40	–	–	–	3.40
Italy	–	–	2.50	8.70	7.20	0.80	22.92	–	–	74.27
Latvia	–	–	–	–	–	–	1.70	–	–	1.70
Lithuania	–	–	–	–	–	–	2.90	–	–	2.90
Luxembourg	0.80	–	0.70	–	–	–	–	–	–	1.50
Netherlands	–	2.24	4.50	–	7.00	1.82	2.97	–	–	18.53
Poland	–	–	0.35	–	0.49	–	7.00	0.21	2.52	10.57
Portugal	–	–	–	–	–	–	–	–	–	2.10

(Continued)

Table 7.4. (Continued)

To	From									Total imports
	Belgium	Denmark	Germany	The Nether-lands	Norway	UK	Russian Fed.	Turkmenistan	Other Europe & Eurasia	
Romania	–	–	1.30	–	–	–	3.95	–	1.00	6.25
Serbia	–	–	–	–	–	–	2.15	–	–	2.15
Slovakia	–	–	–	–	–	–	6.30	–	–	6.30
Slovenia	–	–	–	–	–	–	0.56	–	0.10	1.10
Spain	–	–	–	–	2.12	–	–	–	–	10.74
Sweden	–	0.93	0.15	–	–	–	–	–	–	1.08
Switzerland	–	–	1.20	0.90	0.08	–	0.37	–	0.50	3.05
Turkey	–	–	–	–	–	–	19.65	–	–	25.34
UK	1.80	–	1.00	0.60	14.10	–	–	–	–	17.50
Others	–	–	–	–	0.08	–	1.50	–	–	1.58

Flows are on a contractual basis and may not correspond to physical gas flows in all cases. Cedigaz (provisional).
Data excludes trade within the Former Soviet Union and United Arab Emirates.
Source: Energy Information Administration, USA

Table 7.5. Natural gas trading by countries via pipeline in 2006 in Asia (billions of cubic meter).

To	From							Total imports
	Turkmenistan	Oman	Algeria	Egypt	Indonesia	Malaysia	Myanmar	
Middle East								
Iran	5.80	–	–	–	–	–	–	5.80
Jordan	–	–	–	1.93	–	–	–	1.93
United Arab Emirates	–	1.40	–	–	–	–	–	1.40
Africa								
Tunisia	–	–	1.30	–	–	–	–	1.30
Asia Pacific								
Singapore	–	–	–	–	4.83	1.78	–	6.61
Thailand	–	–	–	–	–	–	8.98	8.98

Flows are on a contractual basis and may not correspond to physical gas flows in all cases.

Source: Cedigaz (provisional).

Data excludes trade within the Former Soviet Union and United Arab Emirates.

7.2 Formation of Natural Gas

There are a number of theories on the formation of natural gas below the earth's crust [3–19]. These theories may be classified into following three categories.

- Thermogenic methane
- Biogenic methane, and
- Abiogenic methane

The thermogenic process is the most widely accepted theory for formation of methane. According to this process, fossil fuels are formed when organic matter is compressed under the earth, at very high pressure for a very long time. As a result, natural gas is usually found with the oil deposits. The amount of methane formation depends on temperature: at low temperatures (shallower deposits), more oil is produced relative to natural gas. At higher temperatures, more natural gas is created as opposed to oil. However, if the deposits are very far underground, they mainly contain natural gas rich in methane. The formation of natural gas and oil in a reservoir is shown in Fig. 7.2.

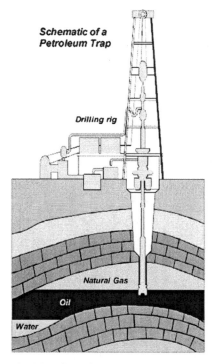

Fig. 7.2. Schematic of a petroleum trap [4].

The transformation of organic matter by microorganisms can lead to the formation of methane. Methane produced in this manner is referred to as biogenic methane, which may be distinguished by its isotopic signature from thermogenic methane [4].

A third way in which methane (and natural gas) may be formed is through abiogenic processes. Extremely deep under the earth's crust, there exist hydrogen-rich gases and carbon molecules, which under certain conditions can chemically react forming methane. A number of researchers have tried to simulate the process in order to verify the theory of abiogenic process for methane formation [5]. However several observations and measurements including high temperature fluid venting from ridges at the middle of the ocean [6], seepages from regions associated with ultramafic rocks on land, fluids from Precambrian shields, and igneous rocks suggest the formation of methane in Earth's crust by abiogenic process.

7.3 Unconventional Sources

Natural gas can also be produced from a number of other unconventional sources [21–33]. These unconventional sources may be divided into six categories:

- Deep natural gas
- Tight natural gas (tight gas sands)
- Gas-containing shales
- Coalbed methane
- Geopressurized zones, and
- Methane hydrates

Among these sources, tight gas sands, gas containing shales, and coalbed methane, are widely used commercially for methane production. Improved exploration and production technologies in the oil and gas industry have made commercial production possible. In Table 7.6 the global unconventional resources for various fossil energy sources is compared. When the gas hydrate is included, the unconventional sources of natural gas are significantly higher than oil or coal.

Discoveries of new conventional natural gas reservoirs are expected to be smaller in size and deeper, and thus more expensive and riskier to develop and produce. The use of unconventional resources is expected to increase dramatically. For example, Canada is a major producer of natural gas from conventional sources. However, as shown in Fig. 7.3 their Reserves/Production ratio is declining steadily. Their production of conventional natural gas peaked in 2000 and has been decreasing ever since. Currently, Canada is exploring production of natural gas from unconventional resources. Unconventional gas will have an important role to play in reducing the gap between demands and declining conventional gas production.

Table 7.6. Global fossil energy reserves, resources, and occurrences in giga tons of oil equivalent (Gtoe).

| | Consumption | | Reserves | Resources | Resource base | Additional occurrences |
	1850–1990	1990				
Oil						
Conventional	90	3.2	150	145	295	
Unconventional	–	–	193	332	525	1,900
Natural gas						
Conventional	41	1.7	141	279	420	
Unconventional	–	–	192	258	450	400
Hydrates	–	–	–	–	–	18,700
Coal	125	2.2	606	2,794	3,400	3,000
Total	256	7.1	1,282	3,808	5,090	24,000

Source: Reference [34].

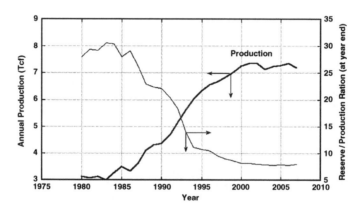

Fig. 7.3. Natural gas production and reserve/production ratio by Canada. Source of data [35, 1].

The USA is experiencing a similar trend. Unconventional gas accounted for 43% of total U.S. natural gas production in 2006. As shown in Fig. 7.4, about 43% of the total natural gas reserve in the USA is from the unconventional sources.

The main sources of unconventional gases in the USA are tight gas sands, coal bed methane and gas shale. Both the National Petroleum Council and US Geological Survey made estimates of these resources. As shown in Table 7.7, there is a significant difference between these two estimates. The difference in the estimates is from the uncertainty and accuracy of the measurement and the models used in the estimation. As shown in Fig. 7.5, currently natural gas from the tight gas sands is the most widely used among these three unconventional resources.

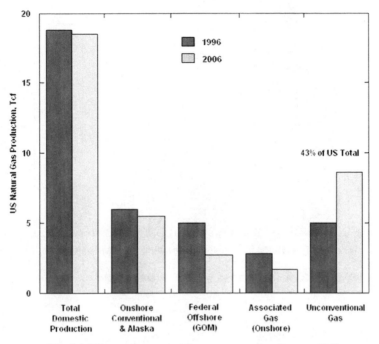

Fig. 7.4. US natural gas serve from unconventional sources [36].

Table 7.7. Comparison of unconventional gas resource estimates in US lower 48 states in trillion cubic feet (Tcf).

	Advanced resources (2006)*		National Petro-leum Council (2003)**	US Geological Survey (2006)
	Proved reserves	Undeveloped resources		
Tight gas sands	73	379	131	177
Coalbed methane	20	73	46	67
Gas shales	12	128	29	60
TOTAL	105		206	304

*With data through 2005; **For accessible undeveloped resources, current technology, with data through 1998; *** Estimates for undeveloped continuous resources with data from 1995–2006. Source: Reference [37].

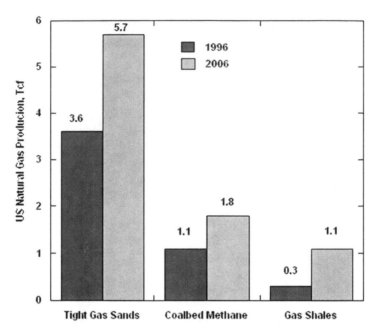

Fig. 7.5. US natural gas production from unconventional sources [36].

7.3.1 Deep Natural Gas

Natural gas that exists at a depth of greater than 15,000 ft is generally called Deep Natural Gas [38–44]. In 2000, the U.S. Geological Survey conducted a study to access undiscovered conventional gas and oil resources in eight regions of the world outside the U.S. The potential reserves that may be available within the next thirty years were studied. This study estimated worldwide natural gas volumes and its distribution at depth >4:5 km (15,000 ft). Two hundred forty-six assessment units in 128 priority geologic provinces, 96 countries, and two jointly held areas were assessed using a probabilistic total petroleum system approach. The distribution of the deep natural gas resources in the USA is given in Table 7.8.

Worldwide estimates of deep gas of undiscovered conventional gas resource outside the U.S. are about 844 trillion cubic feet below 4.5 km (about 15,000 ft). (The U.S. Geological Survey World Petroleum Assessment 2000 Project) and are given in Table 7.9.

Table 7.8. Estimates of undiscovered natural gas by region for depths of 15,000 ft or greater from the 1995 U.S Geological Survey (USGS) National Petroleum Assessment. Data are mean estimates [45].

Region	Conventional gas resources (Bcf)	Continuous-type gas resources (Bcf)	Total gas resources (Bcf)
Alaska	17,936	0	17,936
Pacific	550	2,636	3,186
Rocky Mountains	1,946	55,212	57,158
Colorado Plateau	130	570	700
West Texas-Eastern New Mexico	4,705	0	4,705
Gulf Coast	27,439	0	27,439
Midcontinent	2,264	0	2,264
Eastern	294	0	294
Total	55,264	58,418	113,682

Data includes associated gas from oil accumulations and non associated gas. Onshore regions and state waters only. Unconventional gas includes gas in low-permeability (tight) sandstones. Resource estimates based on current technology case only. Estimates do not include undiscovered gas from small fields (less than 6 Bcf). Refer to Gautier and others (1996) for detailed explanation of assessment.

As can be noted from Table 7.9, the former Soviet Union has the most deep natural gas, followed by Europe. The advancement of technologies for deep drilling, exploration, and extraction is making these sources economical.

7.3.2 Tight Natural Gas

When natural gas is trapped in a very tight formation underground, it is called tight natural gas [47–55]. The basin is unusually impermeable, and includes hard rock or sandstone or limestone formations and non-porous (generally called tight sand). Although a formal definition for "Tight Gas" reservoirs has not been developed, some researchers tried to characterize a tight gas reservoir based on the permeability of gas. Law and Curtis (2002) defined low-permeability (tight) reservoirs as having permeability less than 0.1 milliDarcies (mD). According to the German Society for Petroleum and Coal Science and Technology (DGMK), tight gas reservoirs are those reservoirs with an average effective gas permeability of less than 0.6 mD. Some 'ultra tight' gas reservoirs may have in-situ permeability as low as 0.001 mD.

Table 7.9. Summary data by region for estimated deep undiscovered conventional gas resources in the world from US Geological survey.

Region	Deep AUs/ provinces	Total gas (Tcf) (gas > 4.5 km/gas > 7.5 km)	Total gas (Tcf) (all depths)	Average percent	Average maximum depth of deep gas (ft)	Dominant province(s)	Significant regional example: AU, province, mean undisc. conv. resource, primary reservoir(s)
Former Soviet Union – Region 1	37/12	343/0.5	1,611	21	5,857	North, Middle, and South Caspian Basin provinces	Central Offshore, South Caspian Basin, 71 Tcf, Tertiary shelf turbidites and Jurassic reef carbonates
Mideast-North Africa – Region 2	24/11	131/0	1,370	10	5391	Red Sea Basin, Zagros Fold Belt, Sirte Basin, Rub Al Khali Basin	Paleozoic Reservoirs, Rub Al Khali Basin, 47 Tcf, Permian sandstones
Asia Pacific – Region 3	20/12	38/0.1	379	10	5915	Kutei Basin, Sichuan Basin, Tarim Basin	Tarim Basin Excluding; Marginal Foldbelts; Tarim Basin, 23 Tcf; Ordovician carbonates
Europe – Region 4	18/8	142/0.7	312	46	6500	North Sea Graben, Pannonian Basin, Carpathian-Balkanian Basin, Vestford-Helgeland Basin	Mid-Norway Continental Margin, Vestford-Helgeland, 70 Tcf, mixed clastics-carbonates
N. America Region 5 (excluding USA)	12/4	22/0	155	14	5667	Villahermosa Uplift Alberta Basin	Tamabra-Like Debris-Flow Breccia Limestone Overlying Evaporites, Villahermosa Uplift, 6.9 Tcf; Cretaceous through Tertiary carbonate reservoirs
US portion – Region 5	101/43	55/not calculated for US	259	21	5898	Gulf Coast, Rocky Mts., Northern Alaska	Eastern Thrust Belt, Northern Alaska, 9 Tcf, Mississippian through Early Cretaceous carbonate and clastic reservoirs

Region	Deep AUs/ provinces	Total gas (Tcf) (gas > 4.5 km/gas > 7.5 km)	Total gas (Tcf) (all depths)	Average percent	Average maximum depth of deep gas (ft)	Dominant province(s)	Significant regional example: AU, province, mean undisc. conv. resource, primary reservoir(s)
Central and S. America – Region 6	42/22	88/11	487	18	6425	Eastern Venezuela Basin, Campos Basin, Middle Magdalena, Santa Cruz-Tarija Basin	Sub-Andean Fold and Thrust Belt, Santa Cruz-Tarija Basin, 10 Tcf, Silurian through Tertiary clastic reservoirs
Sub-Saharan Africa –Region 7	10/5	14/0	235	6	5200	West Central-Coastal Niger Delta	Akata Reservoirs, Niger Delta, 8.6 Tcf, Tertiary turbidite reservoirs
South Asia – Region 8	10/7	11/0.1	120	9	6100	Ganges–Brahmaputra Delta, Indus, Bombay	Central Basin, Ganges–Brahmaputra Delta, 5.3 Tcf, Tertiary turbidite sandstone reservoirs
Total	274/124	844/12.4	4928	17	5941		

Source: Reference [46].

Worldwide, tight gas sand resources are speculated to be significant, but no systematic evaluation has been carried out on a global scale. According to an estimate by Holditch [56], worldwide reserve of tight gas may be about 7,406 Tcf (Table 7.10).

Table 7.10. Distribution of worldwide unconventional gas reserves (in Tcf).

Region	Coalbed methane	Shale gas	Tight sand gas	Total
North America	3,017	3,842	1,371	8,228
Latin America	39	2,117	1,293	3,448
Western Europe	157	510	353	1,019
Central and Eastern Europe	118	39	78	235
Former Soviet Union	3,957	627	901	5,485
Middle East and North Africa	0	2,548	823	3,370
Sub-Saharan Africa	39	274	784	1,097
Pacific (Organization for Economic Cooperation and Development)	470	2,313	705	3,487
Other Asia Pacific	0	314	549	862
South Asia	39	0	196	235
WORLD	9,051	16,112	7,046	32,560

Source: References [56, 57].

The Energy Information Administration (EIA) estimated that as of January 1, 2000, 253.83 Tcf of technically recoverable deep natural gas exists in the U.S. This is a significant increase from 1998 estimate which was 37.27 Tcf (Table 7.11). This reserve of tight gas represents over 21% of the total recoverable natural gas in the USA. However, The USDOE, USGS, and other organizations have completed resource assessments of U.S. basins with tight gas accumulations indicating that a vast amount (~6,000 Tcf) of natural gas resources exists. Figure 7.6 shows the tight gas basin location in the USA.

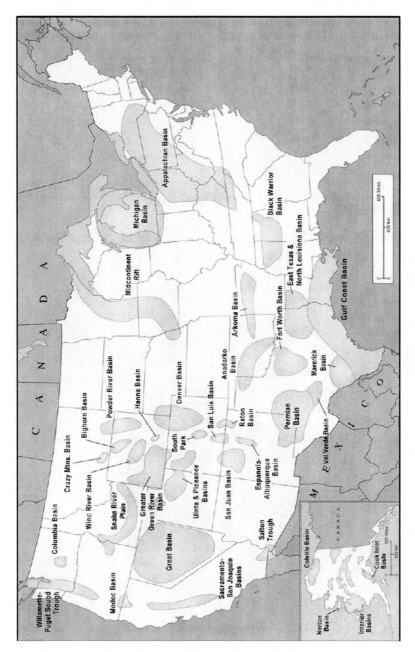

Fig. 7.6. Locations of tight gas basins in the USA [72].

Table 7.11. Tight gas reserve in various basins in the USA.

Tight gas basin	Reserve, billion ft³ (as of 1998)	Tight gas basin	Reserve, billion ft³ (as of 1998)
Arkla Basin	600	Piceance Basin	1,070
East Texas	4,500	Anadarko Basin	2,280
Texas Gulf Coast	3,600	Permian Basin	2,800
Wind River Basin	600	San Juan Basin	8,150
Green River Basin	6,000	Williston Basin	300
Denver Basin	900	Appalachian Basin	4,730
Uinta Basin	740		
Total	36,270		

Source: Reference [58].

Also it may be noted from Fig. 7.7 that some states in the USA are already producing natural gas from these basins.

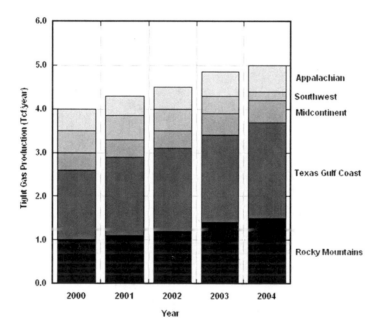

Fig. 7.7. Tight gas production in the USA.

7.3.3 Gas Containing Shales

Shale formations acts both as a source of natural gas and as its reservoir [60, 61]. Natural gas is stored in shale in three forms: free gas in rock pores, free gas in natural fractures, and adsorbed gas on organic matter and mineral surfaces. The process and cost of gas production depend on the shale formation. Recently, advanced drilling, completion, stimulation, and operating technologies have greatly improved the productivity and development economics of gas shale resources. Worldwide estimate of natural gas resources in shales is given in Table 7.12.

Table 7.12. Worldwide estimate of shale gas reserve.

Region	Gas resource in fractured shales (Tcf)
NAM-North America	3,842
LAM-Latin America	2,117
WEU-Western Europe	510
EEU- Eastern Europe	39
FSU-Former Soviet Union	627
MEA-Middle East Africa	2,548
AFR-Africa	274
CPA- Central Pacific	3,528
PAO- Asia and China	2,313
PAS- Other Asia Pacific	314
WORLD	16,112

Source: Reference [57].

Most of the natural gas containing Devonian shale in the U.S. is located around the Appalachian Basin. However, other basins including Michigan basin, Illinois basin, Fort Worth basin, and San Juan Basin are commercially used for shale gas production in the USA .The EIA estimates that there is 55.42 Tcf of technically recoverable shale gas in the USA, representing about 5% of total recoverable resources. The regions in the USA where these basins are located and used for commercial production are shown in Fig. 7.8.

7.3.4 Coal Bed Methane

Many coal seams also contain natural gas, either within the seam itself or in surrounding rocks [62–105]. It is assumed that during the coalification process, as plant materials are progressively converted to coal, large quantities of methane-rich gas is also generated which are stored within the coal. Because of its large internal surface area, coal can store six to seven times more gas than the equivalent rock volume of a conventional gas reservoir.

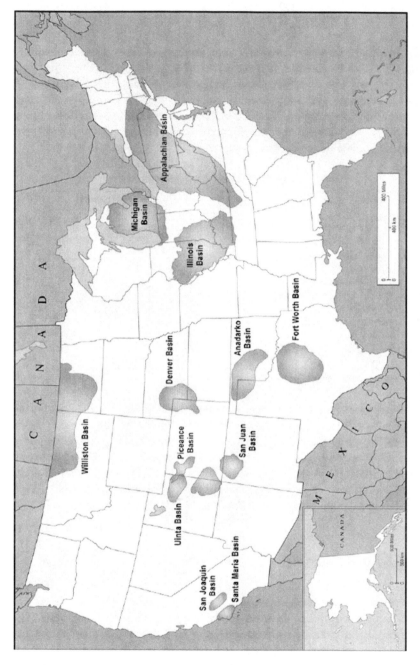

Fig. 7.8. Location of shale gas basins in the USA [72].

The amount of natural gas present in coal increases with coal rank, with depth of the coalbed, and with reservoir pressure. The fractures and pores in coal are generally filled with water. Although the deeper the coalbed, the less water is present, the water becomes more saline. This methane is usually released when coal mining starts. Various phases of coalbed methane production are shown in Fig. 7.9. This methane can be extracted and injected into natural gas pipelines. With the current technology, this methane can be captured or produced economically. However, there are significant environmental challenges, including loss of methane to the atmosphere during underground mining, and disposal of large quantities of water, sometimes saline, that are unavoidably produced with the gas. The coalbed methane is produced by reducing the pressure of the well, and this is generally accomplished by removing water from the coalbed. Figure 7.10 shows general construction of a well for coalbed methane production.

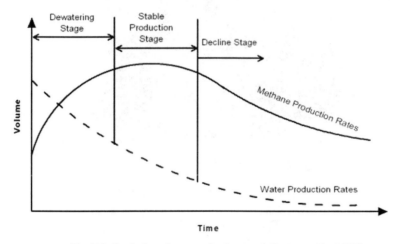

Fig. 7.9. Typical methane production curve from a coalbed [62].

Preliminary worldwide coalbed methane resources are estimated to be in between 5,800 and 24,215 Tcf. The largest potential resources, which also have the largest degree of uncertainty, are in the Former Soviet Union. Estimated resources worldwide are shown earlier in Table 7.10.

The rate of coalbed methane resource development within individual countries will be highly variable due to local economic factors and government energy priorities and policies.

The reserve and production of coal bed methane in the USA are given in Table 7.13.

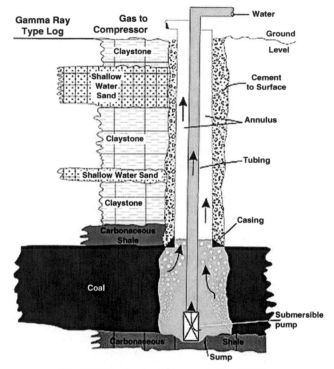

Fig. 7.10. Coalbed methane production [106].

Table 7.13. Coalbed methane reserve in the USA.

Year	Reserve	Production
2000	15,708	1,379
2001	17,531	1,562
2002	18,491	1,614
2003	18,743	1,600
2004	18,390	1,720
2005	19,892	1,732

Source: Reference [107].

7.3.5 Geopressurized Natural Gas

Of all the unconventional sources of natural gas, geopressurized zones are estimated to hold the greatest amount of gas [108–122]. Most of the geopressurized natural gas in the USA is located in the Gulf Coast region. The amount technically recoverable is under dispute, however, it is estimated to be around 1,110 Tcf.

Geopressured reservoirs or aquifers are deep underground reservoirs containing brine. The brine is usually saturated with methane. The methane content could be in the range of 30–80 ft^3 per barrel of reservoir fluid.

7.3.6 Methane Hydrates

Methane hydrates were first discovered in permafrost regions of the Arctic (Fig. 7.11). Methane hydrates (or clathrate hydrates) are ice-like crystalline molecule formed from mixtures of water and methane gas molecules and provide the greatest reservoir for organic carbon on earth (Fig. 7.12). The water (host) molecules, upon hydrogen bonding, form lattice structures with several interstitial cavities. The guest (methane) gas molecules then occupy the lattice cavities, and when a minimum number of cavities are filled, the crystalline structure becomes stable and solid gas hydrates are formed, even at temperatures well above the melting point of water ice. When gas hydrates dissociate (melt), the crystalline lattice breaks down into liquid water (or converts to ice if conditions are below the freezing point of water) and the gas is released [123–126].

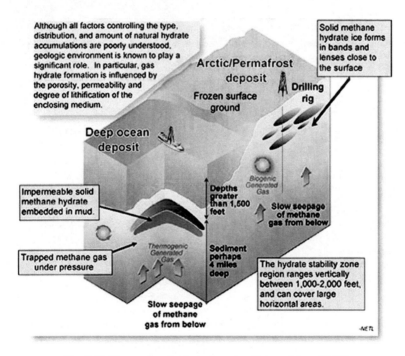

Fig. 7.11. Types of gas hydrate deposits. (Adapted from [127]).

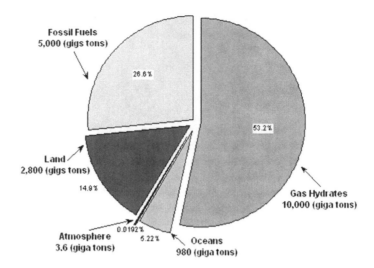

Fig. 7.12. Organic carbon reserve on earth excluding carbon in sediments and rocks. (Printed with permission from [125]).

The two common forms of gas hydrates are known as structures-I and II, which have been investigated by x-ray diffraction methods by von Stackelberg and Müller [126]. These structures are shown in Fig. 7.13.

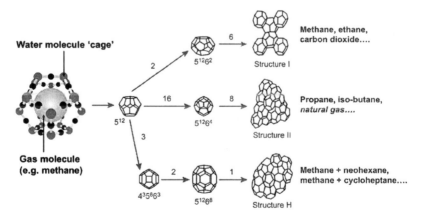

Fig. 7.13. Various types of methane gas hydrates. (Printed with permission from [126]).

Methane forms a **structure I hydrate** with two dodecahedral (20 vertices thus 20 water molecules) and six tetrakaidecahedral (24 water molecules) water cages per unit cell. The hydratation value of 20 can be determined experimentally by MAS NMR [128].

The formation of methane hydrates depends on a host of parameters; presence of free water, temperature, and pressure [129–138]. A phase diagram depicting where methane hydrates may form in the ocean floor is shown in Fig. 7.14.

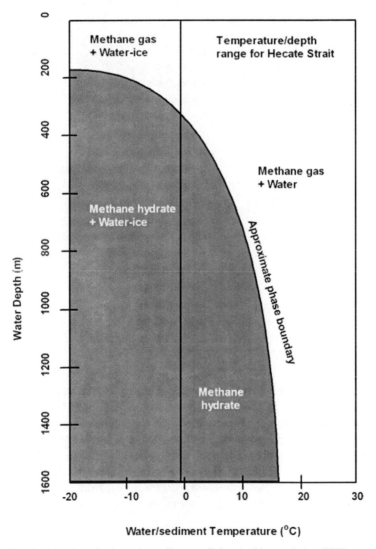

Fig. 7.14. Methane hydrate phase diagram. (Printed with permission [138]).

Estimates of methane hydrate reserve worldwide range anywhere from 7,000 Tcf to over 73,000 Tcf [139–157]. The oceanic deposit is estimated to be 30,000–49,100,000 Tcf, where as in Continental it is estimated to be in the range 5,000–12,000,000 Tcf. It may be noted that the conventional reserve of methane is about 13,000 Tcf. However, The worldwide estimate of methane hydrate reserves is extremely variable. As shown in Table 7.14, the estimate varied from 0.16 to 30,530 Tcf.

Table 7.14. Revised inventory of global estimates of methane in submarine gas hydrate (x 10^{13}).

Best or average value	References
3053	Trofimuk et al. (1973)
1573	Cherskiy and Tsarev (1977)
~ 1550	Nesterov and Salmanov (1981)
1135	Trofimuk et al. (1975)
~120	Trofimuk et al. (1979)
~45.4	Harvey and Huang (1995)
40	Kvenvolden and Claypool (1988)
26.4	Gornitz and Fung (1994)
20	MacDonald (1990), Kvenvolden (1988)
15	Makogon (1981), Trofimuk et al. (1981, 1983a, b), Makogon (1997)
6.8	Holbrook et al. (1996)
4	Milkov et al. (2003)
3.1	McIver (1981)
2.5	Milkov (2004)
>0.2	Soloviev (2002)
>0.016	Trofimuk et al. (1977) [184]

Adapted from [178].

The production of methane from hydrates is challenging and new technologies and production methods need to be developed. USGS scientists believe that we will most likely not see significant worldwide gas production from hydrates for the next 30–50 years. Gas recovery from hydrates is hindered because they occur as a solid in nature and are commonly widely dispersed in hostile Arctic and deep marine environments. However, they also noted that some countries may invest and expedite the production process due to their own need within the next 5–10 years. The detailed estimate of actual reserve has been conducted by few countries so far and is given in Table 7.15.

Table 7.15. National and regional estimates of the amount of gas within hydrates in cubic feet.

Country	Amount of gas in hydrates	Reference
USA	$317,700 \times 10^{12}$	Collett (1995)
Blake Ridge,	635×10^{12}	Dillion et al. (1993)
USA	$2,471 \times 10^{12}$	Dickens et al. (1997)*
North Slope, Alaska	$2,824 \times 10^{12}$	Holbrook al. (1996)*
	$2,012 \times 10^{12}$	Collett (2000)*
	$1,313 \times 10^{12}$	Collett (2000)
	590×10^{12}	Collett (2000)
India	$4,307 \times 10^{12}$	ONGC (1997)
Andaman Sea	$4,307 \times 10^{12}$	ONGC (1997)
Nankai Trough, Japan	$1,765 \times 10^{12}$	MITI/JNOC (1998)

*Includes associated gas [187].

7.4 Composition of Natural Gas

Natural gas mainly consists of methane (CH_4). However, a number of higher hydrocarbons such as ethane, propane, butane, pentane, and hexane along with inert gases including nitrogen and carbon dioxide can be present in the gas stream. A typical composition of natural gas is shown in Table 7.16. The composition can vary, although not significantly, based on its source and supplier. Natural gas may also contain hydrogen sulfide (H_2S) in varying amount and is called "Sour Natural Gas" if the hydrogen sulfide content is greater than 5.7 mg/m^3 at standard pressure and temperature. The sour natural gas needs to be processed further (this is also called sweetening the gas) before the gas can be utilized. Various processes are available for sweetening the gas and are discussed later in this chapter.

Table 7.16. Typical composition of natural gas.

Component	Typical analysis (mol%)	Range (mol%)
Methane	94.9	87.0–96.0
Ethane	2.5	1.8–5.1
Propane	0.2	0.1–1.5
iso-Butane	0.03	0.01–0.3
Normal-butane	0.03	0.01–0.3
iso-Pentane	0.01	Trace–0.14
Normal-pentane	0.01	Trace–0.04
Hexanes plus	0.01	Trace–0.06
Nitrogen	1.6	1.3–5.6
Carbon dioxide	0.7	0.1–1.0

(Continued)

Table 7.16. (Continued)

Component	Typical analysis (mol%)	Range (mol%)
Oxygen	0.02	0.01–0.1
Hydrogen	Trace	Trace – 0.02
Hydrogen sulfide	Trace	0–5%
Nitrogen	Trace	0–5%
Rare gases, Ar, He, Ne, Xe	Trace	
Specific gravity	0.585	0.57–0.62
Gross heating value (MJ/m³), dry basis*	37.8	36.0–40.2

*The gross heating value is the total heat obtained by complete combustion at constant pressure of a unit volume of gas in air, including the heat released by condensing the water vapour in the combustion products (gas, air, and combustion products taken at standard temperature and pressure). In the Union Gas system, the typical sulfur content is 5.5 mg/m³. This includes the 4.9 mg/m³ of sulfur in the odorant (mercaptan) added to gas for safety reasons. The water vapor content of natural gas in the Union Gas system is less than 80 mg/m³, and is typically 16–32 mg/m³.
Source: Union Gas Limited, Ontario, Canada.

7.5 Combustion Properties of Natural Gas

The typical combustion properties of natural gas are shown in Table 7.17. The properties shown are an overall average of the Union Gas system. These values can vary from supplier to supplier.

Table 7.17. Typical combustion properties of natural gas.

Properties	Values
Ignition point	593°C*
Flammability limits	4–16% volume percent in air
Theoretical flame temperature (stoichiometric air/fuel ratio)	1,960°C
Maximum flame velocity	0.3 m/s
Relative density (specific gravity)	0.585
Wobbe index	1,328

7.6 Natural Gas Production

The natural gas that is delivered into our homes begins with the exploration of the earth's surface to locate a reservoir for the natural gas. Once a reservoir is discovered, it goes through a number of processes before it is delivered to homes or customers. These processes may be divided into the following categories:

- Exploration
- Extraction
- Processing
- Transportation
- Storage
- Distribution
- Marketing

7.6.1 Exploration

The search for petroleum or natural gas starts with the geologists, who use surveying and mapping to understand the surface and sub-surface characteristics, to determine which areas are most likely to contain a petroleum or natural gas reservoir [186–192]. Geologists use many tools including the outcroppings of rocks on the surface or in valleys and gorges. Geologic information obtained from the rock cuttings and samples obtained from the digging of irrigation ditches, water wells, and other oil and gas wells are used to determine areas for further exploration.

Geophysicists mainly use three methods for oil and gas exploration: magnetic, gravity, and seismic exploration. The magnetometer and gravity meter are used to locate hidden, subsurface petroleum traps [194]. In seismic exploration, sound is transmitted into the ground by an explosive, such as dynamite, or by a thumper truck. Currently, seismology is the main tool used by geologists to explore an area for petroleum or natural gas [195–204]. Both on-shore and off-shore seismology techniques are available to geologists. Following exploration by these methods, exploratory wells and loggings are done to gain a better understanding of not only of the geology, but also of the total reserve.

7.6.1.1 Magnetometers

In magnetic exploration a magnetometer is used to determine the strength of the earth's magnetic field at a specific point on the earth's surface. Magnetic properties vary based on the composition of the earth's layer. Underground formations can be measured using Magnetometers to generate geological and geophysical data. Magnetometers can measure the small differences in the Earth's magnetic field, which can be determined with an aerial pass of a magnetometer or on the ground using a type of magnetometer called a vertical field balance. From these readings, experts determine if there is oil or gas, because there exists a correlation between low magnetic readings and rocks that contain oil.

7.6.1.2 Gravimeters

Using gravimeters, geophysicists measure and record the difference in the Earth's gravitational field at various underground locations. Minute differences in gravitational field exist due to the different underground formations and rock types. This information can help the geophysicists to determine the existence of potential reservoir for petroleum or natural gas.

Gravitational methods can also be done aerially with a gravimeter or on the ground using a more precise instrument called a gravity gradiometer. The data from gravitational methods is valuable because differences in the gravitational field indicate a difference in the density of the ground which correlates to rocks that contain oil. Both of these methods are relatively low impact system because they only involve either not touching the ground at all, or by setting up stations approximately 100 yards apart using low-impact transportation. Thus the impact of non-seismic techniques is significantly lower than the impact that would be caused by drilling unnecessary wells.

7.6.1.3 Exploratory Wells

Once the survey by various instruments discussed above convince geologists that there are enough indication of a high probability of petroleum formation, exploratory wells are drilled. The presence of suspected oil and gas deposits is generally confirmed by the exploratory (These wells are called wildcat wells) drilling of deep holes. The drill cuttings and fluids are analyzed by geologists to gain a better understanding of the geologic features of the area. Drilling an exploratory well is expensive and also time consuming, since wildcat wells are deeper and drilled in areas having no prior history of oil or gas deposits. Construction of access roads and drill pads are typically required to conduct these exploratory drilling operations increasing the cost of operation. A typical drilling rig is shown in Fig. 7.15.

7.6.2 Logging

Samples collected from the exploratory wells go through a series of tests, generally referred to as "Logging" to allow geologists and drill operators to monitor the progress of the well drilling and to gain a better picture of subsurface formations [205–209]. The quantitative analysis of well logs can provide the following information:

– Porosity
– Water saturation, fluid type (oil/gas/water)
– Lithology

- Permeability
- Hydrocarbons-in-place
- Reserves (the recoverable fraction of hydrocarbons in-place)
- Mapping of reservoir

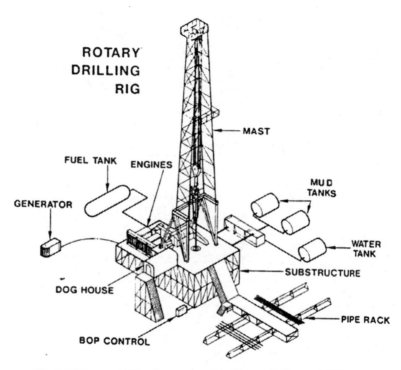

Fig. 7.15. Rotary drilling rig arrangements. Source: Reference [205].

A typical logging system is shown in Fig. 7.16.

There are over 100 different logging tests that can be used to monitor the drilling process and to make decision if the drilling should be continued. The most common types of logs are:

- Standard log
- Resistivity log
- Spontaneous potential log
- Gamma ray log
- Neutron log
- Density log
- Sonic (acoustic) log

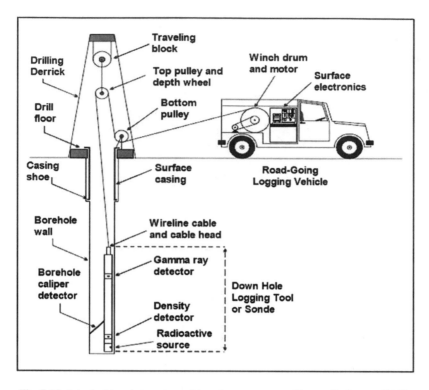

Fig. 7.16. A typical logging system with main components. (Source: Reference [210]).

Standard Log

Standard logging consists of examining and recording the physical properties of the drill cuttings (rock that is displaced by the drilling of the well) and core samples taken from the underground soil. These cuttings and cores are often examined using microscopes with a magnification greater than 2,000 times.

Resistivity Log

This log measures the bulk resistivity of the formation to determine the types of fluids present in the reservoir rocks. Resistivity is a function of porosity and pore fluid in a rock. A non-porous rock or hydrocarbon containing formation has high resistivity. By contrast, if the rock formation is porous and contain saline water, the resistivity will be low. This log is therefore used as an indicator of formation lithology. There are many different types of resistivity logs, which differ mainly in the depth to which the measurements are made. These logs are listed below.

AIT (Array Induction Tool): It measures five depths of investigation.

DIL (Dual Induction Log): This log is used for deep and medium depths of investigation.

DLL (Dual Latero Log): This log is used for deep and medium depths of investigation.

SFL (Spherically Focused Log): This log is used for a shallow depth of investigation.

SGR (Shallow Guard Log): This log is used for a shallow depth of investigation.

Spontaneous Potential (SP) Log

This log provides data on permeability of the rock. The electrical current that occurs naturally between the boreholes drilling fluid and the formation water that is held in pores of the reservoir rock is measured. Porous sandstones have high permeability compared to impermeable shale and thus can distinguish them. The SP log can also be used for locating bed boundaries.

Gamma Ray Log

Rocks contain various naturally occurring radioactive materials that emit gamma rays at various energy levels depending on the type of isotopes present in the rock. In this log the radioactivity of a formation is measured using a gamma detector. Gamma ray logs are one of the most commonly used logs for sequence stratigraphic analysis. Shale commonly have high radioactivity compared to sandstones. Also coarse grain sand, which contains little mud, is less radioactive compared to fine sand that contain significant amount of mud. The gamma ray activity is measured in an API unit, a unit of counting rate for the gamma-ray log. The difference between the high and low radioactivity sections in the API calibration pit is defined as 200 API units. One API unit is defined as the 1/200th of the difference in radioactivity from the gamma ray between zones of high and low radioactivity in the API Gamma Ray calibration pit in Houston, Texas, USA. In shale, radioactivity can be about 200 API units.

Neutron Log

This is also known as compensated neutron log (CNL). A neutron source, typically a californium-252 spontaneous fission source, is placed in the bore hole and a gamma detector picks up the radiation from scattering or capture reactions. The porosity of a formation is measured by using this log. The amount of hydrogen atoms present in the reservoir pores that are filled with either water or hydrocarbon (oil) is measured. The log is calibrated to limestone. The linear limestone porosity units are calibrated using the API Neutron pit in 19% porosity. The water filled limestone is defined as 1000 API units. Along with the density log, the lithology of the formation is determined using the neutron log data.

Density Log

The density log measures the density of the formation rocks for determination of porosity. Different lithologies can also be determined using density log as the density of rocks differs based on its contents, such as 1.2–1.8 g/cm^3 for coal, 2.65 g/cm^3 for pure quartz, and up to 2.75 g/cm^3 for limestone. The density logs generally overestimate the porosity of rocks that contain gas and result in "crossover" of the log curves when paired with neutron logs.

Sonic (Acoustic) Log

This log measures the speed of sound in the formation, which can be correlated to both porosity and lithology of the formation. Sound waves travel faster through high-density shale than through lower-density sandstones. Sonic log value for sandstone is in the range of 51–56 μs/ft.

NMR (Nuclear Magnetic Resonance) Log

This log measures the magnetic response of fluids present in the pore spaces of the reservoir rocks. Both porosity and permeability are determined from the data. The measurements are largely based on the fluid and the pore space characteristics. A better understanding of the fluids and pores is possible compared to other conventional logs like density, neutron, and sonic.

Dipmeter Logs

This log determines the orientations of sandstone and shale beds in the well. The direction and angle of formation dip in relation to the borehole is obtained. The data provides the geologic structure of the formation. The dipmeters can provide a detailed image of the rocks on all sides of the well hole.

Caliper Logging

Caliper logging provides a continuous recording of borehole diameter versus depth. These logs are generally run in uncased wells, but can be also used within casing. Caliper logs are also used to locate caved zones, casing, and the absence of casing; and permit the recognition of mud cake. (i.e., permeable zones).

A number of different logs have been used in the oil and gas industry. These logs are presented in Table 7.18.

Table 7.18. Different types of logs and their purposes.

Log type	Log code	General name for log order	Definition
Electric log	EL	Electric log	Open hole log with an SP curve and typically a non-induced resistivity curve
Induction log	IL	Electric log	SP log with one or more induced resistivity curves (including focused and laterologs)
Micro log	ML	Micro log	Micro-resistivity log
Gamma ray log	GR	Gamma-ray log	Log which only records natural radioactivity (logs with other curves are a different log type)
Neutron log	NTR	Neutron porosity log	Records hydrogen concentration in the formation; usually has a gamma ray curve; does not include density-neutron logs
Density log	DL	Density porosity log	Records electron density in the formation; usually has a gamma ray curve; does not include density-neutron logs
Density-neutron log	DNL	Density porosity log	Porosity log with at least one density curve and at least one neutron curve
Sonic log	SL	Sonic porosity log	Porosity log based on transit time of sound waves through the formation
Magnetic resonance log	MRL	Magnetic resonance porosity log	Porosity log based on measuring the signal generated by polarized hydrogen protons
Computed log	CUL		Any log that attempts to characterize the formation by computer analyses of multiple other logs that have been run in the well
EPT log	EPT		Measures propagation and attenuation of electromagnetic waves through a formation
Dipmeter log	DIP	Dipmeter log	Records the attitude (dip angle and dip direction) of rock layers in the borehole
Gamma ray Spectral log	SPC		Uses gamma ray energy spectrum to record potassium, uranium, and thorium in the formation
Caliper log	CAL		Measures width of the borehole
Fracture ID log	FID		A special presentation of dipmeter micro resistivity measurements that identifies fractures
Borehole imaging log	BIL		High-resolution imaging of borehole circumference using closely spaced log measurements, typically of micro resistivity or sonic transit time

(Continued)

Table 7.18. (Continued)

Log type	Log code	General name for log order	Definition
Production log	PRL	Production log	Any of various logs used in completing a well for production
RFT (repeat formation test) log	RFT		Records formation pressure data (and obtains a small rock sample) of the formation
Temperature log	TMP		Records temperature of drilling mud in the borehole
TVD log	TVD	TVD log	Records position and attitude of borehole in deviated wells

Source: Reference [211].

7.6.3 Extraction

In the extraction phase, the following issues are taken into account.

- Economic considerations
- Permitting, leasing, and royalties
- Technology based on onshore or offshore drilling

If the site and size of the basin is found large enough to be economically feasible, permitting, leasing, and royalty issues are finalized. Finally a decision is made regarding the drilling technology. There are two main types of onshore drilling: Percussion, or 'cable tool' drilling and rotary drilling. Cable tool drilling consists of raising and dropping a heavy metal bit into the ground that punches a hole down through the Earth. Cable tool drilling is usually used for shallow, low pressure formations. In rotary drilling, a sharp rotating metal bit is used to drill through the Earth's crust. This type of drilling is used primarily for deeper wells that may be under high downhole pressure.

7.6.3.1 Well Completion

Before natural gas or oil is extracted from underground, the well must be *completed* for commercial production. The steps involved for completion of a production well are as follows:

- Well casing
- Completion
- Wellhead
- Lifting and well treatment

A series of metal tubes are installed in the freshly drilled hole to strengthen the sides of the well hole, ensuring that no oil or natural gas seeps out of the well hole as it is brought to the surface, and to keep other fluids or gases from seeping into the formation through the well. This process is called the well casing and there are five different types of well casing. They are installed in the following order:

- Conductor casing
- Surface casing
- Intermediate casing
- Liner string
- Production casing

Conductor casing is installed first to prevent the top of the well from caving in and to circulate the drilling fluid up from the bottom of the well. They are generally 20–50 ft long. The surface casing is installed next and fits inside the top of the conductor casing. It can be more than 2,000 ft long, and is smaller in diameter than the conductor casing. Both the conductor and surface casings are cemented into place. The primary objective of surface casing is to prevent fresh water contamination from the drilling activities. The surface casing serves as a conduit for drilling mud returning to the surface, and helps protect the drill hole from being damaged during drilling. Intermediate casing is used to protect the well from various unexpected activities from underground such as pressure change, and saltwater deposit. The intermediate casing may also be cemented into place for added protection. Liner strings are sometimes used instead of intermediate casing and generally are not cemented. Production casing, also known as oil string or long string is installed last. It extends from the surface of the well to the petroleum producing formation. The diameter of the production casing depends on the lifting equipment to be used, the number of completions required, and the possibility of deepening the well at a later time.

7.6.3.2 Completion

There are six types of completion as listed below. The types of completion to be used in any formation depend on the characteristics of the formation and the targeted products.

- Open hole completion
- Conventional perforated completion
- Sand exclusion completion
- Permanent completion
- Multiple zone completion
- Drainhole completion

Open hole completion is the most basic type of completion in which the casing is placed directly in the formation. The end of the casing is open to the formation and no protective filter is installed. The formations that are acid fractured generally use this type of completion.

In conventional perforated completion, the side of the casing is perforated to allow for the flow of hydrocarbons into the well hole. The perforation is carried out in situ using a jet perforating technique. This involves small, electrically ignited charges, lowered into the well. When ignited, these charges penetrate through the casing, cementing, and any other barrier between the formation and the open well forming tiny holes.

If the formation contains large amount of loose sand, sand exclusion completion is used. A screen is used to prevent flow of sand inside the casing. Sand inside the well hole can cause many complications, including erosion of casing and other equipment.

Permanent completion involves permanent installation of the casing, cementing, perforating, and other completion work. This is done only once and can reduce the cost significantly. In this method there is no room for error.

Multiple zone completion is generally used for oil well and if more than two formations are present in close vicinity. This type of completion is preferred if all the formations will be used for production. Oil can be extracted from the formations simultaneously without mixing them, thus reducing the production cost significantly. One of the main challenges is to keep various formations separated.

Drainhole completions are commonly associated with oil wells than with natural gas wells. A horizontal well is drilled from the vertical drill allowing hydrocarbons to drain into the well.

7.6.3.3 Wellhead

Natural gas in the well can be at a pressure well above 20,000 psi. The wellhead consists of various equipment mounted at the opening of the well on the surface that regulate and monitor the extraction of natural gas and oil from the underground formation. These instruments should be capable of withstanding the above pressure. The wellhead consists of three components: the casing head, the tubing head, and the 'Christmas tree'. The casing head generally supports the entire casing and also provides the sealing between casing and the surface. The tubing head provides the sealing between the tubes and also provides the mechanical support to the tubes in the well. The Christmas tree is referred to the various valves and fitting that are used in the casing head and tube head to monitor the flow of the gas or oil on the surface.

7.6.3.4 Lifting and Well Treatment

Once the well is completed, the production of natural gas can proceed. Natural gas flows to the surface due to the pressure difference. Once the flow of natural gas is started, the Most Efficient Recovery (MER) rate is established. As more and more natural gas is extracted from the formation, the production rate of the well decreases. This is known as the decline rate. At this point, lifting equipment and well stimulation may be necessary to maintain the production rate of a well. However, this is generally more common with the oil well or oil wells that have associated natural gas, than with the natural gas only well.

7.6.4 Processing

The natural gas that is fed into the gas pipeline for delivery to the consumer must meet certain specifications in order for the pipeline grid to operate properly. Therefore, natural gas produced at the wellhead, which contains various contaminants and natural gas liquids, must be processed, before delivering to the high-pressure, long-distance pipelines. These specifications are given in Table 7.19. The natural gas processing subject has been discussed in great details in a number of books [211–218].

Table 7.19. Typical composition of natural gas before refining.

Component	Chemical formula	Volume (%)
Methane	CH_4	>85
Ethane	C_2H_6	3-8
Propane	C_3H_8	1–2
Butane	C_4H_{10}	<1
Pentane	C_5H_{12}	<1
Carbon dioxide	CO_2	1–2
Hydrogen sulfide	H_2S	<1
Nitrogen	N_2	1–5
Helium	He	<0.5

If the natural gas does not meet these specifications various operational problems, pipeline deterioration, or even pipeline rupture may occur.

The various processing steps before delivering the natural gas into the pipeline are shown in Fig. 7.17. Some of these steps may be optional depending on the composition of the wellhead gas. The natural gas processing system may be divided into seven major sections.

- Gas-oil separator
- Oil and condensate removal
- Dehydration
- Contaminant removal
- Nitrogen extraction
- Separation of natural gas liquids (NGL)
- Fractionation

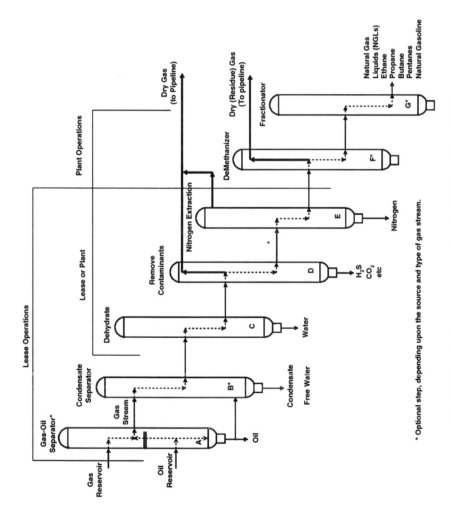

* Optional step, depending upon the source and type of gas stream.

Fig. 7.17. A typical natural gas processing plant. (Adapted from [218]).

7.6.4.1 Gas-Oil Separation

Pressure reduction at the wellhead is generally sufficient for separation of gas from oil using a conventional closed tank. The gas is separated from liquid hydrocarbons (oil) due to the difference in specific gravity. In some cases, however, a multi-stage gas-oil separation process is needed to separate the gas stream from the crude oil. These gas-oil separators are commonly closed cylindrical shells, horizontally mounted with inlets at one end, an outlet at the top for removal of gas, and an outlet at the bottom for removal of oil. Separation is accomplished by alternately heating and cooling by compression of the flow stream through multiple steps. Some water and condensate are also removed by this process. The design of a horizontal separator is shown in Fig. 7.18.

7.6.4.2 Oil and Condensate Removal

Condensates are removed from the gas stream at the wellhead through the use of mechanical separators. The stream can be fed directly into the separator from the wellhead, if the gas-oil separation process is not needed. A Low-Temperature Separator (LTX) is most often used for wells producing high pressure gas along with light crude oil or condensate. These separators use pressure differentials to cool the wet natural gas and separate the oil and condensate. The gas stream enters the processing plant at high pressure (600 lb per in.^{2} gauge (psig) or greater) through an inlet slug catcher where free water is removed from the gas, after which it is directed to a condensate separator. Extracted condensate is routed to on-site storage tanks. The gas stream is rapidly expanded through a choke valve resulting in a decrease in the temperature. As gas cools, liquids present in the stream condensed out from the stream. Often, after liquid removal, the dry gas flows back through the heat exchanger and is warmed by the incoming wet gas. A schematic diagram of a low temperature separator is shown in Fig. 7.19.

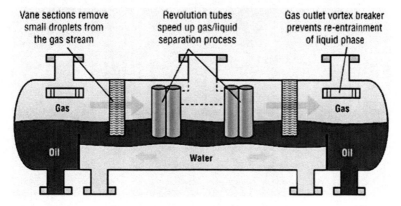

Fig. 7.18. Horizontal dual flow separator [221].

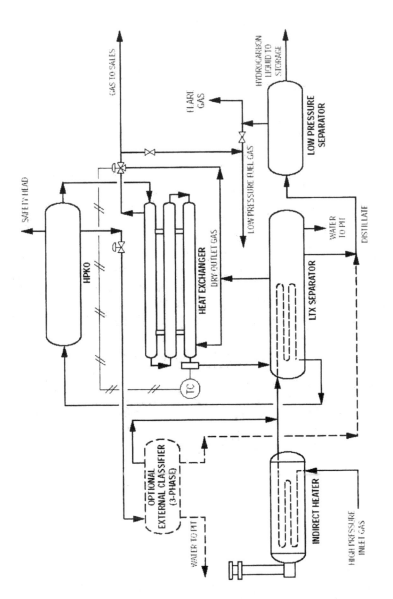

Fig. 7.19. LTX hydrocarbon liquid recovery system [219].

7.6.4.3 Dehydration

The dehydration process is used mainly to eliminate water vapor from the gas stream which may cause the formation of hydrates. Hydrates are solid particles that can cause a number of problems during flow through pipelines including blockage and damage to pressure boosting pumps. Under certain temperature and pressure, methane and other alkanes in the gas stream can form hydrates if free water is present in the gas stream. Two most common methods used by the natural gas industry to remove free water are: the use of ethylene glycol (glycol injection) and solid desiccant dehydration.

Glycol Dehydration (Glycol Injection) [221–240]

Water vapor from the natural gas stream is removed by contacting it with either diethylene glycol (DEG) or triethylene glycol (TEG) in a counter-current contractor. Lean glycol stream containing about 99% glycol is sprayed from the top of the contractor, while the gas stream is fed from the bottom. The water from the wet natural gas stream is absorbed by the glycol. The dry gas from the top of the contractor is send to the next processing unit. The diluted glycol solution (called the rich glycol stream) is fed to another contractor where water vapor is removed by heating the solution while dry air is blown through the contractor to generate the glycol solution to its original concentration. The regenerated glycol solution is recycled back to the first contractor. The schematic diagram of a glycol dehydration system is shown in Fig. 7.20.

One of the concerns with the glycol dehydration system is that the rich glycol stream also contains various impurities along with a small amount of methane. During regeneration of the lean glycol stream, these impurities and methane are released to the atmosphere. The addition of flash tank separator-condensers can recover 90–99% of the dissolved methane. In the flash tank separator the pressure of the glycol stream is reduced suddenly allowing dissolved low boiling point constituents (methane and other hydrocarbons) of the solution to flash or vaporize.

In order to provide good contact between the gas and the liquid, the tower either has trays or packed with the inert packing.

Solid Desiccant Dehydration [241–246]

In this process, natural gas is passed through a tower, from top to bottom, packed with solid desiccants. Typical desiccants used in the natural gas dehydration include activated alumina, granular silica gel or molecular sieve materials. Solid-desiccant dehydrators are generally more effective than glycol dehydrators since a very low dew point of the processed gas can be obtained. These types of

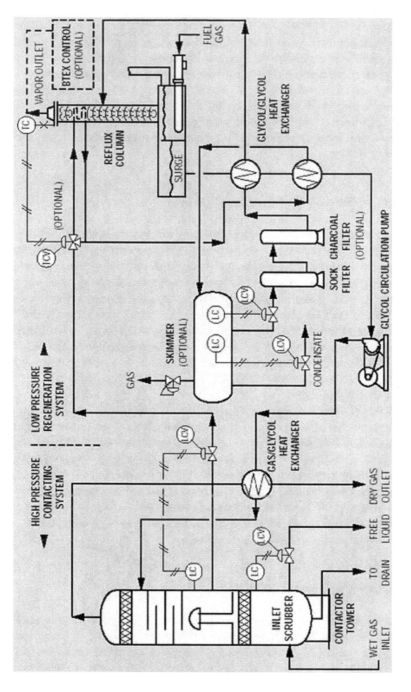

Fig. 7.20. Glycol dehydration system [219].

dehydration systems are best suited for large volumes of gas under very high pressure. They can be used on a pipeline downstream of a compressor station. Generally two or more desiccant beds (towers) are required for continuous operation. After a certain period of time (i.e., after treating certain volume of the natural gas) the bed becomes exhausted. At this point the water content of the treated gas may not meet the required specification, and the gas stream is diverted to the second bed. The exhausted bed needs to be regenerated. To regenerate the desiccant bed, a heated gas, generally air is passed through the desiccant bed removing the water from the desiccant. Following regeneration, the bed is cooled and is ready for the use. A molecular sieve based system developed by UOP is shown in Fig. 7.21.

7.6.4.4 Contaminant and Acid Gas Removal

Hydrogen sulfide (H_2S), CO_2, water vapor, helium, and oxygen present in the natural gas stream must be removed prior to feeding to the pipeline. In the presence of water, CO_2 forms carbonic acid which is corrosive. CO_2 also reduces the BTU value of gas and if the concentration of CO_2 is more than 2–3%, the gas is unmarketable. H_2S is an extremely toxic gas that is also very corrosive to equipment. Amine sweetening processes remove these contaminants so that the gas is marketable and suitable for transportation.

Amine Treatment Process [248–254]

Amine has a natural affinity for both CO_2 and H_2S allowing this to be a very efficient and effective removal process. A number of amine compounds are used for sweetening of the natural gas. Sweetening of natural gas referred to removal of acid gases: H_2S, and CO_2. Each of the amines offers distinct advantages to specific treating problems. These amines are listed below.

MEA (Monoethanolamine)

Mainly used in low pressure natural gas treatment applications requiring stringent outlet gas specifications.

MDEA (Methyldiethanolamine)

It has a higher affinity for H_2S than CO_2 which allows some CO_2 "slip" while retaining H_2S removal capabilities.

DEA (Diethanolamine)

It is used for medium to high pressure treatment facility and does not require reclaiming, as required for MEA and DGA systems.

FORMULATED (SPECIALTY) SOLVENTS

A variety of blended or specialty solvents are available in the market for removal for H_2S and CO_2.

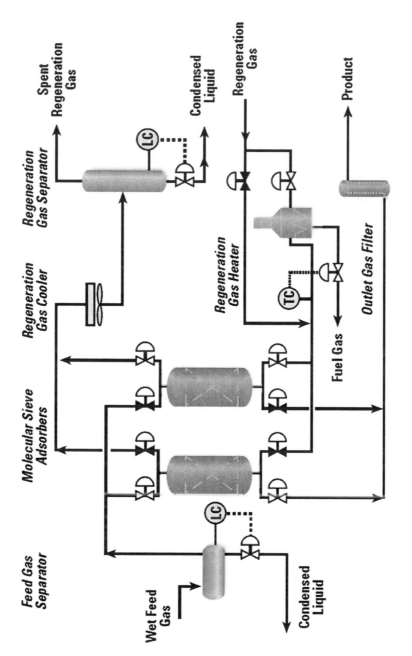

Fig. 7.21. Desiccant based natural gas dehydration system [247].

The reactions of amines with H_2S and CO_2 are summarized below

$$2\ RNH_2 + H_2S = (RNH_3)_2S$$
$$2\ RNH_2 + CO_2 = RNHCOONH_3R$$

where:

R = mono, di, or tri-ethanol

The recovered hydrogen sulfide gas stream may be: (1) vented, (2) flared in waste gas flares or modern smokeless flares, (3) incinerated, or (4) utilized for the production of elemental sulfur using the Claus process or sulfuric acid. If the recovered H_2S gas stream is not to be utilized as a feedstock for commercial applications, the gas is usually passed to a tail gas incinerator in which the H_2S is oxidized to SO_2 and is then released to the atmosphere through a stack.

The gas sweetening process is illustrated in Fig. 7.22. Sour gas enters at the bottom of the contactor or absorber tower and the lean amine solution is sprayed from the top. Purified gas flows from the top of the tower. The amine solution containing the absorbed acid gases is now considered rich stream. The lean amine and rich amine flow through the heat exchanger in counter current direction, heating the rich amine. Rich amine is then further heated in the regeneration still column by steam. The steam rising through the still liberates H_2S and CO_2, regenerating the amine. Steam and acid gases separated from the rich amine are condensed and cooled. The condensed water is separated in the reflux accumulator and returned to the still. Hot, regenerated, lean amine is cooled in a solvent aerial cooler and circulated to the contactor tower, completing the cycle.

Gas Sweetening with Amines

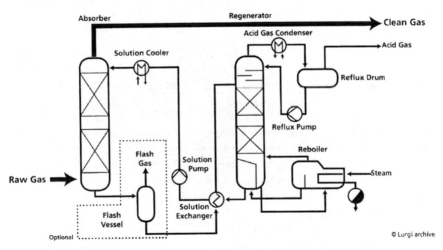

Fig. 7.22. A gas sweetening process flow diagram using amines. (Adapted from Lurgi (1/9/2009) Gas sweetening with amines. www.lurgi.com/website/fileadmin/user_upload/1_PDF/2_Technologie/englisch/10_Aminwaesch en-E.pdf).

7.6.4.5 Nitrogen Extraction

Once hydrogen sulfide and carbon dioxide are removed to the acceptable level, the stream is fed to a Nitrogen Rejection Unit (NRU). The stream could be further dehydrated in a NRU using molecular sieve beds. The nitrogen is cryogenically separated and vented. Another type of NRU unit separates methane and heavier hydrocarbons from nitrogen using an absorbent solvent. The absorbed methane and heavier hydrocarbons are flashed off from the solvent by depressurizing the stream. The liquid from the flash regeneration step is returned to the top of the methane absorber as lean solvent. Helium, if any, can be extracted from the gas stream through membrane diffusion in a Pressure Swing Adsorption (PSA) unit.

7.6.4.6 Natural Gas Liquid Recovery

The NGL can be recovered from the stream using two methods: cryogenic and absorption (non-cryogenic) methods. The absorption and cryogenic expander processes together account for around 90% of total natural gas liquids production.

In the absorption process, extraction is carried out using a lean oil absorption-mechanical refrigeration system. The refrigerated absorption process enhanced the extraction efficiency. Recently, both refrigeration and pre-saturation methods have been developed for further enhancement of the efficiency. The introduction of Joule Thompson valves and turbo expanders in 1960s made significant contributions to the achievement of cryogenic conditions. The use of reflux and the heat integration allowed high NGL recoveries.

7.6.4.7 Oil Absorption Process

In this method, the natural gas is contacted with a lean oil (molecular weight of about 150) in an absorber column at a temperature of about 100°F. An absorbing oil that has high affinity for NGLs is used in the absorption column. The rich oil exiting the bottom of the absorber flows into a rich oil depropanizer which separates the propane and lighter components and returns them to the gas stream. The rich oil is then fractionated in a column, where the NGL's (C_4+) are recovered as an overhead product and the lean oil is recycled to the absorber column. This process allows for the recovery of around 75% of butanes, and 85 – 90% of pentanes and heavier molecules from the natural gas stream. A schematic flow diagram of the system is shown in Fig. 7.23.

Extraction of NGL can be enhanced by using refrigerated low molecular weight oil. The typical temperature with propane refrigerant is about –42°C. A lean oil having molecular weight in the range of 100–110 is generally used in this process. In the refrigerated oil absorption method, total recovery can be more than 90%, and ethane extraction can be around 40%. Extraction of the other, heavier NGLs can be close to 100% using this process. A typical flow diagram of the process is shown in Fig. 7.24.

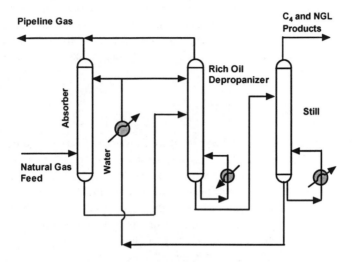

Fig. 7.23. Recovery of NGL using oil absorption method. (Printed with permission from Mehra YR (2004) Market driven evolution of gas processing technologies for NGLs. Advanced Extraction Technologies. http://www.aet.com/gtip1.htm [255]).

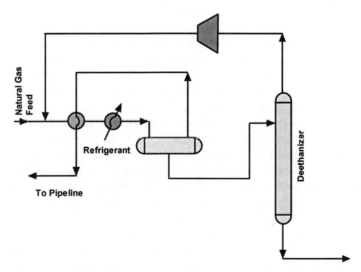

Fig. 7.24. A schematic diagram of a process for enhancement of NGL recovery using refrigeration process. (Printed with permission from Mehra YR (2004) Market driven evolution of gas processing technologies for NGLs. Advanced Extraction Technologies. http://www.aet.com/gtip1.htm [255]).

A number of refrigeration processes have been developed to further lower the temperature. These methods include Cascade Refrigeration Process, Joule Thompson (JT) Expansion Process, and Turbo Expansion Process. Also, several proprietary NGL extraction processes are available in the market. The extraction efficiency was enhanced using various extraction schemes such as lean column reflux and maximum heat integration. The integration between the natural gas recovery process and liquefaction process is possible while maintaining high efficiencies for both the processes.

7.6.4.8 Fractionation

The recovered NGL is further separated into different fractions to increase their product value. The process is called fractionation. The process occurs in stages and in a number of columns connected in series. The liquid feed is heated and fed to a deethanizer. This step separates the ethane from the NGL stream. In the next step, propane is separated in the depropanizer. The Debutanizer is the next step of the process. This step boils off the butanes, leaving the pentanes and heavier hydrocarbons in the NGL stream. Finally, a Butane Splitter or deisobutanizer is used to separate iso- and normal- butanes.

7.6.5 Natural Gas Transport

Natural gas is transported and delivered to the consumer from the production facilities mainly through a complex net work of pipelines. There are essentially three major types of pipelines along the transportation route: the gathering system, the interstate pipeline, and the distribution system. The gathering system consists of low pressure, low diameter pipelines that transport raw natural gas from the wellhead to the processing plant. Pipelines can be characterized as interstate or intrastate. Interstate pipelines carry natural gas across state boundaries, in some cases across the country. Intrastate pipelines, on the other hand, transport natural gas within a particular state. Natural gas pipelines are subject to regulatory oversight, which in many ways determines the manner in which pipeline companies must operate. The USA natural gas pipeline grid includes more than 210 mainline natural gas pipeline systems. In 2005,109 were classified as interstate systems by the Federal Energy Regulatory Commission (FERC). The remaining 101 were intrastate natural gas pipeline systems, whose operations are confined to a single State. The combined natural gas pipeline capacity on mainline intrastate systems is about 33 Bcf/d.

Interstate natural gas pipeline systems account for more than 148 Bcf/d of total USA natural gas transportation capacity and approximately 213,000 miles of pipeline. Furthermore, the top 30 interstate natural gas pipeline companies alone account for more than 78%, or about 115 Bcf/d of the interstate natural gas pipeline capacity [256]. The network of the pipelines in the USA is shown in Fig. 7.25.

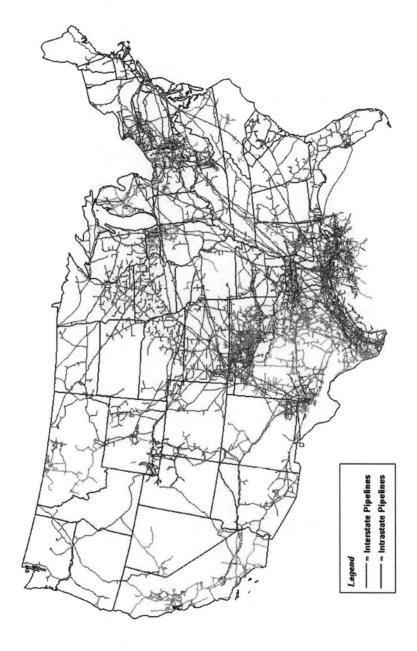

Fig. 7.25. Natural gas pipeline network for distribution of natural gas in the USA. (Adapted from Energy Information Administration, USA).

As can be seen from Fig. 7.26, the pipeline capacity remained more or less stagnant in the USA for the last several years. However, a major expansion is planned over the next several years. The increased capacity will require addition of physical pipeline to the network. The planned addition of pipeline mileage is shown in Fig. 7.27.

The natural gas pipeline network runs through several regions and also the capacity depends on the demand of the particular region. Fig. 7.28 shows the capacity of natural gas pipeline in various regions.

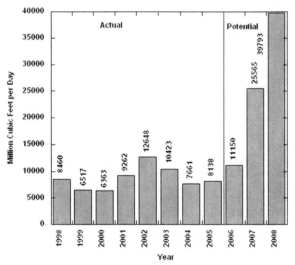

Fig. 7.26. The capacity of the pipeline and expected expansion in the USA for transportation of natural gas.

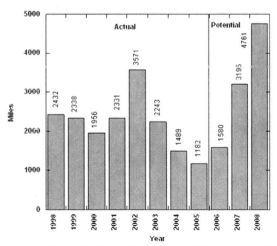

Fig. 7.27. Addition to natural gas pipeline mileage in the USA. (Source: Energy Information Administration, GasTran natural gas transportation information system, Natural gas pipeline projects database).

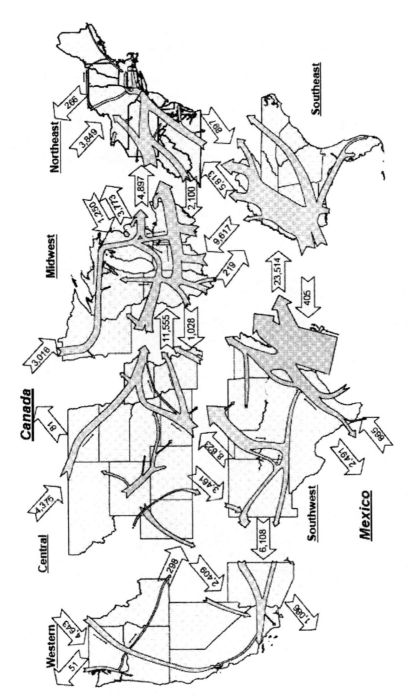

Fig. 7.28. Capacity of natural gas transportation in the North America. (Adapted from Energy Information Administration, USA).

7.6.5.1 International Transportation of Natural Gas

Natural gas is becoming a major energy source through out the world. However, a majority of countries sell their known resources. As a result, the international transportation of natural gas through pipelines is becoming a major method for trading natural gas. In Europe, Russia is the major exporter of natural gas. The pipelines that exists or being planned in Europe for transportation of natural gas are shown in Fig. 7.29. Figure 7.30 shows the pipeline in various parts of Europe. Recently, Europe is planning to transport natural gas from the Fareast through Turkey. The proposed pipeline is shown in Fig. 7.31. Various international pipelines that are under construction or proposed are given in Table 7.20.

Table 7.20. International pipeline under construction or proposed.

Company name	Project name and location	Length (miles)	Cost ($ US million)	In service date
AFRICA				
NNPC/Sonatrach	TransSaharan Gas Ppeline No. Africa-Ben Saf-Almeria, Spain	2,772	$6 billion	Feasibility
Saipem (Shell Dev)	Niger Delta	214	$420	2008
ASIA PACIFIC				
Western Australian Gov Continental Gas Pipeline. Trans	Trans Continental Gas Pipeline Offshore Australia to Hobart	1,827	$3 billion	Feasibility
China National Petroleum Corp.	Xingang Province to Guangzhou,	N/A	N/A	Feasibility
Dampier Bunbury Pipeline Co.	Dampier Bunbury Pipeline expansion	122	$430	2009
PT Perusahaan Gas Negara (PGN)	South to North Samatra	328	$574	2008
	Kepodang-Tambak Lorok	130	$105	
	Sengkang-Makassar Indonesia	173	$110	
	East Java-West, Java	442		2010
	E. Kalamantan to C. Java	768		2010

Company name	Project name and location	Length (miles)	Cost ($ US million)	In service date
PT Perusahaan Gas Negara (PGN)	E. Kalamantan to Central Java	434	$1.6 billion	2007–2008
Soopec	Sichuan Province China	1,008	$4.7 billion	2008
Gas Authority of India	Dahej-Uran Pipeline	310	$330	2007–2009
FSU-EASTERN EUROPE				
Botas, D.E.P.A. & Edison Gas	IGI Pipe line Greece to Italy	504	N/A	2010
FSI Energy	KoRus Sakhalin Pipeline Russia	1,575	$3 billion	N/A
Governments of Hungary/ Croatia	Adriatic Coastto Hungary	214	N/A	Feasibility
KazMunaiGaz	Kazakhstan to china	1,890	N/A	2010
Nabucco Gas Pipeline Int'l. Ltd	Nabucco Pipeline Turkey to Austria	2142	N/A	2011
Starstroi (Sakhalin Energy)	Sakhalin II pipeline	504	N/A	2008
MIDDLE EAST				
Abu Dhabi Gas Industries Co(GASCO)	Habshan–Bu Hasa Pipeline UAE	32	$35	N/A
National Iranian Oil Co	Iran-Pakistan- India Pipeline	1,735	$4 billion	2010
AMEC SPIE Capag	Yemen Gas Pipeline	202	$200	2008
Qatar/ Pakistan*	Gulf South Asia Pipeline Qatar to Pakistan	1,021	$2.7 billion	N/A
WESTERN EUROPE & EU COUNTRIES				
Gassco*	Norway to Sweden	N/A	$1.3 billion	2008

Source: Reference [257].

The exports and imports of natural gas by various countries are given in Appendix VII.

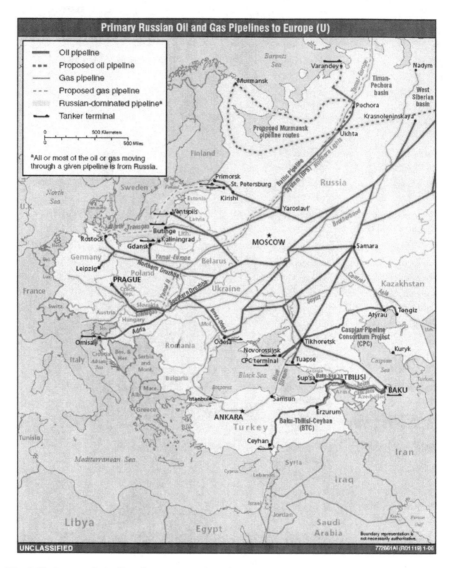

Fig. 7.29. Proposed pipeline for transportation of natural gas. (Adapted from Energy Information Administration, USA, Natural Gas, Russia).

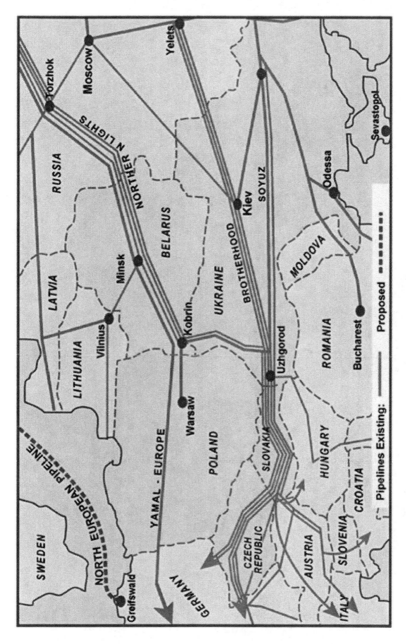

Fig. 7.30. Natural gas pipeline in Europe. (Adapted from Energy Information Administration, USA).

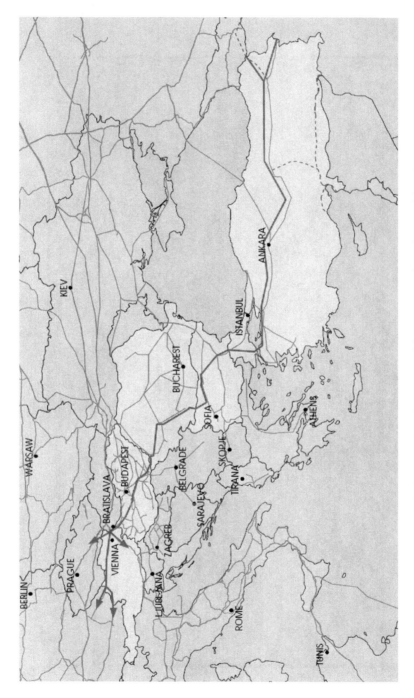

Fig. 7.31. Proposed pipeline through Turkey. (Adapted from Energy Information Administration, USA).

7.6.6 Storage of Natural Gas

Natural gas storage facilities serve two purposes: they provide both the base load requirements and meet the peak load requirements. In order to ensure long term steady and reliable supply of natural gas, it is stored underground. There are three main types of underground storage facilities [258–266]:

- Depleted gas reservoirs
- Aquifers
- Salt caverns

However, mines and hard rock caverns are also considered for storage. These methods are shown in Fig. 7.32.

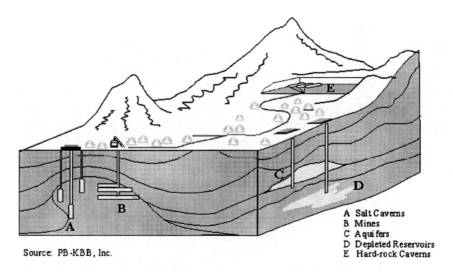

Source: PB-KBB, Inc.

A Salt Caverns
B Mines
C Aquifers
D Depleted Reservoirs
E Hard-rock Caverns

Fig. 7.32. Methods for storage of natural gas [267].

7.6.6.1 Depleted Gas Reservoirs

These are original underground formation basins for natural gas. Once they are depleted, these formations are used for holding or storage of natural gas. Since the extraction network is already in place, the cost of converting a depleted reservoir into a storage facility is very economical. Depleted reservoirs are attractive because their geological characteristics are already well known and a history exists regarding their operation and maintenance.

7.6.6.2 Aquifers

These are underground porous, permeable rock formations that are natural water reservoirs. These formations are reconditioned and used as natural gas storage facilities. However, these aquifers need to be characterized fully, particularly their composition and porosity before reconditioning. Once an aquifer is selected for gas storage, various infrastructures, including extraction equipment, pipelines, dehydration facilities, and compression equipment must be installed. Because of these requirements, aquifers are the least desirable and most expensive type of natural gas storage facility.

7.6.6.3 Salt Caverns

Underground salt formations are another medium for natural gas storage. Salt caverns are highly non-porous and therefore loss of injected natural gas is minimal. The salt cavern storage facilities are typically located between 1,500 and 6,000 ft beneath the surface.

Base load facilities are capable of holding enough natural gas to satisfy long term seasonal demand requirements. Depleted gas reservoirs are the most common type of base load storage facility. These reservoirs are larger; however the amount of natural gas that can be used from them each day is limited. The main objective is to provide steady supply of natural gas.

Table 7.21. Underground storage.

	2000	2001	2002	2003	2004	2005
Total storage capacity	8,240,886	8,415,326	8,207,074	8,205,716	8,255,042	8,268,443
Salt caverns	189,043	218,483	225,958	234,601	239,990	250,532
Aquifers	1,263,711	1,195,141	1,234,007	1,237,132	1,238,158	1,350,689
Depleted fields	6,788,130	7,001,700	6,747,108	6,733,983	6,776,894	6,667,222
Total number of active fields	413	418	407	391	393	394
Salt caverns	28	28	29	30	30	30
Aquifers	49	39	38	43	43	44
Depleted fields	336	351	340	318	320	320

Source: Energy Information Administration, Underground natural gas storage capacity.

Peak load storage facilities, on the other hand, are designed to have high-deliverability for short periods of time. Peak load facilities are intended to meet sudden, short-term demand increases. Salt caverns are the most common type of peak load storage facility, although aquifers may be used to meet these demands as well.

Storage facilities in the USA can be found almost in all the states, but they are most concentrated in the consuming north east region of the country. The underground storage capacity by facility types are listed in Table 7.21. The distribution of these facilities in various states are given in Fig. 7.33.

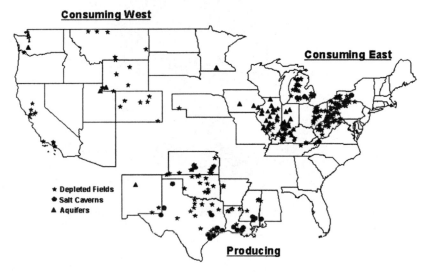

Fig. 7.33. Underground natural gas storage facilities in the lower 48 states. (Source: Energy Information Administration (2004) Gas tran geographic information system Underground Storage Database).

The natural gas is delivered to the consumer from the storage facility rather than from the gas processing plant directly. The natural gas is injected into the underground storage facility to maintain what is known as 'base gas' or 'cushion gas'. This is the volume of gas that must remain in the storage facility to provide the required pressurization to extract the remaining gas. The remaining of the gas may be called the working gas capacity. Working gas is the volume of natural gas in the storage reservoir that can be extracted during the normal operation of the storage facility. This is the natural gas that is being stored and withdrawn; the capacity of storage facilities normally refers to their working gas capacity. Periodically, underground storage facility operators may reclassify portions of working gas as base gas after evaluating the operation of their facilities. The working gas capacity by storage facility is shown in Fig. 7.34. However, as can be seen from Fig. 7.35, for daily use salt cavern and aquifers are used more than depleted reservoirs.

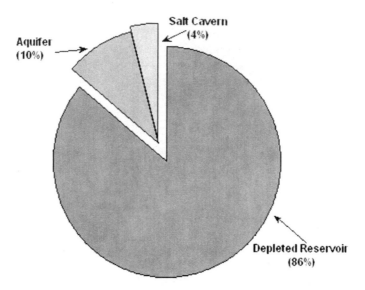

Fig. 7.34. Working gas capacity in the USA Source: Working gas capacity by type of storage. (Source: Energy Information Administration, Natural Gas Storage in the USA, 2001).

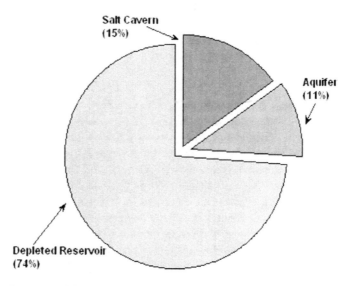

Fig. 7.35. Daily deliverability by type of storage. (Source: Energy Information Administration, Natural Gas Storage in the USA, 2001).

7.6.7 Distribution

Natural gas from intrastate pipeline is delivered to local distribution companies, which is called citigates. The pricing of natural gas is generally determined at this point. The price breakdown is shown in Fig. 7.36. Typically, local distribution companies take ownership of the natural gas at the citygate, and deliver it to each individual customer's location of use. This requires an extensive network of small-diameter distribution pipe.

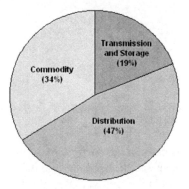

Fig. 7.36. Component of natural gas price. (Source: Energy Information Administration).

Traditionally, local distribution companies have been awarded exclusive rights to distribute natural gas in a specified geographic area. They are also responsible for billing, safety inspection, and providing natural gas hookups for new customers. Local distribution companies must maintain the highest safety standards and are responsible for fixing problems with the distribution network. Some of the safety features that local distribution companies must provide include:

- Leak detection equipment
- Safety education programs
- Technicians on call
- Emergency preparedness
- One call systems

7.6.8 Natural Gas Use

Natural gas provides almost 24% of the total energy need in the USA, which is second to petroleum (39%). Fig. 7.37 shows the contribution of natural gas to the total energy need of the USA.

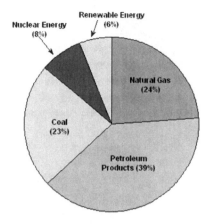

Fig. 7.37. Natural Gas use compare to other energy use. (Source: Energy Information Administration. Annual Energy Outlook 2007).

Natural gas is used basically by all sectors. Fig. 7.38 gives an idea of the proportion of natural gas use per sector. Although the industrial sector uses the greatest proportion of natural gas in the United States, the residential sector and electric power generation using natural gas follow very closely.

The uses of natural gas may be divided into the following categories:

1. Residential uses
2. Commercial uses
3. Industrial uses
4. Natural gas use for vehicles
5. Electricity generation

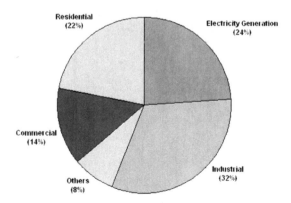

Fig. 7.38. Natural gas use by various sectors in the USA. (Source: Energy Information Administration. Annual Energy Outlook 2007).

7.6.8.1 Residential Uses

One of the main reasons for the wide spread use of natural gas in the residential sector is its cost compared to other sources (Fig. 7.39). The best known uses for natural gas around the home are for heating and cooking. According to the American Gas Association, in 2000, about 51% of homes in the USA (or 49.1 million households) used natural gas for heating. Also a high proportion of new homes are being built with natural gas heating. A report in 2003 by the U.S. Census Bureau on new housing indicated that 70% of single family homes completed in 2003 used natural gas for heating, followed by 27% that used electric heat, and 2% used heating oil. The new generations of natural gas ranges are efficient, economical, and versatile. In addition to heating homes, natural gas can also be used to help cool houses, through natural gas powered air conditioning. Other examples of natural gas appliances include space heaters, clothes dryers, pool and jacuzzi heaters, fireplaces, barbecues, garage heaters, and outdoor lights. All of these appliances offer a safe, efficient, and economical alternative to electricity or other fuel.

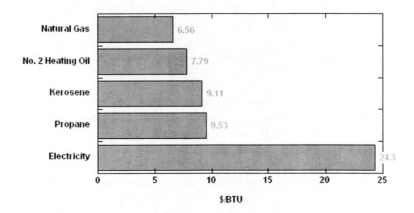

Fig. 7.39. Cost of various energy sources used by residential sector. (Source: US Department of Energy).

7.6.8.2 Commercial Uses

Commercial uses of natural gas are very similar to residential uses. The commercial sector that includes public and private facilities, such as office buildings, schools, churches, hotels, restaurants, and government buildings use significant amount of natural gas. The main uses of natural gas in this sector include space heating, cooking, water heating, and cooling. The percentage usage of various sectors is shown in Fig. 7.40.

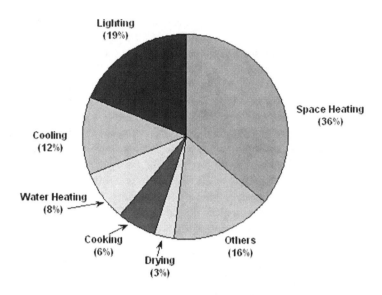

Fig. 7.40. Commercial use of natural gas. (Source: Washington Policy and Analysis, Inc., Fueling the Future 2000).

Natural gas based cooling systems are becoming more popular because of their energy efficiency and also some systems have the capability to enhance indoor air quality. There are three types of natural gas based cooling processes. Engine driven chillers use a natural gas engine and waste heat from the gas engine can be used for heating applications, increasing energy efficiency. The second system is called absorption chillers, which provide cool air by evaporating a refrigerant like water or ammonia. The heat is provided by using natural gas. These absorption chillers are best suited to cooling large commercial buildings, like office towers and shopping malls. The third type of commercial cooling system consists of gas-based desiccant systems. In this system, a desiccant first removes water vapor from the humid air. The humidity of the dry air is then adjusted by spraying water vapor into the stream. The exhausted desiccants are regenerated by using the natural gas. The desiccant can co-adsorb various indoor pollutants along with water vapor, thus enhancing the indoor air quality.

Recently combined heating and power (CHP) or combined cooling, heating and power (CCHP) systems are found to be more energy efficient than the single unit. The energy savings come from the heat that is released from natural gas powered electricity generators. The heat can be harnessed to run space or water heaters, or commercial boilers.

7.6.8.3 Industrial Use

Industry uses energy from various sources, but they are the largest consumer of natural gas, accounting for almost 43% of the total natural gas use (see Fig. 7.41). The graph below shows current as well as projected energy consumption by fuel in the industrial sector.

Natural gas is consumed primarily in the pulp and paper, metals, chemicals, petroleum refining, stone, clay and glass, plastic, and food processing industries. These businesses account for over 84% of all industrial natural gas use. Natural gas is also used for waste treatment and incineration, metals preheating (particularly for iron and steel), drying and dehumidification, glass melting, food processing, and fueling industrial boilers. Other industrial applications of natural gas include infrared heating, direct contact water heating, industrial combined heat and power, and industrial co-firing.

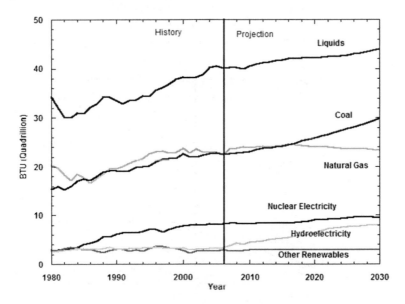

Fig. 7.41. Current and projected use of various energy sources including natural gas by industries. (Source: Energy Information Administration. Annual Energy Outlook 2007 with Projections to 2030).

7.6.8.4 Natural Gas Vehicles [268–272]

According to the Natural Gas Vehicle Coalition, there are currently 130,000 Natural Gas Vehicles (NGVs) on the road in the United States, and more than 2.5 million NGVs worldwide. In fact, the transportation sector accounts for 3% of all natural gas used in the United States. All types of vehicles including passenger cars, trucks, buses, vans, and heavy-duty utility vehicles have been designed and produced to run using natural gas. Despite various advances, a number of disadvantages of natural gas vehicles prevent their mass-production. Limited range, trunk space, higher initial cost, and lack of refueling infrastructure pose impediments to the future spread of natural gas vehicles.

7.6.8.5 Electricity Generation

In 2000, 23,453 MW of new electric capacity was added in the U.S. Of this, almost 95%, or 22,238 MW was generated using natural gas (see Fig. 7.42).

A number of new facilities are 'combined-cycle' units. Both a gas turbine and a steam turbine are used for power generation. The hot gases released from burning natural gas turn a gas turbine and generate electricity. In combined-cycle plants, the waste heat from the gas-turbine is used for generating steam, which is then used to generate electricity using a steam turbine. Because of this efficient use of the heat energy released from the natural gas, combined-cycle plants can achieve 50–60% thermal efficiencies.

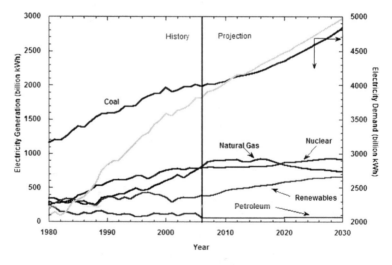

Fig. 7.42. Use of natural gas in electricity generation. (Source: Energy Information Administration. Annual Energy Outlook 2007 with Projections to 2030).

7.6.8.6 Natural Gas Use for Fertilizer Production

About 5–6% of natural gas produced in the world is used for fertilizer production. Most of natural gas is used as feedstock in the production of ammonia, which is next used for production of various nitrogen-fertilizers. There is at present no economic alternative to natural gas as a feedstock. As can be seen from Table 7.22, the cost of using other resources for fertilizer production is significantly higher than natural gas.

Methane (CH_4) in the natural gas is dissociated to produce hydrogen, which is then reacted with nitrogen over a catalyst to produce ammonia (NH_3). Natural gas must be free from any sulfur compounds. If sulfur compounds remain in the natural gas stream, they can poison the catalysts that are used in the remaining steps. Sulfur compounds are removed either by adsorption on activated carbon in the temperature range of 15–50°C or by reaction with a zinc oxide catalyst at 350–400°C. After the sulfur compounds are removed, natural gas is reformed with steam over a nickel catalyst according to the following two reactions to produce Syngas.

$$CH_4 + H_2O - CO + 3H_2$$
$$CO + H_2O - CO_2 + H_2.$$

The exit gas is heated to a temperature in the range of 750 to 850°C and pressurized in the range of about 28–35 atm (415–515 psi) before introducing it in the secondary reformer. Air, which is the source of nitrogen, is introduced in this stage. Oxygen from air reacts with CO releasing heat that drive the second reaction, which generates CO_2. The product of the second reforming stage is a mixture of carbon oxides, H_2, N_2, and other impurities. Carbon oxides are removed next. First CO is converted to CO_2 by the shift reaction, followed by a CO_2 removal step. An iron oxide-chromium oxide catalyst is used in the shift reaction. The CO_2 removal operation is done in two steps – a bulk CO_2 removal in which CO_2 concentration is reduced to a few parts per million and a final purification step. The most common bulk CO_2 removal operation is performed by scrubbing the gas with a methyldiethanolamine or monoethanolamine solution. If an ammonia production plant is associated with a nearby urea plant, the CO_2 may be recovered and used for urea production. The final gas mixture before introducing it into an ammonia production reactor must be ultra-pure. Therefore, any traces of CO_2 and CO must be removed from the gas stream. This is normally done by reacting CO_2 and CO with H_2 gas over a nickel catalyst (the reverse of the reforming reactions) converting them to CH_4. A cryogenic purification method is used to remove the methane from the gas stream. The clean gas mixture containing only N_2 and H_2 is compressed to between 136 and 340 atm (2,000 and 5,000 psi) and then passed over an iron catalyst where the nitrogen and hydrogen react to form ammonia by the following reaction:

$$N_2 + 3H_2 - 2NH_3.$$

After production, ammonia may be used to produce a variety of downstream products, which include ammonium nitrate, ammonium sulfate, nitric acid, and urea.

Table 7.22. Comparison of energy cost for fertilizer production normalized to the cost of natural gas.

Items	Natural gas	Heavy oil	Coal
Energy consumption	1.0	1.3	1.7
Investment cost	1.0	1.4	2.4
Production cost	1.0	1.2	1.7

Source: Reference [273].

7.7 Liquefied Natural Gas (LNG)

LNG is natural gas that is cooled at atmospheric pressure at a temperature -260°F (−161°C). At this condition, it is liquid. The liquefaction is accomplished using a refrigeration process in a plant. The unit where LNG is produced is called a train. Liquefying natural gas reduces its volume by a factor of 610. The reduction in volume makes the gas practical to transport and store. LNG is mostly methane (85–95%) and the rests are ethane, propane and butane (5–15%) A small amount of nitrogen can be also present. Depending on the country of origin, the composition can vary slightly. As a result, its heating value will also change. The composition of LNG based on its origin is given in Table 7.23.

Table 7.23. Variation in the LNG composition based on it origin.

Origin	Methane (%)	Ethane (%)	Propane (%)	Butane (%)	Nitrogen (%)
Algeria	87.6	9.0	2.2	0.6	0.6
Australia	89.3	7.1	2.5	1.0	0.1
Malaysia	89.8	5.1	3.3	1.4	0.3
Nigeria	91.6	4.6	2.4	1.3	0.1
Oman	87.7	7.5	3.0	1.6	0.2
Qatar	89.9	6.0	2.2	1.5	0.4
Trinidad & Tobago	96.9	2.7	0.3	0.1	0.0

Source: Reference [274].

Liquefaction of LNG makes it possible to trade it internationally, since it can be transported in specially built tanks in doublehulled ships to a receiving terminal where it is stored in heavily insulated tanks. The LNG is then sent to regasifiers which turn the liquid back into a gas that enters the pipeline system for distribution to customers as part of their natural gas supply. In the USA, net imports of LNG are expected to increase from 0.6 Tcf in 2004 to more than 6 Tcf in 2025.

This will be almost 21% of total U.S. natural gas demand. As can be seen from Table 7.24, LNG imports to the USA are increasing steadily and it is projected to increase faster in the future.

Table 7.24. LNG import to the USA in the last several years.

Year	Amount of LNG imported (MMcf)	Year	Amount of LNG imported (MMcf)
1990	84,193	2000	226,036
1991	63,596	2001	238,126
1992	43,116	2002	228,730
1993	81,685	2003	506,519
1994	50,778	2004	652,015
1995	17,918	2005	631,260
1996	40,274	2006	583,537
1997	77,778		
1998	85,453		
1999	163,430		

The LNG is imported into the USA from various countries via ships. As can be seen from Fig. 7.42, LNG is imported from a number of countries over the last 30 years, however, the demand increased dramatically in the last several years. This resulted in a new international shipping routes (Fig. 7.43).

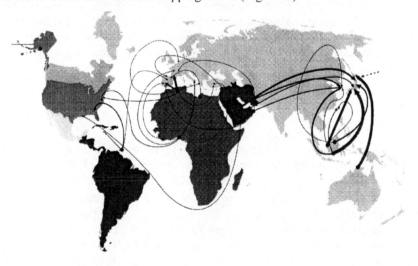

Fig. 7.43. International route of LNG transportation. The thickness of the line represents relative LNG volume movement. (Adapted from [275]).

7.8 Liquefaction Process

The Phillips Cascade and Air Products APCI processes are mostly used for liquefaction of natural gas [276–278]. Several new processes have been recently proposed for liquefaction, and they are:

Axen/IFP (DMR) – LIQUEFIN^{TM} [279–280]
Linde AG (Statoil) – MFC$^{®}$ [281]
Turbo-Expander (BHP)
Blck & Vetch Pritchard Inc. – PRICO$^{®}$ [282]

7.8.1 Phillips Cascade Process

The Phillips cascade process is a three-stage process [283–284]. Three pure components are used for refrigeration; (1) Propane pre-cooling, (2) Ethylene, and (3) Methane. A schematic diagram of the Phillips cascade process is shown in Fig. 7.44. The refrigeration circuits are cascaded to provide maximum LNG production. Each circuit uses two compressors. The LNG from the last-stage flash drum is sent to the tanks by the transfer pumps, where it is stored at about 70 mbar and - 161°C. Advantages of this process are low installation costs, and the use of a two - train - in - one reliability concept. However, the increase use of gas turbines and compressors also increases the maintenance costs.

7.8.2 APCI Process

This process utilizes two cooling stages. In the first stage, propane is used as a cooling fluid and a mixed refrigerant is used in the second stage [285]. Generally a mixture of ethanol, propane, methanol and nitrogen obtained after splitting the C2+ is used as refrigerant. The composition of the mixture of coolants is based on the composition of natural gas in the plant. Natural gas, after passing through the pretreatment systems, is cooled in the propane vaporizer. The pressure of the propane is adjusted so that it remains cool, and no condensation occurs. The second stage is the main cryogenic coolant, which cools the natural gas through a closed circuit of mixed coolants. After liquefying, it is subcooled for storing. A schematic diagram of the process is shown in Fig. 7.45.

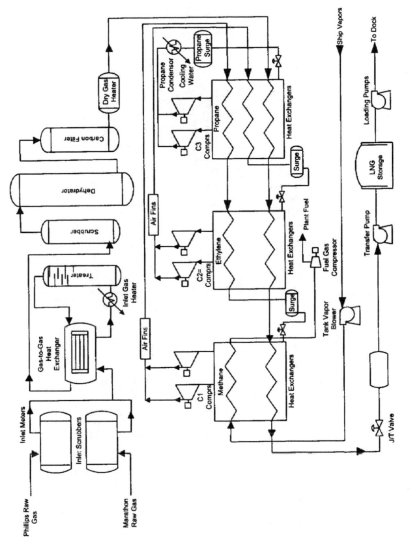

Fig. 7.44. Phillips cascade process for liquefaction of natural gas. (Reprinted with permission from [277]).

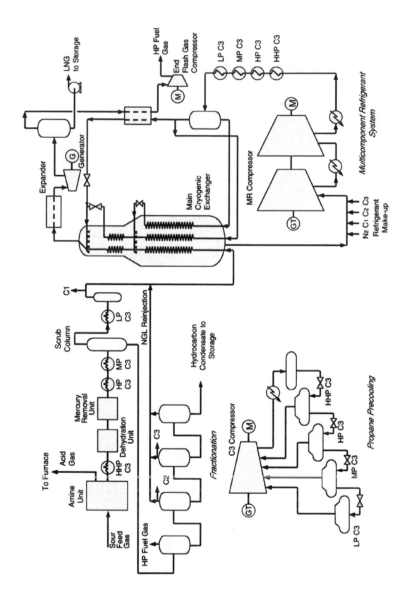

Fig. 7.45. APCI propone precooled mixed refrigerant typical process. (Reprinted with permission from [270]).

7.9 Transportation and Storage of LNG

Specially designed containers are used for shipping of LNG. The majority of the new containers for LNG transportation via sea are in the size range of 120,000–140,000 m^3. New containers with a capacity up to 260,000 m^3 are now currently being constructed by several builders. There are four containment systems in use.

7.9.1 Moss Tanks

These are spherical aluminum tanks and are designed by Moss Maritime, Norway. The cross-sectional view of a Moss tank is shown in Fig. 7.46 and its design characteristics are presented in Fig. 7.47.

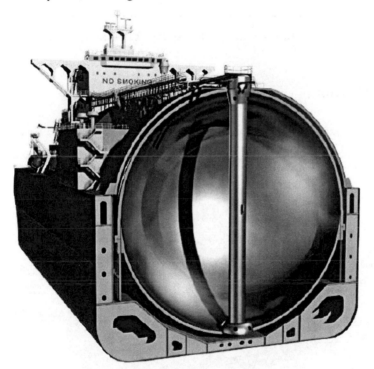

Fig. 7.46. The Kvaerner/Moss Rosenberg tank design for LNG transportation. (Adapted from Frivik P-E (2003) The Importance of Knowledge in the Changing Nature of Natural Gas Supply–Contributions from Academia and Applied Research in Industrial LNG Development. IEA Advisory Group on Oil and Gas Technology. Economic Analysis Division of the International Energy Agency Initiation of Global Dialogue on "the Future of Natural Gas Supply and Use" Exploring the Impact of Financial and Technological Drivers Washington DC, 22 January 2003 [286]).

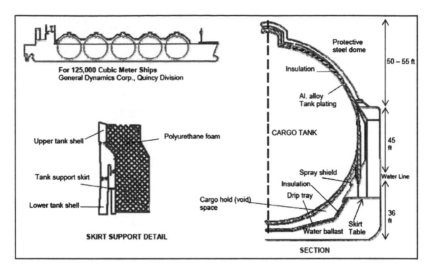

Fig. 7.47. Free standing spherical LNG transportation tank. (Adapted from [287]).

7.9.2 IHI Tanks

The tank is made of aluminum and is built by Ishikawajima-Harima Heavy Industries, Japan. The IHI tank is shown in Fig. 7.48.

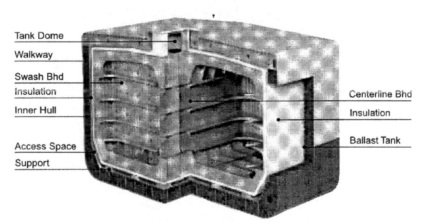

Fig. 7.48. Floating production storage & offloading unit for LNG shipment. (Adapted from [288]).

7.9.3 GT96

The GT96 is designed by Gaz Transports. The tank consists of two membranes: a primary and secondary thin membrane. Both the membranes are made of invar which has negligible thermal contraction in the temperature range the tanks operate. The insulation is made out of plywood boxes filled with perlite. The design features are shown in Fig. 7.49.

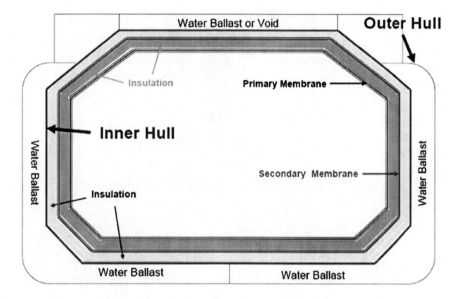

Fig. 7.49. Design features of a membrane tank. (Adapted from [289]).

7.9.4 TGZ Mark III

The TGZ Mark III is a membrane type and is manufactured by Technigaz. The membrane is made out of stainless steel with baffles, which allow the thermal contraction when the tank is cooled down. The interior design of TGZ Mark III tank is illustrated in Fig. 7.50.

7.10 LNG Storage Facility

There are basically two types of LNG (liquid natural gas) storage tanks: above ground, and underground.

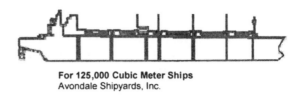

For 125,000 Cubic Meter Ships
Avondale Shipyards, Inc.

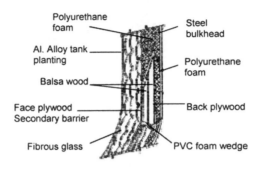

Fig. 7.50. Free standing prismatic LNG tank. (Adapted from [287]).

7.10.1 Underground Storage Tank

The underground storage tanks are composed of continuous diaphragm walls, side walls and base mat slabs, and each tank has different requirements of performances.

7.10.2 Above Ground Storage Tank

There are three types of above ground LNG storage tanks:

Single containment
Double containment
Full containment

A Single containment tank is generally a single tank (Fig. 7.51). In some design an outer container is included. However, only the inner tank is required to meet the low temperature ductility requirements for storage of LNG.

A double containment tank consists of both the inner tank and the outer tank (Fig. 7.52). Both the tanks are capable of independently containing the refrigerated liquid.

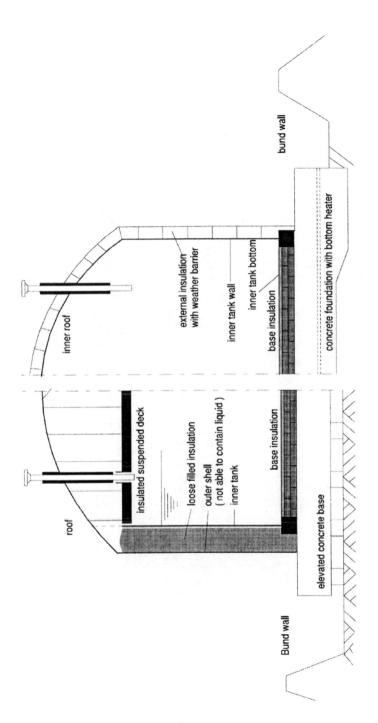

Fig. 7.51. Single containment type LNG storage tank. (Printed with permission [283]).

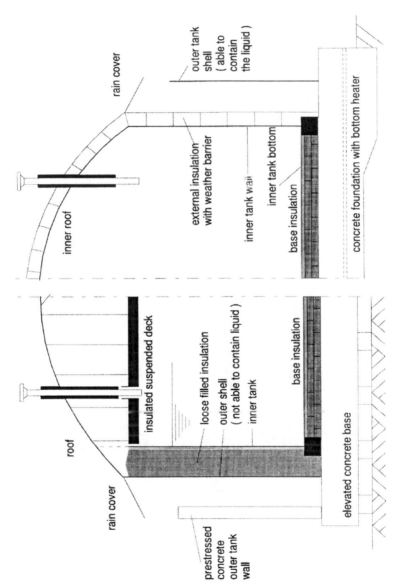

Fig. 7.52. Double containment type LNG storage tank. (Printed with permission from [283]).

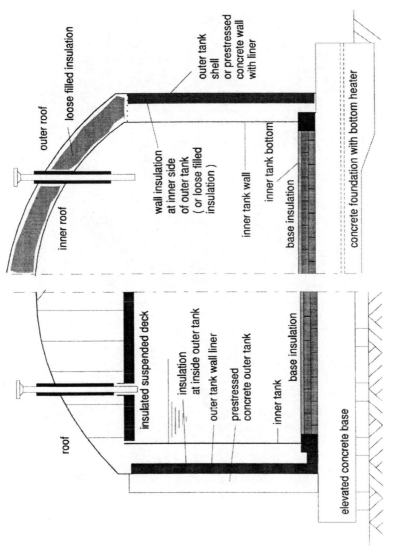

Fig. 7.53. Full containment type LNG storage tank. (Printed with permission from [283]).

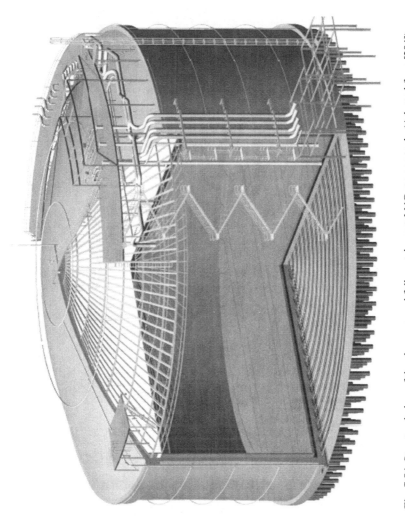

Fig. 7.54. Structural view of the above ground full containment LNG storage tank. (Adapted from [284]).

A full containment tank (Fig. 7.53) is similar in design to the double containment tank. It differs from the double containment tank in that the outer tank of a full containment tank is capable of both containing the refrigerated liquid and controlled venting of the vapor resulting from product leakage in the case of an accident. The structural aspects of the tank are shown in Fig. 7.54. The full containment type is regarded as the most advanced type and can also be constructed, in-ground or under-ground. The inner tank is manufactured with 9% nickel steel and the outer tank is composed of reinforced concrete and pre-stressed concrete. The 9% nickel steel is capable of withstanding cryogenic conditions. The concrete outer tank is designed to resist various external loads including seismic load. Insulating materials are placed between the inner and outer tank to preserve the stored LNG.

References

1. BP statistical Review of World Energy, 2008
2. Energy Information Administration, USA, Report # DOE/EIA -0484, 2006
3. Whiticar MJ, Faber E, Schoell M (1986) Biogenic methane formation in marine and freshwater environments: CO2 reduction vs. acetate fermentation-isotope evidence. Geochem Cosmochim Acta 50: 693–709
4. Horita J, Berndt ME (1999) Abiogenic methane formation and isotopic fractionation under hydrothermal condition. Science 285(5430): 1055–1057
5. Charlou JL, Fouquet Y, Donval J-P, Auzende JM (1996) Mineral and gas chemistry of hydrothermal fluids on an ultrafast spreading ridge: East Pacific Rise, 17° to 19° S (Naudur cruise, 1993) phase separation processes controlled by volcanic and tectonic activity. J Geophys Res 101(B7): 15899–15919
6. Anon (1911) The origin of oil and gas. Pet Rev 24: 303–304, 335
7. Berl E (1934) Origin of asphalts, oil, natural gas and bituminous coal. Science (Washington, DC) 80: 227–228
8. Berl E (1942) Origin of coal, oil and natural gas and their production from plant material. Sci Counsel 7: 35, 57
9. Boreham CJ, Golding SD, Glikson M (1998) Factors controlling the origin of gas in Australian Bowen Basin coals. Org Geochem 29: 347–362
10. Dolenko GN (1989) Origin and petroleum and natural gas and oil and gas accumulation in the Earth's crust. A reply. Izvestiya Akademii Nauk SSSR, Seriya Geologicheskaya: 138–141
11. Dolenko GN (ed) (1978) Origin and Migration of Petroleum and Gas, Kiev, Naukova Dumka
12. Gemp SD (1972) Formation of gas deposits. Geologiya i Geokhimiya Goryuchikh Iskopaemykh No. 30: 62–70
13. Geodekyan AA, Kartsev AA, Yanshin AL (1989) Origin of petroleum and natural gas and oil- and gas accumulation in the Earth's crust. A discussion. Izv. Akad. Nauk SSSR, Ser. Geol. 135–137
14. Haun JD, Lucas GB (1968) Origin and accumulation of natural gas. Memoir – Am Assoc Petrol Geol 2: 1990–1994
15. Kalinko M (1977) Origin of petroleum and natural fossil-fuel gases. Neftyanik: 32–36

16. Kartsev AA, Tabasaranskii ZA, Subbota MI, Mogilevskii GA (1959) Geochemical Methods of Prospecting and Exploration for Petroleum and Natural Gas (Trans. from Russian) California U.P., Cambridge U.P.

17. Lur'e MA, Kurets IZ, Shmidt FK (2003) The possible abiogenic origin of oil and gas. Chem. Technol. Fuels Oils (Translation of Khimiya i Tekhnologiya Topliv i Masel) 39: 1–5

18. Maimin ZL (1989) Recent views or the origin of petroleum and natural gas. Geologiya i Geokhimiya Goryuchikh Iskopaemykh 73: 51–55

19. Stratton MA (1969) Natural Gas; Origin, Location, Composition, Treatment, Uses. (Natural Gas Series, No. 1), 2nd ed. Ministry of Fuel and Power, Victoria

20. Schematic of a petroleum trap. Source: Energy Information Administration, US Department of Energy

21. Bonham LC (1982) The future of unconventional natural gas as an alternative energy resource. Proceedings of the Annual Convention – Indonesian Petroleum Association 11th: 307–322

22. Decrouez D (1990) Nonconventional gas resources and abiogenic gas theory. Gas, Wasser, Abwasser (1969–1990) 70: 204–212

23. Doherty MG (1980) Unconventional gas. IGT GaScope 49: 2–6, 8

24. Doherty MG (1982) Unconventional natural gas resources. Proceedings, Annual Convention – Gas Processors Association 61st: 22–28

25. Terasaki D (2006) The resources of unconventional natural gases and their world supply and demand assumption in future. J Jpn Inst Energy 85: 105–111

26. Stosur G (2007) Global scramble for natural gas and the role of unconventional gas resources. Nafta (Zagreb, Croatia) 58: 559–567

27. Johnson RL, Jr., Hopkins CW, Zuber MD (2000) Technical challenges in the development of unconventional gas resources in Australia. APPEA J 40: 450–468

28. King GR, Ertekin T (1991) State-of-the-art modeling for unconventional gas recovery. SPE Formation Evaluation 6: 63–71

29. Kurosawa A (2007) An analysis of unconventional gas and enhanced coalbed methane in long-term global energy supply. J Jpn Inst Energy: 87–93

30. Miskimins JL (2006) Unconventional natural gas reservoirs: what are the associated challenges? Nafta (Zagreb, Croatia) 57: 495–503

31. Pollastro RM (2007) Total petroleum system assessment of undiscovered resources in the giant Barnett Shale continuous (unconventional) gas accumulation, Fort Worth Basin, Texas. AAPG Bull 91: 551–578

32. Runge HC (1990) Methane-hydrate – a useful source of unconventional natural gases? Forschungsgruppe Wirtsch, Energ Invest, Forschungszentrum Juelich G.m.b.H., Juelich, Germany: 19

33. Warwick PD (2007) Unconventional energy resources and geospatial information: 2006 review. Natural Resources Research (New York) 16: 243–261

34. Jefferson M (2000) Long-term energy scenarios: the approach of the World Energy Council. Int J Global Energy Issues 13(1–3): 2000

35. Canadian Association of Petroleum Producers

36. Kuuskraa VA (2007) A Decade of Progress in Unconventional Gas, Advanced Resources International, OGJ Unconventional Gas Article #1, Arlington, VA, USA

37. Kuuskraa VA, Bank GC (2007) The Unconventional Gas Resource Base, Advanced Resources International, OGJ Unconventional Gas Article #2

38. Dyman TS, Crovelli RA, Bartberger CE, Takahashi KI (2002) Worldwide Estimates of Deep Natural Gas Resources Based on the U.S. Geological Survey World Petroleum Assessment 2000. Resources Research (New York) 11: 207–218
39. Dyman TS, Wyman RE, Kuuskraa VA, Lewan MD, Cook TA (2003) Deep Natural Gas Resources. Natural Resources Research (New York) 12: 41–56
40. Gerling P, Kockel F, Krull P, Stahl WJ (1998) Deep natural gas – the HC potential of pre-Westphalian rocks in North Germany. Proceedings of the World Petroleum Congress 15th: 81–82
41. Graf HG (1976) Ultra deep [natural gas] production. Erdoel-Erdgas-Zeitschrift 92: 423–425
42. Weismann TJ (1999) Reappraisal of deep natural-gas potential in U.S. basins. Book of Abstracts, 218th ACS National Meeting, New Orleans, August 22–26: PETR-038
43. Whiticar MJ, Faber E (eds) (1999) The Search for Deep Gas. Selected papers presented at the I.E.A/BMFT International Workshop, held in Hannover. In: Geol Jahrb, Reihe D, 1999: 107
44. Price LC (1995) Origins, characteristics, controls, and economic viabilities of deep-basin gas resources. Chem Geol 126: 335–349
45. U.S. Geological Survey (USGS) (1995) National Petroleum Assessment
46. Survey World Petroleum Assessment 2000 and the 1995 National Assessment (U.S. Geological Survey World Energy Assessment Team, 2000; Gautier and others, 1996. As reported in Dyman TS, Crovelli RA, Bartberger CE, Takahashi KI (2002) Worldwide estimates of deep natural gas resources based on the U.S. geological survey world petroleum assessment 2000. Natural Resources Research 11(3): 207–218
47. Arevalo Villagran JA (2001) Analysis of long-term behavior in tight gas reservoirs: case histories
48. Behr A, Mtchedlishvili G, Friedel T, Haefner F (2006) Consideration of damaged zone in a tight gas reservoir model with a hydraulically fractured well. SPE Production & Operations 21: 206–211
49. Bruce PL, Hunter JL, Kuhlman RD, Weinheimer DD (1992) New fracturing techniques reduce tight gas sand completion problems. Oil Gas J 90: 72–76
50. Coskuner G (2004) Drilling induced formation damage of horizontal wells in tight gas reservoirs. J Can Pet Technol 43: 13–18
51. Galovic S (1998) Fraced horizontal wells show potential of deep tight gas – Soehlingen Z-10 example. Nafta (Zagreb) 49: 87–91
52. Sieber D, Mauth K (2004) Tight gas well Soehlingen Z15 – application of new frac technology. DGMK Tagungsbericht 2004-2: 57–64
53. Pow M, Kantzas A, Allan V, Mallmes R (1999) Production of gas from tight naturally fractured reservoirs with active water. J Can Pet Technol 38: 38–45
54. Lerche I (2005) Under-pressured and over-pressured tight gas sands: II. Spatially and temporally varying conditions. Energy Exploration Exploitation 23: 169–180
55. Liermann N, Jentsch M (2003) Tight gas reservoirs – natural gas for the future. Erdoel, Erdgas, Kohle 119: 270–273
56. Holditch SA (2006) Tight gas sands. SPE Paper 103356, Distinguished Author Series
57. Rogner H (1997) An assessment of world hydrocarbon resources. Annu Rev Energy Environ 22: 217–262

58. Stevens SH, Kuuskraa J, Kuuskraa V (1998) Unconventional natural gas in the united states: production, reserves, and resource potential (1991-1997). Prepared for: California Energy Commission, Contract No.: 300-97-011, December 1, 1998, http://www.energy.ca.gov/FR99/documents/98-12_STEVENS.PDF

59. Law BE (1993) The relationship between coal rank and spacing: implications for the prediction of permeability in coal. Proceedings of the 1993 International Coalbed Methane Symposium. The University of Alabama, Tuscaloosa, May 17–21: 435–441

60. Hoover KV (1960) Devonian-Mississippian shale sequence in Ohio. OSTI ID: 7329188

61. Milici RC (1993) Autogenic gas (self sourced) from shales – an example from the Appalachian Basin. OSTI ID: 7052186

62. Kuuskraa VA, Brandenberg CF (1989) Coalbed methane sparks a new energy industry. Oil Gas J 87(41): 49–56

63. Abraham KS (2006) Coalbed methane activity expands further in North America. World Oil 226(8): 61–62

64. Boyer CM II (1989) The coalbed methane resource and the mechanisms of gas production. GRI Topical Report GRI 89/0266

65. Carlton DR (2006) Discovery and development of a giant coalbed methane resource, Raton Basin. Las Animas County, southeast Colorado: The Mountain Geologist 43(3): 231–236

66. Deul M, Kim AG (2002) Coal beds: a source of natural gas. Oil Gas J 100(35): 68, 70

67. Eaton SR (2006) Coalbed gas frontier being tapped: AAPG Explorer 27(11): 20, 24, http://www.aapg.org/explorer/2006/11nov/horseshoe_canyon.cfm

68. Gentzis T (2006) Economic coalbed methane production in the Canadian Foothills: solving the puzzle. Int J Coal Geol 65: 79–92

69. Hill R (2002) CBM: converting a resource into energy. World Coal 11: 50–51, 53

70. Law BE (1988) Coal-bed methane. In LB Magoon, ed, Petroleum systems of the United States. USGS Bulletin 1870: 52–53

71. Law BE (1992) Coalbed methane. In LB Magoon, ed, The petroleum system – status of research and methods. U.S. Geological Survey Bulletin 2007: 20–21

72. Law BE (1993) The relationship between coal rank and cleat spacing: implications for the prediction of permeability in coal. Proceedings of the 1993 International CBM Symposium, paper 9341: 435–442

73. Law BE, Rice DD (1993) Coalbed methane – new perspectives on an old source of energy. In S-H Chiang, ed, Coal – energy and the environment. Tenth Annual International Pittsburgh Coal Conference, Proceedings: 316–319

74. Law BE, Rice DD (eds) (1993) Hydrocarbons from coal. AAPG Studies in Geology 38: 400

75. Markowski AK (1993) Coalbed methane: new energy from an old scourge. Pennsylvania Geological Survey, Pennsylvania Geol 24(2): 8–14

76. McKinnon I (2002) Canadian coalbed methane. Oil and Gas Investor 22(3): 56–59

77. Murray DK (2000) CBM in the United States: World Coal March: 61–64

78. Narasimhan KS, Mukherjee AK, Sengupta S, Singh SM, Alam MM (1998) Coalbed methane potential in India. Fuel 22: 1865–1866

79. Palmer ID, Cameron JR, Moschovidis ZA (2006) Permeability changes affect CBM production predictions. Oil Gas J 104(28): 43–50

80. Pinsker LM (2002) Coalbed methane: the future of U.S. natural gas? Geotimes 47(11): 34–35

81. Rice DD, Law BE, Clayton JL (1993) Coalbed gas – an undeveloped resource. In DG Howell, ed, The future of energy gases: USGS Professional Paper 1570: 389–404
82. Rice DD (1997) Coalbed methane – an untapped energy resource and an environmental concern. U.S. Geological Survey, Fact Sheet FS-019-97
83. Riestenberg D, Ferguson R, Kuuskraa VA (2007) Unconventional gas – 3. New plays, prospects, resources continue to emerge. Oil Gas J 105(36): 48–54
84. Rightmire CT (1984) Coalbed methane resource. In CT Rightmire, GE Eddy, JN Kirr, eds, Coalbed methane resources of the United States: AAPG Studies in Geology 17: 1–13
85. Rightmire CT, Choate R (1986) Coal-bed methane and tight gas sands interrelationships. In CW Spencer, RF Mast, eds, Geology of tight gas reservoirs: AAPG Studies in Geology 24: 87–110
86. Rogers RE (1994) Coalbed methane: principles and practice. Prentice Hall, Englewood Cliffs, NJ
87. Saulsberry JL, Schafer PS, Schraufnagel RA (eds) (1996) A guide to coalbed methane reservoir engineering. Chicago, IL, Gas Research Institute
88. Scott AR (1994) Composition of coalbed gases. In Situ 18: 185–208
89. Selden RF (1934) The occurrence of gases in coals. U.S. Bureau of Mines Report of Investigations 3233
90. Sever M (2006) Coalbed gas enters the energy mix. Geotimes 51(9): 30–33
91. Squaret J, Dawson M (2006) Coalbed methane expands in Canada. Oil Gas J 104(28): 37–50
92. von Schoenfeldt H, Zupanik J, Wight DR (2004) Unconventional drilling. University of Alabama, 2004 International Coalbed Methane Symposium Proceedings, paper 0441
93. Warwick PD, Sanfilipo JR, Barker CE, Morris LE (1999) Coal-bed methane in the Gulf Coastal Plain; a new frontier? GSA 31
94. Warwick PD, Breland FC Jr, Ratchford ME, Hackley PC (2004) Coal gas resource potential of Cretaceous and Paleogene coals of the Gulf of Mexico Coastal Plain. In PD Warwick, ed, Selected presentations on coal-bed gas in the eastern United States: U.S. Geological Survey Open-File Report 2004-1273. pubs.usgs.gov/of/2004/1273/2004-1273Warwick.pdf
95. Wheat RW (1999) Coalbed methane potential, core and pilot program. Illinois basin AAPG Bull 83: 1374
96. Wheaton J, Donato T (2004) Coalbed-methane basics: Powder River Basin, Montana. Montana Bureau of Mines and Geology, Information Pamphlet 5
97. Williams P (2004) Alberta's CBM. Oil Gas Investor 24(6): C-9
98. Williams P (2006) Western Canadian CBM. Oil Gas Investor 26(9): 42–51
99. Wyman RE (1984) Gas resources in Elmworth coal seams. In JA Masters, ed, Elmworth – a case study of a deep basin gas field. Canadian Society of Petroleum Geologists Memoir 38: 173–187
100. Yalçin MN, Inan S, Hoşgörmez H, Çetin S (2003) A new Carboniferous coal/shale driven gas play in the western Black Sea region (Turkey). Mar Petrol Geol 19: 1241–1256
101. Zuber MD, Hopkins C (1996) Coalbed methane engineering methods. SPE Short Course Manual, S.A. Holditch & Associates, Inc.

102. Zuber MD (1998) Production characteristics and reservoir analysis of coalbed methane reservoirs. In Lyons PC, ed, Special issue: Appalachian coalbed methane. Int J Coal Geol 38: 27–45

103. Zuber MD, Boyer CM II (2001) Comparative analysis of coalbed methane production trends and variability – impact on exploration and production. Tuscaloosa, Alabama, Proceedings International Coalbed Methane Symposium Paper 136: 245–256

104. Zuber MD, Boyer CM II (2001) Analysis optimizes CBM economics. Am Oil Gas Rep 44(12): 62, 65–67

105. Zuber MD, Boyer CM II (2002) Coalbed-methane evaluation techniques – the current state of the art. J Pet Technol 54(2): 66–68

106. Wyoming State Engineers Office, http://www.wsgs.uwyo.edu/Coal/CBM_Info.aspx

107. Energy Information Administration. Coalbed methane proved reserves and production (Bcf)

108. Doherty MG, Randolph PL, Rogers LA, Poonawala NA (1982) Methane production from geopressured aquifers. JPT, J Pet Technol 34: 1591–1599

109. Dorfman MH (1977) The supply of natural gas from geopressured zones: engineering and costs. Future Supply Nat.-Made Pet. Gas, Tech. Rep., UNITAR Conf. Energy Future, 1st: 873–888

110. Garg SK, Riney TD (1984) Brine and gas recovery from geopressured systems. I. Parametric calculations. S-Cubed, La Jolla, CA

111. Garg SK, Riney TD, Wallace RH, Jr. (1986) Brine and gas recovery from geopressured systems. Geothermics 15: 23–48

112. Jones PH (1977) Gas in geopressured zones. Future Supply Nat.-Made Pet. Gas, Tech. Rep., UNITAR Conf. Energy Future, 1st: 889–911

113. Matthews CS (1980) Gas evolution from geopressured brines. US Department of Energy, Washington, DC

114. Randolph PL (1977) Natural gas content of geopressured aquifers. Inst Gas Technol, Chicago, IL, USA, CONF-771153-P1-14

115. Rogers LA (1981) Coming to a technical understanding of natural gas from geopressured-geothermal aquifers. Geotech Environ Aspects Geopressure Energy Pap Int Conf: 59–67

116. Brown WM (1976) 100,000 Quads of natural gas, HI-2451/3-P, Hudson Institute Paper

117. Griggs J (2005) A reevaluation of geopressurized-geothermal aquifers as an energy source. PROCEEDINGS, Thirtieth Workshop on Geothermal Reservoir Engineering Stanford University, Stanford, California, January 31–February 2, 2005, SGP-TR-176

118. Hise BR (1976) Natural gas from geopressured aquifers. In Natural Gas from Unconventional Geologic Sources. National Academy of Sciences, Washington, DC: 41–63

119. Isokari OF (1976) Natural gas production from geothermal geopressured aquifers. Presented at the 1976 Annual Fall Technical Conference and Exhibition held in New Orleans, Louisiana, October 3–6. Paper SPE 6037

120. Jones PH (1976) Natural gas resources of the geopressured zones in the Northern Gulf of Mexico Basin. In Natural Gas from Unconventional Geologic Sources, National Academy of Sciences, Washington, DC: 17–23

121. Cox JL. (ed) (1983) Natural Gas Hydrates: Properties, Occurrence, and Recovery. Butterworth, Woburn, MA

122. Kaplan IR (ed) (1974) Natural Gases in Marine Sediments. Plenum, New York

123. Sloan ED Jr. (1990) Clathrate Hydrates of Natural Gases. Marcel Dekker, New York

124. Englezos P (1993) Clathrate Hydrates. Ind Eng Chem Res 32: 1251–1274
125. Whiticar MJ (1990) A geochemical perspective of natural gas and atmospheric methane. 14th EAOG Mtg. Paris, 1989. In B Durand (eds) Advances in Organic Geochemistry 1989, Org Geochem. 16: 531–547
126. von Stackelberg M, Müller HR (1954) Center for Gas Hydrate Research, Institute of Petroleum Engineering, Heriot-Watt University, Edinburgh EH14 http://www.pet.hw.ac.uk/research/hydrate/hydrates_what.htm. von Stackelberg M, Müller HR (1954) Feste Gashydrate Z. für Elektrochemie, 58: 25
127. The National Methane Hydrates R&D Program All About Hydrates – Geology of Methane Hydrates, NETL, http://www.netl.doe.gov/technologies/oilgas/FutureSupply/MethaneHydrates/about-hydrates/geology.htm
128. Dec SF, Bowler KE, Stadterman LL, Koh CA, Sloan ED Jr. (2006) Direct measure of the hydration number of aqueous methane. J Am Chem Soc 128(2): 414–415
129. Hyndman RD, Davis EE (1992) A mechanism for the formation of methane hydrate and seafloor bottom-simulating reflectors by vertical fluid expulsion. J Geophys Res 97(B5): 7025–7041
130. Brooks JM, Field ME, Kennicutt MC II (1991) Observations of gas hydrates in marine sediments, offshore northern California. Mar Geol (96): 103–109
131. Claypool GE, Kaplan IR (1974) Methane hydrate phase boundary estimates. The origin and distribution of methane in marine sediments. In Kaplan IR (ed) Natural Gases in Marine Sediments. Plenum Press, New York: 99–139
132. Dickens GR, Quinby-Hunt MS (1994) Methane hydrate stability in seawater. Geophys Res Lett 21: 2115–2118
133. Englezos P, Bishnoy PR (1988) Prediction of gas hydrate formation conditions in aqueous electrolyte solutions. Am Inst Chem Eng J 34: 1718–1721
134. John VT, Papdopolous KD, Holder GD (1985) A generalized model for predicting equilibrium conditions for hydrates. Am Inst Chem Eng J 10: 202–205
135. Seitz JC, Pasteris JD (1990) Theoretical and practical aspects of differential partitioning of gases by clathrate in fluid inclusions. Geochemica et Cosmochemica Acta 54: 631–639
136. Soloviev V, Ginsburg GD (1994) Formation of submarine gas hydrates. Bull Geol Soc Denmark 41: 86–94
137. Dholabhai PD, Englezos P, Kalogerakis N, Bishnoi PR (1991) Equilibrium conditions for methane hydrate formation in aqueous mixed electrolyte solution. Canadian J Chem Eng 69: 800–805
138. Sloan ED (1998) Clathrate Hydrates of Natural Gases, 2nd ed. Marcel Dekker, New York
139. Collett TS (1983) Detection and evaluation of natural gas hydrates from well, logs, Prudhoe Bay, Alaska, Proceedings of the 4th International Conference on Permafrost, Fairbanks, Alaska: 169–174
140. Collett TS (1993) Natural gas hydrates of the Prudhoe Bay and Kuparuk River area, North Slope, Alaska. Am Assoc Pet Geol Bull 77(5): 793–812
141. Collett TS (1993) Natural Gas Production from Arctic Gas Hydrates, United States Government Printing Office, Washington, DC. The Future of Energy Gases, U.S. Geological Survey Professional Paper 1570L 299–311
142. Collett TS, Kuuskraa VA (1998) Hydrates contain vast store of world gas resources. Oil Gas J 90–95 A-3

143. Dillon WP, Myung WL, Fehlhaber K, Coleman DF (1999) Gas hydrates on the Atlantic continental margin of the United States – controls on Concentration, the future of energy gases. U.S. Geological Survey Professional Paper 1570: 313–330

144. Kvenvolden KA, Claypool GE, Thirelkeld CN, Sloan ED (1984) Geochemistry of a natural occurring massive marine gas hydrate. Org Geochem 6: 703–713

145. Kvenvolden KA, McDonald TJ, Thomas J (1985) Gas hydrates of the middle America trench, Initial Reports of the Deep Sea Drilling Project. 84: 667–682

146. Kvenvolden KA (1988) Methane hydrate – a major reservoir of carbon in the shallow geosphere? Chem Geol 71: 41–51 A-6

147. Kvenvolden KA, Grantz A (1990) Gas hydrates of the Arctic Ocean region. Geol Soc Am 1(28): 539–549

148. Kvenvolden KA (1993) A primer on gas hydrates, the future of energy gases. U.S. Geological Survey Professional Paper 1570: 279–291

149. Lorenson TD, Kvenvolden KA (1998) Methane in coastal sea water, sea ice, and bottom sediments. Beaufort Sea, Alaska, Internet: http://geochange.er.usgs.gov/pub/gas_hydrates/OFR_95-70/Core/meta/report.html v. 95–70: 1–13

150. MacDonald GJ (1990) Role of methane clathrates in past and future climates. Clim Change 16: 247–281

151. Max MD, Lowrie A (1996) Oceanic methane hydrates: a "frontier" gas resource. J Pet Geol 19(1): 41–56

152. Schoell M (1988) Multiple Origins of Methane in the Earth. Chem Geol 71: 1–10 A-8

153. Ginsburg GD, Guseynov RA, Dadeshev AA, Ivanova GA, Kazantsev SA, Solov'yev VA, Telepnev EV, Askeri-Nasirov RYe, Yesikov AD, Mal'tseva VI, Mashirov Yu-G, Shabayeva IYu (1992) Gas hydrates of the southern Caspian. Int Geol Rev 34: 765–782

154. Ginsburg GD, Soloviev VA, Cranston RE, Lorenson TD, Kvenvolden KA (1993) Gas hydrates from the continental slope, offshore Sakhalin Island, Okhotsk Sea. Geo-Marine Lett 13: 41–48

155. Kvenholden KA, Barnard LA (1983) Gas hydrates of the Blake Outer Ridge, Site 533. In Sheridan RE, Gradstein F. Initial Reports of the Deep Sea Drilling Project: U.S. Government Printing Office, Washington, DC, 76: 353–365

156. Kvenvolden KA, MacDonald TJ (1985) Gas hydrates of the Middle America Trench-Deep Sea Drilling Project Leg 84. In von HueneR, Aubouin J, eds, Initial Reports of the Deep Sea Drilling Project. U.S. Government Printing Office, Washington, DC 84: 667–682

157. Kvenvolden KA, Kastner M (1990) Gas hydrates of the Peruvian outer continental margin. In Suess ER, von Huene R, eds, Proceedings of the Ocean Drilling Program, Scientific Results. U.S. Government Printing Office, Washington, DC 112: 517–526

158. Trofimuk AA, Cherskiy NV, Tsarev VP (1973) Accumulation of natural gases in zones of hydrate – formation in the hydrosphere. Doklady Akademii Nauk SSSR 212: 931–934

159. Cherskiy NV, Tsarev VP (1977) Evaluation of the reserves in the light of search and prospecting of natural gases from the bottom sediments of the world's ocean. Geologiya i Geofizika 5: 21–31

160. Nesterov II, Salmanov FK (1981) Present and future hydrocarbon resources of the Earth's crust. In: Meyer RG, Olson JC, eds, Long-Term Energy Resources. Pitman, Boston, MA: 185–192

161. Trofimuk AA, Cherskiy NV, Tsarev VP (1975) The reserves of biogenic methane in the ocean. Doklady Akademii Nauk SSSR 225: 936–939
162. Trofimuk AA, Cherskiy NV, Tsarev VP (1979) Gas hydrates – new sources of hydrocarbons. Priroda 1: 18–27
163. Harvey LDD, Huang Z (1995) Evaluation of potential impact of methane clathrate destabilization on future global warming. J Geophys Res 100: 2905–2926
164. Kvenvolden KA, Claypool GE (1988) Gas hydrates in oceanic sediment. USGS Open-File Report 88–216
165. Gornitz V, Fung I (1994) Potential distribution of methane hydrates in the world's oceans. Global Biogeochem Cycles 8: 335–347
166. MacDonald GJ (1990) The future of methane as an energy resource. Annu Rev Energy 15: 53–83
167. Kvenvolden KA (1988) Methane hydrate – a major reservoir of carbon in the shallow geosphere?. Chem Geol 71: 41–51
168. Makogon YF (1981) Perspectives of development of gas hydrate accumulations. Gasovaya Promyshlennost 3: 16–18
169. Trofimuk AA, Makogon YF, Tolkachev MV (1981) Gas hydrate accumulations – new reserve of energy sources. Geologiya Nefti i Gaza 10: 15–22 and (1983) On the role of gas hydrates in the accumulation of hydrocarbons and the formation of their pools. Geologiya i Geofizika 6: 3–15
170. Trofimuk AA, Tchersky NV, Makogon UF, Tsariov VP (1983) Possible gas reserves in continental and marine deposits and prospecting and development methods. In Conventional and Unconventional World Natural Gas Resources. Proceedings of the Fifth IIASA Conference on Energy Resources, International Institute for Applied Systems Analysis, Laxenburg: 459–468
171. Makogon YF (1997) Hydrates of Hydrocarbons, Penn Well, Tulsa, OK
172. Holbrook WS, Hoskins H, Wood WT, Stephen RA, Leg 164 Science Party, Lizarralde D (1996) Methane hydrate and free gas on the Blake Ridge from vertical seismic profiling. Science 273: 1840–1843
173. Milkov AV, Claypool GE, Lee Y-J, Dickens GR, Xu W.ODP Leg 204 Scientific Party, Borowski WS (2003) In situ methane concentrations at Hydrate Ridge offshore Oregon: new constraints on the global gas hydrate inventory from an active margin. Geology 31: 833–836
174. McIver RD (1981) Gas hydrates. In: Meyer RG, Olson JC, eds, Long-Term Energy Resources. Pitman, Boston, MA: 713–726
175. Milkov AV (2004) Global estimates of hydrate-bound gas in marine sediments: how much is really out there? Earth-Sci Rev 66(3–4): 183–197
176. Soloviev VA (2002) Global estimation of gas content in submarine gas hydrate accumulations. Russ Geol Geophys 43: 609–624
177. Trofimuk AA, Cherskiy NV, Tsarev VP (1977) The role of continental glaciation and hydrate formation on petroleum occurrences. In Meyer RF, ed, Future Supply of Nature-made Petroleum and Gas. Pergamon, New York: 919–926
178. Global estimates of hydrate-bound gas in marine sediments: how much is really out there? Alexei V. Milkov Earth-Science Reviews Volume 66, Issues 3–4, August 2004: 183–197 [185]
179. Collett TS (1995) Gas hydrate resources of the United States. National Assessment of United States Oil and Gas Resources, U.S. Geological Survey Digital Data Series 30
180. Oil and natural Gas Commission, India, Bulletin 1997

181. Dillon WP, Lee MW, Fehlhaber K, Coleman DF (1993) Gas hydrates on the Atlantic continental margin of the United States – controls on concentration: The Future of Energy Gases, US Geo Surv Prof paper 1570

182. Dickens GR, Paull CK, Wallace P, the ODP Leg 164 Scientific Party (1997) Direct measurement of in situ methane quantities in a large gas-hydrate reservoir. Nature 385: 426–428

183. Holbrook WS, Hoskins H, Wood WT, Stephen RA, Lizarralde D, Leg 164 Science Party. (1996) Methane hydrate and free gas on the Blake Ridge from vertical seismic profiling. Science 273:1840–1843

184. Collett TS (2000) Natural gas hydrate in oceanic and permafrost environments. In Max MD, ed, Kluwer, Dordrecht, The Netherlands: 123–136

185. Ministry of Economy, Trade and Industry (METI)/Japan National Oil Corporation (JNOC), Report 1998

186. Collett TS (1997) Resource potential of marine and permafrost associated gas hydrates. Oceanic Gas Hydrate: Guidance for Research and Programmatic Development at the Naval Research Laboratory, Proceedings of the Workshop on Naval Research Laboratory Gas Hydrate Research Program, Max MD, Pallenbarg RE, Rath BB, eds. NRL/MR/6100-97-8124. Naval Research Laboratory, Washington, DC: 24–33

187. USGS Geological Research Activities with U.S. Minerals Management Service, Gas Hydrate, http://geology.usgs.gov/connections/mms/joint_projects/methane.htm [167]

188. Abrosimova OO, Guba SV (2006) Use of AVO-analysis in exploration of hydrocarbon reservoirs (as illustrated by West Siberian fields). Geol., Geofiz. Razrab. Neft. Gazov. Mestorozhd. Geologiya, Geofizika i Razrabotka Neftyanykh i Gazovykh Mestorozhdenii: 11–16

189. Enikeeva FK, Khamatdinov RT, Kozhevnikov DA, Miller VV, Polyachenko AL, Ochkur AF (1991) Advances in nuclear geophysics in the USSR: equipment, data processing, and interpretation. Nucl. Tech. Explor. Exploit. Energy Miner. Resour., Proc. Int. Symp.: 353–377

190. Falcon NL (1973) Exploring for oil and gas. Mod. Petrol. Technol., 4th ed.: 26–66

191. Vyas D, Raghavendran K, Balram, Mallika V, Prasad J, Satyanarayana K (2006) Geochemical surface prospecting studies – a case history to predict nature of subsurface hydrocarbons for exploration. J Appl Geochem 8: 288–298

192. Weil W (1986) New method for geophysical and geochemical prospecting for hydrocarbon [petroleum and gas] fields. Technika Poszukiwan Geologicznych 25: 31–36

193. Sassen R (1985) Basic geochemical strategies for hydrocarbon exploration. Oil Gas J 83: 128–132

194. Zhao K-b, Sun C-q (2004) Application of hydrocarbon geochemical exploration technique in natural gas exploration. Shiyou Shiyan Dizhi 26: 574–579, 584

195. Foote RS (1996) Relationship of near-surface magnetic anomalies to oil- and gas-producing areas. AAPG Memoir 66: 111–126

196. Bates R, Lynn H, Simon M (1999) The study of naturally fractured gas reservoirs using seismic techniques. AAPG Bull 83: 1392–1407

197. Fournier F, Borgomano J (2007) Geological significance of seismic reflections and imaging of the reservoir architecture in the Malampaya gas field (Philippines). AAPG Bull 91: 235–258

198. Takahashi I (2006) Issues and status of 3D seismic reservoir property estimation. Sekiyu Gijutsu Kyokaishi 71: 3–10

199. Pecher IA, Holbrook WS (2003) Seismic methods for detecting and quantifying marine methane hydrate/free gas reservoirs. Coastal Systems and Continental Margins 5: 275–294

200. Scheevel JR, Payrazyan K (2001) Principal component analysis applied to 3D seismic data for reservoir property estimation. SPE Reserv Evaluat Eng 4: 64–72

201. Fagin SW (1991) Seismic Modeling of Geologic Structures. Society of Exploration Geophysicists, Tulsa, OK

202. Sheriff RE (1991) Encyclopedic dictionary of exploration geophysics, 3rd ed, Society of Exploration Geophysicists, Tulsa, OK

203. Sheriff RE, Lloyd PG (1995) Exploration Seismology. Cambridge University Press, Cambridge

204. Yilmaz O (2000) Seismic Data Analysis, Volumes 1 and 2. Society of Exploration Geophysicists, Tulsa, OK

205. DEIS (April 2003) Appendix C: Oil and Gas Exploration, Development, and Production, Custer National Forest, Sioux Ranger District Oil & Gas Leasing Analysis. Draft EIS

206. Hearst JR, Nelson PH (1985) Well logging for physical properties. McGraw-Hill, New York

207. Serra OE (1983) Fundamentals of well-log interpretation. Elsevier, New York

208. Rider MH (1986) The geological interpretation of well logs. Wiley, New York

209. Pirson SJ (1963) Handbook of well log analysis for oil and gas formation evaluation. Prentice Hall, Englewood Cliffs, NJ

210. Well log: The bore hole image. www.worldofteaching.com

211. Indiana Geological Survey. Log type geophysical www.igs.indiana.edu/pdms/Help/log_type_geophysical.htm

212. Campbell JM (1976) Gas Conditioning and Processing. Volume I. Phase Behavior, Physical Properties, Energy Changes, Vessel Sizing, Heat Transfer, and Fluid Flow. Campbell Petroleum Series, Norman, OK

213. Katz DLV (1959) Handbook of Natural Gas Engineering. McGraw-Hill, New York

214. Speight JG (1990) Fuel Science and Technology Handbook. Marcel Dekker, New York

215. Maddox RN (1982) Gas Conditioning and Processing. Vol. 4: Gas and Liquid Sweetening. Penn Well Books, Tulsa, OK

216. Rojey A, Jaffret C, Cornot-Gandolphe S, Durand B, Jullian S, Valais M Natural Gas: Production, Processing Transport, Institut Francais Du Petrole Publications

217. Kidnay AJ, Parrish WR (2006) Fundamentals of Natural Gas Processing, CRC Press, Boca Raton, FL

218. Kohl AL, Nielsen R (1997) Gas Purification, 5th ed. Gulf Professional Publishing, Houston, TX

219. Mokhatab S, Poe WA, Speight JG (2006) Handbook of Natural Gas Transmission and Processing, 1st ed. Gulf Professional Publishing, Houston, TX

220. Energy Information Administration Office of Oil and Gas (2006) Natural gas processing: The crucial link between natural gas production and its transportation to market

221. NATCO, Houston, TX, USA

222. Appah D (2001) Use of triethylene glycol to dehydrate natural gas. Global J Pure Appl Sci 7: 331–338

223. Bahadori A, Zeidani K (2006) New equations estimate acid-gas solubility in TEG. Oil Gas J 104: 55–59

224. Gandhidasan P (2003) Parametric analysis of natural gas dehydration by a triethylene glycol solution. Energy Sources 25: 189–201
225. Glaves PS, McKee RL, Kensell WW, Kobayashi R (1983) Glycol dehydration of high-carbon dioxide gas. Proceedings of the Gas Conditioning Conference 33: D1–D11
226. Wichert E, Wichert GC (2004) New charts estimate acid gas solubility in TEG: process engineers can calculate absorption of H2S and CO2 in triethylene glycol to optimize operations. Hydrocarbon Processing 83: 47–48
227. Wieninger P (1991) Operating glycol dehydration systems. Proceedings – Laurance Reid Gas Conditioning Conference 41st: 23–59
228. Howe OG (1955) Reclaim that glycol. Pet Manage Pet Manag 27: D55–56
229. Hubbard RA (1989) Method advanced for evaluating triethylene glycol (TEG) systems. Oil Gas J 87: 47–49, 52
230. Jackson RC (1960) Glycol dehydration systems for natural gas. Proc Gas Conditioning Conf: 3–12
231. Kean JA, Turner HM, Price BC (1991) Structured packing in triethylene glycol dehydration service. Proceedings – Laurance Reid Gas Conditioning Conference 41st: 228–258
232. Laurence LL (1952) Natural-gas dehydration with triethylene glycol. Oil Gas J 50: 76–77
233. Madera M, Hoflinger W, Kadnar R (2003) An update to analytical procedures for quality control of triethylene glycol in natural gas dehydration. Conference Proceedings 53rd: 139–150
234. Nordstad KH, Gjertsen LH, Ophaug J, Lunde O, Roseveare J (2000) A new approach to the use of glycol in low temperature, high-pressure gas processing applications. Proceedings, Annual Convention – Gas Processors Association 79th: 252–264
235. Perry CR (1974) Activated carbon filtration of amine and glycol solutions. Proceedings of the Gas Conditioning Conference 24: H, 1–14
236. Polderman LD (1957) Dehydrating natural gas with glycol. Oil Gas J 55: 106–112
237. Russell GF (1945) Dehydration of natural gas with diethylene glycol. Petroleum Refiner 24: 139–142
238. Senatoroff NK (1945) Dehydration of natural gas at high pressure using diethylene glycol water solution. Gas: 21: 25–26, 28, 30, 33–24, 37
239. Sullivan JH (1952) Dehydration of natural gas by glycol injections. Oil Gas J 50: 70–71
240. Vinokur AE (1981) Extraction of a gas condensate using units for drying natural gas with glycol. Gazovaya Promyshlennost, Seriya: Podgotovka i Pererabotka Gaza i Gazovogo Kondensata (Referativnaya Informatsiya): 1–4
241. Alekseev SZ, Afanas'ev AI, Kislenko NN (2000) Application of new absorbents at gas processing plants. Gazovaya Promyshlennost: 30–31
242. Schulz T (1997) Adsorption plants as an alternative to natural gas processing in underground repositories. DGMK Tagungsbericht 9701: 41–48
243. Schulz T (1998) Adsorption as an alternative to gas conditioning. Int J Hydrocarbon Eng 3: 30, 32–34
244. Victory RM, Harris TB (1970) Recent molecular sieve products and process developments in natural gas processing. Proceedings of the Gas Conditioning Conference: G-1-G-17
245. de Bruijn JNH, Huffmaster MA, van de Graaf JM, van Grinsven PFA, Grootjans H (2002) Maximizing molecular sieve performance in natural gas processing. Annual Convention Proceedings – Gas Processors Association 81st: 209–226

246. Kel'tsev NV, Orazmuradov AO, Khadzhiev MD (1979) Prospects of the use of natural zeolites of Turkmenistan for thorough drying of gases. Izvestiya Akademii Nauk Turkmenskoi SSR, Seriya Fiziko-Tekhnicheskikh, Khimicheskikh i Geologicheskikh Nauk: 124–127

247. Universal Oil Product (1/9/2009) Molsiv Molecular Sieve. Gas Processing. http://www.uop.com/objects/96%20MolecularSieves.pdf

248. Oostwouder S (2000) Successful MDEA conversion. Hydrocarbon Engineering 5: 94, 96, 98–99

249. Bourbonneux G (1999) Acid gas reinjection engineering view point. Gas Cycling: a New Approach, Proceedings of the Seminar, Rueil-Malmaison, France, May 14, 1998: 33–56

250. Briot P, Cadours R, Methivier A (2008) Treatment of natural gas with processing of removed hydrogen sulfide and carbon dioxide impurities, Fr Demande: 25

251. FD Skinner, KE McIntush, MC Murff (1995) Amine-based gas sweetening and claus sulfur recovery process chemistry and waste stream survey. Gas Research Institute, Chicago, IL

252. D Law (1994) New MDEA design in gas plant improves sweetening, reduces CO_2. Oil Gas J 92(35): 83–86

253. JC Polasek, GA Iglesias-Silva, JA Bullin (1992) Using mixed amine solutions for gas sweetening. Proceedings of the 71st GPA Annual Convention, Tulsa, OK: Gas Processors Association: 58–63

254. JD Lawson, AW Garst (1976) Gas sweetening data: equilibrium solubility of hydrogen sulfide and carbon dioxide in aqueous monoethanolamine and aqueous diethanolamine solutions. J Chem Eng Data 21(1): 20–30

255. Mehra YR (2004) Market driven evolution of gas processing technologies for NGLs. Advanced Extraction Technologies. http://www.aet.com/gtip1.htm

256. Energy Information Administration (2006) Natural gas pipeline affiliations database

257. Oildom Publishing Company of Texas, Inc. 2006, Gale, Cengage Learning, 2008

258. Faske B, Schmidt T, Storz M (1993) New approaches in completion of salt caverns for natural gas storage. GWF, Gas- Wasserfach: Gas/Erdgas, 134: 566–573

259. Gumrah F, Izgec O, Gokcesu U, Bagci S (2005) Modeling of underground natural gas storage in a depleted gas field. Sources 27: 913–920

260. Wallmann CF (2002) Development of the underground natural gas storage, Breitbrunn/Eggstatt. Proceedings of the World Petroleum Congress 17th: 475–477

261. Walton KS, LeVan MD (2006) Natural gas storage cycles: influence of nonisothermal effects and heavy alkanes. Adsorption 12: 227–235

262. Schulz T, Rajani J, Brands D (2001) Solving storage problems. Hydrocarbon Eng 6: 55–56, 58–60

263. Sedlacek R (1999) Underground gas storage in Europe. Erdoel, Erdgas, Kohle 115: 537–540

264. Sedlacek R (2006) Underground gas storage in Germany. Erdoel, Erdgas, Kohle 122: 389–390, 392, 394, 396–398, 400

265. Sedlacek R (2007) Underground gas storage in Germany. Erdgas, Kohle 123: 422–432

266. Lux KH, Schmidt T (1993) Optimization of gas storage operations in salt caverns. Part 1. Erdoel, Erdgas, Kohle 109: 125–129

267. Energy Information Administration (2004) Gas tran geographic information system Underground Storage Database

268. Weaver CS (1989) Natural gas vehicles – a review of the state of the art. SAE Technical Paper Doc No. 892133
269. Ishii M, Ishizawa S, Inada E, Idoguchi R, Sekiba T (1994) Experimental studies on a natural gas vehicle. SAE Special Publication, CONF-9410173: 125–135
270. Cook TL, Komodromos C, Quinn DF, Ragan S (1999) Adsorbent storage for natural gas vehicles. Carbon Mater Adv Technol: 269–302
271. Suga T, Knight B, Arai S (1997) Near-zero emissions natural gas vehicle, Honda Civic Gx Document Number: 972643, www. sae.org
272. Menon VC, Komarneni S (1998) Porous adsorbents for vehicular natural gas storage: a review. J Porous Mater 5(1): 43–58
273. European Fertilizer Manufacturers Association (EFMA), Brussels, Belgium
274. Groupe International Des Importateurs De Gaz Natural Liquefie
275. US Department of Energy (2005) Liquefied natural gas: understanding the basic facts. DOE/FE-0489
276. Mokhatab S, Economides MJ (2006) Process selection is critical to onshore LNG economics. Global LNG report, WorldOil Magazine: 227(2)
277. Shukri T (2004) LNG technology selection. Hydrocarbon Engineering 9: 2
278. Smaal A (2003) Liquefaction plants: development of technology and innovation. Paper presented at the 22nd World Gas Conference, Tokyo, Japan
279. Martin P-Y, Pigourier J, Boutelant P (2003) Liquefin: an innovative process to reduce LNG costs. Paper presented at the 22nd World Gas Conference, Tokyo, Japan
280. Fisher B, Boutelant P (2002) A new LNG process is now available. Presented at the GPA Europe Technical Meeting, London, England, Feb. 2002
281. Mølnvik MJ (2003) LNG technologies-State of the art. Statoil, NTNU Global Watch Seminar: Gas Technology, Norway, August 29, 2003
282. Swenson LK (1977) Single mixed refrigerant closed loop process for liquefying natural gas. US Patent 4,033,735 July 5, 1977
283. Houser CG, Yao J, Andress DL, Low WR (1997) Efficiency improvement of open-cycle cascaded refrigeration process. US Patent 5,669,234 September 23, 1997
284. Andress DL, Watkins RJ (2004) Beauty of simplicity: Phillips optimized cascade LNG liquefaction process. AIP Conf Proc 710: 91–100
285. Rentler RJ, Macungie P, Sproul DD (1983) Combined cascade and multi-component refrigeration method with refrigerant intercooling. US Patent 4,404,008 September 13, 1983
286. Frivik P-E (2003) The Importance of knowledge in the changing nature of natural gas supply – contributions from Academia and Applied Research in Industrial LNG Development. IEA Advisory Group on Oil and Gas Technology. Economic Analysis Division of the International Energy Agency Initiation of Global Dialogue on the Future of Natural Gas Supply and Use. Exploring the Impact of Financial and Technological Drivers, Washington DC, January 22, 2003
287. Office of Technology Assessment (1977) Transportation of liquefied natural gas. NTIS PB-273486
288. IHI SPB LNG FPSO, http://www.ihi.co.jp/ihimu/images/seihin/pl15-2.pdf
289. Cushing J (2006) LNG vessel safety and security. DOE LNG forum, Houston, TX, USA

290. Munko B (2007) Economic design of small scale LNG tankers and terminals. LNG Conference Offshore Center, Denmark
291. Yang Y-M, Kim J-H, Seo H-S, Lee K, Yoon I-S (2006) Development of the world's largest above ground full containment LNG storage tank. 23rd World Gas Conference, Amsterdam, The Netherlands

Problems

1.   What are the major factors affecting natural gas prices?
2.   What greenhouse gas emissions are associated with natural gas in the U.S.?
3.   How is natural gas stored? How is LNG used? Why use LNG?
4.   Can the use of natural gas be an answer to global warming?
5.   How feasible is natural gas fueled passenger car?
6.   What are the challenges for use of natural gas in a vehicle?
7.   Does use of natural gas affect the environment?
8.   Does production of natural gas affect the environment?
9.   How is natural gas distributed to consumers?
10. Are there adequate supplies of natural gas to meet future needs?
11. What percentage of natural gas is used for electricity generation? Should we build more power plants based on natural gas? What are the issues?
12. There is an attempt to promote natural gas as an alternative to petroleum. Discuss if this is viable and if there is enough resources to replace petroleum?
13. Discuss various uses of natural gas and how these will be affected if natural gas becomes unavailable at an affordable price.
14. Why it important to dry the natural gas before sending it through pipeline?
15. During natural gas processing various sulfur compounds are removed, but before selling to the consumer again a certain type of sulfur compound is added to the gas. Explain the reasons behind this practice.
16. What are the losses from the storage of natural gas?
17. Methane hydrates are considered as the major source of natural gas in the future. Discuss the issues related to its extraction from its source. What are the likely consequences?

8 PETROLEUM

Abstract

Petroleum dominates the world economy. No other commodity affects everyday life the way petroleum does. Although more than 70% of petroleum is used for transportation, it is an essential raw material for making a variety of products that we use in our everyday life. Petroleum is a complex chemical mixture and its trade and also processing depend on its physical and chemical properties. Crude petroleum pumped out from the underground reservoirs goes through a number of processing steps before the final products are obtained and sold to the public. The main objective of the processing is to maximize the yield of transportation fuels. Exploration, extraction from underground reservoirs, benchmarking and processing of crude petroleum are discussed in this chapter.

8.1 Introduction

The word "petroleum" comes from the Latin words *petra*, (or rock), and *oleum*, (oil). Oil is found in reservoirs in sedimentary rocks. Tiny pores in the rock allowed the petroleum to seep in. These "reservoir rocks" hold the oil like a sponge, confined by other non-porous layers that form a "trap."

According to the most widely accepted theory, oil is composed mainly of hydrocarbons, and was formed millions of years ago in a process that began when aquatic plant and animal remains were covered by layers of sediment – particles of rock and mineral. Over millions of years of extreme pressure and high temperatures, these particles became the mix of liquid hydrocarbons that we know as oil. Different mixes of plant and animal remains, as well as pressure, heat, and time, have caused hydrocarbons to appear today in a variety of forms: crude oil, a liquid; natural gas, a gas; and coal, a solid. Although the major consumption of oil is in transportation sector, as can be seen from Table 8.1, petroleum or oil is the key raw material for a variety of other consumer products.

T.K. Ghosh and M.A. Prelas, *Energy Resources and Systems:*
Volume 1: Fundamentals and Non-Renewable Resources, 383–451.

Table 8.1. Products that use petroleum as the starting raw material for their manufacturing.

Commercial products			
Ink	Dishwashing liquids	Paint brushes	Cameras
Telephones	Toys	Unbreakable dishes	Combs
Insecticides	Antiseptics	Dolls	Dice
Car sound	insulation	Fishing lures	Mops
Deodorant	Tires	Motorcycle helmets	Purses
Linoleum	Sweaters	Tents	Dresses
Refrigerator	linings	Paint rollers	Pajamas
Floor wax	Shoes	Electrician's tape	Pillows
Plastic wood	Model cars	Glue	Candles
Roller-skate	wheels	Trash bags	Ice buckets
Hand Lotion	Clothesline	Dyes	Crayons
Soft contact lenses	Shampoo	Panty hose	Caulking
Food preservatives	Fishing rods	Oil filters	Life jackets
Transparent tape	Anesthetics	Upholstery	Garden hose
Disposable diapers	TV cabinets	Cassettes	Plywood adhesive
Sports car bodies	Salad bowls	House paint	Milk jugs
Electric blankets	Awnings	Ammonia	Sun glasses
Car battery cases	Safety glass	Hair curlers	Cold cream
Synthetic rubber	VCR tapes	Eyeglasses	Antihistamines
Vitamin capsules	Movie film	Ice chests	Slacks
Rubbing alcohol	Loudspeakers	Fertilizers	False teeth
Ice cube trays	Credit cards	Toilet seats	Toothpaste
Insect repellent	Water pipes	Toothbrushes	Golf balls
Roofing shingles	Fishing boots	Wire insulation	Cortisone
Balloons	Shower curtains	Fan belts	Artificial limbs
Umbrellas	Curtains	Heart valves	Parachutes
Beach umbrellas	Detergents	Aspirin	Faucet washers
Putty	Rubber cement	Bandages	Tool racks
Hair coloring	Nail polish	Guitar strings	Tennis rackets
Drinking cups	Petroleum jelly	Luggage	Shoe polish
Yarn	Shower doors	Artificial turf	Lipstick
Golf bags	Vaporizers	Wading pools	Perfume
Roofing	Folding doors	Ballpoint pens	Carpeting
LP records	Hearing aids	Shaving cream	Soap dishes
Skis	Permanent press clothes	Soap dishes	

8.2 Consumption of Oil

No other commodity dominates modern society in the way the oil does. Oil not only drives the global economy, it also controls our life style. Table 8.2 shows the oil consumption by various countries. World oil consumption increased by 2% in 2003, followed by a 4% increase in 2004. The 4% rise in 2004 was the largest yearly increase in a quarter-century. This sudden unexpected increase in oil consumption in 2004 year was due to the rapid growth of oil use in the United States and East Asia, notably China. In 2005, growth of world oil consumption slowed to 1.5%, partly reflecting the restraining effects of higher prices. Nonetheless, the level of oil consumption is still high relative to earlier expectations. The demand is expected to remain strong because its consumption is directly related to the global economy. As can be seen from the table, although the consumption of oil in the USA decreased in 2005, the world consumption increased by 1%. The worldwide crude oil demand for 2006 was estimated to be around 84.83 million barrels a day, or a growth of about 1.5%. Most of the increase in the output came from the OPEC (Organization of the Petroleum Exporting Countries) who pumped additional 170,000 barrels a day in April, increasing its output to 30.04 million barrels a day.

Table 8.2. Oil consumption by the countries (million barrels per day).

	Year					Change 2006 over 2005	2006 share of total
	2002	2003	2004	2005	2006		
USA	19,761	20,033	20,731	20,802	20,589	−1.3%	24.1%
Canada	2,067	2,132	2,248	2,247	2,222	−1.5%	2.5%
Mexico	1,837	1,885	1,919	1,973	1,972	−0.8%	2.2%
Total North America	23,665	24,050	24,898	25,023	24,783	−1.3%	28.9%
Argentina	364	372	394	421	442	5.1%	0.5%
Brazil	2,063	1,985	1,999	2,047	2,097	2.2%	2.4%
Chile	228	229	229	244	248	1.8%	0.3%
Colombia	222	222	223	225	230	2.7%	0.3%
Ecuador	131	137	141	168	180	7.3%	0.2%
Peru	147	140	151	165	160	−3.9%	0.2%
Venezuela	594	479	518	547	565	3.4%	0.7%
Other S. & Cent. America	1,144	1,160	1,170	1,189	1,230	3.4%	1.5%
Total S. & Cent. America	4,892	4,725	4,826	5,006	5,152	2.9%	6.1%
Austria	271	293	285	295	294	−0.2%	0.4%
Azerbaijan	74	86	92	107	96	−10.7%	0.1%

(Continued)

Table 8.2. (Continued)

	Year					Change 2006 over 2005	2006 share of total
	2002	2003	2004	2005	2006		
Belgium & Luxembourg	691	748	785	815	837	2.8%	1.1%
Bulgaria	88	103	103	108	110	1.4%	0.1%
Czech Republic	174	185	203	211	208	−1.1%	0.3%
Denmark	200	193	189	195	201	3.1%	0.2%
Finland	226	239	224	233	225	−4.0%	0.3%
France	1,967	1,965	1,978	1,960	1,952	−0.3%	2.4%
Germany	2,714	2,664	2,634	2,605	2,622	0.9%	3.2%
Greece	414	404	435	432	451	4.7%	0.6%
Hungary	140	132	136	159	160	1.1%	0.2%
Iceland	19	18	20	21	20	−5.5%	–
Republic of Ireland	182	178	185	196	195	−0.6%	0.2%
Italy	1,943	1,927	1,873	1,819	1,793	−1.1%	2.2%
Kazakhstan	193	183	188	208	221	6.0%	0.3%
Lithuania	53	51	55	58	59	0.4%	0.1%
Netherlands	952	962	1,003	1,070	1,057	w	1.3%
Norway	208	219	210	212	217	2.9%	0.3%
Poland	420	435	460	479	502	5.4%	0.6%
Portugal	338	317	322	331	344	4.9%	0.4%
Romania	226	199	230	223	223	−0.4%	0.3%
Russian Federation	2,606	2,622	2,634	2,628	2,735	4.2%	3.3%
Slovakia	76	71	68	81	82	2.8%	0.1%
Spain	1,526	1,559	1,593	1,619	1,602	−0.9%	2.0%
Sweden	317	332	319	315	312	−0.9%	0.4%
Switzerland	267	259	258	262	269	2.5%	0.3%
Turkey	656	668	688	649	617	−4.7%	0.7%
Turkmenistan	86	95	103	110	117	6.3%	0.1%
Ukraine	278	286	293	294	317	8.1%	0.4%
United Kingdom	1,693	1,717	1,764	1,802	1,781	−1.0%	2.1%
Uzbekistan	130	148	134	139	143	3.0%	0.2%
Other Europe & Eurasia	453	495	518	540	558	3.1%	0.7%
Total Europe & Eurasia	19,726	19,905	20,132	20,314	20,482	1.1%	24.9%
Iran	1,429	1,513	1,575	1,607	1,669	3.7%	2.0%
Kuwait	222	238	266	302	275	−10.4%	0.4%
Qatar	79	77	84	98	110	15.0%	0.1%
Saudi Arabia	1,572	1,684	1,805	1,891	2,005	6.2%	2.4%
United Arab Emirates	320	333	355	376	408	7.8%	0.5%
Other Middle East	1,425	1,393	1,407	1,437	1,455	1.2%	1.8%
Total Middle East	5,047	5,238	5,492	5,712	5,923	3.5%	7.2%
Algeria	222	231	240	251	260	4.3%	0.3%
Egypt	534	550	567	623	612	−2.4%	0.7%

	Year					Change 2006 over 2005	2006 share of total
	2002	2003	2004	2005	2006		
South Africa	499	512	523	494	499	0.6%	0.6%
Other Africa	1,254	1,274	1,314	1,362	1,419	4.2%	1.7%
Total Africa	2,510	2,567	2,645	2,731	2,790	2.0%	3.4%
Australia	846	851	854	848	886	4.5%	1.0%
Bangladesh	80	83	83	84	86	1.7%	0.1%
China	5,288	5,803	6,772	6,984	7,445	6.7%	9.0%
China Hong Kong SAR	268	269	314	285	273	−4.3%	0.3%
India	2,374	2,420	2,573	2,569	2,575	0.6%	3.1%
Indonesia	1,115	1,132	1,150	1,168	1,031	−11.9%	1.3%
Japan	5,359	5,455	5,281	5,355	5,164	−3.7%	6.0%
Malaysia	489	480	493	477	499	4.6%	0.6%
New Zealand	141	148	150	154	156	1.6%	0.2%
Pakistan	357	321	325	353	372	5.9%	0.5%
Philippines	332	330	336	314	307	−1.9%	0.4%
Singapore	699	668	748	794	853	7.8%	1.1%
South Korea	2,282	2,300	2,283	2,308	2,312	−0.1%	2.7%
Taiwan	999	1,069	1,084	1,113	1,120	0.7%	1.3%
Thailand	766	836	913	918	926	0.7%	1.1%
Other Asia Pacific	504	509	546	571	584	2.0%	0.7%
Total Asia Pacific	21,898	22,674	23,905	24,294	24,589	1.3%	29.5%
TOTAL WORLD	**77,737**	**79,158**	**81,898**	**83,080**	**83,719**	**0.7%**	**100.0%**
European Union 25 #	14,471	14,546	14,686	14,861	14,865	0.3%	18.2%
European Union 27 #	14,785	14,849	15,019	15,192	15,198	0.3%	18.6%
OECD	47,687	48,289	49,095	49,448	49,041	−0.9%	58.1%
Former Soviet Union	3,667	3,748	3,783	3,819	3,997	4.7%	4.8%
Other EMEs	26,383	27,121	29,021	29,812	3,0682	2.9%	37.1%

OECD-Organization for Economic Co-operation and Development; EME-Established Market Economy
* Inland demand plus international aviation and marine bunkers and refinery fuel and loss. Consumption of fuel ethanol and biodiesel is also included
^ Less than 0.5; w Less than 0.05%.
# Excludes Estonia, Latvia and Lithuania prior to 1985 and Slovenia prior to 1991.
Annual changes and shares of total are calculated using million tonnes per annum figures. Differences between these world consumption figures and world production statistics are accounted for by stock changes, consumption of non-petroleum additives and substitute fuels, and unavoidable disparities in the definition, measurement or conversion of oil supply and demand data.
Source: Reference [1].

World oil production has been able to meet the consumption so far. The increase in production came mainly from the OPEC countries. However, as shown in Table 8.3, the oil production of a number of oil exporting countries is declining. World oil demand is expected to grow from 84.83 million barrels per day in 2006 to 98 million barrels per day in 2015 and 118 million barrels per day in 2030. This increased demand will continue despite the increase in world oil prices that is expected to be 35% higher in 2025 than the current price. Much of the growth in oil consumption is projected for the nations of non-OECD (Organization for Economic Co-operation and Development) Asia, where strong economic growth is expected. Non-OECD Asia (including China and India) accounts for 43% of the total increase in world oil use over the projection period.

Table 8.3. Oil production by various countries in the last several years.

	Year					Change 2006 over 2005	2006 share of total
	2002	**2003**	**2004**	**2005**	**2006**		
USA	7,626	7,400	7,228	6,895	6,871	−0.5%	8.0%
Canada	2,858	3,004	3,085	3,041	3,147	4.4%	3.9%
Mexico	3,585	3,789	3,824	3,760	3,683	−2.1%	4.7%
Total North America	14,069	14,193	14,137	13,695	13,700	0.1%	16.5%
Argentina	818	806	754	725	716	−1.3%	0.9%
Brazil	1,499	1,555	1,542	1,715	1,809	5.5%	2.3%
Colombia	601	564	551	554	558	0.7%	0.7%
Ecuador	401	427	535	541	545	0.7%	0.7%
Peru	98	92	94	111	116	3.5%	0.1%
Trinidad & Tobago	155	164	152	171	174	1.5%	0.2%
Venezuela	2,895	2,554	2,907	2,937	2,824	−3.9%	3.7%
Other S. & Cent. America	152	153	144	142	140	−1.7%	0.2%
Total S. & Cent. America	6,619	6,314	6,680	6,897	6,881	−0.4%	8.8%
Azerbaijan	311	313	315	452	654	44.9%	0.8%
Denmark	371	368	390	377	342	−9.3%	0.4%
Italy	106	107	105	117	111	−5.6%	0.1%
Kazakhstan	1,018	1,111	1,297	1,356	1,426	5.6%	1.7%
Norway	3,333	3,264	3,188	2,969	2,778	−6.9%	3.3%
Romania	127	123	119	114	105	−8.0%	0.1%
Russian Federation	7,698	8,544	9,287	9,552	9,769	2.2%	12.3%
Turkmenistan	182	202	193	192	163	−15.2%	0.2%
United Kingdom	2,463	2,257	2,028	1,809	1,636	−9.6%	2.0%
Uzbekistan	171	166	152	126	125	−0.7%	0.1%
Other Europe & Eurasia	501	509	496	469	454	−2.9%	0.5%
Total Europe & Eurasia	16,281	16,965	17,570	17,533	17,563	0.2%	21.6%

| | Year | | | | | Change 2006 over | 2006 share |
	2002	2003	2004	2005	2006	2005	of total
Iran	3,543	4,183	4,248	4,268	4,343	1.2%	5.4%
Iraq	2,116	1,344	2,030	1,833	1,999	9.0%	2.5%
Kuwait	1,995	2,329	2,482	2,643	2,704	2.4%	3.4%
Oman	900	824	756	779	743	−4.6%	0.9%
Qatar	783	917	990	1,045	1,133	8.1%	1.3%
Saudi Arabia	8,928	10,164	10,638	11,114	10,859	−2.3%	13.1%
Syria	548	527	495	458	417	−8.9%	0.5%
United Arab Emirates	2,324	2,611	2,656	2,751	2,969	7.3%	3.5%
Yemen	457	448	420	426	390	−8.7%	0.5%
Other Middle East	48	48	48	34	32	−7.7%	w
Total Middle East	21,642	23,395	24,764	25,352	25,589	0.7%	31.2%
Algeria	1,680	1,852	1,946	2,016	2,005	−0.3%	2.2%
Angola	905	862	976	1,233	1,409	14.3%	1.8%
Cameroon	75	68	62	58	63	8.6%	0.1%
Chad	-	24	168	173	153	−11.7%	0.2%
Rep. of Congo (Brazzaville)	231	215	216	246	262	6.7%	0.3%
Egypt	751	749	721	696	678	−2.5%	0.8%
Equatorial Guinea	215	247	343	356	358	0.6%	0.5%
Gabon	295	240	235	234	232	−0.9%	0.3%
Libya	1,375	1,485	1,624	1,751	1,835	4.2%	2.2%
Nigeria	2,103	2,263	2,502	2,580	2,460	−4.9%	3.0%
Sudan	233	255	325	355	397	11.8%	0.5%
Tunisia	75	68	72	74	69	−7.1%	0.1%
Other Africa	63	71	75	72	68	−5.3%	0.1%
Total Africa	8,001	8,398	9,263	9,846	9,990	1.4%	12.1%
Australia	731	624	541	554	544	−2.1%	0.6%
Brunei	210	214	210	206	221	7.1%	0.3%
China	3,346	3,401	3,481	3,627	3,684	1.6%	4.7%
India	801	798	816	784	807	3.1%	1.0%
Indonesia	1,288	1,183	1,152	1,129	1,071	−5.3%	1.3%
Malaysia	757	776	793	767	747	−3.1%	0.9%
Thailand	204	236	223	265	286	8.7%	0.3%
Vietnam	354	364	427	398	367	−8.0%	0.5%

(Continued)

Table 8.3. (Continued)

	Year					Change 2006 over 2005	2006 share of total
	2002	2003	2004	2005	2006		
Other Asia Pacific	193	195	186	197	215	8.0%	0.3%
Total Asia Pacific	7,884	7,791	7,829	7,926	7,941	0.1%	9.7%
TOTAL WORLD	**74,496**	**77,056**	**80,244**	**81,250**	**81,663**	**0.4%**	**100.0%**
European Union 25 #	3,203	2,995	2,774	2,535	2,306	−9.0%	2.8%
European Union 27 #	3,331	3,119	2,893	2,649	2,412	−8.9%	2.9%
OECD	21,422	21,156	20,716	19,825	19,398	−2.2%	23.3%
OPEC 11	29,031	30,884	33,175	34,068	34,202	0.2%	41.7%
OPEC 12	29,936	31,746	34,151	35,301	35,611	0.7%	43.5%
Non-OPEC £	35,933	35,673	35,661	35,343	35,162	−0.5%	43.0%
Former Soviet Union	9,533	10,499	11,407	11,840	12,299	3.9%	15.3%

* Includes crude oil, shale oil, oil sands and NGLs (the liquid content of natural gas where this is recovered separately). Excludes liquid fuels from other sources such as biomass and coal derivatives.
^ Less than 0.05; w Less than 0.05%; # Excludes Estonia, Latvia and Lithuania prior to 1985 and Slovenia prior to 1991; £ Excludes Former Soviet Union, includes Angola.
Annual changes and shares of total are calculated using million tonnes per annum figures.
Source: Reference [1].

On the supply side, the production of oil has been constrained by available capacity, natural disasters, and geopolitical developments. In 2003 and 2004, as oil consumption and prices rose briskly, Saudi Arabia and other members of OPEC pumped more oil. OPEC was able to boost production relatively quickly in response to changing market conditions by utilizing production capacity that had been idle. By the end of 2004, however, OPEC's spare production capacity was greatly diminished (Fig. 8.1). As a consequence, OPEC's oil production flattened out over the past year even as oil prices continued to soar. Oil production outside OPEC also leveled off last year, contrary to earlier expectations for continued growth. The projected excess oil production capacity of the world is shown in Fig. 8.2

OPEC has maintained excess capacity of only 1 million to 2 million barrels a day since 2004, down from 4 million in 2001 and 5.6 million in 2002. Although OPEC's excess capacity has rebounded from its 2005 low, the gains are largely in heavy crude oils that can only be processed in specialized refineries. These facilities are running at full capacity, so the added supplies are not relieving a tight market. The latest evidence also suggests OPEC is now restraining its output.

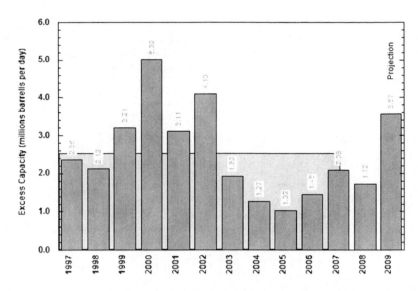

Fig. 8.1. Excess oil production capacity of OPEC and projection for 2009 (Adapted from [2]).

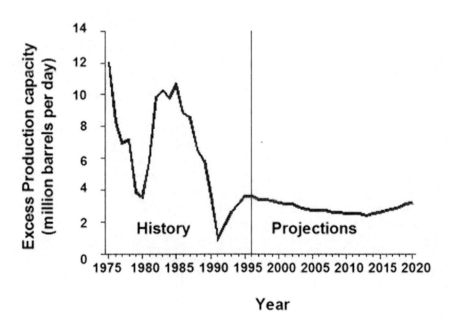

Fig. 8.2. The excess oil production capacity of the world (Adapted from [3]).

Forecasting world oil demand and production is becoming challenging. As shown in Fig. 8.3, among OPEC countries, basically all of the excess production capacity is with Saudi Arabia. The forecast, therefore, depends to a greater extent on the decision of Saudi Arabia's intent on production change.

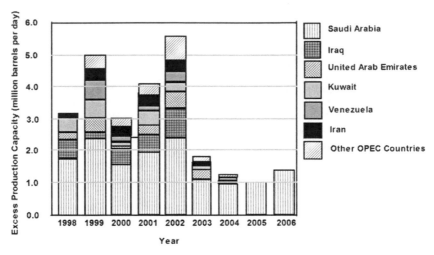

Fig. 8.3. Excess oil production capacities of OPEC countries (Adapted from [2]).

Recently (July 2, 2008), The U.S. Energy Information Administration has lowered its estimate for non-OPEC production in 2010 by 1.1 million barrels per day to 51.8 million barrels per day, from last year's forecast of 52.9 million. At the same time, the EIA lowered its 2010 OPEC production forecast by 400,000 barrels to 37.4 million.

However, it is reported by Associated Press (Abbot S, 07/04/2008) that Saudi Arabia's state-owned oil company, Aramco, is spending $10 billion to build the infrastructure to pump 1.2 million barrels of oil per day by next June from the Khurais field and its two smaller neighbors. This will increase Saudi Arabia's total amount of oil production capacity to 12.5 million barrels per day by the end of 2009; up from a little more than 11 million barrels per day now.

The increased production may not be sufficient to bring down the price of crude oil. Although the consumption of oil is showing decline in the USA, it is increasing in other countries, particularly in China. The annual change in the consumption rate is shown in Fig. 8.4 and the actual consumption is shown in Fig. 8.5.

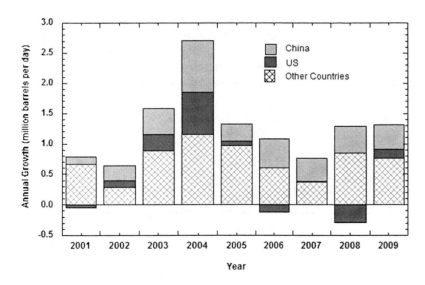

Fig. 8.4. Change in world oil consumption (Adapted from [4]).

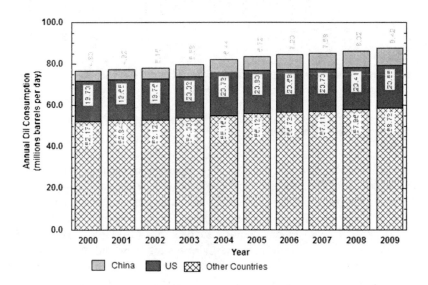

Fig. 8.5. Oil consumption by the USA and China, and rest of the world (Adapted from [4]).

The production of oil is not keeping up with the increasing demand. The world is increasingly becoming dependent on the supply from the OPEC countries. As can be seen from Fig. 8.6, although a number of non-OPEC countries including the USA have increased its production, at the same time the production capacity of a number of major oil producing countries is in a decline.

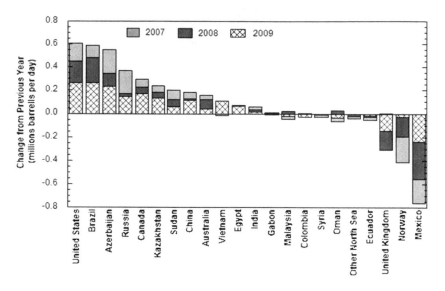

Fig. 8.6. Non-OPEC oil production growth; changes from the previous year (Adapted from [4]).

8.3 Oil Demand by Sectors

Most of the oil in the world is used by the transportation sector, which accounts for more than half of the total use. The industrial sector accounts for about 38% of the oil use, mostly for chemical and petrochemical processes. Consequently, much of the world's incremental oil demand is projected for use in the transportation sector (Fig. 8.7). Unconventional liquids such as gas-to-liquids, coal-to-liquids, ethanol and biodiesel produced from energy crops are expected to share some of the increased demand for transportation fuel; however, oil is still expected to be the major fuel of choice for transportation. An estimate of oil production by various oil producing countries in the future is given in Table 8.4.

In the USA, oil is mainly used for transportation accounting for about 70% of the total consumption. The uses of oil in various sectors in the USA are shown in Fig. 8.8.

Table 8.4. Forecast for future oil production by various oil producing countries.

Region /Country	Annual production				Annual growth		
	2006	2007	2008	2009	2007	2008	2009
OPEC Countries	35.823	35.410	37.096	37.082	-0.414	1.687	-0.014
North America	15.326	15.344	15.278	15.472	0.019	-0.066	0.194
Canada	3.288	3.356	3.416	3.585	0.068	0.060	0.169
Mexico	3.707	3.501	3.189	2.947	-0.206	-0.313	-0.242
United States	8.330	8.487	8.673	8.941	0.157	0.186	0.267
Russia and Caspian Sea	11.890	12.350	12.543	13.071	0.461	0.192	0.528
Russia	9.677	9.876	9.896	10.045	0.199	0.021	0.149
Azerbaijan	0.648	0.849	0.962	1.197	0.201	0.113	0.235
Kazakhstan	1.388	1.445	1.495	1.631	0.057	0.050	0.136
Turkmenistan	0.177	0.180	0.189	0.198	0.003	0.009	0.008
Latin America	4.560	4.597	4.799	5.013	0.037	0.203	0.213
Argentina	0.802	0.791	0.786	0.775	-0.012	-0.005	-0.011
Brazil	2.167	2.277	2.494	2.758	0.110	0.217	0.264
Colombia	0.544	0.543	0.545	0.518	-0.001	0.002	-0.027
Ecuador	0.537	0.512	0.497	0.482	-0.024	-0.015	-0.015
Other Latin America	0.509	0.473	0.477	0.480	-0.036	0.004	0.002
North Sea	4.780	4.544	4.191	4.019	-0.236	-0.352	-0.172
Norway	2.786	2.565	2.398	2.370	-0.221	-0.168	-0.027
United Kingdom	1.602	1.607	1.445	1.301	0.005	-0.162	-0.144
Other Non-OPEC	12.213	12.309	12.636	12.993	0.096	0.326	0.357
World Total	**84.591**	**84.554**	**86.543**	**87.650**	**-0.038**	**1.990**	**1.107**

Source: [BP Statistical Review of World Energy 2008, 2].

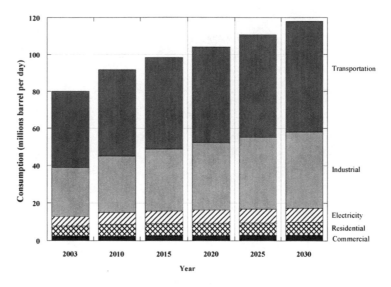

Fig. 8.7. World oil consumption by sectors (Adapted from [5]).

8.4 Exploration, Drilling, and Production

8.4.1 Exploration and Drilling

The search for oil and gas involved exploration both in land and off-shore, followed by drilling of exploratory wells. The methodologies for exploration and drilling techniques have been discussed in Chapter 7.

8.4.2 Production

The basic production steps and well completion are discussed in Chapter 7. The production techniques for oil only wells are discussed below. The naturally occurring pressure in the underground reservoir determines if the reservoir is economically viable. The pressure varies with the characteristics of the trap, the reservoir rock and the production history.

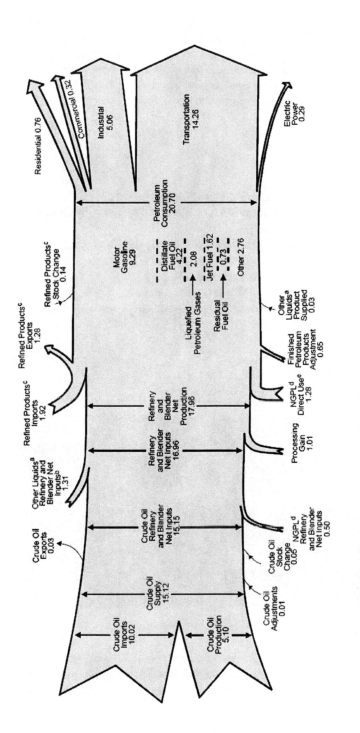

Fig. 8.8. US petroleum flow 2007 (million barrels per day). http://www.eia.doe.gov/emeu/aer/diagram2.html.

[a] Unfinished oils, other hydrocarbons/hydrogen, and motor gasoline and aviation gasoline blending components.

[b] Net imports (1.41) and adjustments (-0.05) minus stock change (0.02) and product supplied (0.03).

[c] Finished petroleum products, liquefied petroleum gases, and pentanes plus.

[d] Natural gas plant liquids.

[e] Production minus refinery input.

Notes: • Data are preliminary. • Values are derived from source data prior to rounding for publication. • Totals may not equal sum of components due to independent rounding.

For most oil wells, the pressure underground is high enough to force the oil to the surface. This is called *natural lift* production methods. Reservoirs in the Middle East tend to be long-lived on natural lift. As the underground pressure in the reservoir dissipates due to continuous extraction, the remaining oil is extracted by means of an *artificial lift*. A pump powered by gas or electricity is used for this purpose. The majority of the oil reservoirs in the United States are produced using some kind of artificial lift.

8.4.2.1 Production by Artificial Lift

The artificial lift methods of producing oil from wells include (1) pumping with sucker rods (2) gas lift (3) hydraulic subsurface pumps (4) electrically driven centrifugal well pumps and (5) swabbing.

About 90% of the wells in the United States are equipped with sucker-rod–type pumps (see Fig. 8.9). This type of pumps is installed at the lower end of the tubing string and is actuated by a string of sucker rods extending from the surface to the subsurface pump [6]. The two common variations are mechanical and hydraulic long-stroke pumping. Other lifting mechanisms are jet pumps, and sonic pumps.

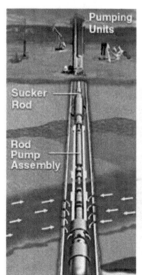

Fig. 8.9. Sucker rod type artificial lift pump for oil production (Printed with permission from [6]).

In the United States, primary production methods, including artificial lift, account for less than 40% of the total oil production. Once the primary production methods even with artificial lift become ineffective, the remaining oil is extracted using "secondary" and/or "tertiary" production methods [7–35]. One common method for secondary production is called water flooding, in which the oil well is flooded using water to displace oil. Water forces the oil to the drilled shaft or "wellbore." Finally, producers may need to turn to "tertiary" or "enhanced" oil recovery methods. These techniques are often centered on increasing the oil's flow characteristics through the use of steam, carbon dioxide and other gases or chemicals. Secondary production methods account for about 50% and tertiary recovery is the remaining 10%.

The reservoir characteristics and the physical properties of the crude oil such as density and viscosity determine the cost of producing oil. These costs can range from $2 per barrel in the Middle East to more than $15 per barrel in some fields in the United States, including capital recovery. Technological advances in exploration, drilling, production methods have made it possible to produce oil cheaper in places such as deepwater Gulf of Mexico, where the production cost is about $10 per barrel.

8.4.2.2 Off-Shore Production

Significant advances have been made in the off-shore drilling and production techniques. In 1978, the greatest off-shore production depth was 300 m. In the 1990s, the crude oil production from the very deep offshore sectors provided stability to the global oil market. By 1998, the depth of the offshore production well was about 1,800 m at Petrobras in the Campos Basin in Brazil. Table 8.5 shows the advances in the deep offshore drilling and production of crude oil.

Table 8.5. Advances in the depth of production from the offshore basins.

Oil field	Location	Year	Depth (m)	
Cognac	Gulf of Mexico	1978	312	Shell Oil
Jolliet	Gulf of Mexico	1989	540	Conoco Inc.
Marlim	Campos Basin, Brazil	1991	752	Petrobras
Marlim 4	Campos Basin, Brazil	1994	1,027	Petrobras
Mensa	Gulf of Mexica	1997	1,650	Shell Oil
Marlim Sul	Campos Basin, Brazil	1997	1,709	Petrobras
Roncador	Campos Basin, Brazil	1999	1,852	Petrobras
Thusder Horse	Gulf of Mexico	2001	5,640 (ft)	BP and Exxon
Tupi	Brazil	2007	>3,000	Petrobras

For oil companies, the next target depth is 3,000 m. Meeting this objective constitutes a major industry challenge for the next 5–10 years.

8.5 Crude Oil Benchmarking

The physical and chemical properties of crude oils generally differ from one field to another field. These properties of the crude oils may even differ over the time from the same field. The quality of the crude oil, i.e., its physical and chemical consistency, is extremely important as it determines not only the crude oil processing (refining) techniques and re-processing necessary to achieve the optimal mix of product output, but also its market price. Price differentials between crude oils actually reflect the relative ease of refining. Based on the physical characteristics of the crude oils they are classified into different categories, which are called Crude Oil Benchmarking [36, 37]. Crude oils of similar quality are often compared to a single representative crude oil, a "benchmark," of the quality class for pricing purposes worldwide. Crude oils are bought and sold in the stock markets as a commodity. The largest markets are in London, New York and Singapore, but crude oil and refined products – such as gasoline (petrol) and heating oil – are bought and sold all over the world.

Benchmarking of crude oils depends mainly on their density and sulfur content. Less dense (or "lighter") crudes generally contain higher percentage of light hydrocarbons. The light hydrocarbons are most desired products as they are higher value products. Lighter crude can be separated (fractionated) by simple distillation process. The denser ("heavier") crude oils require more extensive processing. The products from simple distillation are generally of lower value and require additional processing to produce the desired range of products.

Crude oil is considered "sweet" if it contains less than 0.5% sulfur. Sulfur is generally present as hydrogen sulfide. Small amounts of carbon dioxide may also be present in the crude. Light, sweet crudes are preferred by refiners because of their low sulfur content and relatively high yields of high-value products such as gasoline, diesel fuel, heating oil, and jet fuel. A higher sulfur content is undesirable for both processing and product quality.

Crude oil price Benchmarks were first introduced in the mid-1980s. There are three official benchmarks:

- West Texas Intermediate (WTI)
- Brent Blend
- Dubai Crude

Recently, two other benchmarking are used for trading and pricing purposes; New York Mercantile Exchange, and OPEC Basket.

8.5.1 West Texas Intermediate (WTI)

WTI is used primarily in the U.S. and is very light and very sweet. Its API (American Petroleum Institute) gravity is 39.6° (making it a "light" crude oil), and it contains only about 0.24% of sulfur (making it a "sweet" crude oil). This type of crude is suitable for producing low-sulfur gasoline and low-sulfur diesel. Although the production of WTI crude oil is on the decline, it still is the major benchmark of crude oil in the USA. WTI is generally priced at about a $5 to $6 per-barrel premium to the OPEC Basket price and about $1 to $2 per-barrel premium to Brent, although on a daily basis the pricing relationships between these can vary greatly.

8.5.2 Brent Blend

Brent blend is a mixture of crude oil from 15 different oil fields in the Brent and Ninian systems from the North Sea. Its API gravity is 38.3° (making it a "light" crude oil, but not quite as "light" as WTI), and sulfur content is about 0.37% making it a "sweet" crude oil, but slightly less "sweet" than WTI). Brent blend is ideal for making gasoline and middle distillates, both of which are consumed in large quantities in Northwest Europe, where Brent blend crude oil is typically refined.

Brent blend has become the de facto international oil benchmark. If no other information is given for a particular crude oil, its price is set in comparison to Brent Blend when traded at London's International Petroleum Exchange (IPE) in the UK and other European markets. According to the IPE, Brent blend is used to price two thirds of the worlds internationally traded crude oil supplies. The physical value of North Sea Brent ("dated Brent") is widely used in benchmarking the bulk of oil from the North Sea, West and North Africa, Russia and Central Asia, as well as large volumes from the Middle East heading into western markets.

The production of Brent blend, like WTI, is also on the decline, but it remains the major benchmark for other crude oils in Europe and Africa. Brent blend is generally priced at about a $4 per-barrel premium to the OPEC Basket price or about a $1 to $2 per-barrel below WTI, although on a daily basis the pricing relationships can vary greatly.

8.5.3 Dubai Crude

In the Gulf, Dubai crude is used as a benchmark to price other regional crudes that are sold to Asia. Dubai crude is a medium heavy, low sulfur crude, typical of the grades produced in the Persian Gulf. It is generally sold at a lower price than Brent blend and WTI.

8.5.4 New York Mercantile Exchange

Crude prices on the New York Mercantile Exchange generally refer to light, sweet crude. Oil containing more than 0.5% sulfur by weight is said to be "sour". Not only the US domestic crude, but also a number of foreign crudes are traded based on this benchmarking.

The NYMEX miNY™ crude oil futures contract, designed for investment portfolios, is the equivalent of 500 barrels of crude, 50% of the size of a standard futures contract. The contract is available for trading on the CME Globex® (Chicago Mercantile Exchange) electronic trading platform and clears through the New York Mercantile Exchange clearinghouse.

The Exchange also lists for trading futures contract for Dubai crude oil; a futures contract on the differential between the light, sweet crude oil futures contract and Canadian Bow River crude at Hardisty, Alberta; and futures contracts on the differentials of the light, sweet crude oil futures contract and four domestic grades of crude oil: Light Louisiana Sweet, West Texas Intermediate-Midland, West Texas Sour, and Mars Blend.

8.5.5 OPEC Basket

The Organization of Petroleum Exporting Countries (OPEC) was founded in Baghdad, Iraq, in September 1960, mainly by oil producing countries from Middle East. The objective was to unify and coordinate members' petroleum policies. Since 1982, OPEC also sets crude oil production quotas of its member countries. Current OPEC members include Iran, Iraq, Kuwait, Saudi Arabia, and Venezuela, Qatar, Indonesia, Libya, the United Arab Emirates, Algeria, and Nigeria. Although Iraq remains a member of OPEC, Iraqi production has not been a part of any OPEC quota agreements since March 1998.

OPEC collects pricing data on a "basket" of crude oils from its member countries. OPEC uses the price of this basket to monitor world oil market conditions. From January 1, 1987 to June 15, 2005, OPEC calculated an arithmetic average of seven crude oil streams, including: Algeria's Saharan Blend, Indonesia Minas, Nigeria Bonny Light, Saudi Arabia Arab Light, Dubai Fateh, Venezuela Tia Juana and Mexico Isthmus (a non-OPEC oil) to estimate the OPEC basket price. This average is determined according to the production and exports of each country and is used as a reference point by OPEC to monitor worldwide oil market conditions.

From June 16, 2007, OPEC's reference basket consists of eleven crude streams representing the main export crude of all member countries, weighted according to production and exports to the main markets. The crude oil streams in the basket are:

1. Saharan Blend (Algeria)
2. Minas (Indonesia)
3. Iran Heavy (Islamic Republic of Iran)
4. Basra Light (Iraq)
5. Kuwait Export (Kuwait)
6. Es Sider (Libya)
7. Bonny Light (Nigeria)
8. Qatar Marine (Qatar)
9. Arab Light (Saudi Arabia)
10. Murban (UAE)
11. BCF 17 (Venezuela)

The API gravity for the new Basket is heavier, at 32.7° compared to 34.6° for the previous basket of seven crudes. The sulfur content of the new Reference Basket is 1.77%, making it more sour compared to the previous basket of 1.44%.

8.6 Crude Oil Characterization

A **crude oil assay** is the chemical evaluation of crude oil feedstock by various tests generally carried out in laboratories. Each crude oil type has unique chemical characteristics. No crude oil type is identical. Crude oil assays evaluate whole crude oils and various boiling range fractions of the crude oil. Assay data is used by refineries to determine if a crude oil feedstock is compatible for a particular petroleum refinery. The data also provide important information on the yield, quality, production rate, environmental problems, and marketing. An assay can be customized to meet specific requirements.

A crude oil assay involves a physical distillation of the crude oil to generate specific boiling range fractions ("cuts"). Each of the cuts is analyzed for physical and chemical properties, and basic or detailed information is provided regarding the whole crude properties and the individual cut qualities. The crude oil assay consists of the tests given in Table 8.6 along with the ASTM standards used for these tests. The detail characterization of a typical crude oil is given in Appendix VIII.

Table 8.6. Various test methods for characterization of petroleum.

Petroleum measurement	Unit	EN Test	IP Test	ISO Test	ASTM Test same	ASTM Test similar
Aromatics	% vol				nb. GC/MS	ASTM D5769
Aromatics	dm³/m³			ISO 3837	ASTM D1319	
Aromatics	vol%		IP 156		ASTM D482	
Ash Content	%m/m	EN6245	IP 4	ISO6245		
Benzene	dm³/m³	EN 12177	IP 425			ASTM D3606
Benzene	vol%					
Carbon Residue (Micro)	% m/m	EN10370	IP 398	ISO10370		ASTM D4530
Cetane number	None	EN5165	IP 41	ISO5165	ASTM D613	
Cetane Index	None	EN4264	IP 380	ISO4264	ASTM D4737	
CFPP	°C	EN116	IP 309			ASTM D6371
Cloud Point	°C	EN23015	IP 219	ISO3015		ASTM D2500
Copper corrosion	None	EN2160	IP 154	ISO 2160	ASTM D130	
Density at 15°C	kg/l	EN 3675	IP 160	ISO 3675	ASTM D1298	
Density at 15°C	kg/m³	EN 12185	IP 365	ISO 12185		ASTM D4052
Distillation (Rec. or Evap. Vol%)	°C	EN 3405	IP 123	ISO 3405		ASTM D86
Distillation, % Evap @ T°C	vol%					
Distillation, I.B.P	°C					
Distillation, F.B.P.	°C					
Distillation, Loss	vol%					
Distillation, Recovery	vol%					
Distillation, Residue	vol%					
Doctor test	None		IP 30			ASTM D4952
Existent gums	g/m³	EN 6246	IP 131	ISO6246	ASTM D381	
Existent gums	mg/100 mL		IP 131		ASTM D381	
Flash Point	°C	EN22719	IP404	ISO2719		D93
Induction period (Oxstab)	min.	EN7536	IP 40	ISO 7536	ASTM D525	
Kinematic Viscosity @ T°C	mm²/s	EN3104	IP 71	ISO3104	ASTM D445	
Lead	mg/L	EN 237	IP 428			ASTM D3237
Lubricity	um		IP 450	ISO12156		ASTM D6079

Petroleum measurement	Unit	EN Test	IP Test	ISO Test	ASTM Test same	ASTM Test similar
Mercaptans	mg/kg		IP 342	ISO 3012		ASTM D3227
Octane No. Motor	0	EN 25163	IP 236	ISO 5163	ASTM D2700	
Octane No. Research	0	EN 25164	IP 237	ISO 5164	ASTM D2699	
Olefins	vol%		IP 156	ISO 3837	ASTM D1319	
Olefins	dm^3/m^3					
Oxidation Stability	g/m^3	EN12205	IP 388	ISO12205	ASTM D2274	
Oxygen	%m/m	EN 1601	IP 408		nb. GC OFID	ASTM D5599
Oxygenates	vol%					
Particulate Contamination	mg/kg	EN12662	IP 440			ASTM D6217
Polycyclic Aromatic Hydrocarbons	%m/m	EN12916	IP 391	ISO6591		
Sulfur	% mass or %m/m	EN8754	IP336	ISO8754		ASTM D4294
Sulfur	mg/kg	EN14596	IP 447	ISO14596		ASTM D2622
Sulfur	mg/kg		IP 490			ASTM D5453
Sulfur	mg/kg	EN 24260	IP 243	ISO4260	nb. Wickbold	
Vapor pressure. (RVP, ASVP, DVPE)	kPa	EN 13016	IP 394	ISO3007		ASTM D5191
Vapor pressure. (RVP, ASVP, DVPE)	hPa or mb		IP 69			ASTM D323
Vapor pressure. (RVP, ASVP, DVPE)	mmHg or torr					
Vapor pressure. (RVP, ASVP, DVPE)	kg/m^2					
Vapor pressure. (RVP, ASVP, DVPE)	g/cm^2					
Water Content	%m/m	EN 12937	IP 348	ISO 12937		ASTM D6304

8.7 Crude Oil Refining

Crude oil must be refined in order to produce finished products [38–49]. There are four basic operations that all the refineries perform for production of a variety of products. These are:

- Distillation
- Catalytic Reforming
- Cracking
- Treating

8.7.1 Distillation

The crude oil is heated and fed to a distillation column or tower. A number of such distillation columns are used in a refinery to produce a variety of products. The columns are operated at various temperatures and pressures. Depending on the operating pressure of the columns, they are called atmospheric column (Crude Distillation Unit) or vacuum distillation columns. During distillation, the lightest materials, such as propane and butane, vaporize and are collected from the top of the first atmospheric column. Medium weight materials, that include gasoline, jet and diesel fuels condense in the middle. Heavy materials, called gas oils, condense in the lower portion of the atmospheric column. The heaviest tar-like material, called residuum, is referred to as the "bottom of the barrel", and is collected from the bottom of the column. Products from the top, middle and bottom of the column are transferred to different plants for further refining. A schematic diagram of a refinery for light oils is shown in Fig. 8.10.

The separation of the crude oil into various fractions depends on the temperature at a particular location of the column. Figure 8.11 shows the typical temperature at various locations of an atmospheric distillation column and the corresponding fractions.

The temperature at various locations of the column is maintained by using a variety of techniques. As can be seen from Fig. 8.12 a companion column is used along side the main crude distillation unit where a stream is drawn from the crude distillation column, heated, and again feed back to the crude distillation column. Also, a number of heaters are used to recover the waste heat and to pre-heat the crude oil.

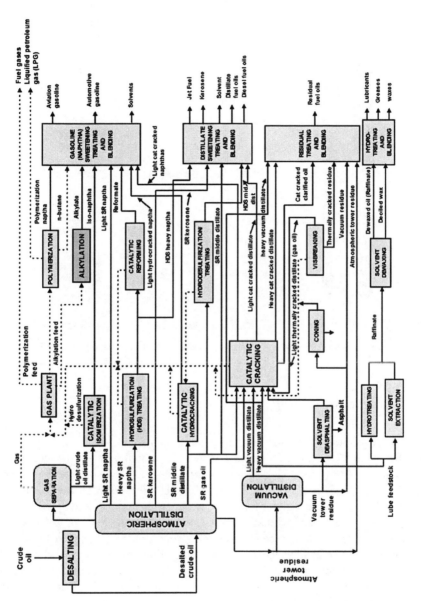

Fig. 8.10. Flow diagram of a crude oil processing refinery (Courtesy of [50]).

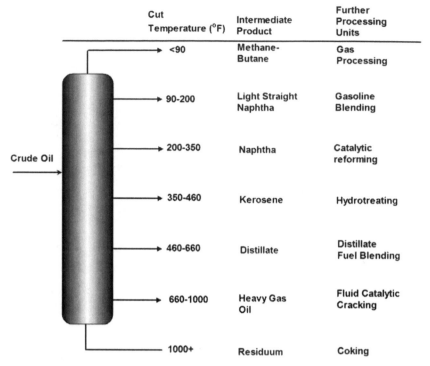

Cut Temperature (°F)	Intermediate Product	Further Processing Units
<90	Methane-Butane	Gas Processing
90-200	Light Straight Naphtha	Gasoline Blending
200-350	Naphtha	Catalytic reforming
350-460	Kerosene	Hydrotreating
460-660	Distillate	Distillate Fuel Blending
660-1000	Heavy Gas Oil	Fluid Catalytic Cracking
1000+	Residuum	Coking

Fig. 8.11. Temperatures and corresponding fractions in the first step of crude oil distillation.

8.7.2 Catalytic Reforming

For use as a gasoline or motor fuel, the octane number of the finished product should be above 87. Catalytic reforming is one of the method used for increasing octane number of gasoline [51–60]. For motor fuel use, the octane number determines the quality of the product as it relates to the combustion characteristics of the fuel. A higher octane number reflects a lower tendency of the hydrocarbon to undergo a rapid, inefficient detonation in an internal combustion engine. The rapid detonation is undesirable as it causes knocking sound in the engine. In the USA, the octane number posted in the gas station is the arithmetic average of the MON (motor octane number which is measured at high engine speeds) and RON (research octane number which is measured at low engine speeds). The RON and MON of some selected hydrocarbons are given in Table 8.7. As can be seen from the table, aromatics have higher octane number and a greater percentage of them are desirable in the finished motor fuel products. The light petroleum distillates (naphtha) are catalytically reformed for the purpose of raising the octane number

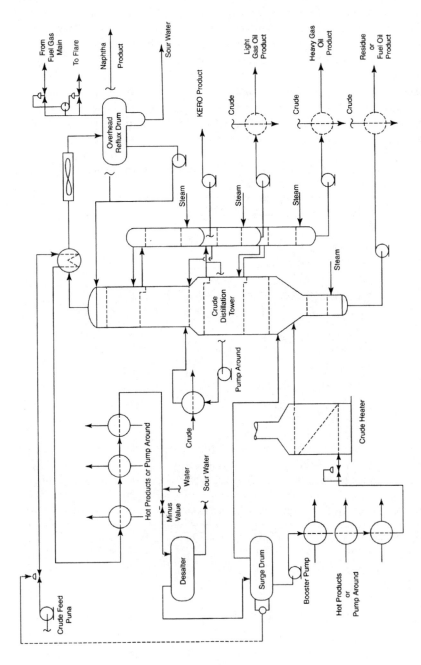

Fig. 8.12. The layout of a typical atmospheric crude oil distillation system (Printed with permission from [49]).

of the hydrocarbon feed stream. Naphtha is contacted with a platinum based catalyst at elevated temperatures (higher than 200°C (400°F)) and hydrogen pressures
ranging from 345 to 3,450 kPa (50–500 psig). The low octane, paraffin-rich naphtha feed is converted to a high octane aromatic rich liquid product. The by-
products of the process are hydrogen and light hydrocarbons. The UOP LLC first
introduced the platinum based catalytic reforming unit (called Platforming™
process) in 1949. Since then significant improvement has been made, particularly
in the catalyst area. The introduction of bimetallic catalysts allows lower pressure,
higher severity operation: ~1,380–2,070 kPa (200–300 psig) at 95–98 octane
number with typical cycle lengths of 1 year.

Table 8.7. Typical Research Octane Number (RON) and Motor Octane Number (MON) of ome
selected hydrocarbons.

Compounds	RON	MON
Paraffins		
n-Heptane	0	0
2-Methylhexane	42.4	46.3
3-Ethylpentane	65.0	69.3
2,4-Dimethylpentane	83.1	83.8
Aromatics		
Toluene	120.1	103.2
Ethylbenzene	107.4	97.9
Isopropylbenzene	113.0	99.3
1-Methyl-3-ethylbenzene	112.1	100.0
1,3,5-trimethylbenzene	>120	>120

Source: Reference [49]

Typical composition of the naphtha stream before and after the catalytic
reforming is given in Table 8.8. The catalytically reformed naphthas are blend
with various other streams to obtain the motor fuel with desired octane number.

Table 8.8. Composition of a typical naphtha stream before and after catalytic reformation.

Compounds	Composition of Typical Naphtha (wt%)	Reformate Composition (wt%)
Aromatics		
Benzene	1.45	3.72
Toluene	4.06	13.97
Ethylbenzene	0.52	3.13
p-Xylene	0.92	3.39
m-Xylene	2.75	7.47
o-Xylene	0.87	4.83

Compounds	Composition of Typical Naphtha (wt%)	Reformate Composition (wt%)
C9+Aromatics	3.31	36.05
Total Aromatics	13.88	72.56
Total Olefins	0.11	0.82
Paraffins and Napthenes		
Propane	0.79	0.00
Isobutane	1.28	0.14
n-Butane	3.43	0.94
Isopentane	5.62	2.52
n-Pentane	6.19	1.74
Cyclopentane	0.64	0.10
C6 Isoparaffins	6.00	3.91
n-Hexane	5.3	1.74
Methylcyclopentane	2.58	0.28
Cyclohexane	3.26	0.03
C7-Isoparaffins	4.55	7.70
n-Heptane	4.65	2.22
C7 Cyclopentanes	2.77	0.33
Methylcyclohexane	7.57	0.04
C8 Isoparaffins	4.24	2.86
n-Octane	3.43	0.62
C8-Cyclopentanes	1.52	0.14
C8 Cyclohexanes	5.23	0.06
C9 Naphthenes	3.63	0.04
C9-Paraffins	5.93	0.90
C10 Naphthenes	1.66	0.04
C10-Paraffins	3.41	0.24
C11 Naphthenes	1.04	0.00
C11-Paraffins	0.53	0.03
Total Paraffins	55.35	25.56
Total Naphthenes	30.7	1.06

Source: Reference [49]

The objective of catalytic reforming is to produce lighter aromatics so that the octane number of the product stream increases. A number of reaction steps take place before the final products are obtained. The reaction steps are shown in Fig. 8.13 and the process flow diagram is shown in Fig. 8.14.

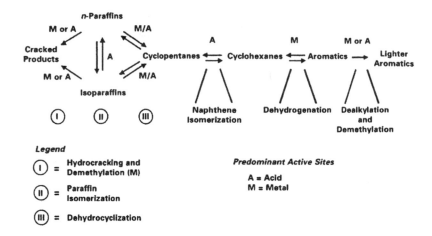

Fig. 8.13. Steps involved in catalytic reforming for production of light aromatics (Adapted from UOP, CCR platforming process for motor fuel production [61]).

Catalysts play an important role in the reforming process. Although platinum is the best catalyst, the cost of platinum makes the process very expensive. A number of non-platinum based catalysts have been developed. Also, zeolite was found to be an excellent support material for a number of active materials such as zinc [62–76]. Several modifications to the process have been made to improve its efficiency [77–81].

8.7.3 Cracking

The objective of the refinery is to maximize the production of transportation fuel; gasoline, jet fuel, and diesel. However, among these three, the greatest demand is for gasoline. The middle distillate, gas oil and residuum are converted into gasoline, jet and diesel fuels in a series of processing plants called cracking units, in which heavy hydrocarbon molecules break down into smaller, lighter ones. There are three applications of the cracking processes and are given in Table 8.9.

Table 8.9. Various objectives of catalyst cracking units.

Applications	Feedstock	Products
Gas oil cracking	Vacuum gas oils	Motor gasoline, LCO and LPG
Resid cracking	Atmospheric resid VGO and vacuum resides	Motor gasoline, LCO, and LPG
Cracking for petrochemicals	Vacuum gas oils and added resides	Light olefins-C_2, C_3, C_4 and aromatics

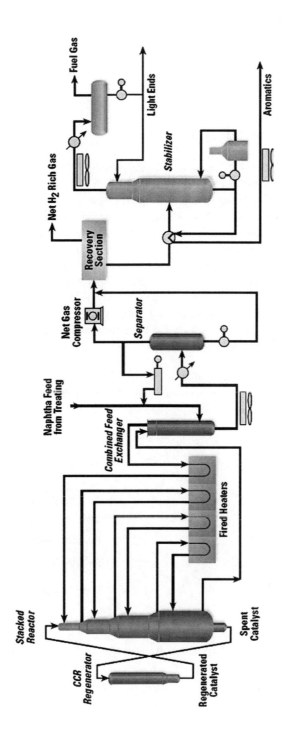

Fig. 8.14. Flow diagram of a catalytic reforming unit (Adapted from UOP, CCR platforming process for motor fuel production [61]).

Three basic cracking processes are used in the refinery to produce transportation fuels.

- Fluid Catalytic Cracking (FCC)
- Hydrocracking
- Coking (Thermal Cracking)

8.7.3.1 Fluid Catalytic Cracking (FCC)

In this process, heavy fractions of vacuum gas oil and resid (boiling point > 344°C (650°F)) are heated at 1,000°F under a vacuum in the presence of a catalyst to produce more valuable products such as Liquefied Petroleum Gas (LPG), gasoline, and diesel fuels [82–131]. A schematic diagram of a catalytic cracking unit (CCU) and a catalyst regeneration unit (CRU) is shown in Fig. 8.15. Catalysts contact the oil near the base of CCU riser where most of the reactions takes place. The reaction products and catalyst are separated in the catalyst/vapor separator. The vapor stream is further cleaned in a cyclone to remove any carried-over catalyst and fed to the main fractionators and the gas plant for separation of the products. The spent catalysts are regenerated by burning off the deposited coke from the catalyst surface and are fed back to the base riser of CCU. Typical CCU undergoes 100–400 such cycles a day.

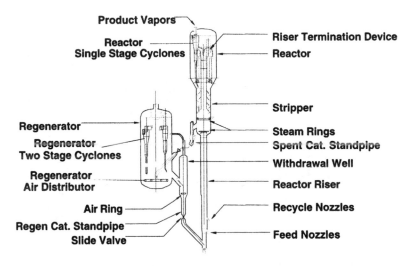

Fig. 8.15. A typical fluid catalytic cracking unit. (From Letzsch W (2006), Fluid catalytic cracking, Chapter 6, Handbook of Petroleum Processing, Eds. Jones DSJ, Pujado PR, Springer, 2006).

The chemical reactions that take place during cracking may be described by the following reactions. The basic reaction paths during fluid catalytic cracking are shown below. The process can be terminated at any point depending on the desired products.

$$Gas\,Oil\,or\,Re\,sid \rightarrow Diesel \rightarrow Gasoline \rightarrow LPG + Coke$$

Paraffin $\rightarrow$ Paraffin + Olefin

C_nH_{2n+2} $\rightarrow$ $C_pH_{2p+2} + C_mH_{2m}$

$C_{10}H_{22}$ (Decane) $\rightarrow$ C_6H_{14} (Hexane) + C_4H_8 (Butylene)

8.7.3.2 Gas Oil Catalytic Cracking

The design and operation of catalytic cracking unit for gas oil is shown in Fig. 8.16. A gas oil cracking unit consists of a feed injection system, reactor riser, riser termination system, and vapor quenching system. The feed, which is in the liquid form, is vaporized upon injection and is contacted with the catalyst. The regenerated and recycled catalyst from the catalyst regenerator is hot; the feed injection system should cool it down as quickly as possible before its contact with the feed. The other feature of the injection system is that it should provide plug flow of the feed. Various feed injection systems, reactor with riser and quench system, and catalyst regenerators are developed to improve the efficiency of the system.

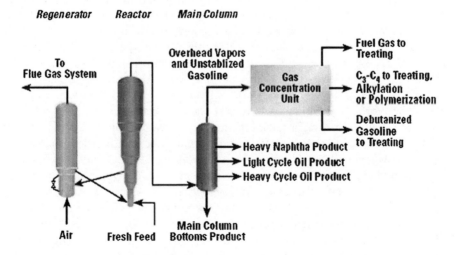

Fig. 8.16. A gas oil cracking unit (From UOP Fluid catalytic cracking unit (FCC) and related processes, UOP [61]).

8.7.3.3 Resid Catalytic Cracking

Refineries are under increasing pressure to process high boiling point feeds and crude oils with high levels of contaminant metals. Reside catalytic cracking process was developed to further process high boiling residue. One of the main issues was development of catalysts. A catalyst should have the following characteristics in order to be effective and economical.

- Capability to passivity contaminant metals such as nickel and vanadium
- Capable of cracking higher boiling range molecules
- A high activity and stability

The catalyst generally used for resid cracking is elite Type Y because of its high hydro-thermal stability, up to a temperature of 1,600°F, three-dimensional structure, average pore diameter of 7.5 A, high activity and selectivity. Elite Type Y resid catalysts offer low production of coke and preservation of elite integrity and activity, and inertness in the presence of high concentrations of nickel and vanadium. A number of companies produce catalysts for RFCC (Resid Fluid Catalytic Cracking) units with varying composition and characteristics.

Although the basic design is the same, resid catalytic cracking units differ based on a specific task that needs to be carried out. The feed injection system should be capable of handling heavier feed which requires more steam for proper dispersion of the feed into the reactor. The main difference of a RFCC with other FCC is in the design of the regenerator. The regenerator should be designed such a way that the regenerated catalyst is cooled down before recycling back to the cracking unit. Either a single stage regenerator with a catalyst cooler or a two-stage regenerator is used. Currently most of the RFCC units employ two-stage regenerator. It not only cools down the catalyst, but a two-stage regenerator produces CO rather than CO_2. This can reduce or even eliminate the need for any heat removal system. Another advantage is that most of the hydrogen (about 80–85% of initial hydrogen content) in the coke can be burnt off in the first stage of the regenerator leaving no carbon on the catalyst surface. The moisture produced during combustion of hydrogen tends to deactivate the catalyst. Therefore, catalysts should be hydro-thermally stable. A typical resid cracker is shown in Fig. 8.17.

Fluid catalytic cracking is one of the main processes for upgrading the product quality and yield. Significant efforts have been directed towards research and process development [82–96]. The catalysts used in the FCC units play a major role. A number of researchers focused their attention on development of new catalysts or modification of existing catalysts [97–112]. Among various catalysts, ZSM based catalysts are explored heavily recently due to its high temperature stability and capability to retain activity [113–118]. One of issues with the FCC process is the regeneration of catalysts for repeated use [119–124]. This will not only extend the life time of the catalyst, but also reduce the operating costs. The riser design of FCC units is important for product quality and yield [125–131].

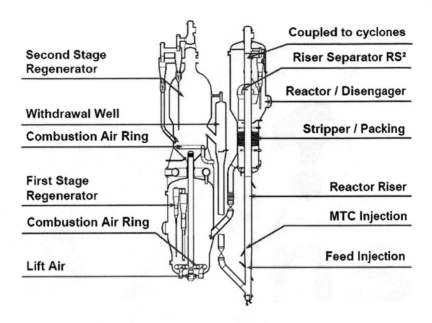

Second Stage Regenerator

Withdrawal Well

Combustion Air Ring

First Stage Regenerator

Combustion Air Ring

Lift Air

Coupled to cyclones

Riser Separator RS²

Reactor / Disengager

Stripper / Packing

Reactor Riser

MTC Injection

Feed Injection

Fig. 8.17. A resid catalytic cracking unit developed by Axens IFP group (From Roux R (2004) A new separator helps FCC adapt to a new refinery-petrochemical role. Axens IFP Group Technologies, PETEM 2004).

8.8 Cracking for Light Olefins and Aromatics

One of the main objectives of cracking heavier feedstock is to produce light olefins, mainly propylene. The demand for propylene as a petrochemical feedstock has increased significantly in recent years.

In 2006, worldwide production of propylene for chemical uses amounted to almost 70,000 metric tons and was valued at roughly $80 billion. Consumption of propylene worldwide is expected to grow at an average annual rate of about 5% over the 5-year period from 2006 to 2011.

The major use of propylene is in the production of polypropylene; almost 61% of the world's propylene was used for polypropylene production in 2006. In Fig. 8.18 the major consumers of propylene are shown. Other uses of propylene include production of acrylonitrile, oxo chemicals, propylene oxide, cumene, isopropyl alcohol and polygas chemicals. Since propylene is an established market, no significant new chemical uses are expected to emerge in the future.

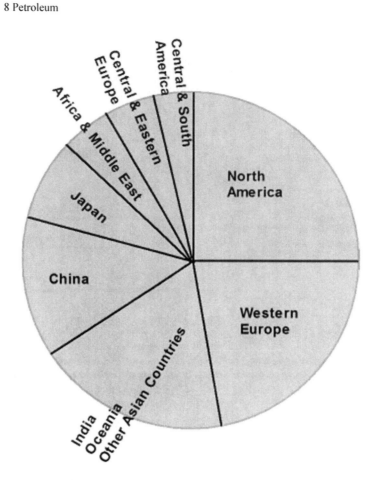

Fig. 8.18. Consumption of propylene in various regions of the world and by some selected countries.

Three major cracking processes; Deep Catalytic Cracking (DCC), Fluid Catalytic Cracking (FCC), and Steam Cracking (SC) are currently used for production of propylene [134–141]. Various products yield by these processes is given in Table 8.10. Although the total product yield by SC is higher than DCC or FCC, the combined aromatic and olefin fractions is higher for DCC process. A schematic diagram of DCC process is shown in Fig. 8.19. The basic operation is the same as that of a gas-oil cracking unit. A number of feedstock can be used in DCC units including vacuum gas oil (VGO), hydrotreated VGO, coker gas oil, and atmospheric resid. Two processes have been developed recently; PetroFCC by UOP and Maxofin by Kellogg Brown & Root-Halliburton to increase the propylene yield from heavy feeds.

Table 8.10. Yield of products by three cracking processes.

Components	DCC	FCC	SC
Paraffins	14.3	28.6	3.5
Olefins	32.4	35.3	13.3
Naphthenes	5.0	9.8	4.1
Aromatics	48.3	26.3	79.1
Aromatics Breakdown			
Benzene	1.9	0.6	37.1
Toluene	9.4	2.4	18.9
C_8	15.6	6.7	13.5
C_9	12.1	12.5	5.4
C_{10}^+	9.3	4.1	4.2
Total	48.3	26.3	79.1

Source: Reference [49].

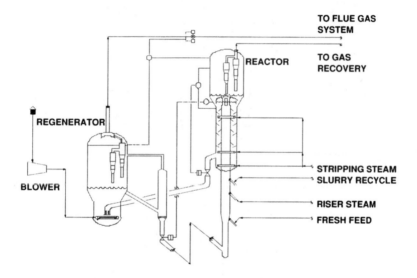

Fig. 8.19. Schematic diagram of a deep catalytic cracking unit (From W. Letzsch, Fluid catalytic cracking, Chapter 6, Handbook of Petroleum Processing, Eds. DSJ Jones and PR Pujado, Springer, 2006 [132]).

The PetroFCC process flow diagram is shown in Fig. 8.20 and the cracking unit is shown in Fig. 8.21. Most of the technologies employed in PetroFCC are adopted from their UOP-FCC units. The spent catalyst is recycled back to the feed riser following regeneration. Interestingly, according to UOP, the spent catalyst is less active, but more selective than the clean regenerated catalyst. The operational conditions of PetroFCC for enhanced olefin productions are; hydrocarbon pressure: 10–30 psia, temperature: 1,000–1,150°F, and shape selective additives: 10–25 wt% of catalyst. The yield of various olefins from PetroFCC is compared with FCC in Table 8.11.

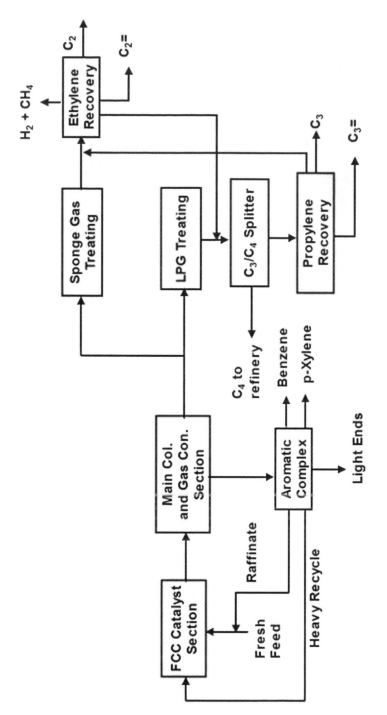

Fig. 8.20. The process flow diagram of a PetroFCC unit.

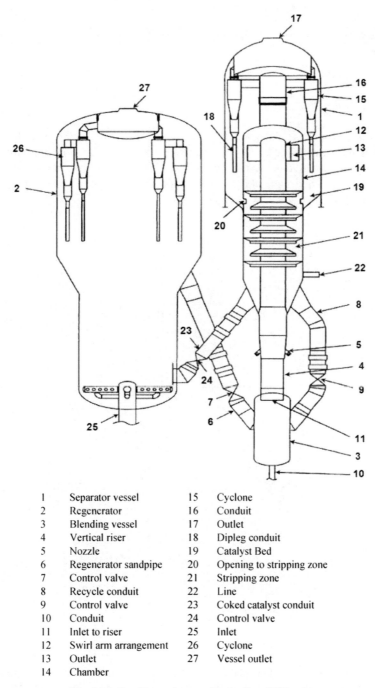

1	Separator vessel	15	Cyclone
2	Regenerator	16	Conduit
3	Blending vessel	17	Outlet
4	Vertical riser	18	Dipleg conduit
5	Nozzle	19	Catalyst Bed
6	Regenerator sandpipe	20	Opening to stripping zone
7	Control valve	21	Stripping zone
8	Recycle conduit	22	Line
9	Control valve	23	Coked catalyst conduit
10	Conduit	24	Control valve
11	Inlet to riser	25	Inlet
12	Swirl arm arrangement	26	Cyclone
13	Outlet	27	Vessel outlet
14	Chamber		

Fig. 8.21. Cracking unit assembly for PetroFCC unit.

Table 8.11. Comparison of yields of various olefins between PetroFCC and FCC processes.

Compounds	PetroFCC	FCC
Propylene	22	4.7
Butylene	14	~6
Ethylene	6	~1
Gasoline	28	53.5

Source: Reference [49].

Maxofin process is designed to maximize propylene production. The main reactor is shown in Fig. 8.22. It has a stacked reactor-regenerator configuration. A special ZSM-5 additive is used along with the FCC catalyst to enhanced propylene selectivity. The yield from the Maxofin process for a gas oil feed operating at three different modes is given in Table 8.12.

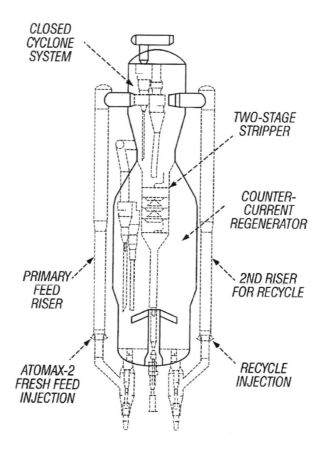

Fig. 8.22. The main reactor of the Maxofin process. (From Tallman MJ, Santner C, Miller RB (2006) Integrated catalytic cracking and steam pyrolysis process for olefins- **US Patent 7,128,827** [142]).

Table 8.12. Yields from Maxofin unit.

	Max C$_3$=	Intermediate	Max Fuels
Recycle	Yes	No	No
ZSM-5	Yes	Yes	No
Riser Temp, oC	538/593	538	538
Yields (wt%)			
C$_2$ Minus	7.6	2.3	2.2
Ethylene	4.3	2.0	0.9
Propylene	18.4	14.4	6.2
Butylene	12.9	12.3	7.3
Gasoline	18.8	35.5	49.8
Coke	8.3	6.4	5.9
Conversion	86.4	87.7	85.4

Source: Reference [49].

8.9 Delayed Coking Unit (Coker)

In a Delayed Coking Unit (Coker), low-value residuum is converted to high-value light products, producing petroleum coke as a by-product by using mainly heat [143–150]. The large residuum molecules are cracked into smaller molecules when the residuum is held in a coke drum at a high temperature for a period of time. Only solid coke remains and must be drilled out from the coke drums. A schematic diagram of the Coker from the UOP is shown in Fig. 8.23.

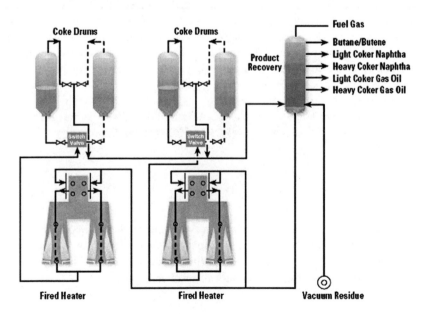

Fig. 8.23. A delayed coking unit developed by UOP.

8.10 Hydrocracking

Hydrocracking utilizes hydrogen gas and a catalyst to modify the residue feed stream into various products [151–172]. Only carbon–carbon bonds are broken and hydrogen immediately saturates any olefins that are formed. Hydrocracking can produce LPG, naphtha, kerosene and distillates and a range of products depending on the type of feed to the unit.

It proceeds by two main reactions: hydrogenation of higher unsaturated hydrocarbons followed by cracking them to the required fuels. The process is carried out by passing oil feed together with hydrogen at high pressure (1,000–2,500 psig, or 7–17 MPa) and moderate temperatures (500–750°F or 260–400°C) into a reactor with a bifunctional catalyst, comprising an acidic solid and a hydrogenating metal component. Gasoline of high octane number is produced, both directly and through a subsequent step such as catalytic reforming; jet fuels may also be manufactured simply by changing conditions with the same catalysts.

Generally, the process is used as an adjunct to catalytic cracking. Oils, which are difficult to convert in the catalytic process because they are highly aromatic and cause rapid catalyst decline, can be easily handled by hydrocracking process. The low cracking temperature and the high hydrogen pressure, which decreases catalyst fouling, make the process more favorable. The most important components in any feed are the nitrogen-containing compounds, since these are severe poisons for hydrocracking catalysts and must be almost completely removed.

The products from hydrocracking units are composed of either saturated or aromatic compounds; no olefins are found. In making gasoline, the lower paraffins formed in the reaction have high octane numbers. The remaining gasoline has excellent properties as a feed to catalytic reforming, producing a highly aromatic gasoline, which easily attains 100 octane number. Another attractive feature of hydrocracking is the low yield of gaseous components, such as methane, ethane, and propane, which are less desirable than gasoline.

A hydrocracking unit may have either a single stage once-through, single stage with recycle, or a two-stage flow scheme. Among these flow schemes both single stage with recycle and two-stage recycle are widely used in the industry.

8.10.1 Single Stage with Recycle

The flow diagram of a single stage with recycle unit is shown in Fig. 8.24. The fresh feed is mixed with the recycled oil, preheated and passed downward through the reactor over the catalyst bed along with hydrogen. The effluent from the reactor goes through a series of separator to recover various product fractions and hydrogen. The recovered hydrogen together with the make up hydrogen is recycled back to the reactor. Both the pre-treatment and cracking are achieved in the same reactor using amorphous catalyst. However most of the units use a pretreatment and a cracking catalyst configuration. The stream first passes through the pre-treatment catalyst where organic sulfur and nitrogen are converted to hydrogen sulfide and ammonia, respectively. No attempt is made to remove hydrogen sulfide and ammonia from the feed stream at this point. The product from the first catalyst bed is passed over the hydrocracking catalyst in the second stage of the reactor where most of the hydrocracking takes place. Hydrogen sulfide and ammonia have little effect on the conversion or yield of the final product. The catalyst for hydrocracking consists of sulfided molybdenum and nickel on alumina support. The reactor operates in the temperature range of 570–800°F (300–425°C) and hydrogen pressures between 1,250 and 2,500 psig (85–170 bar).

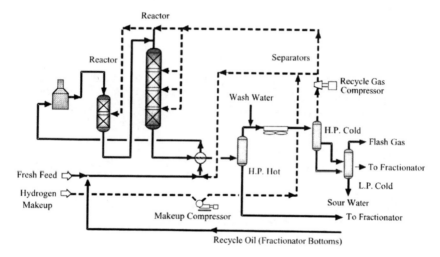

Fig. 8.24. Single stage hydrocracking unit. (From W. Letzsch, Fluid catalytic cracking, Chapter 6, Handbook of Petroleum Processing, Eds. DSJ Jones and PR Pujado, Springer, 2006 [132]).

8.10.2 Two-Stage Process

In the two stage process, the hydrotreatment is carried out in the first stage. Pre-heated feedstock, along with recycled hydrogen is sent to the first-stage reactor, where sulfur and nitrogen compounds are converted to hydrogen sulfide and ammonia over a catalyst. Limited hydrocracking also occurs. A schematic diagram of the two-stage process is shown in Fig. 8.25.

The product stream from the first stage is cooled and liquefied, and thus separates hydrogen sulfide and ammonia. The liquid stream is run through a hydrocarbon separator where it is fractionated with the unconverted oil and is recycled to the second stage. The hydrogen is recycled to the feedstock. Depending on the products desired, the stream is separated into gasoline components, jet fuel, and gas oil fractions. The bottom products are again mixed with a hydrogen stream and charged to the second stage. A higher temperature and pressure is used in the second reactor. The product from the second stage is separated from the hydrogen and charged to the fractionator. Since hydrogen sulfide and ammonia are not present in the feed stream to the second stage reactor, various noble metal or base metal sulfide can be used for hydrocracking. Typical reactions that take place during hydrocracking are given in the handbook [173].

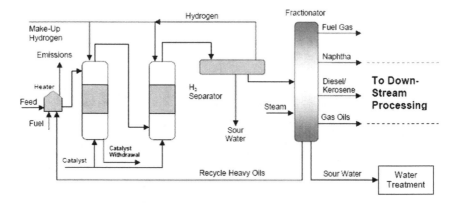

Fig. 8.25. Two stage hydrocracking unit. (Adapted from 2006 Refining Processes Handbook, Hydrocarbon Processing, Gulf Publishing Co. Houston, USA [173]).

8.11 Hydrotreatment

The main objective of hydrotreatment is to remove various undesired compounds such as sulfur, nitrogen, olefins, and aromatics from the petroleum fractions [174–184]. Hydrotreatment is also used to upgrade and to meet the strict product specifications or for use as feedstocks elsewhere in the refinery. The product quality specifications are driven by environmental regulations. A hydrotreatment facility is designed to employ a wide range of operating conditions due to the variation of the type of feed, desired cycle length, and expected quality of the finished product. The following fractions are generally hydrotreated:

- **Naptha:** Pretreatment of the feed prior to catalytic reforming to remove sulfur, nitrogen and metals. The trace metals present in the stream would poison (deactivate) the noble metal catalysts used in the reforming units.
- **Kerosene and Diesel:** Hydrotreatment of this fraction removes sulfur, saturates olefins and some aromatics in the fraction. This upgrades kerosene and diesel in terms of its product quality and stability.
- **Lube oil:** Hydrotreatment improves its viscosity index, color and stability.
- **FCC Feed:** Removal of sulfur and nitrogen compounds through hydrotreatment improves yield, reduces emissions, and extends catalyst life.
- **Resids:** Hydrotreatment removes sulfur compounds and improves its quality as feedstocks.

Although hydrotreatment is used for a variety of applications as described above, the basic flow diagram of the hydrotreatment plant is common. The two major sections of the plant are a high-pressure reactor system (Fig. 8.26) and a low-pressure fractionation system (Fig. 8.27).

The typical operating conditions of a hydrotreatment plant are as follows:

LHSV:	0.2–8.0
H_2 circulation rate:	300–4,000 SCFB (50–675 Nm^3/m^3)
H_2 partial pressure:	200–2,000 psia (14–138 bar)
SOR temperature:	550–700°F (290–370°C)

(LHSV: Liquid Hourly Space Velocity)

The feed and recycled gas (reactants) streams are heated to the desired temperature before introducing them to the top of the reactor. As the reactants flow downward through the catalyst bed, the hydrogenation reactions take place. The effluents from the reactor are forwarded to the fractionation sections where the stream is separated to desired products. The gaseous effluent from the reactor contains H_2 and H_2S. The H_2S is removed from the stream before recycling back to the feed stream. Typical chemical reactions that take place in the reactor are given in [173].

Hydrotreatment catalysts come in different shapes and sizes as shown in Fig. 8.28, however, their basic characteristics are similar. The active component of the catalyst is generally molybdenum sulfide, which is about 25 wt%, of the total mass. The active component is dispersed on an inert support such as γ-alumina. A promoter, which may be up to 25 wt%, is added to the catalyst to enhance the activity of molybdenum sulfide. Both cobalt–molybdenum (Co–Mo) and nickel–molybdenum (Ni–Mo) have been used as a promoter.

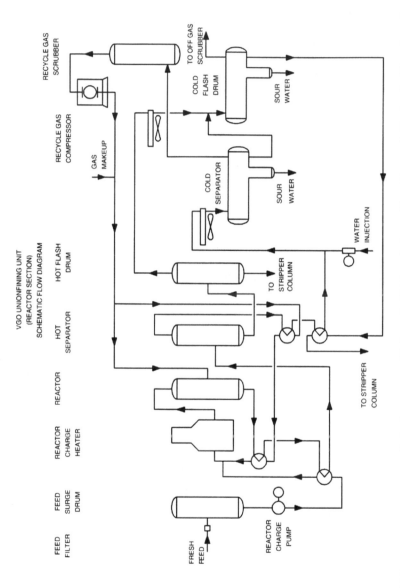

Fig. 8.26. The high pressure reactor system for hydrotreatment (W. Letzsch, Fluid catalytic cracking, Chapter 6, Handbook of Petroleum Processing, Eds. DSJ Jones and PR Pujado, Springer, 2006).

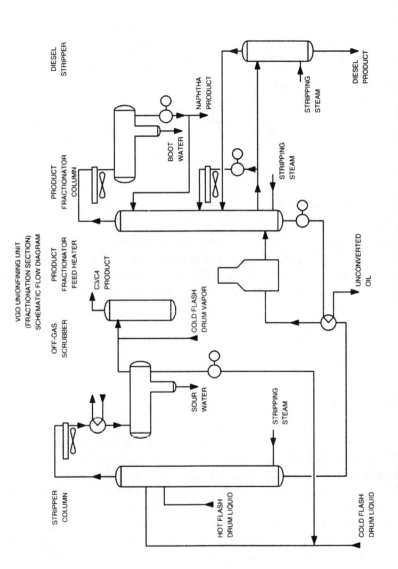

Fig. 8.27. The low pressure fractionation system of the hydrotreatment unit (W. Letzsch, Fluid catalytic cracking, Chapter 6, Handbook of Petroleum Processing, Eds. DSJ Jones and PR Pujado, Springer, 2006).

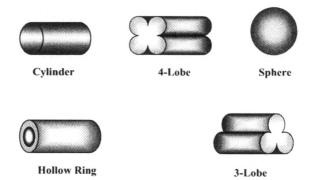

Cylinder   4-Lobe   Sphere

Hollow Ring   3-Lobe

Fig. 8.28. Various shapes of hydrotreatment catalysts. (From W. Letzsch, Fluid catalytic cracking, Chapter 6, Handbook of Petroleum Processing, Eds. DSJ Jones and PR Pujado, Springer, 2006).

8.12 Gasoline Reforming

Gasoline reforming is referred to altering the composition of gasoline to achieve a higher octane rating [185–201]. Various gasoline or motor fuel fractions from different parts of the refinery are further processed to ensure the product quality specifications. Three major processes are used for gasoline reforming:

- Alkylation
- Catalytic olefin condensation
- Isomerization

8.12.1 Alkylation

Alkylation of motor fuel is carried out to produce highly branched C5–C12 isoparaffins (also called alkylate) which are valuable gasoline blending component. Alkylate is an ideal blendstock for making high octane fuel, especially as the alternatives, such as lead additives, are banned and other additives such as MTBE and aromatics are under scrutiny in many countries due to various environmental and health concerns. In this process, C3–C5 olefins along with isobutane are converted to C5–C12 isoparaffins using an acid catalyst. Either a liquid or a solid acid may be used as a catalyst. A number of catalysts including H_2SO_4, HF, H_2SO_4-HSO_3F, HF-BF_3, $AlCl_3$-HCl, trifluoromethane sulfonic acid chloride, Pt-alumina, BF_3 on alumina, zeolites, and ion exchanged resins have been proposed for the alkylation reactions. Among these catalysts, HF [202–206] and H_2SO_4 [207–219] alkylation are most common in the refineries. Recently, UOP has developed a solid catalyst alkylation process (Alkylene^{TM}) that is available for commercial applications. Typical reactions are shown below. The majority of alkylate produced today comes from two routes: sulfuric and hydrofluoric acid catalyzed alkylation. The typical alkylation reactions are shown below.

$$C_4H_{10} \quad + \quad C_4H_8 \quad \xrightarrow{H_2SO_4 \text{ or } HF} \quad 2,2,4 \text{ Trimethylpentane}$$

Isobutane   Butylene   Isooctane

$$C_4H_{10} \quad + \quad C_3H_6 \quad \xrightarrow{H_2SO_4 \text{ or } HF} \quad 2,3 \text{ Dimethylpentane}$$

Isobutane   Propylene

8.12.1.1 Hydrofluoric Acid Alkylation Process

The basic operating principle of sulfuric and hydrofluoric alkylation processes is rather similar. However, sulfuric acid is not as active as hydrofluoric acid as catalyst for the alkylation reaction.

Sulfuric acid alkylation reaction should be carried out at a very low temperature to maintain a low reactor temperature. The sulfuric acid consumption rate during alkylation reaction is over hundred times that of HF.

A schematic flow diagram of the UOP HF Alkylation process is shown in Fig. 8.29. The UOP design is a forced acid and water cooled system. In this process, water is used to remove the heat of reaction. Therefore, the acid requirement is not dependent on the heat removal and the acid use could be reduced significantly. The mixing between the hydrocarbon and the acid is accomplished using a pump, which at the same time can provide necessary inlet pressure for feed nozzles. The feed is introduced in the alkylation reactor as fine droplets. The enhanced dispersion and contact of hydrocarbon and acid contribute an additional 0.2–0.7 octane to the alkylate product. In the last 6 years UOP has licensed 6 new HF units.

8.12.1.2 Sulfuric Acid Alkylation Process

ExxonMobil introduced the stirred auto-refrigerated sulfuric acid alkylation process to maximize the yield. A simplified flow diagram of the process is shown in Fig. 8.30.

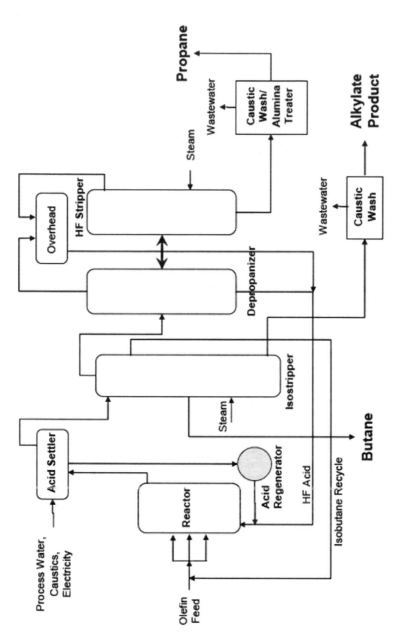

Fig. 8.29. The UOP hydrofluoric acid catalyzed alkylation process (2006 Refining Processes Handbook, Hydrocarbon Processing, 2006 [173]).

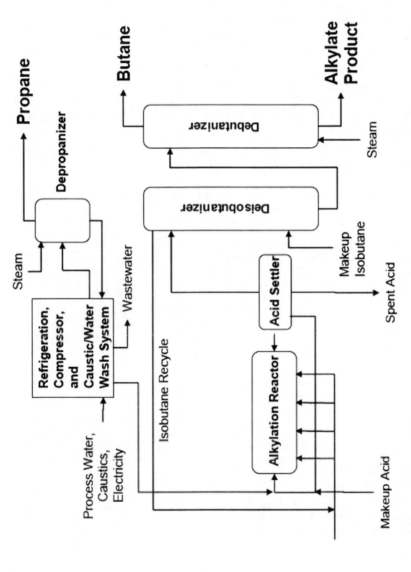

Fig. 8.30. Sulfuric acid catalyzed alkylation process flow diagram (2006 Refining Processes Handbook, Hydrocarbon Processing, 2006 [173]).

In this process, the olefin-recycle isobutane mixture, along with recycle acid and recycle refrigerant, are introduced to the reactor system. An emulsion is created through thorough mixing of reactants and the acid catalyst. The olefins and isobutane react very quickly to form alkylate and release reaction heat. The reaction heat is removed by the auto-refrigeration system by vaporizing some isobutane from the reaction mixture. Just like any other refrigeration system, the iso-butane vapor is compressed, condensed, and returned to the reactor as recycle refrigerant. From the reactor, the emulsion is routed to the settler, where the acid is separated from the hydrocarbon phase, then recycled back to the reactor. The hydrocarbon stream is washed with water to remove acidic components and is fed to the deiso-butanizer. The deisobutanizer bottom stream is split further into normal butane and alkylates products.

A comparison of the two alkylation processes is given in Table 8.13. The HF catalyzed process is cheaper to sulfuric acid process.

Table 8.13. A comparison of alkylation processes.

Process Parameters	Alkylene + Butamer*	HF+ Butamer*	Onsite Regeneration H_2SO_4 +Butamer*
Total feed from FCC, BPSD	7, 064	7, 064	7, 064
C5+ Alkylate	8, 000	7, 990	7, 619
C5+ Alkylate RON	95.0	95.2	95.0
MON	92.9	93.3	92.2
(R+M)/2	94.0	84.3	93.6
C5+ Alkylate D-86, °F			
50%	213	225	216
90%	270	290	296
Economics			
Variable cost of Production, $/bbl**	2.57	0.82	1.37
Fixed cost of production	1.88	2.43	3.53
Total cost of production	4.45	3.25	4.90
EEC, SMM	46.5	40.5	63.3

All cases include a butamer to maximize feed utilization
Raw materials are not included

8.12.2 Isomerization Process

Isomerization of n-butane, n-pentane and n-hexane is carried out into their respective isoparaffins so that substantially higher octane number products are produced.

Isomerization process can also provide additional feedstock for alkylation unit since it converts n-butane into isobutene.

There are two distinct isomerization processes; butane (C4) and pentane/hexane (C5/C6). Butane isomerization produces feedstock for alkylation. Aluminum chloride catalyst and hydrogen chloride are universally used for the low-temperature processes. Platinum or another metal catalyst is used for the higher-temperature processes. In a low-temperature process, the reactor operates at 230–340°F and 200–300 psi. Hydrogen is removed in a high-pressure separator and hydrogen chloride is recovered in a stripper column. The resultant butane mixture is sent to a fractionator (deisobutanizer) to separate n-butane from the isobutane product.

In Pentane/hexane isomerization process, dried and desulfurized feedstock is mixed with a small amount of organic chloride and recycled hydrogen, and then heated in a reactor. The feed next goes to the isomerization reactor where the paraffins are isomerized to isoparaffins in the presence of another catalyst. The reactor effluent is then cooled and separated into a liquid product (isomerate) and a recycle hydrogen-gas stream. The flow diagram of an isomerization unit is shown in Fig. 8.31.

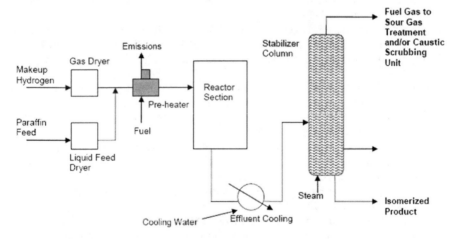

Fig. 8.31. A schematic process flow diagram of the isomerization process (From 2006 Refining Processes Handbook, Hydrocarbon Processing, 2006 [173]).

References

1. BP Statistical Review of World Energy, June 2008
2. Energy Information Administration, Forecasts & Analyses analyses and projections of energy information. http://www.eia.doe.gov/oiaf/forecasting.html
3. Kendell JM (1998) Measures of oil import dependence. Energy Information Administration. http://www.eia.doe.gov/oiaf/archive/issues98/oimport.html

4. Energy Information Administration (2008) Short term energy outlook June 2008. http://www.eia.doe.gov/steo
5. International Energy Outlook (2006) Chapter 3: World oil markets, Report #DOE/EIA-0484
6. Basic Artificial Lift Canadian Oilwell Systems Company Ltd. http://www.coscoesp.com/esp/basic%20artificial%20lift%20tech%20paper/Basic%20Artificial%20Lift.pdf
7. Poettman FH (1974) Secondary and Tertiary Oil Recovery Processes. Interstate Oil Compact Commission, Oklahoma
8. Ali SMF (1966) Growth of steam and hot-water zones in steam injection. Producers Monthly 30: 8–12
9. Chevalier LR, Morris T, Allen C, Lazarowitz V, Fektenberg L (2000) Comparison of primary and secondary surfactant flushing to enhance LNAPL recovery. Soil & Sediment Contamination 9: 425–448
10. Claridge EL (1972) Prediction of recovery in unstable miscible flooding. Society of Petroleum Engineers Journal 12: 143–155
11. Crawford PB (1964) Use of detergents in waterfloods. Producers Monthly 28: 20–21
12. Dawe RA (2000) Reservoir engineering. Modern Petroleum Technology (6th Edition) 1: 207–282
13. Dever CD (1964) Chemical control of mobility–a new dimension in waterflooding. Producers Monthly 28: 13–15
14. Drimus I, Adamache I, Lazescu C (1958) Surfactants [used] in the recovery of crude oil from an artificial core. Buletinul Institutului Politehnic Bucuresti 20: 129–138
15. Farouq Ali SM (1965) Oil recovery by solvent injection. Mineral Ind, Penn State Univ 35: 1–6
16. Fitch RA, Griffith JD (1964) Experimental and calculated performance of miscible floods in stratified reservoirs. J Petroleum Technol 16: 1289–1298
17. Furati KM (1998) History effects on oil recovery efficiency. Journal of Petroleum Science & Engineering 19: 295–308
18. Godbold FS (1965) Inert gas helps recover "Attic" oil. Oil & Gas Journal 63: 133–135
19. Haseltine NG, Beeson CM (1965) Steam injection systems and their corrosion problems. Materials Protection 4: 57–58, 61
20. Hirakawa S, Matsunaga T, Yamaguchi S (1984) Oil recovery by gas injection. Sekiyu Gijutsu Kyokaishi 49: 189–195
21. Ibrahim MNM, Abdullah J, Shuib S, Mizan AM (2004) Secondary recovery performance evaluation of oil reservoir using boundary element method. Journal of Physical Science 14: 41–51
22. Inks CG, Lahring RI (1968) Controlled evaluation of a surfactant in secondary recovery. Journal of Petroleum Technology 20: 1320–1324
23. Kabadi VN (1992) A study of the effects of enhanced oil recovery agents on the quality of Strategic Petroleum Reserves crude oil: Final technical report. In. Dep. Chem. Eng.,North Carolina Agric. Tech. State Univ., Greensboro, NC, USA., p 27
24. Kalaydjian F, Vizika O, Moulu J-C, Munkerud PK (1995) The role of wettability and spreading in gas injection processes under secondary conditions. Geological Society Special Publication 84: 63–71
25. Mack J (1979) Process technology improves oil recovery. Oil & Gas Journal 77: 67–71
26. Marsden SS (1965) Wettability: The elusive key to water flooding. Petrol Engr 37: 82–87

27. Michaels AS, Porter MC (1965) Water-oil displacements from porous media utilizing transient adhesion-tension alterations. AIChE Journal 11: 617–624
28. Moore CR (1983) Well preparation for tertiary production. Proceedings of the Annual Southwestern Petroleum Short Course 30th: 199–205
29. Nicksic SW (1974) Secondary recovery of gas and oil. Energy Sources 1: 237–247
30. Parrish F, Jr., Meadows P (1965) Oil recovery from 17 water-injection projects in Clay, Jack, Montague, and Wise Counties, Tex. Bureau of Mines Report of Investigations No. 6603: 101 pp
31. Paul SE, Bahnmaier EL (1981) Enhanced oil recovery operations in Kansas, 1979. Energy Resources Series 17. In. Kansas Geol Surv, Lawrence, KS, USA
32. Szabo MT, Guilbault LJ, Sherwood NS (1976) Secondary and tertiary recovery of petroleum. Calgon Corp, USA, US Patent 3,948,783
33. Tadema HJ (1963) Research on secondary recovery. Verhandel Kon Ned Geol-Mijnbouwk Genoot, Geol Ser 21: 85–92
34. Tomastik TE (1999) Large potential reserves remain for secondary recovery in Ohio. Oil & Gas Journal 97: 70–72
35. Wiesenthal R (1964) The effect of light-gasoline injection on oil recovery by water flooding. J Petroleum Technol 16: 1307–1315
36. Energy information Administration (July 2006) Pricing Differences Among Various Types of Crude Oil. http://tonto.eia.doe.gov/ask/crude_types1.html
37. James T (2007) Energy Markets: Price Risk Management and Trading. New York: Wiley Finance
38. American Petroleum Institute (1971) Chemistry and Petroleum for Classroom Use in Chemistry Courses. Washington, D.C.: American Petroleum Institute
39. Exxon Company USA (1987) Encyclopedia for the User of Petroleum Products. Lube-text D400. Houston: Exxon Company
40. Hydrocarbon Processing (1988) Refining Handbook. Houston: Gulf Publishing Co
41. Hydrocarbon Processing (1992) Refining Handbook. Houston: Gulf Publishing Co
42. Kutler AA (1969) Crude distillation. Petro/Chem Engineering. New York: John G. Simmonds & Co., Inc.
43. Mobil Oil Corporation (1972) Light Products Refining, Fuels Manufacture. Mobil Technical Bulletin, 1972. Fairfax, Virginia: Mobil Oil Corporation
44. Shell International Petroleum Company Limited (1983) The Petroleum Handbook. Sixth Edition. Amsterdam: Elsevier Science Publishers B.V
45. Speight JG (1980) The Chemistry and Terminology of Petroleum. New York: Marcel Dekker
46. Meyers RA (2004) Handbook of Petroleum Refining Process. New York: McGraw-Hill
47. Gary JH, Handwerk GE, Kaiser MJ (2007) Petroleum Refining: Technology and Economics. Boca Raton, FL: CRC Press
48. Speight JG, Ozum B (1979) Petroleum Refining Processes. New York: Marcel Dekker
49. Jones DSJ, Pujado PP (2006) Handbook of Petroleum Processing. New York: Springer
50. Occupational Safety and Health Administration (OSHA). OSHA Technical Manual Section IV: Chapter 2 Petroleum Refining Processes. www.osha.gov/dts/osta/otm/otm_iv/otm_iv_2.html
51. Greensfelder BS, Archibald RC, Fuller DL (1947) Catalytic reforming. Fundamental hydrocarbon reactions of petroleum naphthas with molybdena-alumina and chromia-alumina catalysts. Chem Eng Progress 43: 561–568

52. Hatch LF (1969) Chemical view of refining. Hydrocarbon Processing (1966–2001) 48: 77–88

53. Kubo T, Hashimoto A (1980) Catalytic reforming. Petrotech (Tokyo, Japan) 3: 721–727

54. Martino G (2001) Catalytic reforming. Petroleum Refining 3: 101–168

55. Burd SD, Jr., Maziuk J (1972) Selectoforming gasoline and LPG [liquefied petroleum gas]. Hydrocarbon Processing (1966–2001) 51: 97–102

56. Elshin AI, Chizhoov AA, Malyuchenko AA, Gurdin VI, Kuks IV, Lesik AT (2001) Reforming of a low-octane middle cut of catalytic cracker gasoline. Neftepererabotka i Neftekhimiya (Moscow, Russian Federation): 13–17

57. Filotti T (1956) The catalytic reforming processes for gasoline. Petrol si Gaze 7: 138–144

58. Gautam R, Bogdan P, Lichtscheidl J (2000) Maximise assets with advanced catalysts. Hydrocarbon Engineering 5: 38,40–42,44

59. Genis O, Simpson SG, Penner DW, Gautam R, Glover BK (2000) Aromatics and catalytic reforming in 2000+. Hydrocarbon Engineering 5: 87–88,90,92–93

60. Schwarzenbek EF (1971) Catalytic reforming. Advances in Chemistry Series 103: 94–112

61. UOP LLC (2009) CCR platforming process for motor fuel production. www.uop.com/objects/CCR%20Platforming.pdf

62. Becker K, Blume H, Klotzsche H (1969) Development of reforming catalysts. Chemische Technik (Leipzig, Germany) 21: 348–353

63. Belyi AS (2005) Reforming Catalysts of the PR Family: Scientific Foundations and Technological Advancement. Kinetics and Catalysis 46: 684–692

64. Chen CY, Zones SI (2001) Reforming of FCC heavy gasoline and LCO with novel borosilicate zeolite catalysts. Studies in Surface Science and Catalysis 135: 4223–4230

65. Day M (2005) Supported metal catalysts in reforming. Catalytic Science Series 5: 187–228

66. Ebeid FM, Habib RM (1974) Comparison between two catalytic reforming catalysts. Proc Iran Congr Chem Eng, 1st 1: 65–73

67. Kravtsov AV, Ivanchina ED, Galushin SV (2000) Testing of commercial gasoline-reforming catalysts. Izvestiya Vysshikh Uchebnykh Zavedenii, Khimiya i Khimicheskaya Tekhnologiya 43: 65–72

68. Maslyanskii GN, Bursian NR, Shipikin VV, Zharkov BB (1966) Regeneration of alumina-platinum reforming catalysts with chlorine. Khimiya i Tekhnologiya Topliv i Masel 11: 1–5

69. Mazhidov A, Abidova MF, Takhirov A (1972) Testing an improved aluminum-molybdenum catalyst during reforming. Uzbekskii Khimicheskii Zhurnal 16: 73–75

70. Moon DJ, Ryu JW (2003) Partial Oxidation Reforming Catalyst for Fuel Cell-Powered Vehicles Applications. Catalysis Letters 89: 207–212

71. Murata K, Saito M, Takahara I, Inaba M (2008) Dramatic improvement of catalyst life by rhodium and cerium additives for Ni-based reforming catalysts. Reaction Kinetics and Catalysis Letters 93: 51–58

72. Pop G, Ganea R, Theodorescu C (2002) Reforming over Zn-zeolite hybrid catalyst. Pre-Print Archive - American Institute of Chemical Engineers, [Spring National Meeting], New Orleans, LA, United States, Mar 11–14, 2002: 717–722

73. Qi A, Wang S, Fu G, Ni C, Wu D (2005) La-Ce-Ni-O monolithic perovskite catalysts potential for gasoline autothermal reforming system. Applied Catalysis, A: General 281: 233–246

74. Ramirez S, Viniegra M, Dominguez JM, Schacht P, De Menorval LC (2000) n-heptane reforming over Pt supported on beta zeolite exchanged with Cs and Li cations. Catalysis Letters 66: 25–32

75. Chen CY, Zones SI (2001) Reforming of FCC heavy gasoline and LCO with novel borosilicate zeolite catalysts. Studies in Surface Science and Catalysis 135: 4223–4230

76. Pop G, Ganea R, Theodorescu C (2002) Reforming over Zn-zeolite hybrid catalyst. Pre-Print Archive - American Institute of Chemical Engineers, [Spring National Meeting], New Orleans, LA, United States, Mar 11–14, 2002: 717–722

77. Schaefer J, Sommer M, Diezinger S, Trimis D, Durst F (2006) Efficiency enhancement in gasoline reforming through the recirculation of reformate. Journal of Power Sources 154: 428–436

78. Senn DR, Lin F-N, Wuggazer T (2000) Improve reforming catalyst performance. World Refining 10: 48–49

79. Suehiro H (1973) Unleaded gasoline and the reforming technology for automotive fuels. Processes and catalysts. Kogyo Reametaru 51: 30–33

80. Tomasik Z, Wrzyszcz J (1960) Catalytic reforming of octane fractions. Chem Stosowana 4: 81–99

81. Schaefer J, Sommer M, Diezinger S, Trimis D, Durst F (2006) Efficiency enhancement in gasoline reforming through the recirculation of reformate. Journal of Power Sources 154: 428–436

82. Avidan AA, Edwards M, Owen H (1990) Innovative improvements highlight FCC's [fluid catalytic cracking] past and future. Oil & Gas Journal 88: 33–36, 38–43, 46–50, 52, 54–38

83. Anderson NK, Sterba MJ (1946) Catalytic cracking unit for the smaller refiner. Petroleum World (Los Angeles) 43: 54–56

84. Carlsmith LE, Johnson FB (1945) Pilot plant development of fluid catalytic cracking. Journal of Industrial and Engineering Chemistry (Washington, D C) 37: 451–455

85. Chen Y-M (2003) Applications for fluid catalytic cracking. Chemical Industries (Dekker) 91: 379–396

86. Edwards M (2006) A question of balance. Hydrocarbon Engineering 11: 46–51

87. Jahnig CE, Martin HZ, Campbell DL (1983) The development of fluid catalytic cracking. ACS Symposium Series 222: 273–291

88. Jahnig CE, Martin HZ, Campbell DL (1984) The development of fluid catalytic cracking. Chemtech 14: 106–112

89. Vermilion WL, Niclaes HJ (1976) Fuel and petrochemicals from fluid catalytic cracking. Large Chem Plants, Proc, Int Symp, 3rd: 69–80

90. Vermilion WL, Niclaes HJ (1977) Petrochemicals from the FCC unit. Hydrocarbon Processing (1966–2001) 56: 193–197

91. Mattox WJ (1950) The fluid catalytic cracking process. Colloid Chemistry 7: 477–495

92. Pryor CC (1944) Latest type fluid catalytic cracking plant in operation. Petroleum Management 15: 61–66

93. Read D, Jr. (1946) Application of fluid catalytic cracking in present refinery operations. Oil & Gas Journal 44: 243–249

94. Redwan DS, Ali SA (1992) Recent advances in fluid catalytic cracking process. Fuel Science & Technology International 10: 141–172

95. Uhl WC (1972) New developments in fluid catalytic cracking. World Petroleum 43: 53–56

96. Vermilion WL, Niclaes HJ (1977) Petrochemicals from the FCC unit. Hydrocarbon Processing (1966–2001) 56: 193–197

97. Turaga UT, Song C (2003) MCM-41-supported Co-Mo catalysts for deep hydrodesulfurization of light cycle oil. Catalysis Today 86: 129–140

98. Andersson S-I, Myrstad T (2001) Optimum properties of RFCC catalysts. Studies in Surface Science and Catalysis 134: 227–238

99. Andersson S-I, Myrstad T (2007) Discrepancies in FCC catalyst evaluation of atmospheric residues. Studies in Surface Science and Catalysis 166: 13–29

100. Arandes JM, Torre I, Castano P, Olazar M, Bilbao J (2007) Catalytic Cracking of Waxes Produced by the Fast Pyrolysis of Polyolefins. Energy & Fuels 21: 561–569

101. Bollas GM, Lappas AA, Iatridis DK, Vasalos IA (2007) Five-lump kinetic model with selective catalyst deactivation for the prediction of the product selectivity in the fluid catalytic cracking process. Catalysis Today 127: 31–43

102. Brown M, Ford J, Cameron A (2006) Fresh catalyst addition system fluid catalytic cracking. Hydrocarbon Engineering 11: 55–56, 58

103. Cao Z, Liu J, Li D (2006) FCC gasoline hydroisomerization over Pt/HZSM-5 catalysts. Petroleum Science and Technology 24: 1027–1042

104. Cerqueira HS, Rawet R, Costa AF (2002) FCC optimization review: catalyst impact on the production chain. Proceedings of the World Petroleum Congress 17th: 25–35

105. Chen Y-M (2006) Recent advances in FCC technology. Powder Technology 163: 2-8

106. Cheng W-C, Habib ET, Jr., Rajagopalan K, Roberie TG, Wormsbecher RF, Ziebarth MS (2008) Fluid catalytic cracking. Handbook of Heterogeneous Catalysis (2nd Edition) 6: 2741–2778

107. Cheng Y, Wu C, Zhu J, Wei F, Jin Y (2008) Downer reactor: From fundamental study to industrial application. Powder Technology 183: 364–384

108. Foskett S (2007) Competitive catalysts. Hydrocarbon Engineering 12: 39–40,42,44–45

109. Komvokis VG, Iliopoulou EF, Vasalos IA, Triantafyllidis KS, Marshall CL (2007) Development of optimized Cu-ZSM-5 deNOx catalytic materials both for HC-SCR applications and as FCC catalytic additives. Applied Catalysis, A: General 325: 345–352

110. Miyazaki H (2007) Fluid catalytic cracking (FCC) advanced catalyst evaluation using a small fluidized bed catalytic cracker. Petrotech (Tokyo, Jpn) 30: 223–226

111. Nee JRD, Harding RH, Yaluris G, et al. (2005) Fluid catalytic cracking (FCC), catalysts and additives. Kirk-Othmer Encyclopedia of Chemical Technology (5th Edition) 11: 678–699

112. Tongue T, Rajagopalan K (2001) Development of fluid cracking catalyst. Preprints – American Chemical Society, Division of Petroleum Chemistry 46: 195–198

113. Biswas J, Maxwell IE (1990) Octane enhancement in fluid catalytic cracking. I. Role of ZSM-5 addition and reactor temperature. Applied Catalysis 58: 1–18

114. Gan J, Wang T, Liu Z, Tan W (2007) Recent progress in industrial zeolites for petrochemical applications. Studies in Surface Science and Catalysis 170B: 1567–1577

115. Haiyan W, Jing Z, Guojing C, Liang Z, Min W, Jun M (2008) Reducing Olefins Content of FCC Gasoline Using a NANO-HZSM-5 Catalyst. Petroleum Science and Technology 26: 499–505

116. Pan H, Wei G, Yuan H, et al. (2007) Studies on catalytic cracking catalyst of hydrocarbons with a new type of zeolite L. Studies in Surface Science and Catalysis 170B: 1392–1398

117. Pappal DA, Schipper PH (1991) Increasing motor octanes by using ZSM-5 in catalytic cracking. Riser pilot plant gasoline composition analyses. ACS Symposium Series 452: 45–55

118. Sanchez-Castillo Marco A, Madon Rostam J, Dumesic James A (2005) Role of rare earth cations in Y zeolite for hydrocarbon cracking. The Journal of Physical Chemistry B 109: 2164–2175

119. Snuggs JF (1947) Regeneration of spent catalyst in fluid-catalytic cracking. Transactions of the ASME 69: 785–788

120. Snuggs JF (1947) Regeneration of spent catalyst in fluid catalytic cracking. Oil & Gas Journal 45: 88–91

121. Upson LL, Rosser FS, Hemler CL, et al. (2005) Fluid catalytic cracking (FCC) units, regeneration. Kirk-Othmer Encyclopedia of Chemical Technology (5th Edition) 11: 700–734

122. Fernandes JL, Pinheiro CIC, Oliveira NMC, Neto AI, Ribeiro FR (2007) Steady state multiplicity in an UOP FCC unit with high-efficiency regenerator. Chemical Engineering Science 62: 6308–6322

123. Fernandes JL, Pinheiro CIC, Oliveira NMC, Inverno J, Ribeiro FR (2008) Model development and validation of an industrial UOP fluid catalytic cracking unit with a high-efficiency regenerator. Industrial & Engineering Chemistry Research 47: 850–866

124. Kumar S, Chadha A, Gupta R, Sharma R (1995) CATCRAK: A process simulator for an integrated FCC-regenerator system. Industrial & Engineering Chemistry Research 34: 3737–3748

125. Gauthier T, Andreux R, Verstraete J, Roux R, Ross J (2005) Industrial development and operation of an efficient riser separation system for FCC units. International Journal of Chemical Reactor Engineering 3: No pp given

126. Jazayeri B (1991) Optimize FCC riser design. Hydrocarbon Processing, International Edition 70: 93–95

127. Atias JA, de Lasa H (2004) Adsorption and catalytic reaction in FCC catalysts using a novel fluidized CREC riser simulator. Chemical Engineering Science 59: 5663–5669

128. Yuan QM, Li CY, Yang CH, Wang YL, Zhang ZT, Shan HH (2007) Studies on conversion of CGO by two-stage riser fluid catalytic cracking. Abstracts of Papers, 233rd ACS National Meeting, Chicago, IL, United States, March 25–29, 2007: PETR-068

129. Yuan Q-M, Wang Y-L, Zhang Z-T, Li C-Y, Yang C-H, Shan H-H (2007) Studies on conversion of coker gas oil by two-staged riser fluid catalytic cracking. Preprints – American Chemical Society, Division of Petroleum Chemistry 52: No pp given

130. Van Landeghem F, Nevicato D, Pitault I, et al. (1996) Fluid catalytic cracking: modeling of an industrial riser. Applied Catalysis, A: General 138: 381–405

131. Bollas GM, Vasalos IA, Lappas AA, Iatridis DK, Voutetakis SS, Papadopoulou SA (2007) Integrated FCC riser-regenerator dynamics studied in a fluid catalytic cracking pilot plant. Chemical Engineering Science 62: 1887–1904

132. Letzsch W (2006) Fluid catalytic cracking, Chap 6, Handbook of Petroleum Processing, Eds. Jones DSJ, Pujado PR, Springer 2006

133. Roux R (2004) A new separator helps FCC adapt to a new refinery-petrochemical role. Axens IFP Group Technologies, PETEM 2004

134. Marui M (2003) UOP propylene production technology. Petrotech (Tokyo, Jpn) 26: 667–673

135. Aitani AM (2004) Advances in propylene production routes. Oil, Gas (Hamburg, Germany) 30: 36–39

136. Corma A, Melo F, Sauvanaud L, Ortega FJ (2004) Different process schemes for converting light straight run and fluid catalytic cracking naphthas in a FCC unit for maximum propylene production. Applied Catalysis, A: General 265: 195–206

137. Watabe M (2007) FCC catalysts and additives for propylene production. Zeoraito 24: 125–132
138. Fujiyama Y, Redhwi HH, Aitani AM, Saeed MR, Dean CF (2005) Demonstration plant for new FCC technology yields increased propylene. Oil & Gas Journal 103: 54–58
139. Imhof P, Rautianinen E, Gonzalez J (2005) Maximising propylene yields. Hydrocarbon Engineering 10: 29–30
140. Kelkar CP, Harris D, Xu M, Fu J (2007) Enhanced propylene production in FCC by novel catalytic materials. DGMK Tagungsbericht 2007 2: 37–44
141. Golden S, Pulley R, Dean CF (2004) Catalyst changes, downstream improvements increase FCC propylene yields. Oil & Gas Journal 102: 44–46,48,50,52–54
142. Tallman MJ, Santner C, Miller RB (2006) Integrated catalytic cracking and steam pyrolysis process for olefins-US Patent 7,128,827
143. Ho TC (1992) Study of coke formation in resid catalytic cracking. Industrial & Engineering Chemistry Research 31: 2281–2286
144. Ho TC (1993) A study of coke formation in resid catalytic cracking. Studies in Surface Science and Catalysis 75: 2551–2554
145. Rossi WJ, Deighton BS, MacDonald AJ (1977) Residuum conversion with Chevron hydrotreating. Proceedings – Refining Department, American Petroleum Institute 56: 397–404
146. Martinez NP, Lujano J, Velasquez J, Mora S, Kizer O (1986) Selection of fluid catalytic cracking catalysts for resid processing. Revista Tecnica INTEVEP 6: 23–30
147. Evans M (2007) From resid to LPG. Part 2. Maximising LPGs from the FCCU. Hydrocarbon Engineering 12: 32–34, 36, 38
148. Evans M (2007) From resid to LPG. Part1: Upgrading resid to transportation fuels. Hydrocarbon Engineering 12: 30–32,34,36
149. Shioiri T (1978) Catalytic cracking of residual oils. Nenryo Kyokaishi 57: 96–105
150. Gupta A, Subba Rao D (2001) Model for the performance of a fluid catalytic cracking (FCC) riser reactor: effect of feed atomization. Chemical Engineering Science 56: 4489–4503
151. Ahmed HS, El-Kady FY (2008) Hydrocracking deasphalted oil from an atmospheric residuum. Energy Sources, Part A: Recovery, Utilization, and Environmental Effects 30: 247–258
152. Alam K, Ahmed S (2007) Preparation of beta zeolite and MCM-41-based hydrocracking catalysts. Preprints – American Chemical Society, Division of Petroleum Chemistry 52: 35–37
153. Bertoncini F, Adam F, Dutriez T, et al. (2008) Toward comprehensive hydrocracking chemistry via breakthrough VGO characterization. Abstracts of Papers, 236th ACS National Meeting, Philadelphia, PA, United States, August 17–21, 2008: PETR-037
154. Bhaskar M, Valavarasu G, Balaraman KS (2003) Advantages of Mild Hydrocracking FCC Feed-A Pilot Plant Study. Petroleum Science and Technology 21: 1439–1451
155. Guan C, Wang Z, Yu S, Guo A, Jiang A (2003) Hydrocracking of atmospheric residue by two-stage suspended bed. Preprints – American Chemical Society, Division of Petroleum Chemistry 48: 110–113
156. Husain S, McComb DW, Perkins JM, Haswell R (2008) Sample preparation and electron microscopy of hydrocracking catalysts. Journal of Physics: Conference Series 126: No pp given
157. Krenzke D, Vislocky J (2007) Cracking catalyst systems. Hydrocarbon Engineering 12: 57–58, 60–63

158. Landau MV, Vradman L, Valtchev V, Lezervant J, Liubich E, Talianker M (2003) Hydrocracking of Heavy Vacuum Gas Oil with a Pt/H-beta-Al2O3 Catalyst: Effect of Zeolite Crystal Size in the Nanoscale Range. Industrial & Engineering Chemistry Research 42: 2773–2782

159. Liu D, Li M-Y, Cui W-L, Zhang S-Y (2008) Study on the structure and activity of dispersed Ni catalyst for slurry bed hydrocracking of residue. Preprints – American Chemical Society, Division of Petroleum Chemistry 53: 172–176

160. Lott R, Lee LK (2003) Upgrading of heavy crude oils and residues with (HC)3TM hydrocracking technology. American Institute of Chemical Engineers, [Spring National Meeting], New Orleans, LA, United States, Mar 30–Apr 3, 2003: 577–593

161. Menoufy MF, Ahmed HS, Mohamed LK (2006) A new approach to residue upgrading. Egyptian Journal of Petroleum 15: 1–10

162. Millan M, Adell C, Hinojosa C, Herod AA, Kandiyoti R (2008) Mechanisms of catalytic activity in heavily coated hydrocracking catalysts. Oil & Gas Science and Technology 63: 69–78

163. Muravyev A, Berutti M (2007) Operator training system for hydrocracking unit: real world questions and answers. AIChE Spring National Meeting, Conference Proceedings, Houston, TX, United States, Apr 22–27, 2007: p81368/81361-p81368/81367

164. Ohtsuka Y, Byambajav E, Tanaka R (2003) Hydrocracking of asphaltenes with metal catalysts supported on mesoporous silica. Abstracts of Papers, 225th ACS National Meeting, New Orleans, LA, United States, March 23–27, 2003: FUEL-051

165. Putek S, Januszewski D, Cavallo E (2008) Upgrade hydrocracked resid through integrated hydrotreating. Hydrocarbon Processing 87: 83–84, 86, 88, 90, 92

166. Rahimi PM, Gentzis T (2003) Thermal hydrocracking of Cold Lake vacuum bottoms asphaltenes and their subcomponents. Fuel Processing Technology 80: 69–79

167. Rashid K (2007) Hydrocracking experience in a Gulf refinery. AIChE Spring National Meeting, Conference Proceedings, Houston, TX, United States, Apr 22–27, 2007: p77732/77731-p77732/77711

168. Sakashita K, Ito K, Asaoka S (2008) Hydrocracking on nanoporous and nano-interface catalyst consisting of nano-oxides and nano-zeolite. Preprints – American Chemical Society, Division of Petroleum Chemistry 53: 1–4

169. Valavarasu G, Bhaskar M, Balaraman KS (2003) Mild Hydrocracking - A Review of the Process, Catalysts, Reactions, Kinetics, and Advantages. Petroleum Science and Technology 21: 1185–1205

170. van Veen JAR, Minderhoud JK, Huve LG, Stork WHJ (2008) Hydrocracking and catalytic dewaxing. Handbook of Heterogeneous Catalysis (2nd Edition) 6: 2778–2808

171. Zhang S, Deng W, Hui L, Dong L, Guohe Q (2008) Slurry-phase Residue Hydrocracking with Dispersed Nickel Catalyst. Energy & Fuels 22: 3583–3586

172. Zhang X, Zhang F, Yan X, et al. (2008) Hydrocracking of heavy oil using zeolites Y/Al-SBA-15 composites as catalyst supports. Journal of Porous Materials 15: 145–150

173. 2006 Refining Processes Handbook, Hydrocarbon Processing, Gulf Publishing Co, Houston, USA

174. Garg S, Bhaskar T, Soni K, et al. (2008) Novel highly active FSM-16 supported molybdenum catalyst for hydrotreatment. Chemical Communications (Cambridge, United Kingdom): 5310–5311

175. Gomez UE, Santos L, Ordonez OD (2007) PCA Reduction in naphtenic base oils by hydrotreatment. Abstracts of Papers, 234th ACS National Meeting, Boston, MA, United States, August 19–23, 2007: PETR-075

176. Narangerel J, Sugimoto Y (2008) Removal of nitrogen compounds before deep hydrotreatment of synthetic crude oils. Journal of the Japan Petroleum Institute 51: 165–173

177. Pinzon MH, Centeno A, Giraldo SA (2006) Role of Pt in high performance Pt-Mo catalysts for hydrotreatment reactions. Applied Catalysis, A: General 302: 118–126

178. Prins R (2008) Hydrotreating. Handbook of Heterogeneous Catalysis (2nd Edition) 6: 2695–2718

179. Putek S, Januszewski D, Cavallo E (2008) Upgrade hydrocracked resid through integrated hydrotreating. Hydrocarbon Processing 87: 83–84, 86, 88, 90, 92

180. Ramirez J, Sanchez-Minero F (2008) Support effects in the hydrotreatment of model molecules. Catalysis Today 130: 267–271

181. Robinson PR (2006) Petroleum processing overview. Practical Advances in Petroleum Processing 1: 1–78

182. Robinson PR, Dolbear GE (2006) Hydrotreating and hydrocracking: fundamentals. Practical Advances in Petroleum Processing 1: 177–218

183. Wiehe IA (2007) The processing of resids and heavy oils. AIChE Spring National Meeting, Conference Proceedings, Houston, TX, United States, Apr 22–27, 2007: p79653/79651–p79653/79615

184. Yoshimura Y, Toba M, Matsui T, et al. (2007) Active phases and sulfur tolerance of bimetallic Pd-Pt catalysts used for hydrotreatment. Applied Catalysis, A: General 322: 152–171

185. Angelescu E, Gurau P, Pogonaru G, Musca G, Pop G, Pop E (1990) Conversion of alkanes into gasoline on ZSM-5 zeolite catalysts. Revue Roumaine de Chimie 35: 229–237

186. Behroozi A, Beitari H, Ghorbanipoor M, Nasrabadi AM (2008) Increase gasoline production – a case study. Hydrocarbon Processing 87: 107–111

187. Chen CY, Zones SI (2001) Reforming of FCC heavy gasoline and LCO with novel borosilicate zeolite catalysts. Studies in Surface Science and Catalysis 135: 4223–4230

188. Davis BH (1992) Clean gasoline reforming with superacid catalysts: Final technical report, September 25, 1990–September 24, 1992. In. Cent. Appl. Energy Res.,Univ. Kentucky, Lexington, KY, USA., p 82

189. Day M (2005) Supported metal catalysts in reforming. Catalytic Science Series 5: 187–228

190. Genis O, Simpson SG, Penner DW, Gautam R, Glover BK (2000) Aromatics and catalytic reforming in 2000+. Hydrocarbon Engineering 5: 87–88, 90, 92–93

191. Ginzel W, Buchsbaum A (1989) Upgrading of FCC (fluidized-bed catalytic cracking) naphtha octanes in the reformer. Erdoel & Kohle, Erdgas, Petrochemie 42: 396–400

192. Hughes TR, Jacobson RL, Tamm PW (1988) Catalytic processes for octane enhancement by increasing the aromatics content of gasoline. Studies in Surface Science and Catalysis 38: 317–333

193. Kolesnikov IM, Zuber VI, Svarovskaya NA, Kolesnikov SI (2008) Reforming of naphtha cut in a fluidized bed of catalysts. Chemistry and Technology of Fuels and Oils 44: 133–138

194. Krishna R, Balamalliah G, Mehrotra RP, et al. (1987) Development of mono- and bimetallic catalysts for reforming of naphtha for production of aromatic concentrates and for high-octane gasoline. Research and Industry 32: 160–168

195. Nelson WL (1967) Hydrocracking. III. How much reforming does heavy hydrocrackate need. Oil & Gas Journal 65: 95

196. Ramage MP, Graziani KR, Schipper PH, Krambeck FJ, Choi BC (1987) KINPTR (Mobil's kinetic reforming model): a review of Mobil's industrial process modeling philosophy. Advances in Chemical Engineering 13: 193–266

197. Schwarzenbek EF (1971) Catalytic reforming. Advances in Chemistry Series 103: 94–112
198. Selakovic OV, Jovanovic MR, Kapor MZ, Markov SB (1996) The effects of catalyst ageing and refreshing on gasoline reforming process. Petroleum and Coal 38: 22–25
199. Senn DR, Lin F-N, Wuggazer T (2000) Improve reforming catalyst performance. World Refining 10: 48–49
200. Sharma N, Murthy KR (1996) Development of reforming catalysts in India: from concept to commercialization. Chemical Industry Digest 9: 99–102, 104–107
201. Tomasik Z, Wrzyszcz J (1960) Catalytic reforming of octane fractions. Chem Stosowana 4: 81–99
202. Kunkel JH (1944) Sun's new 15 plant completes 100-octane conversion program. Petroleum Management 15(7): 82D–98
203. Linn CB, Nebeck HG (1953) The alkylation of hydrocarbons in the presence of hydrogen fluoride. The science of petroleum Pt. II(Sec. 1. Synthetic products of petroleum): 302
204. Kocal JA (1990) Hydrofluoric acid alkylation process. U.S. Patent 4,783,567.
205. Peters WD, Rogers CL (1955) New hydrofluoric acid alkylation process. Petroleum Refiner 34(9): 126–128
206. Simpson MB, Kester M, de Melas F (2008) The world of the end user. ABB and Conoco Phillips; collaboration process. Alkylation with hydrofluoric acid. Chimica e l'Industria (Milan, Italy) 90(1): 42–47
207. (1992) Sulfuric acid alkylation shows promise for upgrading gasoline pentenes. Oil & Gas Journal 90: 72–74
208. Ackerman S, Chitnis GK, McCaffrey DS, Jr. (2001) ExxonMobil sulfuric acid alkylation process. Preprints – American Chemical Society, Division of Petroleum Chemistry 46: 241–245
209. Ackerman S, Chitnis GK, McCaffrey DS, Jr. (2002) ExxonMobil sulfuric acid alkylation process. Pre-Print Archive – American Institute of Chemical Engineers, [Spring National Meeting], New Orleans, LA, United States, Mar 11–14, 2002: 1144–1155
210. Buiter P, Van't Spijker P, Van Zoonen D (1968) Advances in alkylation. World Petrol Congr, Proc, 7th 4: 125–133
211. Chapin LE, Liolios GC, Robertson TM (1985) Which alkylation – hydrofluoric acid or sulfuric acid? Hydrocarbon Processing, International Edition 64: 67–71
212. Davis RE (1978) Improve sulfuric acid alkylation performance. In. R. E. Davis Chem. Corp., Oak Brook, IL, p 39
213. Goldsby AR (1998) Sulfuric acid alkylation process. Book of Abstracts, 215th ACS National Meeting, Dallas, March 29–April 2: PETR-020
214. Grechishkina MI (2004) Experience in designing sulfuric acid alkylation units. Chemistry and Technology of Fuels and Oils (Translation of Khimiya i Tekhnologiya Topliv i Masel) 40: 109–111
215. Khvostenko NN, Lagutenko NM, Kurylev VD, Kirillov DV, Esipko BA (2000) Modernization of a sulfuric acid alkylation unit. Chemistry and Technology of Fuels and Oils (Translation of Khimiya i Tekhnologiya Topliv i Masel) 36: 18–20
216. Kolesov SV, Tsadkin MA, Badikova AD, Rakhmanov RR, Kudasheva FK, Gimaev RN (2002) Sulfuric acid alkylation of isobutane with butylenes in a continuous-flow tubular contactor. Chemistry and Technology of Fuels and Oils (Translation of Khimiya i Tekhnologiya Topliv i Masel) 38: 228–232

217. Mosher AD (1996) Effluent refrigerated sulfuric acid alkylation. Petroleum and Coal 38: 17–28
218. Prochukhan KY, Islamov ER, Nefedova IV, et al. (1999) New method for sulfuric acid alkylation of isoparaffins with olefins. Chemistry and Technology of Fuels and Oils (Translation of Khimiya i Tekhnologiya Topliv i Masel) 35: 65–67
219. Pryor P, Graves D (2001) Improvements in sulfuric acid alkylation technology. Abstracts of Papers, 222nd ACS National Meeting, Chicago, IL, United States, August 26–30, 2001: PETR-038

Listing of Standards

European Standard

EN 116: Diesel and domestic heating fuels – Determination of cold filter plugging point

EN 237: Liquid petroleum products – Petrol – Determination of low lead concentrations by atomic absorption spectrometry

EN 1601: Liquid petroleum products – Unleaded petrol – Determination of organic oxygenate compounds and total organically bound oxygen content by gas chromatography (O-FID)

EN 2160: Petroleum products – Corrosiveness to copper – Copper strip test (ISO 2160:1998)

EN 3104: Petroleum products – Transparent and opaque liquids – Determination of kinematic viscosity and calculation of dynamic viscosity (ISO 3104:1994)

EN 3405: Petroleum products - Determination of distillation characteristics at atmospheric pressure (ISO 3405:2000)

EN 3675: Crude petroleum and liquid petroleum products – Laboratory determination of density – Hydrometer method (ISO 3675:1998)

EN 4264: Petroleum products - Calculation of cetane index of middle-distillate fuels by the four-variable equation (ISO 4264:2007)

EN 5165: Petroleum products – Determination of the ignition quality of diesel fuels – Cetane engine method (ISO 5165:1998). EN ISO 5165:1998

EN 6245: Petroleum products – Determination of ash (ISO 6245:2001) EN ISO 6245:2002

EN 6246: Petroleum products – Gum content of light and middle distillate fuels – Jet evaporation method (ISO 6246:1995)

EN 7536: Petroleum products – Determination of oxidation stability of gasoline – Induction period method (ISO 7536:1994)

EN 8754: Petroleum products – Determination of sulfur content – Energy-dispersive X-ray fluorescence spectrometry (ISO 8754:2003)

EN 10370: Petroleum products – Determination of carbon residue – Micro method (ISO 10370:1993). EN ISO 10370:1995

EN 12177: Liquid petroleum products – Unleaded petrol – Determination of benzene content by gas chromatography. EN 12177:1998/AC:2000

EN 12185: Crude petroleum and petroleum products – Determination of density – Oscillating U-tube method (ISO 12185:1996)

EN 12205: Petroleum products – Determination of the oxidation stability of middle-distillate fuels (ISO 12205:1995)

EN 12662: Liquid petroleum products – Determination of contamination in middle distillates

EN 12916: Petroleum products – Determination of aromatic hydrocarbon types in middle distillates – High performance liquid chromatography method with refractive index detection

EN 12937: Petroleum products – Determination of water – Coulometric Karl Fischer titration method (ISO 12937:2000)

EN 13016-1: Liquid petroleum products – Vapour pressure – Part 1: Determination of air saturated vapour pressure (ASVP) and calculated dry vapour pressure equivalent (DVPE)

EN 13016-2: Liquid petroleum products – Vapour pressure – Part 2: Determination of absolute pressure (AVP) between 40°C and 100°C

EN 14596: Petroleum products – Determination of sulfur content – Wavelength-dispersive X-ray fluorescence spectrometry (ISO 14596:2007)

EN 22719: Petroleum products and lubricants; determination of flash point; Pensky-Martens closed cup method (ISO 2719:1988)

EN 23015: Petroleum products – Determination of cloud point (ISO 3015:1992)

EN 24260: Petroleum products and hydrocarbons – Determination of sulfur content – Wickbold combustion method (ISO 4260:1987)

EN 25163: Motor and aviation-type fuels – Determination of knock characteristics – Motor method

EN 25164: Methods of test for petroleum and its products. Motor fuels. Determination of knock characteristics. Research method (1994)

Institute of Petroleum Standards

IP 4: Petroleum products – Determination of Ash IP 30 (2005)

IP 40: Petroleum products – Determination of oxidation stability of gasoline – Induction period method (1997)

IP 41: Petroleum products – Determination of the ignition quality of diesel fuels – Cetane engine method (1999)

IP 69: Petroleum products – Determination of vapour pressure – Reid method (2001)

IP 71: Section 1: Petroleum products –Transparent and opaque liquids – Determination of kinematic viscosity and calculation of dynamic viscosity. (1995) Section 2: Glass capillary kinematic viscometers – Specifications and operating instructions (1997)

IP 123: Petroleum products – Determination of distillation characteristics at atmospheric pressure (2001)

IP 131: Petroleum products – Gum content of light and middle distillate fuels – Jet evaporation method (1999)

IP 154: Petroleum products – Corrosiveness to copper – Copper strip test (2000)

IP 156: Determination of hydrocarbon types in petroleum products – Fluorescent indicator adsorption method (2008)

IP 160: Crude petroleum and liquid petroleum products – Laboratory determination of density – Hydrometer method IP 219 Cloud Point of Petroleum Products (1999)

IP 236: Petroleum products – Determination of knock characteristics of motor and aviation fuels – Motor method (2006)

IP 237: Petroleum products – Determination of knock characteristics of motor fuels – Research method (2006)

IP 243: Petroleum products and hydrocarbons – Determination of sulfur content – Wickbold combustion method (1994)

IP 309: Diesel and domestic heating fuels – Determination of cold filter plugging point (1999)

IP 336: Petroleum products – Determination of sulfur content – Energy-dispersive-X-ray fluorescence method (2004)

IP 342: Petroleum products – Determination of thiol (mercaptan) sulfur in light and middle distillate fuels – Potentiometric method (2000)

IP 365: Crude petroleum and petroleum products – Determination of density – Oscillating U-tube method (1997)

IP 380: Petroleum products – Calculation of cetane index of middle distillate fuels by the four-variable equation (2008)

IP 388: Petroleum products – Determination of the oxidation stability of middle-distillate fuels (1997)

IP 391: Petroleum products – Determination of aromatic hydrocarbon types in middle distillates – High performance liquid chromatography method with refractive index detection (2007)

IP 394: Liquid petroleum products – Vapour pressure – Part 1: Determination of air saturated vapour pressure (ASVP) (2008)

IP 398: Petroleum products – Determination of carbon residue – Micro method (1996)

IP 408: Liquid petroleum products – Unleaded petrol – Determination of organic oxygenate compounds and total organically bound oxygen content by gas chromatography (O-FID) (1998)

IP 425: Liquid petroleum products – Unleaded petrol – Determination of benzene content by gas chromatography (2001)

IP 428: Liquid petroleum products – Petrol – Determination of low lead concentrations by atomic absorption spectrometry (2006)

IP 440: Liquid petroleum products – Determination of contamination in middle distillates (1999)

IP 447: Petroleum products – Determination of sulfur content – Wavelength-dispersive X-ray fluorescence spectrometry (2008)

IP 450: Diesel fuel – Assessment of lubricity using the high-frequency reciprocating rig (HFRR) – Part I: Test Method (2000)

IP 490: Petroleum products – Determination of sulfur content of automotive fuels – Ultraviolet fluorescence method (ISO 20846:2004) (2005)

International Organization for Standards (ISO)

ISO 2160: Petroleum products – Corrosiveness to copper – Copper strip test   Edition: 3 (1998)

ISO 2719: Determination of flash point – Pensky-Martens closed cup method   Edition: 3 (2002)

ISO 3007: Petroleum products and crude petroleum – Determination of vapour pressure – Reid method (1999)

ISO 3012: Petroleum products – Determination of thiol (mercaptan) sulfur in light and middle distillate fuels – Potentiometric method (1999)

ISO 3015: Petroleum products – Determination of cloud point (1992)

ISO 3104: Petroleum products – Transparent and opaque liquids – Determination of kinematic viscosity and calculation of dynamic viscosity (1994)

ISO 3405: Petroleum products – Determination of distillation characteristics at atmospheric pressure (2000)

ISO 3675: Crude petroleum and liquid petroleum products – Laboratory determination of density – Hydrometer method (1998)

ISO 3837: Liquid petroleum products – Determination of hydrocarbon types – Fluorescent indicator adsorption method (1993)

ISO 4260:   Petroleum products and hydrocarbons – Determination of sulfur content – Wickbold combustion method (1987)

ISO 4264: Petroleum products and hydrocarbons – Determination of sulfur content Wickbold combustion method (2007)

ISO 5163: Petroleum products – Determination of knock characteristics of motor and aviation fuels – Motor method (2005)

ISO 5164: Petroleum products – Determination of knock characteristics of motor fuels – Research method (2005)

ISO 5165: Petroleum products – Determination of the ignition quality of diesel fuels – Cetane engine method (1998)

ISO 6245: Petroleum products – Determination of ash (2001)

ISO 6246: Petroleum products – Gum content of light and middle distillate fuels – Jet evaporation method (1995)

ISO 7536: Petroleum products – Determination of oxidation stability of gasoline – Induction period method (1994)

ISO 8754: Petroleum products – Determination of sulfur content – Energy-dispersive X-ray fluorescence spectrometry (2003)

ISO 10370: Petroleum products – Determination of carbon residue – Micro method (1993)

ISO 12156: Diesel fuel – Assessment of lubricity using the high-frequency reciprocating rig (HFRR) – Part 1: Test method. (2007) Diesel fuel – Assessment of lubricity using the high-frequency reciprocating rig (HFRR) – Part 2: Limit (2006)

ISO 12185: Crude petroleum and petroleum products – Determination of density – Oscillating U-tube method (1996)

ISO 12205: Petroleum products – Determination of the oxidation stability of middle-distillate fuels (1995)

ISO 12937: Petroleum products – Determination of water – Coulometric Karl Fischer titration method (2000)

ISO 14596: Petroleum products – Determination of sulfur content – Wavelength-dispersive X-ray fluorescence spectrometry (2007)

American Society for Testing and Materials (ASTM)

ASTM D86 07 Standard Test Method for Distillation of Petroleum Products at Atmospheric Pressure

ASTM D93 06 Standard Test Methods for Flash Point by Pensky-Martens Closed Cup Tester

ASTM D130 -04 Standard Test Method for Corrosiveness to Copper from Petroleum Products by Copper Strip Test

ASTM D323 06 Standard Test Method for Vapor Pressure of Petroleum Products (Reid Method)

ASTM D381 04 Standard Test Method for Gum Content in Fuels by Jet Evaporation

ASTM D445 04 Standard Test Method for Kinematic Viscosity of Transparent and Opaque Liquids (and the Calculation of Dynamic Viscosity)

ASTM D482 07 Standard Test Method for Ash from Petroleum Products

ASTM D525 01 Standard Test Method for Oxidation Stability of Gasoline (Induction Period Method)

ASTM D613 05 Standard Test Method for Cetane Number of Diesel Fuel Oil

ASTM D1298 99 Standard Test Method for Density, Relative Density (Specific Gravity), or API Gravity of Crude Petroleum and Liquid Petroleum Products by Hydrometer Method

ASTM D1319 03 Standard Test Method for Hydrocarbon Types in Liquid Petroleum Products by Fluorescent Indicator Adsorption

ASTM D1319 03e1 Standard Test Method for Hydrocarbon Types in Liquid Petroleum Products by Fluorescent Indicator Adsorption

ASTM D2274 03 Standard Test Method for Oxidation Stability of Distillate Fuel Oil (Accelerated Method)

ASTM D2500 05 Standard Test Method for Cloud Point of Petroleum Products

ASTM D2622 08 Standard Test Method for Sulfur in Petroleum Products by Wavelength Dispersive X-ray Fluorescence Spectrometry

ASTM D2699 07 Standard Test Method for Research Octane Number of Spark-Ignition Engine Fuel

ASTM D2700 07 Standard Test Method for Motor Octane Number of Spark-Ignition Engine Fuel

ASTM D3227 04 Standard Test Method for (Thiol Mercaptan) Sulfur in Gasoline, Kerosine, Aviation Turbine, and Distillate Fuels (Potentiometric Method)

ASTM D3237 -06 Standard Test Method for Lead in Gasoline by Atomic Absorption Spectroscopy

ASTM D3606 07 Standard Test Method for Determination of Benzene and Toluene in Finished Motor and Aviation Gasoline by Gas Chromatography

ASTM D4052 96(2002)e1 Standard Test Method for Density and Relative Density of Liquids by Digital Density Meter ASTM D4530 07 Standard Test Method for Determination of Carbon Residue (Micro Method)

ASTM D4294 08 Standard Test Method for Sulfur in Petroleum and Petroleum Products by Energy Dispersive X-ray Fluorescence Spectrometry

ASTM D4737 04 Standard Test Method for Calculated Cetane Index by Four Variable Equation

ASTM D4952 02(2007) Standard Test Method for Qualitative Analysis for Active Sulfur Species in Fuels and Solvents (Doctor Test)

ASTM D5191 07 Standard Test Method for Vapor Pressure of Petroleum Products (Mini Method)

ASTM D5453 08 Standard Test Method for Determination of Total Sulfur in Light Hydrocarbons, Spark Ignition Engine Fuel, Diesel Engine Fuel, and Engine Oil by Ultraviolet Fluorescence

ASTM D5769 04 Standard Test Method for Determination of Benzene, Toluene, and Total Aromatics in Finished Gasolines by Gas Chromatography/Mass Spectrometry

ASTM D6079 04 Standard Test Method for Evaluating Lubricity of Diesel Fuels by the High-Frequency Reciprocating Rig (HFRR)

ASTM D6371 05 Standard Test Method for Cold Filter Plugging Point of Diesel and Heating Fuels

ASTM D5599 00 Standard Test Method for Determination of Oxygenates in Gasoline by
Gas Chromatography and Oxygen Selective Flame Ionization Detection

ASTM D6217 98(2003)e1 Standard Test Method for Particulate Contamination in Middle
Distillate Fuels by Laboratory Filtration

ASTM D6304 04 Standard Test Method for Determination of Water in Petroleum Products,
Lubricating Oils, and Additives by Coulometric Karl Fisher Titration

Problems

1. In Table 8.1 is given a list of products which are manufactured from petroleum based products. Is there any alternative route for their manufacturing? Do you think the prices and quality of these products will be the same? What impact will this have on our society.
2. What is crude oil benchmarking? Why it is necessary?
3. Why is it important to characterize crude oil?
4. Is crude oil essential for all types of transportation? Which sector of the transportation system could be run without petroleum and how?
5. What are various processes involved in the processing of crude oil and what are their objectives?
6. Why is crude petroleum separated into various fractions?
7. How dependent is the United States on foreign oil?
8. How many barrels of oil does the United States consume per year?
9. How much oil is produced in Alaska and where does it go?
10. How much petroleum does the United States import?
11. Why don't fuel prices change as quickly as crude oil prices?
12. Do we have enough oil worldwide to meet our future needs?
13. How many gallons of gasoline does one barrel of oil make?
14. What are the differences between various types of crude oil prices?
15. What are the differences among "crude oil", "petroleum products", and "petroleum"?
16. What are the products and uses of petroleum?
17. When was the last refinery built in the United States?
18. Define the octane number? Why is it important?
19. Write a report on the energy requirements for operating a refinery.
20. Write a report on the wastes generated from processing of crude oil.
21. What is the difference between gasoline and diesel fuel?

9 NUCLEAR

Abstract

The world's demand for energy will increase because the quality of living is tied to its consumption and because the world's population is increasing. It is well known that high quality energy sources such as electricity and oil are directly linked to economic growth and quality of life (e.g., access to food, medicine, housing and education). As more countries participate in the benefits of globalization, world energy use will grow. For example, in the past decade prior to the financial collapse of world markets that occurred during October of 2008, two of the world's most populated countries, China and India, had unprecedented economic growth and this played a major role in the price of oil climbing to nearly $150 per barrel during the summer of 2008. The year 2008 also saw an precipitous drop in oil prices as well. It is well known that economic growth is cyclic and that during periods of recession, demand for energy decreases. After October of 2008 the price of oil dropped under $45 dollar per barrel. As of this writing the world was still in the recession of 2008, but history tells us that a recovery will occur and that during the next economic growth period oil prices will once again rise. The other factor which impacts growth in energy demand is growth in population. The US Census Bureau has projected that the world population will increase to 9 billion people by 2042 from approximately 6.6 billion people today. The future holds more uncertainty. The competition for scarce energy resources will only accelerate as more people in the world participate in the economic benefits of globalization and as world population grows.

One of the requirements for sustaining human life and progress is availability of a clean source of energy that does not harm the environment. The release of CO_2 into the atmosphere is the main cause of global warming and various associated climate changes. A major advantage of nuclear energy is that it doesn't put CO_2 into the atmosphere. In addition it provides a steady source of constant electrical power that does not suffer the whim of weather patterns. This is a critical feature because climate change does impact weather patterns. For example, areas

T.K. Ghosh and M.A. Prelas, *Energy Resources and Systems:*
Volume 1: Fundamentals and Non-Renewable Resources, 453–647.

which currently have an abundance of wind or clear skies for solar energy use today may experience a change over the 30 or so year lifetime of a wind farm or a solar energy plant.

Although nuclear energy generates electricity without releasing harmful gases; SO_2, NOx, CO_2, etc, the issues related to spent fuel (nuclear waste) from the nuclear reactors must be addressed. Reprocessing of spent fuels and the use of breeder reactors can substantially minimize its impact and even can lead to zero waste system. In this chapter, the complete nuclear fuel cycle is discussed.

9.1 Introduction

There are two fundamental ways by which energy is released from nuclear reactions: fission and fusion of atomic nuclei. The mass of a nucleus (a nucleus is made up of protons and neutrons) is always less than the sum of the individual masses of the protons and neutrons which constitute it. The difference is a measure of the nuclear binding energy which holds the nucleus together. During either a fission or a fusion reaction part of this binding energy is released and is utilized for electricity generation. This binding energy can be calculated from the Einstein relationship and is discussed below.

In 1905, a young patent clerk in Switzerland developed a theory that would forever change the world. That young patent clerk was Albert Einstein. His theory of relativity is one of the major achievements in modern physics (the other being quantum mechanics).

In the 1880s, Physicists believed that waves require a medium to propagate. Sound waves propagate in air, and waves propagate in water. It was believed that the earth traveled through an "ether wind," which allowed light to propagate through space. American Physicist Albert Abraham Michelson (1852–1931) and American Chemist Edward Williams Morley (1838–1923) designed an experiment that attempted to examine the motion of earth relative to the ether using Michelson's new instrument, an interferometer. The experimental arrangement is shown in Fig. 9.1.

A light beam is split. Part of the beam travels straight and the other part travels 90° up. Michelson and Morley assumed that the speed of light is c and the speed of the ether wind is v. Michelson and Morley reasoned that the part of the beam that travels anti-parallel and then parallel to the ether wind will take a longer time to traverse the distance $2d$, and the time is given by:

$$t_{\downarrow\uparrow} = \frac{d}{c+v} + \frac{d}{c-v} = \frac{2dc}{c^2 - v^2} \tag{9.1}$$

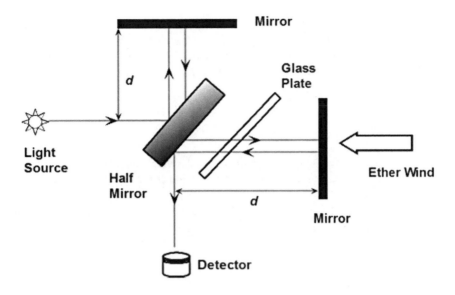

Fig. 9.1. Michelson interferometer.

Likewise along the path perpendicular to the ether wind, the time it takes the beam to traverse the distance $2d$ is given by;

$$t_\perp = \frac{2d}{\sqrt{c^2 - v^2}} \tag{9.2}$$

The ratio of the parallel time to perpendicular time can be represented as:

$$\frac{t_{\downarrow\uparrow}}{t_\perp} = \frac{1}{\sqrt{1 - \dfrac{v^2}{c^2}}} \tag{9.3}$$

If the light source has zero velocity with respect to the ether, then the ratio is 1. If the earth is in motion, the light source should have a velocity with respect to the ether so the ratio should not be 1. The two beams at the detector will then be out of phase and thus will interfere with one another. The interference fringes can then be measured.

Michelson and Morley ran thousands of experiments over many months. In each and every one of their experiments the ratio was 1. They had to conclude that there was no ether wind.

From this work, other physicists tried to explain the result. George Francis FitzGerald (1851–1901), an Irish physicist, developed the idea that objects grew shorter in the direction of their motion because the ether wind would exert a pressure on the body. FitzGerald developed the FitzGerald length contraction formula from this assumption and used it to explain the Michelson–Morley experiment. The length is calculated from the following expression.

$$L = L_o \sqrt{1 - \frac{v^2}{c^2}} \tag{9.4}$$

In Eq. (9.4), L is the length in the moving reference frame and L_o is the length at rest. The problem with the FitzGerald contraction is that when $v > c$, the L is an imaginary number.

Hendrick Antoon Lorentz (1853–1928), a Dutch physicist, extended the work of FitzGerald. He postulated that mass would have to increase with motion and is given below.

$$m = \frac{m_o}{\sqrt{1 - \frac{v^2}{c^2}}} \tag{9.5}$$

Lorentz's work was able to predict the motion of high-speed charged particles in electromagnetic fields. Often times these contractions are called the Lorentz contractions.

Einstein assumed that the relative motion of bodies is impossible to sort out. How does one determine which body is absolutely at rest? The second assumption that he made in his new theory is that the speed of light in a vacuum is a constant regardless of frame of reference. This was a drastic change from the universally accepted Newtonian mechanics. In Newtonian mechanics if I am on a platform moving at the speed of light and I throw an object off that platform with a velocity of the speed of light, then the relative speed of that object to the rest frame is,

$$V = V_1 + V_2 = 2c \tag{9.6}$$

where $V_1 = V_2 = c$

According to Einstein, the velocity of the object would be,

$$V = \frac{V_1 + V_2}{1 + \frac{V_1 V_2}{c^2}} = c \tag{9.7}$$

This forced the object to have a velocity no greater than the speed of light.

Classical physicists believed that mass could not be created or destroyed. But the Lorentz contraction and Einstein's special theory of relativity differed in that mass was increased as velocity increased. The implication of this is very important to nuclear energy. We can make the following approximation (use a Taylor series expansion),

$$\frac{1}{\sqrt{1-\frac{v^2}{c^2}}} \approx 1 + \frac{v^2}{2c^2}$$

(9.8)

So, the mass of a body in motion, m_1, becomes,

$$m_1 = m_o\left(1+\frac{v^2}{2c^2}\right) = m_o + m_o\frac{v_2}{2c^2}$$

(9.9)

The increase in the mass as a result of motion is given by;

$$m = m_1 - m_o = \frac{1}{2}m_o\frac{v^2}{c^2}$$

(9.10)

The term $\frac{1}{2}\,m_o v^2$ is the kinetic energy of the rest mass. This energy is denoted by E, therefore,

$$m = \frac{E}{c^2}$$

(9.11)

This equation can be rearranged to give the mass energy relationship,

$$E = mc^2$$

(9.12)

The implication of this relationship can be seen in the calculation of binding energy of nuclei. If we assume that the mass of an atom is the summation of the mass of its components, then for an oxygen atom, we would assume it has eight neutrons, eight protons and eight electrons. The sum of these components would be,

$$m_{theory}^{oxygen} = 8m_p + 8m_n + 8m_e$$

(9.13)

where m_p, m_n and m_e are the masses of a free proton, neutron and electron. The problem is that the actual mass of an oxygen atom is less than the sum of its components.

$$m^{oxygen}_{experimental} < m^{oxygen}_{theory} \tag{9.14}$$

This mass difference is,

$$\Delta m = m^{oxygen}_{theory} - m^{oxygen}_{experimental} \tag{9.15}$$

The resulting mass change must go into energy according to the mass energy relationship,

$$E = \Delta m c^2 \tag{9.16}$$

This energy is known as the binding energy. In order to break apart the atom into its basic components, an energy equivalent to the binding energy of the atom must be supplied.

By convention, the number of protons in an atom is represented by Z, the number of electrons in an atom is equivalent to the number of protons and thus are represented by Z, the number of neutrons in an atom is represented by N, and the atomic number is the total number of protons and neutrons and is represented by A.

$$A = N + Z \tag{9.17}$$

It is useful to compare the binding energy of all atoms by looking at the binding energy per nucleon (a nucleon is either a proton or neutron). The binding energy per nucleon is given by the following expression.

$$\text{Binding Energy per Nucleon} = \frac{\Delta m C^2}{A} \tag{9.18}$$

We can plot a curve of the binding energy per nucleon for all known atoms as shown in Fig. 9.2.

The binding energy per nucleon curve tells us that the most stable element in the universe is iron. The second law of thermodynamics tells us that all systems tend towards their minimum energy. Therefore,

All matter in the universe will tend towards iron

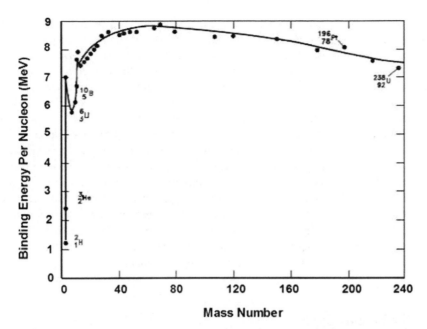

Fig. 9.2. Binding energy per nucleon as a function of mass number for the stable nuclides (Courtesy [1]).

9.2 The Fusion Cycle

According to the modern cosmology, the universe started with the big bang. A point in space with near infinite energy exploded. As the energy wave propagated, it cooled. Light particles such as baryons and leptons formed. Eventually hydrogen began to condense from this energy wave during the cooling process.

The hydrogen began to form density perturbations in space. This spatial variation of mass began to attract other hydrogen particles. The more particles that were attracted to the density variations, the more gravitation attraction there was to bring in more hydrogen. The mass began to build up. Eventually, the mass was large enough to form a proto-star. At this point, nuclear reactions that convert hydrogen into heavier elements produced sufficient energy that the energy produced by the fusion reactions balanced the energy lost by radiation. The mass grew larger and larger and eventually, the fusion energy produced was sufficient to create a high surface temperature and the surface glowed in the visible wavelength (e.g., stars were formed).

Some of the stars that were formed had enormous mass. The hydrogen fuel in these massive stars was consumed at rapid rates. Other elements formed from hydrogen fusion such as helium, and carbon began to fuse to form heavier elements. These fusion reactions created oxygen. Oxygen began to fuse creating silicon. Silicon began to fuse to form iron. The iron core remained inactive since it is the element with the largest binding energy per nucleon. As the iron core of the star grew larger and larger, the star could no longer support the pressure from the surrounding mass. This caused the star to collapse. As the star collapsed upon itself, the outer shells of silicon, oxygen, carbon, helium and hydrogen grew denser. This density increase caused an upsurge of fusion activity that resulted in an explosion. The massive star became a supernova. The massive energy release sent iron, silicon, oxygen, carbon, and helium and hydrogen particles in all directions at very high energy. Some of these particles collided (the supernova was like a massive celestial high-energy accelerator) and underwent complex nuclear reactions. These reactions produced elements heavier than iron. The remnants of the supernova began to condense. New stars were formed along with planets from the debris.

9.3 The Fission Cycle

Among the heavy elements that condensed to form planets was uranium-235. In the late 1930s Enrico Fermi had been bombarding uranium with thermal neutrons (the definition of thermal neutron is discussed later). He believed that he had created an element with an atomic mass of 93. Basically he was right, but his explanation was not very clear.

In 1938, German Physicist Otto Hahn and his coworkers Fritz Straussman performed an experiment planned by Hahn and Lise Meitner in which uranium was bombarded with thermal neutrons. The chemical makeup of the uranium had changed in that presence of barium was found. Because Meitner was a Jewish exile from Germany, Hahn and Straussman, who worked in the Kaiser-Wilhelm-Institut in Germany, could not include Meitner as a co-author of the paper announcing the result. Lise Meitner was widely credited as being the first to recognize that nuclear fission had occurred. She and Otto Frisch developed a proof that fission had occurred in these experiments and published a paper in Nature, January 16, 1939. In their paper they described how barium could be produced in a fission reaction along with krypton and additional neutrons.

Word of the discover spread like wildfire. Niels Bohr went to the US for a conference and discussed the possibility of fission with US physicists. Many of the physicists went back to their laboratories and verified the fission reaction.

Hungarian-American physicist Leo Szilard began to think about the nuclear chain reaction shortly afterwards. He pondered on the implications of the reactions and became concerned. Given that he was a Jewish refugee from Hitler's tyranny, he was fully aware of the danger that the Nazis posed to the world and what it would mean if Hitler was able to develop a weapon based on the nuclear chain reaction. Sizlard discussed his fear with physicist Eugene Paul Wigner and Edward Teller. They decided to bring their concerns to the attention of the US government. In order to do so they needed the help of the world's most prominent scientist, Albert Einstein. They were able to persuade Einstein to write a letter to President Franklin D. Roosevelt. In 1941, Roosevelt agreed to start a massive research program to develop a bomb based on nuclear fission. The order was issued on December 6, 1941, the day before the Japanese attacked Pearl Harbor.

The start of mankind's trek into nuclear energy began with fear while the world was in the death grip of World War II.

Nuclei of atomic mass up to 40 remain stable as the number of protons and the number of neutrons remain equal (Fig. 9.3). The strong force which holds the nucleus together is stronger than the Coulombic force which causes the protons to repel one another. The strong force has a maximum interaction length of about 1–1.5 fm, beyond which it is zero. Additionally, the strong force is repulsive as distances become shorter than 0.1 fm.

A nucleus is on the order of 1 fm in diameter. A proton and a neutron are about 0.01 fm in diameter. The density of nucleons in a nucleus is about constant throughout the volume. The importance of this fairly constant density is that the distance between nucleons remains constant regardless of the number of nucleons in the nucleus.

As the number of protons increases, the Columbic force gets larger and larger. The distances between protons must get larger. Neutrons fill in the space as protons move further apart. Eventually, the number of nucleons fills a volume so large that the strong forces can no longer act. At this point, the number of neutrons becomes larger than the number of protons.

The line of stability shown in Figs. 9.4 and 9.5 is very narrow. If there are fewer neutrons in a nucleus than the line of stability, the nucleus will undergo a radioactive process in which a proton in the nucleus is converted to a neutron and a positron. A positron is a positively charged electron.

$$_N^A X_Z \rightarrow {}_{N+1}^A Y_{Z-1} + \beta^+ + \nu \tag{9.19}$$

where β^+ is a positron and ν is a neutrino.

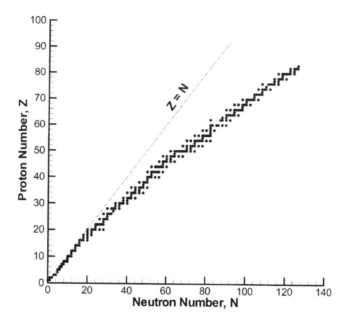

Fig. 9.3. Values of protons and neutrons for 266 stable nuclides. The line Z = N represents number of proton equals to number of neutron.

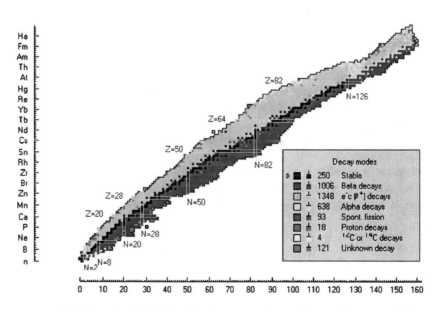

Fig. 9.4. A plot of all 250 stable elements vs. the atomic mass (Courtesy of [2]).

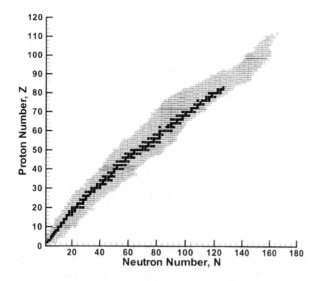

Fig. 9.5. Plot of neutron number versus proton number for all known nuclides (Dark squares represent stable nuclides and light squares represent unstable nuclides (Courtesy of [2]).

In this reaction, the element X is neutron poor and lies above the line of stability. If there are fewer neutrons than the line of stability, the decay mode is β^+. If there are more neutrons than the line of stability, the decay mode is β^-.

$$_N^A XX_Z \rightarrow\ _{N-1}^A YY_{Z+1} + \beta^- + \bar{v} \tag{9.20}$$

where $\bar{v}$ is an antineutrino.

The farther a nucleus is from the line of stability, the faster it decays. In nuclear science, the rate of decay is illustrated by the half life. The half life is the time it takes N radioactive atoms to decay to $0.5N$ radioactive atoms. The decay of radioactive elements is a statistical process. This process can be modeled by a rate equation:

$$\frac{dN}{dt} = -kN \tag{9.21}$$

where k is a decay constant.

The solution to this equation is,

$$N(t) = N(0)e^{-kt} \tag{9.22}$$

The half life can be found by solving,

$$\frac{N\left(t_{1/2}\right)}{N(0)} = 0.5 = e^{-k\,t_{1/2}} \tag{9.23}$$

$$-k\,t_{1/2} = \ln(0.5) \tag{9.24}$$

$$k = \frac{0.693}{t_{1/2}} \tag{9.25}$$

Typically, in nuclear science, the decay rates of nuclei are given in half-lives. From the half-life, the decay constant is calculated using Eq. (9.25).

There are other types of radioactive decay processes. Some heavy nuclei can decay by giving off alpha particles (helium nucleus) and other types of ions.

One of the most interesting processes is fission. Elements like plutonium 238 can spontaneously fission. As discussed, fission is the splitting of a nucleus. On average, each fission gives off more than two neutrons (with a high energy distribution as shown in Fig. 9.6).

$$_N^A X_Z \rightarrow {}_{N1}^{A1}fl_{Z1} + {}_{N2}^{A2}fh_{Z2} + \vartheta n \tag{9.26}$$

where ϑ is the statistical number of neutrons given off per fission. For U-235, ϑ is 2.44.

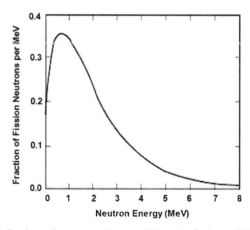

Fig. 9.6. Energy distribution of neutrons given off by the fission of U-235 as calculated (Courtesy [1]).

The release of more than one neutron per fission was key to Leo Szilard's idea of a chain reaction. If you consider neutron bookkeeping, you use one thermal neutron to initiate fission. In the process the fission gives off 2.44 additional neutrons. If each of these neutrons causes fission, then you have 2.44 × 2.44 (5.95) neutrons in the second generation. As you can see, each additional generation would have 2.44 more neutrons than the previous generation. This process is a geometrical process. However, such processes can not be sustained. There are natural processes which will cause the fission rate to plateau.

Nuclear fission occurs in several elements. The reaction begins with the capture of a neutron in the nucleus. In general, the probability of capturing a neutron with a low velocity is higher than capturing a neutron with a high velocity. The energy of a neutron is given by,

$$E_n = \frac{1}{2} m_n v^2 \tag{9.27}$$

where, E_n is the neutron energy (Joules), m_n (kilogram) is the neutron mass and v (meters per second) is the neutron velocity.

Energy is related to temperature. For an individual neutron the temperature/energy relationship is,

$$E_n = kT \tag{9.28}$$

where k is Boltzman;s constant (1.381×10^{-23} J/K) and T is temperature in Kelvin.

Because the energy of a high velocity neutron can be a very small number in Joules, it is common to express particle energy in electron Volts (eV).

$$1 \text{ eV} = 1.6 \times 10^{-19} \text{ J} \tag{9.29}$$

If we want to know the energy of a neutron, which is at room temperature, it can be calculated from Eqs. (9.28) and (9.29). Room temperature is about 20°C or 293 K. So a neutron of temperature 293 K has an energy of:

$$E_{293} = \frac{kT}{1.6 \times 10^{-19}} = \frac{\left(1.38 \times 10^{-23} \times 293\right)}{1.6 \times 10^{-19}} = 0.0253 \text{ eV} \tag{9.30}$$

Figure 9.7 shows the cross section for nuclear fission in U-235 and U-238 as a function of energy. The cross section is a measure of the probability of a reaction. Thus the higher the cross section, the higher is the probability of the reaction. As Fig. 9.7 shows, the cross section for fission in U-235 is very high at low energies. The unit of a barn is used which is 1×10^{-24} cm^2. This is about equal to the cross sectional area of a typical nucleus. The absorption cross sections for all of the elements fall of as $1/v$ (where v is velocity) at energies below 2 eV. For light elements the $1/v$ behavior persists to high energies. For heavy elements there will be sharp peaks at energies above 2 eV which are due to enhanced absorption in the nucleus due to metastable levels. These sharp peaks are called resonances and they occur roughly between 2 eV and 100 KeV. Thermal cross sections are very important to modern light water or heavy water moderated power plants. Table 9.1 tabulates cross sections for important elements at 0.025 eV energies.

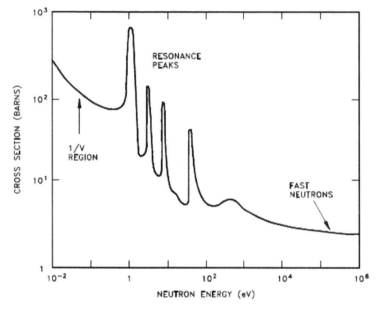

Fig. 9.7. Cross section for neutron capture (n, γ) and fission for U-235 and U-238 as a function of neutron energy (Adapted from [1]).

Table 9.1. Data for interactions with various elements at 0.025 Ev.

Element	Absorption cross section (barns)	Fission cross section (barns)
U-233	579	531
U-235	681	582
Natural U	7.59	4.19
Pu-239	1011	743
Pu-241	1377	1009

The concept of a cross section can be understood by looking at the illustration in Fig. 9.8 shown below,

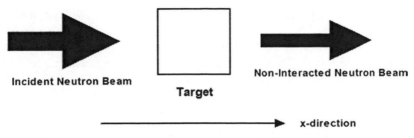

Fig. 9.8. Illustration showing concept of a nucleus cross section. An incident beam of neutrons intersect a target material and the non interacted beam of neutrons exits the target.

In this illustration, an incident beam of neutrons with intensity $I(x)$ (neutrons per square meter per second) strikes the target and the non-interacted neutrons exit the target. The neutron beam intensity is a function of x (meter), $I(x)$ and an equation can be set up to calculate it. We use the cross section to make this calculation by setting up the following relationship,

$$-dI(x) = N\sigma I(x)dx \tag{9.31}$$

where $dI(x)$ is the differential neutron beam intensity at the point x, N is the density of target atoms (atoms per m^3), σ is the cross section (m^2), dx is a differential length.

The solution to this differential equation is,

$$I(x) = e^{(-N\sigma x)} \tag{9.32}$$

Terms can be grouped. The macroscopic cross section Σ is equal to $N\sigma$. Using the macroscopic cross section we can write the equation,

$$-\frac{dI(x)}{I(x)} = \Sigma \, dx \tag{9.33}$$

where this represents the fraction of neutrons at the point x which have interacted in a length of dx.

Thus, the term Σdx represents the probability that a neutron will interact in a length of dx. The macroscopic cross section is the probability per unit path length that a neutron will interact. Thus,

$$\frac{I(x)}{I(0)} = e^{(-\Sigma x)} \tag{9.34}$$

$e^{(-\Sigma x)}$ is the probability that a neutron reaches the point x without interacting with the target.

Define, $p(x)\,dx$ as the probability that a neutron which reaches x has its first interaction in a length dx. The mean free path (λ) is the average distance that a neutron travels before interaction. The mean free path is given by,

$$\lambda = \int_{0}^{\infty} x\,p(x)\,dx = \int_{0}^{\infty} x\,\Sigma\,e^{\Sigma x}\,dx = \frac{1}{\Sigma} \tag{9.35}$$

When a neutron is captured by a nucleus, a compound nucleus is formed. The additional neutron causes instability in the nucleus thus causing it to deform (Fig. 9.9). As the nucleus deforms it begins to split into two pieces. These pieces then emit gamma rays and neutrons leaving behind two fission fragments (Fig. 9.10). The fission fragments typically are unstable and eventually emit radiation over a time scale of seconds to years.

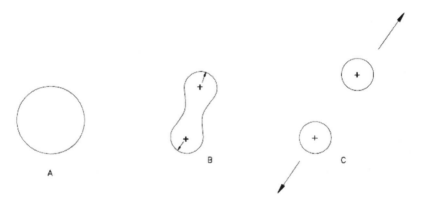

Fig. 9.9. Curve showing the potential energy versus distance of the two components of the compound nucleus as it deforms and splits into two segments. E_A is the activation energy required to split the nucleus into two fragments and the equation is the governing Coulombic repulsion equation (Adapted from [1]).

For fission to occur, it is possible to formulate a model which shows why certain elements fission. Begin by defining Potential energy (V), Kinetic Energy (KE) and total energy $(M_A C^2)$. Total energy is equal to potential energy plus kinetic energy,

$$M_A C^2 = V + KE \tag{9.36}$$

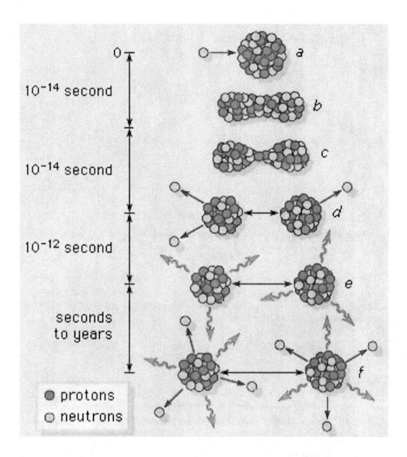

Fig. 9.10. An illustration of the phases of neutron capture leading to fission. In step *a* the neutron is captured by the nucleus. In steps *b* and *c* the nucleus begins to split. In step *d* the fission fragments form and fast neutrons emitted. The fragments promptly emit gamma rays in step *e* as they energetically stabilize. In step *f* the radioactive fission fragments decay (Adapted from [3]).

Therefore,

$$V = M_A C^2 - KE \tag{9.37}$$

Initially, before the two fragments split, the distance between the two fragments is *0* and the *KE* is *0*. As the nucleus begins to deform, energy must be added to the nucleus (E_{crit}) to overcome the strong force. So,

$$V = M_A C^2 + E_{crit} \tag{9.38}$$

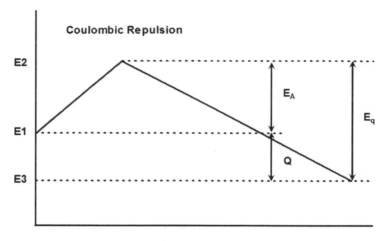

Fig. 9.11. This figure illustrates how the nucleus fissions. *E1* is the total energy of the nucleus before splitting, *E2* is the total energy plus the energy required to overcome the strong force, *E3* is the total energy of the two fission fragments, *Q* is the change in energy from the initial to final state and E_q is the coulomb repulsion energy.

From Fig. 9.11, the Q value is,

$$Q = M_A C^2 - M_{A1} C^2 - M_{A2} C^2 \tag{9.39}$$

where M_{A1} is the mass of the first fission fragment and M_{A2} is the mass of the second fission fragment.

E_{crit} can be estimated as,

$$E_{crit} = E_q - Q \tag{9.40}$$

and E_q by,

$$E_q = \frac{\left(Z_1 Z_2 e^2\right)}{\left(R_1 - R_2\right)} \tag{9.41}$$

where Z_1 is the number of protons in fission fragment 1 and Z_2 is the number of protons in fission fragment 2, e is the charge of a proton, R_1 is the radius of the nucleus before splitting and R_2 is the radius of the nucleus when it begins to split.

The radius of a nucleus is estimated by,

$$R = r_e \frac{A^{1/3}}{2} \tag{9.42}$$

where A is the atomic mass and $r_e = \dfrac{e^2}{m_e C^2}$ and m_e is the mass of an electron.

From Equations (9.41) and (9.42) it can be seen that,

$$E_q = \frac{Z_1 Z_2 e^2}{\left(\dfrac{r_e}{2}\right)\left(A_1^{1/3} + A_2^{1/3}\right)} \tag{9.43}$$

and,

$$E_q = \frac{2m_e C^2 Z_1 Z_2}{\left(A_1^{1/3} + A_2^{1/3}\right)} \tag{9.44}$$

The term $2m_e C^2$ is about 1 MeV. Also it can be assumed for the time being that $Z_1 = Z_2$, therefore,

$$E_q \approx \frac{0.16 Z^2}{A^{1/3}} \tag{9.45}$$

For U-238, $Z = 92$ and $A = 238$, and

$E_q = 218$ MeV

Q for U-238 is about 212 MeV, thus

$E_{crit} \sim 6$ MeV

For lead, Pb-208, $Z = 82$ and $A = 208$. The value of E_q is given by,

$E_q = 182$ MeV

For Pb-208, Q is about 162 MeV, so,

$E_{crit} \sim 20$ MeV

In Table 9.2 is given the E_{crit} and binding energy of the last nucleon for various elements.

Table 9.2. The value of E_{crit} and the binding energy for the last nucleon.

Element	E_{crit} (MeV)	Binding energy last nucleon (MeV)
Th-232	5.9	*
Th-233	6.5	5.1
U-233	5.5	*
U-234	4.6	6.6
U-235	5.75	*
U-236	5.3	6.4
U-238	5.85	*
U-239	5.5	4.9
Pu-239	5.5	*
Pu-240	4.0	6.4

*Binding energy is not relevant for this analysis.

Fission will occur when the binding energy of the last nucleon is greater than E_{crit}. From Table 9.2, this condition applies to U-234, U-236 and Pu-240. Thus the nuclei which capture the neutron to trigger fission are U-233, U-235 and Pu-239. These materials are the primary practical fissile fuels.

The fission fragments do come out as a light fragment and a heavy fragment. However the fragments do not come out as a particular pair of nuclei. They come out in a distribution of paired nuclei. Figure 9.12 shows the distribution of paired nuclei as two distinct peaks.

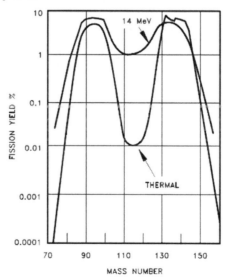

Fig. 9.12. The percent yield of fission fragments manifest as two peaks, one for the heavy fragment and one for the light fragment (Adapted from [3]).

The decay of radioactive fission products produces heat. Albeit, it is a small amount of the total heat produced in an operating nuclear power plant (about 0.7% of the total heat), it is enough heat to require cooling when the reactor is shut down. The Borst-Wheeler formula calculates the decay heat of a reactor after it has shut down,

$$P(t,T) = 4.10 \times 10^{11} \left[t^{-0.2} - (t+T)^{-0.2} \right] \tag{9.46}$$

where $P(t,T)$ is the total power emitted in the form of beta and gamma rays from the decaying fission products in a reactor which has operated T seconds at a power of 1 W, t is the time after shutdown in seconds.

For example, the University of Missouri Research Reactor is the most powerful University operated research reactor in the United States. Its operating power is 10 MW. During a typical week it operates continuously at full power for 150 h. The decay heat 10 s after shutdown can be calculated accurately by the Borst-Wheeler formula,

$T = 150$ h $= 5.4 \times 10^6$ s, thus
$P(10\text{s}, 5.4 \times 10^6 \text{s}) = 2.29 \times 10^{11}$ MeV/s/ W
Decay Heat in Reactor $= 2.29 \times 10^{11}$ MeV/s/W $\times$ 10,000 W
Decay Heat in Reactor $= 2.29 \times 10^{17}$ MeV/s $\times$ 1.6 $\times$ 10^{-13} J/MeV $= 36,640$ W

Once the nucleus fissions, one of the products is neutrons. Depending on which pair of fission fragments come out, the number of neutrons given off can vary. Over a large number of fissions, the statistical average of neutrons given off per event for example is about 2.44 for U-235. The decay chain of U-235 is shown in Fig. 9.13. The neutrons are born at fairly high energies (greater than 1 MeV) and as shown in Fig. 9.12, the energies have a distribution which is dependent on the fission fragment pair.

Nuclear reactors are designed to take advantage of the large cross section at thermal energies. In order to slow down the fast neutrons born in fission, materials have to be used to slow down the fast neutrons. These materials are called moderators and are based on light elements such as graphite, water, beryllium and heavy water.

Reactors are typically designed to use thermal neutrons (with neutron energies below 1 eV) and fast neutrons with energies from about 100 keV up to the top of range of the fission neutron energy spectrum. Thermal cross sections are very important to modern light water or heavy water moderated power plants. Table 9.1 tabulates cross sections for important elements at 0.025 eV energies.

In reality, the reactor materials are not entirely made up of fissile fuels and moderators. There are components such as structural elements, fuel cladding and there is leakage of neutrons from the reactor.

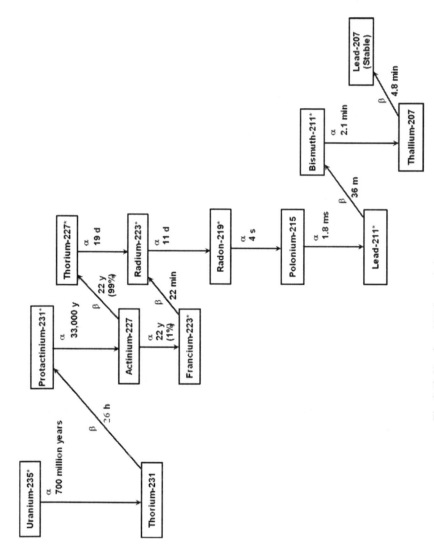

Fig. 9.13. Uranium-235 decay chain.

In reactor physics we describe the above process by the six factor formula.

$$k = \vartheta f p \, \varepsilon \, P_f P_t \tag{9.47}$$

In Eq. (9.47), ϑ is the number of fast neutrons produced by fission with thermal neutrons; f is the fraction of thermal neutrons absorbed in the fuel. Some of the thermal neutrons are absorbed in the fuel and some in the other materials that make up the reactor; p is the resonance escape probability. As the fast neutrons move through materials, there are absorption resonances at high neutron energies (2 to 100,000 eV in the materials that make up the reactor. This is the probability that the fast neutrons will slow down without being absorbed; ε is the fast fission factor. Fast neutrons can produce fission, ε is the number of additional fast neutrons that are created by fast fission; P_f is the probability that a fast neutron stays in the reactor. Some fraction of fast neutrons will leak out of the reactor volume; P_t is the probability that a thermal neutron stays in the reactor. Some fraction of thermal neutrons will leak out of the reactor volume. This process is shown in Fig. 9.14.

The factor k is a means of neutron bookkeeping. k neutrons produced in fission will survive to be absorbed by the fuel and will produce k additional fission reactions. If k is greater to or equal to one, then the reaction is self sustaining. This is a chain reaction. Reactors are designed to have $k > 1$. A nuclear reactor is controlled by the use of control rods. These rods are made up of materials that absorb thermal neutrons. When the control rods are inserted into the nuclear reactor, the k value of the reactor is less than one. When the control rods are taken out of the reactor, $k > 1$ and the reactor is able to undergo a chain reaction. The control rods allow the operator to control the reactor power level and to shut the reactor down.

The k value is a geometrical series which increases rapidly,

Neutrons in Generation $n = k^n$ (9.48)

Figures 9.15 and 9.16 is the neutron production over multiple generations for a k value of 2.44 and 1.1, respectively. Given that the time between generations is on the order of microseconds, and that energy release is directly proportional to the number of neutrons, it can be seen that energy output can multiply rather rapidly over a short period of time.

The total number of fission reactions can be very large in a short amount of time. Even though nuclear science had many applications which had saved millions of lives by the time Word War II started, people associate the word nuclear with nuclear weapons. A nuclear weapon is a formidable device which is designed to have a relatively large value of k for the purpose of releasing as much energy as possible in a short period of time. The weapon is designed to maintain a high k value until the energy released blows the device apart. We can see the potential of the weapon in the following example.

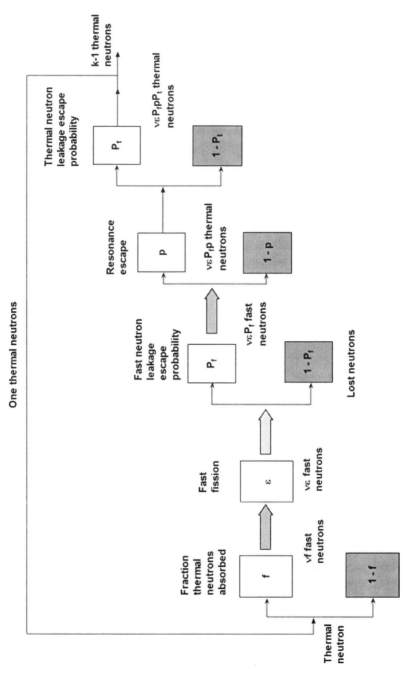

Fig. 9.14. Neutron bookkeeping in a reactor. Printed with permission from Prelas MA, Peck MS (2005) Nonproliferation Issues for Weapons of Mass Destruction. CRC Press [4]

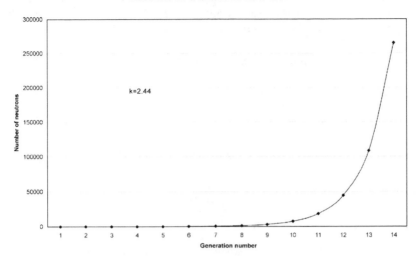

Fig. 9.15. Neutron production from generation to generation for a k value of 2.44 (Printed with permission from [4]).

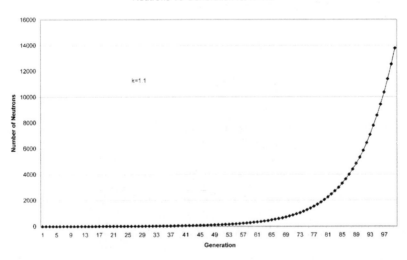

Fig. 9.16. Neutron production from generation to generation for a k value of 1.1 (Printed with permission from [4]).

Consider a nuclear warhead which has a $k = 1.5$ and holds together for 139 neutron generations, what is the total energy released? We begin by looking at the total number of neutrons (TN) that occur in 139 generations,

TN = neutrons in generation 1 + neutrons in gen 2 + ... + neutrons in gen i

$$\text{generation } 0 = n_0$$
$$\text{generation } 1 = n_0 k$$
$$\text{generation } 2 = n_0 k^2$$
$$\text{generation } i = n_0 k^i$$

This is a power series which has an analytical solution,

$$TN(i) = n_0 \left[\frac{k^i - 1}{k - 1} \right]$$

Since each fission will yield v neutrons in a generation the total number of fissions will be,

TF = fissions in generation 1 + fissions in gen 2 + ... + fissions in gen i

$$\text{Fissions in generation } 1 = \frac{n_0 k}{v}$$

$$\text{Fissions in generation } 2 = \frac{n_0 k^2}{v}$$

$$\text{Fissions in generation } i = \frac{n_0 k^i}{v}$$

The formula for the total number of fissions will be,

$$TF(i) = n_0 \frac{\dfrac{k^i - k}{k - 1}}{v}$$

Thus, assuming that $n_0 = 1$, and $v = 2.44$ (for U-235)

$$TF(139) = n_0 \frac{\dfrac{1.5^{139} - 1.5}{1.5 - 1}}{2.44} \sim 2.46 \times 10^{24} \text{ fissions}$$

Each fission gives off about 200 MeV or 3.2×10^{-11} Joules, so the energy produced after 139 generations is,

$$E = 2.46 \times 10^{24} \times 3.2 \times 10^{-11} = 7.9 \times 10^{13} \text{ J}$$

This is a large amount of energy. For an explosive, we can use the relationship that 1,000 t (or a kiloton) of TNT is 4.184×10^{12} Joules. Converting this energy to kilotons of TNT we find,

$$E = 7.9 \times 10^{13}/4.184 \times 10^{12} \sim 18.9 \text{ kt of TNT}$$

Fortunately, it is not easy to design a nuclear weapon. It is a sophisticated device that requires a great deal of technology. For instance, we know that Iraq invested more than 20 billion dollars in its nuclear weapons program and were not even close to getting any significant amounts of fissile materials.

We need to dispel a common concern about the relationship of nuclear weapons to nuclear power. A power nuclear power plant is nothing like a nuclear weapon. A nuclear power plant has a much different design criteria which does not allow large power excursions, thus k is kept at values below 1.1 allowing complete and safe control of the reaction.

It is not an easy task to design a critical assembly ($k > 1$) of fissile materials for a power producing reactor. There is much that goes into the design such as choice of materials, geometry, structural components, moderator, control systems, active safety systems, passive safety systems etc. The US for example requires that nuclear power plants have a negative temperature coefficient which means that the plant will shut itself down if the fuel exceeds a safe temperature. It is beyond the scope of this course to delve into this physics and system details. If the reader has a desire to learn more, there are courses on nuclear reactor engineering, nuclear reactor physics and transport theory that you may wish to take.

In addition to producing power, the fission reaction produces fission products. These products are radioactive (see Fig. 9.17) and produce residual heat even when the reactor is shut down. This residual heat is a problem which must be dealt with in the design of the power plant. The energy that is emitted by fission reactions is shown in Table 9.3.

Table 9.3. Emitted and Recoverable Energy for Fission of U-235

Energy form	Emitted energy, MeV	Recoverable energy, MeV
Fission fragments	168.00	168.00
Fission product decay		
β rays	8.00	8.00
γ rays	7.00	7.00
Neutrinos	12.00	0.00
Prompt γ rays	7.00	7.00
Fission neutrons (kinetic energy)	5.00	5.00
Capture γ rays	0.00	4.00
Total	207.00	200.00

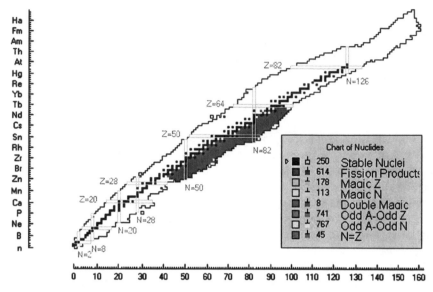

Fig. 9.17. Distribution of fission products. Most of the products are neutron rich and undergo radioactive decay (Courtesy of [2]).

Calculation of the amount of power that fission produces for a given amount of fuel consumed is very large. A simple calculation can be made relating the reactor power (P), to the fuel burnup, and fuel consumption:

$$\text{Fission Rate} = P\ (MW)\ x\ \frac{10^6\ joules}{MW - sec}\ x\ \frac{fission}{E_R\ MeV}\ x\ \frac{MeV}{1.6x10^{-13}\ joule}\ x\ \frac{86400\ sec}{day}$$

$$\text{Fission Rate} = 5.40\ x\ 10^{23}\ \frac{P}{E_R}\ fissions/day$$

The burnup rate can be found by assuming that mass of a fissile nuclei is A,

$$\text{Burnup Rate} = 5.40\ x\ 10^{23}\ \frac{P}{E_R}\ x\ \frac{A}{0.602\ x\ 10^{24}}$$

$$\text{Burnup Rate} = 0.895\frac{PA}{E_R}\ gm\ /\ day$$

For unranium-235, which releases 200 MeV per fission, the burnup rate is,

Burnup Rate = 1.05 P gm/day   (9.49)

So, one MW-day of energy requires about 1 gm of uranium-235 per day.

The fissile material is consumed by both fission reactions and capture reactions (in which fission does not occur). The total absorption rate factor is 1.175. The total consumption rate is:

$$\text{Consumption Rate} = 0.895 \times 1.175 \times \frac{PA}{E_R} \ gm/\ day \qquad (9.50)$$

Consumption Rate = 1.24 gm/day

The unit of megawatt-days per metric tonne of fuel, MWD/t, is used to describe consumption rate. A metric tonne is 1,000 kg or 10^6 gm. If it were possible to fission all uranium-235 the total energy release would be 1 MWD/gm which is equal to 106 MWD/T. The uranium-235 is not all consumed. There are parasitic absorptions that reduce this number slightly to 800,000 MWD/t.

9.4 Uranium Resources

About 439 commercial nuclear power reactors are operating in 30 countries, with 372,000 MWe of total capacity providing 16% of the world's electricity as base-load power (Fig. 9.18). Also there are 284 research reactors in 56 countries, and further 220 reactors that power ships and submarines.

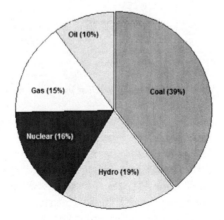

Fig. 9.18. World electricity generation by fuel type.

In Fig. 9.19 the share of electricity generated by nuclear energy by various countries is shown. France is leading all the countries with 80%.

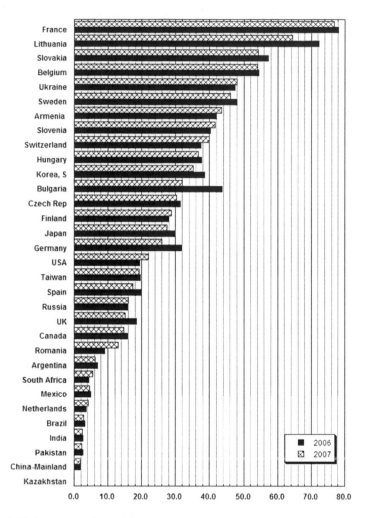

Fig. 9.19. Percentage of electricity generated by nuclear by various countries (Adapted from [5]).

As can be noted from Fig. 9.20, the share of nuclear towards total electricity production is steadily increasing. Interestingly, from 1990 to 2006, world capacity rose by 44 GWe, or 13.5%, due both to net addition of new plants and uprating of some established ones. Total electricity production increased to 757 billion kWh (40%). The relative contributions to this increase were: new construction 36%, uprating 7% and availability increase 57%. Nuclear power reactors that are under construction or planned for the near future are given in Appendix IX.

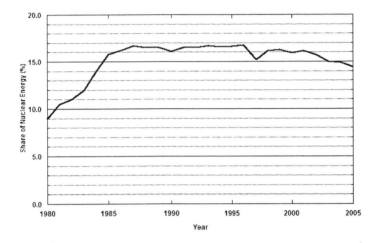

Fig. 9.20. Global share of electricity production by nuclear energy (Adapted from [5]).

The total generation of electricity by nuclear energy is steadily increasing worldwide. These data are shown in Fig. 9.21. A number of nuclear power plants are already under construction. Also several more plants have been planned worldwide which will further increase the share of total electricity production by nuclear energy. The plants under construction and that are planned are given in Appendix IX

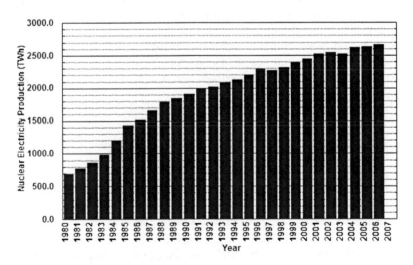

Fig. 9.21. Yearly nuclear electricity production in the world (Adapted from [5]).

9.5 Fuel Cycle

Sustainability of nuclear power production relies heavily upon the closing of the fuel cycle, i.e., reprocessing of the spent fuel. A number of countries including, Japan, France, and Russia have been reprocessing spent fuel from their light water reactor fleet for many years. The United States opted for the once-through cycle in the early 1970s, but has shifted its philosophy in recent years, as fossil fuel prices have continued to soar. Also, India and China are planning to reprocess the spent fuel from the nuclear reactors.

9.5.1 Once-Through Cycle

The fuel cycle begins with mining and milling of uranium, followed by conversion and enrichment. The fuel cycle is described in details later in this chapter. The enriched product is then sent to fabrication. The enriched product can be either in a metal or oxide form. The fuel is encased in a protective barrier known as cladding and arranged such that critical mass can be achieved within a core, under proper conditions. This fuel is then cycled through a reactor core, which usually amounts to three cycles of use, approximately 18 months each. Once the fuel has reached the end of its useful life, it is transferred to a storage pool, where it decays over a period of several years. Dry storage is also available for fuel that has decayed sufficiently and is necessary when spent fuel pools reach their capacity. This is the current stopping point of the current U.S. fuel cycle.

The next step in the once-through cycle would be the shipment of the spent fuel to a permanent repository as high level waste (HLW). However, no repository has been licensed for use and the only active project, Yucca Mountain, still has substantial political and scientific hurdles to overcome. The topic of waste generation and final storage is discussed later.

9.5.2 Closed Fuel Cycle

The front end of the closed fuel cycle is the same as that of the once-through cycle. However, the back end of the closed fuel cycle is substantially different. Instead of simply storing the spent fuel in a High Level Waste (HLW) disposal facility, the fuel is reprocessed for recycle back into the fuel cycle. The reprocessing involves separating the fuel material from the cladding material, retrieving the fissionable and fissile materials from the mixture, mainly plutonium and uranium, for recycle. The rest of the long lived fission products are vitrified for long term storage. The uranium and plutonium can be recycled back into fuel for light water and fast reactor use. Additionally, both thermal reactors and fast breeder reactors can make use of the U-238, which is present in 99% of natural uranium. Thermal reactors will convert some of the U-238 into plutonium some of which is burned during operation of the reactor. About 1/3 of the energy produced in a light water power reactor is derived from the plutonium generated by the converted U-238. Fast breeder reactors on the other hand produce more fissionable material than they consume, providing a more efficient means of uranium use. The fuel-resources for nuclear reactors can be extended if reprocessing and fast breeder reactors are used instead of once-through cycles.

Annual requirements of uranium worldwide for existing power reactors are about 67,000 t of uranium. According to the authoritative "Red Book" [6] produced jointly by the OECD's (Organisation for Economic Co-operation and Development) Nuclear Energy Agency (NEA) and the UN's International Atomic Energy Agency (IAEA), the world's present known economic resources of uranium, exploitable at below $80 per kilogram of uranium, are about 3.5 million tonnes. This amount is therefore enough to last for 50 years at today's rate of usage – a figure higher than many widely used metals. Current estimates of all expected uranium resources (including those not yet economic or properly quantified) are four times as great, representing 200 years' supply at today's rate of usage. It can be seen from Table 9.4 that Australia has a substantial amount (about 23%) of the world's low-cost uranium, followed by Kazakhstan 15%, and Russia 10%.

Table 9.4. Known recoverable resources of Uranium (2007 data).

Country	Tonnes U	% of world	Country	Tonnes U	% of World
Australia	1,243,000	23%	Niger	274,000	5%
Kazakhstan	817,000	15%	Uzbekistan	111,000	2%
Russia	546,000	10%	Ukraine	200,000	4%
Canada	423,000	8%	Jordan	112,000	2%
USA	342,000	6%	India	73,000	1%
South Africa	435,000	8%	China	68,000	1%
Namibial	275,000	5%	Mongolia	62,000	1%
Brazil	278,000	5%	Other	210,000	4%
World total	5,469,000				

Source: World Nuclear Association, London, UK [5]. Reasonably Assured Resources plus Inferred Resources, to US$ 130/kg U, 1/1/07, from OECD/NEA & IAEA, *Uranium 2007: Resources, Production and Demand*, "Red Book" [6].

The amount of uranium that can be extracted from the ores depends on the uranium price. As can be seen from Fig. 9.22, in countries such as the USA and Niger, significant amount of uranium can be recovered at a cost of US$ 130/kg of U.

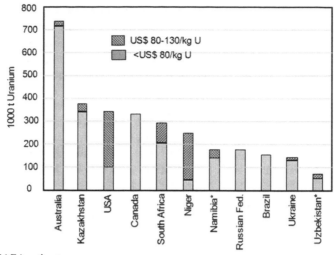

* IAEA estimate

Fig. 9.22. Reasonably Assured Resources plus Inferred Resources, to US$ 130/kg U [6]. Note: The Australian figure had risen to 1,558,000 t U as at August 2007 and other country figures would have risen also, but are not yet published. 1/1/05.

It is expected that the demand for uranium will increase as more and more reactors are constructed worldwide. With this being anticipated, the investment for exploration of uranium resources has increased significantly in recent years (Fig. 9.23).

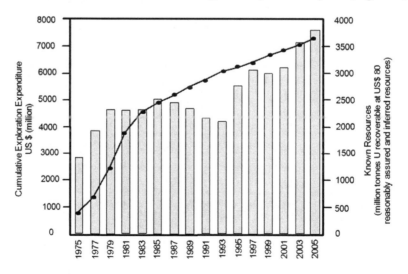

Fig. 9.23. Investment for exploration of uranium (Adapted from [5]).

The IAEA-NEA estimates that if all conventional resources are considered, there are about 10 million tonnes of uranium beyond the 4.7 million tonnes known economic resources, which is enough to go beyond 200 years' at today's rate of consumption. However, if unconventional resources such as phosphate/phosphorite deposits (22 Mt U recoverable as by-product) and seawater (up to 4000 Mt) are considered, the available resources would be even greater. These unconventional resources are currently not economical, but as the price of uranium increases these resources may become attractive.

The use of the fast breeder reactor would increase the utilization of uranium 50-fold or more. This type of reactor can be started up on plutonium derived from conventional reactors and operated in closed circuit with its reprocessing plant. Such a reactor, supplied with natural or depleted uranium for its "fertile blanket", can be operated in such a way that each tonne of ore yields 60 times more energy than a conventional reactor. However, reprocessing and the use of fast breeder reactors can increase the operation of nuclear reactors significantly (Table 9.5).

Table 9.5. Years of uranium availability for nuclear power.

Reactor/Fuel Cycle	Years of 2004 world nuclear electricity generation with identified conventional resources	Years of 2004 world nuclear electricity generation with total conventional resources	Years of 2004 world nuclear electricity generation with total conventional and unconventional resources
Current once through fuel cycle with light water reactors	85	270	675
Pure fast reactor fuel cycle with recycling	5, 000 – 6, 000	16, 000 – 19, 000	40, 000 – 47, 000

The values in the last row assume that fast reactors allow essentially all U-238 to be bred to Pu-239 for fuel, except for minor losses of fissile materials during reprocessing and fuel fabrication. Adapted from Rogner H-H, McDonald A (November 2007) Nuclear Energy - Status and Outlook, 20th World Energy Congress, Rome, Italy [7].

9.6 Uranium Supply and Demand

Uranium is currently extracted in 19 countries, and Canada and Australia account for more than 50% of the worldwide production. Approximately 40,000 tons of uranium is produced each year, supplying approximately 60% of the uranium needed for the existing reactors. The rest of the uranium is made up by secondary uranium sources, such as natural and enriched stockpiles, re-processing of spent fuel and enrichment of uranium tails [7].

Demand for uranium has gone up slowly over the past three decades. The upward trend has been a result of expansion of nuclear power overseas and more recently, the pending demand from mass global expansion of nuclear power. Uranium prices have risen more dramatically in the past few years, generating renewed interest in new exploration. Figure 9.24 shows recent trends in uranium requirements and production.

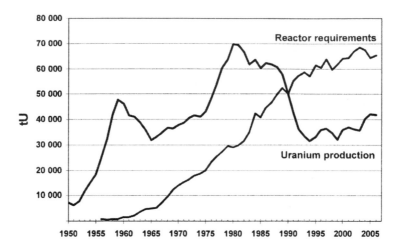

Fig. 9.24. Global Annual Uranium Production and Reactor Requirements, 1950–2006 (Adapted from [7]).

It is assumed that the need of uranium will be between 78,000 and 129,000 t of uranium by 2030 [7] due to proposed and anticipated new reactors. This will certainly force uranium prices up and encourage even more mine developments worldwide.

9.7 Electricity Generation from Nuclear Energy

The steps or processes involved in generation of electricity from nuclear energy may be divided into following categories. This is also called the Nuclear Fuel Cycle.

- Uranium mining and extraction
- Enrichment
- Fuel Fabrication
- Power production
- Waste management
- Spent fuel reprocessing (If the objective is to recycle unused/unburned uranium)

The nuclear fuel cycle is shown graphically in Fig. 9.25.

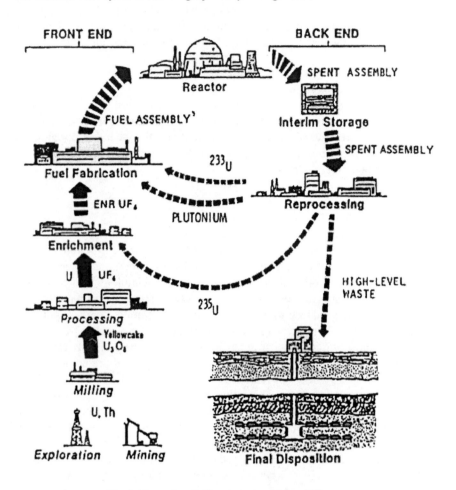

Fig. 9.25. Nuclear fuel cycle (Adapted from [8]).

9.7.1 Uranium Mining and Extraction

Uranium can be found in nature in several ores. Uranium has been found as a significant constituent in about 150 different minerals and in small concentration in another 50 minerals. Primary uranium minerals include uraninite and pitchblende. Other ores from which uranium may be extracted economically include autunite, tobernite, coffinite, and carnotite.

It is estimated that about 90% of world's low-cost uranium reserves are in Canada, South Africa, the United States, Australia, Niger, Namibia, Brazil, Algeria, and France. Sandstone formations in the Colorado Plateau and Wyoming Basin of the western United States also contain significant reserves of uranium.

9.7.1.1 Mining and Milling

Detailed exploration is necessary prior to any major investment being placed in mining. There are several methods of exploration utilized today, including geo-logical mapping, airborne and surface surveys, hydro-chemical sampling, well-logging and botanical methods [9].

Methods of Mining

Open-pit and underground mining remain the dominant extraction methods in most of the world, accounting for 68% of production. Additionally, approximately 11% of uranium is produced from in-situ leaching technology, which is the pre-ferred method in several countries, such as Kazakhstan. The remainder of fresh uranium supply is produced as a by-product material from copper and gold mining and a small amount is produced from water treatment operations [6].

Open-pit and underground mining are essentially the same as that used for other mineral extraction, such as coal. In-situ leaching is a more complex process. Several holes are drilled, approximately 50 ft apart, and a leaching solution is injected into the center hole. This solution consists of water, an oxidant and an ionic complex agent, designed to mobilize and dissolve uranium. The solution is pumped out from the remaining holes and uranium is removed through ion exchange. The stripped solution is re-oxidized and treated for proper pH, and is recycled back into the process. This method is not without problems, as it can con-taminate groundwater, if not performed properly. To prevent this, more water is pumped out than is pumped in, creating a flow away from the water table. Once the mine has been fully utilized, it is flushed with clean water and all holes are plugged. If performed properly, in-situ mining has less environmental impact on mining sites than open-pit or underground mining and is highly effective for extracting uranium.

Following uranium mining from open-pit or underground methods, the ore is crushed, grinded, pulverized into powder and roasted to remove organics. The uranium is removed via ion exchange or solvent extraction. The resulting U_3O_8 product is then dried and packaged as yellowcake into 55 gallon drums for ship-ment to an enrichment facility.

Mining Wastes

Open-pit and underground mining produce significant amounts of tailings from the milling process. All of the material left over after the yellowcake is produced, remains as waste. These tailings typically contain some uranium as well as radon and other decay products. Additionally, the tailings contain acids from the milling process, which can leach out various toxic metal from soil and cause groundwater contamination. Strict enforcement of discharge limits are enforced by the Nuclear Regulatory Commission (NRC) and Environmental Protection Agency (EPA) in the United States.

Mill tailings must be sufficiently contained within tailing ponds, so that acids and radioactive materials do not escape into the environment. Several advances have been made in recent years, considering tailings were not regulated during the early years of uranium production.

In-situ mining also has several disadvantages. Although this type of mining does not produce tailings, the groundwater aquifer near these mines must be restored to similar conditions as they were before in-situ extraction began. This can be a rather challenging undertaking and has been the source of criticism for this method of mining.

Another source of waste generated by all of these mining techniques revolves around the milling treatment and the chemicals involved. Acids are employed for separation of uranium from the ore as well as stripping of resin columns. Additionally, solvent extraction utilizes various chemicals, which must also be disposed of properly.

9.7.2 Conversion and Enrichment

Although the processes involved in conversion and enrichment have not changed much over the past two decades, there are some notable exceptions and future trends.

Prior to fuel enrichment, the U_3O_8 produced in the mill must be purified and converted into uranium hexafluoride (UF_6). UF_6 was chosen as the enrichment compound due to its unique physical and chemical properties. It is a solid at room temperature, and its melting point is 147°F. This is the only compound of uranium which behaves in this fashion and has made it the ideal candidate for enrichment. Properties of various uranium compounds are given in Table 9.6. As can be seen from the table, among all the uranium compounds, only uranium hexafluoride has the melting point that is low enough to use in the separation process.

Table 9.6. Melting points of uranium and uranium compounds.

Uranium compounds	Melting point (°F)
Uranium metal	2071
Diboride	4289
Tetrabromide	960
Tribromide	1346
Dicarbide	4262
Tetrachloride	1094
Trichloride	1548
Hexafluoride	147
Tetrafluoride	1760
Tetraiodide	943
Mononitride	4766
Dioxide	4532
Disulfide	>2012

Source: Adapted from [10].

Various physical forms of UF_6 at various temperatures and pressures are expressed by its phase diagram. The boundaries between solid, liquid, gaseous forms detect the operating conditions. The phase diagram of UF_6 is shown in Fig. 9.26.

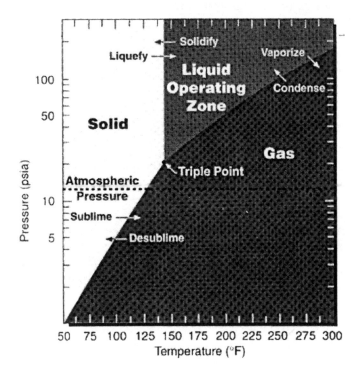

Fig. 9.26. The phase diagram of UF_6 (Adapted from. [10]).

A solvent extraction process, called Plutonium Uranium Extraction (PUREX), is used for extraction and purification of uranium. The PUREX process takes advantage of the preference of uranium to form coordinated compounds within aqueous solutions that can be selectively extracted from the solution by an organic solvents, such as tributyl phosphate (TBP). Uranium is next precipitated out from the solution using ammonium hydroxide. The second method involves using hydrogen peroxide to precipitate out uranium peroxide from weak acid solutions. Steps involved in producing UF_6 from yellowcake are shown in Fig. 9.27, and a simplified diagram of the solvent extraction unit is shown in Figure 9.28. Once these methods have been successfully completed, conversion to UF_6 follows [9].

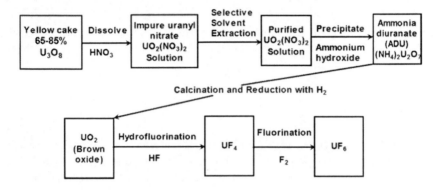

Fig. 9.27. Reactions pathways for UF_6 production (Adapted from [10]).

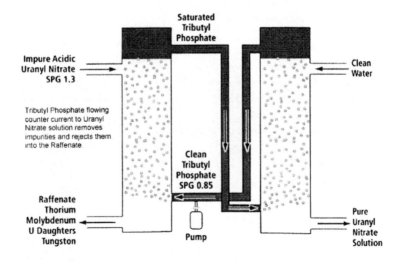

Fig. 9.28. A simplified schematic diagram of the solvent extraction unit (Adapted from [10]).

Uranium diuranate (ADU) that is precipitated out from the solution is converted to UO_2 by calcining it in hydrogen. UO_2 is next converted into UF_6 in two steps. Both steps utilize a fluidized bed reactor, which heats the UO_2 to approximately $1,000°F$ in the presence of HF first and then with F_2. The chemical reaction that takes place is:

$$UO_2 + 4HF \rightarrow 2H_2O + UF_4$$

This UF_4 is next reacted with fluorine gas to form the UF_6 as follows:

$$UF_4 + F_2 \rightarrow UF_6$$

The solvent extraction step removes impurities prior to the reduction step. This results in a very pure form of UF_6 at the end of the fluorination process, leaving a product ready for enrichment [9].

9.7.2.1 Enrichment

The enrichment of uranium refers to the increase in concentration of U-235 isotopes. Depending on the degree of enrichment, its grade varies. Also a number of enrichment processes have been suggested, but only few are used commercially.

Grades
> Highly enriched uranium (HEU)
> Low-enriched uranium (LEU)
> Slightly enriched uranium (SEU)

Methods
> Thermal diffusion
> Gaseous diffusion
> The gas centrifuge
> The Zippe centrifuge
> Aerodynamic processes
> Electromagnetic isotope separation
> Laser processes
> Chemical methods
> Plasma separation

Enrichment Process

Among the methods mentioned above, gaseous diffusion and gas centrifuge methods are most widely used commercially for enrichment of uranium. Laser separation is still in developmental stage, but is likely to compete with gaseous diffusion and gas centrifuge methods in the near future. The United States has relied primarily on the gaseous diffusion method due to its more simplistic design and successful operational history. However, currently, most of the countries preferring gas centrifuge method.

Gaseous Diffusion

The first step in the diffusion process is conversion of solid UF_6 to the gaseous form by heating it above 135°F. It is then forced through a series of porous membranes, which separates U-235 from the U-238. Since U-235 is lighter than U-238, it diffuses at a relatively faster rate than U-238 through the membranes. Figure 9.29 illustrates the diffusion process during uranium enrichment. To achieve a U-235 concentration from its natural 0.7% to 3% to 5%, several thousand stages are connected in series.

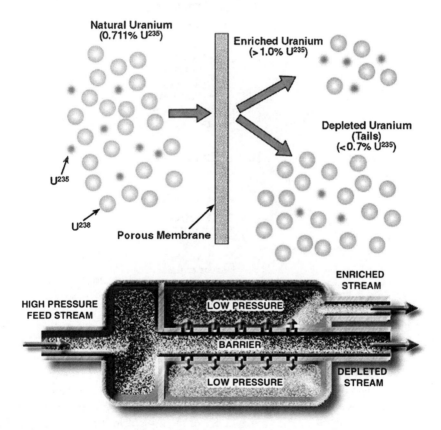

Fig. 9.29. An illustration of gaseous diffusion process for uranium enrichment and a diffusion cell (Adapted from [11]).

Gas Centrifuge

In this method, solid UF_6 is also heated first to form gaseous UF_6, which is then fed into the center of a rotor, spinning at very high velocity, inside a casing held at vacuum. Due to the mass differences, the heavier U-238 tends to separate from the lighter U-235 and is forced outward. The enriched product is then collected from the center and fed into the next centrifuge. The depleted UF_6 is fed back into the system for further separation. In order to achieve U-235 percentages adequate for reactor fuel, several thousand stages must be connected in series. Figure 9.30 illustrates a typical centrifuge unit used for fuel enrichment.

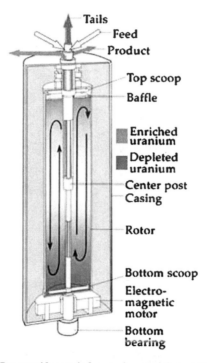

Fig. 9.30. Gas centrifuge unit for uranium enrichment (Adapted from [12]).

The centrifuge technology has been used worldwide with great success. The US Energy Corp (USEC) and AREVA are planning to build a new facility in New Mexico, USA, based on the centrifuge process, and another one near Idaho Falls, ID, USA. One of the big advantages of centrifuge technology is that it has a 5% energy savings over gaseous diffusion. Enrichment plants are extremely energy intensive, and savings from the centrifuge process are very significant. The US project will be the most advanced fuel enrichment plant in the world, employing the new AC100 centrifuge machines. Details of these units are classified, but the USEC expects the plant to produce 3.8 million separative work units (SWU) per year by 2012, using 11,500 machines, once the plant is fully on-line [13].

About 100,000–120,000 SWU is required to enrich the annual fuel loading for a typical 1,000 MWe light water reactor. Enrichment costs are substantially related to electrical energy used. The gaseous diffusion process consumes about 2,500kWh (9,000 MJ) per SWU, while modern gas centrifuge plants require only about 50 kWh (180 MJ) per SWU. Also, the current trend is to use the centrifuge technology over the diffusion technology (Table 9.7).

Table 9.7. Trends in the use of technology for uranium enrichment.

Supply source	2007	2017
Diffusion	25%	0
Centrifuge	65%	96%
HEU ex weapons	10%	4%

Source: Reference [5].

(The Separative Work Unit (*SWU*) is a measure of the work expended during an enrichment process. Uranium enrichment is sold as *SWU*. Higher levels of U-235 require more *SWU*).

The *SWU* may be calculated from the following equation:

$$SWU = P \cdot f(N_p) + W \cdot f(N_w) - F \cdot f(N_f) \tag{9.51}$$

where P is the amount of product, N_p is the product concentration, W is the amount of waste, N_w is the waste concentration, F is the amount of feed, and N_f is the feed concentration, and $f(x)$ is a value function and is defined as:

$$f(x) = (2x - 1)\ln\frac{x}{(1-x)} \tag{9.52}$$

where x is a given concentration.

(The function $f(x)$ is dimensionless. The unit of *SWU* depends on the units of P, W, and F, which are generally expressed in units of kilograms (kg) or tonnes. The *SWU* is expressed as a kg-*SWU* or metric tones-*SWU*. The performance of a centrifuge can be expressed in terms of rate of enrichment, that is, *SWUs* per year or month. Individual centrifuges might be described in terms of kg-SWUs per year. A *SWU* per unit time is referred to, not as separative work, but as separative power).

Laser Separation

This technology differs substantially from the diffusion and centrifuge methods. Although the different isotopes of uranium have identical chemical behavior, their electronic energies are very different, causing them to absorb energy at different wavelength. This is the fundamental basis behind laser technology, enabling isotopic separation. The laser is focused through the target, with the wavelength tuned specifically into that for U-235. The targeted U-235 atoms will lose an electron (ionize), with no affect on the rest of the feed material, mainly U-238. The U-235 is collected in a negatively charged surface in the liquid form, where it runs down to a die cast. The resulting pellets can then be shipped off to fuel fabrication. The tailings, which amount to 30% less than with other methods, are collected and can be disposed of or used in the fast reactor. Advantages of this technology include reduced tailings and laser separation uses just 5% of the energy required by gaseous diffusion [14]. The uranium feed for laser separation is in the metal form, eliminating the hazards associated with UF_6. Figure 9.31 illustrates the laser separation method for uranium enrichment.

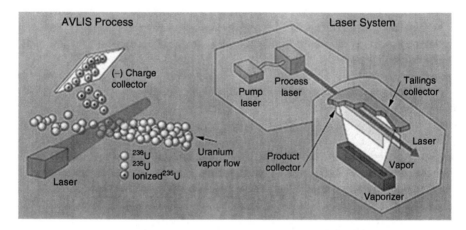

Fig. 9.31. Laser isotope separation method for uranium enrichment [15].

Scientists at Lawrence Livermore National Laboratory had demonstrated production scale capability of this enrichment process. However, the technology was transferred to USEC in the early 1990s, and they discontinued further development of the project in 1999 primarily due to declining uranium prices. Currently, Silex System Ltd, New South Wales, Australia, is further developing a laser based technology based on CRISLA (condensation repression by isotope selective laser activation) for full scale commercial application. The CRISLA process was invented by Dr. Jeff Eerkens, University of Missouri, Columbia, Missouri, USA. GE-Hitachi recently purchased the exclusive rights to the technology and moved the effort to their Wilmington, North Carolina location. Exelon and Entergy, which are the two largest nuclear utility owners in the United States, have signed letters of intent to buy laser-enriched uranium from GE [5].

9.7.2.2 Waste Generated by Enrichment Processes

The tailings of uranium enrichment are a key factor that goes into the price of SWU. Typically, tailings contain 0.2–0.3% by weight of U-235. There is approximately 700 million kilograms of depleted UF_6, containing 475 million kilograms of uranium in the United States. This is stored in 60,000 steel cylinders at the various laboratories and enrichment facilities. Recycling of this depleted UF_6 could be an economical and environmental success, which has been looked into by scientists at Lawrence Livermore National Laboratory [13].

9.7.3 Fuel Fabrication

Fuel fabrication varies greatly from one reactor to another, in terms of fuel and cladding type, fuel enrichment and geometry. The types of commercial reactors currently used for electricity generation are listed below.

- Research reactors
- Pressurized water reactor, (PWR)
- Boiling water reactor (BWR)
- Fast breeder reactor (FBR)
- Pressurized Heavy Water Reactor (PHWR) or CANDU

Fuels are produced in either the metal or ceramic form. Metal fuel has the benefits of higher thermal conductivity and ease of fabrication. Among the drawbacks of metal fuel are lower melting temperatures and its tendency to undergo growth upon irradiation. Ceramic fuels have the benefit of providing good retention of fission products during irradiation; low fabrication costs, and are chemically and structurally stable. Drawbacks include a brittle structure, susceptible to cracking and low thermal conductivity. There has been substantial research and development regarding advanced fuels and will be discussed further later in this chapter.

9.7.3.1 Ceramic Pellet Fuel

Commercial light water and CANDU reactors typically use UO_2 pellet fuel (MO_X fuel can also be used in these reactors). There are wet and dry processes available to convert the enriched UF_6 to ceramic grade UO_2. The three methods that are most widely used are the dry conversion, ammonium diuranate and the ammonium uranyl carbonate routes.

The dry conversion route begins with UF_6 decomposition using superheated steam to form UO_2F_2 particles. The particles then undergo pyrohydrolysis through interaction with steam and hydrogen. All these steps occur within a rotary kiln, which is the most common method of conversion in the U.S. and France [16]. The reactions that take place within the kiln are:

$$UF_6 + 2H_2O \rightarrow UO_2F_2 + 4HF$$
$$UO_2F_2 + H_2O \rightarrow UO_3 + 2HF$$
$$UO_3 + H_2 \rightarrow UO_2 + H_2O$$

The ammonium diuranate route involves hydrolysis of UF_6, filtration of the resulting precipitate and heating to form UO_2. Ammonium hydroxide is mixed in with the feed UF_6 to form the ammonium diuranate, which can readily be filtered, washed to remove as much entrained fluoride as possible and dried to remove moisture and excess ammonia. The product is then passed on to a pyrohydrolysis and reduction furnace, which removes the remaining fluorine and completes conversion to UO_2. The reactions that take place during this process are:

$$UF_6 + 2 H_2O \rightarrow UO_2F_2 + 4HF$$
$$2 UO_2F_2 + 8 HF + 14 NH_4OH \rightarrow (NH_4)_2U_2O_7 + 12 NH_4F + 11 H_2O$$

The ammonium uranyl carbonate route is used by Germany and Sweden. Advantages of this technology include production of a free-flowing, granular UO_2 with uniform particle size. The afore-mentioned method requires compaction and granulation prior to pressing into pellets. The UF_6 feed is heated and directed to a precipitation vessel, which contains a mixture of ammonium hydroxide and ammonium carbonate. The uranium is precipitated out as ammonium uranyl carbonate. The solid is then filtered out of solution, washed with clean ammonium carbonate to remove most of the fluoride, then dried and transferred to a furnace, supplied with hydrogen and steam at 650°C. The remaining fluoride is removed as HF and decomposition of the ammonium uranyl carbonate produces UO_2. The reactions that take place during this process are:

$$UF_6 + 5 H_2O + 10 NH_3 + 3 CO_2 \rightarrow (NH_4)_4UO_2(CO_3)_3 + 6 NH_4F$$
$$(NH_4)_4UO_2(CO_3)_3 + H_2 \rightarrow UO_2 + 3 CO_2 + 4 NH_3 + 3 H_2O$$

Most of the light water fuel used today is in the form of small cylindrical ceramic pellets. Enriched UO_2, from the previously mentioned processes, is mixed with an organic pore-forming agent, which will later decompose during the sintering process. The pores that are formed provide the space for collection of fission products produced during irradiation, preventing fuel growth beyond tolerances. A binding agent is also added to the powder prior to pressing, which results in a "green" pellet prior to sintering. The selection of binding agent is crucial since this determines the amount of handling damage that will occur to the pellet prior to sintering, thus lowering rejection rates. Pressure in the range of 3 to 4 tons/cm^2 is applied to the powder-mixture within a die until the resulting pellet density is approximately 5.5–6.0 g/cm^3. The final process of pellet production is sintering, which is performed in ovens at temperatures of approximately 1750°C [16]. The sintering converts the green pellet into the ceramic fuel with a crystalline grain structure while retaining the original shape. The pellets are then grounded to strict tolerances and the removed material is recycled back into the process.

9.7.3.2 Research Reactor Fuel Assembly

The Training, Research, Isotopes, General Atomics (TRIGA) reactor is the most widely used research reactor throughout the world. It can be built with thermal power levels ranging from 10 kW to 10 MW. A photograph of the fuel pellet and a fuel pin of the TRIGA reactor is shown in Fig. 9.32. Depending on the type of the research reactor, the fuel assembly is also different and is shown in Fig. 9.33.

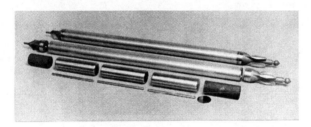

Fig. 9.32. Fuel pellets along with fuel pins used in TRIGA reactor (Printed with permission from [17]).

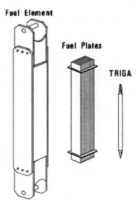

Fig. 9.33. Typical research reactor fuel assembly (Adapted from [18]).

As shown in Fig. 9.34, the assembly of the TRIGA fuel assembly contains a number of other components.

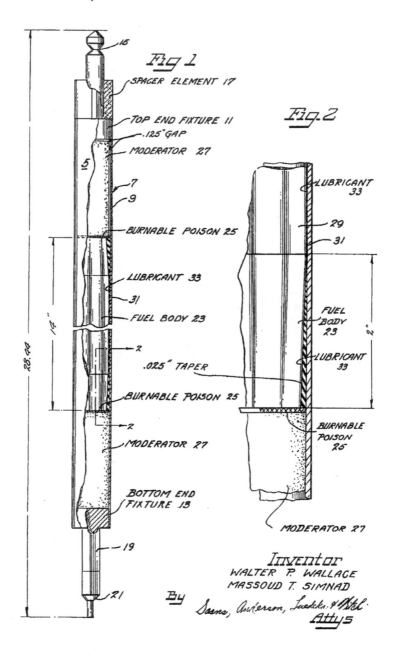

Fig. 9.34. The details of a TRIGA fuel pin design (Adapted from [19]).

9.7.3.3 Light Water Reactor Fuel Assemblies

The fuel assembly for light water reactors starts with the loading of pellets into fuel pins. Several materials have been utilized for these pins, including various alloys of stainless steel and zircoloy. However, zircoloy has become the material of choice due to its high heat transfer capabilities, low absorption cross section and chemical stability when exposed to the coolant and fuel. One end of each pin is welded, and fuel pellets are stacked and a spring holds them in place. This is shown in Fig. 9.35. The pin is evacuated, pressurized with helium and the open end is sealed and welded. PWR fuel pins are pressurized to approximately 2,000 psi and BWR fuel pins are pressurized to approximately half of that. This is due to different operating pressures within the pressure vessels of these reactors.

The loaded fuel pins are arranged into a proper geometry for the respective application. PWR and BWR cores utilize a variety of square fuel pin arrays. A distinct difference lies in the control rod accommodations of the two core designs. PWR assemblies have guide tubes, which allow control rods to slide in and out. BWR control rods are a crucifix shape and are placed in the gaps between assemblies. BWR assemblies are also surrounded by a zircoloy shroud, to prevent coolant mixing between assemblies.

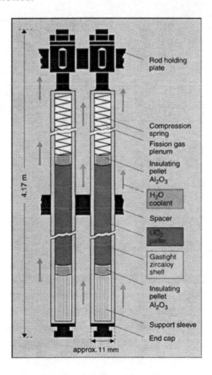

Fig. 9.35. Basic steps in fuel rod and fuel assembly construction (Printed with permission from [20]).

9.7.3.4 CANDU Reactor Fuel Assemblies

CANDU reactors utilize the pressurized water design. The fuel pin design is essentially the same, but the assembly arrangement is different from PWR. A distinct advantage of CANDU reactor design is that it does not require enriched fuel. This drastically reduces the front-end costs associated with fuel production. Natural UO_2 pellets are again stacked into zircoloy pins, with a spring holding them in place. A graphite layer is added to CANDU fuel pins between the pellets and zircoloy pin. The pins are pressurized with helium, welded and leak checked.

Fig. 9.36 shows a CANDU fuel assembly. As can be seen from the figure, it has significantly different arrangement than PWR or BWR fuel assemblies. The circular assemblies are 0.5 m long and are arranged horizontally within the core.

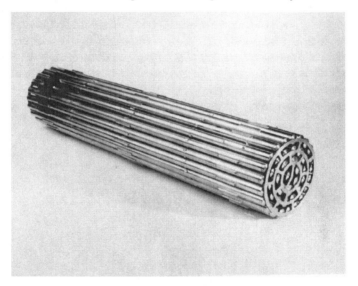

Fig. 9.36. A CANDU fuel assembly (Courtesy of Atomic Energy of Canada Limited, Mississauga, Ontario, Canada).

9.7.3.5 Mixed Oxide (MOX) Fuel Assemblies

The objective of reprocessing is to use separated plutonium as the fuel in the PWR or BWR reactors. Pu-239 is generated in light water reactors, which is a fissile isotope and responsible for approximately 30% of power production in PWR and BWR cores. Spent fuel from these reactors still contains a substantial amount of fissile isotopes, including the Pu-239. During reprocessing of light water spent fuel, Pu-239 is collected and mixed with natural or enriched uranium to produce mixed oxide fuel (MOX). This fuel may contain up to 8% PuO_2 and run in existing PWR cores with up to 30–40% of the MOX fuel. No significant core modifications is necessary [16]. The use of MOX fuel greatly enhances the utilization of reactor fuel beyond the once-through cycle and has been utilized by Japan and France for many years. The United States is currently in the process of licensing a facility for MOX production as a partial solution to the vast supply of spent reactor fuel awaiting disposal.

9.7.3.6 Metal Fuel

Metallic fuel has not been heavily utilized in the past, but may be ready to become more prominent with the development of fast breeder reactors and new pyro-metallurgical procedures, which combine reprocessing and fuel fabrication [21]. Advantages of metal fuel include relative ease of fabrication and its extremely high heat transfer capabilities, as compared with oxide fuels. The main disadvantage of metallic fuels is the low melting temperature, which has been a chief concern of regulatory agencies. However, the very high heat transfer capability of these fuels overcomes the low melting points and ensures fuel stability.

9.7.3.7 Thorium Fuel

Thorium is far more plentiful in nature than uranium. This is especially true in India, where the ratio of thorium to uranium reserves is approximately 6 to 1. India's growth in energy consumption is dramatic, and they have invested substantial resources into finding ways to utilize their thorium reserves. Table 9.8 provides the estimated thorium reserves worldwide at an extraction cost of $80/kg.

Table 9.8. Thorium reserves of various countries [22].

Country	Tonnes	% of world
Australia	452,000	18
USA	400,000	16
Turkey	344,000	14
India	319,000	13
Venezuela	300,000	12
Brazil	221,000	9
Norway	132,000	5
Egypt	100,000	4
Russia	75,000	3
Greenland	54,000	2
Canada	44,000	2
South Africa	18,000	1
Other countries	33,000	1
World total	2,492,000	

RAR + Inferred to USD 80/kg Th
"Source" Data for Australia compiled by [22]

Thorium (Th-232) can be fabricated as an oxide fuel for pellets, micro-particle (for TRISO fuel) or metal fuel. As oxide fuel, thorium can be placed around enriched uranium providing a blanket for the fissile material. The concept is essentially the same as that of a light water breeder reactor. Th-232 is a fertile material and absorbs neutrons to become U-233, which fissions and keeps the chain reaction going. However, Pu-233 is also generated during this process. Also, there are substantial concerns about reprocessing, as U-233 has some intense gamma-emitting daughters with short half-lives.

9.7.3.8 Fuel Cladding

Fuel cladding serves as a protection device for the fuel, provides a barrier for fission products escaping the fuel and acts as a heat transfer surface from the fuel to the coolant. Ideal cladding material must have a small cross section for neutron absorption and interact well with the fuel and coolant. Materials that have been used as cladding include stainless steel and zircoloy, the latter being most heavily utilized for most applications.

Future reactors will need advanced cladding materials, as many of these reactors will subject the fuel to much higher operating temperatures. TRISO fuel, which will be discussed later in this chapter, is well suited for higher operating temperatures. The pyrolytic-carbon layers protect the fuel from the high temperatures and the silicon carbide layer provides the extra fission product barrier. Unlike prior fuel designs, the TRISO fuel cladding is incorporated into the fuel particle itself. The disadvantage of this unique design is the reprocessing challenges this represents, making once-through of TRISO a distinct possibility. Other future reactors concepts do not have cladding at all. Molten fuel concepts have no specific fuel structure and hence, no cladding.

9.8 Uranium Downblending

Uranium used in nuclear weapons is enriched to approximately 93% of U-235, while uranium used in commercial nuclear power plants typically is enriched to 3–5% U-235. Uranium enriched to more than 20% U-235 is called Highly Enriched Uranium (HEU) and can only be used in nuclear weapons and in research reactors. Surplus HEU can, however, be downblended with Low Enriched Uranium (LEU) to make it suitable for use in commercial nuclear fuel.

The downblending only involves uranium. In contrast, plutonium is used for the production of mixed oxide fuel (MOX).

In 1993, the U.S. and Russia signed the US-Russia HEU Agreement, under which Russia was to supply the downblended uranium derived from 500 t of HEU to the USA over a period of about 20 years. While the deliveries under this agreement are still ongoing, the U.S. now have begun downblending some of their own surplus HEU.

9.8.1 Blending Process

In a first step, the HEU and the blendstock have to be converted to the chemical form required for the selected blending process, if not already in the appropriate form. For the downblending process, there exist the following methods:

Mixing of liquids

Uranium in the form of uranyl nitrate hexahydrate (UNH), $UO_2(NO_3)_2 \cdot 6H_2O$, or molten uranium metal are mixed together to form the final mixture.

Mixing of gases

Uranium is converted to uranium hexafluoride (UF_6) and mixed together in the gaseous phase.

The existing commercial downblending facilities in the U.S. (BWXT in Lynchburg, Virginia, and NFS in Erwin, Tennessee) are using the UNH process, while the Russian facilities (in Novouralsk, Seversk, and Zelenogorsk) are using the UF_6 process. Historically, downblending has also been performed at the following DOE nuclear weapons facilities in the U.S.: the Y-12 Plant in Oak Ridge, Tennessee (UNH and molten metal processes), and the Savannah River Site (SRS) in Aiken, South Carolina (UNH process).

After the blending, the material has to be converted to UO_2, before it can be used in the production of commercial nuclear fuel. The blending process has been further described by Arbital and Snider [23].

9.9 Power Production/Burn Up

A nuclear reactor core is composed of a several hundred "assemblies", arranged in a regular array of cells, each cell being formed by a fuel or control rod surrounded, in most designs, by a moderator and coolant, which is water in most reactors.

As the fuel is consumed (under go fission), the old fuel rods must be replaced periodically with fresh ones (this period is called a cycle). The fuel is generally replaced every 18–24 months. Only a part of the assemblies (typically one third) are removed since the fuel depletion is not spatially uniform, and the rest of the fuels are rearranged in the core. The new assemblies are not placed exactly at the same location of the removed ones. Even bundles of the same age may have different burn-up levels, which depends on their previous positions in the core. Thus the available bundles must be arranged in such a way that the yield is maximized, while safety limitations and operational constraints are satisfied. Consequently reactor operators are faced with the so-called optimal fuel reloading problem, which consists in optimizing the rearrangement of all the assemblies, the old and fresh ones, while still maximizing the reactivity of the reactor core so as to maximize fuel burn-up and minimize fuel-cycle costs.

9.10 Types of Nuclear Reactors

9.10.1 Research Reactors

Most research and training reactors are pool type and are not designed for power production. In pool type reactor, the core containing fuel rods and control rods is immersed in an open pool of water. The water under normal pressure acts as neutron moderator, cooling agent and radiation shield. In this type of reactors, operators may work above the reactor safely since water can provide adequate shielding. Pool reactors are used as a source of neutrons and for training, and in rare instances for process heat but not for electricity generation.

Research reactors typically range from 10 kW to 10 MW. Research reactors are simpler than power reactors and operate at lower temperatures. These reactors typically need far less fuel, but more highly enriched uranium, typically up to 20% U-235; although some use 93% U-235. The core is cooled typically by natural or forced convection with water, and a moderator is required to slow down the neutrons and enhance fission. To reduce neutron loss from the core generally a reflector is used. The most common type of research reactor is called TRIGA. A typical TRIGA reactor is shown in Fig. 9.37.

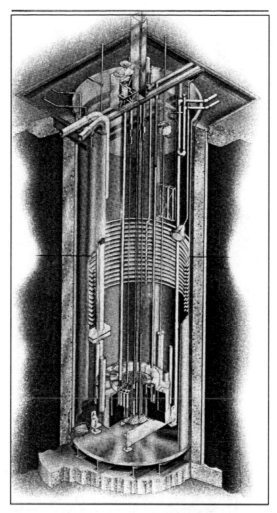

Fig. 9.37. The cutaway view of a 10 kW TRIGA Mark I reactor at San Diego, CA, USA (Printed with permission from [17]).

9.10.2 Commercial Reactors for Electricity Generation

As can be seen from Fig. 9.38, nuclear reactors for electricity generation are continuously undergoing design changes. Several types of the nuclear reactors are in use either commercially or for research purpose. The power reactor deployment timeline is shown in this figure, from past reactors to anticipated future reactors, although it has shifted to the right multiple times.

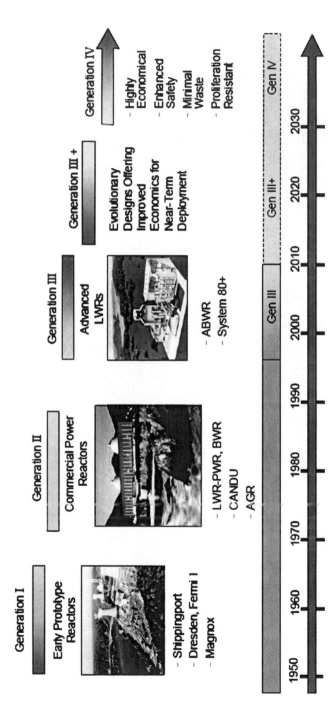

Fig. 9.38. Timeline of deployment of various generations of nuclear power reactor. Adapted from U.S. Department of Energy (2002) A technology roadmap for Generation IV nuclear energy systems. U.S. DOE Nuclear Energy Research Advisory Committee and the Generation IV International Forum, December 2002, GIF-002-00. http://www.ne.doe.gov/GenIV/documents/gen_iv_roadmap.pdf [24].

9.11 Generation II Light Water Reactors

Current nuclear reactors used for power production are Generation II reactors, and 439 reactors are operating worldwide at the present time, with 104 in the U.S. PWRs and BWRs belong to Generation II reactor designs. Several advances have been made over the years in order to increase the efficiency and improve safety. However, the basic design of the reactors has not changed substantially. Although both of these reactor designs utilize water as a moderator and coolant, there are distinct differences between these two reactors.

The light water design necessitates the use of enriched uranium fuel, typically 3–5% U-235. After a typical three cycles of use, the fuel reaches its maximum burn-up and is no longer suitable as fuel for these reactors. The fuel is allowed to decay in spent fuel pools, which provide radiation shielding and decay heat removal capabilities. Once sufficient decay time has been reached, the fuel can be placed in dry storage, sent to a final repository site, or re-processed to retrieve useful fuel isotopes and minimize the high level waste requiring ultimate disposal. Descriptions of Generation II reactors can be found in a number of nuclear engineering text books [25–31] and NRC reactor concept manuals [32–34].

9.11.1 Pressurized Water Reactor (PWR)

Pressurized water reactors (PWR) account for approximately 60% of U.S. operating reactors. The primary coolant system consists of large pumps, which circulate the water through the reactor, where the energy is transferred from the fuel elements to the coolant, then on to a secondary coolant circuit to produce steam. The cooler water is then circulated back to the reactor and the process repeats. Another essential component within the primary coolant system is a high pressure pump, which maintains primary coolant pressure at approximately 2,000 psi. This prevents the coolant from flashing to steam at its normal operating temperature of 600°F .

The steam is used to run both high and low pressure turbines to generate the electricity. The exhausted steam is directed to a condenser, where it is cooled through interactions with a third coolant (usually river or sea water). The condensed secondary water is then pumped back to the steam generator and the cycle repeats.

A schematic flow diagram of a PWR nuclear power plant is shown in Fig. 9.39. The PWR utilizes UO_2 pellets within zircoloy pins. These pins are arranged into a square assembly, typically 14×14 to 18×18 arrays as shown in Fig. 9.40. The assembled core is shown in Fig. 9.41. There are approximately 120–190 of these assemblies in each reactor core. A PWR vessel with the fuel assembly and other accessories is shown in Fig. 9.42.

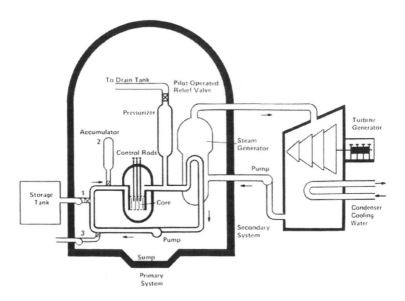

Fig. 9.39. Schematic of a PWR system (Printed with permissionfrom [35]).

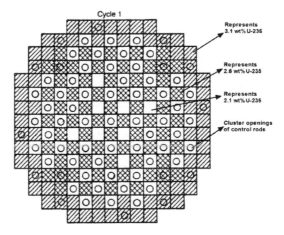

Fig. 9.40. Initial fuel loading of PWR and their arrangements in the fuel assembly (Courtesy of Westinghouse Electric Corp. Printed with permission from [25]).

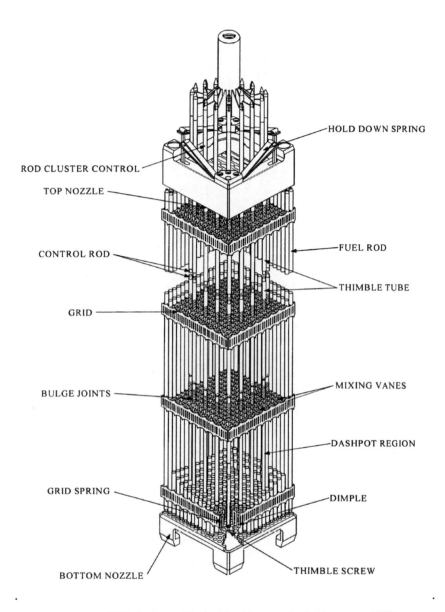

Fig. 9.41. A PWR fuel assembly for 17 × 17 array of rods (Courtesy of [33]).

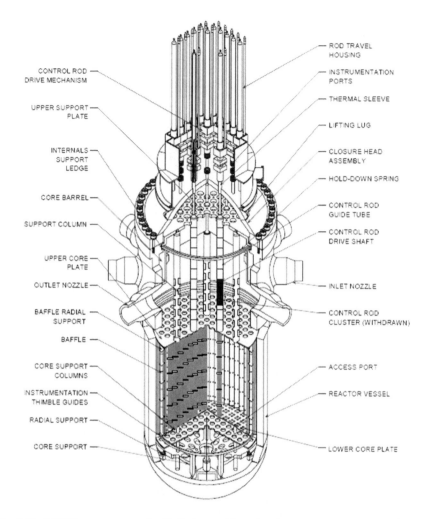

CONTROL ROD
DRIVE MECHANISM

UPPER SUPPORT
PLATE

INTERNALS
SUPPORT
LEDGE

CORE BARREL

SUPPORT COLUMN

UPPER CORE
PLATE

OUTLET NOZZLE

BAFFLE RADIAL
SUPPORT

BAFFLE

CORE SUPPORT
COLUMNS

INSTRUMENTATION
THIMBLE GUIDES

RADIAL SUPPORT

CORE SUPPORT

ROD TRAVEL
HOUSING

INSTRUMENTATION
PORTS

THERMAL SLEEVE

LIFTING LUG

CLOSURE HEAD
ASSEMBLY

HOLD-DOWN SPRING

CONTROL ROD
GUIDE TUBE

CONTROL ROD
DRIVE SHAFT

INLET NOZZLE

CONTROL ROD
CLUSTER (WITHDRAWN)

ACCESS PORT

REACTOR VESSEL

LOWER CORE PLATE

Fig. 9.42. A PWR pressure vessel with fuel assembly and various reactor components (Courtesy of [34]).

9.11.2 Boiling Water Reactor (BWR)

Boiling water reactors (BWR) encompass approximately 40% of operating commercial reactors in the U.S. A schematic diagram of a BWR nuclear power plant is shown in Fig. 9.43. Although water is still utilized as both coolant and moderator, primary coolant is circulated into the pressure vessel and directed to the bottom of the reactor core, similar to PWR designs. However, BWR coolant is at a much lower pressure than their PWR counterparts and mass boiling is allowed in the fuel region. The steam is collected at the top of the pressure vessel, where the quality is increased prior to direct feed into the main turbine for electricity generation. Similarly to a PWR, the exhausted steam is fed through a condenser where secondary water (lake, river, sea water, etc.) cools the primary coolant and condenses it back to a liquid. This liquid is then returned to the pressure vessel and the process repeats.

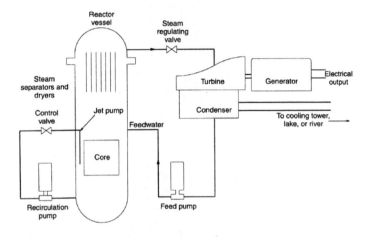

Fig. 9.43. Flow diagram of a BWR direct cycle system (Courtesy of [36]).

BWR fuel consists of oxide pellets in zircoloy pins, arranged in typically 9 × 9 or 10 × 10 arrays, as shown in Fig. 9.44. These assemblies are much smaller and lighter than PWR assemblies, but a far greater number (up to 800) is required to make up the larger BWR core.

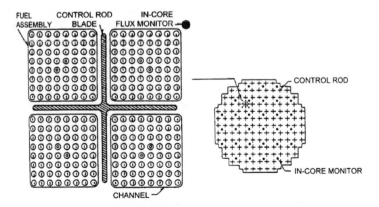

Fig. 9.44. Fuel rod arrangement in a BWR core (Printed with permission from [25]).

The BWR fuel assembly and the cutaway view of the pressure vessel are shown in Figs. 9.45 and 9.46, respectively.

1. Top fuel guide
2. Channel fastener
3. Upper tie plate
4. Expansion spring
5. Locking tab
6. Channel
7. Control rod
8. Fuel rod
9. Spacer
10. Core plate assembly
11. Lower tie plate
12. Fuel support piece
13. Fuel pellets
14. End plug
15. Channel spacer
16. Plenum spring

Fig. 9.45. A BWR fuel assembly (Adapted from [37]).

A set of pumps re-circulates water within the pressure vessel to help pre-heat the incoming coolant water. Start-ups and shut-downs are primarily accomplished by manipulating the control rods into and out of the reactor core, which are inserted through the bottom of the core. In contrast, in a PWR control rods are inserted from the top of the core.

The transfer of heat from one coolant medium to another is a source of efficiency loss in any reactor. Since the BWR design incorporates core cooling and steam generation into one loop, this provides an advantage over the PWR design. BWR pressure vessels are not subjected to higher pressures and do not require the thicker vessel walls, drastically reducing the cost and difficulty of forging. However, these economical advantages are countered by the radiological issues associated with BWR designs. Since the steam is in direct contact with the turbine, it becomes contaminated and requires massive and costly shielding during operation. Accident analysis becomes more challenging as well, since a portion of the primary loop must exit containment to drive the turbine.

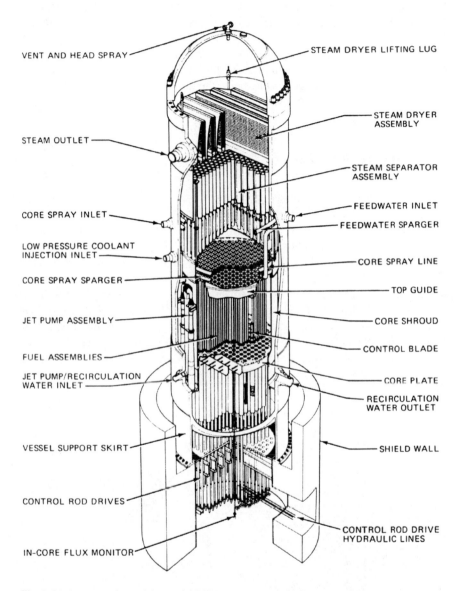

VENT AND HEAD SPRAY

STEAM DRYER LIFTING LUG

STEAM DRYER ASSEMBLY

STEAM OUTLET

STEAM SEPARATOR ASSEMBLY

CORE SPRAY INLET

FEEDWATER INLET

FEEDWATER SPARGER

LOW PRESSURE COOLANT INJECTION INLET

CORE SPRAY LINE

CORE SPRAY SPARGER

TOP GUIDE

JET PUMP ASSEMBLY

CORE SHROUD

FUEL ASSEMBLIES

CONTROL BLADE

JET PUMP/RECIRCULATION WATER INLET

CORE PLATE

RECIRCULATION WATER OUTLET

VESSEL SUPPORT SKIRT

SHIELD WALL

CONTROL ROD DRIVES

CONTROL ROD DRIVE HYDRAULIC LINES

IN-CORE FLUX MONITOR

Fig. 9.46. Cutaway view of the model BWR pressure vessel (Courtesy of GE Nuclear Energy).

A major difference between the PWR and the BWR design is that in the PWR the primary and secondary coolant systems have boundaries between one another, which are not crossed under normal conditions. This allows containment of the PWR primary system within one building and prevents radioactive contamination of the steam turbine. Isolation of the primary coolant within a single containment structure offers an additional benefit with regards to accident analysis, such as a loss of coolant accident.

To reiterate, the PWR design is not without its disadvantages. The pressure vessel of the PWR is thicker and costlier than that of the BWR due to the high pressure of the primary coolant. Additionally, the use of three heat transfer mediums in the PWR lowers the overall plant efficiency.

9.11.3 CANDU Reactors

Heavy water (D_2O) is an extremely good moderator; it slows down neutrons without absorbing them. This efficient use of neutron inventory allows the use of natural uranium to continue the chain reaction, where it otherwise would not be possible with the use of other moderating materials.

As mentioned previously, Canada has a vast supply of uranium deposits and is one of the world's leading suppliers. Canada has never pursued a nuclear weapons program and thus did not feel the need to build a fuel enrichment facility. However, during WWII, Canada assisted the U.S. by developing the first heavy-water moderated reactor in Montreal, which could be used to produce plutonium. After the war ended, Canada continued to develop the heavy water moderated reactor, and it has now evolved into a pressurized heavy water moderated reactor, called the CANada Deuterium Uranium (CANDU) reactor. The reactor system is shown in Fig. 9.47.

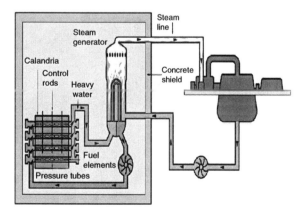

Fig. 9.47. Layout of a CANDU reactor system (Printed with permission from [38]).

The CANDU design is similar to the PWR design in many respects. It is also pressurized to prevent boiling of the coolant and steam generators convert secondary coolant into steam for the turbine. In a CANDU reactor the fuel assembly is horizontally mounted, allowing for fuel bundles to be replaced during operation without any need to shut down the reactor completely. These bundles consist of 37 zircoloy fuel rods, containing uranium oxide pellets. Twelve bundles lie end to end in each channel, and are simply forced out of one end by new bundles being inserted into the opposite end. The inside view of a CANDU is shown in Fig. 9.48.

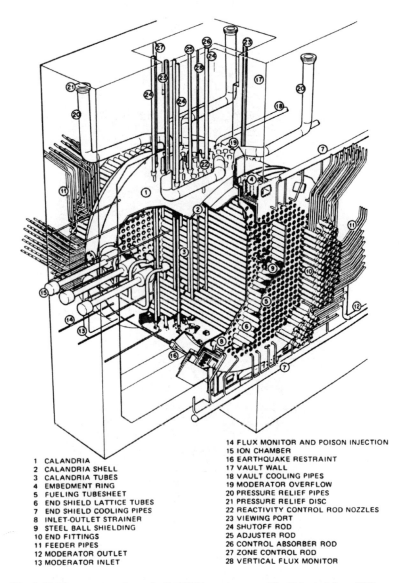

1	CALANDRIA	14	FLUX MONITOR AND POISON INJECTION
2	CALANDRIA SHELL	15	ION CHAMBER
3	CALANDRIA TUBES	16	EARTHQUAKE RESTRAINT
4	EMBEDMENT RING	17	VAULT WALL
5	FUELING TUBESHEET	18	VAULT COOLING PIPES
6	END SHIELD LATTICE TUBES	19	MODERATOR OVERFLOW
7	END SHIELD COOLING PIPES	20	PRESSURE RELIEF PIPES
8	INLET-OUTLET STRAINER	21	PRESSURE RELIEF DISC
9	STEEL BALL SHIELDING	22	REACTIVITY CONTROL ROD NOZZLES
10	END FITTINGS	23	VIEWING PORT
11	FEEDER PIPES	24	SHUTOFF ROD
12	MODERATOR OUTLET	25	ADJUSTER ROD
13	MODERATOR INLET	26	CONTROL ABSORBER ROD
		27	ZONE CONTROL ROD
		28	VERTICAL FLUX MONITOR

Fig. 9.48. The cutaway view of a CANDU reactor assembly (Adapted from [39]).

CANDU technology remains popular within Canada and has been partially adopted in India due to its ability to utilize thorium fuels. Flexible fuel capabilities are one of the chief advantages of this design. Additionally, the ability to re-fuel during operation pushes capacity factors much higher than is usually seen in PWR and BWR designs. Utilizing natural uranium eliminates enrichment costs, drastically reducing the price of fuel. The biggest drawback of the CANDU design is the high cost of heavy water. The CANDU system is shown in Fig. 9.49.

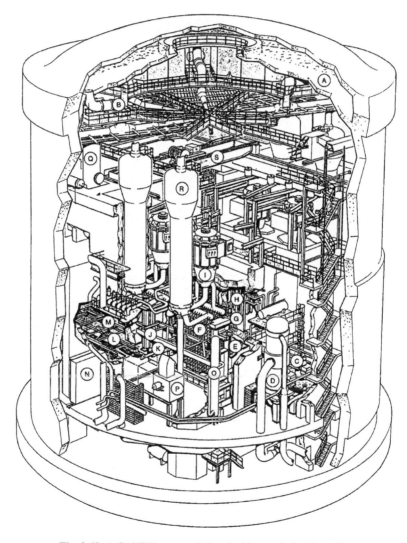

Fig. 9.49. A CANDU reactor (Printed with permission from [35]).

9.11.4 RBMK Reactors

The Russian water-cooled, graphite moderated reactors were developed in the former Soviet Union and 27 have been built and operated (Fig. 9.50). RBMK cores have some similarities to Advanced Gas Reactor (AGR) and BWR designs. The overall layout is similar to an AGR, but each fuel assembly is housed in a pressurized tube, containing light water as a coolant. Despite the pressure, the coolant is allowed to boil and directly feeds the turbine. The fuel is made up of 18 zircoloy rods, containing enriched uranium oxide, to make up a 3.5 m long bundle [16]. The fuel bundles are stacked in the core.

Negative void temperature coefficients are inherent in the design of most nuclear reactors and add a large degree of safety. A detailed analysis of the reactor safety system has been given by IAEA [40]. As temperature rises within the core, the reactor essentially shuts itself down as the void co-efficient takes on a greater influence on core reactivity. This is not the case with the RBMK design, as graphite has a positive void co-efficient and any increase in temperature adds positive reactivity to the core. This design instability became infamous in 1986, when Chernobyl reactor number 4 catastrophically failed, during planned testing, in which operators had disregarded critical operational procedures and safety systems were over-ridden. Since then, the RBMK design has been modified to prevent a similar occurrence. The most significant change has been utilization of higher enriched fuels to help absorb thermal neutrons and create a negative void feedback.

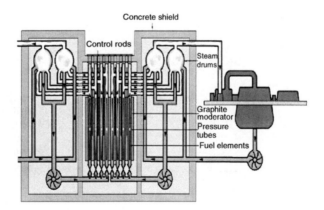

Fig. 9.50. A RBMK reactor system (Printed with permission from [38]).

9.12 Generation III & III+ Reactors

Generation III and III+ reactors are the next generation of reactors, some of which have already been built and are operating worldwide. Industry experience has prompted drastic alterations in the design, construction, licensing and operation of nuclear power plants. In the past, reactors were built to suit individual companies and even individual sites. This will no longer be the case, as each of the next generation designs will be built more modularly, requiring the customers to prepare their sites to suit the reactor design. The shift in design philosophy is intended to reduce construction time and costs, stream-line licensing procedures for regulators and standardize operational procedures.

Many of these new designs have incorporated passive or inherent safety features, some requiring no active controls or operator action to mitigate design accidents. This important characteristic will allow the new reactors to operate more efficiently and produce more power than their predecessors. Additionally, these reactors have been designed for longer operational lifetimes (60 years) and higher fuel burnup. The Generation III and III+ reactors are listed in Table 9.9.

Table 9.9. Generation III and III+ reactors.

Reactor Type	Abbreviation Used	Design life	Vendor
Advanced Boiling Water Reactor	ABWR		General Electric, USA
Advanced Passive-1000	AP1000	60	Westinghouse Electric Co., USA
US Evolutionary Power Reactor	USEPR	60	Areva, France
US Advanced Pressurized Water Reactor	USAPWR	60	Mitsubishi Heavy Industries, Japan
Economic Simplified Boiling Water Reactor	ESBWR		General Electric, USA
Advanced CANDUS Reactor	CANDUACR		Atomic Energy Canada Ltd., Canada
International Reactor Innovative and Secure	IRIS		International Team
System 80+	System 80+		Westinghouse Electric Co., USA

9.12.1 Advanced Light Water Reactors

Several different designs of advanced light water reactor are in the process of being deployed worldwide. A focus will be made on the most likely designs to be deployed and the regions of the world in which they will be located.

Utilities within the U.S. have several designs under consideration, although none have yet been built. NRG Energy and South Texas Project are set to begin construction on the first two new generation reactors in the U.S, and already submitted the combined license application to the NRC. These will be of the advanced boiling water reactor (ABWR) designed by General Electric. This design was selected mainly due to operational experience of the four similar units that have been operating in Japan since 1996, with four more under construction. This is a proven design, which will dramatically reduce the construction time and enhance operational confidence. The ABWR (Figs. 9.51 and 9.52) features internal circulating pumps for improved safety, fully digital control systems and demonstrated reduction in construction and operational costs [41].

ABWR Plant Layout

1. Reactor Pressure Vessel
2. Reactor Internal pumps
3. Fine Motion Control Rod Drives
4. Main Steam Isolation Valves
5. Safety/Relief Valves (SRV)
6. SRV Quenchers
7. Lower Drywell Equipment Platform
8. Horizontal Vents
9. Suppression pool
10. Lower Drywell Flooder
11. Reinforced Containment
    Concrete Vessel
12. Hydraulic Controls Units
13. Control Rod Drive Hydraulic
    System Pumps
14. RHR Heat Exchanger
15. RHR Pump
16. HPCF Pump

17. RCIC Steam Turbine and pump
18. Diesel Generator
19. Standby Gas Treatment Filter
    and Fans
20. Spent Fuel Storage Pool
21. Refueling Platform
22. Shield Blocks
23. Steam Dryer and Separator
    Storage pool
24. Bridge Crane
25. Main Steam Lines
26. Feedwater Lines

27. Main Control Room
28. Turbine-Generator
29. Moisture Separator Reheater
30. Combustion Turbine Generator
31. Air Compressor and Dryers
32. Switchyard

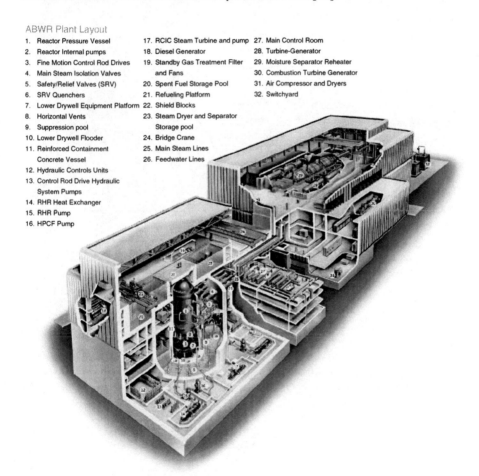

Fig. 9.51. The layout of an ABWR power plant (Courtesy of GE Hitachi Nuclear Energy. www.ge-energy.com/nuclear).

Advanced Boiling Water Reactor Assembly

1. Vessel Flange and Closure Head
2. Vent and Head Spray
3. Steam Outlet Flow Restrictor
4. RPV Stabilizer
5. Feedwater Nozzle
6. Forged Shell Rings
7. Vessel Support Skirt
8. Vessel Bottom Head
9. RIP Penetrations
10. Thermal Insulation
11. Core Shroud
12. Core Plate
13. Top Guide
14. Fuel Supports
15. Control Rod Drive Housings
16. Control Rod Guide Tubes
17. In Core Housing
18. In-Core Insturment Guide Tubes and Stabilizers
19. Feedwater Sparger
20. High Pressure Core Flooder (HPCF) Sparger
21. (HPCF) Coupling
22. Low Pressure Flooder (LPFL)
23. Shutdown Cooling Oulet
24. Steam Separators
25. Steam Dryer
26. Reactor Internal Pumps (RIP)
27. RIP Motor Casing
28. Core and RIP Differential Pressure Line
29. Fine Motion Control Rod Drives
30. Fuel Assemblies
31. Control Rods
32. Local Power Range Monitor

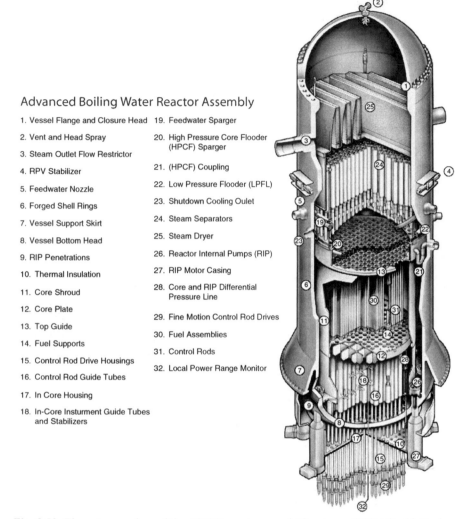

Fig. 9.52. The cutaway view of the ABWR reactor vessel (Courtesy of GE Hitachi Nuclear Energy. www.gepower.com/prod_serv/products/nuclear_energy/en/downloads/abwr_callouts.pdf).

9.12.2 Advanced Passive-1000 Reactor (AP-1000)

Westinghouse has received final design certification from the NRC for its Advanced Passive-1000 (AP-1000) reactor, the first Generation III+ design to do so. The AP-1000 design has improved upon proven PWR technology to include enhanced safety features, as the most serious accidents require no operator action or AC power to shut down the plant or remove decay heat. This AP-1000 (Fig. 9.53) is an 1,100 MWe, scaled-up version of the AP-600 originally designed [42–47]. The steam generators (Fig. 9.54) are located within the containment building. The additional safety features shown in Fig. 9.55 makes it very attractive among other reactor designs.

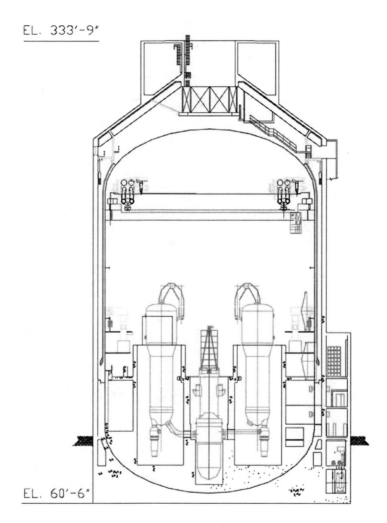

EL. 333'-9"

EL. 60'-6"

Fig. 9.53. AP 1000 reactor pressure vessel assembly (Printed with permission from [47]).

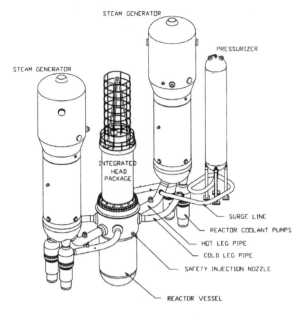

Fig. 9.54. Steam generator assembly of AP1000 (Printed with permission from [47]).

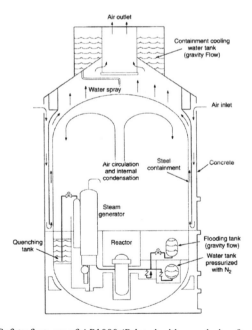

Fig. 9.55. Safety features of AP1000 (Printed with permission from [35]).

9.12.3 Advanced Pressurized Water Reactor (APWR)

Mitsubishi has designed a large 1,700 MWe Advanced PWR (APWR), which boasts one of the largest outputs of any commercial reactor designs to date and is shown in Fig. 9.56. This plant is a larger and more efficient version of the PWR designs currently in operation throughout the U.S. An application for standardized design certification was submitted to the NRC in December, 2007 and is awaiting approval. The fuel assembly of APWR is shown in Fig. 9.57, and the pressure vessel is shown in Fig. 9.58.

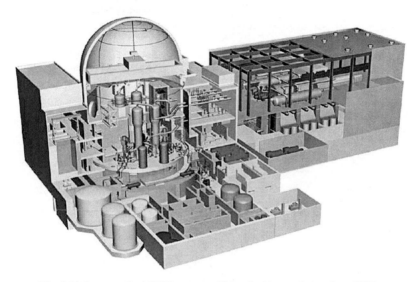

Fig. 9.56. Layout of a APWR systems (Printed with permission from [48]).

9.12.4 Evolutionary Power Reactor (EPR)

France has become the nuclear industry leader over the past two decades. The European Pressurized Reactor (EPR), shown in Fig. 9.59, was designed by Areva, which is a 1,700 MWe unit and uses four redundant safety loops and passive systems. Two of these plants are currently under construction in Europe and more are scheduled for construction worldwide. AREVA has submitted for regulator

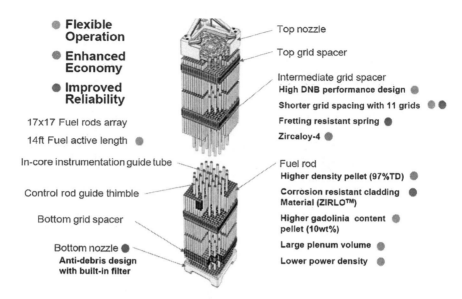

Fig. 9.57. Fuel assembly of USAPWR (Printed with permission from [48]).

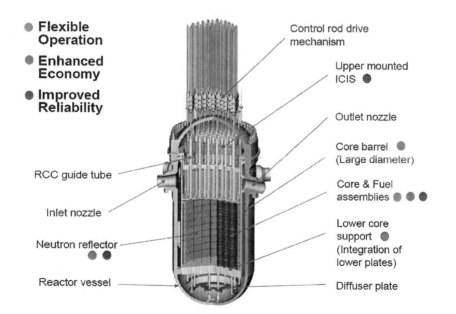

Fig. 9.58. The cutout view of US APWR designed by Mitsubishi Heavy Industries for US market (Printed with permission from [48]).

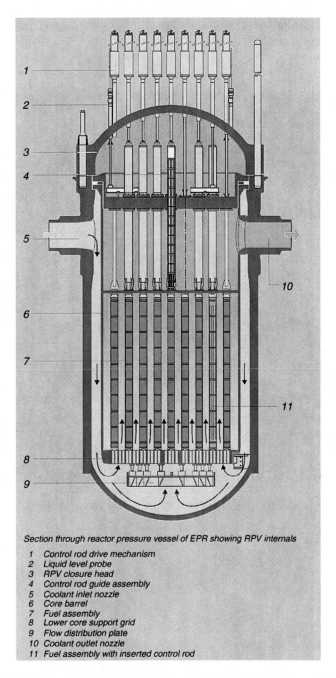

Section through reactor pressure vessel of EPR showing RPV internals

1   Control rod drive mechanism
2   Liquid level probe
3   RPV closure head
4   Control rod guide assembly
5   Coolant inlet nozzle
6   Core barrel
7   Fuel assembly
8   Lower core support grid
9   Flow distribution plate
10 Coolant outlet nozzle
11 Fuel assembly with inserted control rod

Fig. 9.59. Cut out of the EPR pressure vessel. US EPR (Adapted from [49]).

approval in several countries including the USA. This modified design for the
USA has been renamed as the Evolutionary Power Reactor (EPR). The layout for
an USEPR is shown in Fig. 9.60 and the cutaway of the reactor to be used in the
USEPR is shown in Fig. 9.61.

Fig. 9.60. The layout of the US-EPR power plant (Adapted from [49]).

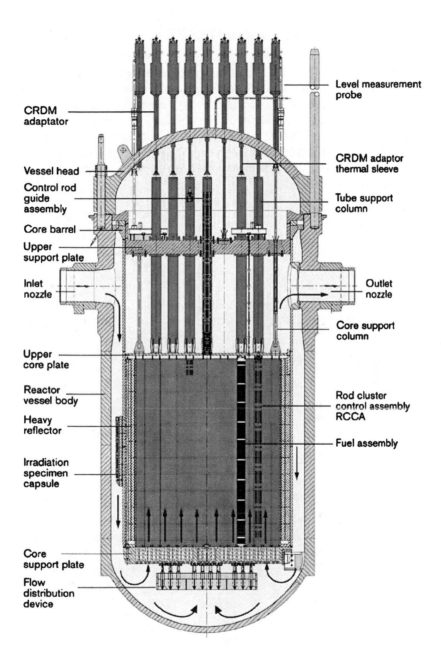

Fig. 9.61. The reactor pressure vessel for US-EPR (Adapted from [49]).

9.12.5 Economic & Simplified Boiling Water Reactor (ESBWR)

General Electric has designed a 1,390 MWe reactor, called the Economic & Simplified Boiling Water Reactor (ESBWR) to compete with other Generation III+ reactors [50–53]. The technical data of an ESBWR system is given in Table 9.10. The ESBWR is designed with natural circulation cooling and will have better safety features then the current BWR (Figs. 9.62–9.64). A comparison of various safety features between BWR and ESBWR is given in Table 9.11. This reactor is behind the ABWR and AP-1000 in terms of projected deployment, but orders have been already placed for the ESBWR.

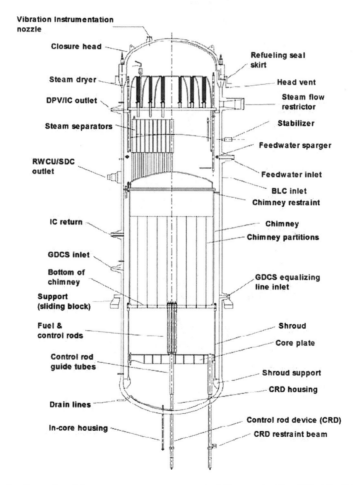

Fig. 9.62. A schematic of the reactor pressure vessel of Economic Simplified Boiling Water Reactor (ESBWR) (Printed with permission from [51]).

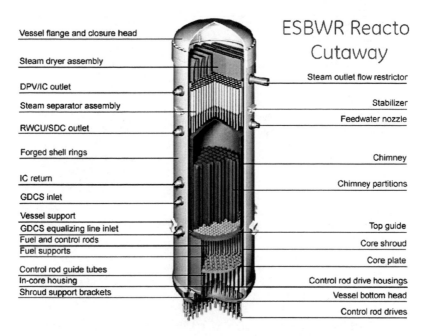

Fig. 9.63. Cutaway of ESBWR reactor (Courtesy of GE Hitachi Nuclear Energy).

Table 9.10. ESBWR, Technical fact sheet

Parameters	Values
Plant life (years)	60
Thermal power	4,500 MW
Electrical power	1,560 MW
Plant efficiency	34.7 %
Reactor type	Boiling water reactor
Core	
Fuel type	Enriched UO_2
Fuel enrichment	4.2% [c]
No. of fuel bundles	1,132
Coolant	Light water
Moderator	Light water
Operating cycle length[a]	12–24 months
Outage duration[b]	~14 days
Percent fuel replaced at refueling	See footnote [d]
Average fuel burnup at discharge	~50,000 MWd/MT
Number of Steam Lines	4
Number of feedwater trains	2
Containment Parameters	
Design temperature	340°F
Design pressure	45 psig

(Continued)

Table 9.10. (Continued)

Parameters	Values
Reactor Parameters	
Design temperature	575°F
Operating temperature	550°F
Design pressure	1,250 psig
Nominal operating pressure	1,040 psia
Feedwater & Turbine Parameters	
Turbine Inlet/Outlet temperature	543/93°F
Turbine Inlet/Outlet pressure	985/0.8 psia
Feedwater temperature	420°F
Feedwater pressure	1,050 psia
Feedwater flow	4.55×104 gpm
Steam mass flow rate	19.31×10^6 lbs/h
Yearly waste generated	
High level (spent fuel)	50 t
Intermediate level (spent resins, filters, etc.) and	1,765 ft^3
Low Level (compactables/non-compactables)	
Waste	

[a]Days of operation between outages; [b]For refueling only
[c] For a 24 month cycle; [d]20% for a 12 month cycle, 42% for a 24 month cycle
Source: Reference [53].

Table 9.11. A comparison of safety features between BWR and ESBWR.

Function	Current BWR reactors safety systems	ESBWR	
		Safety systems	Nonsafety
High-pressure inventory control	Motor and/or steam driven pumps with some vessel inventory loss and containment heat up	Isolation condensers conserve coolant inventory and avoid containment heat up	Multiple motor-driven pumps
Depressurization and low pressure inventory control	Automatic depressurization system with complex cooling water systems	Diverse/redundant automatic depressurization system using pool with gravity flow for inventory control	Diesel generator–driven pumps
Containment decay Heat removal	Diesel generator–driven pumped systems with complex cooling water systems and ultimate heat sink	Completely passive condensers with simple transfer of heat to pools that can boil off to the atmosphere	DG-driven pumps and cooling water
Fission product control and off-site doses	Double containment barriers and motor-driven filter and purge systems	Numerous in-containment natural removal mechanisms	HVAC systems
Severe accident features	Inserting or igniters for hydrogen control and other features to limit corium impact. Containment vent added as backup in ABWR. Lower drywell flooder. External reactor building connection to RPV.	Inert containment	Core catcher and passive lower drywell flooder to limit corium impact and the ability to easily connect portable systems

Source: Reference [52].

9.12.6 International Reactor Innovative & Secure (IRIS) Reactor

International Reactor Innovative & Secure (IRIS) reactor is designed by Westing-house as a modular 335 MWe PWR. The IRIS pressure vessel contains the steam generators and coolant circulating pumps, adding significant accident mitigation features to the design (Fig. 9.64). The design certification for the IRIS is expected in 2010, with a first of a kind plant built by 2015 [54–57].

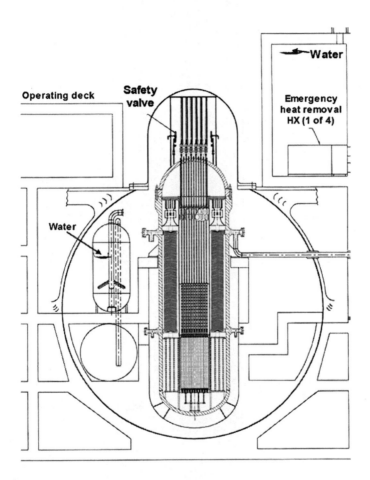

Fig. 9.64. The design of the steel containment building for IRIS system (Printed with permission from [56]).

The layout of the pressure vessel and the power plant are shown in Fig. 9.65 and Fig. 9.66, respectively.

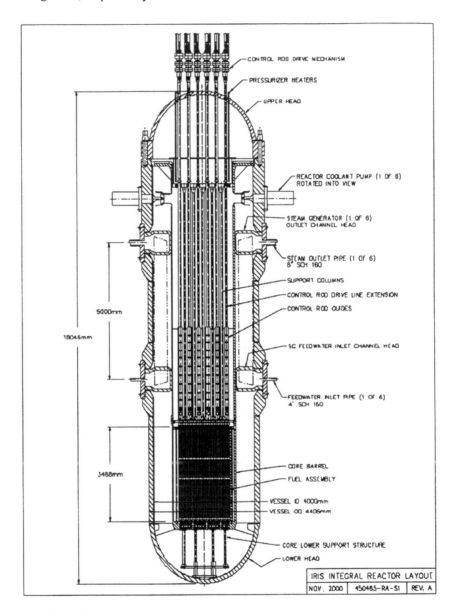

Fig. 9.65. Layout of reactor pressure vessel of IRIS reactor (Adapted from [57]).

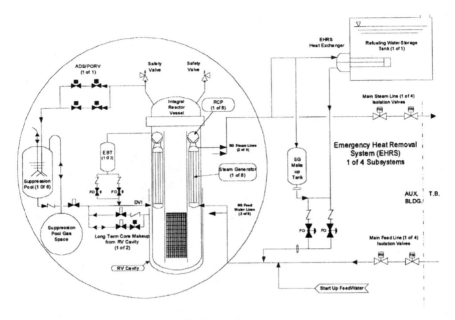

Fig. 9.66. Lyaout of a IRIS plant (Printed with permission from [56]).

9.12.7 APR-1400

South Korea's regulatory agency awarded design certification to the APR-1400 in 2003. This 1,450 MWe design evolved from a U.S. design developed in the 1900's, known as the US System 80+. This design incorporates the common attributes of generation III and III+ reactors in that it utilizes burnable poisons within the fuel to increase burn-up to 60 GWD/t, longer plant lifetime and increased safety features.

9.12.8 VVER-1200

Russia signed an agreement with Natsionalna Elektricheska Kompania and Atom-stroyexport in January 2008 to build two new AES-92 plants in Bulgaria, utilizing VVER-1000 reactors, with a combined output of 2,000 MWe. These reactors are also being built in China and India. Russia has improved upon this design to create the VVER-1200, which has an output of 1150–1200 MWe with higher efficiency and longer anticipated lifetime. Russia is projecting to begin operating these reactors in 2012 and is hoping to connect an additional 20–25 of these reactors to the grid by 2020 [58].

9.13 Advanced Heavy Water Reactors

Canada has designed an upgraded version of the CANDU reactor, called Advanced Canada reactor (ACR), and is shown in Figs. 9.67 and 9.68 that will be a 700 MWe light water-cooled, heavy water-moderated reactor. The ACR will utilize slightly enriched (approximately 2.1%) natural uranium [16]. This is expected to improve the efficiency of the plant and fuel burn-up, reducing the waste generation.

These reactors will also have higher burn-ups than light water reactors and are capable of utilizing spent fuel from a PWR or a BWR. However, the projected 10% increase in burn-up of the light water reactor fuels, may not justify the elaborate systems needed to handle the extremely radioactive feed material. The versatility of the ACR design also includes the ability to employ MOX, thorium and actinides, which is of significant interest to countries housing large stockpiles of plutonium, such as Russia or have large reserves of thorium, such as India.

Due to the light water-cooling of the reactor, some of the negative aspects of the original CANDU design are avoided, such as the constant problem with tritium leaks. Additionally, a slightly negative void co-efficient will be achieved with this design, drastically improving overall reactor safety. As with Generation III+ designs, passive safety features have been included in this design, greatly increasing the margin of safety. Several countries are in the process of certifying this design, such as Canada and the United Kingdom. Several other countries, such as Japan, India, Russia and the U.S. have expressed varying levels of interest in this design.

9.14 Fast Reactors

In order to close the fuel cycle, fast reactors may be essential. Fast reactors are capable of either breeding fissile materials from fertile fuel or burning transuranics (TRU). Fissile Pu and U from nuclear weapons and spent fuel can be utilized for power production. This will also reduce proliferation risk of these materials. Fast reactors are currently being utilized worldwide for research, energy production and waste burning.

Fast reactors are designed differently from thermal reactors. They do not have a moderator, as the slowing of neutrons prior to fission is not required. The coolant for these reactors is a liquid metal, such as sodium, further preventing neutron thermalization. In breeder reactors, the fast neutrons interact with the outer U-238 blanket, which mainly captures the neutrons to eventually form Pu-239, which is fissile. As a result of these interactions, a higher abundance of fissile material results than was present initially, hence the term "breeder reactor". In contrast, burner reactors do not have the fertile blanket, but simply burn off the actinides from the fuel, for example Pu-239 from weapons materials.

As shown in Table 9.12, a number of countries have operating experiences with fast reactors. Japan, France and Russia have dedicated vast resources into these programs, with a notable increase in activity in recent years. Russia has begun construction on the first BN-800 fast reactor, which is an improved version of the BN-600, currently on-line and supplying the most reliable electricity to Russia's grid than any other reactor [5].

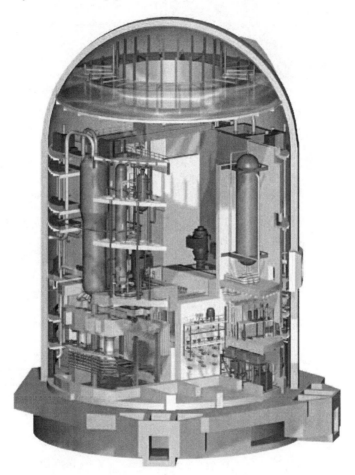

Fig. 9.67. Advanced CANDU reactor (ACR) building curaway (Courtesy of Atomic Energy of Canada Ltd., Mississauga, Ontaria, Canada. www.aecl.ca).

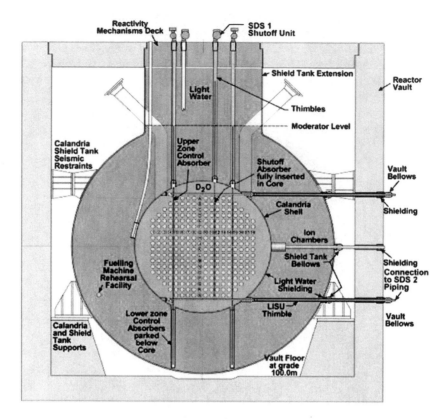

Fig. 9.68. ACR Calandria and shield tank assembly (Printed with permission from [59]).

Table 9.12. Fast neutron reactors.

Reactor location	MWe	MW (thermal)	Operation
USA			
EBR 1	0.2		1951–63
EBR 2	20		1963–94
Fermi 1	66		1963–72
SEFOR		20	1969–72
Fast Flux TF		400	1980–93
UK			
Dounreay FR	15		1959–77
Protoype FR	270		1974–94

Reactor location	MWe	MW (thermal)	Operation
France			
Rapsodie		40	1966–82
Phenix*	250		1973–
Superphenix 1	1240		1985–98
Germany			
KNK 2	21		1977–91
India			
FBTR		40	1985–
Japan			
Joyo		140	1978–
Monju	280		1994–96–?
Kazakhstan			
BN 350*	135		1972–99
Russia			
BR 5/10		5 /10	1959–71, 1973–
BOR 60	12		1969–
BN 600*	560		1980–

Source: Reference [5].

India has made tremendous progress with their fast breeder program, in hopes of successfully sustaining a thorium fuel cycle. A 500 MWe prototype fast breeder began construction in 2004, in Kalpakkam, and is anticipated to begin operation in 2010. This reactor will be fueled with uranium plutonium carbide, with a thorium blanket to breed U-233.

9.15 Gas-Cooled Reactors

Gas-cooled reactors are another design that is likely to be a part of future generation reactors. In the United Kingdom, these reactors are already used commercially. The current versions are graphite moderated and cooled by CO_2. The first generation of gas-cooled reactors utilizes natural uranium metal fuel in a magnesium alloy, hence the name Magnox. The second generation design is called the advanced gas reactor (AGR), which utilizes 2.5% to 3.5% enriched uranium oxide fuel in stainless steel cans [16]. The fuel assembly is shown in Fig. 9.69. The schematic diagram of an AGR based power plant is shown in Fig. 9.70.

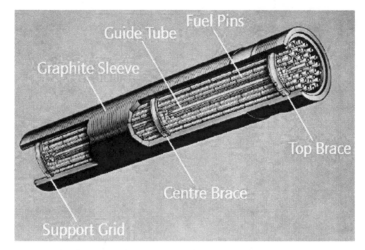

Fig. 9.69. AGR fuel assembly (Courtesy of Westinghouse Electric Corporation).

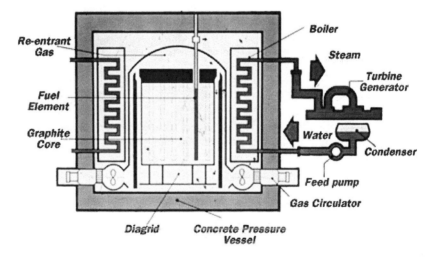

Fig. 9.70. A schematic diagram of the AGR system (Courtesy of British Energy Group).

9.16 Generation IV Reactors

Generation II, III, and III+ reactors are designed to provide a secure and low cost electricity supply to the base load electricity need. However, concerns over energy resource availability, climate change, air quality, green house gas emissions, and energy security provide opportunities for the use of nuclear energy to a broader market. Generation IV systems are intended to be responsive to the needs of this broad range of market in various nations and users. Generation IV reactors can be designed for small output (200 MWe and higher) and as a modular unit with 60–80 years lifetime. Also, Generation IV reactors can be used for hydrogen production. Generation IV systems aim to reduce capital cost, enhance nuclear safety, minimize the generation of nuclear waste, and further reduce the risk of weapons materials proliferation.

In 2001, the Generation IV International Forum (GIF) was established, made up of countries with nuclear power capabilities or interest in future nuclear power utilization. The countries that are participating in the GIF are Argentina, Brazil, Canada, Euratom, France, Japan, South Korea, South Africa, Switzerland, United Kingdom, USA, Russia, and China. The goal of this organization was to identify future reactor designs which would meet four goals; nuclear sustainability, competitiveness, safety & reliability and proliferation resistance. These are shown below in details [24].

Sustainability-1
Generation IV nuclear energy systems will provide sustainable energy generation that meets clean air objectives and provides long-term availability of systems and effective fuel utilization for worldwide energy production.

Sustainability-2
Generation IV nuclear energy systems will minimize and manage their nuclear waste and notably reduce the long-term stewardship burden, thereby improving protection for the public health and the environment.

Economics-1
Generation IV nuclear energy systems will have a clear life-cycle cost advantage over other energy sources.

Economics-2
Generation IV nuclear energy systems will have a level of financial risk comparable to other energy projects.

Safety and Reliability-1
Generation IV nuclear energy systems operations will excel in safety and reliability.

Safety and Reliability-2
Generation IV nuclear systems will have a very low likelihood and degree of reactor core damage.

Safety and Reliability-3
Generation IV nuclear energy systems will eliminate the need for offsite emergency response.

Proliferation Resistance and Physical Protection
Generation IV nuclear energy systems will increase the assurance that they are very unattractive and the least desirable route for diversion or theft of weapons-usable materials, and provide increased physical protection against acts of terrorism.

Six reactors have since been identified by the GIF [24] for detailed study. Some of their operating conditions are shown in Table 9.13.

Table 9.13. Operating parameters of Generation IV reactors.

System	Neutron spectrum	Coolant	Temp.°C	Fuel cycle	Size (MWe)
VHTR (Very high temperature gas reactor)	Thermal	Helium	900–1000	Open	250–300
SFR (Sodium-cooled fast reactor)	Fast	Sodium	550	Closed	30–150, 300–1500, 1000–2000
SCWR (Supercritical water cooled reactor)	Thermal/fast	Water	510–625	Open/closed	300–700 1000–1500
GFR (Gas-cooled fast reactor)	Fast	Helium	850	Closed	1200
LFR (Lead-cooled fast reactor)	Fast	Lead	480–800	Closed	20–180, 300–1200, 600–1000
MSR (Molten salt reactor)	Epithermal	Fluoride salts	700–800	Closed	1000

These reactors share some common attributes and each has their own advantages and disadvantages. All six reactor designs operate at much higher temperatures than those currently operating. This factor alone presents significant challenges to reactor designers. However, as technology progresses, the material problems associated with these designs can be overcome. Additional challenges with regards to financial competitiveness can be overcome as well, once multiple reactors are built, generating experience and increased efficiency. Sustainability is another significant challenge, as operation and electricity generation must be balanced with proliferation resistance. Each of the six designs identified by the GIF must address these issues. The remainder of this section will take a closer look at the six potential generation IV reactor designs and where they might fit into the overall nuclear energy plan.

9.16.1 Gas-Cooled Fast Reactor (GFR)

The design of GFR will be drawn from the GT-MHR design. Helium will be used to cool the reactor core, and the hot helium gas from the reactor will be used in a Brayton cycle to run a gas turbine for higher efficiency. The GFR will utilize a single combined turbine and compressor shaft, and will operate in the fast neutron spectrum, which has the ability to burn fissile and fertile fuels by two orders of magnitude greater than thermal spectrum gas reactors. The design concept of a GFR is shown in Fig. 9.71 and the design parameters are given in Table 9.14.

The GFR reactors will use a special type of fuel called TRISO (TRIstructural ISOtropic). The manufacturing of TRISO particles is discussed later. These particles are extremely hardy, and their reprocessing is going to be challenging. It is expected that the silicon carbide layer that will protect the fuel and provide a barrier for fission products, but may be a problem in reprocessing of the spent fuel. Since closing the fuel cycle is so critical to sustaining nuclear power well into the future, finding fuels which can be reprocessed is essential. The GIF has identified some candidate fuels, which include tightly packed (U, Pu) carbide kernels in a ceramic-ceramic (cercer) arrangement. An alternative option involves larger (U, Pu) carbide kernels with thinner coatings, or cermet fuel. These fuels are still in the initial stages of development and a final decision has not been made. Criteria for successful fuel selection includes the ability to withstand temperatures up to 1,400°C, burn-up to 250 GWD/MTHM, and radiation resiliency up to 100–150 dpa [24]. The timeline associated with this design, set by the GIF, involves the development of laboratory-scale demonstration unit by 2012 and a proto-type by 2025 [60–67].

Table 9.14. A summary of design parameters for GFR.

Reactor parameters	Reference value
Reactor power	600 MWth
Net plant efficiency (direct cycle helium)	48%
Coolant inlet/outlet temperature and pressure	490°C/850°C at 90 bar
Average power density	100 MWth/m3
Reference fuel compound	UPuC/SiC (70/30%) with about 20% Pu content
Volume fraction, Fuel/Gas/SiC	50/40/10%
Conversion ratio	Self-sufficient
Burnup, Damage	5% FIMA; 60 dpa

Source: Reference [24].

9.16.2 Lead-Cooled Fast Reactor (LFR)

The design of LFR, shown in Fig. 9.72, is based on Russian naval and developing (BREST) fast reactor technologies. The operating parameters for a LFR is given in Table 9.15. The LFR reactors can be designed in three different sizes; two of which are for normal in-place utilization and the smallest one would be used as

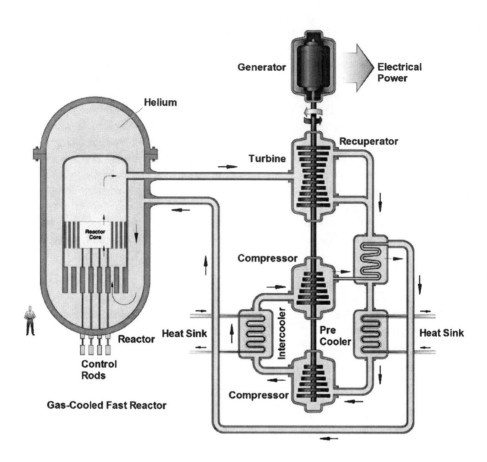

Fig. 9.71. The basic schematic diagram of gas-cooled fast reactor (GFR) system for power generation (Adapted from [24]).

a "battery" offering 15–20 year service and replacement as a cartridge rather than refueling. This could be very attractive to countries without their own nuclear program. The LFR is a fast breeder reactor, cooled by lead or a lead-bismuth mixture. The reactor would have full actinide recycle capability and effectively burn metal alloy or nitride fuel. This would eventually include back-end fuel cycle waste, such as spent light water fuel, zirconium and TRU. Due to the high reactor outlet temperatures (550–880°C), the LFR has the potential for use as hydrogen production unit.

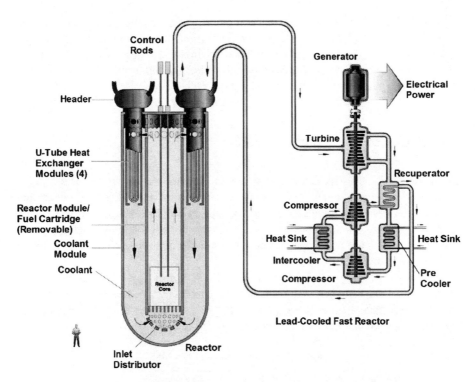

Fig. 9.72. Schematic diagram of a LFR reactor system (Adapted from [24]).

Table 9.15. Various operating conditions for LFR reactor.

Reactor parameters	Reference value			
	Pb-Bi Battery (Nearer Term)	Pb-Bi Module (Nearer term)	Pb-Large (Nearer term)	Pb-Battery (Far term)
Coolant	Pb-Bi	Pb-Bi	Pb	Pb
Outlet Temperature (°C)	~ 550	~ 550	~ 550	750–800
Pressure (atm)	1	1	1	1
Rating (MWh)	125–400	~ 1,000	3,600	400
Fuel	Metal alloy or nitride	Metal alloy	Nitride	Nitride
Cladding	Ferritic	Ferritic	Ferritic	Ceramic coatings or refractory alloys
Average Burn-up (GWD/MTHM)	~ 100	~ 100–150	100–150	100
Conversion ratio	1	~ 1	1.0–1.02	1.0
Lattice	Open	Open	Mixed	Open
Primary flow	Natural	Forced	Forced	Natural
Pin linear heat rate	Derated	Nominal	Nominal	Derated

Source: Reference [24].

The LFR has significant research and development challenges which must be overcome prior to laboratory scale demonstration. The potential for deploying small reactors to developing countries and hydrogen production from the larger version, make this reactor attractive world-wide. Various aspects of LFR design and operation are discussed in these references [68–82].

9.16.3 Molten Salt Reactor (MSR)

Fuels for the MSR reactor is mixed in with a molten salt that also serves as a coolant. The entire mixture is circulated through the primary system, drastically departing from conventional techniques. A second molten salt circuit would remove the heat from the primary salt and transfer it to a gas, which would then turn the turbine on a Brayton cycle. The MSR operates at very high temperatures, and can be used for hydrogen production [83–95].

Although this design, shown in Fig. 9.73, has significant potential, several obstacles remain, including unknowns related to corrosion, radioactive gas build-up, metal clustering in heat exchangers and salt processing/recycling. The parameters suggested for the operation of a MSR is given in Table 9.16.

Table 9.16. Basic parameters of a MSR.

Reactor parameters	Reference value
Net power	1,000 MWe
Power density	22 MWth/m^3
Net thermal efficiency	44–50%
Fuel-salt	
– Inlet temperature	565°C
– Outlet temperature	700°C (850°C for hydrogen production)
– Vapor pressure	<0.1 psi
Moderator	Graphite
Power cycle	Multi-reheat
	Recuperative helium
	Brayton cycle
Neutron spectrum burner	Thermal–actinide

Source: Reference [24].

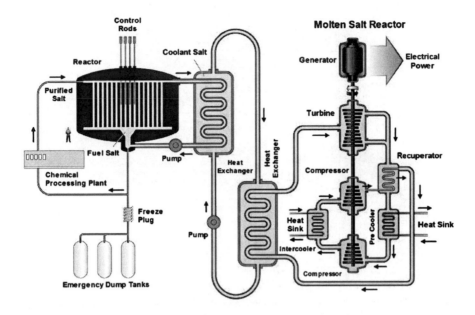

Fig. 9.73. The basic schematic diagram of a molten salt reactor (MSR) system for power generation (Adapted from [24]).

9.16.4 Sodium-Cooled Fast Reactor (SFR)

The SFR reactors have been operated by several countries in the past, but with a limited success. France operated the 1,200 MWe Super Phenix for several years. In the USA, a smaller scale demonstrations unit, EFR-II, was tested to gain a better understanding of the process. There are still significant challenges that need to be addressed before full scale commercialization. The basic plant design is illustrated in Fig. 9.74 and its operating parameters are presented in Table 9.17.

The SFR can utilize MOX or metallic fuel and would consist of sodium bonded plates, which increases the heat transfer capabilities of the fuel, keeping peak temperatures below the fuel melting point. Liquid sodium is circulated across the fuel plates and through an internal heat exchanger, where the heat is transferred to a separate sodium circuit. The secondary circuit is used to produce steam to run a steam turbine. The reactor is kept just above ambient temperature in order to mitigate the consequences of air or water interaction with the sodium. Sodium bonding with the fuel significantly reduces the risk of fuel melting [96–108].

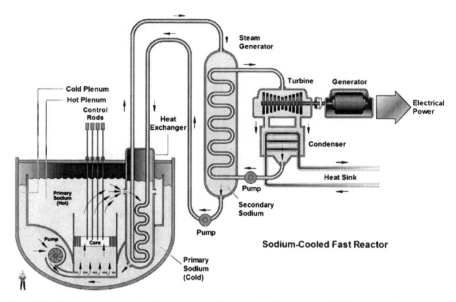

Fig. 9.74. The basic schematic diagram of sodium-cooled fast reactor (SFR) system for power generation (Adapted from [24]).

Table 9.17. Various reactor parameters of a SFR system.

Reactor parameters	Reference value
Outlet temperature	530–550°C
Pressure	~1 atm
Rating	1000–5000 MWth
Fuel	Oxide or metal alloy
Cladding	Ferritic or ODS ferritic
Average burnup	~150–200 GWD/MTHM
Conversion ratio	0.5–1.30
Average power density	350 MWth/m^3

Source: Reference [24].

9.16.5 Supercritical-Water-Cooled Reactor (SCWR)

The SCWR design, shown in Fig. 9.75, builds upon the vast experience gained through current light water reactor operations. The design of these plants would be very similar to Generation II BWR designs.

These reactors would operate at a temperature of approximately 500°C and at a pressure of 25 MPa, producing steam at supercritical conditions. The operating conditions are summarized in Table 9.18. It may be noted that coal-fired power

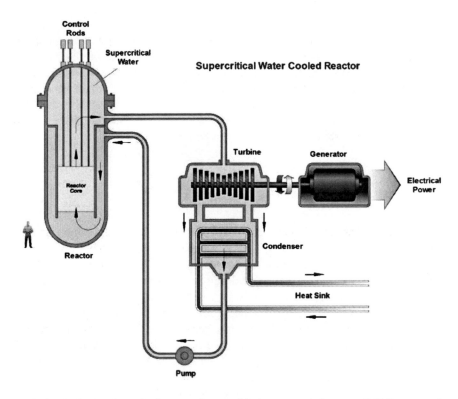

Fig. 9.75. The basic schematic diagram of supercritical water cooled reactor (SCWR) system for power generation (Adapted from [24]).

Table 9.18. Operating parameters of a SCWR system.

Reactor parameters	Reference value
Plant capital cost	$900/KW
Unit power	1,700 MWe
Neutron spectrum	Thermal spectrum
Net efficiency	44%
Coolant inlet and outlet	280°C/510°C/25 MPa
Temperatures and pressure	
Average power density	~100 MWth/m³
Reference fuel	UO2 with austenitic or ferritic-martensitic stainless steel, or Ni-alloy cladding
Fuel structural materials	Advanced high-strength
Cladding structural materials	metal alloys are needed
Burnup/Damage	~45 GWD/MTHM; 10–30 dpa
Safety approach	Similar to ALWRs

Source: Reference [24].

plants are increasing use of supercritical steam to improve the efficiency. This became possible due to advancement in the materials capable of withstanding high temperatures, oxidation and pressures. The entire coolant system of a SCWR plant would be significantly smaller resulting in a smaller containment building, adding to the capital savings. The GIF has acknowledged that the design and licensing of these reactors will be no easy task, due to the material challenges associated with the supercritical coolant. The goal for design completion is 2015 to 2020. Various information of the system is given in these references [109–119].

9.16.6 Very High Temperature Reactor (VHTR)

A schematic diagram of a VHTR based nuclear power plant is shown in Fig. 9.76. Currently, two designs, the PBMR of South Africa, and GT-MHR of General Atomics of the USA are in the most advanced stage of their development. China and Japan are also pursuing their own design of VHTR type system. The reactor would be graphite moderated and helium cooled, operating at temperatures up to 1,000°C. This increase in coolant temperatures is the largest design goal of the VHTR. A major difference in the design between PBMR and GT-MHR is in the fabrication of the fuel, which is discussed below. Both the systems will utilize TRISO fuel, but the geometric design is different. Fuels for this reactor would be similar in design to the GT-MHR concept, with uranium or possibly a (U, Pu) mixture within the fuel assembly. Although the once-through fuel cycle is still the plan, research has been focusing on methods to recycle TRISO fuel. The development of structural materials for the plant that can withstand the extremely high temperatures is one of the challenges before commercialization.

The VHTR project represents a potentially significant leap in nuclear power philosophy. A VHTR system can be used for both electricity generation and hydrogen production with very high efficiency. Among all the Generation IV reactors, VHTRs are most suitable for hydrogen production because of high outlet temperature of the coolant from the reactor. These reactors have the ability to decouple themselves completely from the electric industry if the hydrogen economy materializes. Various operations conditions are summarized in Table 9.19. Discussions on various aspects of VHTRs are provided in these references [120–137].

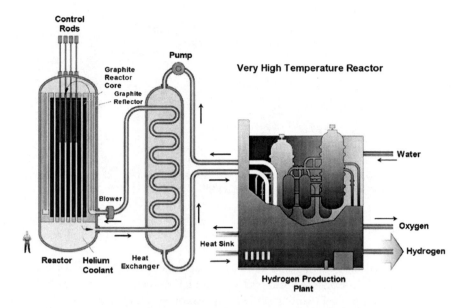

Fig. 9.76. The basic schematic diagram of very high temperature reactor (VHTR) system for power generation (Adapted from [24]).

Table 9.19. Various reactor operating conditions of a VHTR.

Reactor parameters	Reference value
Reactor power	600 MWth
Coolant inlet/outlet temperature	640/1,000°C
Core inlet/outlet pressure	Dependent on process
Helium mass flow rate	320 kg/s
Average power density	6–10 MWth/m^3
Reference fuel compound	ZrC-coated particles in blocks, pins or pebbles
Net plant efficiency	>50%

Source: Reference [24].

All the advanced gas cooled reactors, such as PBMR and GT-HMR, will be using gas turbine to take advantage of the high outlet temperature of the coolant from the reactors. Generally helium is the preferred gas for cooling the reactor. Since, the coolant gas has to be extremely pure, the operation of the gas turbine is expected to be easier and more efficient. The overall plant efficiency for electricity generation is expected to be above 50%. The plant efficiency for various type of reactors is shown in Fig. 9.77.

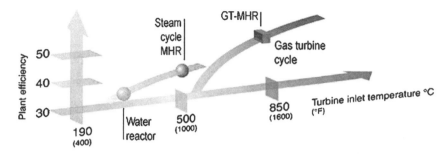

Fig. 9.77. A comparison of plant efficiency of various types of advanced gas cooled reactor based power plants (Printed with permission from [138]).

9.16.6.1 TRISO Fuel

The VHTRs will utilize micro-particles of Pu or U coated with several layers of inert materials as fuels. These fuels are called TRISO fuel. This fuel design consists of a small enriched uranium or thorium kernel surrounded by porous carbon layer, which retains the majority of fission products during irradiation. A pyrolytic carbon layer surrounds the inner carbon layer to improve thermal stability. Structural and chemical stability is guaranteed by a silicon carbide layer, which provides an impenetrable barrier to fission products and minor actinides. A final layer of graphite surrounds the silicon carbide. The structure of an individual TRISO fuel is shown in Fig. 9.78.

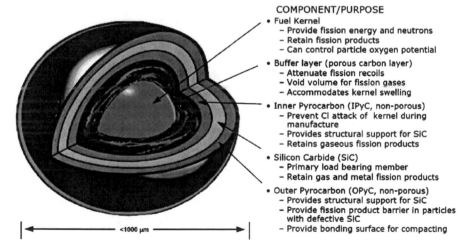

Fig. 9.78. Triso Fuel Particle Structure (Adapted from [139]).

In PBMR fuel design, approximately 15,000 TRISO particles are then mixed with a resin and graphite powder, pressed, and sintered to make a sphere of about 6 cm in diameter. Each sphere contains about 9 g of enriched uranium. The final fuel assembly is shown in Fig. 9.79 and the distribution of TRISO particles inside the fuel assembly is shown in Fig. 9.80.

Fig. 9.79. The PBMR fuel assembly containing TRISO particles (Printed with permission from [140]).

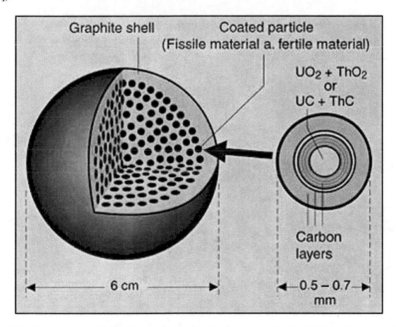

Fig. 9.80. Distribution of TRISO particles inside the fuel assembly for PBMR (Printed with permission from [140]).

For GT-MHR, the TRISO particles are compacted in the form of a cylinder. Several cylinders are used to make the fuel pin, which are then inserted inside the channels of a graphite block. The structure of the fuel assembly is shown in Fig. 9.81.

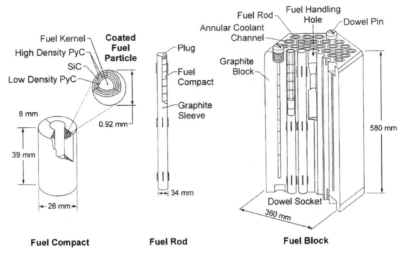

Fig. 9.81. The fuel assembly for GT-MHR (Printed with permission from [141]).

One of the advantages of TRISO fuel is that various types of fissile materials may be used to prepare the TRISO particles. The fissile materials that can be used are shown in Fig. 9.82.

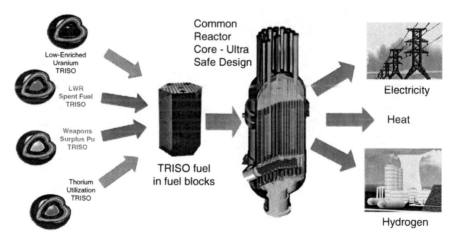

Fig. 9.82. Types of fissile materials that can be used in TRISO fuels (Printed with permission from [142]).

The fuel or UO₂ kernels for TRISO Particles are produced via a sol-gel method. The process flow diagram is described in Fig. 9.83. The process begins with the combining of cooled acid-deficient uranyl nitrate with an equimolar mixture of hexamethylenetetramine (HMTA) and urea. This forms the feed, which is then dispersed as droplets into a gelation column containing hot silicone oil. The spheres that form in the process are separated from the oil and washed with carbon tetrachloride to remove any adhering oil. They are further washed with ammonium hydroxide to remove ammonium nitrate and the unreacted HMTA and urea. The resulting gel spheres are dried and the NH_4NO_3 content is reduced by a factor of 1000, to ensure their survival [143] during sintering process. This reduction process represents the majority of the waste production for the sol-gel internal gelation process.

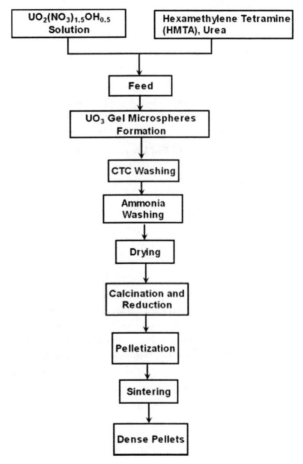

Fig. 9.83. Flow sheet for the preparation of UO₂ kernels via internal gelation process (Printed with permission from [143]).

The fuel kernels are next coated with a variety of layers in a fluidized bed by the chemical vapor deposition method. These individual TRISO particles are used to make the fuel assembly described above.

TRISO fuel has been considered in a variety of applications for advanced fuel designs. Various aspects of TRISO fuel design, properties, and characteristics are given in these references [144–160]. Uranium can be substituted for plutonium and TRU from reprocessed waste fuel. Several hundred thousand pebbles are arranged in a similar fashion to a gumball machine, which makes up the reactor core. Advantages of TRISO fuel include the capability of achieving a high burnup and the ability to operate in much higher temperatures, increasing plant efficiency.

9.16.6.2 PBMR and GT-MHR

The two most advanced designs of VHTRs are the Pebble Bed Modular Reactor (PBMR) [161–179] and the Gas Turbine Modular Helium Reactor (GT-MHR) [180–200].

A schematic diagram of the PBMR system is shown in Fig. 9.84. A pilot-scale project is being directed at Koeberg, South African, headed by the South African utility Eskom. A number of other countries are involved with the project including the USA, China, France, and Germany. The helium gas will be used as coolant. The high temperature helium gas will run the gas turbine for electricity generation, following which it will be feed back to the reactor. The cold leg (inlet side) and hot leg (outlet side) of the coolant will be approximately 500°C and 900°C, respectively [201].

The core of the reactor will consist of TRISO pebbles, essentially dumped into the pressure vessel with a fixed central graphite column for increased neutron reflection. The gas will be cycled through a series of compressors to raise pressure, prior to entering the top of the core. The gas flows through TRISO particles, picking up the heat from the fuel, expands and depressurizes across the turbines, where electricity is generated.

The development of GT-MHR is a collaborative project between the U.S., Russia and Japan. The reactor will be built modularly as a 300 MWe unit for disposal of surplus materials from Russian nuclear weapons program (Fig. 9.85). It will be capable of providing highly efficient electrical power, in the neighborhood of 48%.

The core of these reactors consists of hexagonal graphite blocks, with holes drilled for fuel, helium flow and burnable poisons. TRISO particles are bonded together with carbonaceous matrix, into rod-shaped compacts, which are loaded into graphite blocks. Each core has 1,020 fuel blocks, containing approximately 20.4 billion TRISO particles.

Two pressure vessels are required for the GT-MHR, due to the extremely high temperatures of the helium coolant (approximately 1,560°C). The first vessel contains the reactor. The second is the power conversion vessel, which contains the turbine, compressors and compact heat exchangers. This design utilizes the high

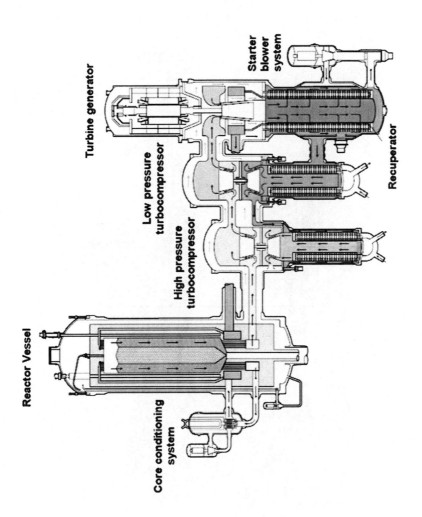

Fig. 9.84. Basic PBMR Design. Printed with permission Weil J (November 2001) Pebble-bed design returns. IEEE Spectrum, 37 – 40 [201].

temperature gas in a Brayton cycle, and will result in an overall plant efficiency near 50% [202]. Various specially designed components such as heater system (Fig. 9.86), helium gas compressors (Fig. 9.87) needed to be designed for the GT-MHR system.

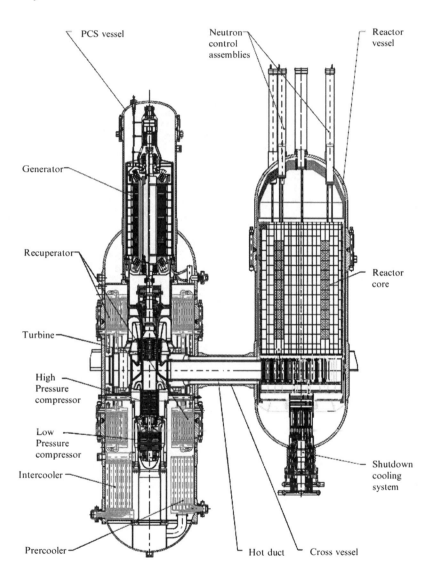

Fig. 9.85. GT-MHR reactor module arrangement (Printed with permission from [203]).

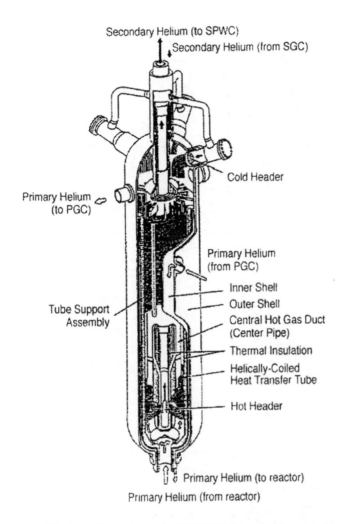

Secondary Helium (to SPWC)

Secondary Helium (from SGC)

Cold Header

Primary Helium (to PGC)

Primary Helium (from PGC)

Inner Shell

Outer Shell

Central Hot Gas Duct (Center Pipe)

Thermal Insulation

Helically-Coiled Heat Transfer Tube

Hot Header

Tube Support Assembly

Primary Helium (to reactor)

Primary Helium (from reactor)

Fig. 9.86. Heater system for GT-MHR (Printed with permission from [204]).

Japan and China are also pursuing their own design of high temperature gas reactors. These designs are still in the preliminary stage, however, the basic module has been designed and also tested to gain better understanding of the operation and operating parameters. The Japanese design is called HTTR and the main reactor design is shown in Fig. 9.88. The complete layout of the power plant is given in Fig. 9.89. The core design and layout of the fuel rods in the core is shown in Fig. 9.90.

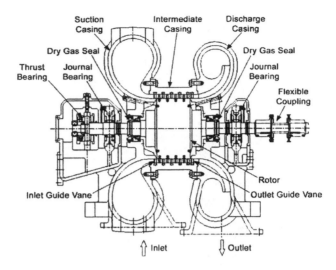

Fig. 9.87. Helium compressor for GT-MHR (Printed with permission from [204]).

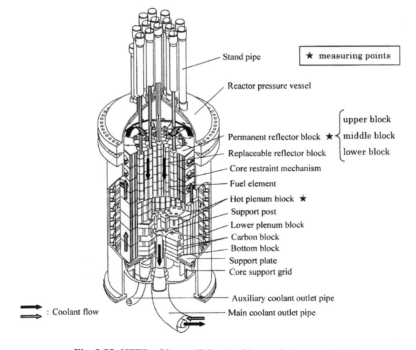

Fig. 9.88. HTTR of Japan (Printed with permission from [205]).

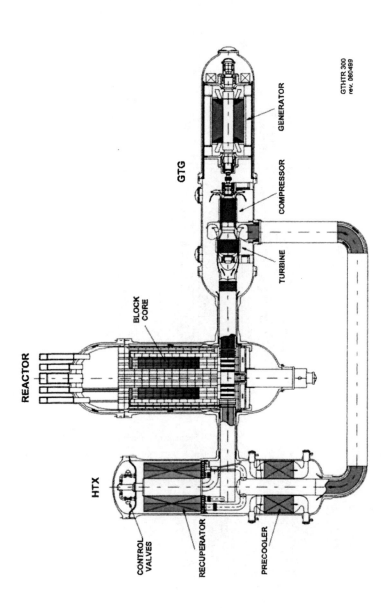

Fig. 9.89. System arrangement. Printed with permission Takamatsu K, Nakagawa S, Takeda T (2006) Development of core dynamics analysis of coolant flow reduction tests of HTTR. Proceedings HTR2006: 3rd International Topical Meeting on High Temperature Reactor Technology October 1-4, 2006, Johannesburg, South Africa Paper No. C00000174 [205].

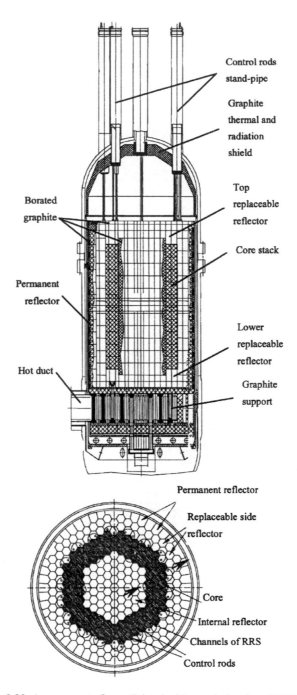

Control rods
stand-pipe

Graphite
thermal and
radiation
shield

Top
replaceable
reflector

Core stack

Borated
graphite

Permanent
reflector

Lower
replaceable
reflector

Graphite
support

Hot duct

Permanent reflector

Replaceable side
reflector

Core

Internal reflector

Channels of RRS

Control rods

Fig. 9.90. Arrangement of core (Printed with permission from [202]).

The Chinese unit is called HTR-10. The Chinese design has already gone through two generations. The latest modular design is shown in Fig. 9.91.

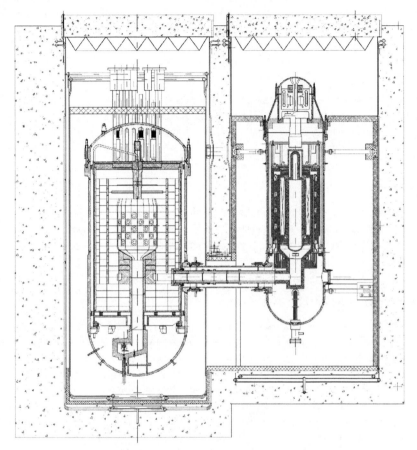

Fig. 9.91. HTR-10 of China (Printed with permission from [142]).

9.17 Waste Management

A discussion of nuclear energy is never complete without addressing the nuclear waste issues. "The main objective of radioactive waste management is to deal with radioactive waste in a manner that protects human health and the environment now and in the future without imposing undue burdens on future generations." (The Principles of Radioactive Waste Management, Safety Series No. 111-F, IAEA, Vienna 1995).

Radioactive waste consists of a variety of materials having different physical and chemical properties and containing different types of radioactivity. There are no international standard definitions of waste, although the IAEA has proposed three categories; each nation tends to develop its own classification system. (Classification of Radioactive Waste, A Safety Guide. A Publication in the Radwaste Programme. Safety Series No. 111-G-1.1, IAEA 1994). The classifications of nuclear waste according to the IAEA are as follows:

1. Exempt Waste (EW)
2. Low-Intermediate Level Waste (LILW)
   (a) Low-Intermediate Level Waste-Short Lived (LILW-SL)
   (b) Low-Intermediate Level Waste-Long Lived (LILW-LL)
3. High Level Waste (HLW)

Exempt Waste (EW)

This is radioactive waste that can be safely disposed of with ordinary refuse. In the UK it is called Very low-level waste (VLLW) and is defined as a waste of activity less than 400 kBq (~ 10 μCi)/0.1 m^3 of waste or single items of less than 40 kBq activity.

Low-Intermediate Level Waste (LILW)

The LILW consists of trash and debris from routine operations such as used ion exchange resins and filter cartridges, and decommissioning. It is primarily low level concentration beta/gamma contamination, but may include alpha contaminated material. It does not usually require special handling, unless contaminated with alpha emitters. There is little heat output from this category of waste.

The LILW is further divided into two categories: LILW-SL, and LILW-LL. The LILW-SL contains radionuclides with a half life of less than 30 years. If the half life is greater than 30 years, it is classified as LILW-LL. Fuel reprocessing wastes, such as the canning materials contain long-lived species of radionuclides. Some countries, notably the US and Canada do not use this classification category. However, France uses the IAEA classification. Although the UK uses the IAEA classification, they retained Low Level Waste and Intermediate Level Waste distinctions.

In the UK, LLW is defined as that waste with a radioactive content exceeding 400 kBq in any 0.1 m^3 and 40 kBq per article (unless the activity is due to carbon-14 or tritium, in which case the limits are a factor of ten greater) but not exceeding 4GBq/te of alpha radioactivity, or 12 GBq/te of beta/gamma radioactivity.

The ILW is defined as that waste with a radioactive content exceeding that of LLW, and does not require heat dissipation to be taken into account in the design of storage or disposal facilities.

High-level waste (HLW)

Depending on the strategy adopted for the back end of the fuel cycle, HLW may comprise either spent fuel or the highly active raffinate resulting from the first stage of fuel reprocessing. This raffinate is often immobilized in a suitable matrix for eventual disposal - glass and synroc are two examples of such a matrix. It contains high concentrations of beta/gamma emitting fission products and alpha emitting actinides. HLW is de facto a long-lived waste type and requires remote handling due to the radiation levels. In some countries the definition of HLW encompasses spent-fuel.

In the UK, HLW is defined as that waste in which the temperature may rise significantly as a result of the radioactivity, so that this factor has to be taken into account in designing storage or disposal facilities.

Some countries choose to categories alpha bearing waste separately. For example in the USA, Transuranic Waste (TRU) is defined as the waste containing more than 100 nanocuries of alpha-emitting transuranic isotopes, with half lives greater than 20 years, per gram of waste.

Such wastes are generated in research laboratories, fuel fabrication plants and reprocessing plants. Some alpha waste is classed as LLW, but hulls, caps and fins from reprocessing plants would be classed as ILW.

The nuclear waste classification in the USA is given in Table 9.20

Radioactive waste is produced by a number of sources, but by far the largest quantities – in terms of both radioactivity and volume – are generated by the commercial nuclear power plants, military nuclear weapons production facilities, and by nuclear fuel cycle activities to support these industries such as uranium mining and processing.

Although all elements up to and including uranium are found in nature, no elements with atomic numbers greater than uranium – that is, no transuranic elements – are naturally occurring. All transuranic elements are unstable and many of them are alpha-emitters with very long half-lives.

In both commercial and military sectors, some of the radioactive wastes generated are mixed with hazardous substances, such as organic solvents or other toxic, but non-radioactive chemicals. In the case of such wastes, the radioactive components of mixed wastes are regulated under the Atomic Energy Act by the Nuclear Regulatory Commission for commercial sources, and by the Department of Energy for military sources. The hazardous components, however, are subject to regulation by the Environmental Protection Agency according to an environmental law known as the Resource Conservation and Recovery Act (RCRA).

NARM wastes (Naturally-Occurring and Accelerator-Produced Radioactive Materials) are not consistently regulated under any current federal standard. NARM includes such materials as radium-226 and thorium-230 produced outside the nuclear fuel-cycle, and radionuclides produced by particle accelerators. NARM wastes are generated by both federal and non-federal facilities.

Table 9.20. Classification of radioactive wastes in the USA.

Category of radioactive waste	Definition
High-Level Waste (HLW)	1. Spent Fuel: irradiated commercial reactor fuel 2. Reprocessing Waste: liquid waste from solvent extraction cycles in reprocessing. Also the solids into which liquid wastes may have been converted. NOTE: The Department of Energy defines HLW as reprocessing waste only, while the Nuclear Regulatory Commission defines HLW as spent fuel and reprocessing waste.
Transuranic Waste (TRU)	Waste containing elements with atomic numbers (number of protons) greater than 92, the atomic number of uranium. (Thus the term "transuranic," or "above uranium.") TRU includes only waste material that contains transuranic elements with half-lives greater than 20 years and concentrations greater than 100 nanocuries per gram. If the concentrations of the half-lives are below the limits, it is possible for waste to have transuranic elements but not be classified as TRU waste.
Low-Level Waste (LLW)	Defined by what it is not. It is radioactive waste not classified as high-level, spent fuel, transuranic or byproduct material such as uranium mill tailings. LLW has four subcategories: Classes A, B, C, and Greater-Than Class-C (GTCC), described below. On average, Class A is the least hazardous while GTCC is the most hazardous.
Class A	On average the least radioactive of the four LLW classes. Primarily contaminated with "short-lived" radionuclides. (average concentration: 0.1 curies/ft^3)
Class B	May be contaminated with a greater amount of "short-lived" radionuclides than Class A. (average concentration: 2 curies/ft^3)
Class C	May be contaminated with greater amounts of long-lived and short-lived radionuclides than Class A or B. (average concentration: 7 curies/ft^3)
GTCC	Most radioactive of the low-level classes (average concentration: 300–2,500 curies/ft^3) (The 300 figure is based on the 1985 inventory. The higher figure represents anticipated inventory in 2020, including some decommissioning wastes.)

9.17.1 Spent Reactor Fuel

Spent reactor fuel is classified as high level waste (HLW) and there are significant concerns with the storage, transportation and handling of this material. The fuel consists of uranium, plutonium, fission products, transuranics (TRU) and various other minor actinides. The isotopic content of spent fuel will be discussed later in this chapter. The heat generation and radio-toxicity, which remain a problem for hundreds of thousands of years, are two major concerns when dealing with spent fuel. Mainly two steps are involved in the management of spent fuel; (1) Temporary on-site storage and (2) Permanent underground storage in geological repository or reprocessing.

9.17.1.1 Temporary Storage

Once fuel rods are permanently removed from the reactor, it must remain immersed in water for removal of heat that is released from continuing radioactive decay. Special spent fuel pools, adjacent to the reactors, offer temporary storage for fuel rods. Specially designed racks are used for the storage. These racks consist of neutron absorbing materials, such as Boral, and are designed and arranged in a manner to ensure that the criticality would not be achieved. The spent fuel pools also offer shielding from the highly radioactive fuel assemblies.

Storage of spent fuel on-site was never intended to be a long-term solution. However, in the USA, utilities have been forced to store all of their spent fuel and await for a permanent underground geological repository. France, Japan, Russia and the U.K., on the other hand, are reprocessing the spent fuel. Prior to 1977, when the USA deferred reprocessing indefinitely, utilities operated under the assumption that the government would receive spent fuel a few years after irradiation. Most reactor spent fuel pools were only designed to store spent fuel rods from five years of operation. However, the permanent repository in the USA is not ready for accepting these fuels rods forcing the utilities to find alternate methods for long-term storage. Table 9.21 shows the number of fuel assemblies currently stored on-sites in the USA.

Table 9.21. U.S. Storage of Spent Fuel as of 2002.

Reactor type	Number of assemblies		
	Stored at reactor sites	Stored at Away from reactor facilities	Total
Boiling-Water Reactor	90,398	2,957	93,355
Pressurized-Water Reactor	69,800	491	70,291
High-Temperature Gas Cooled Reactor	1,464	744	2,208
Total	161,662	4,192	165,854
In Metric Tonnes of Uranium (MTU)			
Boiling-Water Reactor	16,153.6	554.0	16,707.6
Pressurized-Water Reactor	30,099.0	192.6	30,291.6
High-Temperature Gas Cooled Reactor	15.4	8.8	24.2
Total	46,268.0	755.4	47,023.4

MTU = Metric tonnes of uranium.
A number of assemblies discharged prior to 1972, which were reprocessed, are not included in this table (no data is available for assemblies reprocessed before 1972). Totals may not equal sum of components because of independent rounding.
Source: Reference [206].

Two options are currently being adopted by utilities within the U.S., while awaiting a final solution from the government. The first involves installation of additional storage rack capacity within the existing spent fuel pools, shown in Fig. 9.92. Most nuclear power utilities have adopted this option; with 90% of spent fuel is currently being stored in these racks. The second option involves storage of spent fuel on site in dry storage containers, but housed away from the reactors as shown in Fig. 9.93.

Fig. 9.92. Typical spent fuel pool (Courtesy of [8]).

Fig. 9.93. Typical dry storage casks and storage area (Courtesy of U.S. Department of Energy, Office of Civilian Radioactive Waste Management).

The Nuclear Regulatory Commission (NRC) has licensed several different designs of dry storage containers. Some these containers can be used for both storage and eventual transportation. The NRC has also licensed some dry storage designs for compacting of fuel assemblies. This involves disassembling the fuel for more compacted arrangement of the fuel pins within the container. Spatial savings of 2 to 1 can be achieved with these designs, reducing the number of storage casks needed. However, this method does create separate HLW, from the remaining fuel assembly structure, which must be adequately stored for eventual disposal.

Following adequate decay of fuel elements, the fuel cycle can take one of two directions. As previously mentioned, some countries have chosen to close or partially close their fuel cycles through reprocessing of the spent fuel, leaving a more concentrated high level waste form. Others have chosen a once-through fuel cycle, in which entire spent fuel assemblies are sent to a final high level waste repository.

9.17.1.2 Repository

The option of burial of HLW within a deep underground repository has been heavily explored by several countries. Finland, Canada, France, Sweden and the U.S. all have waste management plans that include final repository utilization. These plans are in various stages of development and contention.

Challenges associated with repository design include the need to adequately protect the fuel encapsulations from corrosion, moisture and seismic anomalies, while keeping heat generation of these packages below set standards. For Yucca Mountain, temperature limits include those at the drift wall must be kept below 200°C and those midway between the drifts cannot exceed the boiling point of water. The standards and limits imposed on these repositories are for a minimum of 10,000 years [207].

9.17.2 US Repository

Following adoption of the Nuclear Waste Policy Act in 1982, each nuclear utility in the U.S. has been paying $0.001/kW-h into the Nuclear Waste Fund. This fund was created as an agreement with the Department of Energy to accept spent nuclear fuels from utilities for final disposal in a government operated repository. Yucca Mountain, shown in Fig. 9.94, was selected due to the arid climate in this region, stability of the earth formation and remoteness of the site. The spent fuel casks will be stored in several tunnels as shown in Fig. 9.95. However, the project has been plagued with one setback after another and the planned acceptance of fuel is already 10 years beyond the initial contracted date.

The NRC has reviewed the environmental impact statement, which was submitted by the DOE. The DOE plans to submit a license request by June of 2008, although funding shortcomings have forced site layoffs, potentially affecting the associated timeline shown in Fig. 9.96.

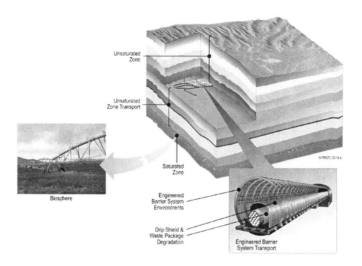

Fig. 9.94. Proposed Layout of Yucca Mountain Repository, an artist's impression (Courtesy of U.S. Department of Energy, Office of Civilian Radioactive Waste Management).

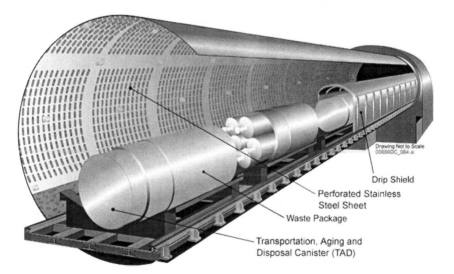

Fig. 9.95. The storage arrangement of spent fuel casks in Yucca Mountain (Courtesy of U.S. Department of Energy, Office of Civilian Radioactive Waste Management).

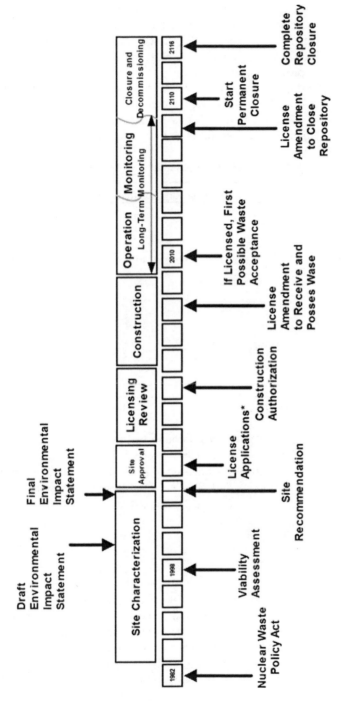

Fig. 9.96. Proposed timeline for operation of Yucca Mountain repository.

Disposal of HLW is a necessary part of any nuclear power program. However, issues surrounding the Yucca Mountain project have the potential to pose the greatest threat to a nuclear renaissance in the United States, but at the same time these issues are significant reasons for the U.S. shift from once-through fuel cycle philosophy to that of reprocessing and recycle.

France, Japan, Russia, India and the U.K. all have reprocessing production capabilities (Table 9.22). MOX fuel has been cycled into CANDU and light water reactor cores up to 30% loading. Although this still represents a small fraction of world spent fuel utilization, it offers significant and valuable operational experience.

Table 9.22. Spent fuel processing capacity around the world.

Type of fuel	Reprocessing facility	Capacity (in tones)	
	France, La Hague	1700	
	UK, Sellafield (THORP)	900	
LWR fuel:	Russia, Ozersk (Mayak)	400	
	Japan (Rokkasho)	800	
	Total approx		3800
	UK, Sellafield	1500	
Other nuclear fuels:	India	275	
	Total approx		1750
Total civil capacity			5550

Sources: References [5, 208].

Finland and Sweden have adopted once-through fuel cycle policies, electing to earmark their spent fuel for final disposal within a repository. Significant advances have been made towards repository construction in Finland, with expected license submittal in 2012 and operation in 2020. Sweden is in the process of identifying a repository site.

9.17.3 Spent Fuel Transfer

Whether a country chooses a closed or open fuel cycle, eventually the spent fuels need to be transferred from the reactor site to a central reprocessing facility or repository. This is a routinely performed operation in some countries such as France, Japan and the U.K. Although the U.S. is not reprocessing spent commercial reactor fuel, thousands of spent fuel shipments have taken place over the last thirty years. Most of these shipments were carried out between reactors, owned by the same utility, in order to share spent fuel storage space [209]. There have also been multiple shipments of spent fuel to research and test facilities. Finally, research and test reactors have continued to ship their spent fuel to government disposal facilities.

9.17.3.1 Transportation

The two common methods of transporting commercial spent nuclear fuels are by railcar and over the road by trucks. Fuels are loaded into the casks underwater with careful documentation to ensure the correct fuel assemblies are removed. The containers are also sealed underwater prior to removal from the storage pond. Once the cask has been removed from the water, it must be extensively cleaned to remove any surface contamination. The cask is then loaded onto its respective transport vehicle. Throughout this process, continuous radiation monitoring is performed to ensure personnel are protected. Prior to shipment, a final radiation and contamination survey must be performed to ensure the package is safe for shipment.

Oversight of these shipments is the responsibility of the NRC in partnership with the Department of Transportation (DOT). Each of these government organizations have extensive procedures set up to ensure safe shipment of spent fuel. The department of transportation also performs rigorous inspections of the transport vehicle prior to shipment.

Cask Design

The design of spent fuel shipment casks must pass rigorous testing prior to licensing (Fig. 9.97). The casks designed for over the road shipment typically weigh 25–40 t. Railcar casks weigh up to 120 t, offering significantly higher volume for spent fuel. The truck casks can carry approximately 6 t of spent fuel, while the rail casks can carry approximately 20 t. Worldwide, approximately 80,000 t of spent fuel has been shipped with zero release to the environment.

As can be seen in Fig. 9.97, these cask designs incorporate inner and outer steel shells for structural integrity. Lead shells provide both gamma shielding and further structural integrity. These packages also have a water layer to provide neutron shielding.

Certification of these shipping casks is a rigorous procedure and meant to ensure the casks will maintain their structural integrity under extreme adverse conditions. Testing that has been performed includes crash tests, where a tractor trailer truck, carrying a fuel cask, is slammed into a concrete wall at 61 and 84 mph. A locomotive was slammed broadside into a cask, mounted on a truck at 80 mph.

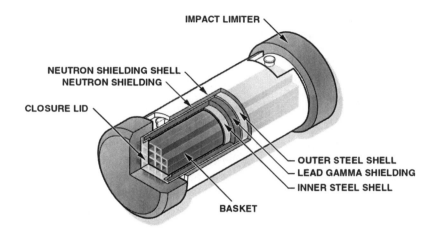

Typical Specifications
Gross Weight (including fuel): 250,000 pounds (125 t)
Cask Diameter: 8 ft
Overall Diameter (including Impact Limiters): 11 ft
Overall Length (including Impact Limiters): 25 ft
Capacity: Up to 26 PWR or 61 BWR fuel assemblies

(a) Generic Rail Cask

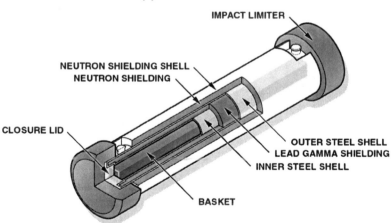

Typical Specifications
Gross Weight (including fuel): 50,000 pounds (25 t)
Cask Diameter: 4 ft
Overall Diameter (including Impact Limiters): 6 ft
Overall Length (including Impact Limiters): 20 ft
Capacity: Up to 4 PWR or 9 BWR fuel assemblies

(b) Generic Truck Cask

Fig. 9.97. Spent fuel shipping casks for railcar and truck (Courtesy of U.S. Nuclear Regulatory Commission).

The crash-fire test involved slamming a railcar, containing a cask, into a massive concrete barrier at 81 mph, subsequently subjecting it to a jet-fuel fire for 125 min. Finally, drop tests were conducted where a cask was dropped from certain heights onto un-yielding surfaces and sharp objects, ensuring the cask was exposed to its most vulnerable points. During all these tests, there was no release of radioactive materials, however, some exterior damage was noted.

Certification of these shipping casks is a rigorous procedure and meant to ensure the casks will maintain their structural integrity under extreme adverse conditions. Testing that has been performed includes crash tests, where a tractor trailer truck, carrying a fuel cask, is slammed into a concrete wall at 61 and 84 mph. A locomotive was slammed broadside into a cask, mounted on a truck at 80 mph. The crash-fire test involved slamming a railcar, containing a cask, into a massive concrete barrier at 81 mph, subsequently subjecting it to a jet-fuel fire for 125 min. Finally, drop tests were conducted where a cask was dropped from certain heights onto un-yielding surfaces and sharp objects, ensuring the cask was exposed to its most vulnerable points. During all these tests, there was no release of radioactive materials; however, some exterior damage was noted.

In addition to two methods mentioned, there have been approximately 300 sea voyages of spent fuel, carrying 8,000 t of spent fuel and other HLW. Special ships have been designed and certified to Irradiated Nuclear Fuel Class 3 (INF-3) standards. These ships are jointly owned by International Nuclear Services Limited, Japanese utilities and Areva. Fuel cask and special shipment designs are illustrated by Figs. 9.98 and 9.99, respectively.

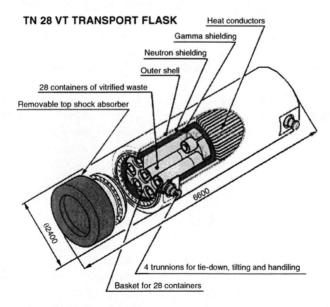

Fig. 9.98. Cutaway view of transportation flask for sea-shipping (Courtesy of [5]).

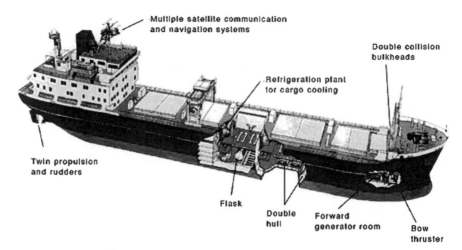

Fig. 9.99. Spent fuel shipping vessel (Courtesy of [5]).

Several elaborate safety systems are incorporated, such as double hulls, with impact resistant materials between them, twin engines operating independently as well as duplication and separation of all essential systems [210].

9.17.3.2 Security & Logistical Concerns

Shipment of spent fuel is a well-coordinated event, subject to extensive procedural compliance and intense security. Although details of spent fuel shipments are only available on a "need to know" basis, the code of federal regulations offers general guidance. Local law enforcement officials are included in the planning stage of fuel shipments, representing a significant faction of the response, in the event of an emergency.

The NRC also mandates the establishment of a security organization for each shipment, including armed escorts and a movement control center, set up as a focal point for any concern related to the shipment. The control center is also responsible for tracking the shipment and coordinating a response to any contingencies or emergencies [210].

9.18 Conditions of Spent Fuel

Prior to discussing spent fuel reprocessing techniques, it is necessary to take a look at the general conditions of spent fuel. Two general areas of concern related to spent fuel are the isotopic content of the fuel and the amount of decay time accumulated since irradiation. These factors affect the method and timeframe associated with fuel reprocessing.

9.18.1 Isotopic Composition

The isotopic composition of spent nuclear fuel is a product of its burn-up, decay time, initial enrichment and fuel arrangement within the reactor. A host of radio nuclides are present in the fuel immediately following irradiation, although many of these products decay away fairly quickly. Spent fuel from a typical light water reactor contains 95.6% uranium (<1% U235), 2.9% stable fission products, 0.9% plutonium, 0.3% cesium & strontium, 0.1% iodine & technetium, 0.1% other long-lived fission products and 0.1% minor actinides. Table 9.23 lists most common isotopes. A more detailed list of isotopes present in the spent fuel is given by the DOE [211].

Table 9.23. Long-lived fission products from 1,000 MWe reactors, 150 days after discharge.

Isotopes	PWR (Fuel: Uranium, 3.3% U235)	PWR (Fuel: Uranium and recycled Plutonium)	HTGR (Fuel: U235, thorium, and recycled Uranium)	LMFBR (Fuel: Uranium and recycled Plutonium)
Volatile Fission Products, Ci/year				
H3	$1.88 \cdot 10^4$	$2.47 \cdot 10^4$	$1.03 \cdot 10^4$	$1.98 \cdot 10^4$
Kr85	$3.00 \cdot 10^5$	$1.87 \cdot 10^5$	$4.90 \cdot 10^5$	$1.59 \cdot 10^5$
I129	1.02	1.31	1	0.742
Nonvolatile Fission Products, Ci/year				
Sr89	$2.65 \cdot 10^6$	$1.84 \cdot 10^6$	$3.18 \cdot 10^6$	$2.16 \cdot 10^6$
Sr90	$2.09 \cdot 10^6$	$1.24 \cdot 10^6$	$2.32 \cdot 10^6$	$8.93 \cdot 10^5$
Y91	$4.39 \cdot 10^6$	$3.24 \cdot 10^6$	$4.10 \cdot 10^6$	$3.92 \cdot 10^6$
Zr95	$7.54 \cdot 10^6$	$6.95 \cdot 10^6$	$5.24 \cdot 10^6$	$8.53 \cdot 10^6$
Nb95	$1.60 \cdot 10^7$	$1.30 \cdot 10^7$	$9.86 \cdot 10^6$	$1.60 \cdot 10^7$
Tc99	$3.90 \cdot 10^2$	$3.95 \cdot 10^2$	$2.70 \cdot 10^2$	$3.11 \cdot 10^2$
Ru103	$2.41 \cdot 10^6$	$2.70 \cdot 10^6$	$7.02 \cdot 10^5$	$3.39 \cdot 10^6$
Ru106	$1.12 \cdot 10^7$	$1.86 \cdot 10^7$	$9.26 \cdot 10^6$	$1.94 \cdot 10^7$
Cs134	$5.83 \cdot 10^6$	$5.09 \cdot 10^6$	$5.52 \cdot 10^6$	$4.86 \cdot 10^5$
Cs137	$2.92 \cdot 10^6$	$3.00 \cdot 10^6$	$2.42 \cdot 10^6$	$2.37 \cdot 10^6$
Ce141	$1.53 \cdot 10^6$	$1.42 \cdot 10^6$	$1.19 \cdot 10^6$	$1.40 \cdot 10^6$
Ce144	$2.25 \cdot 10^7$	$1.79 \cdot 10^7$	$1.43 \cdot 10^7$	$1.65 \cdot 10^7$
Rare Earths	$2.42 \cdot 10^7$	$2.15 \cdot 10^7$	$3.02 \cdot 10^7$	$4.01 \cdot 10^7$
Total	$1.14 \cdot 10^8$	$1.24 \cdot 10^8$	$1.02 \cdot 10^8$	$1.26 \cdot 10^8$

Source: Reference [211].

9.18.2 Decay Time

Decay of spent fuel (Fig. 9.100) is a pre-requisite of reprocessing, although some methods of reprocessing are less sensitive to prior decay of radionuclides. There are four primary reasons why decay of spent fuel for certain period of time is allowed prior to shipment. Decay of I-131 reduces the quantities of radioiodine released during reprocessing. Decay of Xe-133 leaves Kr-85 as the only radio-active noble gas that will be released during reprocessing. Decay of U-237 elimi-nates the need for remote handling of the purified uranium product, following reprocessing [211]. Finally, reduction in radioactive fission product activity simpli-fies fuel shipment and reduces radiological damage to the organic solvents used in the aqueous methods during reprocessing.

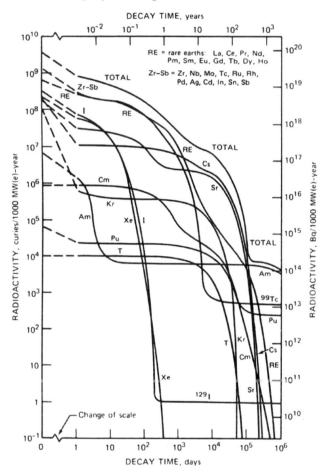

Fig. 9.100. Decay of radioactivity of irradiated fuel for 1 Year in a 1,000 MWe PWR (Printed with permission from [212]).

Most reactors operating today have an abundance of spent fuel, which has decayed for many years. This is especially true in the U.S., where many of the utilities have been storing fuel, in anticipation of government acceptance, for several decades. Generally, the decay of spent fuel beyond the first 5 years is not needed for reprocessing.

9.18.3 Reprocessing & Recycle

The uranium contained in the spent fuels is still available for further energy production. However, in order to obtain the remainder of the fuel's potential energy output, the fuel must first be reprocessed. Several methods of fuel reprocessing have been utilized and a number of new methods are in various stages of development. The fundamental concept behind each of these techniques is to extract useful isotopic content from spent fuel while minimizing HLW that must be sent to a final repository and preventing nuclear proliferation. Transmutation technologies appear to have a significant role to play in HLW management and are also described in the following section.

9.19 Reprocessing of Spent Fuel

The reprocessing step of the fuel cycle "back-end" is already being utilized in France, Japan, Russia and the U.K. Although the rate of spent fuel reprocessing is not yet at the level of spent fuel production in these countries, they have a significant political and technological advantages over countries that are developing commercial experience with reprocessing, such as the United States. The recently renewed interest world-wide in closing the fuel cycle, has resulted in increased research and development of reprocessing technologies.

Closing the fuel cycle is one of the primary goals of next generation nuclear technologies. The two fundamental areas currently undergoing extensive research are spent fuel partitioning and transmutation. Several methods have been developed, throughout the history of nuclear power, to effectively separate available fissile material from the waste. Additionally, methods of reducing the toxicity and volume of HLW must be identified, considering the limitations and availability of final repositories.

9.19.1 Partitioning

Spent fuel treatment technologies have been in development since the beginning of nuclear power. Initially, the goal of these technologies was the development of nuclear weapons, which led to various reprocessing technologies currently being employed, as well as those still under development. As previously discussed, spent fuel consists mainly of U-238. The remainder is made up of fission products, plutonium and other actinides (Fig. 9.101).

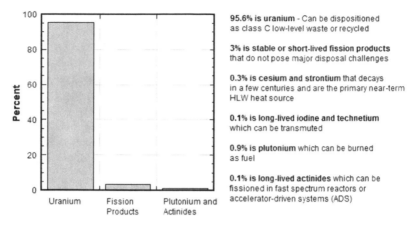

Fig. 9.101. Major constituents of spent fuel following typical power plant irradiation (Adapted from [211]).

The reason for substantial interest in developing reprocessing techniques is clear from Fig. 9.101. Aqueous methods of spent fuel reprocessing have been utilized for several decades, for both civilian and defense programs. With priorities shifting to fuel conservation, waste reduction and proliferation resistance, development of more effective aqueous and non-aqueous techniques of spent fuel partitioning are underway.

9.19.2 Decladding

Prior to all aqueous reprocessing techniques, the fuel cladding must be separated from the fuel material. The two common methods of decladding are chemical and mechanical decladding. Chemical decladding is most effective with fuels in which the fuel is bonded to the cladding material. Mechanical decladding is more suited for unbonded fuel designs, such as pellet fuels and Magnox fuels. Both of these methods are discussed below.

9.19.2.1 Chemical Decladding

In order to expose the fuel for reprocessing, the cladding is dissolved using a solvent. This method is the preferred method for bonded cladding, as separation of the two materials would be impractical through mechanical means. However, the products generated by reactions during chemical decladding consume more storage space than the original cladding material, and is highly radioactive for some time.

Some of the first nuclear reactors in the U.S. utilized uranium metal slugs, bonded to aluminum-silicon alloy that are encased in aluminum cans. The aluminum can and bonding material were dissolved in hot, aqueous sodium hydroxide solution, containing sodium nitrate to prevent hydrogen build-up [211]. The chemical reaction is:

$$Al + 0.85\ NaOH + 1.05\ NaNO_3 \rightarrow NaAlO_2 + 0.9\ NaNO_2 + 0.15\ NH_3 + 0.2\ H_2O$$

Two processes, called The Zirflex and Sulfex processes, were designed for zircoloy and stainless steel claddings, respectively. Both of these processes were developed prior to optimization of mechanical decladding techniques and were never put into large scale production. The Sulflex process that uses sulfuric acid can attack the fuel itself. With the advances in mechanical methods of decladding, the chemical methods for these fuels were abandoned.

9.19.2.2 Mechanical Decladding

The mechanical decladding method has become the preferred method worldwide for exposing the fuels during reprocessing reactions. This method involves transverse chopping and sawing with shears and saws, as well as longitudinal slitting and extrusion of the fuel pins.

The transverse shearing method is most preferred, as saws tend to leave a larger quantity of fine waste, difficult to collect. Additionally, this method does not require prior fuel bundle disassembly into individual pins. The shears simply cut right through the entire assembly.

With Magnox fuel, unbonded aluminum cladding is removed via longitudinal extrusion through a steel die. The uranium metal rod is admitted through the die, scrapping off the cladding as it passes through. This method is not appropriate for pellet fuels, as they would break apart and jam the process [211].

During the de-cladding procedure, steps must be taken to treat the off-gases from these methods. The fuel cladding will contain up to 10% of the krypton and xenon gases, as well as some C14 in the form of CO_2, tritium, iodine and other volatile fission products. Techniques have been developed to treat these off-gases, as environmental standards no longer allow direct venting, as was done in the past. Among these methods, voloxidation, developed by the Oak Ridge National Laboratory is most widely used to remove tritium and other fission products. The basis of the voloxidation process is to oxidize spent oxide fuel at low temperatures (about 500°C) in order to remove tritium and increase the dissolution rate during aqueous processing. Advanced voloxidation not only performs these functions but also removes and collects specific fission products such as krypton, xenon, cesium, rubidium, iodine, technetium, molybdenum, and ruthenium. During oxidation of the fuel in a rotating kiln, U_3O_8 swells and pulverizes. This releases the tritium, which is exposed to oxidizing gases and is converted to tritiated water, which is collected, allowed to decay and is finally disposed [211]. Krypton, xenon and iodine are trapped for storage, greatly reducing the gaseous effluent radioactivity from reprocessing facilities.

9.19.2.3 Fuel Dissolution

The fundamental goal of fuel dissolution is to completely transfer it into solution. Depending on the decladding method, various forms of waste remediation are need on the remaining cladding. The inventory and accountability of fuel materials are maintained to ensure nonproliferation of the radioactive materials.

The aqueous methods used for reprocessing of spent fuels rely heavily upon nitric acid as a dissolution agent. As the fuel is being dissolved, oxygen is added directly to the dissolver to prevent the formation of gaseous reaction products, such as hydrogen. The reactions taking place for uranium dissolution are [211]:

$$3 \ UO_2 + 8 \ HNO_3 \rightarrow 3 \ UO_2(NO_3)_2 + 2 \ NO + 4 \ H_2O$$
$$UO_2 + 4 \ HNO_3 \rightarrow UO_2(NO_3)_2 + 2 \ NO2 + 2 \ H_2O$$
$$2 \ UO_2 + 4 \ HNO_3 + O_2 \rightarrow 2 \ UO_2(NO_3)_2 + 2 \ H_2O$$

Within oxide fuels, plutonium dissolves as a mixture of hexavalent and tetravalent plutonyl nitrates, both of which can be extracted from solution. Most of the fission products dissolve fully into solution, although higher burn-up fuels can leave behind some solid fission products, such as molybdenum and zirconium. Extensive research and experience have gone into determining the most effective balance between acid concentration and dissolution rates. Additional steps are taken during dissolution to prevent the formation of a critical mass by the fissile materials present in the solution. This is avoided by controlling the quantity of fissile material dissolved, adding soluble neutron absorbers and ensuring that the geometry of the dissolving unit will not allow attaining the criticality.

9.19.3 Aqueous Methods

France, Russia, Japan and the U.K. have developed extensive reprocessing facilities, using the aqueous process Purex. This process has evolved from the early aqueous methods, used in nuclear weapons development program in the U.S.

9.19.3.1 Bismuth Phosphate

Bismuth phosphate process was the first method utilized by the U.S. for extraction of plutonium, which coprecipitated plutonium (tetra or trivalent states) with $BiPO_4$. Uranium remained in its soluble hexavalent state in the solution, thus facilitated the extraction of plutonium only. The reduction of plutonium was carried out via a series of oxidation and reduction reactions. This method produced kilograms of 99.9% purity plutonium [213].

9.19.3.2 Redox

The Redox was first solvent extraction method developed, also by the U.S. The process has an advantage over the co-precipitation method, in that it can be continuously operated, rather than the batch technique of the bismuth phosphate process. Another advantage of this technique was its ability to extract uranium, in addition to the plutonium.

Methyl isobutyl ketone (hexone) is used as the solvent in this process, which is also used to purify uranium from mining ores. Hexone, immiscible with water, selectively extracts uranyl and plutonyl nitrates from the solution, if sufficiently high nitrate ion concentration is maintained. Aluminum nitrate was used to maintain the desired nitrate ion concentrations.

The first phase of this process involves converting plutonium into hexavalent plutonyl nitrate, which is the valence state of plutonium with the highest distribution coefficient in hexone. The hexavalent uranium and plutonium nitrates are extracted into the hexone solvent. Fission products are scrubbed from the solvent using aluminum nitrate, sodium nitrate and sodium dichromate. Plutonium is then converted to its inextractable trivalent phase, while keeping uranium in the hexone. This allows separation of the plutonium from the uranium. Nitric acid is used to strip the uranium back to the aqueous liquid, where it could be further decontaminated from fission products.

9.20 Purex

Although the Redox process was able to effectively separate out uranium and plutonium from fission products, tributylphosphate (TBP) was found to be more effective as a solvent. The TBP is far less flammable and less susceptible to degradation in the presence of nitric acid, as opposed to hexone. It is widely available in very pure form, and at reasonable costs. Unlike the Redox process, nitric acid can be used as the salting agent, greatly reducing the volume of waste. Utilizing this new solvent, the Purex (**P**lutonium **UR**anium **EX**traction) process was developed. All of the current commercial reprocessing facilities use some variation of the Purex process. General description of the PUREX process is discussed in these references [214–220]. The PUREX has undergone numerous modifications that include process flow diagram, equipment, instruments, solvents, and recovery of products [221–269]. The process has been also extended to other systems such as thorium fuel cycle, high burn fuel, and fast reactor fuels [270–275].

Following de-cladding and dissolution, the first step of the Purex process is primary decontamination. The process begins with an extracting section, in which uranium and plutonium are removed from the 6–8M nitric acid solution, through countercurrent contact with the 30% TBP in n-dodecane [211]. Fission products typically have lower distribution coefficients than uranium and plutonium, which keeps the majority of these fission products in the aqueous solution. In the scrubbing section of primary decontamination, nitric acid is used to remove the small amount of fission products carried over into the solvent. The primary decontamination phase of the Purex process separates 99–99.9% of fission products from the uranium and plutonium. The extraction of uranium and plutonium follows following reactions [276].

$$UO_2{}^+(aq) + 2\ NO_3{}^-(aq) + 2\ TBP(org) \leftrightarrow UO_2(NO_3)_2(TBP)_2(org)$$
$$Pu_4{}^+(aq) + 4\ NO_3{}^-(aq) + 2\ TBP(org) \leftrightarrow Pu(NO_3)_4(TBP)_2(org)$$

Plutonium is reduced to its trivalent state using Fe^{2+}, U^{4+}, hydroxylamine, or cathodic reduction. The trivalent plutonium is inextractable by TBP, migrating to the aqueous phase, while the uranium remains in the extractable hexavalent condition. Thus plutonium exists in the aqueous phase and the uranium exists in the organic phase. The basic separation mechanism is shown in Fig. 102.

The separated plutonium, leaving the partitioning step, still contains approximately 1% of uranium, along with a small amount of fission products. Plutonium is further purified by two additional cycles of solvent extraction. Plutonium along with its impurities is converted back to tetravalent and is extracted again with the uranium leaving behind other fission products in the solution. It is then separated from the uranium. Purified plutonium is not allowed to build up at reprocessing sites due to the proliferation risk associated with this material. In commercial facilities, it is immediately fabricated into MOX fuel, thereby, greatly reducing the proliferation risks.

Uranium must also be purified, after leaving the partitioning step of the Purex process. This is accomplished by scrubbing it with 0.01M nitric acid, and transferring it back to the aqueous phase. Further solvent extractions with TBP are performed, while leaving the remaining plutonium in the aqueous phase. Prior to acceptance as feed material at enrichment plants, the purified uranium must meet a set of limits on radioactivity.

The typical Purex reprocessing method is shown in Fig. 9.103, however, a number of variations of the basic process have been developed. The process also generates a large amount of acidic-nonradioactive and radioactive wastes. The amount of both wastes has been reduced over the years, since it became more efficient and through recycling of the various chemicals. Another criticism of the process revolves around the separation of purified plutonium, which represents a significant proliferation risk. The new separation technologies are focusing on simultaneous recovery of plutonium and uranium so that plutonium becomes useless as weapon grade material. In the USA, these processes are called **UR**anium **EX**traction (UREX). Several versions of the UREX processes called UREX+1, UREX+2, etc. have been developed, each has its own objectives.

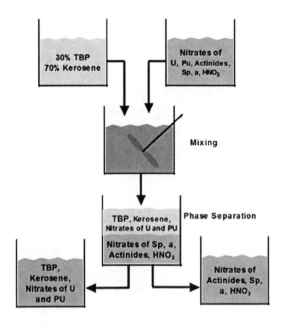

Fig. 9.102. Uranium and plutonium separation mechanism.

9.21 URanium EXtraction (UREX)+ Process

The decladding and dissolution steps for the UREX processes are essentially the same as that of the Purex process. However, a lower concentration of nitric acid could be used than used in the Purex process. A number of variations of UREX processes have been developed to separate various streams further. These processes are called UREX-1, UREX-1a, etc and are listed in Table 9.24. The TBP remains the solvent, but the UREX+ method of partitioning does not separate out pure plutonium from Np or other TRU, thereby making it extremely unattractive as weapon grade plutonium. Other goals of the UREX+ program were to separate out many of the heat producing and highly radioactive fission products. This would help reduce off-site dose to personnel and reduce the volume of HLW that must be sent to the final repository. The final Pu/Np product from the UREX+3 process is very close to a conventional MOX fuel, which might make NRC approval easier [24].

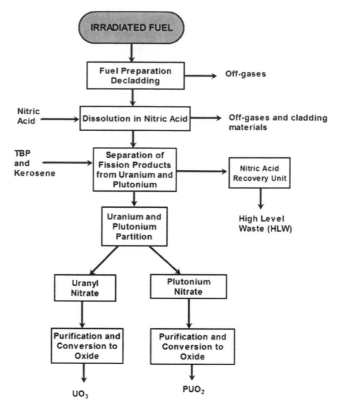

Fig. 9.103. Typical Purex Flow Sheet.

Table 9.24. UREX+ Processes under development [277].

Process	Product						
	# 1	# 2	# 3	# 4	# 5	# 6	# 7
UREX+1	U	Tc	Cs/Sr	TRU/Ln	FP		
UREX+1a	U	Tc	Cs/Sr	TRU	FP/Ln		
UREX+1b	U	Tc	Cs/Sr	U/TRU	FP/Ln		
UREX+2	U	Tc	Cs/Sr	Pu/Np	Am/Cm/Ln	FP	
UREX+2a	U	Tc	Cs/Sr	U/Pu/Np	Am/Cm/Ln	FP	
UREX+3	U	Tc	Cs/Sr	Pu/Np	Am/Cm	FP/Ln	
UREX+3a	U	Tc	Cs/Sr	U/Pu/Np	Am/Cm	FP/Ln	
UREX+4	U	Tc	Cs/Sr	Pu/Np	Am	Cm	FP/Ln
UREX+4a	U	Tc	Cs/Sr	U/Pu/Np	Am	Cm	FP/Ln

In all cases, iodine is removed as an off-gas from the dissolution process

Processes are designed for the generation of no liquid high level wastes

U: Uranium (contributor to dose rate, and the mass and volume of high level wastes

Tc: Technetium (long lived fission product, minor contributor to long term dose

Cs/Sr: Cesium and strontium (primary short term heat generators, affect waste from loading and repository drift loading

TRU: Transuranic elements; Pu-Plutonium, Np-Neptunium, Am-Americium, Cm-Curium (primary long term dose rate contributors)

Ln: Lanthanide (rare earth) fission products

FP: Fission products other than cesium, strontium, technetium, iodine, and lanthanides

Argonne National Laboratory (ANL) has conducted laboratory scale demonstrations of the UREX+1a and UREX+3 processes. It is expected that these two versions of UREX processes will be developed to full scale commercial plants first. The description of the UREX+ process is based on the laboratory scale demonstrations by the ANL and the basic flow diagram is shown in Figs. 9.104–9.108.

Following dissolution, a reductant/complexant is added to the nitric acid in the scrub to limit the extractability of Pu and Np [278]. TBP in n-dodecane is introduced as the extractant that removes U and Tc from the remaining fission products and TRU. The next stage strips Tc from the product and the final stage strips the U from the final waste stream, which would be recycled back into the process. The three stages of separation were performed through the use of multistage centrifugal contactors, as shown in Fig. 9.109.

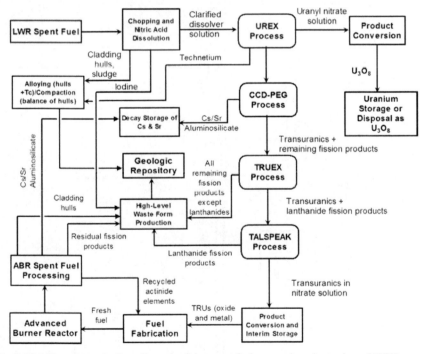

Fig. 9.104. The schematic flow diagram of the spent fuel processing plant using a UREX process (Adapted from [277]).

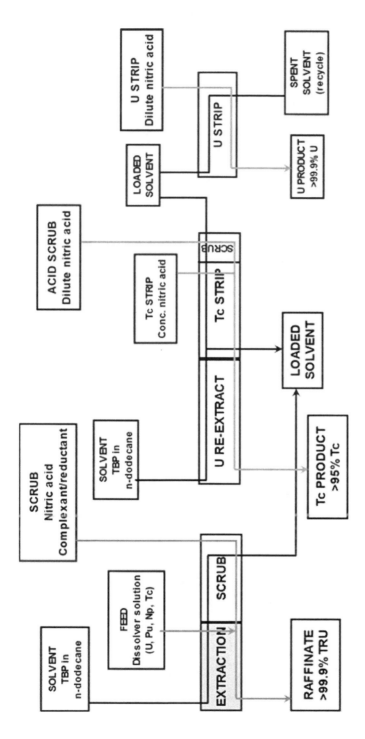

Fig. 9.105. A flow diagram of the uranium extraction unit. (From [279]).

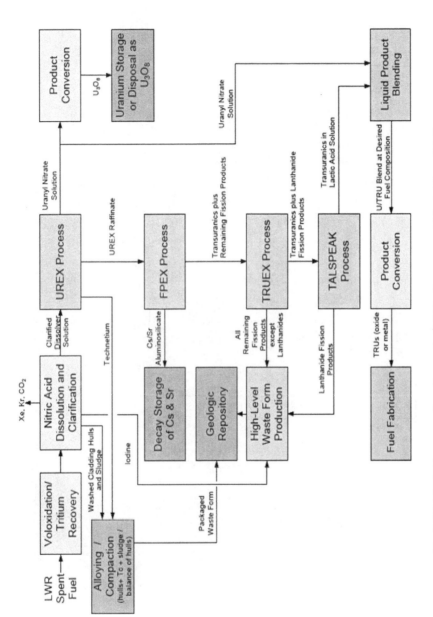

Fig. 9.106. UREX+1a process flow diagram for GNEP reference case. (Adapted from [277]).

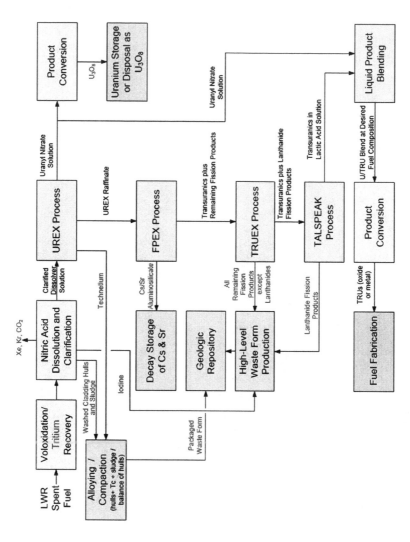

Fig. 9.107. Wastes and storage products generated from UREX+1a process. These are shown in red (Adapted from [277]).

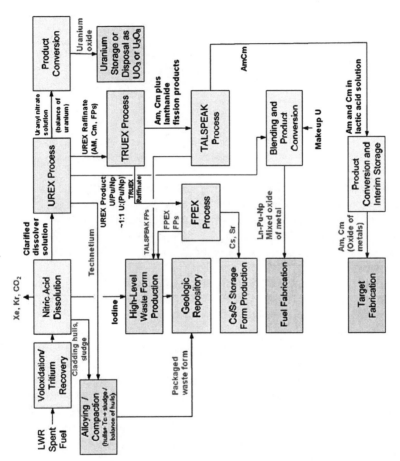

Fig. 9.108. UREX+3 process flow diagram. (Adapted from [277]).

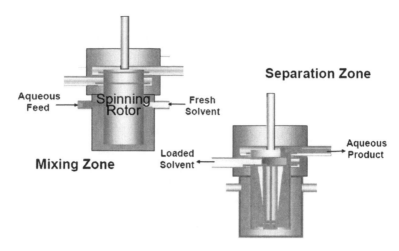

Fig. 9.109. Multistage centrifugal contactor (Adapted from [279]).

The raffinate from the initial Urex process is then fed directly into the CCD-PEG phase of partitioning, which is primarily focused on removing Sr and Cs. The solvent is a mixture of chlorinated cobalt dicarbollide (CCD), which is selective for Cs and polyethylene glycol (PEG), which is selective for Sr. The various stages involved in scrubbing and stripping the Sr and Cs from the feed stream are illustrated in Fig. 9.110.

The raffinate from the CCD-PEG phase is fed into the NPEX (Neptunium (**NP**) **EX**traction process) phase of the overall process, which is designed to remove Pu and Np. Volume reduction between these two phases would be necessary, as the reductant/complexant employed in the initial process, must be destroyed prior to the NPEX phase. Otherwise, the Pu and Np would not be extractable and would fail to separate from the feed. The solvent for the NPEX phase is also TBP in n-dodecane. Through a series of extraction, scrubbing and stripping, the Np and Pu are separated together from the feed, which can then be sent for fuel fabrication.

The raffinate of the NPEX phase is fed directly into the TRUEX (Trans-uranic (**TRU**) **EX**traction) phase, shown in Fig. 9.111. A 0.2M CMPO (octyl-N-diisobutylcarboylmethyl-phosphine oxide) and 1.4M TBP diluted by n-dodecane, is utilized as the extractant. TRUEX is capable of separating out Am, Cm, rare earth elements and residual Pu and Np [278]. First impurities in oxalic acid are removed using moderately concentrated nitric acid. The product of the TRUEX phase is fed directly into the Cyanex 301 phase, which is designed to separate out the rare earth elements from Am and Cm. The chemical formula of Cyanex 301 is bis(2,4,4-trimethylpentyl)dithiophosphinic acid. The Cyanex 301 is diluted by TBP and n-dodecane [278] prior to its use.

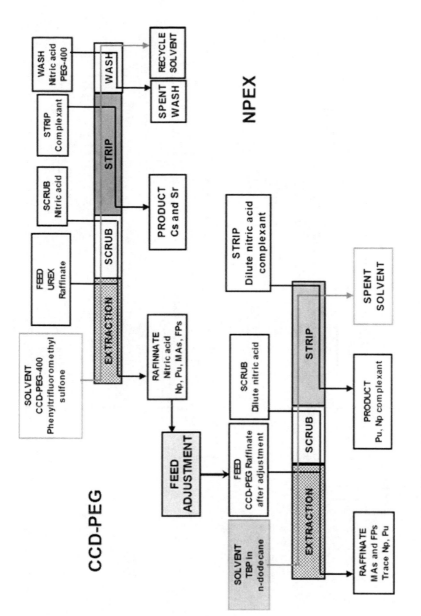

Fig. 9.110. CCD-PEG & NPEX Sections of UREX+3 Spent Fuel Reprocessing Method. (Adapted from [278]).

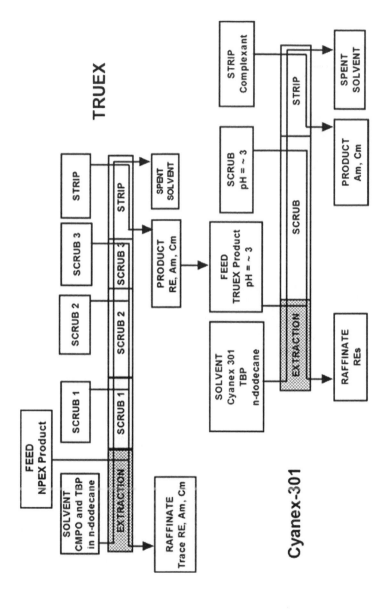

Fig. 9.111. TRUEX and Cyanex 301 Sections of UREX+3 Spent Fuel Reprocessing Method. (Adapted from [278]).

The use of an UREX process is expected to reduce the waste generation significantly. The projected amounts of wasted from various streams are given in Table 9.25.

Table 9.25. UREX+1a/+3 processes: Projected waste generation for every 100 t of spent fuel processed waste [280].

Waste stream	Waste composition	Category	Volume, m^3
Uranium	U_3O_8 powder	Storage	18
Cesium/Strontium	Cs/Sr Aluminosilicate	Storage	1.1
Hulls + Tc, sludge	Zr-Fe based alloy	HLW	0.6
Compacted hulls	Non-TRU Zr	HLW	6.1
U losses	Borosilicate glass	HLW	1.0–3.4
TRU losses	Borosilicate glass	HLW	0.06
Iodine	Potassium iodate	HLW	0.018
Krypton	Zeolite/aluminosilicate	HLW	0.014
Tritium	Grout	HLW	<0.01
Lanthanide FPs	LABS glass	HLW	0.31
Carbon-14	Sodium carbonate	HLW	0.034

9.22 Non-aqueous Methods

Spent fuel can also be reprocessed by non-aqueous methods [281, 282]. The three main methods are the fluoride volatility method, molten-salt, and electrochemical separation processes. The last two methods are also called pyroprocessing. Most non-aqueous techniques can handle spent fuel with much shorter decay times, as compared to aqueous techniques. Since there is no solvent, radiolysis and heat are of no concern. In fact, the heat generated by the spent fuel can help sustain the high temperatures needed for some of these techniques. Non-aqueous techniques can substantially reduced neutron moderation, as compared with their aqueous counterparts. Therefore, development of a critical mass, within the reprocessing equipment, is less of a concern. These facilities have the advantage of being more compact and could potentially generate less waste.

These methods are not without their disadvantages. Pyroprocesses require extremely high temperatures, and, therefore, high temperature material compatibility. Also, with the exception of fluoride volatility, these processes might not be able to fully decontaminate the spent fuel handling materials during reprocessing. This adds significant complexity to the processes, since all handling techniques must be performed in heavily shielded hot-cells.

9.22.1 Fluoride Volatility Process

In this method, uranium, plutonium and neptunium are converted to their volatile hexafluorides, to separate them from other materials as well as each other which can then be recycled [283–298]. Fluoride volatility method is most effective when fuels contain little plutonium or neptunium because the fluorides PuF_6 and NpF_6 are less stable than UF_6. The volatility of these fluorides is given in Table 9.26.

Table 9.26. Melting/Boiling point of several fluoridesflurodies.

Flouride compounds	Melting/Boiling point
UF_6	329.69 K
NpF_6	328.33 K
PuF_6	335.31 K

A process flow sheet for fluoride volatility process is shown in Fig. 9.112.

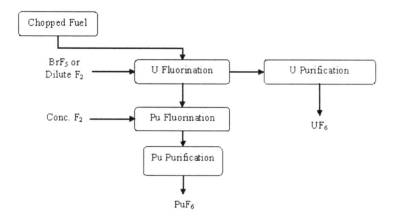

Fig. 9.112. A basic flow diagram of fluoride volatile process.

A hybrid recycle system, called Fluorex process, has been developed by Hitachi Inc, Japan, which combined both aqueous and non-aqueous methods. Fluoride volatility and solvent extraction are applied as shown in Fig 9.113. Spent fuel from thermal reactors is sheared and their cladding material is removed by a pyrolysis method, such as the AIROX process. In AIROX process, holes are drilled in the fuel cladding and the fuel is subjected to cycling oxidation and reduction cycles. The U_3O_8 expands due to oxidation of UO_2 causing the fuel to break apart Fluorination and purification of most of the uranium is carried out by applying the fluoride volatility method in a compact facility. About 10% of the residues, including the plutonium, can be treated by the well-established Purex method. The recovered fuels can be used as MOX fuels [299].

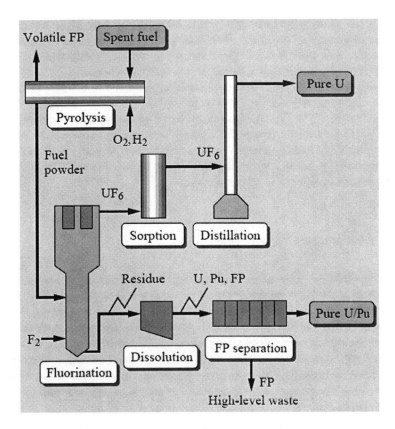

Fig. 9.113. The hybrid fluoride volatile process, called Fluorex, for dry reprocessing of spent fuel (Printed with permission from [299]).

9.22.2 Molten-Salt Process

Since the 1960s, many experiments have been carried out to determine the feasibility of molten salt processes for fuel reprocessing. Two basic systems have been developed and tested in the U.S. These include the mixed fluoride salt system and the chloride eutectic salt as an ionic solvent in pyrochemical reprocessing techniques.

The Molten Salt Reactor Experiment (MSRE) was conducted by Oak Ridge National Laboratory (ORNL). The MSRE provided the basis for a number of new processes later on. A mixed fluoride molten salt was used as a coolant, as well as a fuel and blanket system. The mixture was consisted of BeF_2, LiF, ThF_4, and UF_4, that effectively extracted bred Pu-233 from the salt phase into liquid bismuth by reduction with lithium metal [300]. A stream was diverted away from the main salt loop for fission product removal through processing with high concentrations of lithium. The purified salt stream was then re-directed back to the main salt loop. Uranium was separated as UF_6, after fluorination with hydrofluoride and fluorine gas. This uranium product could be recycled for enrichment.

Another method utilized transport of actinides between two magnesium alloys, one containing copper and the other containing zinc, for separation of various components. The difference in chemical potential between plutonium and uranium allowed separation of the two in the alloys. A decontamination factor of 100 is possible [300]. The noble elements are kept in the copper alloy, with the reactive fission products contained within the zinc phase of the system. This method has the potential for reprocessing of metallic fuels.

9.22.3 Electrochemical Process

The electrochemical form of pyroprocessing, also referred to as electrorefining, has been employed for reprocessing of spent fuels. The Integral Fast Reactor (IFR) program in the U.S. was developed for spent fuel processing from the Experimental Breeder Reactor (EBR-II). Although electrochemical processes are similar to the salt transport process described early, the driving force between the anode and cathode is electrical potential between the two electrodes. The electrical potential can be controlled accurately to selectively prevent reduction of certain elements into the salt. By varying electrical potential, along with multiple units, various compounds can be sequentially separated from each other. Very high purity products can be obtained from this system.

Argonne National Laboratory used the electrochemical and pyrometallurgical techniques for reprocessing of spent EBR-II metallic fuel. The system is shown in Fig. 9.114. The uranium metal fuel was placed into a cadmium anodic basket, where it dissolved into a LiCl–KCl eutectic salt mixture. An electric potential was created through the salt, causing the actinides to deposit in a molten cadmium cathode. This formed an intermetallic compound, which caused an increase in the chemical free energy of the heavy metal, that was sufficient to increase the dissolution potential of uranium causing it to migrate and collect on the solid cathode. As uranium depleted in the bath, the voltage increased in the system, which acted as a signal to change out the solid cathode, in preparation for plutonium deposit.

By changing the solid cathodes at the onset of the voltage rise, plutonium could be separated from uranium. The noble metal fission products did not oxidize at the anode, and remained within the cadmium anode. The more reactive fission products remained in the salt phase. Cadmium and salt phases could be processed by distilling cadmium and regenerating the salt through stripping with Li/Cd alloy. The fission products are disposed of as a high level waste. This process can be utilized for LWR oxide fuels with a reduction step in the beginning to convert the oxide to metallic form prior to electrorefining.

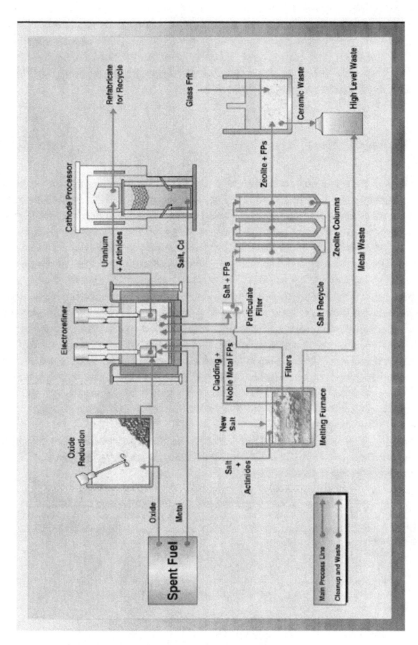

Fig. 9.114. Pyroprocessing Technique Developed by Argonne National Lab. (Adapted from [301]).

The pyroprocesses are limited in their uses due to material incompatibility problems associated with corrosion and high temperature degradation. These processes will require further development for Generation IV systems. Several countries, including the U.S., Japan, France, Russia and Spain have on-going research in this area in support of global nuclear waste remediation and Generation IV reactor implementation program [302–306].

9.23 Thorium Fuel Cycle

Aqueous and non-aqueous techniques that are described earlier can also be used for reprocessing of spent fuels from the thorium fuel cycle. The Thorium Extraction (Thorex) process, shown in Fig. 9.115, was developed by ORNL in the 1950s, for extraction of uranium and thorium from spent thorium fuel. Similar to Purex, a 30% TBP in n-dodecane is utilized as the solvent. Thorium has a much lower distribution coefficient between an aqueous solution and TBP as compared to uranium or plutonium. As a result, the thorium has to be forced into the organic TBP phase with the use of a salting agent. During early development of the process, aluminum nitrate was used as the salting agent. However, this increased the volume of high level wastes. Nitric acid was substituted as the salting agent, which became a more effective solution. Another key difference in the Thorex process compared to Purex process is that if the percentage of thorium in the extractant is too high, a third organic phase will form, greatly reducing the amount of thorium extracted in the TBP phase. This is prevented by adding highly concentrated HNO_3 to the bottom of the thorium extraction stage, where the thorium concentration is the lowest.

A two-stage Thorex process (Table 9.27) is also under development for high burn-up (on the order of 100,000 MWd/MT) fuels, expected from the HTGR or Thorium High Temperature Reactor (THTR) [307, 308].

Table 9.27. Recommended thorex concentrations for high burn-up fuel [308].

Process stream	Concentration	Relative flowrates
Extraction		
Feed	1.0 M Th; 0.5–1.0 M HNO_3	1.0
Scrub	0.1 M HNO_3	1.0
Salting agent	13.0 M HNO_3	0.2
Solvent	30% TBP/Dodecane	9.0
Partitioning		
Feed	0.15 M Th; 0.2 M HNO_3	6.0
Strip	0.5 M HNO_3	5.0
Scrub	30% TBP/Dodecane	1.0
U-Stripping		
Strip	0.3 M HNO_3	5.0

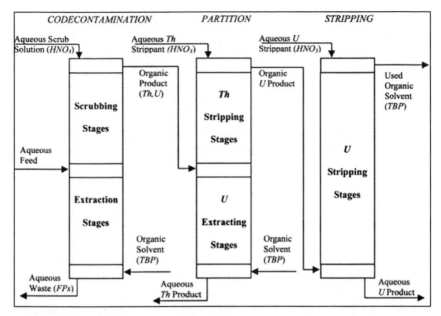

Fig. 9.115. Basic thorex flow sheet for spent thorium fuel reprocessing (Printed with permission from [307]).

Among various reprocessing technologies that are being considered, a Thorium Molten Salt Reactor (TMSR) is also under consideration. Since the thorium cycle produces fewer actinides during irradiation, which contribute heavily to the high level radioactivity in the salt, it is an attractive alternative to uranium fuel. Reprocessing of the fuel would be through pyrochemical techniques in the molten salt, similar to those previously described. This would act to decontaminate the produced U-233, as part of new fuel preparation [309].

9.24 Waste Treatment/Recycling

The greatest challenge to the sustainability of nuclear power is waste management. This has always been the Achilles heal for the nuclear industry and is the greatest source of fear among the general public. Every aspect of the fuel cycle generates some form of radioactive and/or otherwise hazardous waste, which must be disposed of properly.

High level waste is certainly the most problematic, as it includes radioactive material with very long half-lives and emits high levels of ionizing radiation. Finding ways to adequately reprocess, transmutate, store or some combination of all of these methods, is the top priority for governments and utilities. Deep underground repositories, such as the Yucca Mountain Project in the USA, are potentially capable of storing this material until the radiotoxicity is sufficiently depleted. The long term storage introduces a number of uncertainties, public acceptance, and policy issues. Although reprocessing of spent fuels will reduce the volume for permanent storage, a number of non-radioactive waste stream are also generated during reprocessing that must be treated before disposal to meet local, state, and federal regulations regarding discharge to the environment. The waste forms throughout the fuel cycle are discussed below, and the methods by which these wastes are minimized and disposed of are also described. Much of this technology is still in the experimental stage, although some methods are simply building upon older processes.

9.24.1 Fuel Cycle Front-End

Waste associated with the front-end of the fuel cycle includes wastes from mining, milling, conversion and fabrication processes. The government regulations regarding disposal of these non-radioactive wastes are becoming more stringent. In the USA, both the Nuclear Regulatory Commission (NRC) and Environmental Protection Agency (EPA) are involved in regulation of these wastes. Companies are also developing new technologies and putting efforts in place to minimize the generation of these wastes. Table 9.28 illustrates the efforts in place to minimize waste.

Table 9.28. Waste minimization categories in the fuel cycle front-end [310].

Process	Arisings	Source reduction	Recycle and reuse	Waste management optimization
Refining	Drums		●	
	Insolubles	●		●
	Liquid effluents	●	●	
	Sludges	●		●
	Liquid nitrates		●	
	Solvents		●	
Conversion	Solid calcium fluoride	●		●
	Radioactive sludges			●
	Non radioactive sludges	●	●	
	Hydrogen fluoride		●	
Enrichment	Uranium contaminated soilds		●	●
	Depleted uranium		●	
Fuel Fabrication	Ammonium fluoride solution		●	
	Ammonium nitrate solution		●	
	Magnesium fluoride		●	●
	Graphite		●	●
	Hydrogen fluoride	●	●	
	Extraction residues	●	●	
	Sludges	●		
	Zircaloy	●		

Process	Arisings	Source reduction	Recycle and reuse	Waste management optimization
	Stainless Steel	●		
	Miscellaneous metal scrap	●		●
	Ventilation filter	●		●
	Mixed combustible materials	●		

9.24.2 Mining & Milling Waste

Both open-pit and underground mining of uranium essentially produce the same basic types of hazardous waste. These include waste rock from the mining, tailings from milling, industrial waste and waste water. In-situ mining does not have the waste rock or tailings problem, but the leaching solution can contaminate groundwater and must be avoided.

Waste rock may contain traces of oxidizing minerals, which can form acids, when mixed with water. This is a hazard common to any open-pit or underground mining operation. The waste rock of uranium mines will still have traces of uranium, although too low for economic retrieval. In the past, waste rock was not of particular concern. However, new regulations require further treatment before disposal on mining sites so that the acid leached compounds do not enter the groundwater. Some of the remedial methods include processing of the waste rock with the ore, disposal as mine backfill, placed in flooded out mine pits, or covered with topsoil and re-vegetated, if the hazard is sufficiently low [311].

In the milling operation, sulfuric acid is used to leach the ore. After extraction of uranium compounds, the remaining impurities left in the sulfuric acid solution are neutralized with lime and blended with the waste rock to form tailings. The tailings contain all of the radioactive decay chain elements from uranium, shown in Fig. 9.116, as well as the chemical additives from the milling process.

Some tailings were used as backfill, although the milling operation adds mass, resulting in a larger amount of waste than can be occupied by the mine pit. Some tailings have been used to dam valleys to form tailings ponds. Natural lakes have also been used as tailings ponds. Some operations have simply piled the tailings to form mountains of waste. This has been especially problematic in arid regions of the southwest, where winds have blown across dry tailings piles and spread contamination over large distances. Others storage facilities have leached out acid, causing contamination of local streams and ground water. Some tailings have been utilized for construction material for homes and businesses.

New government regulations no longer allow past tailings storage practices. The tailing disposal areas must have liners with drains in appropriate places prior to tailings loading. After the tailings have been loaded, an engineered cover is placed on the tailings pile, to prevent the spread of contamination through the air. Tailings are also placed back into the mines from which they came.

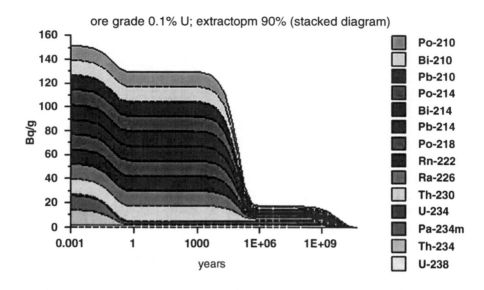

ore grade 0.1% U; extractopm 90% (stacked diagram)

Legend:
- Po-210
- Bi-210
- Pb-210
- Po-214
- Bi-214
- Pb-214
- Po-218
- Rn-222
- Ra-226
- Th-230
- U-234
- Pa-234m
- Th-234
- U-238

Fig. 9.116. Uranium Tailings Activity for ore grade 0.1% U after 90% extraction (Adapted from [312]).

An open pit uranium mining activity is shown in Fig. 9.117.

However, much more advanced efforts are taken to ensure groundwater does not flow through the tailings and cause contamination. In-situ mining, illustrated in Fig. 9.118, has several advantages over open-pit and underground mining, with regards to waste management. There are no tailings or waste rock associated with this type of mining. About 5% of the radioactivity within the ore reaches the surface, reducing dose to personnel. However, there is an inherent risk of contamination of groundwater aquifer, when leaching solution is pumped out to the surface. However, Cochran and Tsoulfanidis [9] noted that Texas has been using in-situ techniques for over 20 years, with no groundwater contamination.

Typically, sulfate is added to the leaching solution to form an acidic solution, which will dissolve the target ore. However, carbonates should be used, if there is too much limestone in the soil. This solution is hard-piped into the mine, then pumped back out through a central return, where it is sent off to a set of ion exchangers for uranium extraction. This cycle continues until the levels of uranium become uneconomical to extract. The leaching solution is then neutralized and allowed to evaporate. Clean water is pumped underground through the system until contamination levels are within acceptable standards. The groundwater aquifers are monitored at all times to ensure that no migration of leaching agents, and if any, immediate actions are taken to correct the situation. A summary of treatments of mining wastes has been provided by IAEA [314].

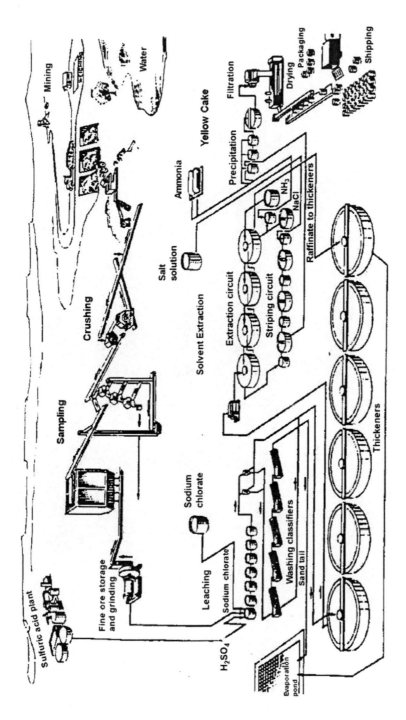

Fig. 9.117. Typical Uranium Strip-Mining or Underground Mining Operation. (Adapted from [313]).

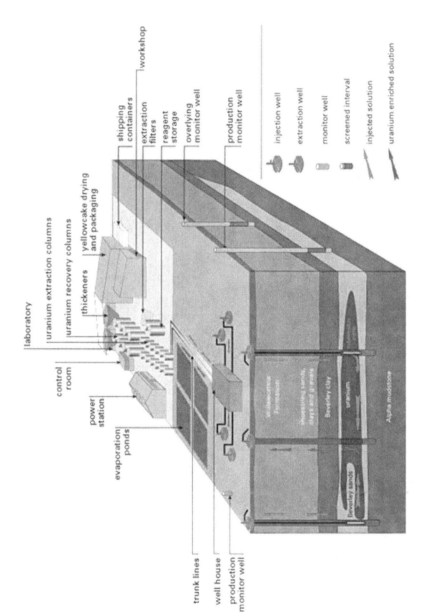

Fig. 9.118. In-situ leaching of uranium. (Adapted from [208]).

9.24.3 Conversion & Enrichment Waste

During conversion of yellowcake to UF_6 and subsequent enrichment, nonradio-active but significant amount of hazardous wastes are generated. The organic phase contains about 95 g uranium/L, and the raffinate contains 0.1 g uranium/L. The uranium is back-extracted into the aqueous phase by stripping it with 0.01M nitric acid.

   The uranyl nitrate is then converted to UO_3, through concentration and denitration methods. The remaining raffinate is neutralized with lime, prior to drying and disposal. Water, nitric acid and nitrogen oxides are released in these steps and can be recycled back into the feed stream.

   During conversion of yellowcake to UF_6, volatile fluorides of silicon, sulfur and boron are generated. These gases are removed with the excess HF through a combination of scrubbing with water, and aqueous KOH. The scrubbed solution is neutralized with lime for disposal or condensed to produce dilute HF for reuse in the system.

   Conversion of UF_4 to UF_6 is accomplished through a reaction with fluorine at 425°C to 535°C in a fluid-bed reactor charged with CaF_2 to improve heat transfer. The product gas is passed through a cold-trap to condense out UF_6, and the excess fluorine is passed through a clean-up reactor, where it reacts with UF_4 to produce additional UF_6.

   Once the product reaches its target enrichment, it is converted to UO_2 for fuel fabrication feed material. The waste from this process is in the form of depleted $^{238}UF_6$. This is converted to metallic form for use in military applications, such as armor-piercing munitions.

Fuel Fabrication Waste

The UF_6 can be converted to UO_2, the feed material for fuel fabrication, by one of the following three methods (Fig. 9.119). The first method involves hydrolyzing UF_6 in water, then adding ammonia to precipitate out ammonium diuranate, which is reduced to UO_2 with hydrogen at high temperatures. The second method combines UF_6, CO_2 and NH_3 in water to form ammonium uranyl carbonate. This is combined with steam and hydrogen at 500–600°C. The third method involves reducing and hydrolyzing the UF_6 with hydrogen and steam, forming UO_2 and HF. The resulting HF can be neutralized with lime for disposal, or diluted and returned to the conversion stream.

   Fuel fabrication plants produce a significant amount of waste, although the majority is in the form of metallic scrap, which has significant value and is recycled back into the process. Most of the chemical waste formed in the fabrication plant is from the afore-mentioned conversion of UF_6 to UO_2 and are listed in Table 9.29. Chemical recovery methods of these chemicals are shown in Fig. 9.120.

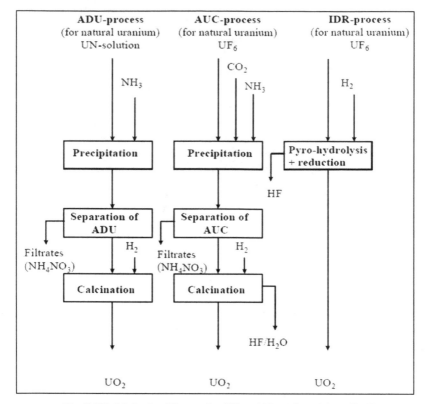

Fig. 9.119. Methods of Converting UF$_6$ to UO$_2$ (Adapted from [310]).

Table 9.29. Typical hazardous, non-radioactive, chemicals generated from the fuel fabrication systems for a 1,000 t U throughput facility.

Arising	Quantity	Classification	Process/Origin
Ammonia fluoride solution	4,000 m^3	By-product	AUC
Ammonia nitrate solution	5,000 m^3	By-product	AUC/ADU
Extraction residues	10 m^3	Material for treatment	AUC/ADU
Sludges	1 m^3	Material for treatment	AUC/ADU
Hydrogen fluoride	1,000 t	By-product	IDR
Magnesium fluoride	450 t	By-product	Magnox
Graphite	350 t	Material for treatment	Magnox
Zircaly	1 t	Material for treatment	Water reactor fuel
Stainless steel	1 t	Material for treatment	Gas cooled reactor
Miscellaneous metal scrap	40 t	Material for treatment	All
Ventilation filters	100–200 m^3	Material for treatment	All
Mixed combustible material	300 m^3	Material for treatment	All

Source: Reference [310].

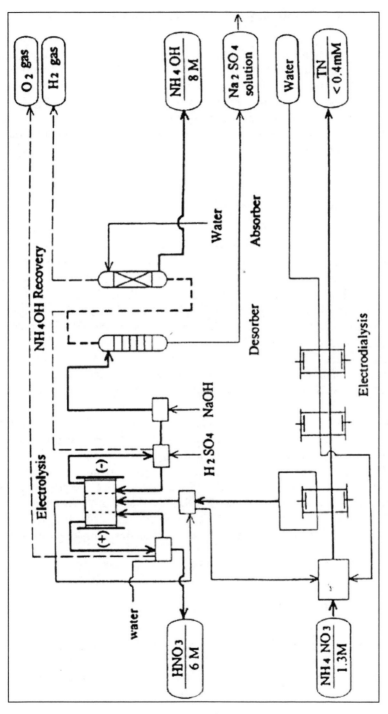

Fig. 9.120. Nitric Acid and Ammonia Recovery from the Fuel Fabrication Process. (Adapted from [310]).

9.25 Separation Technologies in Waste Management

Wastes formed during reprocessing activities contain significant amount of nitrate, acid and radioactive sludge. Effective partitioning of this waste can reduce the volume of radioactive and heat-producing wastes. A number of methods were developed for remediation of these types of wastes, particularly for that generated from the US military nuclear weapons program currently stored at the Hanford site. A number of these processes are further developed to apply to civilian wastes and are discussed below.

9.25.1 Transuranic Extraction (TRUEX)

This solvent extraction technique was designed for separation of transuranic (TRU) elements such as Np, Pu, Am and Cm, from aqueous nitrate or chloride waste streams. Each of the aqueous reprocessing methods results in waste streams for which the TRUEX technique would be beneficial. Reduction of TRU from the waste stream, greatly reduces the radio-toxicity of the waste, making long-term disposal significantly less demanding. The flow diagram of the TRUEX process is shown in Fig. 9.121.

The solvent used in the TRUEX process is a mixture of 0.2M octyl-(phenyl)-N, N-diisobutylcarbamoyl-methylphosphine oxide (CMPO) and 1.4M TBP in n-dodecane [316, 317]. Three scrubbing sections are incorporated in this process. The first scrub uses oxalic acid to remove impurities from the solvent. The second unit uses moderately concentrated nitric acid to scrub the oxalic acid from the solvent. The final scrubbing section uses dilute nitric acid to lower TRU concentrations in the solvent, making it more conducive for stripping.

The TRUEX process has been demonstrated under laboratory conditions as a part of UREX+ process at the Argonne National Laboratory. The product stream contained 3.4% Tc, 0.02% Pu, less than 2% Np, less than 0.04% Am and less than 1.2% of Cm in the laboratory testing [278]. The process needs further development since some of the TRU elements were still at undesirable levels for repository disposal.

9.25.2 Strontium Extraction (SREX) Process

For the first 50 to 100 years, following spent fuel discharge from a reactor, one of the primary sources of decay heat is Sr-90. Effective partitioning of Sr and Cs, from the fuel, would cause a significant decrease in the decay heat, produced by the fuel. As shown in Fig. 9.122, this will have significant effect on the repository capacity.

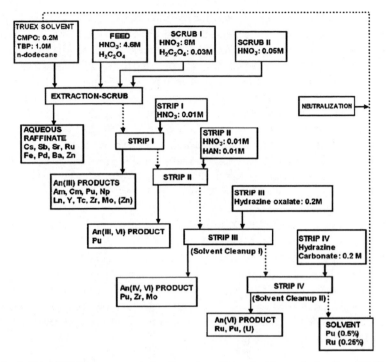

Fig. 9.121. TRUEX waste separation flow sheet (Printed with permission from [315]).

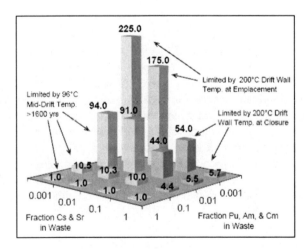

Fig. 9.122. Volume reduction due to reprocessing of spent fuel (Adapted from [278]).

As a result, Cs and Sr are targeted for removal and several processes have been evaluated. The Idaho National Engineering and Environmental Laboratory (INEEL) is developing a strontium Extraction (SREX) process. A schematic diagram of the process is shown in Fig. 9.123. The process is consisted of 24 contractors or stages as shown by number in the flow sheet. The flow sheet consisted of an extraction section, a 2.0 M HNO_3 scrub section to remove extracted K from the SREX solvent, a 0.05 M HNO_3 strip section for the removal of Sr from the SREX solvent, a 0.1 M ammonium citrate strip section for the removal of Pb from the SREX solvent, and a 3.0 M HNO_3 equilibration section. TBP was added to the solvent as a phase modifier to prevent third-phase formation and a paraffinic hydrocarbon was used as a diluent. This process has been tested in several laboratories and is envisioned as becoming a portion of the Purex or UREX+ flow sheets, or it can also be used as a stand-alone process.

The solvent used in the SREX process is the crown ether 0.15M 4,4(5),di-(t-butylcyclohexano)-18-crown-6($DtBuCH_{18}C_6$) and a 1.5M TBP in an Isopar-L® dilluent, which has proven to be highly selective for strontium in aqueous solution [318]. A high level of strontium separation can be achieved, approaching greater than 99.99% recovery of Sr. The process can also remove Pb by more than 94%. The TBP also removed Pu and U in excess of 99%. However, disadvantages of this process include the cost of the reagent and the chemical and radiolytic degradation of the crown ether [318].

9.25.3 CCD-PEG

The CCD-PEG process, shown in Fig. 9.124, has been developed and tested, along with the UREX+ process for removal of Cs and Sr together from the solution. This process has proven highly efficient for removing Cs and Sr from the UREX+ waste stream, if the nitric acid concentration is less than 1M.

The solvent is chlorinated cobalt dicarbollide (CCD) and polyethylene glycol (PEG) in a phenyltrifluoromethyl sulfone diluent. The Cs and Sr are extracted into the solvent, along with any barium or rubidium that may be present in the stream. During the laboratory demonstration of the process, Cs and Sr were stripped from the solvent using guanidine carbonate diethylenetriamine pentaacetic acid (DTPA) solution. A new, regenerable, stripping agent based on methylamine carbonate is under investigation, which is expected to generate less organic waste and simplify solidification of the resulting waste [320].

As nitric acid concentration increases, there is a corresponding reduction in the Cs and Sr distribution coefficient, illustrated in Fig. 9.125. This reduction is significant if the nitric acid concentration is greater than 1M [318–320].

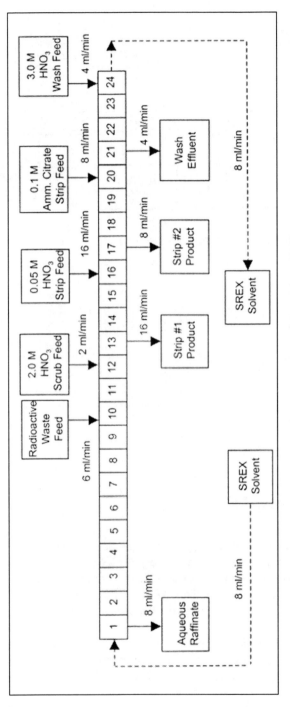

Fig. 9.123. SREX Flow Sheet. (Adapted from [310]).

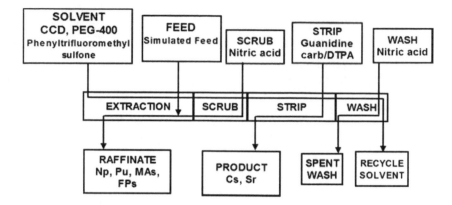

Fig. 9.124. CCD-PEG Flow Sheet (Printed with permission from [320]).

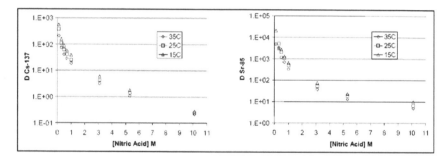

Fig. 9.125. CCD-PEG distribution coefficients as a function of nitric acid concentration (Printed with permission from [320]).

9.25.4 TALSPEAK

The chemical behavior of actinides and lanthanides is very similar, which makes their separation from each other extremely difficult. The most successful method of separation to date is the use of Trivalent Actinide Lanthanide Separation by Phosphorus-Reagent Extraction from Aqueous Komplexes (TALSPEAK) process. The process may be divided into two categories: (1) Direct process and (2) Indirect process.

In the direct TALSPEAK process, shown in Fig. 9.126, the lanthanides are selectively separated from the actinides, which remain in the aqueous phase. The lanthanides can then be stripped from the solvent for waste disposal. The indirect

TALSPEAK process extracts both lanthanides and actinides from solution. The actinides are then selectively stripped from the lanthanides into a complexant solution [321]. Although TALSPEAK has shown good separation capabilities, the acidity of the solvent must be very low. Therefore, the feed acidity must be adjusted to the desired level prior to feeding to the extraction unit. Another difficulty includes limited metal ion loading in the solvent making its cleaning process expensive [322].

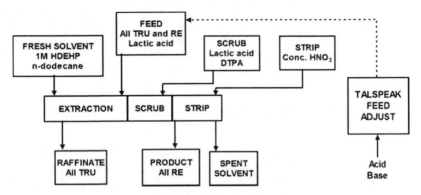

Fig. 9.126. TALSPEAK flow sheet (Adapted from [323]).

Several processes are under development for actinide stripping from solvents, following co-extraction with lanthanides. These methods include DIDPA (the name was derived from the solvent used in the process, diisodecylphosphoric acid), SETFICS (**SE**paration of **T**rivalent **F**-elements **I**ntrogroup by **C**MPO **S**olvent) and PALADIN developed by CEA, France). Similarly, processes are being developed for direct actinide extraction from lanthanides, called Selective Actinides Extraction (SANEX) processes. The SANEX process includes CYANEX 301 (the process is based on a resin called CYANEX from Cytec Industries Inc., NJ, USA), DIAMEX (diamide extraction) and ALINA (Actinide Lanthanide Intergroup separation from Acidic solutions) processes [322].

9.25.5 Ion Exchange

Ion exchange processes have been in use for several decades for nuclear waste separation. Both organic and inorganic resins are available for treatment of nuclear wastes. Highly selective organic resins have been developed, providing excellent partitioning of various radionuclides including Cs and Sr. Examples include a substituted diphosphonic acid resin for efficient separation of heavy metal cations from liquid waste and a resin, with crown ether as the functional group, for Sr separation from aqueous solution. A number of these resins are found to be effective in strong nitric acid solutions. The waste streams of the current aqueous reprocessing techniques often have strong nitric acid concentrations.

The inorganic resins have high capacity for some radioactive elements, chemical stability and resistant to radiolysis. Silicotitanates, zeolites, titanium phosphate and some types of clay are among the materials currently being developed. Another key benefit of inorganic resin is the potential for transforming them directly into ceramic materials. This ceramic waste form has the potential for direct disposal in a repository, although substantial testing must still be performed to determine the long-term retention capabilities of the resin [324, 325].

9.25.6 Thorium Reprocessing Waste

Although thorium fuel represents a significant departure from uranium and plutonium fuels, the reprocessing techniques are essentially the same. Thorex reprocessing utilizes the same TBP solvent to extract uranium and thorium from a nitric acid solution. Thorium reprocessing does involve additional stripping steps, which does result in an increased volume of waste. However, as previously described, both the solvent and solution can be recycled back into earlier stages of the process. Essentially, thorium reprocessing does not represent a major departure from Purex methods, with regards to waste generation.

9.26 Non-fuel Materials

The main focus of spent fuel reprocessing has been on partitioning and waste treatment of the fuel material. However, the majority of fuel assembly material consists of cladding and other structural materials. These components represent a large volume of the high level waste generated in nuclear reactors and must be properly disposed of.

Chemical de-cladding methods result in the dissolution of the cladding into solution. Following successful partitioning efforts, the cladding remains in solution, with the fission products and other waste elements. This waste solution is then sent off for treatment, which may include evaporation, vitrification, cementation or some combination of these processes.

Mechanical de-cladding leaves behind fuel hulls, end-fittings, fragments and fine residue, from the chopping and shearing mechanisms. A series of nitric acid dissolutions are performed, in order to leach out all remaining fuel, from the structural materials. The bulk metal waste is then rinsed and stored in drums. This material is then crushed into discs and dried with hot inert gas. The discs are stacked into the final waste canister and an upper cap is seal-welded in place. These canisters, shown in Fig. 9.127, are then sent to temporary storage facilities, awaiting final repository availability. The plant layout of the LaHague Reprocessing Facility currently operating in France is shown in Fig. 9.128.

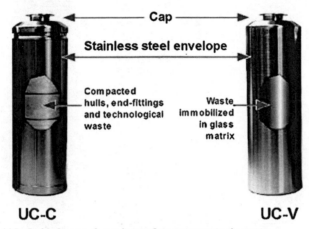

UC-C: Universal canister for compacted waste
UC-V: Universal canister for vitrified waste

Fig. 9.127. Universal canister for compacted waste (Printed with permission from [326]).

Recycling of the spent fuel hulls has been studied under the sponsorship of the U.S. Department of Energy. The sol-gel process used to form TRISO particles, could also transform the TRU product from the UREX+ processes into a cermet fuel. The zircoloy is pulverized into powder and heated to approximately 900°C to transform ZrH_2 to metallic Zr according the following reaction:

$$ZrH_2 \rightarrow Zr + H_2$$

The resulting two zircoloy and TRU products are combined to form an oxide fuel, which could be utilized in certain generation IV reactors [327].

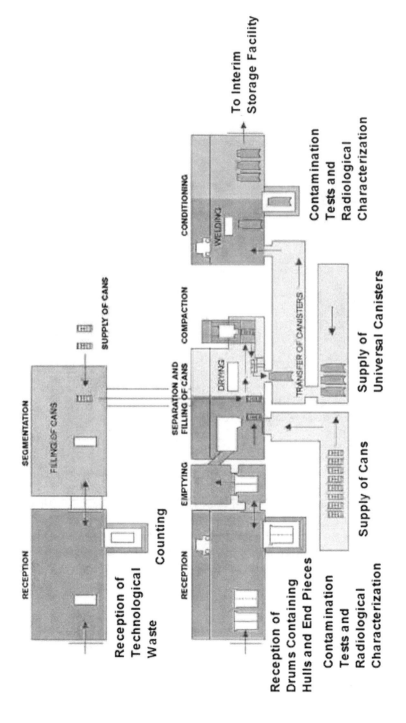

Fig. 9.128. LaHague Spent Fuel Hull/End-fitting Processing Facility. (Printed with permission from [326]).

9.27 Transmutation

The radiotoxicity of a number of radionuclides present in the waste can be reduced significantly by transmutation as shown in Fig. 9.129.

Transmutation describes both the fission of actinide materials in spent fuel as well as converting radioactive materials into stable nuclides, through neutron capture. This process takes place in any nuclear reactor, although the extent of the transmutation is highly dependent on the type of reactor and fuel. Conventional light water reactors produce Pu-239 by transmutation, which accounts for up to 30% of power production. However, the capture and fission cross sections for most non-fissile materials are very low in the thermal range, making light water reactors inefficient transmutation systems.

The effectiveness of transmutation depends on fast reactors or accelerator driven systems. An example of transmutation reaction is neutron capture of Tc-99 [328]. As shown in Fig. 9.130, the transmutation can reduce the radiotoxicity significantly within a relatively short period of time compared to storing in a repository.

$$Tc\text{-}99 + n \rightarrow Tc\text{-}100 \rightarrow \beta\text{- decay} \rightarrow Ru\text{-}100 + n \rightarrow Ru\text{-}101 + n \rightarrow Ru102(stable)$$

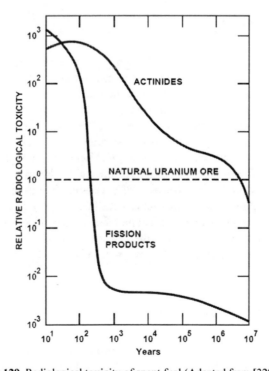

Fig. 9.129. Radiological toxicity of spent fuel (Adapted from [329]).

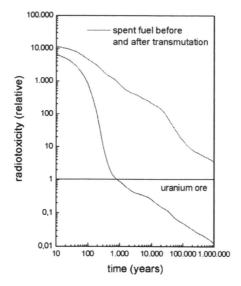

Fig. 9.130. Radiotoxicity effect of transmutation on 1 t of SNF (Adapted from [330]).

9.27.1 Fast Reactors

Several countries are heavily involved in development of fast reactor technology, including the U.S., France, Japan, Russia and the U.K. These reactors represent high potential for both energy production and waste transmutation in the future.

Many of the target isotopes for transmutation have relatively large cross sections in the epithermal and fast neutron ranges. Fast reactors operate with neutrons in these ranges and have very high fluxes, as compared to their light water counterparts. This makes the fast reactor much more efficient at converting target material into their respective product material. Additionally, the by-product heat can be utilized for energy production. Burning of excess plutonium or breeding from fertile uranium are other benefits, available with fast reactors. Many of the countries developing these reactors have envisioned fast burner reactors adjacent to light water reactors to complete a closed fuel cycle. Although high level waste would still be generated, the volume and toxicity would be greatly reduced.

9.27.2 Accelerator Technology

Accelerator-driven transmutation systems, shown in Fig. 9.131, have become the focus of extensive research world-wide and considered to be the preferred method of waste transmutation by several countries. The principle behind this technology is the production of a high-energy, high-current proton beam. Negatively charged hydrogen ions are accelerated into a thin metal foil, where the electrons are stripped and a proton beam emerges. These protons are accelerated and directed towards a high atomic number target material for spallation. The spallation target is surrounded by actinide fuel, which is the transmutation material. This can also consist of fresh spent reactor fuel, from light water reactors. In principle, this technology could convert all TRU waste into relatively short-lived fission products, while yielding some energy production as a by-product [328, 332].

This technology has been pursued by several nuclear-capable countries and is at the fore-front of advanced transmutation technology. Several modification of the process is underway to address the use of thorium fuel, pure TRU targets, TRU and Pu targets as well as the fresh spent fuel. With the advances in cyclotron and accelerator technology, the accelerator driven systems could become large enough to become commercial scale power plants.

9.28 Direct Use of Spent PWR fuel in CANDU (DUPIC)

Another method of spent fuel disposal that has undergone substantial research and development in Canada and South Korea is the direct use of PWR fuel in CANDU reactors, called DUPIC process (Direct Use of spent PWR fuel In CANDU). The basic objective is the utilization of PWR fuel, which has reached its useful life in light water cooled reactors, but still has sufficient fuel remaining for CANDU operation. The oxide fuel is separated from the fuel assemblies; no dissolution of the fuel is necessary. The fuel is generally run through a die and stripped of the cladding material. The fuel material is grounded into powder form and can be mixed with fresh uranium, prior to pelletizing. The fuel is then re-loaded into pins and loaded into a CANDU reactor, arranged in a different orientation than a regular CANDU reactor.

Significant challenges are associated with the DUPIC fuel design. Every stage of this process must be performed remotely, as spent reactor fuel radiation levels are extremely hazardous. Loading of the fuel is also a major challenge, as fresh fuel is typically air-loaded and does not represent a radiation hazard, which is not the case with DUPIC fuel. The most likely solution will be to load the fuel backwards, from the spent fuel pool, thereby providing the necessary shielding. However, several logistical and equipment modifications are necessary to ensure the neutronics and plant safety.

The DUPIC method of spent fuel mitigation remains a promising technique. South Korea has tested smaller versions of these assemblies in their research reactor program and produced full-size DUPIC fuel assemblies [331].

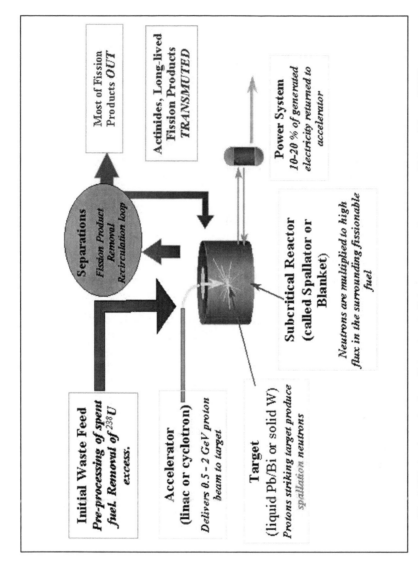

Fig. 9.131. A schematic view of. Accelerator-Driven transmutation system. (Adapted from [330]).

9.29 Waste Vitrification

Three methods have been explored for long-term waste immobilization, which include cementation, bituminization and vitrification. Cementation and bituminization have both been utilized heavily for low and intermediate level wastes. Cementation is a relatively easy and inexpensive method, but is not suitable for liquid wastes. Bitumen is more capable of suspending liquid or gel wastes and has lower leaching rates than cementation. However immobilization of waste in glass by vitrification is considered to be most preferred method.

Waste vitrification, illustrated in Fig. 9.132, is a mature technology, having been utilized by countries with extensive reprocessing experience, such as France and the U.K. [333]. This is a two-step operation. The first step involves evaporation and calcination of the waste solution in a heated, rotating tube. This is followed by the addition of glass forming compounds or glass frit to the calciner for vitrification. Borosilicate glass is the primary type currently in use, which is made up of 80% SiO_2 (silica), B_2O_3 (boric anhydride), Al_2O_3 (alumina) and Na_2O (sodium oxide). The glass and waste calcine are then heated to 1150°C and poured into a final waste canister, with a capacity of 400 kg. The canister is sealed with a welded cover and allowed to cool in dry storage, awaiting final repository availability. In France, 4,000 t of glass has been produced in this manner and an additional 2,000 t has been produced in the U.K.

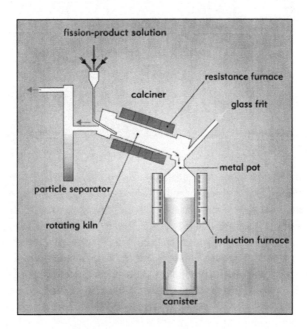

Fig. 9.132. HLW vitrification diagram (Printed with permission from [333]).

In the USA, a HLW vitrification demonstration plant was constructed in the West Valley, NY. In this demonstration plant over 9.32 million curies of cesium137/strontium-90 (approximately 85% of the total estimated curie inventory) removed from an underground waste storage tanks, leaving only tank heel wastes remaining to be removed for processing. In the demonstration project, 211 canisters of borosilicate waste glass were produced. Each canister holds approximately 2,000 kg of glass and has a contact dose rate of nearly 2,700 rem per hour. The project encompassed waste mobilization and transfer, slurry feed preparation, joule-heated melter operation, canister handling and temporary storage, and melter off-gas treatment [334].

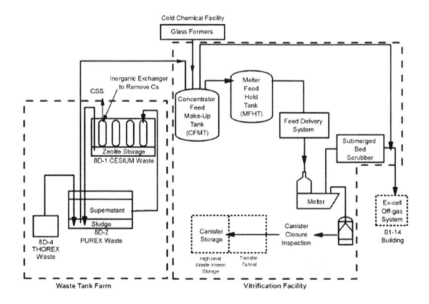

Fig. 9.133. The flow diagram of the West valley, NY, USA HLW vitrification demonstration plant (Adapted from [334]).

The future of nuclear power is certainly bright. Evidence of a nuclear renaissance is seen throughout the nuclear community. Nuclear power is experiencing a global resurgence because energy is key to the future economic development of nations. For example, China has made a decision to invest in its energy infrastructure to continue its economic growth by building 100 nuclear power plants by the year 2020. The U.S. has created the global nuclear energy partnership (GNEP) designed to develop new nuclear recycling and power technologies, in conjunction with several countries. New nuclear power plants are being constructed worldwide. The NRC is reviewing nine new nuclear power plant designs for licensing. Nuclear engineering departments are experiencing higher enrollment numbers, as demand for graduates has risen dramatically. The next generation of nuclear reactors will expand upon the knowledge gained thus far and help improve Generation IV designs. Through the use of new reactors and fuel designs as well as spent fuel partitioning and transmutation, nuclear power will prove to be a sustainable and reliable source of energy, well into the future.

References

1. US Department of Energy (1993) DOE Fundamentals Handbook, Nuclear Physics and Reactor Theory: Volume 1 and 2. DOE-HDBK 1019/1-93
2. National Nuclear Data Center. Chart of nuclides. Brookhaven National Laboratory. http://www.nndc.bnl.gov/chart/
3. Heeger K (2008) Fission and nuclear energy Lecture 21 University of Wisconsin.
4. Prelas MA, Peck MS (2005) Nonproliferation Issues for Weapons of Mass Destruction. CRC Press, New York, USA
5. World Nuclear Association, London, UK
6. NEA/IAEA (OECD Nuclear Energy Agency and International Atomic Energy Agency), 2006: Uranium 2005: Resources, Production and Demand. A joint report by the OECD Nuclear Energy Agency and the International Atomic Energy Agency Publication No. 6098. OECD, Paris (2006).
7. Rogner H-H, McDonald A (November 2007) Nuclear Energy - Status and Outlook, 20th World Energy Congress, Rome, Italy
8. U.S. Nuclear Regulatory Commission, 2008.
9. Cochran R, Tsoulfanidis N (1999) The Nuclear Fuel Cycle: Analysis and Management, 2nd Edition. American Nuclear Society, La Grange Park, Illinois.
10. Argonne National Laboratory. Depleted UF_6 management information network. http://web.ead.anl.gov/uranium/index.cfm. 12/18/2008.
11. U.S. Nuclear Regulatory Commission. Fact sheet on uranium enrichment. http://www.nrc.gov/reading-rm/doc-collections/fact-sheets/enrichment.html. 12/18/2008.
12. Wood HG, Glaser A, Kemp RS (2008) The gas centrifuge and nuclear weapons proliferation. Physics Today September: 40–15
13. USEC. http://www.usec.com/v2001_02/HTML/Aboutusec_enrichment.asp.
14. Heller A (May 2000) Laser Technology Follows in Lawrence's Footsteps. Science and Technology Review. https://www.llnl.gov/str/str2000.html.
15. Hargrove S (May 2000) Laser Technology Follows in Lawrence's Footsteps. Science and Technology Review. www.llnl.gov/str/Hargrove.html.
16. Wilson PD (1996) The Nuclear Fuel Cycle. Oxford University Press, New York.
17. Fouquet DM, Razvi J, Whittemore WL (November 2003) TRIGA research reactors: A pathway to the peaceful applications of nuclear energy. Nuclear News: 46–56.
18. US DOE, National Transportation Program. Spent nuclear fuel and high-level radioactive waste transportation. http://www.nti.org/e_research/official_docs/doe/spent_nuc_feul.pdf.
19. Wallace WP, Simnad MT (1964) Fuel element. U.S. Patent No. 3,119,747, January 28, 1964.
20. European Nuclear Society. Fuel rod. www.euronuclear.org/info/encyclopedia/f/fuel-rod.htm. 12/18/2008

21. Keiser DD, Jr., Kennedy JR, Hilton BA, and Hayes SL (2008) The development of metallic nuclear fuels for transmutation applications: Materials challenges. JOM Journal of the Minerals, Metals and Materials Society 60(1): 29–32

22. OECD (Organisation for Economic Co-operation and Development) (2006) Red Book Retrospective. A review of uranium resources, production and demand from 1965 to 2003.

23. Arbital JG, Snider JD (1996) Technology for down-blending weapons grade uranium into commercial reactor-usable uranium. Nuclear Materials Management - Annual Meeting 25: 890–895

24. U.S. Department of Energy (2002) A technology roadmap for Generation IV nuclear energy systems. U.S. DOE Nuclear Energy Research Advisory Committee and the Generation IV International Forum, December 2002, GIF-002-00. http://www.ne.doe.gov/GenIV/documents/gen_iv_roadmap.pdf

25. Stacey WM (2001) Nuclear Reactor Physics. Wiley-Interscience, New York

26. J. Kenneth Shultis and Richard E. Faw (2007) Fundamentals of Nuclear Science and Engineering, 2nd Ed. CRC Press, New York, USA

27. Lamarsh JR, Baratta AJ (2001) Introduction to Nuclear Engineering 3rd Ed. Addison-Wesley Series in Nuclear Science and Engineering. Prentice Hall, Upper Saddle River, NJ

28. Hore-Lacy I (2006) Nuclear Energy in the 21st Century. World Nuclear University Press/Academic Press, London, UK

29. Bodansky, D (1996) Nuclear Energy: Principles, Practices, and Prospects. American Institute of Physics. Woodbury, NY

30. Knief RA (1992) Nuclear Engineering: Theory and Technology of Commercial Nuclear Power, Taylor and Francis

31. Glasstone S, Sesonske A (1994) Nuclear Reactor Engineering, 4th Ed. Chapman and Hall, New York

32. USNRC Technical Training Center. Boiling water reactor systems, Reactor Concepts Manual, Nuclear Regulatory Commission). http://www.nrc.gov/reading-rm/basic-ref/teachers/01.pdf

33. USNRC Technical Training Center. Nuclear power for electrical generation, Reactor Concepts Manual, Nuclear Regulatory Commission). http://www.nrc.gov/reading-rm/basic-ref/teachers/03.pdf

34. USNRC Technical Training Center. Pressurized water reactor system, Reactor Concepts Manual, Nuclear Regulatory Commission). http://www.nrc.gov/reading-rm/basic-ref/teachers/04.pdf

35. Murray RL (2007) Nuclear Reactors. Kirk-Othmer Encyclopedia of Chemical technology. Wiley, Malden, MA.

36. Nuclear Energy Institute, Washington D.C., USA

37. General Electric (3/30/2009) BWR/6 fuel assemblies and Control rod module. www.nucleartourist.com/images/bwrfuel1.jpg

38. The Institute of Engineering and Technology. Nuclear Reactor Type. www.theiet.org/factfiles.

39. Assessment and management of ageing of major nuclear power plant components important to safety: CANDU reactor assemblies. IAEA-TECDOC-1197, 2001. http://www.pub.iaea.org/MTCD/publications/PDF/te_1197_prn.pdf)

40. IAEA (International Atomic Energy Agency) (2005) Accident analysis for nuclear power plants with graphite moderated boiling water RBMK reactors. Safety Report Series No. 43.
41. Advanced Boiling Water Reactor Fact Sheet. http://www.gepower.com/prod_serv/products/nuclear_energy/en/downloads/abwr_fs.pdf.
42. AP1000 at a Glance. http://ap1000.westinghousenuclear.com/ap1000_glance.html
43. Long LB, Cummins WE, Winters JW. (2006) AP1000 Design for Security 2006 International congress on advances in nuclear power plants - ICAPP'06, Reno-Nevada USA, June 4-8 2006
44. Kasper K (2006) New Nuclear Options-The AP1000. Health Physics 90(6):519-520
45. AP1000 Design Control Document (2004) Revision 14, September 2004 (Revision 0 sent to NRC March 2002).
46. Matzie RA (2008) AP1000 will meet the challenges of near-term deployment. Nuclear Engineering and Design 238(8): 1856–1862
47. Schulz TL (2006) Westinghouse AP1000 advanced passive plant. Nuclear Engineering and Design 236: 1547–1557
48. Mitsubishi Heavy Industries, Ltd., DOE Technical Session, UAP-HF-07063-12, June 29, 2007).
49. US EPR, Areva. http://www.areva-np.com/us/liblocal/docs/EPR/U.S.EPRbrochure_1.07_FINAL.pdf).
50. Gamble RE, Hinds DH, Hucik SA, Maslak CE (2006) ESBWR... An Evolutionary Reactor Design Conference: 2006 International congress on advances in nuclear power plants – ICAPP'06, Reno – Nevada, USA, June 4–8, 2006. Proceedings of the 2006 international congress on advances in nuclear power plants – ICAPP '06
51. Cheng YK, Shiralkar BS, Marquino W (2005) Performance analyses of ESBWR ECCS and containment systems. Proceedings of ICAPP '05 Seoul Korea Paper 5485
52. Hinds D, Maslak C (January 2006) Next-generation nuclear energy: ESBWR. Nuclear News: 35–40
53. ESBWR, Technical fact sheet (http://www.energetics.com/pdfs/nuclear/esbwr.pdf)
54. Carelli MD, Conway LE, Oriani L, Petrović B, Lombardi CV, Ricotti ME,Barroso ACO, Collado JM, Cinotti L, Todreas NE, Grgić D, Moraes MM, Boroughs RD, Ninokata H, Ingersoll DT, Oriolo F (2004) The design and safety features of the IRIS reactor. Nuclear Engineering and Design 230(1–3): 151–167
55. Carelli MD, Petrovic B, Ferroni P (2007) IRIS safety-by-design and its implication to lessen emergency planning requirements. International Journal of Risk Assessment and Management 8(1–2): 123–136
56. Carelli MD, Conway L, Oriani L, Lombardi C, Ricotti M, Barroso A, Collado J, Cinotti L, M. Moraes M, Kozuch J, Grgic D, Ninokata H, Boroughs R, Ingersoll D, Oriolo F, Carelli MD (2003) The design and safety features of the Iris reactor. 11th International Conference on Nuclear Engineering Tokyo, Japan, April 20–23, 2003 ICONE11- 36564
57. Paramonov DV, Carelli MD, Miller K, Lombardi CV, Ricotti ME. Todreas NE, E. Greenspan E, Yamamoto K, Nagano A, Ninokata H, J. Robertson J, Oriolo F. IRIS reactor development. http://www2.ing.unipi.it/dimnp/CD/supporto/pdf/oriolo03.pdf.
58. Natsionalna Elektricheska Kompania Joint Press Release (2008). http://www.nek.bg/cgi-bin/index.cgi?l=2&d=1254
59. Hedges K (2002) The advanced CANDU reactor (ACR): Ready for the emerging market. ANES 2002 Symposium, October 16–18, 2002, Miami, FL

60. Lennox TA, Banks DM, Gilroy JE, Sunderland RE (1998) Gas cooled fast reactors. Trans. ENC 98 IV, TAL/005392

61. Melese-d'Hospital G, Simon RH (1977) Status of gas-cooled fast breeder reactor programs. Nuclear Engineering and Design 40: 5–12

62. Dostal V, Hejzlar P, Driscoll MJ, Todreas NE (2002) A supercritical CO2 gas turbine power cycle for next generation nuclear reactors. 10th International Nuclear Conference on Engineering (ICONE 10), Arlington, Virginia, USA, April 14–18, 2002

63. Martin P, Chauvin N, Garnier JC, Masson M, Brossard P, Gas cooled fast reactor system: Major objectives and options for reactor, fuel and fuel cycle. Proceedings of GLOBAL 2005 Tsukuba, Japan, October 9–13, 2005 Paper No. IL002

64. Anzieu P, Mizuno T, Okano Y, Aida T (2005) Conceptual core design studies of helium cooled fast reactor with coated particle fuel, Paper 5197, 2005 International Congress on Advances in Nuclear Power Plants (ICAPP '05)

65. Wei TYC, Rouault J (2003) Development of Generation IV advanced gas-cooled reactors with hardened/fast neutron spectrum. Transactions of the American Nuclear Society 88: 683–684

66. Cheng LY, Ludewig H (2007) 2400MWt gas-cooled fast reactor DHR studies status update. Brookhaven National Laboratory Report No. BNL–78166-2007

67. Meyer MK, Fielding R, Gan J (2007) Fuel development for gas-cooled fast reactors. Journal of Nuclear Materials 371(1–3): 281–287

68. Cinotti L, Smith CF, Sienicki JJ, Aït Abderrahim H, Benamati G, Locatelli G, Monti S. Wider H, Struwe D, Orden A (2007) The potential of the LFR and the ELSY project. 2007 International Congress on Advances in Nuclear Power Plants (ICAPP '07). Book of Abstracts, ICAPP 2007 Nice, France, May 13–18. Paper 7585

69. Yu YH, Son HM, Lee IS, Suh KY, (2006) Optimized battery-type reactor primary system design utilizing lead, Paper 6148, 2006 International Congress on Advances in Nuclear Power Plants (ICAPP'06)

70. Hwang IS, (2006) A sustainable regional waste transmutation system: PEACER, Plenary Invited Paper, 2006 International Congress on Advances in Nuclear Power Plants (ICAPP'06)

71. Kim WJ, Kim TW, Sohn MS, Suh KY (2006) Supercritical carbon dioxide Brayton power conversion cycle design for optimized battery-type integral reactor system, Paper 6142, 2006 International Congress on Advances in Nuclear Power Plants (ICAPP'06)

72. Zrodnikov AV, Toshinsky GI, Komlev OG, Dragunov YG, Stepanov VS, Klimov NN, Kpytov II, Krushelnitsky VN, Use of multi-purpose modular fast reactors SVBR-75/100 in market conditions, Paper 6023, 2006 International Congress on Advances in Nuclear Power Plants (ICAPP'06)

73. Cinotti L, Fazio C, Knebel J, Monti S, Abderrahim HA, Smith C, Suh K (2006) Lead-cooled fast reactor, FISA 2006, Luxembourg, 13–16 March 2006. UCRL-CONF-221396

74. Sienicki JJ, Moisseytsev AV (2005) SSTAR lead-cooled, small modular fast reactor for deployment at remote sites - system thermal hydraulic development, Paper 5426, 2005 International Congress on Advances in Nuclear Power Plants (ICAPP'05)

75. Azzati A, Benamati G, Gessi A, Long B, Scadozzo G (2004) Corrosion behaviour of steels in flowing LBE at low and high oxygen concentration. Journal of Nuclear Materials 335: 169–173

76. Nishi Y, Kinoshita I (2003) Experimental study on gas lift pump performance in lead-bismuth eutectic, ICAPP03-3055, 2003 International Congress on Advances in Nuclear Power Plants (ICAPP'03)

77. Toshinsky GI, Grigoriev OG, Efimov EI, Leonchuk MP (2002) Safety aspects of the SVBR-75/100 reactor, NEA Workshop on Advanced Nuclear Safety Issues and Research Needs, February 18–20, 2002, Paris, France

78. Adamov EO, Orlov VV, Filin A (2001) Final report on the ISTC Project 1418: Naturally safe lead-cooled fast reactor for large scale nuclear power, Moscow

79. Smith CF, Halsey WG, Brown NW, Sienicki JJ, Moisseytsev A, Wade DC (2008) SSTAR: The US lead-cooled fast reactor (LFR). Journal of Nuclear Materials 376(3): 255–259

80. Lamont A, Brown N (2005) An economic analysis of GEN-IV lead cooled fast reactor. American Nuclear Society Transactions: 49–50

81. Allen TR, Crawford DC (2007) Lead-cooled fast reactor systems and the fuels and materials challenges. Science and Technology of Nuclear Installations 2007: 1–9

82. Wider HU, Carlsson J, Loewen E (2005) Renewed interest in lead cooled fast reactors. Progress in Nuclear Energy 47(1–4): 44–52

83. Mitachi K, Yamamoto T, Yoshioka R (2007) Three-region core design for 200-MW(electric) molten-salt reactor with thorium-uranium fuel. Nuclear Technology 158(3): 348–357

84. Hron MJ, Juricek V, Kyncl J, Mikisek M, Rypar V (2007), MSR – SPHINX concept program EROS (Experimental zero power salt reactor SR-0). The proposed experimental program as a basis for validation of reactor physics methods. 2007 International Congress on Advances in Nuclear Power Plants (ICAPP '07). Paper 7424

85. Lecarpentier D (2006) Contribution aux travaux sur la transmutation des déchets nucléaires, voie des réacteurs a sel fondu : le concept amster, aspect physique et sûreté (Contribution to the work on radioactive waste transmutation, molten salt reactors : The Amster concept, physical aspects and safety), Doctoral dissertation, Conservatoire national des arts et métiers, Paris

86. Mathieu L, Heuer D, Brissot R, Le Brun C, Liatard E, Loiseaux JM, Méplan O, Merle-Lucotte E, Nuttin A, Wilson J, Garzenne C, Lecarpentier D, Walle E (2006) The thorium molten salt reactor: moving on from the MSBR. Progress in Nuclear Energy 48(7): 664–679

87. Forsberg C, Peterson P (2004) An advanced molten salt reactor using high-temperature reactor technology. 2004 International Congress on Advances in Nuclear Power Plants (ICAPP '04)

88. Forsberg C (2004) Molten Salt Reactor Technology Gaps, 2004 International Congress on Advances in Nuclear Power Plants (ICAPP '04)

89. Ignatiev V, Feynberg O, Mjasnikov A, Zakirov R (2003) Reactor physics and fuel cycle analysis of a molten salt advanced reactor transmuter. 2003 International Congress on Advances in Nuclear Power Plants (ICAPP '03)

90. MacPherson HG (1985) The molten salt reactor adventure. Nuclear Science and Engineering 90: 374–380

91. Mitachi K, Yamamoto T, Yoshioka R (2005) Performance of a 200 MWe molten-salt reactor operated in thorium-uranium fuel-cycle. Proceedings of GLOBAL 2005 Tsukuba, Japan, Oct 9–13, 2005 Paper No. 089

92. Forsberg CW, Peterson PF, Pickard PS (2002) Molten-salt-cooled advanced high-temperature reactor for production of hydrogen and electricity. Nuclear Technology 144(3): 289–302
93. Kazuo F, Hiroo N, Yoshio K, Koushi M, Ritsuo Y, Akira F, Yuzuru S, Kazuto A (2005) New primary energy source by thorium molten-salt reactor technology. Electrochemistry 73(8): 552–563
94. Merle-Lucotte E, Heuer D, Allibert M, Ghetta V, Brun CL, Mathieu L, Brissot R, Liatard E (2007) Optimized transition from the reactors of second and third generations to the thorium molten salt reactor. ICAPP 2007. International Congress on Advances in Nuclear Power Plants, Nice : France" May 13–18, 2007 Paper 7186
95. DeWitte J, Goede T, Perfetti C, Plower T, Wayson M (2007) Design analysis of an advanced molten salt burner reactor. American Nuclear Society Transactions.
96. Chikazawa Y, Okano Y, Konomura M, Sawa N, Shimakawa Y, Tanaka T (2007) A compact loop-type fast reactor without refueling for a remote area power source. Nuclear Technology 157(2): 120–131
97. Hahn D, Kim Y, Kim S, Lee J, Lee Y, Jeong H (2007) Conceptual design features of the KALIMER-600 sodium cooled fast reactor. Global 2007, Boise, USA, September 9–13, 2007
98. Niwa H, Aoto K, Morishita M (2007) Current status and perspective of advanced loop type fast reactor in fast reactor cycle technology development project. Global 2007, Boise, USA, September 9–13, 2007
99. Sienicki J, Moisseytsev A, Cho D, Momozaki Y, Kilsdonk D, Haglund R, Reed C, Farmer M (2007) Supercritical carbon dioxide brayton cycle energy conversion for sodium-cooled fast reactors/advanced burner reactors. Global 2007, Boise, USA, September 9–13, 2007
100. Zaetta A, Dufour Ph, Pruhliere G, Rimpault G, Thevenot C, Tommasi J, Varaine F (2007) Innovating core design for sodium cooled fast reactors of fourth generation. Paper 7383, ICAPP 2007, Nice, France, May 13–18, 2007
101. Chang Y, Konomura M, Lo Pinto P (2005) A case for small modular fast reactor. Global 2005, Tsukuba, Japan, October 9–13, 2005
102. Hahn D, Kim Y, Kin S, Lee J, Lee Y (2005) Design concept of KALIMER-600. Global 2005, Tsukuba, Japan, October 9–13, 2005
103. Kotake S, Sakamoto Y, Ando M, Tanaka T (2005) Feasibility study on commercialized fast reactor cycle systems/current status of the SFR system design. Global 2005, Tsukuba, Japan, October 9–13, 2005
104. Mizuno T, Ogawa T, Naganuma M, Aida T (2005) Advanced oxide fuel core design study for SFR in the feasibility study in Japan. Global 2005, Tsukuba, Japan, October 9–13, 2005
105. Lefevre JC, Mitchell CH, Hubert G (1996) European fast reactor design. Nuclear Engineering Design 162(2–3): 133–143
106. Chang YI (1992) A next-generation concept: The integral fast reactor (IFR), USDOE Report, Argonne National Laboratory Report No. ANL/CP-75894, CONF-9204157-1
107. Hishida M, Kubo S, Konomura M, Toda M (2007) Progress on the plant design concept of sodium-cooled fast reactor. Journal of Nuclear Science and Technology 44(3): 303–308
108. Crawford DC, Porter DL, Hayes SL (2007) Fuels for sodium-cooled fast reactors: US perspective. Journal of Nuclear Materials 371(1–3): 202–231

109. Yoo J, Ishiwatari Y, Oka Y, Yang J, Liu J (2007) Subchannel analysis of supercritical light water-cooled fast reactor assembly. Nuclear Engineering and Design 237: 1096–1105

110. Mori M, Maschek W, Rineiski A (2006) Heterogeneous cores for improved safety performance: A case study: The supercritical water fast reactor. Nuclear Engineering and Design 236(14–16): 1573–1579

111. Yoo J, Ishiwatari Y, Oka Y, Liu J (2006) Conceptual design of compact supercritical water-cooled fast reactor with thermal hydraulic coupling. Annals of Nuclear Energy 33: 945–956

112. Yoo J, Ishiwatari Y, Liu J (2005) Composite core design of high power density supercritical water cooled fast reactor. Global 2005, Tsukuba, Japan, October 9–13, 2005, Paper No. 246

113. Mori M (2005) Core design analysis of the supercritical water fast reactor. Forschungszentrum Karlsruhe in der Helmholtz-Gemeinschaft, Wissenschaftliche Berichte FZKA 7160

114. Mori M, Maschek W, Laurien E, Morita K (2003) Monte-Carlo/Simmer-III reactivity coefficients calculations for the supercritical water fast reactor. Global 2003, New Orleans, Louisiana, November 16–21, 2003, Paper No. 87753

115. Mukohara T, Koshizuka S, Oka Y (1999) Core design of a high-temperature fast reactor cooled by supercritical light water. Annals of Nuclear Energy 26: 1423–1436

116. Oka Y, Kozhizuka S (1998) Conceptual design study of advanced power reactors. Progress in Nuclear Energy 32: 163–177

117. Lee JH, Oka Y, Koshizuka S (1999) Safety system consideration of supercritical water cooled fast reactor with simplified PSA. Reliability Engineering and System Safety 64: 327–338

118. MacDonald PE (2002) Feasibility study of supercritical light water cooled reactors for electric power production. Nuclear Energy Research Initiative Project 2001-001, Westinghouse Electric Co. Grant Number: DE-FG07-02SF22533, Final Report INEEL/EXT-04-02530

119. Granovskii M, Dincer I, Rosen MA, Pioro I (2008) Thermodynamic analysis of the use a chemical heat pump to link a supercritical water-cooled nuclear reactor and a thermochemical water-splitting cycle for hydrogen production. Journal of Power and Energy Systems 2(2): 756–767

120. Oh, C (2007) Power cycle and stress analyses for high temperature gas-cooled reactor. International Congress on Advances in Nuclear Power Plants (ICAPP 2007)

121. Sterbentz JW (2007) Low-enriched very high temperature reactor core design, 2007 International Congress on Advances in Nuclear Power Plants (ICAPP 2007)

122. Vilim RB (2007) Interface design studies for the production of hydrogen using the VHTR coupled to the HTSE process, 2007 International Congress on Advances in Nuclear Power Plants (ICAPP 2007)

123. Billot P, Hittner D, Vasseur P (2006) Outlines of the French R&D Program for the development of High and Very High Temperature Reactor. Third International Topical Meeting on High Temperature Reactor Technology, October 1–4, 2006, Johannesburg, South Africa

124. Fütterer MA, Toscano E, Bakker K, Berg G, Marmier A (2006) Irradiation results of AVR fuel pebbles at increased temperature and burn-up in the HFR petten. Proceedings HTR 2006, Third International Topical Meeting on High Temperature Reactor Technology, October 1–4, 2006, Johannesburg, South Africa

125. Greyvenstein R, Correia M, Kriel W (2006) South Africa's opportunity to maximize the role of nuclear power in a global hydrogen economy. Third International Topical Meeting on High Temperature Reactor Technology, October 1–4, 2006, Johannesburg, South Africa

126. Hittner D, Bogusch E, Besson D (2006) RAPHAEL A European Project for the development of HTR/VHTR technology for industrial process heat supply and cogeneration. Third International Topical Meeting on High Temperature Reactor Technology, October 1–4, 2006, Johannesburg, South Africa

127. Hu S, Liang X, Wei L, (2006) Commissioning and operation experience and safety experiment at HTR-10. Third International Topical Meeting on High Temperature Reactor Technology, October 1–4, 2006, Johannesburg, South Africa

128. Lee Y-W, Park J-Y, Kim YK, Jeong BG, Kim YM (2006) Development of HTGR coated particle fuel technology in Korea. Third International Topical Meeting on High Temperature Reactor Technology, October 1–4, 2006, Johannesburg, South Africa

129. Takamatsu K, Nakagawa S, Takeda T (2006) Development of core dynamics analysis of coolant flow reduction tests of HTTR. Third International Topical Meeting on High Temperature Reactor Technology, October 1–4, 2006, Johannesburg, South Africa

130. Tsvetkov PV (2006) Coupled hybrid Monte Carlo - deterministic analysis of VHTR configurations with advanced actinide fuels. Paper ICAPP-6400, 2006 International Congress on Advances in Nuclear Power Plants (ICAPP'06)

131. Kim TK, Taiwo TA, Hill RN, Stillman A (2005) Spent nuclear fuel characterization for the VHTR. Global 2005, Tsukuba, Japan, October 9–13, 2005, Paper 67

132. Jones AR (1975) Very high temperature reactor (VHTR) technology. 10th Rec Intersoc Energy Convers Eng Conf: 329–337

133. Taketoshi A, Sadao S, Yutaro T (1977) Studies on design principles and criteria of fuels and graphites for experimental multipurpose very high temperature reactor. Report JAERI-M-7415

134. Katsuichi I (1982) Development of fuel for VHTR (Very High Temperature Reactor). Genshiryoku Kogyo 28(8): 53–57

135. Shigeru Y, Shuichi M, Osamu S, Yoshihiro T, Yasuyuki N, Takao N, Kazuo Y, Seiichi U (1987) The study on the role of veryhightemperature reactor and nuclear process heat utilization in future energy systems. Implication in energy, economy, and environment of Japan. Nippon Genshiryoku Kenkyusho JAERI-M, JAERI-M-87-187

136. Christine M (2008) Using genetic algorithms to optimize the helium loop of a very high temperature reactor. Nuclear Technology 162(3): 323–332

137. Shohei U, Jun A, Atsushi Y, Hideharu I, Tomoo T, Kazuhiro S (2008) Fabrication of uniform ZrC coating layer for the coated fuel particle of the very high temperature reactor. Journal of Nuclear Materials 376(2): 146–151.

138. Areva http://www.arevaresources.ca/nuclear_energy/datagb/actualites/gtmhr.htm

139. Venneri F (2005) Destruction of nuclear waste and recycle of resources using MHR technology. IAEA, Trieste 2005

140. http://coal2nuclear.com/2%20TRISO_nuclear_fuel.htm#Chapter_Two,_Part_Two

141. Takamatsu K, Nakagawa S, Takeda T (2006) Development of core dynamics analysis of coolant flow reduction tests of HTTR. Proceedings HTR2006: 3rd International Topical Meeting on High Temperature Reactor Technology, October 1–4, 2006, Johannesburg, South Africa, Paper No. C00000174.

142. Baldwin DE, Campbell M, Ellis C, Richards M, Shenoy A (2007) MHR design, technology and applications. ICENES 2007 Conference, Istanbul, June 03–08

143. Kumar A, Vittal Rao TV, Mukherjee SK, Vaidya VN (2006) Recycling of chemicals from alkaline waste generated during preparation of UO_3 microspheres by sol gel process. Journal of Nuclear Material 350(1): 254–263.

144. Brooks LH (1969) HTGR [high temperature gas reactor] fuel reprocessing: head-end treatment of experimental small scale HTGR fuel elements. In. Gulf Gen. At., Inc., San Diego, CA, USA: 32

145. Byster SE (1980) Dissolution of HTGR TRISO beads by the alkali fluoride fusion method. In. New Brunswick Lab, US DOE, Argonne, IL,USA: 9

146. Chernikov A, Kosukhin V (2008) Deposition of ZrC coats on UO2 particles using the chloride process. Nuclear Engineering and Design 238: 2861–2865

147. Chernikov AS, Lyutikov RA, Kurbakov SD, Repnikov VM, Khromonozhkin VV, Solov'ev GI (1991) Behavior of HTGR coated fuel particles in high-temperature tests. Energy (Oxford, United Kingdom) 16: 295–308

148. Contescu CI, Baker FS, Hunt RD, Collins JL, Burchell TD (2008) Selection of water-dispersible carbon black for fabrication of uranium oxicarbide microspheres. Journal of Nuclear Materials 375: 38–51

149. Kikuchi T, Tobita T, Ikawa K (1984) Uranium contamination in coating and in matrix material of unirradiated coated particle fuel. Journal of Nuclear Science and Technology 21: 233–242

150. Kurata Y, Ikawa K, Iwamoto K (1981) Fission product release from TRISO-coated uranium dioxide particles at 1940 to 2320 DegC. Journal of Nuclear Materials 98: 107–115

151. Lee J-H, Shim J-B, Kim E-H, Yoo J-H, Park S-W, Snyder CT (2008) A feasibility study for the development of alternative methods to treat a spent TRISO fuel. Nuclear Technology 162: 250–258

152. Lobach SY, Knight TW, Jacob NP, Athon CE (2007) Advanced TRISO fuels with zirconium carbide for high temperature reactors. Global 2007: Advanced Nuclear Fuel Cycles and Systems, Boise, ID, United States, Sept 9–13, 2007: 9–14

153. Long EL, Jr., Tiegs TN, Robbins JM, Kania MJ (1981) Performance of HTGR biso- and triso-coated fertile particles irradiated in capsule HT-34. In. Oak Ridge Natl. Lab., Oak Ridge, TN, USA., p 71

154. Lopez-Honorato E, Meadows PJ, Xiao P, Marsh G, Abram TJ (2008) Structure and mechanical properties of pyrolytic carbon produced by fluidized bed chemical vapor deposition. Nuclear Engineering and Design 238: 3121–3128

155. Ogawa T, Fukuda K (1992) Zirconium carbide coated particle fuel development. In. Japan Atomic Energy Res Inst, Tokai, Japan.: 554–560

156. Pappano PJ, Burchell TD, Hunn JD, Trammell MP (2008) A novel approach to fabricating fuel compacts for the next generation nuclear plant (NGNP). Journal of Nuclear Materials 381: 25–38

157. Stansfield OM, Homan FJ, Simon WA, Turner RF (1983) Interaction of fission products and silicon carbide in TRISO fuel particles: a limiting HTGR design parameter. In. GA Technol. Inc., San Diego, CA, USA., p 9

158. Steward KP (1968) Coating contamination in TRISO fuel particles. In. Gulf Gen. At. Inc., San Diego, CA, USA., p 21

159. Tan L, Allen TR, Hunn JD, Miller JH (2008) EBSD for microstructure and property characterization of the SiC-coating in TRISO fuel particles. Journal of Nuclear Materials 372: 400–404

160. Verfondern K, Nabielek H (1985) PANAMA, a computer code to predict TRISO particle failure under accident conditions. In. Kernforschungsanlage Juelich G.m.b.H., Juelich, Fed. Rep. Ger., p 110

161. Charlier C, Fagerholm R, Slabber J, Shayi JL (2007) Safeguarding the Pebble Bed Modular Reactor: a new challenge for the IAEA. Annual Meeting Proceedings of the Institute of Nuclear Materials Management 48th: 244/241–244/248

162. Dardour S, Nisan S, Charbit F (2007) Utilisation of waste heat from GT-MHR and PBMR reactors for nuclear desalination. Desalination 205: 254–268

163. Gittus JH (1999) The ESKOM pebble bed modular reactor. Nuclear Energy (British Nuclear Energy Society) 38: 215–221

164. Greene CA, Muscara J, Srinivasan M (2003) Materials research needs for advanced reactors. In. Office of Nuclear Regulatory Research, U.S. Nuclear Regulatory Commission, USA., pp 85–96

165. Greyvenstein R, Correia M, Kriel W (2008) South Africa's opportunity to maximise the role of nuclear power in a global hydrogen economy. Nuclear Engineering and Design 238: 3031–3040

166. Hevia F, Slabber J (2005) Pebble bed modular reactor. Nuclear Espana 255: 26–30

167. Ion S, Nicholls D, Matzie R, Matzner D (2003) Pebble Bed Modular Reactor, the first generation IV reactor to be constructed. World Nuclear Association Annual Symposium: No pp given

168. Kemm K (1999) Development of the South African Pebble Bed Modular Reactor system. Uranium Institute Annual International Symposium [online computer file] 24th: No pp given

169. Koster A, Matzie R, Matzner D (2004) Pebble-bed modular reactor: a generation IV high-temperature gas-cooled reactor. Proceedings of the Institution of Mechanical Engineers, Part A: Journal of Power and Energy 218: 309–318

170. Koster A, Matzner HD, Nicholsi DR (2003) PBMR design for the future. Nuclear Engineering and Design 222: 231–245

171. McLaughlin DF, Paletta SA, Lahoda EJ, Kriel W, Nigra MM, McLaughlin GT (2005) Hydrogen costs for the PBMR thermal reactor and the westinghouse process. AIChE Annual Meeting, Conference Proceedings, Cincinnati, OH, United States, Oct 30–Nov 4, 2005: 581b/581–581b/521

172. Nicholls DR (1997) The pebble bed modular reactor. Nuclear Engineer (Institution of Nuclear Engineers) 38: 105–107

173. Nicholls DR (2000) Status of the pebble bed modular reactor. Nuclear Energy (British Nuclear Energy Society) 39: 231–236

174. Nicholls DR (2002) Small nuclear reactors: the PBMR. Energia (Madrid, Spain) 166: 35–40

175. Nicholls DR (2002) The pebble bed modular reactor. South African Journal of Science 98: 31–35

176. Reitsma F (2004) The pebble bed modular reactor layout and neutronics design of the equilibrium cycle. PHYSOR-2004, Physics of Fuel Cycles and Advanced Nuclear Systems: Global Developments, Chicago, IL, United States, Apr 25–29, 2004: 96100/96101–96100/96111

177. Rubin O, Venter M, Jordaan J (2006) The control of the PBMR nuclear power unit. Proceedings of the 2006 International Congress on Advances in Nuclear Power Plants, Embedded Topical Meeting, Reno, NV, United States, June 4–8, 2006: 139–144

178. van der Merwe JJ, Venter JH (2006) HTR fuel design, qualification and analyses at PBMR. PHYSOR-2006: Advances in Nuclear Analysis and Simulation, American Nuclear Society's Topical Meeting on Reactor Physics, Vancouver, BC, Canada, Sept 10–14, 2006: c021/021–c021/010

179. Walter A, Schulz A, Lohnert G (2006) Comparison of two models for a pebble bed modular reactor core coupled to a Brayton cycle. Nuclear Engineering and Design 236: 603–614

180. Alberstein D (1997) Weapons grade plutonium destruction in the gas turbine modular helium reactor (GT-MHR). NATO ASI Series, Series 1: Disarmament Technologies 15: 135–146

181. Alberstein D, Neylan AJ (1996) Plutonium disposition in the gas turbine modular helium reactor (GT-MHR). ICONE-4, Proceedings of the ASME/JSME International Conference on Nuclear Engineering, 4th, New Orleans, Mar 10–14, 1996 4: 535–547

182. Baxi CB, Shenoy A, Kostin VI, (2008) Evaluation of alternate power conversion unit designs for the GT-MHR. Nuclear Engineering and Design 238: 2995–3001

183. Gorelov IN, Kiryushin AI, Kodochigov NG, Kuzavkov NG, Sukharev YP (1998) The gas turbine-modular helium reactor (GT-MHR) for electricity generation and plutonium consumption. Atomic Energy (New York)(Translation of Atomnaya Energiya) 83: 877–881

184. Kodochigov NG, Kuzavkov NG, Sukharev YP, Ghudin AG, Shenoy AS (1998) The gas turbine-modular helium reactor program for efficient disposition of weapons plutonium. In. OKBM, N. Novgorod, Russia, pp 81–91

185. La Bar MP, Simon WA (1997) The modular helium reactor for the twenty-first century. Uranium and Nuclear Energy 22nd: 47–58

186. LaBar MP, Shenoy AS, Simon WA, Campbell EM (2004) The gas-turbine modular helium reactor. Nuclear Energy (British Nuclear Energy Society) 43: 165–175

187. Lecomte M, Bandelier P (2003) Desalinated water production optimisation using a high temperature reactor in a cogeneration mode. International Journal of Nuclear Desalination 1: 95–103

188. Lee K-H, Kim K-S, Noh J-M, Zee S-Q (2006) IAEA GT-MHR benchmark calculations using the HELIOS/MASTER code package. PHYSOR-2006: Advances in Nuclear Analysis and Simulation, American Nuclear Society's Topical Meeting on Reactor Physics, Vancouver, BC, Canada, Sept 10–14, 2006: b082/081–b082/089

189. McDonald CF, Silady FA, Wright RM, Kretzinger KF, Haubert RC (1994) GT-MHR helium gas turbine power conversion system design and development. Proceedings of the American Power Conference 56: 518–523

190. Neylan AJ, Shenoy A, Silady FA, Dunn TD (1995) GT-MHR design, performance and safety. In. General Atomics, San Diego, CA, USA., pp 136–147

191. Neylan AJ, Simon WA (1996) Status of the GT-MHR. JAERI-Conf 96-010: 89–96

192. Ohashi K, Okamoto F, Hayakawa H (2000) Modular high temperature reactor (Modular HTR) contributing the global environment protection. Progress in Nuclear Energy 37: 307–312

193. Palmer DJ, Kumar S (2005) The helium reactor and fuel cell combined cycle. Nuclear Future 1: 57–60

194. Penfield SR, Jr., Pause GR, Burger JM, Zugibe KJ (1994) Economic potential of the gas turbine modular helium reactor. Proceedings of the American Power Conference 56: 59–64

195. Rodriguez C, Zgliczynski J, Pfremmer D (1995) GT-MHR operations and control. In. Neth., pp 159–172
196. Silberstein AJ (1998) The Gas Turbine Modular Helium Reactor. An international project to develop a safe, efficient, flexible product. In. Framatome, Paris La Defense, Fr., pp 93–102
197. Talamo A (2006) Advanced in-core fuel cycles for the gas turbine-modular helium reactor. Ph.D. thesis , KTH Royal Institute of Technology, Stockholm, Sweden, p 219
198. Talamo A (2006) Studies on the feasibility of the LWRs waste-thorium in-core fuel cycle in the gas turbine-modular helium reactor. Journal of Nuclear Science and Technology (Tokyo, Japan) 43: 1379–1394
199. Talamo A, Gudowski W (2005) Performance of the gas turbine-modular helium reactor fueled with different types of fertile TRISO particles. Annals of Nuclear Energy 32: 1719–1749
200. Zgliczynski JB, Silady FA, Neylan AJ (1994) The gas turbine-modular helium reactor (GT-MHR), high efficiency, cost competitive, nuclear energy for the next century. Proc Int Top Meet Adv React Saf 2: 628–635
201. Weil J (November 2001) Pebble-bed design returns. IEEE Spectrum, 37–40
202. Kodochigov N, Sukharev Yu, Marova E, Ponomarev-Stepnoy N, Glushkov E, Fomichenko P (2003) Neutronic features of the GT-MHR reactor. Nuclear Engineering and Design 222(2–3): 161–171
203. Ballot B (2002) Presentation of the present HTR concepts and large associated facilities, HTR/ECS 2002 High Temperature Reactor School, Cadarache, France, November 4–8, 2002
204. Takizuka T (2004) Reactor technology development under the HTTR project. The 1st COE-INES International Symposium, INES-1, Tokyo, Japan, October 31–November 4, 2004
205. Takamatsu K, Nakagawa S, Takeda T (2006) Development of core dynamics analysis of coolant flow reduction tests of HTTR. Proceedings HTR2006: 3rd International Topical Meeting on High Temperature Reactor Technology, Johannesburg, South Africa, October 1–4, 2006, Paper No. C00000174
206. Energy Information Administration (2002) Form RW-859, "Nuclear Fuel Data"
207. OECD/NEA 2006 Nuclear Energy Data, Nuclear Eng. International handbook 2007
208. World Nuclear Association, London, UK. OECD/NEA 2006 Nuclear Energy Data, Nuclear Eng. International handbook 2007
209. Uranium Information Centre Limited, Transport of Radioactive Materials, Nuclear Issues Briefing Paper #51, February 2008
210. 10 CFR 73.26. Transportation physical protection systems, subsystems, components, and procedures. http://www.nrc.gov/reading-rm/doc-collections /cfr/part073/part073-0026.html
211. U.S. Department of Energy, Science and Technology (2003) Report to Congress on Advanced fuel cycle initiative: the future path for advanced spent fuel treatment and transmutation research
212. Benedict M, Pigford T, Wolfgang L (1981) Nuclear Chemical Engineering. 2nd Ed. McGraw-Hill, New York
213. Pigford TH (1974) Environmental aspects of nuclear energy production. Ann Rev Nucl Sci 24: 515–557
214. Choppin GR, Khankhasayev M (1999) Chemical Separation Technologies and Related Methods of Nuclear Waste Management. Kluwer, Dordrecht: 1–16

215. Cairns RC (1964) Recovering of spent nuclear fuels: processing. Atomic Power: 57–77
216. Finsterwalder L (1975) Reprocessing technology. In Ges Wiederaufarbeit Kernbrennstoffen mbH, Eggenstein-Leopoldshafen, Fed Rep Ger: 12
217. Geier RG (1979) Purex process solvent: literature review. In Rockwell Hanford Operations, Rockwell Int Corp, Richland, WA, USA: 185
218. Huppert KL (1977) Present state of reprocessing. In Ges Wiederaufarbeitung Kernbrennst mbH, Eggenstein-Leopoldshafen, Fed Rep Ger: 24
219. Mailen JC (1981) Interpretation of the extraction mechanism of the Purex and Thorex processes from kinetics data. Separation Science and Technology 16: 1373–1387
220. McKibben JM (1984) Chemistry of the Purex process. Radiochimica Acta 36: 3–15
221. Beary MM (1970) Solvent improvement resulting from the use of NPH [normal paraffin hydrocarbon mixture] in the Hanford Purex plant. In Atl Richfield Hanford Co, Richland,WA, USA: 9
222. Bray LA (1967) Recovery of cesium from Purex alkaline waste with a synthetic zeolite. In Battelle-Northwest, Richland, WA, USA: 16
223. Chaugule GA, Singh RK, Gurba PB, Bajpai DD, Shukla JP, Sundaresan M (1995) Application of sequential solvent extraction process for the removal of major actinides from acidic high-level liquid waste. NUCAR 95: Proceedings of Nuclear and Radiochemistry Symposium, Kalpakkam, India, February 21–24:158–159
224. Ertel D (1976) Equipment and instrumentation of a laboratory for Purex process analytical chemistry. Des Equip Hot Lab, Proc Symp: 159–164
225. Godfrin J, Mousty F, Planson J, Toussaint J (1980) Separation scheme for high-level nuclear effluent actinides. OXAL process. In CCE, Ispra, Italy: 225–245
226. Gupta KK, Thomas G, Kulkarni PG, Varadarajan N, Singh RK (1995) Evaluation of Duolite S-861 resin for the removal of dissolved TBP from aqueous PUREX process streams. Part II. NUCAR 95: Proceedings of Nuclear and Radiochemistry Symposium, Kalpakkam, India, February 21–24, 1995: 198–199
227. Henrich E, Bauder U, Marquardt R, Druckenbrodt WG, Wittmann K (1986) A new concept for product refining in the Purex process. Atomkernenergie/Kerntechnik 48: 241–245
228. Horner DE (1969) Use of ferrous nitrate as a plutonium reductant for partitioning plutonium and uranium in Purex processes. In Oak Ridge Nat Lab, Oak Ridge, TN, USA: 17
229. Horwitz EP, Kalina DG, Diamond H, Vandegrift GF, Schulz WW (1985) The TRUEX process - a process for the extraction of the transuranic elements from nitric acid wastes utilizing modified PUREX solvent. Solvent Extraction and Ion Exchange 3: 75–109
230. Itoh Y, Kamei K, Hotoku S, Asakura T, Mineo H, Uchiyama G (2002) Development of solvent washing process using butylamine compounds. JAERI-Conf 2002-004: 603–608
231. Jackson RR, Walser RL (1977) Purex process operation and performance, 1970 Thoria Campaign. In Atl Richfield Hanford Co, Richland, WA, USA: 194
232. Kaneko H, Muramoto H, Takeda H, Hoshino T, Segawa T (1980) Iodine removal in the Purex reprocessing process. Fast React Fuel Reprocess, Proc Symp: 185–194
233. Katoh N, Kiyose R, Yamamoto Y (1975) Multivariable cascade control of the Purex process. Journal of Nuclear Science and Technology 12: 53–60

234. Kumar S, Koganti SB (2002) Simulation study of tritium extraction behaviour in PUREX process. In Indira Gandhi Centre for Atomic Research, Tamil Nadu, India: 1–17

235. Kumar SV, Nadkarni MN, Ramanujam A, Venkatesan M, Gopalakrishnan V, Kazi JA (1974) Tail end purification of uranium in the purex process. In Fuel Reprocess Div, Bhabha At Res Cent, Bombay, India: 11

236. Mendel JE (1965) Laboratory studies on the use of uranium(IV) as a plutonium reductant in a Purex process. United States Atomic Energy Commission [Unclassified and Declassified Reports Published by the Atomic Energy Commission and Its Contractors] HW-82103: 13 pp

237. Mineo H, Uchiyama G, Hotoku S, Asakura T, Kihara T (1999) Spent fuel test of an advanced PUREX process: PARC. Global '99: "Nuclear Technology – Bridging the Millennia", Proceedings of the International Conference on Future Nuclear Systems, Jackson Hole, WY, United States, Aug: 725–731

238. Navratil JD, Leebl RG (1978) Modified Purex process for the separation and recovery of plutonium-uranium residues. In Rocky Flats Plant, At Int Div, Golden, CO, USA: 19

239. Ojima H (2008) Outline of the nuclear fuel cycle. In Nuclear Fuel Cycle Engineering Laboratories, Tokai Research and Development Center, Japan Atomic Energy Agency, Tokai-mura, Naka-gun, Ibaraki-ken, Japan: 1–28

240. Petrich G (1983) Computer-simulation of the PUREX process. Nukleare Entsorgung 2: 317–332

241. Petrich G, Kolarik Z (1981) The 1981 Purex distribution data index. In Kernforschungszent Karlsruhe GmbH, Karlsruhe, Fed Rep Ger: 108

242. Rainey RH (1965) Hydrogen reduction of Pu(IV) to Pu(III). Nuclear Applications & Technology 1: 310–311

243. Ramaniah MV, Rao CL, Pisharody KPR, Jadhav AV, Vishwanatha A (1967) Laboratory studies on the use of uranium(IV) in the Purex process. II. Use of uranium(IV) as the reductant for plutonium. Proc Nucl Radiat Chem Symp, 3rd: 343–350

244. Ramaniah MV, Rao CL, Pisharody KPR, Jadhav AV, Viswanatha A (1967) Laboratory studies on the use of uranium(IV) in the Purex process. I. Preparation of uranium(IV) solutions. Proc Nucl Radiat Chem Symp, 3rd: 335–342

245. Richardson GL, Swanson JL (1975) Plutonium partitioning in the Purex process with hydrazine-stabilized hydroxylamine nitrate. In Hanford Eng Dev Lab, Richland, WA, USA: 92

246. Sakurai S, Nakajima K, Tachimori S (1995) Feasibility study of utilization of organic diluent containing boron in Purex process. Proceedings of the International Conference on Nuclear Criticality Safety, 5th, Albuquerque, Sept 17–21, 1995 2: 7 22–27 27

247. Salomon L, Eschrich H, Humblet L (1976) Treatment and disposal of tributyl phosphate-kerosene waste by the Eurowatt process. Nucl Energy Maturity, Proc Eur Nucl Conf 8: 224–236

248. Salomon L, Lopez-Menchero E (1970) Optimization of the aqueous processing of irradiated fuel from nuclear power reactors. Use of uranium(IV) nitrate as reductant in a Purex type processing plant. Industrial & Engineering Chemistry Process Design and Development 9: 345–358

249. Sawant RM, Rastogi RK, Chaudhuri NK (1998) Study of the extraction of U(IV) relevant to PUREX process. Journal of Radioanalytical and Nuclear Chemistry 229: 203–206

250. Schultz WS (1969) DBBP [dibutylbutyl phosphonate] solvent extraction recovery of neptunium and plutonium from purex 1WW solution. In. Battelle-Northwest, Richland, WA, USA: 47

251. Schulz WW (1967) Trilaurylamine extraction of neptunium and plutonium from Purex process waste. Industrial & Engineering Chemistry Process Design and Development 6: 115–121

252. Schulz WW (1970) Macroreticular ion exchange resin cleanup of Purex process tributyl phosphate solvent. In Atlantic Richfield Hanford Co., Richland, WA, USA: 26

253. Segawa T (1967) Reprocessing of nuclear fuel in the World and Japan. Genshiryoku Kogyo 13: 17–22

254. Srinivasan N, Laxminarayanan TS, Balasubramanian GR, Kapoor SC, Ramaniah MV (1968) Studies on the use of uranium(IV) as a reductant for plutonium in purex process. In Fuel Reprocess Div, Bhabha At Res Centre, Bombay, India: 50

255. Srinivasan N, Laxminarayanan TS, Balasubramanian GR (1968) Use of uranium(IV) as a reductant for plutonium in Purex process. In Bhabha At Res Centre, Bombay, India: 16

256. Starks JB (1977) Purex process. In. Savannah River Plant, E I DuPont de Nemours and Co., Aiken, SC, USA: 41

257. Stevenson CE, Paige DM (1967) Research and development on aqueous processing. Reactor and Fuel-Processing Technology 10: 241–252

258. Stieglitz L, Becker R (1983) Chemical and radiolytic solvent degradation in the PUREX process. Nukleare Entsorgung 2: 333–350

259. Taylor RJ, Fox OD, Sarsfield MJ, Carrott MJ, Mason C, Woodhead DA, Maher CJ, Steele H, Koltunov VS (2007) Fundamental chemical kinetic and thermodynamic data for Purex process models. Global 2007: Advanced Nuclear Fuel Cycles and Systems, Boise, ID, United States, Sept 9–13, 2007: 180–181

260. Thompson MC (1977) Solvent extraction of enriched uranium fuels at the Savannah River Plant. In. Savannah River Lab, EI duPont de Nemours and Co, Aiken, SC, USA: 21

261. Uchiyama G, Asakura T, Hotoku S, Fujine S (1997) Long-lived nuclides separation techniques for advancing Purex process. Proceedings of the International Conference on Radioactive Waste Management and Environmental Remediation, 6th, Singapore, Oct 12–16, 1997: 255–260

262. Uchiyama G, Mineo H, Asakura T, Hotoku S, Iizuka M, Fujisaki S, Isogai H, Itoh Y, Hosoya N (2002) PARC process as advanced PUREX process. JAERI-Conf 2002-004: 197–204

263. Uchiyama G, Mineo H, Hotoku S (2000) PARC process for an advanced PUREX process. Progress in Nuclear Energy 37: 151–156

264. Venkatesan M, Ravi TN, Govindan P, Raman VR (1995) Laboratory studies on restoring solvent in Purex process. NUCAR 95: Proceedings of Nuclear and Radiochemistry Symposium, Kalpakkam, India, Feb 21–24, 1995: 166–167

265. Wallwork AL, Bothwell P, Birkett JE, Denniss IS, Taylor RJ, May I (2001) The development of chemical flowsheets for an advanced purex process. Solvent Extraction for the 21st Century, Proceedings of ISEC '99, Barcelona, Spain, July 11–16, 1999 2: 1463–1467

266. Walser RL (1970) Hanford Purex plant experience with reductants. In Atl Richfield Hanford Co, Richland, WA, USA: 25

267. Wang J, Chen J (2007) The application of N,N-Dimethyl-3-Oxa-Glutaramic acid (DOGA) in the PUREX process. Global 2007: Advanced Nuclear Fuel Cycles and Systems, Boise, ID, United States, September 9–13: 1131–1136

268. Wilhite RN (1966) Evaluation of commercial n-paraffin mixtures for Purex diluent. In Savannah River Lab, El duPont de Nemours and Co, Aiken, SC, USA: 7

269. Zhang A, Hu J, Zhang X, Wang F (2002) Hydroxylamine derivative in the Purex Process. Journal of Radioanalytical and Nuclear Chemistry 253: 107–113

270. Baumgaertner F (1976) The Purex process for the reprocessing of nuclear fuels with high plutonium content and high burn-up. Kerntechnik (1959–1978) 18: 245–252

271. Bondin VV, Gavrilov PM, Revenko YuA, Zilberman BYa, Romanovskij VN, Fedorov YuS, Shadrin AYu, Kudryavcev EG, Haperskaja AV (2007) Simplified PUREX process-perspective SNF reprocessing technologie for the plant of the next generation. Global 2007: Advanced Nuclear Fuel Cycles and Systems, Boise, ID, United States, Sept 9–13, 2007: 1484–1489

272. Boudry JC, Miquel P (1974) Adaptation of the Purex process to the reprocessing of fast reactor fuels. In CEN Commis Energ At, Fontenay-aux-Roses Fr: 19

273. Boudry JC, Miquel P (1974) Adaptation of the Purex process to the reprocessing of fast reactor fuels. Proc Int Solvent Extr Conf 2: 1551–1567

274. Endo H, Kamiya M, Shinoda Y, Ojima H (1997) Advanced fuel recycle system concept on PUREX process and MOX fuel fabrication. ICONE-5, Proceedings of the International Conference on Nuclear Engineering, 5th, Nice, May 25–29, 1997: 2211/2211–2211/2218

275. Faugeras P, Bourgesois M, Talmont X (1971) Processing of highly irradiated fuels. Technical situation and future prospects. Purex process and dry process. In CEN Commis Energ At, Fontenay-aux-Roses Fr: 16

276. Paiva A, Malik P (2004) Recent advances on the chemistry of solvent extraction applied to the reprocessing of spent nuclear fuels and radioactive wastes. Journal of Radioanalytical and Nuclear Chemistry 261(2): 485–496

277. Laidler JL (2007) GNEP spent fuel processing: waste stream and disposition options. Nuclear Waste technical Review Board Meeting, Washington D.C. May 15, 2007

278. Vandegrift GF, Regalbuto MC, Aase SB, Arafat HA, Bakel AJ, Bowers DL, Byrnes JP, Clark MA, Emery JW, Falkenberg JR, Lohman AVG, Hafenrichter D, Leonard RA, Pereira C, Quigley KJ, Tsai Y, Vander Pol MH, Laidler JJ (2004) Lab-Scale demonstration of the UREX+ process. Wm'04 Conference, February 29–March 4, 2004, Tucson, AZ WM-4323

279. Pereira C, Vandegrift GF, Regalbuto MC, Bakel A, Bowers D, Byrnes JP, Clark MA, Emery JW, Falkenberg JR, Hafenrichter L, Krebs JF, Leonard R, Maggos LE, Quigley KJ, Laidler JJ (2006) Preliminary results of the lab- scale demonstration of the UREX+1a process using spent nuclear fuel. 2006 AIChE National Meeting November 15, 2006

280. Pereira C, Vandegrift GF, Regalbuto MC, Bakel A, Bowers D, Byrnes JP, Clark MA, Emery JW, Falkenberg JR, Hafenrichter L, Krebs JF, Leonard R, Maggos LE, Quigley KJ, Laidler JJ (2006) Preliminary Results of the Lab- Scale Demonstration of the UREX+1a Process Using Spent Nuclear Fuel. 2006 AIChE National Meeting November 15, 2006

281. Coops MS, Bowersox DF (1984) Nonaqueous processing methods. In Los Alamos Natl Lab, Los Alamos, NM, USA: 12

282. Coops MS, Sisson DH (1982) The potential of pyroprocessing for partitioning Purex wastes. Radioactive Waste Management 6: 333–347

283. Amamoto I, Sato K, Terai T (2006) Behavior of FPs and TRU in a fluoride volatility process. Special Publication – Royal Society of Chemistry 305: 578–580

284. Carr WH, King LJ, Kitts FG, McDuffee WT, Miles FW (1971) Molten-salt fluoride volatility pilot plant. Recovery of enriched uranium from aluminum-clad fuel elements. In Oak Ridge Natl Lab, Oak Ridge, TN, USA: 78

285. Cathers GI, Carr WH, Lindauer RB, Milford RP, Whatley ME (1958) Recovery of uranium from highly irradiated reactor fuel by a fused-salt fluoride-volatility process. Proceedings of the United Nations International Conference on the Peaceful Uses of Atomic Energy 17: 473–479

286. Chijiya M (1976) Studies on fluoride volatility process for the reprocessing of LMFBR fuels. In Sci Technol Agency, Tokyo, Japan: 3

287. Corbin O, Vanderchmitt A, Lucas M (1980) Ruthenium in fuel reprocessing by fluoride volatility process. (II). Ruthenium species appearing in fluorination step as identified by thermochromatography and IR measurements. Journal of Nuclear Science and Technology 17: 443–447

288. Dem'yanovich MA, Prusakov VN, Skiba OV (1982) Fluorination of irradiated uranium-plutonium oxide fuel in the flame reactor. In Nauchno-Issled Inst At Reakt, Dimitrovgrad, USSR: 12

289. Holmes JT, Stethers H, Barghusen JJ (1965) Engineering development of a fluid-bed fluoride volatility process. II. Pilot-scale studies. Nuclear Applications & Technology 1: 301–309

290. Jonke AA (1968) Development of volatility processes for thermal and fast reactor fuels. In Argonne Nat Lab, Argonne, IL, USA: 65–78

291. Levitz NM (1968) Fluoride volatility processes-fluorination of uranium and plutonium. In Argonne Nat Lab, Argonne, IL, USA: 18–41

292. Matsuda M, Sato N, Kirishima A, Tochiyama O (2007) Fluorination behavior of UO_2F_2 in the presence of F_2 and O_2. Global 2007: Advanced Nuclear Fuel Cycles and Systems, Boise, ID, United States, September 9–13:1474–1476

293. Mecham WJ, Liimatainen RC, Kessie RW, Seefeldt WB (1957) Decontamination of irradiated uranium by fluoride volatility process. Chem Eng Progr 53: 72F–77F

294. Reas WH (1967) Fluoride volatility processes. Application to commercial nuclear fuel recovery. In Gen Elec Co, Santa Clara, CA, USA: 342–360

295. Schmets J (1970) Reprocessing of spent nuclear fuels by fluoride volatility processes. Atomic Energy Review 8: 3–126

296. Shimada S, Okumura I, Higashi K (1973) Experimental study on fluoride volatility process for thorium fuels. Journal of Nuclear Science and Technology 10: 689–695

297. Standifer RL (1970) Fluidized-bed fluoride volatility pilot plant for plutonium purification. Chemical Engineering Progress, Symposium Series 66: 198–207

298. Thompson MA, Marshall RS, Standifer RL (1969) Pilot plant experience on volatile fluoride reprocessing of plutonium. In Rocky Flats Div, Dow Chem Co, Golden, CO, USA: 163–176

299. Fukasawa T, Umehara H, Matsuda M (2001) Nuclear fuel cycle technology for a long-term stable supply of energy. Hitachi Review 50(3): 89–94

300. National Research Council (1996) Nuclear Wastes, Technologies for Separations and Transmutation, Appendix D. National Academy Press, Washington DC

301. Chang YI (2002) Advanced nuclear system for the 21st century. US-Japan Workshop: Nuclear Energy in a New Era, Washington D. C., April 29–30, 2002
302. Akabori M, Hayashi H, Minato K (2005) Pyrochemical properties of actinides elements. Japan Atomic Energy Research Institute. http://typhoon.jaea.go.jp/nucef2005/abstracts/S4_R1-2-akabori.pdf
303. Inoue T (2002) Actinide recycling by pyro-process with metal fuel FBR for future nuclear fuel cycle system. Progress in Nuclear Energy 40(3–4): 547–554
304. Kinoshita K, Inoue T, Fusselman S, Grimmett DL, Krueger CL, Storvick S (2003) Electrodeposition of uranium and transuranic elements onto solid cathode in LiCl-KCl/Cd system for pyrometallurgical partitioning. Journal of Nuclear Science and Technology 40(7): 524–530
305. Usami T, Kurata M, Inoue T, Sims HE, Beetham SA, Jenkins JA (2002) Pyrochemical reduction of uranium dioxide and plutonium dioxide by lithium metal. Journal of Nuclear Materials 300(1): 15–26
306. Nawada H, Fukuda K (2005) Role of pyro-chemical processes in advanced fuel cycles. Journal of Physics and Chemistry of Solids 66: 647–651
307. Zabunoglu OH, Akbas T (2003) Flow sheet calculations in Thorex method for reprocessing Th-based spent fuels. Nuclear Engineering and Design 219(1): 77–86
308. Zimmer E, Merz E. Chemical processing of HTR fuels applying either Thorex or Purex flow sheets, IAEA Published Conference Article, http://www.iaea.org/OurWork/ST/NE/inisnkm/nekr/htgr/fulltext/iwggcr8_26.pdf
309. Le Brun C (2007) Molten salts and nuclear energy production. Journal of Nuclear Materials 360(1): 1–5
310. International Atomic Energy Agency (1999) Minimization of waste from uranium purification, enrichment and fuel fabrication. IAEA-TECDOC-1115
311. Frost S (1998) Waste Management in the uranium mining industry. The Uranium Institute 23rd Annual International Symposium, London
312. Diehl P (2004) Uranium mining and milling wastes: An introduction, WISE Uranium Project
313. U.S. Environmental Protection Agency, Technical Resource Document (1995) Extraction and beneficiation of ores and minerals 5: Uranium
314. International Atomic Energy Agency (2004) Treatment of liquid effluent from uranium mines and mills. IAEA-TECDOC-1419, Report of a Coordinated Research Project 1996–2000
315. Ozawa M, Koma Y, Nomura K, Tanaka Y (1998) Separation of actinides and fission products in high-level liquid wastes by the improved TRUEX process. Journal of Alloys and Compounds 271–273: 538–543
316. Law J, Herbst R, Todd T (2002) Integrated AMP-PAN, TRUEX, and SREX testing. II. Flowsheet testing for separation of radionuclides from actual acidic radioactive waste. Separation Science and Technology 37(6): 1353–1373
317. Noyes R (1995) Nuclear Waste Cleanup Technology and Opportunities. Noyes Publications
318. Law JD, Brewer KN, Herbst RS, Todd TA, Wood DJ (1999) Development and demonstration of solvent extraction processes for the separation of radionuclides from acidic radioactive waste. Waste Management 19(1): 27–37
319. US Department Energy, Office of Science and Technology (1998) TRUEX/SREX demonstration: Innovative technology summary report. DOE/EM-0419

320. Todd TA, Law JD, Herbst RS, Meikrantz DH, Peterman DR, Riddle CL, Tillotson RD (2005) Advanced technologies for the simultaneous separation of cesium and strontium from spent nuclear fuel. WM-5083, Waste Management 2005 Conference February 27–March 3 Tucson AZ

321. Swanson J, Pereira C, Vandegrift GF (2002) Preliminary evaluation of solvent-extraction and/or ion-exchange process for meeting aaa program multi-tier systems recovery and purification goals. Argonne National Lab ANL-02/29

322. Madic C (2001) Overview of the hydrometallurgical and pyro-metallurgical processes studied worldwide for the partitioning of high active nuclear wastes. Transactions of the 6th International Exchange Meeting, "Actinides and Fission Product Partitioning and Transmutation", Madrid, Spain, December 11–13, 2000

323. Pereira C, Vandegrift GF, Regalbuto MC, Bakel A, Bowers D, Byrnes JP, Clark MA, Emery JW, Falkenberg JR, Hafenrichter L, Leonard R, Quigley KJ, VanderPol MH, Laidler JJ (2005) Preliminary results of the lab-scale demonstration of the UREX+1a process using spent nuclear fuel. 2005 AIChE National Meeting, November 3

324. Logsdail DH, Mills AL (Eds) (1985) Solvent Extraction and Ion Exchange in the Nuclear Fuel Cycle. Society of Chemical Industry, Ellis Horwood, Chichester

325. Ojovan M, Lee W (2005) An Introduction to Nuclear Waste Immobilisation. Elsevier, Oxford

326. Thomasson J, Barithel S, Cocaud A, Derycke P, Pierre P (2003) The Universal canister strategy in spent fuel reprocessing: UC-C a real industrial improvement. WM' 03 Conference, February 23-27, 2003, Tucson, AZ. http://www.wmsym.org/abstracts/2003/194.pdf

327. MdDeavitt SM, Parkison A, Totemeier AR, Wegener JJ (2007) Fabrication of cermet nuclear fuels designed for the transmutation of transuranic isotopes, materials science forum 561–565: 1733–1736

328. Nuttall W (2005) Nuclear Renaissance Technologies and Policies for the Future of Nuclear Power. Institute of Physics Publishing, Bristol

329. Chang YI (2002) Advanced nuclear system for the 21st century. US–Japan Workshop: Nuclear Energy in a New Era, Washington D. C., April 29–30, 2002

330. Schenkel R, Magill J, Glatz J-P, Mayer K (2003) Partitioning and Transmutation – Technical Feasibility, Proliferation Resistance and Safeguardability, IAEA-SM-367/15/03

331. World Nuclear Association, Accelerator-driven nuclear energy. http://www.world-nuclear.org/info/inf35.html

332. Gudowski W, Why accelerator driven transmutation of wastes enable future nuclear power http://www.neutron.kth.se/publications/conference_papers/W_Gudowski_FR202_1.P DF. 12/14/2008

333. Moncouyoux J, Nabot J (2002) Waste vitrification: More than one string to its bow. Nuclear Energy Division, Commissariat a l'Energie Atomique, CLEFS CEA No 46, Spring, 2002 http://www.cea.fr/var/cea/storage/static/gb/library/Clefs46/pdfg/14-wastevitrification.pdf

334. Hamel WF, Jr., Valenti PJ, Elliott DI (1999) Completion of the first phase of HLW vitrification at the west valley demonstration project. WM'99 Conference, February 28–March 4, 1999

Problems

1. A wise man once did a great service for his king. His king was so pleased that he offered the wise man anything that he wanted. The wise man told the king that he wanted a grain of rice. The king said that this is not a sufficient reward so the wise man said he also wanted two grains of rice tomorrow. The king said that this was not sufficient so he implored the wise man to take more. The wise man thought and said he would like double grains of rice from the day before for 30 days. So on day 3 the total grains would be 4, on day 4 the total grains would be 8 and so on until day 30. The king expressed his surprise that the wise man wanted to little. Was the king right? How many pounds of rice would it take to fill the wise man's request? An average grain of rice weighs 25 mg and there are 454 g in a pound.
2. What is the yield in kiloton when U-235 fissions with a k = 2 for 88 generations?
3. A nuclear power reactor operates for 1 year at 3×10^9 watts thermal. When the reactor shuts down for refueling after 1 year, what is the decay heat?
4. What is E_q, E_{crit} and Q for (a) U-233, (b) Pu-239, (c) U-235.
5. What is the mean free path for a 1 MeV neutron in metallic U-235? Density of Uranium is 18.95 g per cubic centimeter. Avogadro's number is 6.02×10^{23} atoms g-mole^{-1}.
6. What is the mean free path for a 0.025 eV neutron in metallic U-235? Density of Uranium is 18.95 g per cubic centimeter. Avogadro's number is 6.02×10^{23} atoms g-mole^{-1}.
7. What is the mean free path for a 0.25 eV neutron in metallic natural uranium? Density of uranium is 18.95 g per cubic centimeter. Avogadro's number is 6.02×10^{23} atoms g-mole^{-1}.
8. What is the mean free path for a 0.25 eV neutron in metallic plutonium-239? Density of plutonium is 19.84 g per cubic centimeter. Avogadro's number is 6.02×10^{23} atoms g-mole^{-1}.
9. What is the mean free path for a 0.25 eV neutron in metallic U-233? Density of uranium is 18.95 g per cubic centimeter. Avogadro's number is 6.02×10^{23} atoms g-mole^{-1}.
10. What is the temperature in Kelvin for a 1 MeV neutron?
11. Plot the number of atoms of Kr-85 as they decay over a 10-year period. Kr-85 has a half-life of 10.76 years.
12. Polonium-210 decays with a half-life of 138.376 days. The decay product is a 5.407 MeV alpha particle. What is the thermal power of 1 kg of Po-210? After 1 year, what is the thermal power of the 1 kg of Po-210?
13. How much uranium do all 439 nuclear reactors in the world consume in a year?
14. How much energy from the known uranium reserves could be generated in a once through fuel cycle?
15. How much energy from the known uranium reserves could be generated if the fuel is recycled?
16. How much energy from the known thorium reserves could be generated in a once through fuel cycle?
17. How much energy from the known thorium reserves could be generated if the fuel is recycled?
18. Why can fast reactors breed plutonium?

19. How much fissile fuel does a three-gigawatt thermal nuclear power plant use in its fifty-year lifetime? Assume an average capacity factor of 90%.

20. By what factor does the total energy content in the world's uranium and thorium reserves compare to the total energy content of the world's fossil fuel reserves?

21. Is reprocessing of spent fuel a technical or a political issue? Is there technology available to reprocess spent fuel?

22. What are the main objections to reprocessing of spent fuel?

23. What is the difference between reprocessing and recycling?

24. Is it possible to generate zero waste from a nuclear power plant using all the existing technologies?

25. What is the difference between PUREX and UREX processes?

26. Write a report on fast reactors.

27. Compare SWU for various uranium enrichment processes.

10 HUBBERT PEAK THEORY

Abstract

M. King Hubbert made a bold prediction in 1956 that oil production in the U.S. lower 48 states would peak in the early 1970s. His prediction was based on mathematical analysis of the time histories of cumulative discoveries, production, and remaining reserves for a finite resource. His methodology was later applied to global oil production and other finite resources such as coal, natural gas, uranium, and other mineral.

10.1 Introduction

Hubbert developed his model based on two basic considerations [1]:

1. For a finite resource of fixed amount, at time $t = 0$ and $t =$ infinite, the production rate will be zero. Time, $t = 0$, refers to the reference time, when the resource is just being started to be consumed. All the fixed resources will be eventually exhausted; theoretically this time should be $t =$ infinite. However for all practical purpose this time is finite.
2. The second consideration is based on the following mathematical formulation:

Hubbert used Fig. 10.1 as a guide to develop his famous peak-oil production curve. The actual production data up to year 1955 provided the basic trend or slope of the initial part of the production curve. Based on the estimated ultimate reserved at that time, Hubbert constructed a series of curves, matching the area under the curve with the total estimated ultimate reserve. Recognizing that the peak-oil production will last for several years, Hubbert adjusted the maximum in the curve. Instead of making the maximum a sharp point, he flattened the top.

T.K. Ghosh and M.A. Prelas, *Energy Resources and Systems:*
Volume 1: Fundamentals and Non-Renewable Resources, 649–676.
© Springer Science + Business Media B.V. 2009

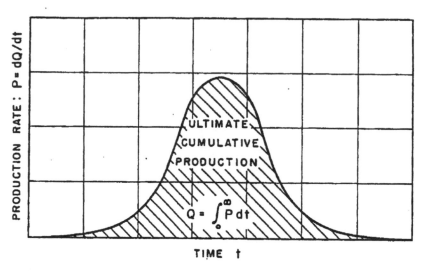

Fig. 10.1. The distribution of production rate over time used by Hubbert for predicting how long production of a finite source will continue before becoming zero [1].

The curve plotted by Hubbert in 1956 is compared with the actual production data in Fig. 10.2 and as can be seen from the figure, the prediction was fairly close. Since his prediction, a number of researchers tried to predict peak-oil production using more detailed mathematical formulations.

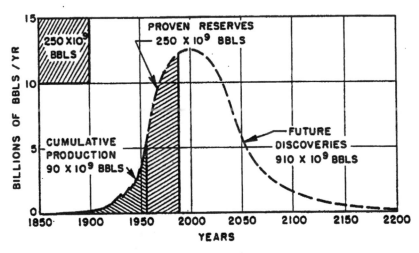

Fig. 10.2. Comparison of actual production rate data with the prediction made by Hubbert in 1956 [1].

10.2 Development of the Theory

A fundamental mathematical basis for the prediction of peak oil production is described below [2]. A mass balance equation for cumulative discoveries, production, and remaining reserves may be written as:

$$Q_d = Q_p + Q_r \qquad (10.1)$$

where, Q_d = Cumulative total discovered resources
Q_p = Cumulative production
Q_r = Remaining proved reserves (which have not been employed for production)

Assuming that Q_d, Q_p and Q_r are continuous functions of time, the rate of change of these quantities can be expressed by taking the derivative of Eq. (10.1) with respect to time and is given by:

$$\frac{dQ_d(t)}{dt} = \frac{dQ_p(t)}{dt} + \frac{dQ_r(t)}{dt} \qquad (10.2)$$

When a resource is first discovered, the amount of which is given by $Q_d(t)$ will rise exponentially from zero value. The reason for this exponential growth is that intensive exploration occurs and more and more discoveries of the resources are made within a very short time period. As shown in Fig. 10.3, as the remaining undiscovered pockets of the resource become harder to find, $Q_d(t)$ finally tapers off.

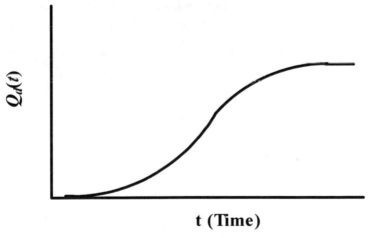

t (Time)

Fig. 10.3. The behavior of cumulative discovery data of a finite resource.

The actual cumulative discoveries of oil in the USA and the world are shown in Fig. 10.4. It can be seen from the figure that discoveries of oil have slowed down. No major discoveries of oil have been reported in the USA for last several years. Similarly, the discoveries in other parts of the world are rather small. No giant or supergiant oil fields have been discovered either in the last several years.

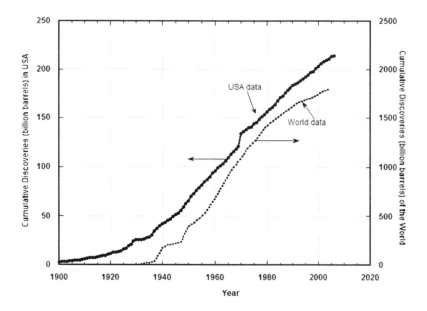

Fig. 10.4. Cumulative discoveries of crude oil in the USA and World [3–5].

The exponential growth rate is driven by consumers who demand more and more of the resources as new ways of using the resource are developed. The behavior of $Q_d(t)$ as a function of time can be described by a logistics curve. The initial growth of $Q_d(t)$ follows the Malthus equation from population growth studies and is given by:

$$\frac{dQ_d}{dt} = k_1 Q_d \tag{10.3}$$

where k_1 is a constant. The solution of Eq. (10.3) is given by:

$$Q_d(t) = Q_d(0)e^{k_1 t} \tag{10.4}$$

Since Q_d is finite, there is a fixed amount of total discoverable reserve for any finite resource. If this is denoted by $Q_d(\infty)$, then

$$Q_d(\infty) - Q_d(t) = \text{total resources that remain to be discovered.}$$

The Malthus equation works well during the growth phase but does not describe the tapering off phase. Equation (10.3) may be modified to describe the entire process by using the Verhulst equation, which is given by:

$$\frac{dQ_d(t)}{dt} = k_2 Q_d(t)[Q_d(\infty) - Q_d(t)] \tag{10.5}$$

If it is assumed that $k_2 Q_d(\infty) = k$, then Eq. (10.5) applies for early times. Equation (10.5) implies that the rate of change in $Q_d(t)$ is proportional to both the instantaneous value of the discovered resources and to the amount of remaining resource.

Equation (10.5) can be rearranged to provide;

$$\frac{1}{Q_d(\infty)} \frac{dQ_d(t)}{dt} = k_2 \frac{Q_d(t)}{Q_d(\infty)}[Q_d(\infty) - Q_d(t)] \tag{10.6}$$

Further rearrangement provides;

$$\frac{1}{Q_d(\infty)} \frac{dQ_d(t)}{dt} = k_2 Q_d(\infty) \frac{Q_d(t)}{Q_d(\infty)} \left[1 - \frac{Q_d(t)}{Q_d(\infty)} \right] \tag{10.7}$$

By replacing; $k_2 Q_d(\infty) = k$

$$\frac{1}{Q_d(\infty)} \frac{dQ_d(t)}{dt} = k \frac{Q_d(t)}{Q_d(\infty)} \left[1 - \frac{Q_d(t)}{Q_d(\infty)} \right] \tag{10.8}$$

By defining $\frac{Q_d(t)}{Q_d(\infty)} = f(t)$ fraction of total discovered resources at time t,

Equation (10.8) may be rewritten as:

$$\frac{df(t)}{dt} = k f(t)[1 - f(t)] \tag{10.9}$$

Equation (10.9) is rearranged in the following manner for solution

$$\frac{df(t)}{f(t)[1 - f(t)]} = k \, dt \tag{10.10}$$

The left hand side of Eq. (10.10) is rearranged as follows:

$$\frac{df(t)}{f(t)} + \frac{df(t)}{1-f(t)} = k\,dt \tag{10.11}$$

Integration of Eq. (10.11) from $t = t_1$ where $f(t_1)$ is known to a value $t = t$ where $f(t)$ is unknown provides:

$$\int_{t_1}^{t}\frac{df(t)}{f(t)} + \int_{t_1}^{t}\frac{df(t)}{1-f(t)} = \int_{t_1}^{t}k\,dt \tag{10.12}$$

or,

$$\ell n\left[\frac{f(t)}{f(t_1)}\right] - \ell n\left[\frac{1-f(t)}{1-f(t_1)}\right] = k\left(t-t_1\right) \tag{10.13}$$

$$\frac{f(t)}{f(t_1)}\left[\frac{1-f(t_1)}{1-f(t)}\right] = e^{k(t-t_1)} \tag{10.14}$$

Substituting, $f(t) = \dfrac{Q_d(t)}{Q_d(\infty)}$

$$\frac{Q_d(t)}{Q_d(\infty)} = \frac{\left[\dfrac{Q_d(t_1)}{Q_d(\infty)}\right]}{\left[\dfrac{Q_d(t_1)}{Q_d(\infty)} + \left[1 - \dfrac{Q_d(t_1)}{Q_d(\infty)}\right]e^{-k(t-t_1)}\right]} \tag{10.15}$$

Discovery of a resource leads to cumulative production utilization $Q_p(t)$. The value of $Q_p(t)$ will follow $Q_d(t)$ but will have a time lag Δt. The cumulative discovery and production of United States oil is shown in Fig. 10.5. The reason for this is that it takes time to get the resource to the consumer. In the USA, this lag time or $\Delta t = 10.5$ years.

An expression for cumulative production, $Q_p(t)$, can be obtained by shifting time by Δt, and is given below.

$$\frac{Q_p(t)}{Q_d(\infty)} = \frac{\left[\dfrac{Q_d(t_1)}{Q_d(\infty)}\right]}{\left[\dfrac{Q_d(t_1)}{Q_d(\infty)} + \left[1 - \dfrac{Q_d(t_1)}{Q_d(\infty)}\right]e^{-k(t-t_1-\Delta t)}\right]} \qquad (10.16)$$

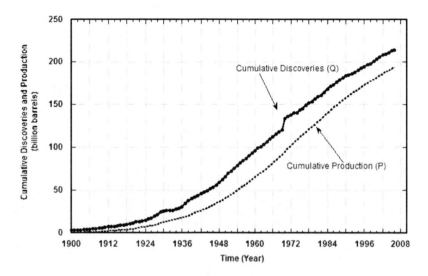

Fig. 10.5. Cumulative discovery and cumulative production curves for the USA showing that the discovery curve can be shifted by 10.5 years to obtain production curve [4].

It may be noted that in Eq. (10.16), $Q_d(\infty)$ should be the same as $Q_p(\infty)$, since ultimately all the reserve oil will be used up. Also, $Q_d(t_1)$ may be replaced by $Q_p(t_1)$. The value of $Q_p(t_1)$ refers to cumulative production in the year t_1. The expression for $Q_p(t)$ becomes

$$\frac{Q_p(t)}{Q_p(\infty)} = \frac{\left[\dfrac{Q_p(t_1)}{Q_p(\infty)}\right]}{\left[\dfrac{Q_p(t_1)}{Q_p(\infty)} + \left[1 - \dfrac{Q_p(t_1)}{Q_p(\infty)}\right]e^{-k_p(t-t_1)}\right]} \qquad (10.17)$$

The value of k_p should be determine the same way as k in Eq. (10.15).

The discovery rate, $\dfrac{dQ_d(t)}{dt}$, can be obtained by differentiating Eq. (10.15) with respect to time (t) and is given by:

$$\frac{dQ_d(t)}{dt} = Q_d(\infty)\frac{Q_d(t_1)}{Q_d(\infty)}\frac{k\left(1 - \dfrac{Q_d(t_1)}{Q_d(\infty)}\right)e^{-k(t-t_1)}}{\left[\dfrac{Q_d(t_1)}{Q_d(\infty)} + \left(1 - \dfrac{Q_d(t_1)}{Q_d(\infty)}\right)e^{-k(t-t_1)}\right]^2} \tag{10.18}$$

The production rate, $\dfrac{dQ_p(t)}{dt}$, can be also calculated from Eq. (10.18) by shifting t by Δt, and is given by:

$$\frac{dQ_p(t)}{dt} = Q_d(\infty)\frac{Q_d(t_1)}{Q_d(\infty)}\frac{k\left(1 - \dfrac{Q_d(t_1)}{Q_d(\infty)}\right)e^{-k(t-t_1-\Delta t)}}{\left[\dfrac{Q_d(t_1)}{Q_d(\infty)} + \left(1 - \dfrac{Q_d(t_1)}{Q_d(\infty)}\right)e^{-k(t-t_1-\Delta t)}\right]^2} \tag{10.19}$$

Therefore, the rate of change for reserves is given by:

$$\frac{dQ_r(t)}{dt} = \frac{dQ_d(t)}{dt} - \frac{dQ_p(t)}{dt} \tag{10.20}$$

Because of time delay Δt, the function $Q_r(t)$ will increase, pass through a maximum, and then decay to zero.

Plots of the rate of discovery, $\dfrac{dQ_d(t)}{dt}$, the rate of production, $\dfrac{dQ_p(t)}{dt}$, and rate of change of reserves, $\dfrac{dQ_r(t)}{dt}$ versus time (in years) show the behavior of these functions. These plots are shown in Figs. 10.6 and 10.7 using some arbitrary data.

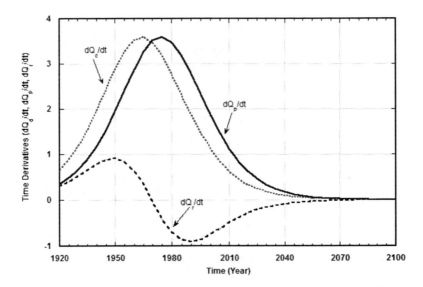

Fig. 10.6. A plot showing behavior of time derivatives of cumulative discovery, production, and reserve.

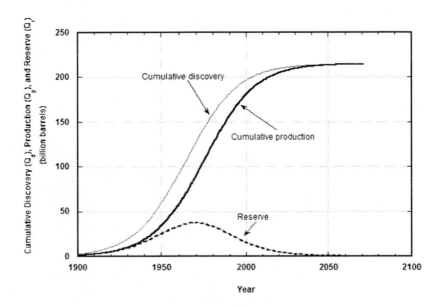

Fig. 10.7. A plot showing ultimate behavior of cumulative discovery, production, and reserve.

Problem 10.1

Estimate United States peak-oil production year and how long the oil will last.

Data:

The following data are necessary to make such an estimate and prediction.

Annual oil discovery data.
Annual oil production data.

From these two sets of data, the following set of data are obtained.

Cumulative discovery data (Q_d)

The data is generally given as proved reserves.
$t_1 = 1965$
$t_2 = 1975$
$Q_d(\infty) = 215$ billion barrels
$Q_d(t_1) = 109.54$ billion barrels
$Q_d(t_2) = 143.87$ billion barrels

In order to calculate k, first $f(t_1)$ and $f(t_2)$ are calculated from $\dfrac{Q_d(t)}{Q_d(\infty)} = f(t)$ as follows:

$$f(t_1) = \frac{Q_d(t_1)}{Q_d(\infty)} = \frac{109.54}{215} = 0.5094 \; ; \; f(t_2) = \frac{Q_d(t_2)}{Q_d(\infty)} = \frac{143.87}{215} = 0.6692$$

Eq. (10.15) can be rearranged as follows to obtain k;

$$k = \frac{\ln\left[\dfrac{f(t_2)[1 - f(t_1)]}{f(t_1)[1 - f(t_2)]}\right]}{(t_2 - t_1)} = 0.0666443$$

A plot of US cumulative discovery (Q_d), cumulative production (Q_p), and reserve (Q_r) is shown in Fig. 10.8. As can be seen from this figure, the US data is following the same behavior as shown in Fig. 10.7.

This value of k is next used to predict $\dfrac{dQ_p(t)}{dt}$ or the annual production rate from Eq. (10.19) and is compared with the actual production rate in Fig. 10.9.

A good match of the predicted data with the actual data could be obtained. Equation (10.19) can be used to predict the annual production rate beyond the year of the available data. The plot in Fig. 10.9 suggests that the peak oil production took place around 1975 and the US oil production will approach zero around 2050.

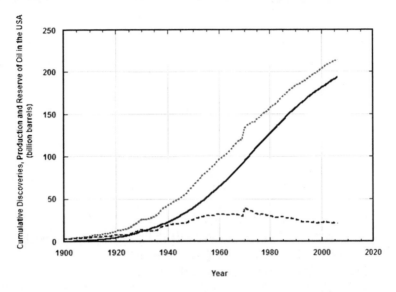

Fig. 10.8. A plot showing cumulative discovery, production, and reserve oil data for the USA [4].

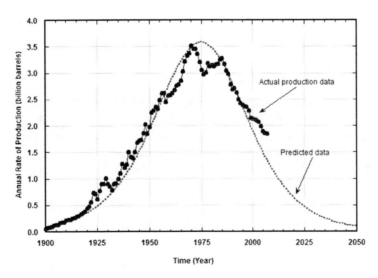

Fig. 10.9. A comparison of predicted annual production data from Eq. (10.19) with that of actual production data for the USA.

10.3 Gaussian Distribution for Peak Oil Prediction

Bartlett [6] noted that the Gaussian distribution can be applied to the annual production vs. time. He suggested the following expression for the Gaussian distribution curve.

$$P = -\frac{dQ}{dt} = \left[\frac{Q_\infty}{S(2\pi)^{1/2}}\right] e^{\left[-\frac{(t_m - t)^2}{2S^2}\right]} \tag{10.21}$$

In this equation, P represents the production of oil per year and contains three adjustable parameters: Q_∞, t_m, and S.

where

t	=	Date (year)
t_m	=	The date of the maximum of the Gaussian Hubbert curve
P	=	The production of oil in barrels per year (bbl/year)
Q	=	The estimated amount of oil remaining in the ground (bbl).
Q_∞	=	The integrated total production (bbl) as the time t approaches infinity; this is the estimated ultimate recovery (EUR)
W	=	The full width at half-height of the Gaussian
W	=	[(8 ln2)0.5 S] = 2.355 : : : S, where S is a convenient width parameter

The parameters for the Gaussian distribution that provided the best fit to the data for the production of oil in the U.S. assuming that $Q_\infty = 222.2 \times 10^9$ barrel or 222.2 billion barrels, are as follows:

Ultimate Resource Q_∞ (bbl) = 222.2 x 10^9
Year (date) of maximum t_m = 1975.6
S (width parameter), year = 27.56

The analysis by Bartlett suggests that approximately three fourths (77%) of the EUR, ($Q_\infty = 222.2 \times 10^9$ bbl) in the 50 states had been produced by the end of 1995. This EUR gives a best fit that is significantly larger than the value found by Hubbert (1982), who based his analysis on U.S. production data for the lower 48 states through 1980. Hubbert's EUR was 161.8×10^9 (see Fig. 10.10).

10.4 Linearization of Hubbert Peak Oil Theory

Several researchers [7–10] employed another approach to predict the peak oil production year using the following linearization techniques. The production rate P is expressed as follows:

$$P = \frac{dQ_p}{dt} = bQ_d(\infty) \frac{e^{b(t-t_m)}}{\left[1 + e^{b(t-t_m)}\right]^2} \tag{10.22}$$

$$Q_p = \frac{Q_d(\infty)}{1 + e^{b(t-t_m)}} \tag{10.23}$$

$$P = bQ_p - b\frac{Q_p^{\;2}}{Q_d(\infty)} \tag{10.24}$$

$$P = bQ_p\left(1 - \frac{Q_p}{Q_d(\infty)}\right) \tag{10.25}$$

$$\frac{P}{Q_p} = b - \frac{b}{Q_d(\infty)}Q_p \tag{10.26}$$

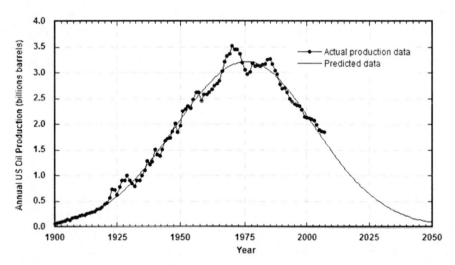

Fig. 10.10. The data for the production of oil in the U.S. are shown, along with the primary Gaussian. This is the Gaussian that has the smallest RMSD and hence is the best fit to the data [6].

A plot of P/Q_p versus Q_p should result in a straight line. The intercept of the line will provide the value of b, and $Q_d(\infty)$ could be calculated from the slope. For the US oil, this plot is shown in Fig. 10.11.

In order to generate the entire curve for annual production rate versus time, $1/P$ that represents year per billion barrels is calculated from the following expression.

$$\frac{1}{P} = \frac{1}{\left[bQ_p \left(1 - \dfrac{Q_p}{Q_d(\infty)} \right) \right]} \tag{10.27}$$

This is done by increasing or decreasing Q_p by increments of one (billion barrel) unit from cumulative production at a specified year. In order to compute, the US peak oil production year, the cumulative production for 1993 was used. The Q_p = 165 billion barrels by 1993. Now the cumulative production can be either increased by one or decreased by one and Eq. (10.27) could be used to calculate $1/P$. Then for each value of P, a year-fraction, i.e. how long it took to produce each billion barrel unit is determined and a plot of P versus year-fraction provided the Fig. 10.12.

From Fig. 10.11, the value of b was found to be 0.064. Also, the plot suggests the ultimate recovery of $Q_d(\infty)$ is 212 billion barrels. The year 1993 when the cumulative production was 165 billion barrels was chosen as the starting point for the calculation. Next, Q_p in 1993 (165 billion barrels) is increased by 1 to 166 billion barrels and Eq. (10.27) provides $1/P$ = 0.432. This suggests that 0.432 fraction year was needed to produce 1 billion barrels. Otherwise, the cumulative production of 166 billion barrels occurred in 1993.432 year. Similarly, Q_p in 1993 (165 billion barrels) could be reduced by one to 164 billion barrels, and $1/P$ was found to be 0.419. This suggests that cumulative production of 164 billion barrels occurred in year 1992.581. The entire plot is shown in Fig. 10.12.

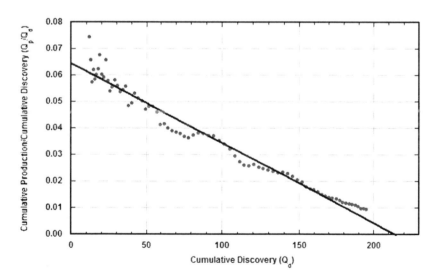

Fig. 10.11. A linearized plot of cumulative production and discovery data according to Eq. (10.26).

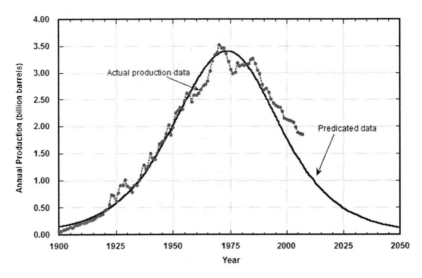

Fig. 10.12. Prediction of annual production data for the USA using linearization method using Eq. (10.27).

10.5 World Peak Oil Forecast

The methods described above are also used to predict when world oil production will peak (see Fig. 10.13).

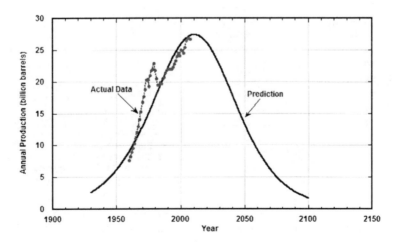

Fig. 10.13. Prediction of oil production peaking in the world using Eq. (10.19) [3].

Bartlett [6] used the Gaussian distribution approach to predict the oil production peak year. An equation similar to Eq. (10.21) was used to generate the world oil production curve and is shown in Fig. 10.14.

Laherrere [10] used 2,000 giga-barrel as the estimated ultimate recovery of crude oil in the world to estimate the peak year for oil production (Fig. 10.15). He used Hubbert style approach for the estimation. It may be interesting to note that

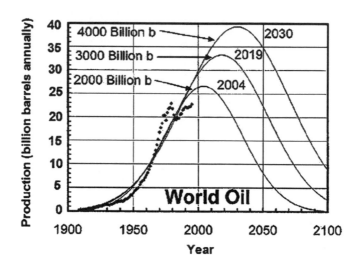

Fig. 10.14. Estimate of world peak year for oil production using Gaussian curve by Bartlett (Printed with permission from [6]).

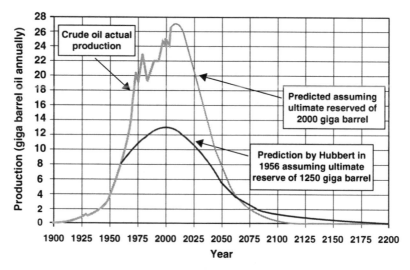

Fig. 10.15. The estimate of peak year for world oil production by Laherrere [10] and comparison with Hubbert's prediction assuming EUR of 2,000 giga-barrel (Printed with permission).

the peak year estimated by Hubbert using the less world reserve of oil was almost the same as that suggested by Laherrere. Extensive exploration in the 1960–1970s led to significant increase in the reserve, however, the oil consumption rate also increased almost proportionally leading to the same peak year as suggested by Hubbert. The cumulative discovery and production oil in the world is shown in Fig. 10.16.

Most studies estimate that oil production will peak sometime between 2010 and 2040, although many of these projections cover a wide range of time, including two studies for which the range extends into the next century. Figure 10.17 shows the estimates of studies examined by US Government Accountability Office (GAO-07-283) [12].

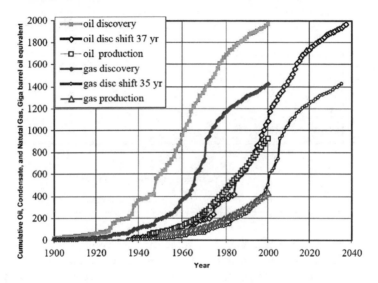

Fig. 10.16. World cumulative discovery and production of conventional oil and condensate, and natural gas (Printed with permission from [11]).

According to the GAO [12], "Key uncertainties in trying to determine the timing of peak oil are the (1) amount of oil throughout the world; (2) technological, cost, and environmental challenges to produce that oil; (3) political and investment risk factors that may affect oil exploration and production; and (4) future world demand for oil. The uncertainties related to exploration and production also make it difficult to estimate the rate of decline after the peak.

Another key difference between the studies is in how much oil they assume is still in the ground. Some studies consider a peak in conventional oil (crude oil of all grades), while other studies consider a peak in total oil, including conventional and nonconventional (meaning tar sands and oil shale) oils. Because of these differences in the peak concept used in the various studies, we have not attempted to

References

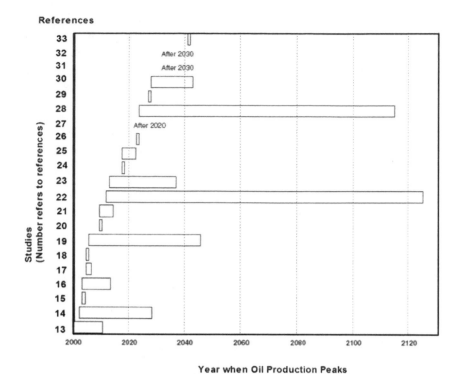

Fig. 10.17. Estimates of when oil production will peak in the world by various researchers and organizations (From GAO report GAO-07-283 [12]).

define a peak as either a peak in conventional oil or conventional plus nonconventional oils. Instead, we have focused on identifying key factors that cause uncertainty in the timing of the peak. These factors would cause such uncertainty regardless of whether the peak concept focused on conventional or total oil.

Estimates of how much oil remains in the ground are highly uncertain because much of these data are self-reported and unverified by independent auditors; many parts of the world have yet to be fully explored for oil; and there is no comprehensive assessment of oil reserves from nonconventional sources. This uncertainty surrounding estimates of oil resources in the ground comprises the uncertainty surrounding estimates of proven reserves as well as uncertainty surrounding expected increases in these reserves and estimated future oil discoveries.

The Oil and Gas Journal and World Oil, two primary sources of proven reserves estimates, compile data on proven reserves from national and private company sources. Some of this information is publicly available from oil companies that are subject to public reporting requirements – for example, information provided by companies that are publicly traded on U.S. stock exchanges that are subject to the filing requirements of U.S. federal securities laws. Information filed pursuant to these laws is subject to liability standards, and, therefore, there is a strong incentive for these companies to make sure their disclosures are complete and accurate. On the other hand, companies that are not subject to these federal securities laws, including companies wholly owned by various OPEC countries where the majority of reserves are located, are not subject to these filing requirements and their related liability standards. Some experts believe OPEC estimates of proven reserves to be inflated. For example, OPEC estimates increased sharply in the 1980s, corresponding to a change in OPEC's quota rules that linked a member country's production quota in part to its remaining proven reserves. In addition, many OPEC countries' reported reserves remained relatively unchanged during the 1990s, even as they continued high levels of oil production. For example, IEA reports that reserves estimates in Kuwait were unchanged from 1991 to 2002, even though the country produced more than eight billion barrels of oil over that period and did not make any important new oil discoveries".

The report by GAO also noted that "There is no universally agreed-upon definition of conventional oil. The Oil and Gas Journal includes Canadian oil sands in its estimates. IEA classifies oil sands as nonconventional, and, therefore, since we are using the IEA classification throughout this report, we have removed the Oil and Gas Journal estimate of 174 billion barrels of oil from the Canadian oil sands data. USGS experts emphasized the importance of these oil sands in future oil production and stated that in their view, these resources are now considered to be conventional".

Although it is projected that oil production by non-OPEC countries will increase, the analysis of reserve and production of these countries shows that non-OPEC and non-Former Soviet Union Countries (non-FSU) have already peaked and are currently declining (Fig. 10.18). The analysis was carried out by Werner and Schindler [34] as reported by Johnson et al. [35].

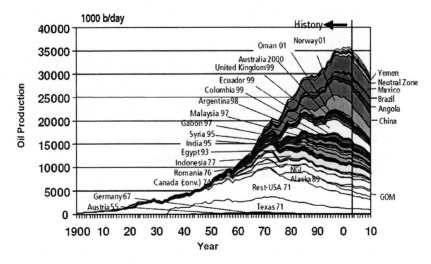

Fig. 10.18. Non-OPEC, non-FSU oil production has peaked and is declining [34, 35].

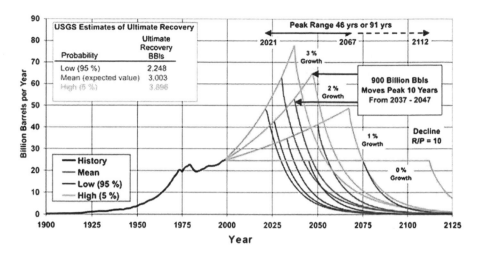

Fig. 10.19. Energy Information Administration world conventional oil production scenarios [36].

1. This summary graph shows all 12 long-term production scenarios based on the 4 annual production growth rates (0, 1, 2, and 3 percent) and the 3 USGS technically recoverable oil resource volumes (2,248, 3,003, and 3,896 billion barrels) equivalent to the 95% probable, mean (expected value), and a 5% probable volumes.
2. The estimated peak year of production ranges from 2021 to 2067 (a span of 46 years) for the 1%, 2%, and 3% per year growth rates and the three resources volumes. Including the 0% growth rate extends the estimated production peak range to 2112 (a span of 91 years). For the mean resource and 2% production growth rate scenario, which reflect the expected resource volume and the recently experienced production growth rate, the peak occurs in 2037.
3. Market feedback mechanisms might smooth and flatten the sharp production peaks as the actual production paths play out, moving the peaks earlier in time.
4. The peak year would be delayed by discovery of a larger recoverable conventional resource base than is currently estimated, or it could occur earlier with accelerated production rates. It may also vary as global oil demand varies. For example, if demand for oil weakens for economic reasons or because substitutes for conventional oil gain market share, the conventional oil production growth rate may decline and result in a later peak.

10.6 Peak Coal Production Forecast

Although it is assumed that a number of countries have significant reserve of coal, the coal production is expected to peak rather sooner. The Hubbert model was used by several researchers to estimate the peak time for the production of US coal. These predictions are shown in Figs. 10.20, 10.21, and 10.22.

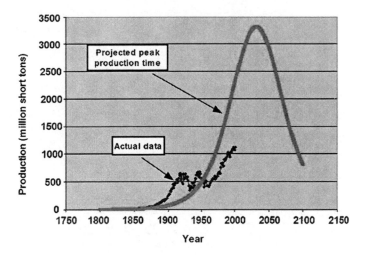

Fig. 10.20. Actual U.S. Coal Production and a Fitted Hubbert Curve (Printed with permission from [37]).

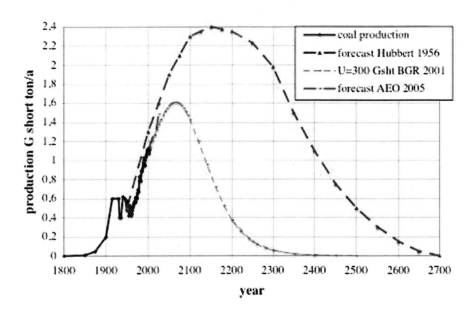

Fig. 10.21. US coal production data and estimate of year for peak production by Laherrere using 300 giga short ton of ultimate coal reserve (Printed with permission from [10]).

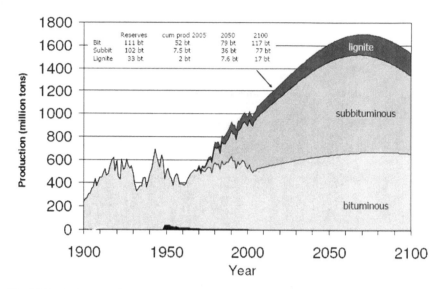

Fig. 10.22. Coal production in the USA: Forecast for the future based on proved reserve, recoverable reserve and estimated recoverable reserve (Printed with permission from [38]).

The Hubbert model or the variation of it has been used to fit the coal production data of various countries. From the fitting of data, the year when the production of coal peak in these countries is estimated and are shown in Figs. 10.23–10.26.

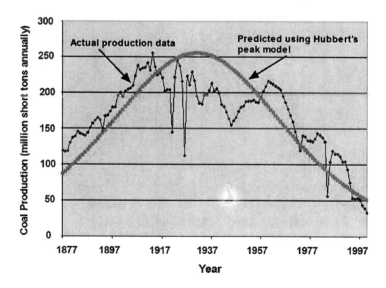

Fig. 10.23. UK coal production and Hubbert peak model (Printed with permission from [37]).

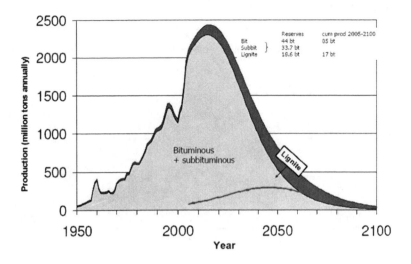

Fig. 10.24. Estimates of future coal production of China based on present reserve estimates (Printed with permission from [38]).

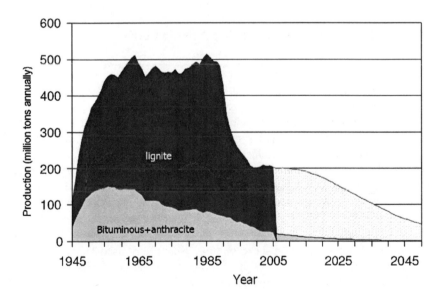

Fig. 10.25. Germany coal production: History and forecast based on proved reserve (Printed with permission from [38]).

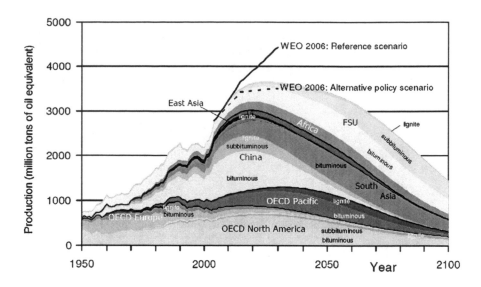

Fig. 10.26. Coal production in the world: History and estimates for the future based on present proved reserve (Printed with permission from [38]).

10.7 Peak Production Forecast for Natural Gas

The Hubbert peak theory is also used to estimate natural gas availability in the future. A similar approach as described for crude oil production can be taken. As shown in Fig. 10.27, the creaming curve for US natural gas is reaching a plateau. The cumulative natural gas discovery curve can be shifted by a certain time period to match the cumulative production curve (Fig. 10.28). However, as shown in Fig. 10.29, the US natural gas production might have peaked already.

The Hubbert theory proposed in 1956 for predicting the time for peak production of a finite resource has been used rather successfully for predicting peak oil production in the USA and other countries. Hubbert [40] provided further insight of the theory in 1982. For a finite resource, it is important to forecast how long the resource will be available. The availability of crude oil has significant implication to a number of areas including the economy, technology used in the industries, transportation sectors, and the life style. Studies have been undertaken by various governments, companies, and organization to estimate and provide a better forecast of peak oil production for a region, country, or the world [41–49].

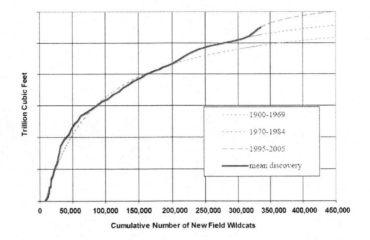

Fig. 10.27. US conventional natural gas creaming curve (Printed with permission from [39]).

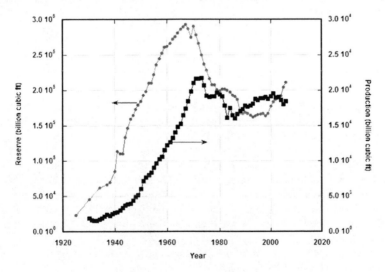

Fig. 10.28. Annual reserve and production curves for natural gas in the USA.

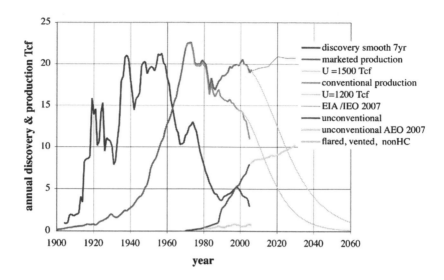

Fig. 10.29. Estimation of future US production of natural gas modeled by Laherrere (Printed with permission from [39]).

References

1. Hubbert MK (1956) Nuclear energy and fossil fuel. Spring Meeting of the Southern District, American Petroleum Institute, San Antonio, TX, March 7–9, 1956. Publication No. 95, Shell Development Co., 1956.
2. Penner SS, Icerman L (1974–1976) Energy. Addison-Wesley.
3. BP Statistical Review of World Energy June 2008.
4. US Energy Information Administration (2008) http://tonto.eia.doe.gov/dnav/pet/hist/rcrr01nus_1a.htm
5. Association for the Study of Peak Oil and Gas (ASPO) (Aleklett K, 2004) IEA accepts peak oil. http://www.peakoil.net/uhdsg/weo2004/AnalysisWorldEnergy Outlook2004.pdf. 12/12/2008.
6. Bartlett AA (2000) An analysis of US and world oil production pattern using Hubbert-style curve. Mathematical Geology 32(1): 1–17.
7. Deffeyes K (2005) Beyond Oil - The view from Hubbert's peak. New York: Hill and Wang.
8. Staniford S (2005) When does Hubbert linearization work? http://www.theoildrum.com/story/2005/9/29/3234/46878.
9. Tao Z, Li M (2007) System dynamics model of Hubbert peak for China's oil. Energy Policy 35(4): 2281–2286.
10. Laherrere J (2005) Forecasting production from discovery, ASPO Lisbon, May 19–20, http://www.oilcrisis.com/laherrere/lisbon.pdf.

11. Laherrere J (2001) Forecasting future production from past discovery. OPEC and the global energy balance: towards a sustainable energy future, Vienna Sept. 28–29, 2001.
12. US GAO (United States Governmental Accountability Office) (2007) CRUDE OIL: Uncertainty about Future Oil Supply Makes It Important to Develop a Strategy for Addressing a Peak and Decline in Oil Production. GAO-07-283.
13. Ivanhoe LF (November 1996) Updated Hubbert curves analyze world oil supply. World Oil 217: 91–94.
14. Bartlett AA (2000) An analysis of U.S. and world oil production patterns using Hubbert-Style curves. Mathematical Geology 32(1): 1–17.
15. Deffeyes KS (November 11, 2002) World's oil production peak reckoned in near future. Oil and Gas Journal 100(46): 46–48.
16. Volvo (2005) Future Fuels for Commercial Vehicles.
17. Bakhtiari AMS (April 26, 2004) World Oil Production Capacity Model Suggests Output Peak by 2006–2007. Oil and Gas Journal.
18. Duncan RC (2000) Peak Oil Production and the Road to the Olduvai Gorge. Pardee Keynote Symposia. Geological Society of America, Summit 2000.
19. Greene DL, Hopson JL, Li J (2003) Running Out Of and Into Oil: Analyzing Global Oil Depletion and Transition Through 2050. Oak Ridge National Laboratory, Department of Energy, Oak Ridge.
20. Campbell CJ (July 14, 2003) Industry Urged to Watch for Regular Oil Production Peaks, Depletion Signals. Oil and Gas Journal.
21. Merril Lynch (October 2005) Oil Supply Analysis.
22. Ministére de l'Economie Des Finances et de l'Industrie (2005) L'industrie pétrolière en 2004.
23. International Energy Agency (2004) World Energy Outlook 2004. Paris France: 101–103.
24. Laherrère J (2003) Future Oil Supplies. Seminar Center of Energy Conversion, Zurich.
25. Gerling P, Remple H, Schwartz-Schampera, Thielemann UT (2004) Reserves, Resources and Availability of Energy Resources. Federal Institute for Geosciences and Natural Resources, Hanover, Germany.
26. Edwards JD (August 1997) Crude oil and alternative energy production forecasts for the twenty-first century: the end of the hydrocarbon era. American Association of Petroleum Geologists Bulletin 81(8).
27. Cambridge Energy Research Associates, Inc (May 2005) Worldwide Liquids Capacity Outlook to 2010, Tight Supply or Excess of Riches.
28. Wood JH, Long GR David F (2004) Morehouse. Long Term World Oil Supply Scenarios. Energy Information Administration.
29. Total (2004) Sharing Our Energies: Corporate Social Responsibility Report 2004.
30. Shell International. Energy Needs (2001) Choices and Possibilities: Scenarios to 2050. Global Business Environment.
31. Directorate-General for Research Energy (2003) World Energy, Technology and Climate Policy Outlook: WETO 2030. European Commission, EUR 20366.
32. Exxon Mobil (November 2005). The Outlook for Energy: A View to 2030. Corporate Planning. Washington, D.C.
33. Parker HW (February 25, 2002) Demand, supply will determine when world oil output peaks. Oil and Gas Journal.
34. Werner Z, Schindler J (July 15, 2002) Future World Oil Supply, International Summer School, Salzburg.

35. Johnson HR, Crawford PM, Bunger JW (March 2004) Strategic significance of America's oil shale resource. Volume I Assessment of strategic issues. Office of Naval Petroleum and Oil Shale Reserves U.S. Department of Energy Washington, D.C.
36. Wood J, Long G (2000) EIA, Long Term World Oil Supply (A Resource Base/ Production Path Analysis) 07/28/2000. http://tonto.eia.doe.gov/ftproot/presentations/long_term_supply/sld001.htm
37. Vaux G (2004) The peak in U.S. coal production. www.fromthewilderness.com.
38. Energy Watch Group (July 2007) Coal: Resources and Future Production. EWG Paper No. 1/07.
39. Laherrere J (August 20, 2007) North America natural gas discovery and production. http://www.oilcrisis.com/laherrere/NAm-NG2007.pdf
40. Hubbert MK (1982) Techniques of prediction as applied to production of oil and gas. US Department of Commerce, NBS Special Publication 631, 1–121.
41. Hirsch RL, Bezdec R, Wendling R. Peaking of world oil production: impacts, mitigation and risk management. 2005. DOE report, http://www.netl.doe.gov/publications/others/pdf/Oil_Peaking_NETL.pdf
42. USGS, 2000. US Geological Survey World Petroleum Assessment. http://pubs.usgs.gov/dds/dds-060/
43. Maugeri L. The Age of Oil: The Mythology, History and Future of the World's Most Controversial Resource, 2006. ISBN: 0275990087.
44. Association for the study of Peak oil and Gas (ASPO), 2007 (accessed) www.peakoil.net
45. Cambridge Energy Research Associates, Inc. (2006) Why the "peak oil" theory falls down: myths, legends, and the future of oil resources. CERA, Cambridge, MA.
46. Lea R (2008) The days of cheap oil have gone, but the peak oil theory is far too bleak. Public Health 122(7): 667–668.
47. Guseo R, Dalla Valle A, Guidolin M (2007) World oil depletion models: Price effects compared with strategic or technological interventions. Technological Forecasting and Social Change 74(4): 452–469.
48. Cooper CJ (2007) Energy and transport issues for Gauteng, South Africa. Journal of Energy in Southern Africa 18(2): 11–15.
49. Brandt AR (2007) Testing Hubbert. Energy Policy 35(5): 3074–3088.

Problems

1. Discuss the strength and weakness of Hubbert peak oil theory.
2. Discuss the strength and weakness of linearization of Hubbert theory, and the Gaussian distribution approach.
3. Explain how the peak oil production timing might affect the economy and the social and political scenarios at the local, national and international level.
4. Apply peak oil theory to other finite resources: (a) uranium (b) silicon. When do the peak occur?
5. Evaluate the databases for oil, natural gas, and coal for reserves and production. Point out any discrepancies that you find.

Appendix I

Energy Versus GDP for Various Countries

Table I.1. The energy use and its relationship to GDP of some selected countries.

Primary energy consumption						
Mtoe	**2007**	**2007 Share of world total (%)**	**2007 GDP**	**2007 Share of world total**	**GDP per capita ($US)**	**Energy use per capita (toe)**
USA	23,61.4	21.3	13,811,200	25.4	46,000	7.77
China	1,863.4	16.8	3,280,053	6.0	5,300	1.40
Russian Federation	692.0	6.2	1,291,011	2.4	14,600	4.92
Japan	517.5	4.7	4,376,705	8.1	33,800	4.07
India	404.4	3.6	1,170,968	2.2	2,700	0.35
Canada	321.7	2.9	1,326,376	2.4	38,200	9.69
Germany	311.0	2.8	3,297,233	6.1	34,400	3.78
France	255.1	2.3	2,562,288	4.7	33,800	3.98
South Korea	234.0	2.1	969,795	1.8	24,600	4.75
Brazil	216.8	2.0	1,314,170	2.4	9,700	1.13
United Kingdom	215.9	1.9	2,727,806	5.0	35,300	3.54
Iran	182.9	1.6	270,937	0.5	12,300	2.78
Italy	179.6	1.6	2,107,481	3.9	31,000	3.09
Saudi Arabia	167.6	1.5	381,683	0.7	20,700	5.95
Mexico	155.5	1.4	893,364	1.6	12,500	1.41
Spain	150.3	1.4	1,429,226	2.6	33,700	3.71
Ukraine	136.0	1.2	140,484	0.3	6,900	2.96
South Africa	127.8	1.2	277,581	0.5	10,600	2.92
Australia	121.8	1.1	821,716	1.5	37,500	5.91
Taiwan	115.1	1.0		0.0	29,800	0
Indonesia	114.6	1.0	432,817	0.8	3,400	5.02
Turkey	101.7	0.9	657,091	1.2	9,400	0
Poland	94.4	0.9	420,321	0.8	16,200	0.48
The Netherlands	91.8	0.8	754,203	1.4	38,600	0
Thailand	85.6	0.8	245,818	0.5	8,000	1.42
Argentina	73.7	0.7	262,331	0.5	13,000	2.45
Belgium & Luxembourg	73.6	0.7	448,560	0.8	36,500	5.51

Primary energy consumption						
Mtoe	2007	2007 Share of world total (%)	2007 GDP	2007 Share of world total	GDP per capita ($US)	Energy use per capita (toe)
Venezuela	71.4	0.6	228,071	0.4	12,800	0
Egypt	63.2	0.6	128,095	0.2	5,400	1.31
United Arab Emirates	60.9	0.5	129,702	0.2	55,200	0
Kazakhstan	60.2	0.5	103,840	0.2	2,000	1.81
Pakistan	58.3	0.5	143,597	0.3	2,600	7.07
Malaysia	57.4	0.5	180,714	0.3	14,400	2.70
Singapore	53.4	0.5	161,347	0.3	48,900	0.77
Sweden	50.2	0.5	444,443	0.8	36,900	13.18
Uzbekistan	49.6	0.4	22,308	0.0	2,200	3.92
Norway	45.0	0.4	381,951	0.7	55,600	0.35
Czech Republic	43.3	0.4	168,142	0.3	24,400	2.27
Romania	39.7	0.4	165,980	0.3	11,100	11.59
Algeria	34.7	0.3	135,285	0.2	8,100	5.55
Greece	34.1	0.3	360,031	0.7	30,500	1.75
Austria	32.6	0.3	377,028	0.7	39,000	9.69
Colombia	30.0	0.3	171,979	0.3	7,200	4.23
Switzerland	28.9	0.3	415,516	0.8	39,800	1.79
Chile	28.6	0.3	163,915	0.3	14,400	1.03
Finland	27.4	0.2	246,020	0.5	35,500	3.18
China Hong Kong SAR	26.5	0.2	206,706	0.4	42,000	3.97
Kuwait	25.4	0.2	102,095	0.2	55,300	0.67
Philippines	24.9	0.2	144,129	0.3	3,300	3.82
Belarus	24.5	0.2	44,771	0.1	10,200	1.74
Hungary	24.5	0.2	138,182	0.3	19,500	5.23
Turkmenistan	24.4	0.2		0.0	9,200	3.78
Portugal	24.0	0.2		0.0	21,800	9.77
Qatar	22.6	0.2	42,463	0.1	75,900	0.27
Bulgaria	20.4	0.2	39,549	0.1	11,800	2.53
Bangladesh	20.3	0.2		0.0	1,400	2.47
Denmark	18.2	0.2		0.0	37,400	4.72
Slovakia	17.5	0.2	45,451	0.1	19,800	2.24
New Zealand	17.4	0.2		0.0	27,300	24.31
Republic of Ireland	15.0	0.1		0.0	45,600	2.81
Peru	13.8	0.1		0.0	7,600	0.13

Mtoe	2007	2007 Share of world total (%)	2007 GDP	2007 Share of world total	GDP per capita ($US)	Energy use per capita (toe)
Primary energy consumption						
Azerbaijan	12.5	0.1	31,248	0.1	9,000	3.31
Ecuador	10.6	0.1	44,184	0.1	7,100	3.22
Lithuania	9.0	0.1	38,328	0.1	16,700	4.17
Other Africa	118.8	1.1		0.0		3.62
Other Middle East	114.8	1.0		0.0		0.47
Other S. & Cent. America	107.9	1.0		0.0		1.53
Other Asia Pacific	87.3	0.8		0.0		0.76
Other Europe & Eurasia	81.9	0.7		0.0		2.53
Total Asia Pacific		3,801.8	34.3			
Total Europe & Eurasia		2,987.5	26.9			
Total North America		2,838.6	25.6			
Total Middle East		574.1	5.2			
Total S. & Cent. America		552.9	5.0			
Total Africa		344.4	3.1			
Total World		**11,099.3**	**100.0**			

In this review, primary energy comprises commercially traded fuels only. Excluded, therefore, are fuels such as wood, peat and animal waste which, though important in many countries, are unreliably documented in terms of consumption statistics. Also excluded are winds, geothermal and solar power generation.

Mtoe (million tonnes of oil equivalent); toe: tones of oil equivalent.

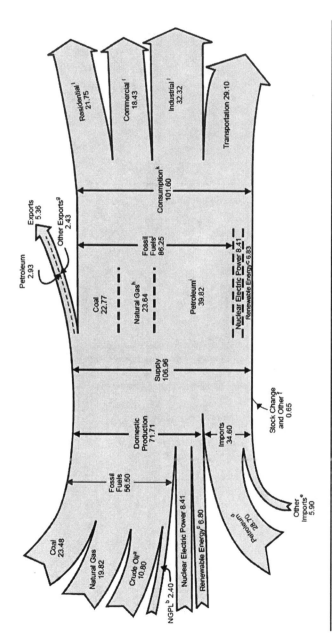

Fig. I.1. Energy flow diagram of the USA in 2007. Energy Information Administration USA

[a] Includes lease condensate.

[b] Natural gas plant liquids.

[c] Conventional hydroelectric power, biomass, geothermal, solar/photovoltaic, and wind.

[d] Crude oil and petroleum products. Includes imports into the Strategic Petroleum Reserve.

[e] Natural gas, coal, coal coke, fuel ethanol, and electricity.

[f] Adjustments, losses, and unaccounted for.

[g] Coal, natural gas, coal coke, and electricity.

[h] Natural gas only; excludes supplemental gaseous fuels.

[i] Petroleum products, including natural gas plant liquids, and crude oil burned as fuel.

[j] Includes 0.03 quadrillion Btu of coal coke net imports.

[k] Includes 0.11 quadrillion Btu of electricity net imports.

[l] Primary consumption, electricity retail sales, and electrical system energy losses, which are allocated to the end-use sectors in proportion to each sector's share of total electricity retail sales. See Note, "Electrical Systems Energy Losses," at end of Section 2.

Notes: • Data are preliminary. • Values are derived from source data prior to rounding for publication. • Totals may not equal sum of components due to independent rounding.

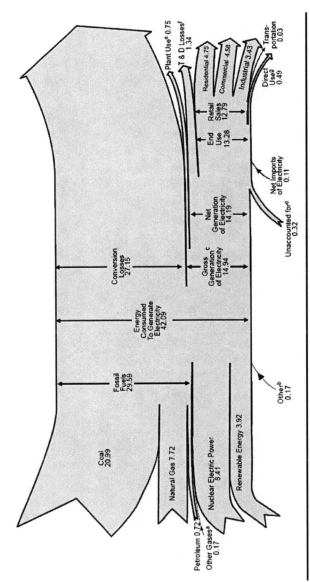

Fig. I.2. Electricity flow in the USA in 2007. Energy Information Administration USA.

a Blast furnace gas, propane gas, and other manufactured and waste gases derived from fossil fuels.

b Batteries, chemicals, hydrogen, pitch, purchased steam, sulfur, miscellaneous technologies, and non-renewable waste (municipal solid waste from non-biogenic sources, and tire-derived fuels).

c Estimated as net generation divided by 0.95.

d Data collection frame differences and nonsampling error. Derived for the diagram by subtracting the "T & D Losses' estimate from "T & D Losses and Unaccounted for' derived from Table 8.1.

e Electric energy used in the operation of power plants, estimated as 5 percent of gross generation.

f Transmission and distribution losses (electricity losses that occur between the point of generation and delivery to the customer) are estimated as 9 percent of gross generation.

g Use of electricity that is 1) self-generated, 2) produced by either the same entity that consumes the power or an affiliate, and 3) used in direct support of a service or industrial process located within the same facility or group of facilities that house the generating equipment. Direct use is exclusive of station use.

Notes: • Data are preliminary. • See Note, 'Electrical System Energy Losses,' at the end of Section 2. • Values are derived from source data prior to rounding for publication. • Totals may not equal sum of components due to independent rounding.

Table I.2. Electricity generation by countries (Terawatt-hours)

Countries	2006	2007	Change 2007 over 2006 (%)	2007 Share of total (%)
US	4,266.3	4,367.9	2.4	22.0
Canada	592.0	602.4	1.8	3.0
Mexico	244.9	253.7	3.6	1.3
Total North America	**5,103.3**	**5,224.0**	**2.4**	**26.3**
Argentina	117.1	120.8	3.1	0.6
Brazil	419.3	433.6	3.4	2.2
Chile	57.6	60.1	4.5	0.3
Colombia	52.3	53.6	2.5	0.3
Venezuela	119.8	124.9	4.3	0.6
Other S. & Cent. America	232.6	240.4	3.3	1.2
Total S. & Cent. America	**998.8**	**1,033.5**	**3.5**	**5.2**
Austria	63.4	63.7	0.5	0.3
Azerbaijan	24.5	21.8	−11.1	0.1
Belarus	31.9	31.9	−	0.2
Belgium & Luxembourg	93.3	95.5	2.3	0.5
Bulgaria	45.8	43.7	−4.7	0.2
Czech Republic	84.3	88.1	4.6	0.4
Denmark	45.6	39.2	−14.0	0.2
Finland	82.2	81.2	−1.2	0.4
France	571.1	566.5	−0.8	2.8
Germany	636.8	636.5	w	3.2
Greece	66.5	67.8	2.0	0.3
Hungary	35.9	40.0	11.5	0.2
Iceland	9.5	11.7	22.7	0.1
Republic of Ireland	27.0	27.2	0.5	0.1
Italy	314.1	314.4	0.1	1.6
Kazakhstan	71.7	76.1	6.2	0.4
Lithuania	12.5	14.0	12.3	0.1
The Netherlands	98.8	103.4	4.6	0.5
Norway	121.7	137.7	13.2	0.7
Poland	161.7	159.3	−1.5	0.8
Portugal	51.1	53.6	5.0	0.3
Romania	62.7	60.6	−3.4	0.3
Russian Federation	996.0	1,014.9	1.9	5.1

Countries	2006	2007	Change 2007 over 2006 (%)	2007 Share of total (%)
Slovakia	31.4	28.0	−11.0	0.1
Spain	308.2	322.3	4.6	1.6
Sweden	142.4	149.2	4.7	0.7
Switzerland	64.1	68.0	6.1	0.3
Turkey	176.0	191.0	8.5	1.0
Turkmenistan	13.3	14.0	5.0	0.1
Ukraine	192.1	195.1	1.6	1.0
United Kingdom	398.3	397.5	−0.2	2.0
Uzbekistan	49.4	49.4	–	0.2
Other Europe & Eurasia	161.1	163.6	1.5	0.8
Total Europe & Eurasia	**5,244.5**	**5,326.8**	**1.6**	**26.8**
Iran	183.4	193.3	5.4	1.0
Kuwait	40.2	41.5	3.3	0.2
Qatar	15.4	16.3	6.0	0.1
Saudi Arabia	183.7	190.1	3.5	1.0
United Arab Emirates	66.2	70.8	7.0	0.4
Other Middle East	171.9	180.1	4.8	0.9
Total Middle East	**660.8**	**692.1**	**4.7**	**3.5**
Algeria	35.0	36.7	4.8	0.2
Egypt	110.7	119.0	7.5	0.6
South Africa	249.0	261.5	5.0	1.3
Other Africa	186.9	195.5	4.6	1.0
Total Africa	**581.6**	**612.6**	**5.3**	**3.1**
Australia	259.5	257.3	−0.8	1.3
Bangladesh	23.9	25.5	6.5	0.1
China	2,834.4	3,277.7	15.6	16.5
China Hong Kong SAR	38.6	38.9	0.9	0.2
India	726.7	774.7	6.6	3.9
Indonesia	129.1	147.0	13.9	0.7
Japan	1,139.8	1,160.0	1.8	5.8
Malaysia	100.8	105.0	4.1	0.5
New Zealand	43.0	43.4	0.9	0.2
Pakistan	96.2	97.1	0.9	0.5
Philippines	56.8	59.6	5.0	0.3

Countries	2006	2007	Change 2007 over 2006 (%)	2007 Share of total (%)
Singapore	35.9	37.5	4.3	0.2
South Korea	415.9	440.0	5.8	2.2
Taiwan	235.1	260.7	10.9	1.3
Thailand	138.7	147.0	6.0	0.7
Other Asia Pacific	124.7	134.3	7.7	0.7
Total Asia Pacific	**6,399.2**	**7,005.7**	**9.5**	**35.2**
TOTAL WORLD	**18988.1**	**19894.8**	**4.8%**	**100.0%**
Of which: European Union[a]	3,369.9	3,387.6	0.5	17.0
OECD	10,545.0	10,766.5	2.1	54.1
Former Soviet Union	1,455.5	1,482.6	1.9	7.5
Other EMEs	6,987.7	7,645.6	9.4	38.4

[a]Based on gross output.

Appendix II

Property Classes Table

Table II.1. MACRS property classes table.

IRS asset classes	Asset description	ADS class life	GDS class life
00.11	Office furniture, fixtures, and equipment	10	7
00.12	Information systems: computers/peripherals	6	5
00.22	Automobiles, taxis	3	5
00.241	Light general-purpose trucks	4	5
00.25	Railroad cars and locomotives	15	7
00.40	Industrial steam and electric distribution	22	15
01.11	Cotton gin assets	10	7
01.21	Cattle, breeding or dairy	7	5
13.00	Offshore drilling assets	7.5	5
13.30	Petroleum refining assets	16	10
15.00	Construction assets	6	5
20.10	Manufacture of grain and grain mill products	17	10
20.20	Manufacture of yarn, thread, and woven fabric	11	7
24.10	Cutting of timber	6	5
32.20	Manufacture of cement	20	15
20.1	Manufacture of motor vehicles	12	7
48.10	Telephone distribution plant	24	15
48.2	Radio and television broadcasting equipment	6	5
49.12	Electric utility nuclear production plant	20	15
49.13	Electric utility steam production plant	28	20
49.23	Natural gas production plant	14	7
50.00	Municipal wastewater treatment plant	24	15
80.00	Theme and amusement park assets	12.5	7

The deprecation deduction for automobiles is limited to $7,660 (maximum) the first tax year, $4,900 the second, $2,950 the third year, and $1,775 per year in subsequent years.

Table II.2. Property class.

Class of property	Items included
3-year property	Tractor units, racehorses over 2 years old, and horses over 12 years old when placed in service, Special handling devices for food and beverage manufacture. Special tools for the manufacture of finished plastic products, fabricated metal products, and motor vehicles Property with ADR class life of 4 years or less
5-year property	Automobiles, taxis, buses, trucks, computers and peripheral equipment, office machinery (faxes, copiers, calculators, etc.), and any property used in research and experimentation. Also includes breeding and dairy cattle. Information Systems; Computers/Peripherals Aircraft (of non-air-transport companies) Computers Petroleum drilling equipment Property with ADR class life of more than 4 years and less than 10 years
7-year property	Office furniture and fixtures, and any property that has not been designated as belonging to another class. All other property not assigned to another class Office furniture, fixtures, and equipment Property with ADR class life of more than 10 years and less than 16 years
10-year property	Vessels, barges, tugs, similar water transportation equipment, single-purpose agricultural or horticultural structures, and trees or vines bearing fruit or nuts. Assets used in petroleum refining and certain food products Vessels and water transportation equipment Property with ADR class life of 16 years or more and less than 20 years
15-year property	Depreciable improvements to land such as shrubbery, fences, roads, and bridges. Telephone distribution plants Municipal sewage treatment plants Property with ADR class life of 20 years or more and less than 25 years
20-year property	Farm buildings that are not agricultural or horticultural structures. Municipal sewers Property with ADR class life of 25 years or more
27.5-year property	Residential rental property
39-year property	Nonresidential real estate, including home offices. (Note that the value of land may not be depreciated)

Table II.3. MACRS applicable percentage for property class.

Recovery year	3-Year property	5-Year property	7-Year property	10-Year property	15-Year property	20-Year property
1	33.33	20.00	14.29	10.00	5.00	3.750
2	44.45	32.00	24.49	18.00	9.50	7.219
3	14.81*	19.20	17.49	14.40	8.55	6.677
4	7.41	11.52*	12.49	11.52	7.70	6.177
5		11.52	8.93*	9.22	6.93	5.713
6		5.76	8.92	7.37	6.23	5.285
7			8.93	6.55*	5.90*	4.888
8			4.46	6.55	5.90	4.522
9				6.56	5.91	4.462*
10				6.55	5.90	4.461
11				3.28	5.91	4.462
12					5.90	4.461
13					5.91	4.462
14					5.90	4.461
15					5.91	4.462
16					2.95	4.461
17						4.462
18						4.461
19						4.462
20						4.461
21						2.231

The 3-, 5-, 7-, and 10-year classes use 200% and the 15- and 20-year classes use 150% declining balance depreciation.

All classes convert to straight-line depreciation in the optimal year, shown with an asterisk (*).

A half-year depreciation is allowed in the first and last recovery years.

If more than 40% of the year's MACRS property is placed in service in the last 3 months, then a mid-quarter convention must be used with depreciation tables that are not shown here.

Source: U.S. Department of the Treasury, Internal Revenue Service Publication 946, *How to Depreciate Property*. Washington, DC: U.S. Government Printing Office.

Appendix III

Unit Conversion Table

Table III.1. Unit conversions.

Unit	To Convert	Multiply By
Acceleration of free fall, standard (g_n)	m /s^2	9.806 65
Acre (based on U.S. survey foot)	m^2	$4.046\ 873 \times 10^3$
Acre foot (based on U.S. survey foot)	m^3	$1.233\ 489 \times 10^3$
Ampere hour (A h)	Coulomb (C)	3.6×10^3
Angström (Å)	m	1.0×10^{-10}
Angström (Å)	nm	1.0×10^{-1}
Atmosphere, standard (atm)	Pascal (Pa)	$1.013\ 25 \times 10^5$
Atmosphere, technical (at)	Pascal (Pa)	$9.806\ 65 \times 10^4$
Bar (bar)	Pascal (Pa)	1.0×10^5
Barn (b)	m^2	1.0×10^{-28}
Barrel (bbl) [for petroleum, 42 gallons (U.S.)]	m^3	$1.589\ 873 \times 10^{-01}$
Barrel (bbl) [for petroleum, 42 gallons (U.S.)]	Liter (L)	$1.589\ 873 \times 10^2$
British thermal unit$_{IT}$ (Btu$_{IT}$)	Joule (J)	$1.055\ 056 \times 10^3$
British thermal unit$_{th}$ (Btu$_{th}$)	Joule (J)	$1.054\ 350 \times 10^3$
British thermal unit (mean) (Btu)	Joule (J)	$1.055\ 87 \times 10^3$
Btu$_{IT}$ ·ft/(h ft^2 °F)	W/(m K)	1.730 735
Btu$_{th}$ ft/(h ft^2· °F)	W/(m K)	1.729 577
Btu$_{IT}$/ft^3	J/m^3	$3.725\ 895 \times 10^4$
Btu$_{th}$/ft^3	J/m^3	$3.723\ 403 \times 10^4$
Btu$_{IT}$/h	Watt (W)	$2.930\ 711 \times 10^{-1}$
Btu$_{th}$/h	Watt (W)	$2.928\ 751 \times 10^{-1}$
Btu$_{IT}$/(h· ft^2 °F)	W/(m^2 K)	5.678 263
Btu$_{th}$/(h ft^2 °F)	W/(m^2 K)	5.674 466
Btu$_{th}$/min	Watt (W)	$1.757\ 250 \times 10^1$
Btu$_{IT}$/lb	J/kg	2.326×10^3
Btu$_{th}$/lb	J/kg	$2.324\ 444 \times 10^3$
Btu$_{IT}$/s	Watt (W)	$1.055\ 056 \times 10^3$
Btu$_{th}$/s	Watt (W)	$1.054\ 350 \times 10^3$
Btu$_{IT}$/ft^2	J/m^2	$1.135\ 653 \times 10^4$
Btu$_{th}$/ft^2	J/m^2	$1.134\ 893 \times 10^4$
Btu$_{IT}$/(ft^2 s)	W/m^2	$1.135\ 653 \times 10^4$
Btu$_{th}$/(ft^2 s)	W/m^2	$1.134\ 893 \times 10^4$
Bushel (U.S.) (bu)	m^3	$3.523\ 907 \times 10^{-02}$
Bushel (U.S.) (bu)	L	$3.523\ 907 \times 10^1$
Calorie$_{IT}$ (cal$_{IT}$)	Joule (J)	4.1868
Calorie$_{th}$ (cal$_{th}$)	Joule (J)	4.184
Calorie (cal) (mean)	Joule (J)	4.190 02

Unit	To Convert	Multiply By
$cal_{th}/(cm\ s\ °C)$	W/(m K)	$4.184\quad 10^2$
cal_{IT}/g	J/kg	4.1868×10^3
cal_{th}/g	J/kg	4.184×10^3
$cal_{IT}/(g\ °C)$	J/(kg K)	4.1868×10^3
$cal_{th}/(g\ °C)$	J/(kg K)	4.184×10^3
$cal_{IT}/(g\ K)$	J/(kg K)	4.1868×10^3
$cal_{th}/(g·\ K)$	J/(kg K)	4.184×10^3
calorie$_{th}$ per second (cal_{th}/s)	Watt (W)	4.184
cal_{th}/cm^2	J/m^2	4.184×10^4
$cal_{th}/(cm^2\ s)$	W/m^2	4.184×10^4
Carat, metric	Gram (g)	2.0×10^{-01}
Centimeter of mercury (0 °C)	Pascal (Pa)	$1.333\ 22 \times 10^3$
Centimeter of water (4 °C)	Pascal (Pa)	$9.806\ 38 \times 10^1$
Centipoise (cP)	Pascal second (Pa s)	1.0×10^{-03}
Centistokes (cSt)	m^2/s	1.0×10^{-06}
Chain (based on U.S. survey foot) (ch)	m	$2.011\ 684 \times 10^1$
Cord (128 ft^3)	m^3	3.624 556
Cubic feet (ft^3)	m^3	$2.831\ 685 \times 10^{-02}$
Cubic feet/sec (ft^3/s)	m^3/s	$2.831\ 685 \times 10^{-02}$
Cup (U.S.)	m^3	$2.365\ 882 \times 10^{-04}$
Cup (U.S.)	Liter (L)	$2.365\ 882 \times 10^{-01}$
Curie (Ci)	Becquerel (Bq)	3.7×10^{10}
Darcy	m^2	$9.869\ 233 \times 10^{-13}$
Debye (D)	Coulomb meter (C m)	$3.335\ 641 \times 10^{-30}$
Temperature, (°C)	Kelvin (K)	T (K) = t (°C)+ 273.15
Temperature, (°F)	(°C)	T (°C) = [t (°F) - 32)]/1.8
Temperature (°F)	Kelvin (K)	T (K) = [t (°F) + 459.67)]/1.8
Temperature (°R)	Kelvin (K)	T (K) = [T (°R)]/1.8
Dyne (dyn)	Newton (N)	1.0×10^{-05}
Dyne centimeter (dyn cm)	Newton meter (N m)	1.0×10^{-07}
Dyne per square centimeter (dyn/cm^2)	Pascal (Pa)	1.0×10^{-01}
Electronvolt (eV)	Joule (J)	$1.602\ 177 \times 10^{-19}$
erg (erg)	Joule (J)	1.0×10^{-07}
erg per second (erg/s)	W	1.0×10^{-07}
Faraday (based on carbon 12)	Coulomb (C)	$9.648\ 531 \times 10^4$
Fathom (based on U.S. survey foot) [7]	Meter (m)	1.828 804
Fermi	Meter (m)	1.0×10^{-15}
Fermi	Femtometer (fm)	1.0
Fluid ounce (U.S.) (fl oz)	(m^3)	$2.957\ 353 \times 10^{-05}$
Fluid ounce (U.S.) (fl oz)	Milliliter (mL)	$2.957\ 353 \times 10^1$
Foot (ft)	Meter (m)	3.048×10^{-01}
Foot (U.S. survey) (ft) [7]	Meter (m)	$3.048\ 006 \times 10^{-01}$
Foot per second (ft/s)	m/s	3.048×10^{-01}
Foot poundal	Joule (J)	$4.214\ 011 \times 10^{-02}$
Foot pound-force (ft· lbf)	Joule (J)	1.355 818

Unit	To Convert	Multiply By
ft ·lbf/s	Watt (W)	1.355 818
gal (Gal)	m/s^2	1.0×10^{-02}
Gallon (gal)	m^3	$4.546\ 09 \times 10^{-03}$
[Canadian and U.K. (Imperial)]		
Gallon (gal)	Liter (L)	4.546 09
[Canadian and U.K. (Imperial)]		
Gallon (U.S.) (gal)	m^3	$3.785\ 412 \times 10^{-03}$
Gallon (U.S.) (gal)	Liter (L)	3.785 412
Gallon (U.S.) per minute (gpm)	m^3/s	$6.309\ 020 \times 10^{-05}$
(gal/min)		
Gallon (U.S.) per minute (gpm)	L/s	$6.309\ 020 \times 10^{-02}$
(gal/min)		
Gamma (γ)	Tesla (T)	1.0×10^{-09}
Gauss (Gs, G)	Tesla (T)	1.0×10^{-04}
Grain (gr)	Milligram (mg)	$6.479\ 891 \times 10^{1}$
g/cm^3	kg/m^3	1.0×10^{3}
Hectare (ha)	m^2	1.0×10^{4}
Horsepower (550 ft lbf/s) (hp)	Watt (W)	$7.456\ 999 \times 10^{2}$
Horsepower (boiler)	W	$9.809\ 50 \times 10^{3}$
Horsepower (electric)	W	7.46×10^{2}
Horsepower (metric)	W	$7.354\ 988 \times 10^{2}$
Horsepower (U.K.)	W	7.4570×10^{2}
Horsepower (water)	W	$7.460\ 43 \times 10^{2}$
Inch (in)	cm	2.54
Inch of mercury (32 °F)	Pascal (Pa)	$3.386\ 38 \times 10^{3}$
Kelvin (K)	(°C)	T (°C) = T (K) - 273.15
Kilogram-force (kgf)	Newton (N)	9.806 65
km/h	m/s	$2.777\ 778 \times 10^{-01}$
Kilowatt hour (kW h)	Joule (J)	3.6×10^{6}
Knot (nautical mile per hour)	m/s	$5.144\ 444 \times 10^{-01}$
Light year (l.y.)	m	$9.460\ 73 \times 10^{15}$
Liter (L)	m^3	1.0×10^{-03}
Micron (μ)	m	1.0×10^{-06}
Micron (μ)	Micrometer (μm)	1.0
Mile (mi)	m	$1.609\ 344 \times 10^{3}$
Mile (mi)	km	1.609 344
Mile (mi)	m	$1.609\ 347 \times 10^{3}$
(based on U.S. survey foot)		
Mile, nautical	m	1.852×10^{3}
Mile per gallon (U.S.) (mpg)	km/L	$4.251\ 437 \times 10^{-01}$
(mi/gal)		
Mile per hour (mi/h)	km/h	1.609 344
Millibar (mbar)	Pascal (Pa)	1.0×10^{2}
Ohm centimeter ($\Omega \cdot$ cm)	Ohm meter ($\Omega \cdot$ m)	1.0×10^{-02}

Unit	To Convert	Multiply By
Ounce (fl oz) [Canadian and U.K. fluid (Imperial)]	m^3	$2.841\ 306 \times 10^{-05}$
Ounce (fl oz) [Canadian and U.K. fluid (Imperial)]	Milliliter (mL)	$2.841\ 306 \times 10^{1}$
Ounce (fl oz) (U.S. fluid)	m^3	$2.957\ 353 \times 10^{-05}$
Pint (U.S. dry) (dry pt)	m^3	$5.506\ 105 \times 10^{-04}$
Pint (U.S. dry) (dry pt)	Liter (L)	$5.506\ 105 \times 10^{-01}$
Pint (U.S. liquid) (liq pt)	m^3	$4.731\ 765 \times 10^{-04}$
Pint (U.S. liquid) (liq pt)	Liter (L)	$4.731\ 765 \times 10^{-01}$
Poise (P)	Pascal second (Pa s)	1.0×10^{-01}
Pound (avoirdupois) (lb)	kg	$4.535\ 924 \times 10^{-01}$
Pound-force (lbf)	Newton (N)	$4.448\ 222$
lbf/ft^2	Pascal (Pa)	$4.788\ 026 \times 10^{1}$
psi (pound-force per square inch) (lbf/in^2)	Pascal (Pa)	$6.894\ 757 \times 10^{3}$
Quad (10^{15} Btu$_{IT}$)	Joule (J)	$1.055\ 056 \times 10^{18}$
Quart (U.S. dry) (dry qt)	m^3	$1.101\ 221 \times 10^{-03}$
Quart (U.S. dry) (dry qt)	Liter (L)	$1.101\ 221$
Quart (U.S. liquid) (liq qt)	m^3	$9.463\ 529 \times 10^{-04}$
Quart (U.S. liquid) (liq qt)	Liter (L)	$9.463\ 529 \times 10^{-01}$
rad (absorbed dose) (rad)	Gray (Gy)	1.0×10^{-02}
rem (rem)	Sievert (Sv)	1.0×10^{-02}
Revolution (r)	Radian (rad)	$6.283\ 185$
Revolution per minute (rpm) (r/min)	Radian per second (rad/s)	$1.047\ 198 \times 10^{-01}$
Roentgen (R)	Coulomb per kilogram (C/kg)	2.58×10^{-04}
rpm (revolution per minute) (r/min)	Radian per second (rad/s)	$1.047\ 198 \times 10^{-01}$
Square foot (ft^2)	m^2	$9.290\ 304 \times 10^{-02}$
Square mile (mi^2) (based on U.S. survey foot)	m^2	$2.589\ 998 \times 10^{6}$
Square mile (mi^2) (based on U.S. survey foot)	km^2	$2.589\ 998$
Square yard (yd^2)	m^2	$8.361\ 274 \times 10^{-01}$
Stokes (St)	m^2/s	1.0×10^{-04}
Therm (EC)	Joule (J)	$1.055\ 06 \times 10^{8}$
Therm (U.S.)	Joule (J)	$1.054\ 804 \times 10^{8}$
Ton, assay (AT)	kg	$2.916\ 667 \times 10^{-02}$
Ton, assay (AT)	g	$2.916\ 667 \times 10^{1}$
Ton, metric (t)	kg	1.0×10^{3}
Tonne (called "metric ton" in U.S.) (t)	kg	1.0×10^{3}
Ton of refrigeration (12,000 Btu$_{IT}$/h)	Watt (W)	$3.516\ 853 \times 10^{3}$
Ton of TNT (energy equivalent)	Joule (J)	4.184×10^{9}
Ton, short (2,000 lb)	Kilogram (kg)	$9.071\ 847 \times 10^{2}$
torr (Torr)	Pascal (Pa)	$1.333\ 224 \times 10^{2}$

Unit	To Convert	Multiply By
W/cm^2	W/m^2	1.0×10^4
W/in^2	W/m^2	$1.550\,003 \times 10^3$
W s	Joule (J)	1.0
Yard (yd)	Meter (m)	9.144×10^{-01}

Appendix IV

Steam Properties

Table IV.1. Saturated water–pressure table.

Pressure P (kPa)	Saturation Temperature T (°C)	Specific volume (m³/kg)		Internal energy (kJ/kg)		Enthalpy (kJ/kg)		Entropy (kJ/kg K)	
		Sat. liquid v_f	Sat. vapor v_e	Sat. liquid u_f	Sat. vapor u_e	Sat. liquid h_f	Sat. vapor h_e	Sat. liquid s_f	Sat. vapor s_e
0.6113	0.01	0.001000	206.14	0	2375.3	0.00	2501.4	0.0000	9.1562
1.0	6.98	0.001000	129.21	29.3	2385.0	29.30	2514.2	0.1059	8.9756
1.5	13.03	0.001001	87.98	54.71	2393.3	54.71	2525.3	0.1957	8.8279
2.0	17.50	0.001001	67.00	73.48	2399.5	73.48	2533.5	0.2607	8.7237
2.5	21.08	0.001002	54.25	88.48	2404.4	88.49	2540.0	0.3120	8.6432
3.0	24.08	0.001003	45.67	101.04	2408.5	101.05	2545.5	0.3545	8.5776
4.0	28.96	0.001004	34.80	121.45	2415.2	121.46	2554.4	0.4226	8.4746
5.0	32.88	0.001005	28.19	137.81	2420.5	137.82	2561.5	0.4764	8.3951
7.5	40.29	0.001008	19.24	168.78	2430.5	168.79	2574.8	0.5764	8.2515
10	45.81	0.001010	14.67	191.82	2437.9	191.83	2584.7	0.6493	8.1502
15	53.97	0.001014	10.02	225.92	2448.7	225.94	2599.1	0.7549	8.0085
20	60.06	0.001017	7.649	251.38	2456.7	251.40	2609.7	0.8320	7.9085
25	64.97	0.001020	6.204	271.9	2463.1	271.93	2618.2	0.8931	7.8314
30	69.10	0.001022	5.229	289.2	2468.4	289.23	2625.3	0.9439	7.7686
40	75.87	0.001027	3.993	317.53	2477.0	317.58	2636.8	1.0259	7.67
50	81.33	0.001030	3.240	340.44	2483.9	340.49	2645.9	1.0910	7.5939
75	91.78	0.001037	2.217	384.31	2496.7	384.39	2663.0	1.2130	7.4564
0.1	99.63	0.001043	1.694	417.36	2506.1	417.46	2675.5	1.3026	7.3594
0.125	105.99	0.001048	1.3749	444.19	2513.5	444.32	2685.4	1.374	7.2844

Pressure P (kPa)	Saturation Temperature T (°C)	Specific volume (m³/kg)		Internal energy (kJ/kg)		Enthalpy (kJ/kg)		Entropy (kJ/kg K)	
		Sat. liquid v_f	Sat. vapor v_g	Sat. liquid u_f	Sat. vapor u_g	Sat. liquid h_f	Sat. vapor h_g	Sat. liquid s_f	Sat. vapor s_g
0.150	111.37	0.001053	1.1593	466.94	2519.7	467.11	2693.6	1.4336	7.2233
0.175	116.06	0.001057	1.0036	486.8	2524.9	486.99	2700.6	1.4849	7.1717
0.200	120.23	0.001061	0.8857	504.49	2529.5	504.7	2706.7	1.5301	7.1271
0.225	124	0.001064	0.7933	520.47	2533.6	520.72	2712.1	1.5706	7.0878
0.250	127.44	0.001067	0.7187	535.1	2537.2	535.37	2716.9	1.6072	7.0527
0.275	130.6	0.00107	0.6573	548.59	2540.5	548.89	2721.3	1.6408	7.0209
0.300	133.55	0.001073	0.6058	561.15	2543.6	561.47	2725.3	1.6718	6.9919
0.325	136.3	0.001076	0.562	572.9	2546.4	573.25	2729	1.7006	6.9652
0.350	138.88	0.001079	0.5243	583.95	2548.9	584.33	2732.4	1.7275	6.9405
0.375	141.32	0.001081	0.4914	594.4	2551.3	594.81	2735.6	1.7528	6.9175
0.40	143.63	0.001084	0.4625	604.31	2553.6	604.74	2738.6	1.7766	6.8959
0.45	147.93	0.001088	0.414	622.77	2557.6	623.25	2743.9	1.8207	6.8565
0.50	151.86	0.001093	0.3749	639.68	2561.2	640.23	2748.7	1.8607	6.8213
0.55	155.48	0.001097	0.3427	655.32	2564.5	665.93	2753	1.8973	6.7893
0.60	158.85	0.001101	0.3157	669.9	2567.4	670.56	2756.8	1.9312	6.76
0.65	162.01	0.001104	0.2927	683.56	2570.1	684.28	2760.3	1.9627	6.7331
0.70	164.97	0.001108	0.2729	696.44	2572.5	697.22	2763.5	1.9922	6.708
0.75	167.78	0.001112	0.2556	708.64	2574.7	709.47	2766.4	2.02	6.6847
0.80	170.43	0.001115	0.2404	720.22	2576.8	721.11	2769.1	2.0462	6.6628
0.85	172.96	0.001118	0.227	731.27	2578.7	732.22	2771.6	2.071	6.6421
0.90	175.38	0.001121	0.215	741.83	2580.5	742.83	2773.9	2.0946	6.6226

Pressure P (kPa)	Saturation Temperature T (°C)	Specific volume (m³/kg)		Internal energy (kJ/kg)		Enthalpy (kJ/kg)		Entropy (kJ/kg K)	
		Sat. liquid v_f	Sat. vapor v_g	Sat. liquid u_f	Sat. vapor u_g	Sat. liquid h_f	Sat. vapor h_g	Sat. liquid s_f	Sat. vapor s_g
0.95	177.69	0.001124	0.2042	751.95	2582.1	753.02	2776.1	2.1172	6.6041
1.00	179.91	0.001127	0.19444	761.68	2583.6	762.81	2778.1	2.1387	6.5865
1.10	184.09	0.001133	0.17753	780.09	2586.4	781.34	2871.7	2.1792	6.5536
1.20	187.99	0.001139	0.16333	797.29	2588.8	798.65	2784.8	2.2166	6.5233
1.30	191.64	0.001144	0.15125	813.44	2591.0	814.93	2787.6	2.2515	6.4953
1.40	195.07	0.001149	0.14084	828.70	2592.8	830.30	2790.0	2.2842	6.4693
1.50	198.32	0.001154	0.13177	843.16	2594.5	844.89	2792.2	2.3150	6.4448
1.75	205.76	0.001166	0.11349	876.46	2597.8	878.50	2796.4	2.3851	6.3896
2.00	212.42	0.001177	0.09963	906.44	2600.3	908.79	2799.5	2.4474	6.3409
2.25	218.45	0.001187	0.08875	933.83	2602.0	936.49	2801.7	2.5035	6.2972
2.50	223.99	0.001197	0.07998	959.11	2603.1	962.11	2803.1	2.5547	6.2575
3.00	233.90	0.001217	0.06668	1004.78	2604.1	1008.42	2804.2	2.6457	6.1869
3.50	242.60	0.001235	0.05707	1045.43	2603.7	1049.75	2803.4	2.7253	6.1253
4	250.40	0.001252	0.04978	1082.31	2602.3	1087.31	2801.4	2.7964	6.0701
5	263.99	0.001286	0.03944	1147.81	2597.1	1154.23	2794.3	2.9202	5.9734
6	275.64	0.001319	0.03244	1205.44	2589.7	1213.35	2784.3	3.0267	5.8892
7	285.88	0.001351	0.02737	1257.55	2580.5	1267.00	2772.1	3.1211	5.8133
8	295.06	0.001384	0.02352	1305.57	2569.8	1316.64	2758.0	3.2068	5.7432
9	303.40	0.001418	0.02048	1350.51	2557.8	1363.26	2742.1	3.2858	5.6722
10	311.06	0.001452	0.018026	1393.04	2544.4	1407.56	2724.7	3.3596	5.6141
11	318.15	0.001489	0.015987	1433.7	2529.8	1450.1	2705.6	3.4295	5.5527

Pressure P (kPa)	Saturation Temperature T (°C)	Specific volume (m³/kg)		Internal energy (kJ/kg)		Enthalpy (kJ/kg)		Entropy (kJ/kg K)	
		Sat. liquid v_f	Sat. vapor v_e	Sat. liquid u_f	Sat. vapor u_e	Sat. liquid h_f	Sat. vapor h_e	Sat. liquid s_f	Sat. vapor s_e
12	324.75	0.001527	0.014263	1473.0	2513.7	1491.3	2684.9	3.4962	5.4924
13	330.93	0.001567	0.012780	1511.1	2496.1	1531.5	2662.2	3.5606	5.4323
14	336.75	0.001611	0.011485	1548.6	2476.8	1571.1	2637.6	3.6232	5.3717
15	342.24	0.001658	0.010337	1585.6	2455.5	1610.5	2610.5	3.6848	5.3098
16	347.44	0.001711	0.009306	1622.7	2431.7	1650.1	2580.6	3.7461	5.2455
17	352.37	0.001770	0.008364	1660.2	2405.0	1690.3	2547.2	3.8079	5.1777
18	357.06	0.001840	0.007489	1698.9	2374.3	1732.0	2509.1	3.8715	5.1044
19	361.54	0.001924	0.006657	1739.9	2338.1	1776.5	2464.5	3.9388	5.0228
20	365.81	0.002036	0.005834	1785.6	2293.0	1826.3	2409.7	4.0139	4.9269
21	369.89	0.002207	0.004952	1842.1	2230.6	1888.4	2334.6	4.1075	4.8013
22	373.80	0.002742	0.003568	1961.9	2087.1	2022.2	2165.6	4.3110	4.5327
22.09	374.14	0.003155	0.003155	2029.6	2029.6	2099.3	2099.3	4.4298	4.4298

Table IV.2. Saturated water–temperature table.

Temperature T (°C)	Saturation Pressure (kPa)	Specific volume (m³/kg)		Internal energy (kJ/kg)		Enthalpy (kJ/kg)		Entropy (kJ/kg K)	
		Sat. liquid v_f	Sat. vapor v_e	Sat. liquid u_f	Sat. vapor u_e	Sat. liquid h_f	Sat. vapor h_e	Sat. liquid s_f	Sat. vapor s_e
0.01	0.6113	0.001000	206.14	0.00	2375.3	0.00	2501.4	0.0000	9.1562
5	0.8721	0.001000	147.12	20.97	2382.3	20.98	2510.6	0.0761	9.0257
10	1.2276	0.001000	106.38	42.00	2389.2	42.01	2519.8	0.1510	8.9008
15	1.7051	0.001001	77.93	62.99	2396.1	62.99	2528.9	0.2245	8.7814
20	2.339	0.001002	57.79	83.95	2402.9	83.96	2538.1	0.2966	8.6672
25	3.169	0.001003	43.36	104.88	2409.8	104.89	2547.2	0.3674	8.5580
30	4.246	0.001004	32.89	125.78	2416.6	125.79	2556.3	0.4369	8.4533
35	5.628	0.001005	25.22	146.67	2423.4	146.68	2565.3	0.5053	8.3531
40	7.384	0.001008	19.52	167.56	2430.1	167.57	2574.3	0.5725	8.2570
45	9.593	0.001010	15.26	188.44	2436.8	188.45	2583.2	0.6387	8.1648
50	12.349	0.001012	12.03	209.32	2443.5	209.33	2592.1	0.7038	8.0763
55	15.758	0.001015	9.568	230.21	2450.1	230.23	2600.9	0.7679	7.9913
60	19.940	0.001017	7.671	251.11	2456.6	251.13	2609.6	0.8312	7.9096
65	25.03	0.001020	6.197	272.02	2463.1	272.06	2618.3	0.8935	7.8310
70	31.19	0.001023	5.042	292.95	2469.6	292.98	2626.8	0.9549	7.7553
75	38.58	0.001026	4.131	313.90	2475.9	313.93	2643.7	1.0155	7.6824
80	47.39	0.001029	3.407	334.86	2482.2	334.91	2635.3	1.0753	7.6122
85	57.83	0.001033	2.828	355.84	2488.4	355.90	2651.9	1.1343	7.5445
90	70.14	0.001036	2.361	376.85	2494.5	376.92	2660.1	1.1925	7.4791

Temperature T (°C)	Saturation Pressure (kPa)	Specific volume (m³/kg)		Internal energy (kJ/kg)		Enthalpy (kJ/kg)		Entropy (kJ/kg K)	
		Sat. liquid v_f	Sat. vapor v_g	Sat. liquid u_f	Sat. vapor u_g	Sat. liquid h_f	Sat. vapor h_g	Sat. liquid s_f	Sat. vapor s_g
20	2.339	0.001002	57.79	83.95	2402.9	83.96	2538.1	0.2966	8.6672
25	3.169	0.001003	43.36	104.88	2409.8	104.89	2547.2	0.3674	8.5580
30	4.246	0.001004	32.89	125.78	2416.6	125.79	2556.3	0.4369	8.4533
35	5.628	0.001006	25.22	146.67	2423.4	146.68	2565.3	0.5053	8.3531
40	7.384	0.001008	19.52	167.56	2430.1	167.57	2574.3	0.5725	8.2570
45	9.593	0.001010	15.26	188.44	2436.8	188.45	2583.2	0.6387	8.1648
50	12.349	0.001012	12.03	209.32	2443.5	209.33	2592.1	0.7038	8.0763
55	15.758	0.001015	9.568	230.21	2450.1	230.23	2600.9	0.7679	7.9913
60	19.940	0.001017	7.671	251.11	2456.6	251.13	2609.6	0.8312	7.9096
65	25.03	0.001020	6.197	272.02	2463.1	272.06	2618.3	0.8935	7.8310
70	31.19	0.001023	5.042	292.95	2469.6	292.98	2626.8	0.9549	7.7553
75	38.58	0.001026	4.131	313.90	2475.9	313.93	2643.7	1.0155	7.6824
80	47.39	0.001029	3.407	334.86	2482.2	334.91	2635.3	1.0753	7.6122
85	57.83	0.001033	2.828	355.84	2488.4	355.90	2651.9	1.1343	7.5445
90	70.14	0.001036	2.361	376.85	2494.5	376.92	2660.1	1.1925	7.4791
95	84.55	0.001040	1.982	397.88	2500.6	397.96	2668.1	1.2500	7.4159
100	0.10135	0.001044	1.6729	418.94	2506.5	419.04	2676.1	1.3069	7.3549
105	0.12082	0.001048	1.4194	440.02	2512.4	440.15	2683.8	1.3630	7.2958
110	0.14327	0.001052	1.2102	461.14	2518.1	461.30	2691.5	1.4185	7.2387
115	0.16906	0.001056	1.0366	482.30	2523.7	482.48	2699.0	1.4734	7.1833
120	0.19853	0.001060	0.8919	503.50	2529.3	503.71	2706.3	1.5276	7.1296

Temperature T (°C)	Saturation Pressure (kPa)	Specific volume (m³/kg)		Internal energy (kJ/kg)		Enthalpy (kJ/kg)		Entropy (kJ/kg K)	
		Sat. liquid v_f	Sat. vapor v_g	Sat. liquid u_f	Sat. vapor u_g	Sat. liquid h_f	Sat. vapor h_g	Sat. liquid s_f	Sat. vapor s_g
125	0.2321	0.001065	0.7706	524.74	2534.6	524.99	2713.5	1.5813	7.0775
130	0.2701	0.001070	0.6685	546.02	2539.9	546.31	2720.5	1.6344	7.0269
135	0.3130	0.001075	0.5822	567.35	2545.0	567.69	2727.3	1.6870	6.9777
140	0.3613	0.001080	0.5089	588.74	2550.0	589.13	2733.9	1.7391	6.9299
145	0.4154	0.001085	0.4463	610.18	2554.9	610.63	2740.3	1.7907	6.8833
150	0.4758	0.001091	0.3928	631.68	2559.5	632.20	2746.5	1.8418	6.8379
155	0.5431	0.001096	0.3468	653.24	2564.1	653.84	2752.4	1.8925	6.7935
160	0.6178	0.001102	0.3071	674.87	2568.4	675.55	2758.1	1.9427	6.7502
165	0.7005	0.001108	0.2727	696.56	2572.5	697.34	2763.5	1.9925	6.7078
170	0.7917	0.001114	0.2428	718.33	2576.5	719.21	2768.7	2.0419	6.6663
175	0.8920	0.001121	0.2168	740.17	2580.2	741.17	2773.6	2.0909	6.6256
180	1.0021	0.001127	0.19405	762.09	2583.7	763.22	2778.2	2.1396	6.5857
185	1.1227	0.001134	0.17409	784.10	2587.0	785.37	2782.4	2.1879	6.5465
190	1.2544	0.001141	0.15654	806.19	2590.0	807.62	2786.4	2.2359	6.5079
195	1.3978	0.001149	0.14105	828.37	2592.8	829.98	2790.0	2.2835	6.4698
200	1.5538	0.001157	0.12736	850.65	2595.3	852.45	2793.2	2.3309	6.4323
205	1.7230	0.001164	0.11521	873.04	2597.5	875.04	2796.0	2.3780	6.3952
210	1.9062	0.001173	0.10441	895.53	2599.5	897.76	2798.5	2.4248	6.3585
215	2.104	0.001181	0.09479	918.14	2601.1	920.62	2800.5	2.4714	6.3221
220	2.318	0.001190	0.08619	940.87	2602.4	943.62	2802.1	2.5178	6.2861
225	2.548	0.001199	0.07849	963.73	2603.3	966.78	2803.3	2.5639	6.2503

Temperature T (°C)	Saturation Pressure (kPa)	Specific volume (m³/kg)		Internal energy (kJ/kg)		Enthalpy (kJ/kg)		Entropy (kJ/kg K)	
		Sat. liquid v_f	Sat. vapor v_e	Sat. liquid u_f	Sat. vapor u_e	Sat. liquid h_f	Sat. vapor h_e	Sat. liquid s_f	Sat. vapor s_e
230	2.795	0.001209	0.07158	986.74	2603.9	990.12	2804.0	2.6099	6.2146
235	3.060	0.001219	0.06537	1009.89	2604.1	1013.62	2804.2	2.6558	6.1791
240	3.344	0.001229	0.05976	1033.21	2604.0	1037.32	2803.8	2.7015	6.1437
245	3.648	0.001240	0.05471	1056.71	2603.4	1061.23	2803.0	2.7472	6.1083
250	3.973	0.001251	0.05013	1080.39	2602.4	1085.36	2801.5	2.7927	6.0730
255	4.319	0.001263	0.04598	1104.28	2600.9	1109.73	2799.5	2.8383	6.0375
260	4.688	0.001276	0.04221	1128.39	2599.0	1134.37	2796.9	2.8838	6.0019
265	5.081	0.001289	0.03877	1152.74	2596.6	1159.28	2793.6	2.9294	5.9662
270	5.499	0.001302	0.03564	1177.36	2593.7	1184.51	2789.7	2.9751	5.9301
275	5.942	0.001317	0.03279	1202.25	2590.2	1210.07	2785.0	3.0208	5.8938
280	6.412	0.001332	0.03017	1227.46	2586.1	1235.99	2779.6	3.0668	5.8571
285	6.909	0.001348	0.02777	1253.00	2581.4	1262.31	2773.3	3.1130	5.8199
290	7.436	0.001366	0.02557	1278.92	2576.0	1289.07	2766.2	3.1594	5.7821
295	7.993	0.001384	0.02354	1305.20	2569.9	1316.30	2758.1	3.2062	5.7437
300	8.581	0.001404	0.02167	1332.00	2563.0	1344.00	2749.0	3.2534	5.7045
305	9.202	0.001425	0.019948	1359.30	2555.2	1372.40	2738.7	3.3010	5.6643
310	9.856	0.001447	0.018350	1387.10	2546.4	1401.30	2727.3	3.3493	5.6230
315	10.547	0.001472	0.016867	1415.50	2536.6	1431.00	2714.5	3.3982	5.5804
320	11.274	0.001499	0.015488	1444.60	2525.5	1461.50	2700.1	3.4480	5.5362
330	12.845	0.001561	0.012996	1505.30	2498.9	1525.30	2665.9	3.5507	5.4417
340	14.586	0.001638	0.010797	1570.30	2464.6	1594.20	2622.0	3.6594	5.3357

Temperature T (°C)	Saturation Pressure (kPa)	Specific volume (m³/kg)		Internal energy (kJ/kg)		Enthalpy (kJ/kg)		Entropy (kJ/kg K)	
		Sat. liquid v_f	Sat. vapor v_e	Sat. liquid u_f	Sat. vapor u_e	Sat. liquid h_f	Sat. vapor h_e	Sat. liquid s_f	Sat. vapor s_e
350	16.513	0.001740	0.008813	1641.90	2418.4	1670.60	2563.9	3.7777	5.2112
360	18.651	0.001893	0.006945	1725.20	2351.5	1760.50	2481.0	3.9147	5.0526
370	21.03	0.002213	0.004925	1844.00	2228.5	1890.50	2332.1	4.1106	4.7971
374.14	22.09	0.003155	0.003155	2029.60	2029.6	2099.30	2099.3	4.4298	4.4298

Table IV.3. Properties of superheated steam.

Temp (°C)	0.01 MPa (Sat. temp 45.81°C)				0.05 MPa (Sat. temp 81.33°C)				0.1 MPa (Sat. temp 99.63°C)			
	v	u	h	s	v	u	h	s	v	u	h	s
Sat.	14.674	2437.9	2584.7	8.1502	3.24	2483.9	2645.9	7.5939	1.694	2506.1	2675.5	7.3594
50	14.869	2443.9	2592.6	8.1749								
100	17.196	2515.5	2687.5	8.4479	3.418	2511.6	2682.5	7.6947	1.6958	2506.7	2676.2	7.3614
150	19.512	2587.9	2783.0	8.6882	3.889	2585.6	2780.1	7.9401	1.9364	2582.8	2776.4	7.6143
200	21.825	2661.3	2879.5	8.9038	4.356	2659.9	2877.7	8.1580	2.172	2658.1	2875.3	7.8343
250	24.136	2736.0	2977.3	9.1002	4.82	2735.0	2976.0	8.3556	2.406	2733.7	2974.3	8.0333
300	26.445	2812.1	3076.5	9.2813	5.284	2811.3	3075.5	8.5373	2.639	2810.4	3074.3	8.2158
400	31.063	2968.9	3279.6	9.6077	6.209	2968.5	3278.9	8.8642	3.103	2967.9	3278.2	8.5435
500	35.679	3132.3	3489.1	9.8978	7.134	3132.0	3488.7	9.1546	3.565	3131.6	3488.1	8.8342
600	40.295	3302.5	3705.4	10.1608	8.057	3302.2	3705.1	9.4178	4.028	3301.9	3704.4	9.0976

Temp (°C)	0.01 MPa (Sat. temp 45.81°C)				0.05 MPa (Sat. temp 81.33°C)				0.1 MPa (Sat. temp 99.63°C)			
	v	u	h	s	v	u	h	s	v	u	h	s
700	44.911	3479.6	3928.7	10.4028	8.981	3479.4	3928.5	9.6599	4.49	3479.2	3928.2	9.3398
800	49.526	3663.8	4159.0	10.6281	9.904	3663.6	4158.9	9.8852	4.952	3663.5	4158.6	9.5652
900	54.141	3855.0	4396.4	10.8396	10.828	3854.9	4396.3	10.0967	5.414	3854.8	4396.1	9.7767
1,000	58.757	4053.0	4640.6	11.0393	11.751	4052.9	4640.5	10.2964	5.875	4052.8	4640.3	9.9764
1,100	63.372	4257.5	4891.2	11.2287	12.674	4257.4	4891.1	10.4859	6.337	4257.3	4891.0	10.1659
1,200	67.987	4467.9	5147.8	11.4091	13.597	4467.8	5147.7	10.6662	6.799	4467.7	5147.6	10.3463
1,300	72.602	4683.7	5409.7	11.5811	14.521	4683.6	5409.6	10.8382	7.26	4683.5	5409.5	10.5183

Temp (°C)	0.2 MPa				0.3 MPa				0.4 MPa			
	v	u	h	s	v	u	h	s	v	u	h	s
Sat.	0.8857	2529.5	2706.7	7.1272	0.6058	2543.6	2725.3	6.9919	0.4625	2553.6	2738.6	6.8959
150	0.9596	2576.9	2768.8	7.2795	0.6339	2570.8	2761.0	7.0778	0.4708	2564.5	2752.8	6.9299
200	1.0803	2654.4	2870.5	7.5066	0.7163	2650.7	2865.6	7.3115	0.5342	2646.8	2860.5	7.1706
250	1.1988	2731.2	2971.0	7.7086	0.7964	2728.7	2967.6	7.5166	0.5951	2726.1	2964.2	7.3789
300	1.3162	2808.6	3071.8	7.8926	0.8753	2806.7	3069.3	7.7022	0.6548	2804.8	3066.8	7.5662
400	1.5493	2966.7	3276.6	8.2218	1.0315	2965.6	3275.0	8.0330	0.7726	2964.4	3273.4	7.8985
500	1.7814	3130.8	3487.1	8.5133	1.1867	3130.0	3486.0	8.3251	0.8893	3129.2	3484.9	8.1913
600	2.013	3301.4	3704.0	8.7770	1.3414	3300.8	3703.2	8.5892	1.0055	3300.2	3702.4	8.4558
700	2.244	3478.8	3927.6	9.0194	1.4957	3478.4	3927.1	8.8319	1.1215	3477.9	3926.5	8.6987
800	2.475	3663.1	4158.2	9.2449	1.6499	3662.9	4157.8	9.0576	1.2372	3662.4	4157.3	8.9244
900	2.705	3854.5	4395.8	9.4566	1.8041	3854.2	4395.4	9.2692	1.3529	3853.9	4395.1	9.1362
1,000	2.937	4052.5	4640.0	9.6563	1.9581	4052.3	4639.7	9.4690	1.4685	4052.0	4639.4	9.3360
1,100	3.168	4257.0	4890.7	9.8458	2.1121	4256.8	4890.4	9.6585	1.584	4256.5	4890.2	9.5256
1,200	3.399	4467.5	5147.5	10.0262	2.2661	4467.2	5147.1	9.8389	1.6996	4467.0	5146.8	9.7060
1,300	3.63	4683.2	5409.3	10.1982	2.4201	4683.0	5409.0	10.0110	1.8151	4682.8	5408.8	9.8780

Temp (°C)	0.01 MPa (Sat. temp 45.81°C)				0.05 MPa (Sat. temp 81.33°C)				0.1 MPa (Sat. temp 99.63°C)			
	0.5 MPa				0.6 MPa				0.8 MPa			
	v	u	h	s	v	u	h	s	v	u	h	s
Sat.	0.3749	2561.2	2748.7	6.8213	0.3175	2567.4	2756.8	6.7600	0.2404	2576.8	2769.1	6.6628
200	0.4249	2642.9	2855.4	7.0592	0.352	2638.9	2850.1	6.9665	0.2608	2630.6	2839.3	6.8158
250	0.4744	2723.5	2960.7	7.2709	0.3938	2720.9	2957.2	7.1816	0.2931	2715.5	2950.0	7.0384
300	0.5226	2802.9	3064.2	7.4599	0.4344	2801.0	3061.6	7.3724	0.3241	2797.2	3056.5	7.2328
350	0.5701	2882.6	3167.7	7.6329	0.4742	2881.2	3165.7	7.5464	0.3544	2878.2	3161.7	7.4089
400	0.6173	2963.2	3271.9	7.7938	0.5137	2962.1	3270.3	7.7079	0.3843	2959.7	3267.1	7.5716
500	0.7109	3128.4	3483.9	8.0873	0.592	3127.6	3482.8	8.0021	0.4433	3126.0	3480.6	7.8673
600	0.8041	3299.6	3701.7	8.3522	0.6697	3299.1	3700.9	8.2674	0.5018	3297.9	3699.4	8.1333
700	0.8969	3477.5	3925.9	8.5952	0.7472	3477.0	3925.3	8.5107	0.5601	3476.2	3924.2	8.3770
800	0.9896	3662.1	4156.9	8.8211	0.8245	3661.8	4156.6	8.7367	0.6181	3661.1	4155.6	8.6033
900	1.0822	3853.6	4394.7	9.0329	0.9017	3853.4	4394.4	8.9486	0.6761	3852.8	4393.7	8.8153
1,000	1.1747	4051.8	4639.1	9.2328	0.9788	4051.5	4638.8	9.1485	0.734	4051.0	4638.2	9.0153
1,100	1.2672	4256.3	4889.9	9.4224	1.0559	4256.1	4889.6	9.3381	0.7919	4255.6	4889.1	9.2050
1,200	1.3956	4466.8	5146.6	9.6029	1.133	4466.5	5146.3	9.5185	0.8497	4466.1	5145.9	9.3855
1,300	1.4521	4682.5	5408.6	9.7749	1.2101	4682.3	5408.3	9.6906	0.9076	4681.8	5407.9	9.5575

Temp (°C)	1.0 MPa				1.2 MPa				1.4 MPa			
	v	u	h	s	v	u	h	s	v	u	h	s
Sat.	0.19444	2583.6	2778.1	6.5865	0.16333	2588.8	2784.4	6.5233	0.14084	2592.8	2790.0	6.4693
200	0.2060	2621.9	2827.9	6.6940	0.16930	2612.8	2815.9	6.5898	0.14302	2603.1	2803.3	6.4975
250	0.2327	2709.9	2942.6	6.9247	0.19234	2704.2	2935.0	6.8294	0.16350	2698.3	2927.2	6.7467
300	0.2579	2793.2	3051.2	7.1229	0.2138	2789.2	3045.8	7.0317	0.18228	2785.2	3040.4	6.9534
350	0.2825	2875.2	3157.7	7.3011	0.2345	2872.2	3153.6	7.2121	0.2003	2869.2	3149.5	7.1360
400	0.3066	2957.3	3263.9	7.4651	0.2548	2954.9	3260.7	7.3774	0.2178	2952.5	3257.5	7.3026
500	0.3541	3124.4	3478.5	7.7622	0.2946	3122.8	3476.3	7.6759	0.2521	3121.1	3474.1	7.6027

Temp (°C)	0.01 MPa (Sat. temp 45.81°C)				0.05 MPa (Sat. temp 81.33°C)				0.1 MPa (Sat. temp 99.63°C)			
	v	u	h	s	v	u	h	s	v	u	h	s
600	0.4011	3296.8	3697.9	8.0290	0.3339	3295.6	3696.3	7.9435	0.2860	3294.4	3694.8	7.8710
700	0.4478	3475.3	3923.1	8.2731	0.3729	3474.4	3922.0	8.1881	0.3195	3473.6	3920.8	8.1160
800	0.4943	3660.4	4154.7	8.4996	0.4118	3659.7	4153.8	8.4148	0.3528	3659.0	4153.0	8.3431
900	0.5407	3852.2	4392.9	8.7118	0.4505	3851.6	4392.2	8.6272	0.3861	3851.1	4391.5	8.5556
1,000	0.5871	4050.5	4637.6	8.9119	0.4892	4050.0	4637.0	8.8274	0.4192	4049.5	4636.4	8.7559
1,100	0.6335	4255.1	4888.6	9.1017	0.5278	4254.6	4888.0	9.0172	0.4524	4254.1	4887.5	8.9457
1,200	0.6798	4465.6	5145.4	9.2822	0.5665	4465.1	5144.9	9.1977	0.4855	4464.7	5144.4	9.1262
1,300	0.7261	4681.3	5407.4	9.4543	0.6051	4680.9	5407.0	9.3698	0.5186	4680.4	5406.5	9.2984

Temp (°C)	1.6 MPa				1.8 MPa				2.0 MPa			
	v	u	h	s	v	u	h	s	v	u	h	s
Sat.	0.12380	2596.0	2794.0	6.4218	0.11042	2598.4	2797.1	6.3794	0.09963	2600.3	2799.5	6.3409
225	0.13287	2644.7	2857.3	6.5518	0.11673	2636.6	2846.7	6.4808	0.10377	2628.3	2835.8	6.4147
250	0.14184	2692.3	2919.2	6.6732	0.12497	2686.0	2911.0	6.6066	0.11144	2679.6	2902.5	6.5453
300	0.15862	2781.1	3034.8	6.8844	0.14021	2776.9	3029.2	6.8226	0.12547	2772.6	3023.5	6.7664
350	0.17456	2866.1	3145.4	7.0694	0.15457	2863.0	3141.2	7.0100	0.13857	2859.8	3137.0	6.9563
400	0.19005	2950.1	3254.2	7.2374	0.16847	2947.7	3250.9	7.1794	0.15120	2945.2	3247.6	7.1271
500	0.2203	3119.5	3472.0	7.5390	0.19550	3117.9	3469.8	7.4825	0.17568	3116.2	3467.6	7.4317
600	0.2500	3293.3	3693.2	7.8080	0.2220	3292.1	3691.7	7.7523	0.19960	3290.9	3690.1	7.7024
700	0.2794	3472.7	3919.7	8.0535	0.2482	3471.8	3918.5	7.9983	0.2232	3470.9	3917.4	7.9487
800	0.3086	3658.3	4152.1	8.2808	0.2742	3657.6	4151.2	8.2258	0.2467	3657.0	4150.3	8.1765
900	0.3377	3850.5	4390.8	8.4935	0.3001	3849.9	4390.1	8.4386	0.2700	3849.3	4389.4	8.3895
1,000	0.3668	4049.0	4635.8	8.6938	0.3260	4048.5	4635.2	8.6391	0.2933	4048.0	4634.6	8.5901
1,100	0.3958	4253.7	4887.0	8.8837	0.3518	4253.2	4886.4	8.8290	0.3166	4252.7	4885.9	8.7800
1,200	0.4248	4464.2	5143.9	9.0643	0.3776	4463.7	5143.4	9.0096	0.3398	4463.3	5142.9	8.9607
1,300	0.4538	4679.9	5406.0	9.2364	0.4034	4679.5	5405.6	9.1818	0.3631	4679.0	5405.1	9.1329

Temp (°C)	0.01 MPa (Sat. temp 45.81°C)				0.05 MPa (Sat. temp 81.33°C)				0.1 MPa (Sat. temp 99.63°C)			
	2.5 MPa				*3.0 MPa*				*3.5 MPa*			
	v	u	h	s	v	u	h	s	v	u	h	s
Sat.	0.07998	2603.1	2803.1	6.2575	0.06668	2604.1	2804.2	6.1869	0.0507	2603.7	2803.4	6.1253
225	0.08027	2605.6	2806.3	6.2639								
250	0.08700	2662.6	2880.1	6.4085	0.07058	2644.0	2855.8	6.2872	0.05872	2623.7	2829.2	6.1749
300	0.09890	2761.6	3008.8	6.6438	0.08114	2750.1	2993.5	6.5390	0.06842	2738	2977.5	6.4461
350	0.10976	2851.9	3126.3	6.8403	0.09053	2843.7	3115.3	6.7428	0.07678	2835.3	3104.0	6.6579
400	0.12010	2939.1	3239.3	7.0148	0.09936	2932.8	3230.9	6.9212	0.08453	2926.4	3222.3	6.8405
450	0.13014	3025.5	3350.8	7.1746	0.10787	3020.4	3344.0	7.0834	0.09196	3015.3	3337.2	7.0052
500	0.13993	3112.1	3462.1	7.3234	0.11619	3108.0	3456.5	7.2338	0.09918	3103.0	3450.9	7.1572
600	0.15930	3288.0	3686.3	7.5960	0.13243	3285.0	3682.3	7.5085	0.11324	3282.1	3678.4	7.4339
700	0.17832	3468.7	3914.5	7.8435	0.14838	3466.5	3911.7	7.7571	0.12699	3464.3	3908.8	7.6837
800	0.19716	3655.3	4148.2	8.0720	0.16414	3653.5	4145.9	7.9862	0.14056	3651.8	4143.7	7.9134
900	0.21590	3847.9	4387.6	8.2853	0.17980	3846.5	4385.9	8.1999	0.15402	3845.0	4384.1	8.1276
1,000	0.2346	4046.7	4633.1	8.4861	0.19541	4045.4	4631.6	8.4009	0.16743	4044.1	4630.1	8.3288
1,100	0.2532	4251.5	4884.6	8.6762	0.21098	4250.3	4883.3	8.5912	0.18080	4249.2	4881.9	8.5192
1,200	0.2718	4462.1	5141.7	8.8569	0.22652	4460.9	5140.5	8.7720	0.19415	4459.8	5139.3	8.7000
1,300	0.2905	4677.8	5404.0	9.0291	0.24206	4676.6	5402.8	8.9442	0.20749	4675.5	5401.7	8.8723

Temp (°C)	4.0 MPa				4.5 MPa				5.0 MPa			
	v	u	h	s	v	u	h	s	v	u	h	s
Sat.	0.04978	2602.3	2801.4	6.0701	0.04406	2600.1	2798.3	6.0198	0.03944	2597.1	2794.3	5.9734
275	0.05457	2667.9	2886.2	6.2285	0.0473	2650.3	2863.2	6.1401	0.04141	2631.3	2838.3	6.0544
300	0.05884	2725.3	2960.7	6.3615	0.05135	2712.0	2943.1	6.2828	0.04532	2698.0	2924.5	6.2084
350	0.06645	2826.7	3092.5	6.5821	0.0584	2817.8	3080.6	6.5131	0.05194	2808.7	3068.4	6.4493
400	0.07341	2919.9	3213.6	6.7690	0.06475	2913.3	3204.7	6.7047	0.05781	2906.6	3195.7	6.6459
450	0.08002	3010.2	3330.3	6.9363	0.07074	3005.0	3323.3	6.8746	0.06330	2999.7	3316.2	6.8186

Temp (°C)	0.01 MPa (Sat. temp 45.81°C)				0.05 MPa (Sat. temp 81.33°C)				0.1 MPa (Sat. temp 99.63°C)			
	v	u	h	s	v	u	h	s	v	u	h	s
500	0.08643	3099.5	3445.3	7.0901	0.07651	3095.3	3439.6	7.0301	0.06857	3091.0	3433.8	6.9759
600	0.09885	3279.1	3674.4	7.3688	0.08765	3276.0	3670.5	7.3110	0.07869	3273.0	3666.5	7.2589
700	0.11095	3462.1	3905.9	7.6198	0.09847	3459.9	3903.0	7.5631	0.08849	3457.6	3900.1	7.5122
800	0.12287	3650.0	4141.5	7.8502	0.10911	3648.3	4139.3	7.7942	0.09811	3646.6	4137.1	7.7440
900	0.13469	3843.6	4382.3	8.0647	0.11965	3842.2	4380.6	8.0091	0.10762	3840.7	4378.8	7.9593
1,000	0.14645	4042.9	4628.7	8.2662	0.13013	4041.6	4627.2	8.2108	0.11707	4040.4	4625.7	8.1612
1,100	0.15817	4248.0	4880.6	8.4567	0.14056	4246.8	4879.3	8.4015	0.12648	4245.6	4878.0	8.3520
1,200	0.16987	4458.6	5138.1	8.6376	0.15098	4457.5	5136.9	8.5825	0.13587	4456.3	5135.7	8.5331
1,300	0.18156	4674.3	5400.5	8.8100	0.16139	4673.1	5399.4	8.7549	0.14526	4672.0	5398.2	8.7055

Temp (°C)	6.0 MPa				7.0 MPa				8.0 MPa			
	v	u	h	s	v	u	h	s	v	u	h	s
Sat.	0.03244	2589.7	2784.3	5.8892	0.02737	2580.5	2772.1	5.8133	0.02352	2569.8	2758.0	5.7432
300	0.03616	2667.2	2884.2	6.0674	0.02947	2632.2	2838.4	5.9305	0.02426	2590.9	2785.0	5.7906
350	0.04223	2789.6	3043.0	6.3335	0.03524	2769.4	3016.0	6.2283	0.02995	2747.7	2987.3	6.1301
400	0.04739	2892.9	3177.2	6.5408	0.03993	2878.6	3158.1	6.4478	0.03432	2863.8	3138.3	6.3634
450	0.05214	2988.9	3301.8	6.7193	0.04416	2978.0	3287.1	6.6327	0.03817	2966.7	3272.0	6.5551
500	0.05665	3082.2	3422.2	6.8803	0.04814	3073.4	3410.3	6.7975	0.04175	3064.3	3398.3	6.7240
550	0.06101	3174.6	3540.6	7.0288	0.05195	3167.2	3530.9	6.9486	0.04516	3159.8	3521.0	6.8778
600	0.06525	3266.9	3658.4	7.1677	0.05565	3260.7	3650.3	7.0894	0.04845	3254.4	3642.0	7.0206
700	0.07352	3453.1	3894.2	7.4234	0.06283	3448.5	3888.3	7.3476	0.05481	3443.9	3882.4	7.2812
800	0.0816	3643.1	4132.7	7.6566	0.06981	3639.5	4128.2	7.5822	0.06097	3636.0	4123.8	7.5173
900	0.08958	3837.8	4375.3	7.8727	0.07669	3835.0	4371.8	7.7991	0.06702	3832.1	4368.3	7.7351
1,000	0.09749	4037.8	4622.7	8.0751	0.08350	4035.3	4619.8	8.0020	0.07301	4032.8	4616.9	7.9384
1,100	0.10536	4243.3	4875.4	8.2661	0.09027	4240.9	4872.8	8.1933	0.07896	4238.6	4870.3	8.1300
1,200	0.11321	4454.0	5133.3	8.4474	0.09703	4451.7	5130.9	8.3747	0.08489	4449.5	5128.5	8.3115

Temp (°C)	0.01 MPa (Sat. temp 45.81°C)				0.05 MPa (Sat. temp 81.33°C)				0.1 MPa (Sat. temp 99.63°C)			
	v	u	h	s	v	u	h	s	v	u	h	s
1300	0.12106	4669.6	5396.0	8.6199	0.10377	4667.3	5393.7	8.5475	0.09080	4665.0	5391.5	8.4842

Temp (°C)	9.0 MPa				10.0 MPa				12.5 MPa			
	v	u	h	s	v	u	h	s	v	u	h	s
Sat.	0.02048	2557.8	2742.1	5.6772	0.018026	2544.4	2724.7	5.6141	0.013495	2505.1	2673.8	5.4624
325	0.02327	2646.6	2856.0	5.8712	0.019861	2610.4	2809.1	5.7568				
350	0.02580	2724.4	2956.6	6.0361	0.02242	2699.2	2923.4	5.9443	0.016126	2624.6	2826.2	5.7118
400	0.02993	2848.4	3117.8	6.2854	0.02641	2832.4	3096.5	6.2120	0.02000	2789.3	3039.3	6.0417
450	0.03350	2955.2	3256.6	6.4844	0.02975	2943.4	3240.9	6.4190	0.02299	2912.5	3199.8	6.2719
500	0.03677	3055.2	3386.1	6.6576	0.03279	3045.8	3373.7	6.5966	0.02560	3021.7	3341.8	6.4618
550	0.03987	3152.2	3511.0	6.8142	0.03564	3144.6	3500.9	6.7561	0.02801	3125.0	3475.2	6.6290
600	0.04285	3248.1	3633.7	6.9589	0.03837	3241.7	3625.3	6.9029	0.03029	3225.4	3604.0	6.7810
650	0.04574	3343.6	3755.3	7.0943	0.04101	3338.2	3748.2	7.0398	0.03248	3324.4	3730.4	6.9218
700	0.04857	3439.3	3876.5	7.2221	0.04358	3434.7	3870.5	7.1687	0.03460	3422.9	3855.3	7.0536
800	0.05409	3632.5	4119.3	7.4596	0.04859	3628.9	4114.8	7.4077	0.03869	3620.0	4103.6	7.2965
900	0.05950	3829.2	4364.8	7.6783	0.05349	3826.3	4361.2	7.6272	0.04267	3819.1	4352.5	7.5182
1,000	0.06485	4030.3	4614.0	7.8821	0.05832	4027.8	4611.0	7.8315	0.04658	4021.6	4603.8	7.7237
1,100	0.07016	4236.3	4867.7	8.0740	0.06312	4234.0	4865.1	8.0237	0.05045	4228.2	4858.8	7.9165
1,200	0.07544	4447.2	5126.2	8.2556	0.06789	4444.9	5123.8	8.2055	0.05430	4439.3	5118.0	8.0937
1,300	0.08072	4662.7	5389.2	8.4284	0.07265	4460.5	5387.0	8.3783	0.05813	4654.8	5381.4	8.2717

Temp (°C)	15 MPa				17.5 MPa				20 MPa			
	v	u	h	s	v	u	h	s	v	u	h	s
Sat.	0.010337	2455.5	2610.5	5.3098	0.007920	2390.2	2528.8	5.1419	0.005834	2293.0	2409.7	4.9269
350	0.011470	2520.4	2692.4	5.4421								
400	0.015649	2740.7	2975.5	5.8811	0.012447	2685.0	2902.9	5.7213	0.009942	2619.3	2818.1	5.5540

Temp (°C)	0.01 MPa (Sat. temp 45.81°C)				0.05 MPa (Sat. temp 81.33°C)				0.1 MPa (Sat. temp 99.63°C)			
	v	u	h	s	v	u	h	s	v	u	h	s
450	0.018445	2879.5	3156.2	6.1404	0.015174	2844.2	3109.7	6.0184	0.012695	2806.2	3060.1	5.9017
500	0.02080	2996.6	3308.6	6.3443	0.017358	2970.3	3274.1	6.2383	0.014768	2942.9	3238.2	6.1401
550	0.02293	3104.7	3448.6	6.5199	0.019288	3083.9	3421.4	6.4230	0.016555	3062.4	3393.5	6.3348
600	0.02491	3208.6	3582.3	6.6776	0.02106	3191.5	3560.1	6.5866	0.018178	3174.0	3537.6	6.5048
650	0.02680	3310.3	3712.3	6.8224	0.02274	3296.0	3693.9	6.7357	0.019693	3281.4	3675.3	6.6582
700	0.02861	3410.9	3840.1	6.9572	0.02434	3398.7	3824.6	6.8736	0.02113	3386.4	3809.0	6.7993
800	0.03210	3610.9	4092.4	7.2040	0.02738	3601.8	4081.1	7.1244	0.02385	3592.7	4069.7	7.0544
900	0.03546	3811.9	4343.8	7.4279	0.03031	3804.7	4335.1	7.3507	0.02645	3797.5	4326.4	7.2830
1,000	0.03875	4015.4	4596.6	7.6348	0.03316	4009.3	4589.5	7.5589	0.02897	4003.1	4582.5	7.4925
1,100	0.04200	4222.6	4852.6	7.8283	0.03597	4216.9	4846.4	7.7531	0.03145	4211.3	4840.2	7.6874
1,200	0.04523	4433.8	5112.3	8.0108	0.03876	4428.3	5106.6	7.9360	0.03391	4422.8	5101.0	7.8707
1,300	0.04845	4649.1	5376.0	8.1840	0.04154	4643.5	5370.5	8.1093	0.03636	4638.0	5365.1	8.0442

Temp (°C)	25 MPa				30 MPa				35 MPa			
	v	u	h	s	v	u	h	s	v	u	h	s
375	0.001973	1798.7	1848.0	4.0320	0.001789	1737.8	1791.5	3.9305	0.001700	1702.9	1762.4	3.8722
400	0.006004	2430.1	2580.2	5.1418	0.002790	2067.4	2151.1	4.4728	0.002100	1914.1	1987.6	4.2126
425	0.007881	2609.2	2806.3	5.4723	0.005303	2455.1	2614.2	5.1504	0.003428	2253.4	2373.4	4.7747
450	0.009162	2720.7	2949.7	5.6744	0.006735	2619.3	2821.4	5.4424	0.004961	2498.7	2672.4	5.1962
500	0.011123	2884.3	3162.4	5.9592	0.008678	2820.7	3081.1	5.7905	0.006927	2751.9	2994.4	5.6282
550	0.012724	3017.5	3335.6	6.1765	0.010168	2970.3	3275.4	6.0342	0.008345	2921.0	3213.0	5.9026
600	0.014137	3137.9	3491.4	6.3602	0.011446	3100.5	3443.9	6.2331	0.009527	3062.0	3395.5	6.1179
650	0.015433	3251.6	3637.4	6.5229	0.012596	3221.0	3598.9	6.4058	0.010575	3189.8	3559.9	6.3010
700	0.016646	3361.3	3777.5	6.6707	0.013661	3335.8	3745.6	6.5606	0.011533	3309.8	3713.5	6.4631
800	0.018912	3574.3	4047.1	6.9345	0.015623	3555.5	4024.2	6.8332	0.013278	3536.7	4001.5	6.7450
900	0.021045	3783.0	4309.1	7.1680	0.017448	3768.5	4291.9	7.0718	0.014883	3754.0	4274.9	6.9386

Temp (°C)	0.01 MPa (Sat. temp 45.81°C)				0.05 MPa (Sat. temp 81.33°C)				0.1 MPa (Sat. temp 99.63°C)			
	v	u	h	s	v	u	h	s	v	u	h	s
1,000	0.023100	3990.9	4568.5	7.3802	0.019196	3978.8	4554.7	7.2867	0.016410	3966.7	4541.1	7.2064
1,100	0.02512	4200.2	4828.2	7.5765	0.020903	4189.2	4816.3	7.4845	0.017895	4178.3	4804.6	7.4037
1,200	0.02711	4412.0	5089.9	7.7605	0.022589	4401.3	5079.0	7.6692	0.019360	4390.7	5068.3	7.5910
1,300	0.02910	4626.9	5354.4	7.9342	0.024266	4616.0	5344.0	7.8432	0.020815	4605.1	5333.6	7.7653

Temp (°C)	40 MPa				50 MPa				60 MPa			
	v	u	h	s	v	u	h	s	v	u	h	s
375	0.001640	1677.1	1742.8	3.8290	0.001559	1638.6	1716.6	3.7639	0.001508	1609.4	1699.5	3.7141
400	0.001907	1854.6	1930.9	4.1135	0.001730	1788.1	1874.6	4.0031	0.001635	1745.4	1843.4	3.9318
425	0.002532	2096.9	2198.1	4.5029	0.002007	1959.7	2060.0	4.2734	0.001815	1892.7	2001.7	4.1626
450	0.003693	2365.1	2512.8	4.9459	0.002486	2159.6	2284.0	4.5884	0.002085	053.9	2179.0	4.4121
500	0.005622	2678.4	2903.3	5.4700	0.003892	2525.5	2720.1	5.1726	0.002956	2390.6	2567.9	4.9321
550	0.006984	2869.7	3149.1	5.7785	0.005118	2763.6	3019.5	5.5485	0.003956	2658.8	2896.2	5.3441
600	0.008094	3022.6	3346.4	6.0144	0.006112	2942.0	3247.6	5.8178	0.004832	861.1	3151.2	5.6452
650	0.009063	3158.0	3520.6	6.2054	0.006965	3093.5	3441.8	6.0342	0.005593	3028.8	3364.5	5.8829
700	0.009941	3283.6	3681.2	6.3750	0.007727	3230.5	3616.8	6.2189	0.006272	3177.2	3553.5	6.0824
800	0.011523	3517.8	3978.7	6.6662	0.009076	3479.8	3933.6	6.5290	0.007459	3441.5	3889.1	6.4109
900	0.012962	3739.4	4257.9	6.9150	0.010283	3710.3	4224.4	6.7882	0.008505	3681.0	4191.5	6.6805
1,000	0.014324	3954.6	4527.6	7.1356	0.011411	3930.5	4501.1	7.0146	0.009480	3906.4	4475.2	6.9127
1,100	0.015642	4167.4	4793.1	7.3364	0.012496	4145.7	4770.5	7.2184	0.010409	4124.1	4748.6	7.1195
1,200	0.016940	4380.1	5057.7	7.5224	0.013561	4359.1	5037.2	7.4058	0.011317	4338.2	5017.2	7.3083
1,300	0.018229	4594.3	5323.5	7.6969	0.014616	4572.8	5303.6	7.5808	0.012215	4551.4	5284.3	7.4837

v: Specific volume (m³/kg); u: Internal energy (kJ/kg); h: Enthalpy (kJ/kg); s: Entropy (kJ/kg K)

Table IV.4. Properties of compressed liquid.

Temp (°C)	5 MPa				10 MPa				15 MPa			
	v	u	h	s	v	u	h	s	v	u	h	s
sat.	0.0012859	1147.8	1154.2	2.9202	0.0014524	1393.0	1407.6	3.3596	0.0016581	1585.60	1610.5	3.6848
0	0.0009977	0.0	5.0	0.0001	0.0009952	0.1	10.0	0.0002	0.0009928	0.15	15.1	0.0004
20	0.0009995	83.7	88.7	0.2956	0.0009972	83.4	93.3	0.2945	0.0009950	83.06	98.0	0.2934
40	0.0010056	167.0	172.0	0.5705	0.0010034	166.4	176.4	0.5686	0.0010013	165.76	180.8	0.5666
60	0.0010149	250.2	255.3	0.8285	0.0010127	249.4	259.5	0.8258	0.0010105	248.51	263.7	0.8232
80	0.0010268	333.7	338.9	1.0720	0.0010245	332.6	342.8	1.0688	0.0010222	331.48	346.8	1.0656
100	0.001041	417.5	422.7	1.3030	0.0010385	416.1	426.5	1.2992	0.0010361	414.74	430.3	1.2955
120	0.0010576	501.8	507.1	1.5233	0.0010549	500.1	510.6	1.5189	0.0010522	498.40	514.2	1.5145
140	0.0010768	586.8	592.2	1.7343	0.0010737	584.7	595.4	1.7292	0.0010707	582.66	598.7	1.7242
160	0.0010988	672.6	678.1	1.9375	0.0010953	670.1	681.1	1.9317	0.0010918	667.71	684.1	1.9260
180	0.001124	759.6	765.3	2.1341	0.0011199	756.7	767.8	2.1275	0.0011159	753.76	770.5	2.1210
200	0.001153	848.1	853.9	2.3255	0.001148	844.5	856.0	2.3178	0.0011433	841.00	858.2	2.3104
220	0.0011866	938.4	944.4	2.5128	0.0011805	934.1	945.9	2.5039	0.0011748	929.90	947.5	2.4953
240	0.0012264	1031.4	1037.5	2.6979	0.0012187	1026.0	1038.1	2.6872	0.0012114	1020.80	1039.0	2.6771
260	0.0012749	1127.9	1134.3	2.8830	0.0012645	1121.1	1133.7	2.8699	0.0012550	1114.60	1133.4	2.8576
280					0.0013216	1220.9	1234.1	3.0548	0.0013084	1212.50	1232.1	3.0393
300					0.0013972	1328.4	1342.3	3.2469	0.0013770	1316.60	1337.3	3.2260
320									0.0014724	1431.10	1453.2	3.4247
340									0.0016311	1567.50	1591.9	3.6546

v: Specific volume (m^3/kg); u: Internal energy (kJ/kg); h: Enthalpy (kJ/kg); s: Entropy (kJ/kg)

Temp (°C)	20 MPa				30 MPa				50 MPa			
	v	u	h	s	v	u	h	s	v	u	h	s
sat.	0.002036	1785.6	1826.3	4.0139								
0	0.0009904	0.2	20.0	0.0004	0.0009856	0.3	29.8	0.0001	0.0009766	0.20	49.0	0.0014
20	0.0009928	82.8	102.6	0.2923	0.0009886	82.2	111.8	0.2899	0.0009804	81.00	130.0	0.2848
40	0.0009992	165.2	185.2	0.5646	0.0009951	164.0	193.9	0.5607	0.0009872	161.86	211.2	0.5527
60	0.0010084	247.7	267.9	0.8206	0.0010042	246.1	276.2	0.8154	0.0009962	242.98	292.8	0.8052
80	0.0010199	330.4	350.8	1.0624	0.0010156	328.3	358.8	1.0561	0.0010073	324.34	374.7	1.0440
100	0.0010337	413.4	434.1	1.2917	0.001029	410.8	441.7	1.2844	0.0010201	405.88	456.9	1.2703
120	0.0010496	496.8	517.8	1.5102	0.0010445	493.6	524.9	1.5018	0.0010348	487.65	539.4	1.4857
140	0.0010678	580.7	602.0	1.7193	0.0010621	576.9	608.8	1.7098	0.0010515	569.77	622.4	1.6915
160	0.0010885	665.4	687.1	1.9204	0.0010821	660.8	693.3	1.9096	0.0010703	652.41	705.9	1.8891
180	0.001112	751.0	773.2	2.1147	0.0011047	745.6	778.7	2.1024	0.0010912	735.69	790.3	2.0794
200	0.0011388	837.7	860.5	2.3031	0.0011302	831.4	865.3	2.2893	0.0011146	819.70	875.5	2.2634
220	0.0011695	925.9	949.3	2.4870	0.001159	918.3	953.1	2.4711	0.0011408	904.70	961.7	2.4419
240	0.0012046	1016.0	1040.0	2.6674	0.001192	1006.9	1042.6	2.6490	0.0011702	990.70	1049.2	2.6158
260	0.0012462	1108.6	1133.5	2.8459	0.0012303	1097.4	1134.3	2.8243	0.0012034	1078.10	1138.2	2.7860
280	0.0012965	1204.7	1230.6	3.0248	0.0012755	1190.7	1229.0	2.9986	0.0012415	1167.20	1229.3	2.9537
300	0.0013596	1306.1	1333.3	3.2071	0.0013307	1287.9	1327.8	3.1741	0.0012860	1258.70	1323.0	3.1200
320	0.0014437	1415.7	1444.6	3.3979	0.0013997	1390.7	1432.7	3.3539	0.0013388	1353.30	1420.2	3.2868
340	0.0015684	1539.7	1571.0	3.6075	0.001492	1501.7	1546.5	3.5426	0.0014032	1452.00	1522.1	3.4557
360	0.0018226	1702.8	1739.3	3.8772	0.0016265	1626.6	1675.4	3.7494	0.0014838	1556.00	1630.2	3.6291
380					0.0018691	1781.4	1837.5	4.0012	0.0015884	1667.20	1746.6	3.8101

Appendix V

Thermal Conductivity of Building Materials

Table V.1. Thermal conductivity of building materials.

Material	Bulk density kg·m⁻³	Thickness mm	Mean temperature °C	Delta T K	Thermal conductivity W·m⁻¹·K⁻¹	Material source
Acoustic Spray Insulation	334	25.96	23.1	13.4	0.0488	National Gypsum Co.
Acrylic Plastic	1191	12.67	49.1	7.3	0.162	Rohm & Haas Co.
Alumina Powder	382	24.97	54	12.5	0.0765	NBS
Aluminum Foil	41	24.82	21.2	12.5	0.18	
Anti-Sweat Compound	855	12.22	19.5	2.7	0.134	NBS, Chemistry Division
Asbestos Cement	1427	17.06	39.2	4.3	0.355	Asbestos Products Company
Asbestos Insulation	259	29.09	23.2	13.5	0.0529	Union Asbestos & Rubber Co. (Pittsburgh Corning Corp.)
Asbestos Paper	364	25.02	21.4	7.1	0.0593	Ruberoid Co.
Asphalt	629	25.58	55	13.3	0.0918	American Gilsonite Co.
Bone Char	1041	24.73	53.8	12	0.125	
Brick	785	29.21	26.7	N.A.	0.209	Cannon Brick Co.
Carpet	188	16.69	24.2	13.6	0.0609	
Cellular Alykyd-Isocyanate	84	22.17	23	13.3	0.0378	NOPCO Chemical Co.
Cellular Cellulose Acetate	N.A.	25.7	21.7	13.2	0.0503	
Cellular Glass	151	24.67	11.1	13.5	0.0631	Pittsburgh Corning Corp.
Cellular Ionomer	40	10.58	4.3	7.9	0.0397	Gilman Brothers Co.
Cellular Plastic	129	17.84	4.7	13.9	0.0365	U.S. Rubber Co.
Cellular Polyethylene	45	12.44	4.4	7.9	0.0468	Dow Chemical Co.
Cellular Polystyrene	16	17.87	24.1	13.6	0.039	
Cellular Polystyrene, Expanded	30	25.12	33.7	11.5	0.0654	Dow Chemical Co.
Cellular Polystyrene, Expanded	18	10.39	4.4	7.8	0.0325	Western Insulfoam Co.
Cellular Polystyrene, Expanded	25	26.57	12.3	14.3	0.0355	U.S. Army Engineer R&D Laboratory
Cellular Polystyrene, Extruded	N.A.	24.81	24	13.2	0.0359	Dow Chemical Co.
Cellular Polystyrene, Extruded	35	31.64	14.9	7.7	0.0306	Philips Research Laboratory GmbH
Cellular Polyurethane	56	26.58	23.4	13.8	0.0196	Union Carbide Chemicals Co.
Cellular Polyvinyl Chloride	74	27.85	12.4	14.4	0.0356	B.F. Goodrich

Material	Bulk density kg·m⁻³	Thick-ness mm	Mean temperature °C	Delta T K	Thermal conductivity W·m⁻¹·K⁻¹	Material source
Cellulose	39	27.06	23.5	13	0.0371	National Cellulose Corp.
Cellulose	49	26.6	23.5	12.9	0.0392	U.S. Insulation Sales Corp.
Cellulose Acetate	84	28.35	34.1	10.7	0.058	E.I. du Pont de Nemours & Co.
Ceramic Fiber	331	25.38	21.5	13.4	0.0902	Owens-Illinois Glass Company, Kaylo Division
Concrete	1579	25.07	19.5	9.3	0.61	NBS
Concrete	1593	23.23	26.9	3.7	0.572	U.S. Maritime Commission
Concrete	1825	23.57	26.1	2.8	0.751	U.S. Maritime Commission
Concrete	1754	22.61	26.5	2.4	0.849	U.S. Maritime Commission
Corkboard	N.A.	24.13	25.6	N.A.	0.0477	Brazil
Corkboard	295	12.66	23.2	5.5	0.0444	Armstrong Cork Co.
Corkboard	295	12.66	32.7	16	0.0453	Armstrong Cork Co.
Cotton	16	25.03	21.7	13.2	0.0362	Insulation Industries, Inc.
Cotton	9.9	25.46	21.5	13.2	0.0411	Janesville Cotton Mill
Cotton	19	25.38	21.3	13.3	0.0373	Sears Roebuck
Cotton	216	N.A.	36.1	N.A.	0.0534	U.S. Department of Agriculture
Cotton	14	25.91	35.7	N.A.	0.042	U.S. Department of Agriculture
Cotton	10	25.65	35.8	N.A.	0.0433	U.S. Department of Agriculture
Cotton Burr	124	25.35	38.6	11.8	0.0523	
Cotton Gauze	190	23.15	23.1	13.4	0.0387	
Cotton Linter	530	2.98	20.1	5	0.0698	
Diatomaceous Earth	154	24.91	54.2	12.4	0.0479	Johns Manville
Diatomaceous Earth	269	14.22	36.9	N.A.	0.0586	Silicair Co.
Diphenylamine	1128	25.51	24.5	9.8	0.171	
Epoxy Resin	1194	24.84	55	12.5	0.217	Sandia Corporation
Epsom Salt	912	25.2	40.9	9.2	0.207	
Fabric	1001	14.32	36.4	5.8	0.138	
Feathers	25	19.76	25	11.9	0.0345	
Felt	392	22.22	36.6	N.A.	0.0626	
Felt	151	22.72	24.2	13.6	0.0556	(Dynatech Corporation)

Material	Bulk density kg·m^{-3}	Thick-ness mm	Mean temperature °C	Delta T K	Thermal conductivity W·m^{-1}·K^{-1}	Material source
Fiberboard	311	13.1	23.8	13.3	0.0599	Agasote Millboard Co.
Fiberboard	416	N.A.	23.9	N.A.	0.0649	United Refrig. Mfg. Co.
Fiberboard	283	12.04	22	10.3	0.0525	Baltimore Lumber Company
Fiberboard	234	24.43	21.3	12.8	0.0508	Flintkote Co.
Fiberboard, Cane	203	25.46	23.3	13.3	0.0531	National Gypsum Co.
Fiberboard, Cane	255	24.57	22.5	13.9	0.0506	Grasas Vegetales Cubanas
Fiberboard, Coconut	304	18.97	35	7.3	0.0721	Strawick Corporation
Fiberboard, Straw	248	25.75	20.9	12.4	0.0761	Plastergon Wallboard Co.
Fiberboard, Vegetable	279	13.18	33.8	N.A.	0.0526	Fir-Tex Insulating Board Co.
Fiberboard, Wood	298	12.24	28.6	5.9	0.0503	U.S. Gypsum Co.
Fiberboard, Wood	258	13.75	31.5	6.4	0.0513	Masonite Corp.
Fiberboard, Wood	314	12.7	33.2	N.A.	0.0537	National Gypsum Co.
Fiberboard, Wood	301	13.54	31.9	N.A.	0.0547	Johns Manville
Fumed Silica	317	25.39	47	12.7	0.0261	Corning Glass Works
Glass	2218-	24.05	24.2	13.4	0.958	Owens Corning Fiberglas Corp.
Glass Fiber Blanket	13	25.64	22.1	13.3	0.0377	Owens Corning Fiberglas Corp.
Glass Fiber Blanket	13	25.75	22.4	13.6	0.0377	Owens Corning Fiberglas Corp.
Glass Fiber Board	137	25.54	23.9	13.5	0.0326	Owens Corning Fiberglas Corp.
Glass Pellet	N.A.	25.91	34.6	N.A.	0.08	
Greenstone	2991	24.68	11.3	1.2	2.06	
Hardboard, Wood	1046	21.57	3	11.5	0.162	Masonite Corp.
Honeycomb Panel	84	26.38	21.7	13.2	0.0529	
Hulls	144	25.27	32.3	13.2	0.0523	Planter Peanut Co.
Infusorial Earth	N.A.	15.88	32.2	N.A.	0.332	
Insulating Cement	501	25.91	27.8	N.A.	0.0894	Crossfield Products
Insulating Cement	319	24.38	33.5	7.5	0.087	Industrials, Inc.
Insulation Panel	81	32.16	26.4	13.5	0.039	Frosted Foods Insulation
Leather	582	7.92	51.7	9.6	0.0748	
Linoleum Cork	463	6.58	20.9	N.A.	0.07	
Marble	2709	22.92	15.9	5.7	1.75	

Material	Bulk density kg·m⁻³	Thickness mm	Mean temperature °C	Delta T K	Thermal conductivity W·m⁻¹·K⁻¹	Material source
Mica	1345	12.83	13.9	4.6	0.241	Baldwin Hill Co.
Mineral Wool	390	22.05	35.3	12.1	0.0508	Owens Corning Fiberglas Corp.
NBS Fibrous Glass	151	24.04	22.8	12.3	0.0334	NBS, Leather Section
NBS Gum Rubber	953	8.19	46.5	4.4	0.144	Gaylord Container Corp.
Paper	690	24.81	20.5	13	0.0808	Gaylord Container Corp.
Paper	256	27.41	37.1	N.A.	0.0437	Waldort Paper Prod. Co.
Particle Board	691	29.27	54.8	12.8	0.142	
Perlite	56	25.41	37.7	11.4	0.0429	Silbrico Corporation
Perlite	147	25.4	21.7	12.7	0.0532	Silbrico Corporation
Perlite	87	25.65	51.9	12.4	0.0556	Atlantic Perlite Co.
Petroleum Coke	1326	25.09	50.6	2.2	1.03	
Phenol Formaldehyde	1355	8.43	13	4	0.201	Westinghouse Electric Corp.
Plaster	815	19.25	19	10.4	0.182	National Gypsum Co.
Plaster	724	25.49	25.9	10.1	0.219	Great Lakes Carbon Corp.
Plaster	1776	26.08	19.2	2.8	0.801	Great Lakes Carbon Corp.
Plastic	1430	14.55	51.9	9.8	0.315	E.I. du Pont de Nemours & Co.
Plastic	1174	5.23	52.4	6.7	0.332	Southern Research Institute
Plastic	1200	25.25	54.4	12.8	0.218	Goodyear Tire & Rubber Co.
Plastic	1780	20.5	16.2	7.2	0.245	Formica Insulation Co.
Plastic, Reinforced Fiber	1828	28.51	54.2	7.5	0.397	Continental-Diamond Fiber Corp.
Plywood	542	37.56	13.4	12.7	0.107	Weyerhaeuser Co.
Poly(methyl) Methacrylate	1175	6.21	12.8	3.7	0.16	E.I. du Pont de Nemours & Co.
Polyester	153	25.08	21.9	13.4	0.053	Monsanto Chemical Co.
Polyester	163	24.65	21.8	13.3	0.0487	NBS
Polyethylene	335	26.41	24.2	13.5	0.0682	U.S. Industrial Chemical Co.
Polytetrafluoroethylene	2156	6.54	54.4	6	0.254	E.I. du Pont de Nemours & Co.
Polyvinyl Chloride	1560	13.31	33	7.4	0.162	U.S. Naval Ordnance Laboratory
Potting Material	994	25.57	26.2	10	0.184	Westinghouse Electric Corp.
Protexulate Powder	976	27.74	23.7	13.2	0.115	
Rock Wool	43	26.4	24.1	13.3	0.0383	Rock Wool Mfg. Co.

Material	Bulk density kg· m⁻³	Thick-ness mm	Mean temperature °C	Delta T K	Thermal conductivity W· m⁻¹· K⁻¹	Material source
Rockboard	1022	11.63	17.3	4.9	0.219	U.S. Rockboard Corp.
Rubber	978	12.67	-1	7.5	0.147	Goodyear Tire & Rubber Co.
Rubber	158	25.49	36.7	11.7	0.0477	U.S. Rubber Co.
Rubber	9.8	25.08	27.7	11.8	0.0358	Goodyear Tire & Rubber Co.
Rubber Tile	1871	26.18	-2.1	5.8	0.434	Armstrong Cork Co.
Rubber, Buna S	76	25.91	34.3	11	0.0332	Great American Industries, Inc., Rubatex Division
Rubber, Neoprene	1417	24.44	17.9	7.4	0.305	(Potomac Rubber Co.)
Rubber, Pure Gum	972	24.08	23.9	13.5	0.157	(National Gypsum Co.)
Rubber, Pure Gum	976	23.93	24	13.4	0.156	Arthur D. Little, Inc.
Rubber, Pure Gum	963	26.21	54.4	12.7	0.162	(Dynatech Corporation)
Rubber, Silicone	1215	12.62	47.7	5.3	0.245	Dow Corning Corp.
Rubber, Silicone	1384	24.19	54.7	8	0.317	(Potomac Rubber Co.)
Rubber, Silicone	1499	13.03	52.7	3.8	0.381	General Electric Company
Rubber, Silicone	1273	12.84	53.6	5.3	0.271	John G. Shelby Co., Inc.
Rubber, Silicone	1366	13.88	20.8	4.9	0.316	Dow Corning Corp. (Green Rubber Co.)
Rubber, Silicone	1860	24.33	24.1	2.4	1.1	National Beryllia Corporation
Rubber, Silicone	N.A.	12.86	22.7	9	0.397	Rohm & Haas Co.
Rubber, Silicone	681	25.04	21.1	12.2	0.131	NASA
Rubber, Silicone	1046	25.12	23.9	13.5	0.165	Dow Corning Corp.
Rubber, Silicone	1046	25.01	24	13.6	0.165	Dow Corning Corp.
Rubber, Silicone	1172	6.98	24.2	3.2	0.234	McDonnell-Douglas Corporation
Rubber, Sponge	78	25.12	26.1	16.5	0.0328	Great American Industries, Inc.
Rubber-Cement Insulation	1088	25.25	54.2	8.3	0.269	Waterproof Insulation Corp.
Sand, Ottawa Silica	1615	25.54	49.3	8	0.306	Ottawa-Silica Co.
Silica Aerogel	73	24.91	21.9	13.4	0.0237	Monsanto Chemical Co.
Slag Wool	118	25.91	41.3	N.A.	0.0398	Rock Fleece Corp.
Soap Powder	754	26.52	24	13.5	0.122	
Soil	2146	38.1	24.3	N.A.	1.54	

Material	Bulk density kg· m⁻³	Thickness mm	Mean temperature °C	Delta T K	Thermal conductivity W· m⁻¹· K⁻¹	Material source
Straw	N.A.	22.76	4.9	13.6	0.0467	North Dakota Research Foundation
Vermiculite	216	25.65	27.8	N.A.	0.0646	Zonolite Co.
Vermiculite Board	253	24.64	24.8	N.A.	0.102	Armco Int'l Corp.
Viscose Sponge	53	25.07	N.A.	N.A.	0.0482	E.I. du Pont de Nemours & Co. (DuPont Rayon Co.)
Wax	1546	25.08	26	11.3	0.128	Halowax Corp.
Wood	94	25.4	35.5	11.1	0.0464	
Wood Fiber Blanket	29	21.84	35	10.5	0.0396	Masonite Corp.
Wood-Cement	423	25.91	37.9	N.A.	0.0913	Celotex Co.
Wool	109	24.49	4.4	13.4	0.0328	Philip Carey Mfg. Co. (Association of American Railroads)
Zirconia	485	25.73	22.7	13.7	0.0619	

Source: NIST Heat Transmission Properties of Insulating and Building Materials Database

Appendix VI

Exports and Imports of Coal by Countries

Coal to Liquid Plants Planned

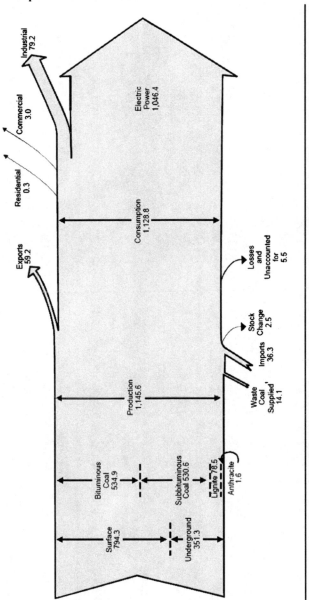

' Includes fine coal, coal obtained from a refuse bank or slurry dam, anthracite culm, bituminous gob, and lignite waste that are consumed by the electric power industrial sectors.

Notes: • Production categories are estimated; other data are preliminary. • Values are derived from source data prior to rounding for publication. • Totals may not equal sum of components due to independent rounding.

Fig. VI.1. Flow of coal in the USA (Energy Information Administration, Annual energy review 2007).

Table VI.1. Imports and exports of coal by various countries.

Country	Production in trillion BTU	Imports in trillion BTU	Exports in trillion BTU	Apparent consumption in trillion BTU	Total recoverable coal in million short tons	BTU value of coal in thousands BTU per short ton	Total Recoverable coal in trillion BTU	Years of coal remained at the current rate of consumption
Canada	1,524.293	588.541	687.181	1,431.272	7,251	20,951	151916.6	99.7
Mexico	221.828	186.640	0.079	403.377	1,335	17,519	23385.9	105.4
United States	23,789.510	1,007.035	1,303.749	22,507.970	270,718	20,310	5498284.9	231.1
Argentina	1.131	32.337	6.682	25.407	467	22,300	10422.7	9211.4
Brazil	81.349	360.941	1.155	441.134	11,148	11,574	129027.3	1586.1
Chile	11.203	123.796	1.132	133.868	1,302	25,664	33410.3	2982.3
Colombia	1,725.098	0	1,616.474	108.624	7,287	24,568	179036.5	103.8
Peru	0.467	32.300	0	32.767	1,168	26,458	30914.9	66250.0
Puerto Rico	0	38.435	0	38.435		–		
Venezuela	226.863	0.487	225.221	2.129	528	27,592	14568.7	64.2
Albania	1.009	0.137	0	1.146	875	8,886	7777.4	7708.7
Austria	0	149.513	0.168	159.346	22	–		
Belgium	0.746	222.181	33.332	196.166		*24,175*	0.0	0.0
Bosnia and Herzegovina	132.892	0.092	0	132.983		13,218	0.0	0.0
Bulgaria	175.601	61.541	0.630	236.512	2,411	6,251	15070.4	85.8
Croatia	0	22.402	0	22.402	43	–		
Cyprus	0	1.307	0	1.307		–		
Czech Republic	815.798	71.680	125.366	767.434	6,120	11,698	71592.7	87.8
Denmark	0	212.238	2.730	209.392		–		

Country	Production in trillion BTU	Imports in trillion BTU	Exports in trillion BTU	Apparent consumption in trillion BTU	Total recoverable coal in million short tons	BTU value of coal in thousands BTU per short ton	Total Recoverable coal in trillion BTU	Years of coal remained at the current rate of consumption
Finland	0	184.105	0	209.949		–		
Former Serbia and Montenegro	347.007	22.980	3.001	366.985	18,288	8,076	147696.1	425.6
France	0	568.920	23.156	592.082	17	–		
Germany	2,181.497	1,168.727	8.492	3,335.581	7,428	9,891	73475.1	33.7
Greece	327.423	13.597	0.433	343.904	4,299	4,524	19450.0	59.4
Hungary	84.421	63.575	11.612	137.643	3,700	7,695	28476.7	337.3
Iceland	0	4.224	0	4.224		–		
Ireland	0	82.919	0.194	80.426	15	–		
Italy	1.852	672.491	6.349	668.063	37	24,001	899.5	485.7
Luxembourg	0	4.461	0	4.461		–		
Macedonia	41.605	3.175	0	44.780		6,425	0.0	0.0
Netherlands	0	462.136	133.218	314.487	548	–		
Norway	65.717	25.882	63.368	28.466	6	25,369	139.8	2.1
Poland	2,651.364	135.804	553.516	2,300.382	15,432	15,494	239109.4	90.2
Portugal	0	147.094	0	139.320	40	–		
Romania	274.352	76.129	0.918	349.562	545	7,102	3867.3	14.1
Slovakia	24.255	149.910	4.074	170.539	190	9,997	1895.5	78.1
Slovenia	53.997	22.495	0.313	76.179	303	10,835	3284.5	60.8
Spain	288.444	580.149	31.561	777.613	584	14,185	8287.3	28.7
Sweden	0	89.385	0.781	95.157	1	–		

Country	Production in trillion BTU	Imports in trillion BTU	Exports in trillion BTU	Apparent consumption in trillion BTU	Total recoverable coal in million short tons	BTU value of coal in thousands BTU per short ton	Total Recoverable coal in trillion BTU	Years of coal remained at the current rate of consumption
Switzerland	0	4.978	0.252	4.782		–		
Turkey	608.464	348.943	0	959.614	4,614	8,509	39260.6	
United Kingdom	446.627	1,296.428	15.589	1,689.652	243	22,411	5434.9	12.2
Estonia	118.209	4.221	1.079	121.351		7,559	0.0	0.0
Georgia	0.166	0.304	0	0.471		16,774	0.0	0.0
Kazakhstan	1,762.350	27.034	523.284	1,266.100	34,479	16,599	572306.3	324.7
Kyrgyzstan	4.759	11.094	0.129	15.724	895	13,748	12305.8	2586.0
Latvia	0	3.756	0	3.756		–		
Lithuania	0	10.230	0	10.230		–		
Moldova	0	2.445	0	2.445		–		
Russia	6,143.047	593.405	2,181.760	4,554.692	173,074	19,029	3293495.2	536.1
Tajikistan	1.609	0.211	0.018	1.801		16,774	0.0	0.0
Ukraine	1,343.790	274.955	149.258	1,469.487	37,647	19,753	743627.7	553.4
Uzbekistan	45.585	0.423	0.467	44.476	4,409	13,229	58329.6	1279.6
Iran	38.948	11.787	1.281	49.453	462	23,245	10736.2	275.7
Israel	0	331.108	0	317.646		–		
Lebanon	0	5.508	0	5.508				
Algeria	0	10.614	0	10.614	44	–		
Botswana	23.983	0.051	0	24.035	44	23,245	1024.9	42.7
Congo (Kinshasa)	3.113	4.832	0	7.945	97	22,776	2209.4	709.7

Country	Production in trillion BTU	Imports in trillion BTU	Exports in trillion BTU	Apparent consumption in trillion BTU	Total recoverable coal in million short tons	BTU value of coal in thousands BTU per short ton	Total Recoverable coal in trillion BTU	Years of coal remained at the current rate of consumption
Egypt	0.615	39.952	12.158	28.409	23	23,245	538.1	875.0
Mozambique	1.393	0	0.821	0.572	234	22,565	5273.2	3785.7
Niger	4.561	0	0	4.561	77	23,245	1793.6	393.3
Nigeria	0.205	0	0	0.205	209	23,245	4868.4	23750.0
South Africa	5,738.113	27.402	1,917.534	3,847.982	53,738	21,302	1144739.1	199.5
Swaziland	7.959	0	2.316	5.642	229	23,245	5329.7	669.7
Tanzania	1.742	0	0	1.742	220	23,245	5124.7	2941.2
Zambia	5.999	0	0.295	4.204	11	22,304	245.9	41.0
Zimbabwe	92.603	1.316	5.215	88.155	553	24,371	13486.2	145.6
Australia	8,572.514	0	5,915.119	2,466.607	86,531	20,431	1767923.3	206.2
Bangladesh	0	14.577	0	14.577		–		
Bhutan	1.307	1.281	0.922	1.666		23,245	0.0	0.0
Burma (Myanmar)	28.944	0	24.739	4.205	2	18,945	41.8	1.4
China	52,803.472	793.958	1,702.600	52,031.825	126,215	20,150	2543246.0	48.2
Hong Kong	0	292.158	0.179	291.978		–		
India	8,203.105	1,255.961	33.571	9,425.496	101,903	16,444	1675669.7	204.3
Indonesia	4,955.250	0	4,395.713	559.537	5,476	23,245	127296.9	25.7
Japan	0	4,669.882	59.257	4,627.030	396	–		
Korea, North	841.931	10.976	63.572	789.336	661	21,513	14228.6	16.9
Korea, South	52.948	1,998.969	0	2,215.316	88	17,009	1499.9	28.3

Country	Production in trillion BTU	Imports in trillion BTU	Exports in trillion BTU	Apparent consumption in trillion BTU	Total recoverable coal in million short tons	BTU value of coal in thousands BTU per short ton	Total Recoverable coal in trillion BTU	Years of coal remained at the current rate of consumption
Laos	3.364	0	1.500	1.864		10,174	0.0	
Malaysia	14.605	251.971	0.313	266.263	4	20,259	89.3	
Mongolia	86.892	0	18.886	68.622		9,996	0.0	0.0
Nepal	0.300	7.250	0	7.550	1	22,678	25.0	83.3
New Zealand	162.994	0	78.660	86.880	629	25,640	16138.3	99.0
Pakistan	93.855	68.637	0	162.491	3,362	16,910	56853.4	605.8
Philippines	47.142	194.808	0	241.950	260	18,129	4716.2	100.0
Taiwan	0	1,733.974	0	1,733.974	1	–		
Thailand	230.422	251.255	0	481.676	1,493	10,961	16359.8	71.0
Vietnam	953.735	6.906	524.220	436.421	165	–		
World Total	**128,497.191**	**22,352.119**	**22,475.592**	**127,547.635**	**1,000,912**			

Table VI.2. Coal to Liquid plants under consideration or planned in the USA

Project Lead	Project Partners	Location	Feedstock	Status	Capacity	Cost
American Clean Coal Fuels	None cited	Oakland, IL	Bituminous	Feasibility	25,000	N/A
Synfuels Inc.	GE, Haldor-Topsoe, NACC, ExxonMobil	Ascension Parish, LA	Lignite	Feasibility	N/A	$5 billion
DKRW Advanced Fuels	Rentech, GE	Medicine Bow, WY	Bituminous	Design (2011)	13,000 bpd	$1.4 billion
DKRW Advanced Fuels	Rentech, GE, Bull Mountain Land Company	Roundup, MT	Sub-bituminous/ Lignite	Feasibility	22,000 bpd	$1–1.5 billion
AIDEA	ANRTL, CPC	Cook Inlet, AK	Sub-bituminous	Feasibility	80,000 bpd	$5–8 billion
Mingo County	Rentech	WV	Bituminous	Feasibility	20,000 bpd	$2 billion
WMPI	Sasol, Shell, DOE	Gilberton, PA	Anthracite	Design	5,000 bpd	$612 million
Rentech/Peabody	N/A	MT	Sub-bituminous/ lignite	Feasibility	10,000–30,000 bpd	N/A
Rentech/Peabody	N/A	Southern IL, Southwest IN, Western KY	Bituminous	Feasibility	10,000–30,000 bpd	N/A
Rentech*	Kiewit Energy Company, WorleyParsons	East Dubuque, IL	Bituminous	Construction (2010)	1,800 bpd*	$800 million
Rentech	Adams County	Natchez, MS	Coal/Petcoke	Feasibility	10,000 bpd	$650–750 million
Rentech	Baard Energy	Wellsville, OH	Sub-bituminous	Feasibility	35,000 bpd	$4 billion
Headwaters	Hopi Tribe	AZ	Bituminous	Feasibility	10,000–50,000 bpd	N/A
Headwaters	NACC, GRE, Falkirk	ND	Lignite	Feasibility	40,000 bpd	$3.6 billion

Table VI.2. Coal to Liquid plants under consideration or planned worldwide

Country	Owner/Developer	Capacity (bpd)	Status
South Africa	Sasol	150,000	Operational
China	Shenhua	20,000 (initially)	Construction Operational in 2007–2008
China	Lu'an Group	~3,000–4,000	Construction
China	Yankuang	40,000 (initially) 180,000 planned	Construction
China	Sasol JV (2 studies)	80,000 (each plant)	Planning
China	Shell/Shenhua	70,000–80,000	Planning
China	Headwaters/UK Race Investment	Two 700-bpd demo plants	Planning
Indonesia	Pertamina/Accelon	~76,000	Construction
Australia	Anglo American/Shell	60,000	Planning
Australia	Altona Resources plc, Jacobs Consultancy, MineConsult	45,000	Planning
Philippines	Headwaters	50,000	Planning
New Zealand	L&M Group	50,000	Planning

Appendix VII

Exports and Imports of Dry Natural Gas in the World

Table VII.1. World Dry Natural Gas Supply and Disposition, Most Recent Annual Estimates, 2006.

Country	Dry gas production	Imports	Exports	Apparent consumption
Canada	6,548	341	3,606	3,307
Mexico	1,741	353	12	2,200
United States	18,476	4,186	724	21,653
North America	**26,765**	**4,879**	**4,342**	**27,160**
Argentina	1,628	64	217	1,475
Bolivia	461	0	381	79
Brazil	349	334	0	683
Chile	67	196	0	264
Colombia	255	0	0	255
Cuba	14	0	0	14
Dominican Republic	0	9	0	9
Ecuador	10	0	0	10
Peru	63	0	0	63
Puerto Rico	0	25	0	25
Trinidad and Tobago	1,287	0	574	713
Uruguay	0	4	0	4
Venezuela	918	0	0	918
Central & South America	**5,053**	**632**	**1,172**	**4,513**
Albania	1	0	0	1
Austria	64	362	93	306
Belgium	0	622	0	616
Bosnia and Herzegovina	0	14	0	14
Bulgaria	0	198	0	198
Croatia	56	41	0	96
Czech Republic	7	346	4	328
Denmark	368	0	185	180
Finland	0	168	0	168
Former Serbia and Montenegro	7	76	0	83
France	43	1,751	35	1,759

Country	Dry gas production	Imports	Exports	Apparent consumption
Germany	692	3,310	411	3,524
Greece	1	116	0	117
Hungary	109	412	5	502
Ireland	18	148	0	166
Italy	388	2,733	13	2,984
Luxembourg	0	50	0	50
Macedonia	0	4	0	4
Netherlands	2,732	889	1,930	1,690
Norway	3,196	0	2,966	230
Poland	212	386	2	574
Portugal	0	148	0	147
Romania	441	219	0	660
Slovakia	7	245	20	232
Slovenia	0.1	39	0	39
Spain	2	1,215	0	1,161
Sweden	0	34	0	34
Switzerland	0	117	0	117
Turkey	32	1,067	0	1,101
United Kingdom	2,819	744	360	3,202
Europe	**11,195**	**15,454**	**6,026**	**20,284**
Armenia	0	57	0	57
Azerbaijan	241	158	0	399
Belarus	6	735	0	741
Estonia	0	52	0	52
Georgia	0.4	49	0	50
Kazakhstan	906	459	268	1,097
Kyrgyzstan	1	26	0	27
Latvia	0	67	0	67
Lithuania	0	103	0	103
Moldova	2	92	0	94
Russia	23,167	1,847	8,416	16,598
Tajikistan	1	44	0	45
Turkmenistan	2,232	0	1,593	639
Ukraine	689	1,872	0	2,560
Uzbekistan	2,216	0	447	1,769
Eurasia	**29,460**	**5,561**	**10,723**	**24,298**
Bahrain	400	0	0	400
Iran	3,835	205	201	3,839
Iraq	64	0	0	64
Israel	34	0	0	34

Country	Dry gas production	Imports	Exports	Apparent consumption
Jordan	11	68	0	79
Kuwait	441	0	0	441
Oman	837	0	457	380
Qatar	1,790	0	1,098	693
Saudi Arabia	2,594	0	0	2,594
Syria	221	0	0	221
United Arab Emirates	1,723	49	250	1,522
Yemen	0	0	0	0
Middle East	**11,952**	**322**	**2,006**	**10,268**
Algeria	3,079	0	2,175	904
Angola	24	0	0	24
Cameroon	1	0	0	1
Congo (Brazzaville)	6	0	0	6
Congo (Kinshasa)	0	0	0	0
Cote d'Ivoire (Ivory-Coast)	46	0	0	46
Egypt	1,596	0	597	999
Equatorial Guinea	46	0	0	46
Gabon	4	0	0	4
Libya	523	0	297	226
Morocco	2	0	0	2
Mozambique	58	0	7	51
Nigeria	1,006	0	621	386
Senegal	2	0	0	2
South Africa	102	7	0	109
Tanzania	5	0	0	5
Togo	0	0	0	0
Tunisia	90	46	0	136
Africa	**6,591**	**53**	**3,697**	**2,947**
Afghanistan	1	0	0	1
Australia	1,509	49	578	1,012
Bangladesh	541	0	0	541
Brunei	487	0	346	141
Burma (Myanmar)	445	0	317	128
China	2,067	33	106	1,993
Hong Kong	0	106	0	106
India	1,098	282	0	1,380
Indonesia	2,016	0	1,215	802
Japan	174	3,130	0	3,247
Korea, South	18	1,165	0	1,137

Country	Dry gas production	Imports	Exports	Apparent consumption
Malaysia	2,190	0	1,053	1,136
New Zealand	145	0	0	149
Niue	0	0	0	0
Pakistan	1,112	0	0	1,112
Papua New Guinea	5	0	0	5
Philippines	78	0	0	78
Samoa	0	0	0	0
Singapore	0	233	0	233
Taiwan	15	360	0	375
Thailand	859	317	0	1,176
Vietnam	201	0	0	201
Asia & Oceania	**12,962**	**5,676**	**3,616**	**14,956**
World Total	**103,977**	**32,578**	**31,582**	**104,425**

Source: Energy Information Administration, Office of Energy Markets and End Use, International Energy Statistics Team.

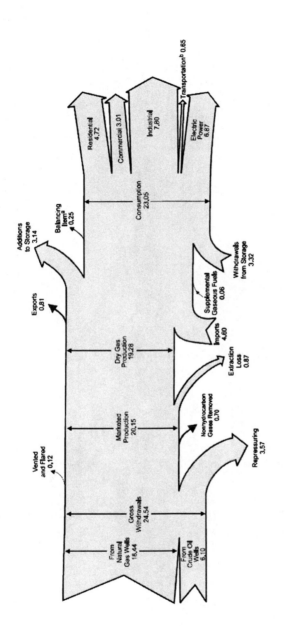

Fig. VII.1. Flow of natural gas in the USA (Energy Information Administration, Annual Energy Review 2007).

[a] Quantities lost and imbalances in data due to differences among data sources.
[b] Natural gas consumed in the operation of pipelines (primarily in compressors), and as fuel in the delivery of natural gas to consumers; plus a small quantity used as vehicle fuel.

Notes: • Data are preliminary. • Values are derived from source data prior to rounding for publication. • Totals may not equal sum of components due to independent rounding.

Appendix VIII

Selected Giant Oil Fields and Their Size

Table VIII.1. Selected giant and supergiant oil fields.

Oil Field	Country	Year discovered	Estimated Reserves (billions of barrel)
Carioca	Brazil	2008	10–33
Sugar Loaf	Brazil	2008	25–40
Tupi	Santos Basin, Brazil	2007	5–8
Bohai	China	2007	7.5
Azadegan	Iran	2004	26
Ferdows/Mound/Zagheh	Iran	2003	38
Kashagan	Kazakhstan	2000	30
White Tiger	Viet nam	1996	5
Priobskoye	West Siberia, Russia	1982	13
Tengiz	Kazakhstan	1979	15–26
Cantarell	Mexico	1976	35–18
Fyodorovskoye	West Siberia, Russia	1971	11
Prudhoe Bay	Alaska, United States	1969	13
Lyantorskoye	West Siberia, Russia	1966	13
Zakum	Abu Dhabi, UAE	1965	12
Samotlor	West Siberia, Russia	1965	14–16
Serir	Libya	1961	12–6.5
Ahwaz	Iran	1958	10.1
Rumaila	Iraq	1953	17
Safaniya-Khafji	Saudi Arabia/Neutral Zone	1951	30
Romashkino	Volga-Ural, Russia	1948	16–17
Ghawar	Saudi Arabia	1948	75–83
Burgan	Kuwait	1938	66–72
Agha Jari	Iran	1937	8.7
Kirkuk	Iraq	1927	8.5
Chicontepec	Mexico	1926	6.5–19
Bolivar Coastal	Venezuela	1917	30–32
Aghajari	Iran	1938	14
Ahvaz	Iran		17
Azadegan	Iran		3–6
Gachsaran	Iran	1928	15
Marun	Iran	1964	16
Mesopotamian Foredeep Basin	Kuwait		66–72
Minagish	Kuwait		2
Raudhatain	Kuwait		11
Sarir	Libya	1961	12.6
Kashagan	Kazakhstan	2000	30
Daqing	China	1959	16

Giant Field: a giant oil or gas field is considered to be one for which the estimate of ultimately recoverable oil is 500 million bbl of oil or gas equivalent. Gas is converted to oil at a ratio of 6,000 cu ft/bbl. Some fields are, therefore, giants only because their combined amounts of oil- and gas-equivalent total at least 500 million bbl, and not because either resource is that great by itself.

Supergiant: 5,000 to 50,000 MMBOE (http://www.wri.org/wri/climate/jm_oil_006.html)

Megagiant: 50,000+ MMBOE (http://www.wri.org/wri/climate/jm_oil_006.html)

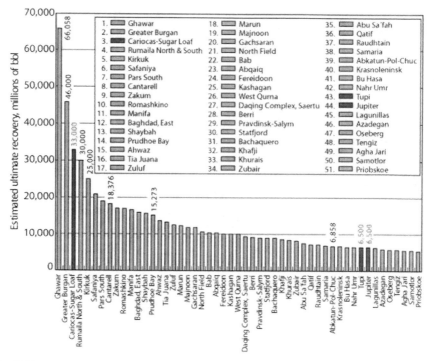

Fig. VIII.1. World oil and condensate field ranking (Printed with permission from Berman A (November 2008) What's new in exploration. WorldOil.com (The oilfield information sources) 229(2)).

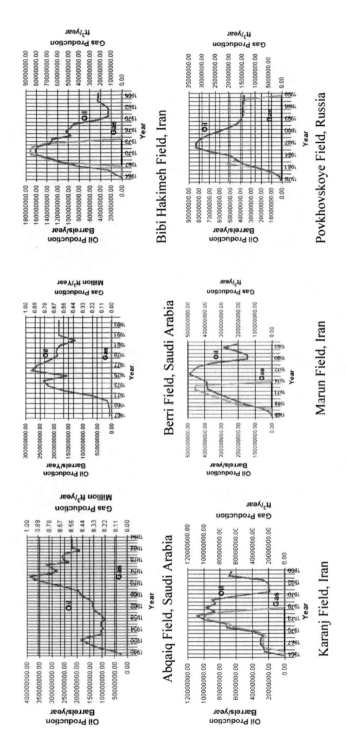

Fig. VIII.2. Oil and gas production profiles of six giant/super giant oil fields (Adapted from Simmons MR, The worlds giant oil fields. Simmons and Company International).

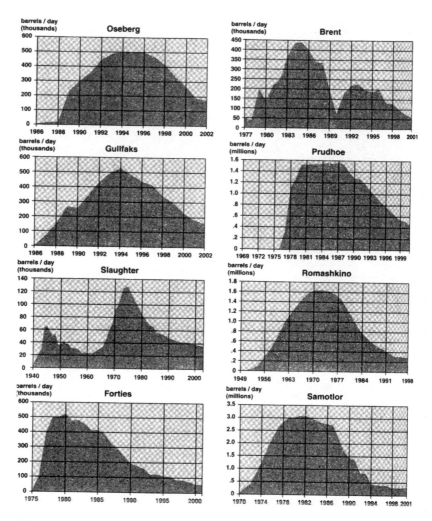

Fig. VIII.3. Production profiles of eight giant/supergiant oil fields (Printed with permission from Simmons MR (2005) Twilight in the Desert. Wiley).

Example of Characterization of Crude Oil

Table VIII.2. A sample crude oil characterization report[a]

Distillate fraction	Whole crude oil	Light hydro-carbons[b]	Light naphtha	Inter-mediate naphtha	Heavy naphtha	Light kerosene	Heavy kerosene
BOILING RANGE, °C	FULL	IBP-nC4	iC5-82.2	82.2–129.4	129.4–176.7	176.7–218.3	218.3–260.0
BOILING RANGE, °F	FULL	IBP-nC4	iC5-180	180–265	265–350	350–425	425–500
Start of Cut, Vol% (Wt%)	0.0 (0.0)	0.0 (0.0)	5.3 (3.8)	15.2 (12.3)	28.8 (25.1)	41.3 (37.3)	51.7 (47.6)
End of Cut, Vol% (Wt%)	100.0 (100.0)	5.3 (3.8)	15.2 (12.3)	28.8 (25.1)	41.3 (37.3)	51.7 (47.6)	63.3 (59.6)
Yield of Cut, Vol% (Wt%)	100.0 (100.0)	5.3 (3.8)	9.9 (8.5)	13.6 (12.8)	12.5 (12.2)	10.4 (10.3)	11.6 (12.0)
Gravity, API @ 15.6°C	47.2	119.6	78.4	60.6	53.5	49.7	43.3
Gravity, Specific @ 15.6 °C	0.7918	0.5636	0.6741	0.7366	0.7649	0.7809	0.8095
Total Sulfur, Wt%	0.044		0.0005	0.0006	0.005	0.009	0.019
Mercaptan Sulfur, WPPM	14.0		1.0	2.0	2.5	1.9	
H₂S Content, WPPM	<1		<1	<1	<1	<1	
Total Nitrogen, WPPM	471		0.1	0.1	0.8	1.8	5.4
Basic Nitrogen, WPPM				<1			
Reid Vapor Pressure, PSI	9.17		10.18				
Paraffins, Vol%			81.0	51.2	60.3	62.9	
Naphthenes, Vol%			17.1	42.8	25.8	27.5	
Aromatics, Vol%			1.9	6.0	13.9	9.6	9.5
Octane, Research - Clear			67.7	57.5			
Octane, Motor - Clear			70.3	54.8			

Distillate fraction	Whole crude oil	Light hydrocarbons[b]	Light naphtha	Inter-mediate naphtha	Heavy naphtha	Light kerosene	Heavy kerosene
Freeze Point, °C[j]					No FP @ -73	-45.2	-23.1
Smoke Point, MM					25	20	16
Cloud Point, °C						-43.9	-26.1
Flash Point, TC, °C						29.4	
Flash Point, PM, °C	<Room Temp						78.9
Neut. Number, mgm KOH/gm	0.01						0.01
Cu Strip Corrn, 3 h @ 100°C						4A	4A
Cetane (Engine)						48.3	49.5
Naphthalenes, Vol%						0.31	3.39
Viscosity, cSt @ -20.0°C	2.20						
Viscosity, cSt @ 20.0°C	1.90						9.30
Viscosity, cSt @ 40.0°C							1.97
Viscosity, cSt @ 50.0°C	—	ASTM DISTILLATION DATA:					
K Factor	12.0	IBP	-0.6	93.4	139.4	178.5	217.0
Pour Point, °C	3.0	5%, °C	26.1	98.2	143.7	186.2	228.0
Micro Carbon Residue, Wt%	0.64	10%, °C	27.8	98.6	144.7	186.7	229.8
Salt, g/bbl	32.50	20%, °C	33.9	100.1	145.7	189.3	231.9
BS&W, Vol%	0.05	30%, °C	36.1	101.4	147.1	189.5	232.9

Distillate fraction	Whole crude oil	Light hydrocarbons[b]	Light naphtha	Intermediate naphtha	Heavy naphtha	Light kerosene	Heavy kerosene
Vanadium, WPPM	1.0	40%, °C	58.1	102.9	148.5	191.7	234.7
Nickel, WPPM	2.0	50%, °C	59.9	104.7	150.2	192.3	236.3
Iron, WPPM	3.0	60%, °C	63.3	106.6	152.2	194.6	237.8
Ethane & Lighter, GC, LV%	0.12	70%, °C	66.5	109.0	154.7	196.4	239.6
Propane, GC, LV%	1.28	80%, °C	70.1	112.0	157.8	198.9	242.4
Iso-Butane, GC, LV%	1.40	90%, °C	80.9	116.7	162.6	202.8	246.5
N-Butane, GC, LV%	2.49	95%, °C	86.1	120.5	166.6	206.4	249.8
Iso-Pentane, GC, LV%	1.99	EP	91.7	127.7	181.6	217.4	257.4
N-Pentane, GC, LV%	1.95	Recovery	100.0	99.7	98.5	98.2	98.6
C6's & Heavier, GC, LV%	90.77	Method	GC Sim Dist	D-86	D-86	D-86	D-86

Fraction	Light atmospheric gas oil	Heavy atmospheric gas oil	Light vacuum gas oil	Intermediate vacuum gas oil	Heavy vacuum gas oil	Vacuum residuum	Light vacuum residuum
BOILING RANGE, °C	260.0–301.7	301.7–343.3	343.3–390.6	390.6–482.2	482.2–565.6	565.6–EP	343.3–EP
BOILING RANGE, °F	500–575	575–650	650–735	735–900	900–1050	1050–EP	650–EP
Start of Cut, Vol% (Wt%)	63.3 (59.6)	73.9 (70.6)	82.6 (79.9)	89.5 (87.5)	96.5 (95.5)	98.6 (98.1)	82.6 (79.9)
End of Cut, Vol% (Wt%)	73.9 (70.6)	82.6 (79.9)	89.5 (87.5)	96.5 (95.5)	98.6 (98.1)	100 (100.0)	100 (100)
Yield of Cut, Vol% (Wt%)	10.6 (11.0)	8.7 (9.3)	6.9 (7.6)	7.0 (8.0)	2.1 (2.6)	1.4 (1.9)	17.4 (20.1)

Fraction	Light atmospheric gas oil	Heavy atmospheric gas oil	Light vacuum gas oil	Intermediate vacuum gas oil	Heavy vacuum gas oil	Vacuum residuum	Light vacuum residuum
Gravity, API @ 15.6°C	41.3	37.7	34.0	25.5	15.4	3.8	24.9
Gravity, Specific @ 15.6°C	0.8189	0.8363	0.8550	0.9013	0.9632	1.0458	0.9047
Total Sulfur, Wt%	0.030	0.070	0.117	0.218	0.296	0.466	0.164
Total Nitrogen, WPPM	39	158	480	1584	4681	4800	2407
Basic Nitrogen, WPPM	30	86	207	560	1317		
Cloud Point, °C	1.7	13.9	26.1	41.1	>48.9		
Pour Point, °C	-3.0	0.0	25.0	38.0	43.3	>48.9	35.0
Aromatics, FIA Vol%	12.4	10.3					
Total Aromatics, Wt% (Iatro)			14.3	23.8	64.8		
Polar Aromatics, Wt% (Iatro)			2.2	4.0	23.3		
Freeze Point, °C	-0.7	16.4					
Smoke Point, MM	20	22					
Flash Point, PM, °C	98.9	126.7					
Bromine No.	0.5	1.4	2.3	5.0	12.4		
Cetane Number (Engine)	67.6	70.0					
Cetane Index (Calculated)	60.2	59.8	57.7	44.7			
K Factor			12.1	12.0	11.7	~11.5	
Viscosity, CST @ 40.0°C	3.21	5.27	9.13	45.79	770.33		57.79

Fraction	Light atmospheric gas oil	Heavy atmospheric gas oil	Light vacuum gas oil	Intermediate vacuum gas oil	Heavy vacuum gas oil	Vacuum residuum	Light vacuum residuum
Viscosity, CST @ 100.0°C	1.28	1.79	2.57	6.34	31.13	17030.0	7.83
Viscosity, CST @ 121.1°C				29.28 @ 50°C	369.2 @ 50°C	2190.7	36.9 @ 50°C
Viscosity, CST @ 148.9°C						310.4	
Viscosity Index			112	81	50		
Neut. Number, ^{i}mg KOH/g	0.04	0.08	0.19	0.13	0.10		0.14
Micro Carbon Residue, Wt%			0.00	0.13	1.03	27.00	3.06
Refractive Index, @ 70°C	1.4355	1.4442	1.4538	1.4819	1.5247		
Vanadium, WPPM					<1	11.0	
Nickel, WPPM					<1	105.0	
Iron, WPPM					1	344.0	
Sodium, WPPM					0.5	1.78	
Pentane Insolubles, Wt%						15.38	
Toluene Insolubles, Wt%						0.02	
N-Heptane Insolubles, Wt%						6.29	
Asphaltenes, Wt%						6.27	
ASTM Distillation, °C, IBP	261.3	298.6	336.7	402.2	(4)		

Fraction	Light atmospheric gas oil	Heavy atmospheric gas oil	Light vacuum gas oil	Intermediate vacuum gas oil	Heavy vacuum gas oil	Vacuum residuum[d]	Light vacuum residuum[d]
ASTM Distillation, °C, 5%	269.0	305.2	342.2	415.6	(4)		
ASTM Distillation, °C, 10%	270.9	307.9	351.7	418.3	(4)		
ASTM Distillation, °C, 20%	273.3	310.7	358.3	421.7	(4)		
ASTM Distillation, °C, 30%	274.9	312.2	362.8	425.0	(4)		
ASTM Distillation, °C, 40%	276.2	313.4	365.0	427.8	(4)		
ASTM Distillation, °C, 50%	277.4	314.5	368.3	431.7	(4)		
ASTM Distillation, °C, 60%	279.0	315.9	371.1	437.2	(4)		
ASTM Distillation, °C, 70%	280.6	317.2	375.0	443.9	(4)		
ASTM Distillation, °C, 80%	282.8	319.1	378.3	453.3	(4)		
ASTM Distillation, °C, 90%	286.5	322.3	382.2	467.2	(4)		
ASTM Distillation, °C, 95%	289.7	325.1	387.2	478.3	(4)		
ASTM Distillation, °C, EP	292.8	327.6	392.2	490.6	(4)		

Fraction	Light atmospheric gas oil	Heavy atmospheric gas oil	Light vacuum gas oil	Intermediate vacuum gas oil	Heavy vacuum gas oil	Vacuum residuum	Light vacuum residuum
Distillate Recovery, Vol%	97.6	98.4	99.0	99.0	(4)		
ASTM Distillation Method	D-86	D-86	D-1160	D-1160	D-1160		

SUMMARY OF GC ANALYSES, LV%	LT NAPHTHA	WHOLE CRUDE
Ethane & Lighter	0.00	0.12
Propane	0.00	1.28
Iso-Butane	0.30	1.40
N-Butane	1.15	2.49
Iso-Pentane	16.49	1.99
N-Pentane	15.46	1.95
Cyclopentane	1.85	0.18
Iso-Hexanes		2.48
N-Hexane		1.95
Methyl Cyclopentane		0.96
Cyclohexane		1.11
Benzene		0.24
C7 Paraffins		3.79
C7 Naphthenes		3.63

NOTES:

This crude oil sample was obtained from Texaco Deep Star's Agbami-2 well, Off-shore Nigeria, on December 26, 1999. It was sampled at the Stock Tank Separator Oil Line, DST-1, on the Glomar Explorer, and represents production from the 16.5_AG_10 Sand formation.

SUMMARY OF GC ANALYSES, LV%

	WHOLE CRUDE
Toluene	0.63
C8 Paraffins	4.76
C8 Naphthenes	1.97
C8 Aromatics	1.17

GC ANALYSES OF NAPHTHA FRACTIONS, WT% [c]

	LIGHT NAPHTHA	INTERMEDIATE NAPHTHA	HEAVY NAPHTHA
Ethane & Lighter	0.00	0.00	0.00
Propane	0.00	0.00	0.00
Isobutane	0.25	0.00	0.00
N-Butane	1.00	0.00	0.00
Isopentane	15.28	0.00	0.00
N-Pentane	14.47	0.00	0.00
2,2-Dimethyl Butane	2.05	0.00	0.00
Cyclopentane	2.06	0.00	0.00
2,3-Dimethyl Butane	2.45	0.00	0.00
2-Methylpentane	12.13	0.00	0.00
3-Methylpentane	7.74	0.00	0.00
N-Hexane	16.46	1.86	0.00
Methyl Cyclopentane	8.40	1.56	0.00
2,2-Dimethyl Pentane	0.83	0.33	0.00
Benzene	2.50	0.47	0.00

NOTES:

GC ANALYSES, Continued

	LIGHT NAPHTHA [e]
2,5-Dimethyl Hexane	0.00
3,3-Dimethyl Hexane	0.00
C-1-T-2-4-Trimethyl Cyclopentane	0.00
T-1-C-2-3-Trimethyl Cyclopentane	0.00
2,3,4-Trimethyl Pentane	0.00
Toluene	0.00
2,3-Dimethyl Hexane	0.00
1,1,2-Trimethyl Cyclopentane	0.00
2-Methyl Heptane	0.00
4-Methyl Heptane	0.00
3,4-Dimethyl Hexane	0.00
C,C-1,2,4-Trimethyl Cyclopentane	0.00
3-Methyl Heptane	0.00
C-1,3-Dimethyl Cyclohexane	0.00
T-1,4-Dimethyl Cyclohexane	0.00

SUMMARY OF GC ANALYSES, LV%	LT NAPHTHA	WHOLE CRUDE	NOTES:	
2,4-Dimethyl Pentane	0.87	0.00	1,1-Dimethyl Cyclohexane	0.00
2,2,3-Trimethyl Butane	0.20	0.00	2,2,5-Trimethyl Hexane	0.00
Cyclohexane	7.44	0.00	C-1,3-Ethylmethyl Cyclopentane	0.00
3,3-Dimethyl Pentane	0.30	0.00	T-1,3-Ethylmethyl Cyclopentane	0.00
1,1-Dimethyl Cyclopentane	0.57	0.00	T-1,2-Ethylmethyl Cyclopentane	0.00
2-Methyl Hexane	1.69	0.00	1,1-Ethylnmethyl Cyclopentane	0.00
2,3-Dimethyl Pentane	0.56	0.00	T-1,2-Dimethyl Cyclohexane	0.00
C-1,3-Dimethyl Cyclopentane	0.55	0.00	C-1,2-Dimethyl Cyclohexane	0.00
3-Methyl Hexane	1.20	0.00	Ethyl Cyclohexane	0.00
T-1,3-Dimethyl Cyclopentane	0.51	0.00	N-Octane	0.00
T-1,2-Dimethyl Cyclopentane	0.50	0.00	Ethyl Benzene	0.00
3-Ethyl Pentane	0.00	0.00	Meta & Para-Xylene	0.00
2,2,4-Trimethyl Pentane	0.00	0.00	Ortho-Xylene	0.00
N-Heptane	12.07	0.00	Total C9 Paraffins	0.00
C-1,2-Dimethyl Cyclopentane	0.93	0.00	Total C9 Cycloparaffins	0.00
Methyl Cyclohexane	17.68	0.00	Total C9 Aromatics	0.00
1,1,3-Trimethyl Cyclopentane	0.97	0.00	C10 & Heavier	0.00
Ethyl Cyclopentane	1.48	0.00		
2,4-Dimethyl Hexane	1.04	0.00	TOTAL	100.00

	Total sulfur in crude, wt%	Total nitrogen in crude, wppm	Api gravity @ 15.6°C	Carbon residue in crude, wt%	Total c5's in crude, lv%	Vanadium in crude, wppm	Nickel in crude, wppm	Iron in crude, wppm
Light Hydrocarbons			4.5		3.16			
Light Naphtha	0.000	0.0	6.7					
Intermediate Naphtha	0.000	0.0	7.8					
Heavy Naphtha	0.001	0.1	6.5					
Light Kerosene	0.001	0.2	5.1					
Heavy Kerosene	0.002	0.6	5.2					
Light Atmospheric Gas Oil	0.003	4.3	4.5					
Heavy Atmospheric Gas Oil	0.006	14.7	3.5					
Light Vacuum Gas Oil	0.009	36.5	2.6	0.00				
Intermediate Vacuum Gas Oil	0.017	126.7	2.0	0.01				
Heavy Vacuum Gas Oil	0.008	121.7	0.4	0.03		<1	<1	<1
Vacuum Residuum	0.009	91.2	0.1	0.51		0.2	2.0	6.5
TOTAL RECOVERY	0.057	396	48.9	0.55	3.16	0.2	2.0	7.0
RAW CRUDE	0.044	471	47.2	0.64	3.94	1.0	2.0	3.0
% RECOVERY	130.4	84.1		86.0	80.3	–	–	–
CRUDE OIL CLASS: [h]	PARAFFIN BASE							
SOURCE COUNTRY:	NIGERIA							

FOOTNOTES TO METHOD III-E EVALUATION

[a] While every effort is made to verify the accuracy of the data contained in this assay, Motiva Enterprises LLC shall have no responsibility and makes no warranty concerning the accuracy of such data and shall further have no responsibility or liability for any direct, or incidental loses or damages resulting from the use of this evaluation or the information contained therein.   MOTIVA ENTERPRISES LLC MAKES NO WARRANTY, COVENANT OR REPRESENTATION WHATSOEVER WITH RESPECT TO THIS EVALUATION, OR TO THE INFORMATION AND DATA CONTAINED THEREIN, AND HEREBY EXPRESSLY DISCLAIMS ANY AND ALL WARRANTIES OR REPRESENTATIONS, EITHER EXPRESS OR IMPLIED, AS TO THE FITNESS FOR A PARTICULAR PURPOSE, QUALITY, CONDITION,SUITABILITY, MERCHANTABILITY, OR PERFORMANCE OF THIS EVALUATION, AND THE INFORMATION AND DATA ON WHICH IT IS BASED, OR OF THE SERVICES AND WORKMANSHIP RENDERED IN CONNECTION THEREWITH.

[b] Light Hydrocarbon (IBP-C4) yields and constituency are determined by the gas chromatographic analysis of the Whole Crude Oil.

[c] Calculated value.

[d] Insufficient sample volume available for testing.

[e] Test results unavailable at the time of report; will be reported by subsequent memorandum when obtained.

[f] The Polar Aromatics contents of these fractions were developed from Iatroscan TLC analysis. Among other compounds, the class includes the thiophenes, nitrogen heterocycles, and naphthenic acids.

[g] This TBP table is calculated assuming linearity between adjacent TBP cut-points, and will not necessarily correspond to similar tables generated by other calculation methods.

[h] Crude oil classification based on criteria outlined in Bureau of Mines Report of Investigations #3279, 1935.

[i] To avoid possible understatement of the Neut Numbers due to reaction of the naphthenic acids with the metallurgy of the fractionation unit, these tests were determined on distilled-in-glass samples.

[j] "No FP @ −73" signifies that no Freeze Point formed before the minimum test temperature of −73°C was reached. "No Cld @ Pour" signifies that no Cloud Point formed prior to the sample reaching it's pour point temperature. "Too Dark" signifies that the sample is insufficiently transparent to allow any cloud point formation to be observed. "Too Heavy for Test" signifies that the sample's viscosity is beyond the range of the test method.

Source: Chevron Co.

TEST	METHOD	TEST	METHOD
Aromatics (FIA), Vol%	ASTM D-1319	Iron, WPPM	X-Ray WDF
Aromatics (HTA), Vol%	AC-PIONA-GC	K Factor	Texaco Design Data Book
Aromatics, Total & Polar, Wt%[f]	Iatroscan TLC/FID	Neut. Number, mgm KOH/g	ASTM D-664
Bromine Number	ASTM D-1159	Nickel, WPPM	X-Ray WDF
BS&W, Vol%	ASTM D-1796	Nitrogen, Basic, WPPM	TEXACO SP-337
Calcium, WPPM	X-Ray WDF	Nitrogen, Total, WPPM	ASTM D-5762
Carbon Residue, Micro, Wt%	ASTM D-4530	Octane, Motor	ASTM D-2700
Cetane Number, Engine	ASTM D-613	Octane, Research	ASTM D-2699
Chlorine, WPPM	X-Ray WDF	Paraffins (HTA), Vol%	AC-PIONA-GC
Cloud Point, °C	ASTM D-5771	Pour Point, °C	ASTM D-5950
Cu Strip Corr, 3 h @ 100°C	ASTM D-130	Refractive Index @ 70 °C	ASTM D-1747
Cycloparaffins (HTA), Vol%	AC-PIONA-GC	Reid Vapor Pressure	ASTM D-5482
Flash Point, PM, °C	ASTM D-93	Salt Content, g/bbl	X-Ray WDF
Flash Point, TC, °C	ASTM D-56	Smoke Point, mm	ASTM D-1322
Freeze Point, °C	ASTM D-2386	Sodium, WPPM	ASTM D-3605
Gravity, API @ 15.6°C	ASTM D-287	Sulfur, Mercaptan, WPPM	ASTM D-3227
Gravity, Specific @ 15.6°C	ASTM D-70	Sulfur, Total, Wt%	ASTM D-2622(X-Ray)
H$_2$S Content, WPPM	ASTM D-3227	Vanadium, WPPM	X-Ray WDF
Insolubles, Heptane, Wt%	IP-143 (Modified)	Viscosity Index	ASTM D-2270
Insolubles, Pentane, Wt%	IP-143 (Modified)	Viscosity, Kinematic, Cst	ASTM D-445
Insolubles, Toluene, Wt%	IP-143 (Modified)	Crude Oil Fractionation	ASTM D-2892 (Modified)
			ASTM D-5236 (Modified)

INCREMENTAL TRUE BOILING POINT YIELD STRUCTURE, VOLUME % (WEIGHT %)[a]

Cumulative Volume % @
Specified Temperature, °C

°C	0	5	55	10	60	15	65	20	70	25	75	30	80	35	85	40	90	45	95
0	–	–	–	–	–	–	–	–	–	5.3	–	6.2	–	7.0	–	7.9	–	8.8	–
										(3.8)		(4.5)		(5.3)		(6.0)		(6.8)	
50	9.6	–	10.5	–	11.4	–	12.2	–	13.1	–	14.0	–	14.8	–	16.0	–	17.4	–	18.9
	(7.5)		(8.3)		(9.0)		(9.7)		(10.5)		(11.2)		(12.0)		(13.1)		(14.4)		(15.8)
100	20.3	21.8	–	23.2	–	24.7	–	26.1	–	27.5	–	29.0	–	30.3	–	31.6	–	32.9	–
	(17.1)	(18.5)		(19.8)		(21.2)		(22.6)		(23.9)		(25.3)		(26.5)		(27.8)		(29.1)	
150	34.2	–	35.6	–	36.9	–	38.2	–	39.5	–	40.9	–	42.1	–	43.4	–	44.6	–	45.9
	(30.4)		(31.7)		(33.0)		(34.3)		(35.6)		(36.9)		(38.1)		(39.4)		(40.6)		(41.8)
200	47.1	48.4	–	49.6	–	50.9	–	52.2	–	53.6	–	55.0	–	56.3	–	57.7	–	59.1	–
	(43.1)	(44.3)		(45.5)		(46.8)		(48.1)		(49.5)		(51.0)		(52.4)		(53.8)		(55.3)	
250	60.5	–	61.9	–	63.3	–	64.6	–	65.8	–	67.1	–	68.4	–	69.7	–	70.9	–	72.2
	(56.7)		(58.2)		(59.6)		(60.9)		(62.2)		(63.6)		(64.9)		(66.2)		(67.5)		(68.8)
300	73.5	74.6	–	75.6	–	76.7	–	77.7	–	78.8	–	79.8	–	80.9	–	81.9	–	82.8	–
	(70.2)	(71.3)		(72.5)		(73.6)		(74.7)		(75.8)		(76.9)		(78.0)		(79.2)		(80.2)	
350	83.6	–	84.3	–	85.0	–	85.8	–	86.5	–	87.2	–	88.0	–	88.7	–	89.4	–	89.8
	(81.0)		(81.8)		(82.6)		(83.4)		(84.2)		(85.0)		(85.8)		(86.6)		(87.4)		(87.9)
400	90.2	90.6	–	91.0	–	91.4	–	91.7	–	92.1	–	92.5	–	92.9	–	93.3	–	93.7	–
	(88.3)	(88.8)		(89.2)		(89.6)		(90.1)		(90.5)		(90.9)		(91.4)		(91.8)		(92.3)	
450	94.0	–	94.4	–	94.8	–	95.2	–	95.6	–	95.9	–	96.3	–	96.6	–	96.7	–	96.8
	(92.7)		(93.1)		(93.6)		(94.0)		(94.4)		(94.9)		(95.3)		(95.6)		(95.7)		
500	96.9	97.1	–	97.2	–	97.3	–	97.5	–	97.6	–	97.7	–	97.8	–	98.0	–	98.1	–
	(96.1)	(96.2)		(96.4)		(96.5)		(96.7)		(96.8)		(97.0)		(97.1)		(97.3)		(97.5)	
550	98.2	–	98.3	–	98.5	–	98.6	–	–	–	–	–	–	–	–	–	–	–	–
	(97.6)		(97.8)		(97.9)		(98.1)													

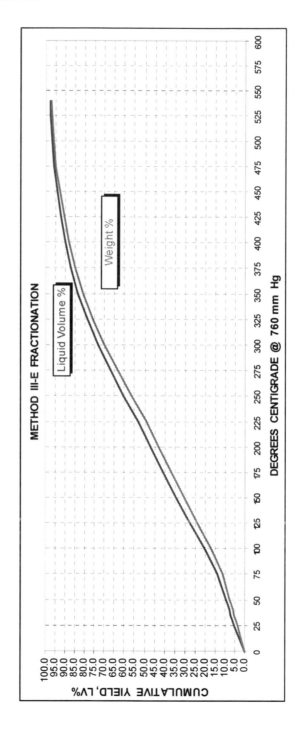

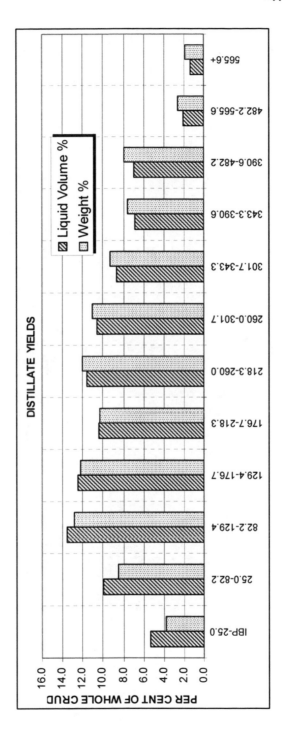

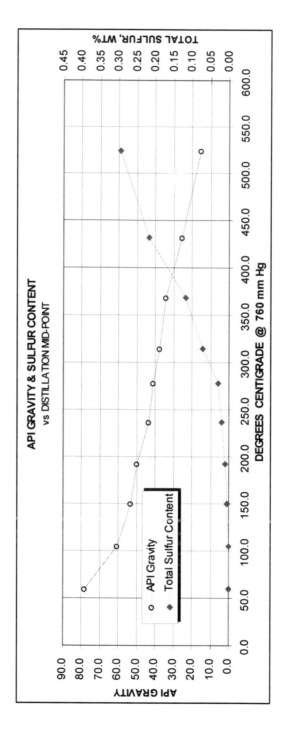

°F	Mid-point of IIIE Cut, F	Mid-Point of Dist, C	Dist Method	Stem Corr Factor	Corr Dist Mid-point, C
IBP-C4					
C5-180	138	60	SD	0	60
180–265	223	105	D-86	0	105
265–350	308	150	D-86	0	150
350–425	388	192	D-86	0	192
425–500	463	236	D-86	0	236
500–575	538	277	D-86	0	277
575–650	613	315	D-86	0	315
650–735	693	368	D1160	0	368
735–900	818	432	D1160	0	432
900–1050	975	524	D1160	0	524
1050+					

	MBP, C	API	Sulfur
C5-180	59.9	78.4	0.001
180–265	104.7	60.6	0.001
265–350	150.2	53.5	0.005
350–425	192.3	49.7	0.009
425–500	236.3	43.3	0.019
500–575	277.4	41.3	0.030

°F	Mid-point of IIIE Cut, F	Mid-Point of Dist, C	Dist Method	Stem Corr Factor	Corr Dist Mid-point, C
575–650	314.5	37.7	0.070		
650–735	368.3	34.0	0.117		
735–900	431.7	25.5	0.218		
900–1050	523.9	15.4	0.296		

975   523.89

YIELD STRUCTURE			
Fraction, °C	Fraction, °C	LV%	Wt%
IBP–25.0	25.0	5.3	3.8
25.0–82.2	82.2	9.9	8.5
82.2–129.4	129.4	13.6	12.8
129.4–176.7	176.7	12.5	12.2
176.7–218.3	218.3	10.4	10.3
218.3–260.0	260.0	11.6	12.0
260.0–301.7	301.7	10.6	11.0
301.7–343.3	343.3	8.7	9.3
343.3–390.6	390.6	6.9	7.6
390.6–482.2	482.2	7.0	8.0

TBP CHART DATA		
Degrees C	Wt% Off	LV% Off
-1	0.0	0.0
25	3.8	5.3
30	4.5	6.2
35	5.3	7.0
40	6.0	7.9
45	6.8	8.8
50	7.5	9.6
75	11.2	14.0
100	17.1	20.3

°F	Mid-point of IIIE Cut, F	Mid-Point of Dist, C
125	23.9	27.5
150	30.4	34.2
175	36.9	40.9
200	43.1	47.1
225	49.5	53.6
250	56.7	60.5
275	63.6	67.1
300	70.2	73.5
325	75.8	78.8
350	81.0	83.6
375	85.0	87.2
400	88.3	90.2
425	90.5	92.1
450	92.7	94.0
475	94.9	95.9
500	96.1	96.9
525	96.8	97.6
540	97.3	98.0
565	98.1	98.6

Stem Corr Factor	Corr Dist Mid-point, C		
482.2–565.6	565.6	2.1	2.6
565.6+		1.4	1.9
343.3+		17.4	20.1
Lt Hydro API		119.56	
TOTAL		100.0	100.0

This crude oil sample was obtained from Texaco Deep Star's Agbami-2 well, Off-shore Nigeria, on December 26, 1999.	Whole Crude Oil	Test methods
Gravity, API @ 15.6°C	47.2	ASTM D-287
Gravity, Specific @ 15.6°C	0.7918	ASTM D-70
Total Sulfur, Wt%	0.044	ASTM D-2622 (X-Ray WDF)
Mercaptan Sulfur, WPPM	14	ASTM D-3227
Total Nitrogen, WPPM	471	ASTM D-5762
Reid Vapor Pressure, psi	9.2	ASTM D-5482
Flash Point, PM, °C	<Room Temp	ASTM D-93
Pour Point, °C	3.0	ASTM D-5950
Viscosity, CST @ 40.0°C	1.90	ASTM D-445
Neut. Number, mgm KOH/g	0.01	ASTM D-664
Micro Carbon Residue, Wt%	0.64	ASTM D-4530
Salt Content, g/bbl (lbs/1,000 bbl)	(71.6)	X-Ray WDF
BS&W, LV%	0.05	ASTM D-1796
Vanadium, WPPM	1	X-Ray WDF
Nickel, WPPM	2	X-Ray WDF
Iron, WPPM	3	X-Ray WDF
538°C Resid, Wt%	3.3	ASTM D-1160 (Modified)
538°C Resid, LV%	2.4	ASTM D-1160 (Modified)
H2S Content, WPPM	<1	ASTM D-3227

This crude oil sample was obtained from Texaco Deep Star's Agbami-2 well, Off-shore Nigeria, on December 26, 1999.	Whole Crude Oil	Test methods
Ethane & Lighter, LV%	0.12	Gas Chromatography (Internal Std)
Propane, LV%	1.28	"
iso-Butane, LV%	1.40	"
n-Butane, LV%	2.49	"
iso-Pentane, LV%	1.99	"
n-Pentane, LV%	1.95	"
C6's & Heavier, LV%	90.77	"
Distillation, °C, IBP	2.2	GC High Temp Simulated Distillation (AC Hi Temp)
Distillation, °C, 5%	45.0	"
Distillation, °C, 10%	88.9	"
Distillation, °C, 15%	115.0	"
Distillation, °C, 20%	133.9	"
Distillation, °C, 25%	148.9	"
Distillation, °C, 30%	162.8	"
Distillation, °C, 35%	176.1	"
Distillation, °C, 40%	195.0	"
Distillation, °C, 45%	215.0	"
Distillation, °C, 50%	232.8	"
Distillation, °C, 55%	247.8	"

This crude oil sample was obtained from Texaco Deep Star's Agbami-2 well, Off-shore Nigeria, on December 26, 1999.

	Whole Crude Oil	Test methods	
Distillation, °C, 60%	263.9	" " "	
Distillation, °C, 65%	282.8	" " "	
Distillation, °C, 70%	300.0	MONITORING PROGRAM YIELD STRUCTURE, WT% (GC SIM DIST)	
Distillation, °C, 75%	316.1		
Distillation, °C, 80%	341.1	IBP–176.7°C Gas & Naphtha	35.2
Distillation, °C, 85%	368.9	176.7–260.0°C Kerosene	23.6
Distillation, °C, 90%	402.8	260.0–343.3°C Atm Gas Oil	21.6
Distillation, °C, 95%	447.0	343.3–538°C Vac Gas Oil	18.4
Recovery, Wt% @ °C	99 @ 544.0	538 °C+ Vacuum Resid	1.2

Appendix IX

Nuclear Power Plants Under Construction or Planned in the World

Table IX.1. Nuclear power plants under construction or planned.

COUNTRY	Nuclear Electricity Generation 2007		Reactors Operable Dec 2008		Reactors Under Construction December 2008		Reactors Planned December 2008		Reactors Proposed December 2008		Uranium Requirement, 2008
	Billion kWh	% e	No.	MWe	No.	MWe	No.	MWe	No.	MWe	tonnes U
Argentina	6.7	6.2	2	935	1	692	1	740	1	740	123
Armenia	2.35	43.5	1	376	0	0	0	0	1	1,000	51
Bangladesh	0	0	0	0	0	0	0	0	2	2,000	0
Belarus	0	0	0	0	0	0	2	2,000	2	2,000	0
Belgium	46	54	7	5,728	0	0	0	0	0	0	1,011
Brazil	11.7	2.8	2	1,901	0	0	1	1,245	4	4,000	303
Bulgaria	13.7	32	2	1,906	0	0	2	1,900	0	0	261
Canada	88.2	14.7	18	12,652	2	1,500	3	3,300	6	6600	1,665
China	59.3	1.9	11	8,587	9	8,700	24	24,940	76	62,600	1,396
Czech Republic	24.6	30.3	6	3,472	0	0	0	0	2	3,400	619
Egypt	0	0	0	0	0	0	0	0	1	1,000	0
Finland	22.5	29	4	2,696	1	1,600	0	0	1	1,000	1,051
France	420.1	77	59	63,473	1	1,630	0	0	1	1,600	10,527
Germany	133.2	26	17	20,339	0	0	0	0	0	0	3,332
Hungary	13.9	37	4	1,826	0	0	0	0	2	2,000	271
India	15.8	2.5	17	3,779	6	2,976	10	9,760	15	11,200	978
Indonesia	0	0	0	0	0	0	2	2,000	4	4,000	0
Iran	0	0	0	0	1	915	2	1,900	1	300	143
Israel	0	0	0	0	0	0	0	0	1	1,200	0
Italy	0	0	0	0	0	0	0	0	10	17,000	0
Japan	267	27.5	55	47,577	2	2,285	11	14,945	1	1,100	7,569

COUNTRY	Nuclear Electricity Generation 2007		Reactors Operable Dec 2008		Reactors Under Construction December 2008		Reactors Planned December 2008		Reactors Proposed December 2008		Uranium Requirement, 2008
	Billion kWh	% e	No.	MWe	No.	MWe	No.	MWe	No.	MWe	tonnes U
Kazakhstan	0	0	0	0	0	0	2	600	2	600	0
Korea DPR (North)	0	0	0	0	0	0	1	950	0	0	0
Korea RO (South)	136.6	35.3	20	17,716	3	3,000	5	6,400	2	2,700	3,109
Lithuania	9.1	64.4	1	1,185	0	0	0	0	2	3,400	225
Mexico	9.95	4.6	2	1310	0	0	0	0	2	2,000	246
Netherlands	4.0	4.1	1	485	0	0	0	0	0	0	98
Pakistan	2.3	2.34	2	400	1	300	2	600	2	2,000	65
Poland	0	0	0	0	0	0	0	0	5	10,000	0
Romania	7.1	13	2	1,310	0	0	2	1,310	1	655	174
Russia	148	16	31	21,743	8	5,980	11	12,870	25	22,280	3,365
Slovakia	14.2	54	5	2,094	2	840	0	0	1	1,200	313
Slovenia	5.4	42	1	696	0	0	0	0	1	1,000	141
South Africa	12.6	5.5	2	1,842	0	0	3	3,565	24	4,000	303
Spain	52.7	17.4	8	7,448	0	0	0	0	0	0	1,398
Sweden	64.3	46	10	9,016	0	0	0	0	0	0	1,418
Switzerland	26.5	43	5	3,220	0	0	0	0	3	4,000	537
Thailand	0	0	0	0	0	0	2	2,000	4	4,000	0
Turkey	0	0	0	0	0	0	2	2,400	1	1,200	0
Ukraine	87.2	48	15	13,168	0	0	2	1,900	20	27,000	1,974
UAE	0	0	0	0	0	0	3	4,500	11	15,500	0

COUNTRY	Nuclear Electricity Generation 2007		Reactors Operable Dec 2008		Reactors Under Construction December 2008		Reactors Planned December 2008		Reactors Proposed December 2008		Uranium Requirement, 2008
	Billion kWh	% e	No.	MWe	No.	MWe	No.	MWe	No.	MWe	tonnes U
United Kingdom	57.5	15	19	11,035	0	0	0	0	6	9,600	2,199
USA	806.6	19.4	104	100,845	0	0	12	15,000	20	26,000	18,918
Vietnam	0	0	0	0	0	0	2	2000	8	8,000	0
WORLD**	2608	15	439	373,676	39	33,018	106	117,825	270	266,275	64,615

This table includes only those future reactors envisaged in specific plans and proposals and expected to be operating by 2030. Longer-range estimates based on national strategies, capabilities and needs may be found in the WNA Nuclear Century Outlook. The WNA country papers linked to this table cover both areas: near-term developments and the prospective long-term role for nuclear power in national energy policies.

Operating = Connected to the grid.
Building/Construction = first concrete for reactor poured, or major refurbishment under way.
Planned = Approvals, funding or major commitment in place, mostly expected in operation within 8 years, or construction well advanced but suspended indefinitely.
Proposed = Specific program or site proposals, expected operation within 20 years. Planned and Proposed are generally gross MWe.
TWh = Terawatt-hours (billion kilowatt-hours). MWe = Megawatt net (electrical as distinct from thermal). kWh = kilowatt-hour.

64,615 tU = 76,200 t U₃O₈.

** The world total includes six reactors operating on Taiwan with a combined capacity of 4,916 MWe, which generated a total of 39 billion likowatt-hour in 2007 (accounting for 19.3% of Taiwan's total electricity generation). Taiwan has two reactors under construction with a combined capacity of 2,600 MWe.

Sources: Reactor data: WNA to 30/11/08.; IAEA- for nuclear electricity production & percentage of electricity (% e) 5/08.; WNA: Global Nuclear Fuel Market (reference scenario) - for U

Appendix X

Data for Prediction of Peak Oil Production Year by the Hubbert Theory

Table X.1. Oil production and discovery data for US.

Year	Annual oil production (billion barrels)	Cumulative production (billion barrels)	Cumulative discovery (billion barrels)
1900	0.063621	0.063621	2.9636
1901	0.069389	0.13300	3.1330
1902	0.088767	0.22180	3.4218
1903	0.10046	0.32220	3.7222
1904	0.11708	0.43930	4.0393
1905	0.13472	0.57400	4.3740
1906	0.12649	0.70050	4.5005
1907	0.16610	0.86660	4.7666
1908	0.17853	1.0452	5.0452
1909	0.18317	1.2283	5.4283
1910	0.20956	1.4379	5.9379
1911	0.22045	1.6583	6.6583
1912	0.22294	1.8813	7.2813
1913	0.24845	2.1297	7.6297
1914	0.26576	2.3955	7.7955
1915	0.28110	2.6766	8.1766
1916	0.30077	2.9774	8.8774
1917	0.33532	3.3127	9.2127
1918	0.35593	3.6686	9.8686
1919	0.37837	4.0470	10.747
1920	0.44293	4.4899	11.690
1921	0.47218	4.9621	12.762
1922	0.55753	5.5196	13.120
1923	0.73241	6.2520	13.852
1924	0.71394	6.9660	14.466
1925	0.62037	7.5863	16.086
1926	0.77087	8.3572	17.157
1927	0.90113	9.2583	19.758
1928	0.90147	10.160	21.160
1929	1.0073	11.167	24.367
1930	0.89801	12.065	25.665
1931	0.85108	12.916	25.916
1932	0.78516	13.701	26.001
1933	0.90566	14.607	26.607
1934	0.90807	15.515	27.692
1935	0.99394	16.509	28.909
1936	1.0985	17.608	30.670
1937	1.2777	18.885	34.392
1938	1.2133	20.098	37.446

Year	Annual oil production (billion barrels)	Cumulative production (billion barrels)	Cumulative discovery (billion barrels)
1939	1.2643	21.363	39.846
1940	1.5032	22.866	41.891
1941	1.4042	24.270	43.829
1942	1.3855	25.656	45.739
1943	1.5056	27.161	47.225
1944	1.6779	28.839	49.292
1945	1.7137	30.553	51.380
1946	1.7334	32.286	53.160
1947	1.8570	34.143	55.631
1948	2.0202	36.164	59.444
1949	1.8419	38.005	62.654
1950	1.9736	39.979	65.247
1951	2.2477	42.227	69.695
1952	2.2898	44.516	72.478
1953	2.3571	46.874	75.819
1954	2.3150	49.189	78.750
1955	2.4844	51.673	81.685
1956	2.6173	54.290	84.725
1957	2.6169	56.907	87.207
1958	2.4490	59.356	89.892
1959	2.5746	61.931	93.650
1960	2.5749	64.506	96.119
1961	2.6218	67.128	98.886
1962	2.6762	69.804	101.19
1963	2.7527	72.556	103.53
1964	2.7868	75.343	106.33
1965	2.8485	78.192	109.54
1966	3.0278	81.219	112.67
1967	3.2157	84.435	115.81
1968	3.3290	87.764	118.47
1969	3.3718	91.136	120.77
1970	3.5175	94.654	133.65
1971	3.4539	98.107	136.17
1972	3.4554	101.56	137.90
1973	3.3609	104.92	140.22
1974	3.2026	108.13	140.38
1975	3.0568	111.18	143.87
1976	2.9762	114.16	145.10
1977	3.0093	117.17	148.95
1978	3.1782	120.35	151.70
1979	3.1213	123.47	153.28
1980	3.1464	126.61	156.42
1981	3.1286	129.74	159.17
1982	3.1567	132.90	160.76
1983	3.1710	136.07	163.81
1984	3.2497	139.32	167.77
1985	3.2746	142.60	171.01
1986	3.1683	145.76	172.65
1987	3.0474	148.81	176.07
1988	2.9791	151.79	178.61

Year	Annual oil production (billion barrels)	Cumulative production (billion barrels)	Cumulative discovery (billion barrels)
1989	2.7788	154.57	181.07
1990	2.6847	157.25	183.51
1991	2.7070	159.96	184.64
1992	2.6246	162.59	186.33
1993	2.4990	165.08	188.04
1994	2.4315	167.52	189.97
1995	2.3943	169.91	192.26
1996	2.3660	172.28	194.29
1997	2.3548	174.63	197.18
1998	2.2819	176.91	197.95
1999	2.1467	179.06	200.82
2000	2.1307	181.19	203.23
2001	2.1175	183.31	205.75
2002	2.0971	185.40	208.08
2003	2.0735	187.48	209.37
2004	1.9833	189.46	210.83
2005	1.8901	191.35	213.11
2006	1.8623	193.21	214.19
2007	1.8484		

Table X.2. Discovery and production data for world crude oil.

Year	Discovery (billion barrels) Annual	Cumulative	Year	Production (billion barrels) Annual	Cumulative
1932	9.0	9.0	1960	7.6613	7.6613
1933	4.0	13.0	1961	8.1943	15.323
1934	4.5	17.5	1962	8.8877	23.517
1935	3.0	20.5	1963	9.5374	32.405
1936	5.0	25.5	1964	10.286	41.942
1937	5.5	31.0	1965	11.070	52.228
1938	42.0	73.0	1966	12.030	63.298
1939	42.5	115.5	1967	12.917	75.329
1940	52.0	167.5	1968	14.100	88.246
1941	18.0	185.5	1969	15.220	102.35
1942	16.0	201.5	1970	16.750	117.57
1943	5.0	206.5	1971	17.710	134.32
1944	3.0	209.5	1972	18.765	152.03
1945	7.4	216.9	1973	20.323	170.79
1946	7.6	224.5	1974	20.338	191.11
1947	7.0	231.5	1975	19.283	211.45
1948	49.0	280.5	1976	20.929	230.73
1949	53.0	333.5	1977	21.794	251.66
1950	54.0	387.5	1978	21.958	273.46
1951	19.5	407.0	1979	22.875	295.42
1952	16.0	423.0	1980	21.739	318.29
1953	26.0	449.0	1981	20.458	340.03
1954	20.0	469.0	1982	19.509	360.49
1955	28.0	497.0	1983	19.440	380.00

	Discovery (billion barrels)		Year	Production (billion barrels)	
Year	Annual	Cumulative		Annual	Cumulative
1956	24.0	521.0	1984	19.892	399.44
1957	35.0	556.0	1985	19.699	419.33
1958	40.0	596.0	1986	20.513	439.03
1959	40.5	636.5	1987	20.670	459.54
1960	42.0	678.5	1988	21.422	480.21
1961	44.0	722.5	1989	21.823	501.63
1962	50.0	772.5	1990	22.079	523.46
1963	41.0	813.5	1991	21.969	545.54
1964	50.0	863.5	1992	21.944	567.51
1965	48.5	912.0	1993	21.962	589.45
1966	47.5	959.5	1994	22.302	611.41
1967	32.0	991.5	1995	22.769	633.71
1968	30.5	1022.0	1996	23.269	656.48
1969	30.4	1052.4	1997	23.995	679.75
1970	29.5	1081.9	1998	24.444	703.75
1971	40.5	1122.4	1999	24.061	728.19
1972	37.0	1159.4	2000	24.999	752.25
1973	38.5	1197.9	2001	24.857	777.25
1974	24.0	1221.9	2002	24.517	802.11
1975	26.5	1248.4	2003	25.349	826.62
1976	31.0	1279.4	2004	26.466	851.97
1977	37.0	1316.4	2005	26.941	878.44
1978	38.0	1354.4	2006	26.842	905.38
1979	36.0	1390.4	2007	26.744	932.22
1980	26.0	1416.4			
1981	24.0	1440.4			
1982	20.0	1460.4			
1983	20.0	1480.4			
1984	22.0	1502.4			
1985	21.0	1523.4			
1986	20.5	1543.9			
1987	18.0	1561.9			
1988	16.2	1578.1			
1989	17.5	1595.6			
1990	16.5	1612.1			
1991	20.0	1632.1			
1992	17.0	1649.1			
1993	16.0	1665.1			
1994	9.0	1674.1			
1995	8.5	1682.6			
1996	9.0	1691.6			
1997	9.0	1700.6			
1998	9.5	1710.1			
1999	14.0	1724.1			
2000	18.0	1742.1			
2001	17.5	1759.6			
2002	13.0	1772.6			
2003	9.0	1781.6			
2004	9.0	1790.6			

Table X.3. Calculated values for linearized Hubbert plot.

Q	P	1/P	Year	Q	P	1/P	Year
1	0.063903	15.64868	1881.272	47	2.348668	0.425773	1953.881
2	0.127201	7.8616	1896.921	48	2.384102	0.419445	1954.307
3	0.189892	5.266144	1904.782	49	2.418931	0.413406	1954.726
4	0.251978	3.968596	1910.048	50	2.453154	0.407639	1955.14
5	0.313459	3.190215	1914.017	51	2.486771	0.402128	1955.547
6	0.374333	2.671418	1917.207	52	2.519783	0.39686	1955.95
7	0.434602	2.300956	1919.879	53	2.552189	0.391821	1956.346
8	0.494265	2.023206	1922.18	54	2.583989	0.386999	1956.738
9	0.553322	1.807264	1924.203	55	2.615183	0.382382	1957.125
10	0.611774	1.63459	1926.01	56	2.645772	0.377962	1957.508
11	0.66962	1.493384	1927.645	57	2.675755	0.373726	1957.886
12	0.72686	1.37578	1929.138	58	2.705132	0.369668	1958.259
13	0.783495	1.276332	1930.514	59	2.733904	0.365777	1958.629
14	0.839524	1.191152	1931.79	60	2.762069	0.362047	1958.995
15	0.894947	1.117385	1932.981	61	2.78963	0.358471	1959.357
16	0.949764	1.052893	1934.099	62	2.816584	0.35504	1959.715
17	1.003976	0.99604	1935.152	63	2.842933	0.351749	1960.07
18	1.057582	0.945553	1936.148	64	2.868676	0.348593	1960.422
19	1.110582	0.900429	1937.093	65	2.893813	0.345565	1960.771
20	1.162977	0.859863	1937.994	66	2.918344	0.34266	1961.116
21	1.214765	0.823204	1938.854	67	2.94227	0.339874	1961.459
22	1.265948	0.789922	1939.677	68	2.96559	0.337201	1961.799
23	1.316526	0.759575	1940.467	69	2.988305	0.334638	1962.136
24	1.366498	0.731798	1941.226	70	3.010413	0.33218	1962.471
25	1.415863	0.706283	1941.958	71	3.031916	0.329824	1962.803
26	1.464624	0.682769	1942.664	72	3.052814	0.327567	1963.133
27	1.512778	0.661035	1943.347	73	3.073105	0.325404	1963.46
28	1.560327	0.640891	1944.008	74	3.092791	0.323333	1963.786
29	1.60727	0.622173	1944.649	75	3.111871	0.32135	1964.109
30	1.653607	0.604738	1945.271	76	3.130345	0.319454	1964.43
31	1.699339	0.588464	1945.876	77	3.148214	0.31764	1964.75
32	1.744465	0.573242	1946.464	78	3.165477	0.315908	1965.067
33	1.788985	0.558976	1947.038	79	3.182134	0.314255	1965.383
34	1.8329	0.545584	1947.597	80	3.198186	0.312677	1965.697
35	1.876208	0.53299	1948.142	81	3.213631	0.311174	1966.01
36	1.918911	0.521129	1948.675	82	3.228472	0.309744	1966.321
37	1.961009	0.509942	1949.196	83	3.242706	0.308384	1966.631
38	2.0025	0.499376	1949.706	84	3.256334	0.307094	1966.939
39	2.043386	0.489384	1950.206	85	3.269357	0.305871	1967.247
40	2.083666	0.479923	1950.695	86	3.281775	0.304713	1967.552
41	2.123341	0.470956	1951.175	87	3.293586	0.30362	1967.857
42	2.16241	0.462447	1951.646	88	3.304792	0.302591	1968.161
43	2.200873	0.454365	1952.108	89	3.315392	0.301623	1968.463
44	2.23873	0.446682	1952.563	90	3.325386	0.300717	1968.765
45	2.275982	0.439371	1953.009	91	3.334775	0.29987	1969.066
46	2.312627	0.432409	1953.449	92	3.343558	0.299083	1969.366

Q	P	1/P	Year	Q	P	1/P	Year
93	3.351735	0.298353	1969.665	142	3.010413	0.33218	1984.504
94	3.359306	0.29768	1969.963	143	2.988305	0.334638	1984.836
95	3.366272	0.297065	1970.261	144	2.96559	0.337201	1985.171
96	3.372632	0.296504	1970.558	145	2.94227	0.339874	1985.508
97	3.378386	0.295999	1970.854	146	2.918344	0.34266	1985.848
98	3.383535	0.295549	1971.15	147	2.893813	0.345565	1986.191
99	3.388078	0.295153	1971.446	148	2.868676	0.348593	1986.536
100	3.392015	0.29481	1971.741	149	2.842933	0.351749	1986.885
101	3.395347	0.294521	1972.036	150	2.816584	0.35504	1987.237
102	3.398072	0.294285	1972.33	151	2.78963	0.358471	1987.592
103	3.400192	0.294101	1972.625	152	2.762069	0.362047	1987.95
104	3.401707	0.29397	1972.919	153	2.733904	0.365777	1988.312
105	3.402615	0.293892	1973.213	154	2.705132	0.369668	1988.678
106	3.402918	0.293865	1973.507	155	2.675755	0.373726	1989.048
107	3.402615	0.293892	1973.8	156	2.645772	0.377962	1989.421
108	3.401707	0.29397	1974.094	157	2.615183	0.382382	1989.799
109	3.400192	0.294101	1974.388	158	2.583989	0.386999	1990.182
110	3.398072	0.294285	1974.682	159	2.552189	0.391821	1990.569
111	3.395347	0.294521	1974.977	160	2.519783	0.39686	1990.961
112	3.392015	0.29481	1975.271	161	2.486771	0.402128	1991.357
113	3.388078	0.295153	1975.566	162	2.453154	0.407639	1991.76
114	3.383535	0.295549	1975.861	163	2.418931	0.413406	1992.167
115	3.378386	0.295999	1976.157	164	2.384102	0.419445	1992.581
116	3.372632	0.296504	1976.453	**165**	**2.348668**	**0.425773**	**1993**
117	3.366272	0.297065	1976.749	166	2.312627	0.432409	1993.432
118	3.359306	0.29768	1977.046	167	2.275982	0.439371	1993.872
119	3.351735	0.298353	1977.344	168	2.23873	0.446682	1994.318
120	3.343558	0.299083	1977.642	169	2.200873	0.454365	1994.773
121	3.334775	0.29987	1977.941	170	2.16241	0.462447	1995.235
122	3.325386	0.300717	1978.241	171	2.123341	0.470956	1995.706
123	3.315392	0.301623	1978.542	172	2.083666	0.479923	1996.186
124	3.304792	0.302591	1978.844	173	2.043386	0.489384	1996.676
125	3.293586	0.30362	1979.146	174	2.0025	0.499376	1997.175
126	3.281775	0.304713	1979.45	175	1.961009	0.509942	1997.685
127	3.269357	0.305871	1979.754	176	1.918911	0.521129	1998.206
128	3.256334	0.307094	1980.06	177	1.876208	0.53299	1998.739
129	3.242706	0.308384	1980.367	178	1.8329	0.545584	1999.285
130	3.228472	0.309744	1980.676	179	1.788985	0.558976	1999.844
131	3.213631	0.311174	1980.986	180	1.744465	0.573242	2000.417
132	3.198186	0.312677	1981.297	181	1.699339	0.588464	2001.005
133	3.182134	0.314255	1981.609	182	1.653607	0.604738	2001.61
134	3.165477	0.315908	1981.924	183	1.60727	0.622173	2002.232
135	3.148214	0.31764	1982.24	184	1.560327	0.640891	2002.873
136	3.130345	0.319454	1982.557	185	1.512778	0.661035	2003.534
137	3.111871	0.32135	1982.877	186	1.464624	0.682769	2004.217
138	3.092791	0.323333	1983.198	187	1.415863	0.706283	2004.923
139	3.073105	0.325404	1983.521	188	1.366498	0.731798	2005.655
140	3.052814	0.327567	1983.847	189	1.316526	0.759575	2006.415
141	3.031916	0.329824	1984.174	190	1.265948	0.789922	2007.204

Q	P	1/P	Year	Q	P	1/P	Year
191	1.214765	0.823204	2008.028	202	0.611774	1.63459	2020.871
192	1.162977	0.859863	2008.887	203	0.553322	1.807264	2022.678
193	1.110582	0.900429	2009.788	204	0.494265	2.023206	2024.701
194	1.057582	0.945553	2010.733	205	0.434602	2.300956	2027.002
195	1.003976	0.99604	2011.73	206	0.374333	2.671418	2029.674
196	0.949764	1.052893	2012.782	207	0.313459	3.190215	2032.864
197	0.894947	1.117385	2013.9	208	0.251978	3.968596	2036.833
198	0.839524	1.191152	2015.091	209	0.189892	5.266144	2042.099
199	0.783495	1.276332	2016.367	210	0.127201	7.8616	2049.96
200	0.72686	1.37578	2017.743	211	0.063903	15.64868	2065.609
201	0.66962	1.493384	2019.236				

INDEX